Rick Steves'®

GERMANY

2010

MUNICH

1. Alte Pinakothek
2. Asamkirche
3. Bavarian National Museum
4. Beer and Oktoberfest Museum
5. To Chinese Tower Beer Garden
6. Cuvilliés Theater
7. Damenstift Church
8. Deutsches Museum
9. English Garden
10. Frauenkirche
11. Fünf Höfe Shops
12. Glyptothek
13. Haus der Kunst
14. Hofbräuhaus
15. Jewish History Museum
16. Kunsthalle
17. Marienplatz
18. Munich City Museum
19. Museum Brandhorst
20. To Museum of Transportation
21. Neue Pinakothek
22. New Town Hall & Glockenspiel
23. Odeonsplatz
24. Old Town Hall
25. Pinakothek der Moderne
26. Residenz Museum
27. Residenz Treasury
28. St. Michael's Church
29. St. Peter's Church
30. Viktualienmarkt

BERLIN

1. Alexanderplatz
2. Bauhaus Archive
3. Bebelplatz
4. Berlin Cathedral
5. Berlin Wall Documentation Center
6. Brandenburg Gate
7. Egyptian/Neues Museums
8. Erotic Art Museum
9. Europa Center
10. Gemäldegalerie
11. Gendarmenmarkt
12. German Cathedral
13. German History Museum
14. German Resistance Memorial
15. Hackesche Höfe
16. Hauptbahnhof (Main Train Station) & EurAide
17. Jewish Museum Berlin
18. KaDeWe Department Store
19. Kaiser Wilhelm Memorial Church
20. Käthe Kollwitz Museum
21. Kennedys Museum
22. Memorial to the Murdered Jews of Europe
23. Museum of Arts and Crafts
24. Museum of The Wall at Checkpoint Charlie
25. Musical Instruments Museum
26. Natural History Museum
27. Neue Wache Memorial
28. New National Gallery
29. New Synagogue
30. Old National Gallery
31. Pergamon Museum
32. Philharmonic Concert Hall
33. Potsdamer Platz & Sony Center
34. Reichstag
35. Spree River Cruises
36. Topography of Terror
37. TV Tower
38. Victory Column
39. Zoo

CONTENTS

Germany

Deutschland

Germany is blessed with some of
Europe's most high-powered sights.
There's spectacular scenery—the jagged
Alps, flower-filled meadows, rolling hills
of forests and farms, and rivers such as
the raging Rhine and moseying Mosel.
Germany has hundreds of castles, some
ruined and mysterious; others stout,
crenellated, and imposing; and still others
right out of a Disney fairy tale. In this
land of the Protestant Reformation—and
Catholic Counter-Reformation—churches
and cathedrals are another forte. Austere
Lutheran houses of worship tower
silently next to exuberantly overripe
Baroque churches, dripping with
curlicues.

Deutschland is energetic, efficient, and organized. It's
Europe's muscleman, both economically and wherever
people line up (Germans have a reputation for pushing
ahead). It's the European Union's most populous country
and biggest economy, with a geographic diversity and
cultural richness that draw millions of visitors every year.

Germany's dark side is recalled in eerie Nazi remnants
(stern office buildings, thoughtfully presented "documentation
centers," haunting concentration camps) and chilling reminders of the Cold War (embodied in a few quickly disappearing

sites—such as scant fragments of the notorious Berlin Wall). And of course there are the cultural clichés—kept alive more by tradition-loving Germans than by tourist demand. The country is dotted with idyllic half-timbered villages where you can enjoy strudel at the bakery or sip a stein of beer while men in lederhosen play oompah music. Peruse a wonderland of chocolates, stock up on Hummels and cuckoo clocks, and learn how to polka.

All of this stands at sharp contrast with the "real" Germany of today. Despite its respect for the past, this is a truly 21st-century country. At the forefront of human progress, Germany is a world of high-tech trains, gleaming cities, social efficiency, and world-class museums celebrating history's greatest cultural achievements.

Modern Germany bustles. Its cities hold 75 percent of its people, and average earnings are among the highest in the world. Most workers get at least a month of paid vacation, and during the other 11 months, this land the size of Montana creates a Gross Domestic Product (GDP) that's about one-quarter of the United States'. Germany has risen from the ashes of World War II to become the world's fifth-largest industrial power.

People all over the world enjoy the fruits of Germany's labor. Their cars are legendary—BMW, Mercedes-Benz, Volkswagen, Audi, and Porsche. We talk on German mobile phone networks (T-Mobile), ride German elevators and trains (ThyssenKrupp and Siemens AG), take German medicines

(Bayer), use German cosmetics (Nivea)...and eat German goodies (Haribo's Gummi Bears).

Germany beats out all but two countries in production of books, Nobel laureates, and professors. In the world of physics, there's Einstein's Relativity, Planck's constant, and the Heisenberg Uncertainty Principle. German inventions range from Gutenberg's printing press to Zeppelin's zeppelins to Roentgen's X-rays to Daimler's and Benz's cars to Geiger's counter. Musically, Germany dominated the scene for more than two centuries—Bach, Beethoven, Brahms, Handel, Pachelbel, Wagner, and more. Germans have a reputation as profound analytical thinkers, sprouting philosophers such as Kant, Hegel, Nietzsche, Marx, and Engels.

Germany is geographically big (compared to other European countries) but closely knit by transportation. Its autobahns—miles and miles of high-quality freeway—are

Germany Almanac

Official Name: Bundesrepublik Deutschland, or simply Deutschland.

Population: Germany's 82 million people (more than three times the population of Texas) are largely of Teutonic DNA (88 percent), plus a small but significant minority (2.4 percent) of Turkish-descended citizens. A third of Germans are Catholic, and a third are Protestant. About 4 percent are Muslim; the remainder are unaffiliated.

Latitude and Longitude: 51°N and 9°E. The latitude is similar to Alberta, Canada.

Area: At 138,000 square miles, Germany is slightly smaller than Montana and about half the size of Texas. It's bordered by nine countries.

Geography: The terrain gradually rises—from flat land in the north to the rugged Alps in the south, culminating in the 9,700-foot Zugspitze mountain. The climate is temperate.

Biggest Cities: The capital city of Berlin has 3.4 million people, followed by Hamburg's 1.7 million and Munich's 1.5 million.

Economy: With a GDP of $2.75 trillion—similar to America's Midwest states combined—Germany is Europe's largest economy. Still, the GDP per capita is approximately $35,000, or about 25 percent less than America's. It's one of the world's most advanced economies, producing steel, cars, chemicals, pharmaceuticals, consumer electronics, and more. Germany also has around 1,300 breweries, but much of the production is consumed domestically. Germany trades almost equally with a half-dozen neighboring countries, and the United States.

Since the 1990 reunification, Germany's economy has been burdened by the cost (about $80 billion a year) of integrating the former East Germany into the modern West. Germany's expensive social security system gets even costlier as the population ages. Thanks to powerful trade unions, workers get good benefits. Unemployment hovers around 8 percent.

Government: In the 2005 elections, Angela Merkel became Germany's first woman chancellor. After the 2009 elections, the conservative Merkel became the head of a big-business-friendly coalition government that leans slightly to the right. A small but powerful minority party, the Greens, presses the pro-environment agenda. Germany's chancellor, similar to the prime minister in other countries, is not elected directly by the people but is the head of the lead party in parliament. The less-powerful president (Horst Köhler) is also elected by parliament. The legislative branch includes the Bundestag (613 seats, elected by both direct and proportional representation) and the Bundesrat (69 votes by local officials of Germany's 16 states).

Flag: Deutschland's flag is composed of three horizontal bands of (from top to bottom) black, red, and gold.

The Average *Deutscher*: The average German is 43 years old—six years older than the average American—has 1.4 kids, and will live to be 79. He or she lives in a household with two other people, watches 2.5 hours of TV a day, and spends 20 minutes reading the daily newspaper. The average German drinks a pint of beer every 32 hours, which is slightly less than the average Irish or Czech.

famous (or notorious) for their no-speed-limit system (more fully explained on page 615). InterCityExpress (ICE) trains zip by at up to 200 miles per hour, linking major cities quickly and efficiently.

As a nation, Germany is less than 140 years old ("born" in 1871), quite young compared to most of its European neighbors. In medieval times, there were 300 countries in what is now Germany, each with its own weights, measures, coinage, king, and lottery. By 1850, the number had dropped to a still formidable 35 countries. Today's Germany is a federation of states, each with its own cultural identity and customs.

Traditionally—and in some ways even today—German culture divides at a sort of North-South Mason-Dixon Line.

Northern Germany was barbarian, is predominantly Protestant, and tackles life aggressively, while southern Germany (Bavaria) was Roman, is largely Catholic, and enjoys a more relaxed tempo. The romantic American image of Germany is beer-and-pretzel Bavaria (probably because that was "our" sector after the war). This historic North-South division is growing less pronounced as Germany becomes a more mobile society.

Germany's roots run deep. Thoughtful travelers can easily trace the country's history in their sightseeing. Find Germany's Roman roots at the impressive Porta Nigra Gate and Basilica of scenic Trier. When Rome fell, German lands fragmented into hundreds of small feudal kingdoms, each with its own castle—many of which still dot the German countryside today. Magnificent Gothic cathedrals like the one in Köln attest to the faith of medieval people. As Germany's economy recovered, it became Europe's trade and transportation hub. Prosperous cities sprung up along the Romantic Road—today's prime tourist trail.

It was from Germany that a humble monk named Martin Luther rocked Europe with religious reform, and you'll see monuments, cities, and churches associated with him. Meanwhile, German Catholics decorated their churches (including the glorious Wieskirche) and palaces (in Munich and Würzburg) in the ornate Baroque/Rococo style, giving a glimpse of the heaven that awaited the faithful. Germany became a Europe-wide battleground for Protestants and Catholics in the Thirty Years' War that was duked out in towns such as Rothenburg (which today is besieged by tourists).

In the 1800s, Germany unified politically, and it became a cultural powerhouse. European nobles flocked to Baden-Baden's casino and thermal baths, while composer Richard Wagner spun operatic tales about German folk legends at the castle of Neuschwanstein with his friend "Mad" King Ludwig II.

Germany's prosperity ended in the humiliating defeat of World War I. You can see the rising specter of Hitler and Nazism at the Nürnberg Rally Grounds (where huge propaganda events were staged, now home to an excellent museum documenting the Nazis' rise to power), at Berlin's Reichstag (whose destruction helped the Nazis take control), and the sobering concentration camp museum at Dachau (one of many places where the Nazis snuffed out their opposition). Germany's utter destruction in World War II is evident in the skylines of today's cities. Some, like Munich and Dresden, were rebuilt in a faux-Baroque style, while Frankfurt sprouted skyscrapers.

At war's end, Germany was divided East-West between the victorious Allies, and the Cold War set in (1945–1990). In Berlin, you can see a few surviving stretches of the Wall that divided the country, and the famous Checkpoint Charlie that controlled the East-West flow. Even today, Eastern cities such as Dresden and Görlitz bear the scars and stunted growth of Soviet occupation. Some friction still exists between the residents of the former East Germany ("Ossies" in impolite slang) and those from West Germany ("Wessies"). Two decades after reunification, and despite billions of dollars of economic aid, the East lags behind the West, with a higher unemployment rate (about double the West's), lower income, potholed infrastructure,

and a few old-timers who miss the good old Red days.

Many visitors can't help but associate Germany with its dark Nazi past. But while a small neo-Nazi skinhead element still survives in the back alleys of German society, for the most part the nation has evolved into a surprisingly progressive, almost touchy-feely place. A genuine sense of responsibility for World War II and the Holocaust pervades much of German society. If you visit a concentration camp memorial, you'll likely see several field-trip groups of German teens visiting there to learn the lessons of the past.

Germany was a founding member of the European Union, and continues to lead the way in creating a healthy Europe for the future—with peace, unity, tolerance (e.g., legalized gay marriage), and human rights as its central motivations. It's the world's second-biggest foreign-aid donor, after the US. Even to a skeptical visitor, it's clear that most Germans are trying to make up for the ugliness their ancestors subjected Europe to not so long ago.

How does a country achieve such robust economic and social success, despite losing two world wars? This is a country of "Type A" personalities. Bold, brassy Germans typically aren't shy to speak their minds. Their directness (some might say "bluntness") is refreshing to some, and startling to others. At least you'll know where you stand. People who enjoy trains that run on time are perfectly suited for travel in everything-has-its-place Germany. Those who like to play it fast and loose might find that improvisation has its limits here.

Paradoxically, the ultra-efficient Germans also have a weak spot for Hummel-esque quaintness and a sentimentality for their own history. They love nature. They love to go a-wandering along a mountain path with their hiking sticks, rucksacks, and state-of-the-art gear. Dramatic cable cars whisk visitors to sweeping cut-glass panoramas. Learn the word *schön*—beautiful—because you'll hear it often, from little old ladies and grown men alike as they survey beautiful vistas of their homeland. They're also prone to get misty-eyed when, after a glass or two of white wine, they and their mates start singing a traditional song from their youth. Cutesy traditions are respected and celebrated. Germans wear dirndls and

lederhosen on holidays, erect maypoles in spring, decorate Christmas trees and host exuberant Christmas markets in winter, and frequent Oktoberfest-type beer halls year-round.

Germans love to travel, through their own country and beyond. They're cosmopolitan and outward-looking. Two-thirds speak at least one other language (mostly English), and they enjoy watching TV and movies beamed in from other countries. Watch out—they may know American politics and history better than you do. They're products of high-quality schools that put kids on either fast or slow tracks, depending on ability and desire. To move on to college, they must pass a major SAT-like test. Once there, the university system is top-quality...with tuition of only a few hundred dollars a semester.

Germans aren't all work and no play. All Europeans love watching sports, but Germans actually play them. More than six million are registered to play *Fussball* (soccer) every year in the official league. There's a big following for pro soccer Bundesliga, and Germany is always a strong contender for the World Cup and Euro Cup championship tournaments (runners-up in the 2008 Euro Cup).

Motorsports are big time, especially Formula One—the European answer to NASCAR—where racing legend Michael Schumacher is one of the world's highest-paid athletes. In the Olympics (winter and summer), Germany is consistently one of the world's top medal-finishers. Just try to keep up with them on one of their summer luge courses *(Sommerrodelbahn)* that allow amateur thrill-seekers to scream down a mountain at top speed.

As Germany speeds into the future, it's faced with a number of challenges—none bigger than immigration. After World War II, Germany needed cheap blue-collar laborers to help rebuild, and they welcomed in many Turkish people as *Gastarbeiters* (guest workers). While many earned money and went home, many others married, had kids, and stayed. Today, more than 10 million immigrants (12 percent of Germany's population) live within its borders—more than every country but the US and Russia. Of these, 2.3 million are Turks, most of whom are Muslims—not always the easiest fit within a traditionally Christian nation.

Germany today is trying to stay competitive in the global

marketplace while maintaining generous social services. Neo-Nazism is a festering sore, and there's a declining birthrate (one of the world's lowest). And its enormous appetite for energy is increasingly at odds with its love for the environment (the government is working to phase out nuclear power and invest in sustainable energy).

After the end of World War II, as the US evolved from an occupying force to a close ally, the two countries gradually built a strong relationship. Today more than 100,000 Americans live in Germany (many of them at US military bases, such as Ramstein near the Rhine). Americans generally find Germany to be one of Europe's most accessible nations. It's efficient, the people are almost aggressively welcoming, the language barrier is minimal...and the German roots that pervade America's melting pot don't hurt matters, either. (More than 15 percent of Americans have some German ancestry—more than any other background.)

Germany today is reunited, a nation of cutting-edge industry, medieval castles, speedy autobahns, old-time beer halls, modern skyscrapers, and the best wurst. This young country with a long past continues to make history.

INTRODUCTION

This book focuses on Germany's top big-city, small-town, and rural destinations. It then gives you all the information and opinions necessary to wring the maximum value out of your limited time and money. If you plan a month or less in Germany and have a normal appetite for information, this book is all you need. If you're a travel-info fiend, this book sorts through all the superlatives and provides a handy rack upon which to hang your supplemental information.

Experiencing Europe's culture, people, and natural wonders economically and hassle-free has been my goal through three decades of traveling, tour guiding, and travel writing. With this new edition, I pass on to you the lessons I've learned, updated for your trip in 2010.

The German destinations covered in this book are balanced to include a comfortable mix of cities and villages, mountaintop hikes and forgotten Roman ruins, sleepy river cruises and sky-high gondola rides. I've also included a taste of neighboring Austria, with side-trips into Tirol and Salzburg. While you'll find the predictable biggies (such as Rhine castles and chunks of the Berlin Wall), I've also mixed in a healthy dose of Back Door intimacy (a soak in a Black Forest mineral spa, a beer with Bavarian monks, and a thrilling mountain luge). I've been selective, including only the most exciting sights. For example, of the many castles in the Mosel Valley, I guide you to the best: Burg Eltz.

The best is, of course, only my opinion. But after spending half of my adult life exploring and researching Europe, I've developed a sixth sense for what travelers enjoy. The places featured in this book will make anyone want to yodel.

About This Book

Rick Steves' Germany 2010 is your friendly Franconian, your German in a jam, a tour guide in your pocket. The book is organized by destination, each one a mini-vacation on its own—filled with exciting sights, strollable neighborhoods, homey and affordable places to stay, and memorable places to eat. This book is updated every year in person, but even with annual updates, things change. For the latest, visit www.ricksteves.com/update, and for reports and experiences—good and bad—from fellow travelers, check www.ricksteves.com/feedback.

In the following chapters, you'll find these sections:

Planning Your Time suggests a schedule with thoughts on how best to use your limited time.

Orientation includes specifics on public transportation, helpful hints, local tour options, easy-to-read maps, and tourist information (abbreviated **TI** in this book).

Sights, described in detail, are rated:

▲▲▲—Don't miss.

▲▲—Try hard to see.

▲—Worthwhile if you can make it.

No rating—Worth knowing about.

Self-Guided Walks take you through interesting neighborhoods, with a personal tour guide in hand.

Sleeping describes my favorite hotels, from good-value deals to cushy splurges.

Eating serves up a range of options, from inexpensive pubs to fancy restaurants.

Connections outlines your options for traveling to destinations by train, bus, and plane. In car-friendly regions, I've included route tips for drivers.

The **German History** chapter introduces you to some of the key people and events in this nation's complicated past, making your sightseeing that much more meaningful.

The **appendix** is a traveler's tool kit, with telephone tips, useful phone numbers, transportation basics (on trains, buses, car rentals, driving, and flying), recommended books and films, a festival list, climate chart, handy packing checklist, a hotel reservation form, and German survival phrases.

Browse through this book and select your favorite sights. Then have a *wunderbar* trip! Traveling like a temporary local and taking advantage of the information here, you'll get the absolute most out of every mile, minute, and euro. I'm happy you'll be visiting places I know and love, and meeting some of my favorite German people.

Planning

This section will help you get started on planning your trip—with advice on trip costs, when to go, and what you should know before you take off.

Travel Smart

Your trip to Germany is like a complex play—easier to follow and to really appreciate on a second viewing. While no one does the same trip twice to gain that advantage, reading this book in its entirety before your trip accomplishes much the same thing.

Design an itinerary that enables you to visit the various sights at the best possible times. Note holidays, festivals, and days when sights are closed. Sundays have the same pros and cons as they do for travelers in the US (special events, limited hours, banks and many shops closed, limited public transportation, no rush hour). Saturdays are virtually weekdays, with earlier closing hours and no rush hour. Popular destinations are even more popular on weekends.

Be sure to mix intense and relaxed periods in your itinerary. To maximize rootedness, minimize one-night stands. It's worth a long drive after dinner to be settled into a town for two nights. Hotels are also more likely to give a good price to someone staying more than one night. Every trip (and every traveler) needs at least a few slack days (for picnics, laundry, people-watching, and so on). Pace yourself. Assume you will return.

Reread this book as you travel, and visit local TIs. Upon arrival in a new town, lay the groundwork for a smooth departure; write down (or print out from an online source) the schedule for the train or bus you'll take when you depart. Drivers can study the best route to their next destination.

While traveling, take advantage of the Internet and phones to make your trip run smoothly. By going online (at Internet cafés or your hotel) and using the phone, you can get tourist information, learn the latest on sights (special events, tour schedules, etc.), book tickets and tours, make reservations, reconfirm hotels, research transportation connections, and keep in touch with loved ones.

Connect with the culture. Set up your own quest for the best beer-and-bratwurst, castle, cathedral, or whatever. Enjoy the hospitality of the Germanic people. Slow down and be open to unexpected experiences. Ask questions—most locals are eager to point you in their idea of the right direction. Keep a notepad in your pocket for organizing your thoughts. Wear your money belt, and learn the local currency and how to estimate prices in dollars. Those who expect to travel smart, do.

Germany at a Glance

▲▲▲Munich Lively city with a traffic-free center, excellent museums, Baroque palaces, stately churches, rowdy beer halls, convivial beer gardens, and beautiful parks (such as the English Garden)—plus the sobering concentration camp memorial at nearby Dachau.

▲▲▲Bavaria and Tirol Pair of Alps-straddling regions (one in Germany, the other in Austria) boasting the fairy-tale castles of Neuschwanstein, Hohenschwangau, and Linderhof; inviting villages such as the handy home base Füssen, Austrian retreat Reutte, and adorable Oberammergau; the towering Zugspitze and its high-altitude lifts; and hiking, luge, and other mountain activities.

▲▲▲Salzburg and Berchtesgaden Austrian musical mecca for fans of Mozart and *The Sound of Music*, offering a dramatic castle, concerts, Baroque churches, and an old town full of winding lanes; plus nearby Berchtesgaden, soaked in alpine scenery and Nazi history.

▲▲Baden-Baden and the Black Forest High-class resort/spa town of Baden-Baden, with decadent bath experiences, a peaceful riverside stroll, and a grand casino; lively university city of Freiburg and cozy village of Staufen; and a thickly forested countryside rife with healthy hikes, folk museums, cute hamlets, and cream cakes.

▲▲Rothenburg and the Romantic Road Well-preserved medieval city full of half-timbered buildings and cobbled lanes surrounded by intact and walkable medieval walls; jumping-off point for the "Romantic Road" scenic route through lovely countryside and time-passed villages, including Dinkelsbühl and Nördlingen.

▲Würzburg Residenz complex (with a palace, manicured gardens, and dazzling Rococo chapel) and lively wine bars and restaurants.

Trip Costs

Five components make up your trip cost: airfare, surface transportation, room and board, sightseeing and entertainment, and shopping and miscellany.

Airfare: A basic round-trip US-to-Frankfurt flight costs $800–1,200, depending on where you fly from and when (cheaper in winter). Always consider saving time and money in Europe by flying "open jaw"—into one city and out of another—for example, into Frankfurt and out of Berlin.

Surface Transportation: For a three-week whirlwind trip of all my recommended destinations, allow $650 per person for

▲**Frankfurt** Europe's bustling banking center, offering a stunning skyscraper skyline and a look at today's Germany.

▲▲**Rhine Valley** Mighty river steeped in legend, where storybook half-timbered villages (including charming home-base towns Bacharach and St. Goar) cluster under imposing castles, such as Rheinfels and Marksburg.

▲▲**Mosel Valley** Peaceful meandering river lined with tiny wine-loving cobbled towns, such as handy Cochem and quaint Beilstein, plus my favorite European castle, Burg Eltz.

▲**Trier** Germany's oldest city, with a lively pedestrian zone and imposing Roman monuments, including the Porta Nigra gate.

▲**Köln** Spectacular Gothic cathedral looming above a busy, museum-packed riverside city.

▲▲**Nürnberg** City with old-fashioned sandstone core and great museums, along with reminders of the Nazi past thoughtfully presented on the outskirts of town.

▲**Dresden** Art-filled city offering exquisite museums, Baroque palaces, a delightful riverside promenade, and hard memories of a notorious WWII firebombing.

▲**Görlitz** Undiscovered town on the Polish border, filled with architectural gems.

▲▲▲**Berlin** Germany's vibrant and now-reunited capital, featuring world-class museums, gleaming modern architecture, and trendy nightlife, along with evocative monuments and memories of The Wall that once divided the city and country.

public transportation (trains and buses) or $800 per person for a car (based on two people sharing a three-week rental), including parking, gas, and insurance. Leasing is worth considering for trips of two and a half weeks or more. Car rental and leases are cheapest when reserved from the US. Train passes are normally sold only outside of Europe. You may save money by simply buying tickets as you go (see "Transportation" in the appendix).

Room and Board: You can thrive in Germany on an average of $120 a day per person for room and board (less in small towns, more in big cities such as Berlin). A $120-a-day budget allows an average of $15 for lunch, $20 for dinner, $5 for beer and *Eis* (ice cream), and $80 for lodging (based on two people splitting the cost of a $160 double room that includes breakfast). That's doable. Students and tightwads eat and sleep on $50 a day ($25 per hostel bed, $25 for meals and snacks).

Sightseeing and Entertainment: In big cities, figure $12–20 per major sight (Munich's Deutsches Museum-$12, Berlin's Museum of The Wall-$18), $5–7 for minor ones, and $25–50 for bus tours and splurge experiences (such as concert tickets, alpine lifts, and conducting the beer-hall band). An overall average of $30 a day works for most. Don't skimp here. After all, this category is the driving force behind your trip—you came to sightsee, enjoy, and experience Germany.

Shopping and Miscellany: Figure $3 per postcard, coffee, beer, and ice-cream cone. Shopping can vary in cost from nearly nothing to a small fortune. Good budget travelers find that this category has little to do with assembling a trip full of lifelong and wonderful memories.

Sightseeing Priorities

Depending on the length of your trip, and taking geographic proximity into account, the following are my recommended priorities.

3 days:	Munich, Bavarian castles
5 days, add:	Rhine Valley, Rothenburg
7 days, add:	More of Bavaria and Tirol, side-trip to Salzburg
10 days, add:	Berlin
14 days, add:	Baden-Baden, Black Forest, Dresden
17 days, add:	Nürnberg, Mosel Valley, Trier
21 days, add:	Würzburg, and slow down
More time:	Choose among Frankfurt, Köln, and Görlitz

(The itinerary and map on pages 8 and 9 include everything on this list.)

When to Go

The "tourist season" runs roughly from May through September. Book ahead for the holidays that occur throughout the year (see "Major Holidays and Weekends").

Summer has its advantages: the best weather, snow-free alpine trails, very long days (light until after 21:00), and the busiest schedule of tourist fun.

Travel during "shoulder season" (May, June, Sept, and early Oct) is easier and can be a bit less expensive. Shoulder-season travelers usually enjoy smaller crowds, decent weather, the full range of sights and tourist fun spots, and the ability to grab a room almost whenever and wherever they like—often at a flexible price. Also, in fall, fun harvest and wine festivals enliven many towns and villages, while forests and vineyards display beautiful fiery colors.

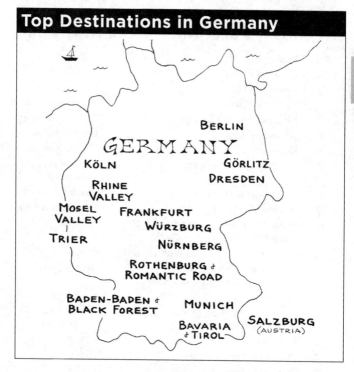

Top Destinations in Germany

GERMANY

BERLIN
KÖLN
GÖRLITZ
DRESDEN
RHINE VALLEY
MOSEL VALLEY
FRANKFURT
WÜRZBURG
TRIER
NÜRNBERG
ROTHENBURG & ROMANTIC ROAD
BADEN-BADEN & BLACK FOREST
MUNICH
BAVARIA & TIROL
SALZBURG (AUSTRIA)

Winter travelers find concert seasons in full swing, with absolutely no tourist crowds, but some accommodations and sights are either closed or run on a limited schedule. Confirm your sightseeing plans locally, especially when traveling off-season. The weather can be cold and dreary, and nightfall draws the shades on sightseeing well before dinnertime. But dustings of snow turn German towns and landscapes into a wonderland, and December offers the chance to wander through Germany's famous Christmas markets. (For more information, see the climate chart in the appendix.)

Know Before You Go

Your trip is more likely to go smoothly if you plan ahead. Check this list of things to arrange while you're still at home.

You need a **passport**—but no visa or shots—to travel in Germany. You may be denied entry into certain European countries if your passport is due to expire within three to six months of your ticketed date of return. Get it renewed if you'll be cutting it close. It can take up to six weeks to get or renew a passport (for more on passports, see www.travel.state.gov). Pack a photocopy of your passport in your luggage in case the original is lost or stolen.

Germany's Best Three-Week Trip by Car

Day	Plan	Sleep in
1	Fly into Frankfurt, pick up car, to Rhine	Bacharach
2	Rhine Valley	Bacharach
3	To Mosel Valley	Beilstein or Trier
4	Mosel Valley and/or Trier	Beilstein or Trier
5	To Baden-Baden	Baden-Baden
6	Relax and soak in Baden-Baden	Baden-Baden
7	Drive through the Black Forest	Staufen or Freiburg
8	To Bavaria and Tirol	Füssen or Reutte
9	Bavaria/Tirol and castles	Füssen or Reutte
10	More Bavaria/Tirol, then to Munich	Munich
11	Munich	Munich
12	More Munich, or side-trip to Salzburg	Munich
13	To Dachau, then follow Romantic Road to Rothenburg	Rothenburg
14	Rothenburg	Rothenburg
15	To Würzburg, drop off car*, then train to Nürnberg	Nürnberg or Würzburg
16	Nürnberg	Nürnberg
17	Train to Dresden	Dresden
18	Train to Berlin	Berlin
19	Berlin	Berlin
20	Berlin	Berlin
21	Fly home	

*After Day 15, you're visiting well-connected cities, making a car unnecessary. Drop the car in Würzburg to save several days of car-rental costs and parking fees.

Smaller Towns vs. Bigger Towns: This itinerary (especially the first half) is heavy on half-timbered villages—a German specialty. But for some, a little cuteness goes a long way. Plan your overnights to either maximize or reduce quaintness. For example, for Days 3-4, 7, and 15, you can opt for smaller towns (Beilstein, Staufen, and the mid-size town of Würzburg) or bigger, more bustling cities (Trier, Freiburg, and Nürnberg).

With Less Time: This trip can be pared down to two weeks by making the following changes: Skip the Mosel (a sleepier version of the Rhine), and go directly from the Rhine to Baden-Baden. From Baden-Baden, head straight for Füssen/Reutte instead of overnighting in Staufen/Freiburg. Skip the Salzburg side-trip; choose between Würzburg and Nürnberg, and stay just one night there; and reduce the stay in Berlin to two nights.

With More Time: Berlin and Salzburg are each easily worth another day. Depending on your interests, you could stay a day in Frankfurt (upon arrival); add another day for the Rhine to visit Köln from Bacharach; and see the town of Görlitz as a side-trip from Dresden (or as a detour en route to Berlin).

By Train: This itinerary is designed to be done by car, but could be done by train with some modifications: Skip the southern Black Forest and take the train from Baden-Baden to Munich, which works well as a home base for visiting Bavaria and Salzburg. Then take the train or bus to Rothenburg; from there, Würzburg, Nürnberg, and Dresden are all on the way to Berlin. Or, for the best of both worlds, consider using trains to connect major cities, and then renting a car strategically to explore worthwhile countryside regions (such as Bavaria/Tirol).

INTRODUCTION

Major Holidays and Weekends

Popular places are even busier on weekends, and holidays can bring many businesses to a grinding halt. Plan ahead and reserve your accommodations and transportation well in advance. Mark these dates in red on your travel calendar: New Year's Day, Easter (April 4 in 2010), Oktoberfest in Munich (Sept 18–Oct 3 in 2010), Christmas, December 26, and New Year's Day. Also check the list of festivals and holidays on page 622 of the appendix.

Book your rooms well in advance if you'll be traveling during peak season or any major **holidays,** such as Oktoberfest (see "Major Holidays and Weekends" sidebar). Check if you'll be visiting **Frankfurt** and **Köln** during convention season (see pages 321 and 422), and consider changing your dates in those cities to avoid the highest hotel rates.

To get tickets to **Neuschwanstein Castle** in peak season, you can email, go online, or phone ahead (a minimum of 24 hours before your visit) to avoid long lines (see page 114 for tips).

Sign up in advance if you'd like a free **Munich BMW Factory tour** (see page 74).

To see **Dresden's Historic Green Vault,** book your tickets ahead (ideally six months before)—or take your chances with same-day tickets (see page 470).

Tickets for the music-packed **Salzburg Festival** (late July through August) can go fast. Consider buying tickets ahead if there's a specific event you want to see (for details, see page 172).

Call your **debit- and credit-card companies** to let them know the countries you'll be visiting so that they won't deny your international charges. Confirm your daily withdrawal limit; consider asking to have it raised so you can take out more cash at each ATM stop. Ask about international transaction fees.

If you're interested in **travel insurance**, do your homework before you buy. Compare the cost of the insurance to the likelihood of your using it and your potential loss if something goes wrong. For details on the many kinds of travel insurance, see www .ricksteves.com/plan/tips/insurance.htm.

If you're planning on **renting a car** in Germany, bring your US driver's license.

Because **airline carry-on restrictions** are always changing, visit the Transportation Security Administration's website (www .tsa.gov/travelers) for an up-to-date list of what you can bring on the plane with you...and what you have to check. Remember to arrive with plenty of time to get through security.

Practicalities

Emergency Telephone Numbers: Dial 112 for police or medical emergencies.

Time: In Germany—and in this book—you'll use the 24-hour clock. It's the same through 12:00 noon, then keep going: 13:00, 14:00, and so on. For anything over 12, subtract 12 and add p.m. (14:00 is 2:00 p.m.).

Germany, like most of continental Europe, is generally six/nine hours ahead of the East/West Coasts of the US. The exceptions are the beginning and end of Daylight Saving Time: Europe "springs forward" the last Sunday in March (two weeks after most of North America), and "falls back" the last Sunday in October (one week before North America). For a handy online time converter, try www.timeanddate.com/worldclock.

Business Hours: In Germany, most shops are open from about 9:00 until 18:00–20:00 on weekdays, but close early on Saturday (generally between 12:00 and 17:00, depending on whether you're in a town or a big city), and are almost always closed on Sunday. By law, stores must close by 22:00, but very few stay open that late. The law makes an exception for shops in train stations, which often have grocery stores that are open long hours. Bank hours vary depending on where you are: They generally open Monday–Friday around 9:00, and close anywhere between 15:00 and 19:00. Some branches close for an hour or two at lunchtime. Catholic regions, including Bavaria, shut down during religious holidays. Turkish-owned shops are often open later than other stores. Many museums and sights are closed on Monday.

Watt's Up? Europe's electrical system is different from North America's in two ways: the shape of the plug (two round prongs) and the voltage of the current (220 volts instead of 110 volts). For your North American plug to work in Europe, you'll need an adapter, sold inexpensively at travel stores in the US. As for the voltage, most newer electronics or travel appliances (such as hair dryers, laptops, and battery chargers) automatically convert the voltage—if you see a range of voltages printed on the item or its plug (such as "110–220"), it'll work in Europe. Otherwise, you can buy a converter separately in the US (about $20).

Discounts: While discounts are not listed in this book, seniors (age 60 and over), students with International Student Identification Cards, teachers with proper identification, and youths under 18 often get discounts—but you have to ask. To get a teacher or student ID card, visit www.statravel.com or www.isic.org.

News: Americans keep in touch via the *International Herald Tribune* (published almost daily throughout Europe and online at

INTRODUCTION

Where Do I Find Information On...?

Credit Card Theft   See page 14.
Packing Light   See the packing list on page 627.
Phoning   See page 598.
Language   See page 629.
Making Hotel Reservations   See page 21.
Tipping   See page 14.
Tourist Information Offices See page 597.
Updates to This Book   See www.ricksteves.com/update

www.iht.com). Other newsy sites are http://news.bbc.co.uk and www.europeantimes.com. Every Tuesday, the European editions of *Time* and *Newsweek* hit the stands with articles of particular interest to travelers in Europe. Sports addicts can get their daily fix online or from *USA Today*. Many hotels have CNN or BBC television channels.

Money

This section offers advice on getting cash, using credit and debit cards, dealing with lost or stolen cards, and tipping.

Cash from ATMs

Throughout Germany, cash machines (ATMs) are the standard way for travelers to get local currency. Bring plastic—credit and/or debit cards. It's smart to bring two cards, in case one gets demagnetized or eaten by a temperamental machine. As an emergency backup, bring several hundred dollars in hard cash (in $20 bills rather than hard-to-exchange $100 bills).

Avoid using currency exchange booths (lousy rates and/or outrageous fees); if you have foreign currency to exchange, take it to a bank. Don't use traveler's checks—they're a waste of time (long waits at slow banks) and a waste of money in fees.

You'll find cash machines all over Germany, always open and providing quick transactions. To withdraw money, you'll need a debit card (ideally with a Visa or MasterCard logo for maximum usability), plus a PIN code. Know your PIN code in numbers; there are only numbers—no letters—on European keypads.

Before you go, verify with your bank that your card will work overseas, and alert them that you'll be making withdrawals in Europe; otherwise, the bank may not approve transactions if it perceives unusual spending patterns. (Your credit-card company may do the same thing—let them know your travel plans, too.)

Exchange Rate

1 euro (€) = about $1.40

To convert prices in euros to dollars, add about 40 percent: €20 = about $28, €50 = about $70. (To get the latest rate and print a cheat sheet, see www.oanda.com.) Just like the dollar, the euro is broken down into 100 cents. You'll find coins ranging from 1 cent to 2 euros, and bills from 5 euros to 500 euros.

So that €65 German cuckoo clock is about $90.

Also ask about international transaction fees; see "Credit and Debit Cards," below.

The German word for "cash machine" is *Geldautomat* (*Bankomat* in Austria). When using a cash machine, try to take out large sums of money to reduce your per-transaction bank fees. If the machine refuses your request, try again and select a smaller amount (some cash machines limit the amount you can withdraw—don't take it personally). If that doesn't work, try a different machine.

To keep your cash safe, use a money belt—a pouch with a strap that you buckle around your waist like a belt, and wear under your clothes. Thieves target tourists. A money belt provides peace of mind, allowing you to carry lots of cash safely. Don't waste time every few days tracking down a cash machine—withdraw a week's worth of money, stuff it in your money belt, and travel!

Credit and Debit Cards

Many shops and restaurants in Germany don't accept plastic, except for the local "EC" cards (a type of debit card with a chip). Those that do take cards more commonly accept Visa and MasterCard than American Express. While many hotels in this book accept credit cards, you'll need local cash for most other purchases (in small bills—break large bills at a bank or larger store). If receipts show your credit-card number, don't toss these thoughtlessly.

Fees: Credit- and debit-card transactions—whether used for purchases or ATM withdrawals—often charge additional, tacked-on "international transaction" fees of up to 3 percent plus $5 per transaction. Note that if you use a credit card for ATM transactions, it's technically a "cash advance" rather than a "withdrawal"—and subject to an additional cash-advance fee.

To avoid unpleasant surprises, call your bank or credit-card company before your trip to ask about these fees. Ask your bank if it has agreements with any German bank for lower withdrawal fees. If the fees are too high, consider getting a card just for your trip: Capital One (www.capitalone.com) and most credit unions have low-to-no international transaction fees.

If merchants offer to convert your purchase price into dollars (called dynamic currency conversion, or "DCC"), refuse this "service." You'll pay even more in fees for the expensive convenience of seeing your charge in dollars.

Damage Control for Lost Cards

If you lose your credit, debit, or ATM card, you can stop people from using it by reporting the loss immediately to the respective global customer-assistance centers. Call these 24-hour US numbers collect: Visa (410/581-9994), MasterCard (636/722-7111), and American Express (623/492-8427).

At a minimum, you'll need to know the name of the financial institution that issued you the card, along with the type of card (classic, platinum, or whatever). Providing the following information will allow for a quicker cancellation of your missing card: full card number, whether you are the primary or secondary cardholder, the cardholder's name exactly as printed on the card, billing address, home phone number, circumstances of the loss or theft, and identification verification (your birth date, your mother's maiden name, or your Social Security number—memorize this, don't carry a copy). If you are the secondary cardholder, you'll also need to provide the primary cardholder's identification-verification details. You can generally receive a temporary card within two or three business days in Europe.

If you promptly report your card lost or stolen, you typically won't be responsible for any unauthorized transactions on your account, although many banks charge a liability fee of $50.

Tipping

Tipping in Germany isn't as automatic and generous as it is in the US, but for special service, tips are appreciated, if not expected. As in the US, the proper amount depends on your resources, tipping philosophy, and the circumstance, but some general guidelines apply.

Restaurants: Tipping is an issue only at restaurants that have table service. If you order your food at a counter, don't tip.

At German restaurants that have a wait staff, a service charge is generally included in the bill, although it's common to round up after a good meal (usually 5–10 percent; so, for an €18.50 meal, pay €20). Give the tip directly to your server. Rather than leaving coins, Germans usually pay with paper, saying how much they'd like the bill to be. For example, for an €8.10 meal, hand over a €20 bill and say *"Neun Euro"*—"Nine euros"—to include a €0.90 tip and get €11 change.

Taxis: To tip the cabbie, round up. For a typical ride, round up about 5–10 percent (to pay a €4.50 fare, give €5; for a €28 fare, give €30). If the cabbie hauls your bags and zips you to the airport to help you catch your flight, you might want to toss in a little more. But if you feel like you're being driven in circles or otherwise ripped off, skip the tip.

Special Services: It's thoughtful to tip a couple of euros to someone who shows you a special sight and who is paid in no other way. Tour guides at public sights often hold out their hands for tips after they give their spiel; if I've already paid for the tour, I don't tip extra unless they've really impressed me (€1–2). At hotels, porters expect a euro for each bag they carry (another reason to pack light). Leaving the maid a euro per overnight at the end of your stay is a nice touch. In general, if someone in the service industry does a super job for you, a tip of a couple of euros is appropriate... but not required.

When in doubt, ask. If you're not sure whether (or how much) to tip for a service, ask your hotelier or the TI; they'll fill you in on how it's done on their turf.

Getting a VAT Refund

Wrapped into the purchase price of your German souvenirs is a Value-Added Tax (VAT) of 19 percent. If you make a purchase of more than a certain amount (€25 in Germany) at a store that participates in the VAT-refund scheme, you're entitled to get most of that tax back. (An exception is if the merchant ships the purchase to your non-European home—in that case, they're not even required to charge VAT.) Getting your refund is usually straightforward and, if you buy a substantial amount of souvenirs, well worth the hassle. You'll need to:

Get the paperwork. Have the merchant completely fill out the necessary refund document, called a "Tax-Free Shopping Cheque." You might be asked for your passport at the store.

Get your stamp at the border or airport. Process your cheque(s) at your last stop in the EU (e.g., at the airport) with the customs agent who deals with VAT refunds. It's best to keep your purchases in your carry-on for viewing, but if they're too large or dangerous (such as knives) to carry on, track down the proper customs agent to inspect them before you check your bag. You're not supposed to use your purchased goods before you leave. If you show up at customs wearing your new lederhosen, officials might look the other way—or deny you a refund.

Collect your refund. You'll need to return your stamped document to the retailer or its representative. Many merchants work with a service, such as Global Refund (www.globalrefund.com) or Premier Tax Free (www.premiertaxfree.com), which have offices at major airports, ports, or border crossings. These services, which extract a 4 percent fee, can refund your money immediately in your currency of choice or credit your card (within two billing cycles). If the retailer handles VAT refunds directly, it's up to you to contact the merchant for your refund. You can mail the documents from home, or quicker, from your point of departure (using a stamped, addressed envelope you've prepared or one that's been provided by the merchant). You'll then have to wait—it could take months.

Customs for American Shoppers

You are allowed to take home $800 worth of items per person duty-free, once every 30 days. The next $1,000 is taxed at a flat 3 percent. After that, you pay the individual item's duty rate. You can also bring in duty-free a liter of alcohol (slightly more than a standard-size bottle of wine; you must be at least 21), 200 cigarettes, and up to 100 non-Cuban cigars. You may take home vacuum-packed cheeses; dried herbs, spices, or mushrooms; and canned fruits or vegetables, including jams and vegetable spreads. Baked goods, candy, chocolate, oil, vinegar, mustard, and honey are OK. Fresh fruits or vegetables are not. Meats, even if canned, are generally not allowed. Remember that you'll need to carefully pack any bottles of wine and other liquid-containing items in your checked luggage, due to the three-ounce limit on liquids in carry-on baggage. To check customs rules and duty rates before you go, visit www.cbp.gov, and click on "Travel," then "Know Before You Go."

Sightseeing

Sightseeing can be hard work. Use these tips to make your visits to Germany's finest sights meaningful, fun, efficient, and painless.

Plan Ahead

Set up an itinerary that allows you to fit in all your must-see sights. For a one-stop look at opening hours in the bigger cities, see the "At a Glance" sidebars. Most sights keep stable hours, but you can easily confirm the latest by checking their website or asking at the local TI.

Don't put off visiting a must-see sight—you never know when a place will close unexpectedly for a holiday, strike, or restoration. If you'll be visiting during a holiday, find out if a particular sight will be open by phoning ahead or visiting its website.

When possible, visit major sights first thing (when your energy is best) and save other activities for the afternoon. Hit the highlights first, then go back to other things if you have the stamina and time.

Going at the right time can also help you avoid crowds. This book offers tips on specific sights, such as Neuschwanstein Castle. Make reservations when possible, or try visiting very early, at lunch, or very late. Evening visits are usually peaceful, with fewer crowds.

Study up. To get the most out of the self-guided walks and sight descriptions in this book, read them before your visit.

In some cities, you can buy a combo-ticket for discounted entry to two or more sights. I've noted these in this book. If you'll be visiting several castles in Bavaria—including two of "Mad" King Ludwig's castles, and those in Munich, Würzburg, Nürnberg, and more—look into the **Bavarian Castles Pass,** which can save you a lot of money (14 days, €20/1 person, €36/2 adults plus children; described on page 98).

At Sights

All sights have rules, and if you know about these in advance, they're no big deal.

At churches—which often offer interesting art (usually free) and a cool, welcome seat—a modest dress code (no bare shoulders or shorts) is encouraged.

Some important sights have metal detectors or conduct bag searches that will slow your entry. Major museums and sights require you to check daypacks and coats. They'll be kept safely. If you have something you can't bear to part with, stash it in a pocket or purse. To avoid checking a small backpack, carry it under your arm like a purse as you enter. From a guard's point of view, a backpack is generally a problem, while a purse is not.

Photography is sometimes banned at major sights. Look for signs or ask. If cameras are allowed, video cameras are as well, but flashes or tripods usually are not. Flashes damage oil paintings and distract others in the room. Even without a flash, a handheld camera will take a decent picture (or you can buy postcards or posters at the museum bookstore).

Museums sometimes have special exhibits in addition to their permanent collection. Some exhibits are included in the entry price; others come at an extra cost (which you may have to pay even if you don't want to see the exhibit).

Many sights rent audioguides, which generally offer excellent recorded descriptions in English (about $7.50). If you bring along your own pair of headphones and a Y-jack, you can sometimes share one audioguide with your travel partner and save money. Guided tours in English are most likely to occur during peak season (some are free, while others can cost up to $12). Tours can range widely in quality.

Expect changes—artwork can be on tour, on loan, out sick, or shifted at the whim of the curator. To adapt, pick up any available free floor plans as you enter. Ask the museum staff if you can't find a particular piece.

Major sights often have an on-site café or cafeteria (usually a good place to rest and have a snack or light meal). The WCs at many sights are free and clean. Many places sell postcards that highlight their attractions. Before you leave, scan the postcards and thumb through the biggest guidebook (or skim its index) to be sure you haven't overlooked something that you'd like to see.

Most sights stop admitting people 30–60 minutes before closing time, and some rooms close early (often 45 minutes before the actual closing time). Guards usher people out, so don't save the best for last.

Every sight or museum offers more than what is covered in this book. Use the information in this book as an introduction—not the final word.

Sleeping

I favor accommodations (and restaurants) handy to your sight-seeing activities. Rather than list hotels scattered throughout a city, I choose two or three favorite neighborhoods and recommend the best accommodations values in each, from $20 bunk beds to fancy-for-my-book $250 doubles.

While accommodations in Germany are fairly expensive, they are normally very comfortable and come with breakfast. Plan on spending $110–150 per hotel double in big cities, and $60–90 in towns and in private homes.

A triple is much cheaper than a double and a single. Single travelers save money at B&Bs (called *Pension*s in Germany), where the single price is often little more than half the double-room price. Hotels, in contrast, charge almost as much for a single room as for a double. Hostels and dorms always charge per person. Especially in private homes, where the boss changes the sheets, people staying several nights are most desirable. One-night stays are sometimes charged extra.

I look for places that are friendly; clean; a good value; located in a central, safe, quiet neighborhood; English-speaking; and not mentioned in other guidebooks. I'm more impressed by a handy location and a fun-loving philosophy than hair dryers and shoe-shine machines.

I also like local character and simple facilities that don't cater to American "needs." Obviously, a place meeting every criterion is rare, and all of my recommendations fall short of perfection—sometimes miserably. But I've listed the best values for each price category, given the above criteria. The very best values are family-run places with showers down the hall and no elevator.

Sleep Code

(€1 = about $1.40, country code: 49)
To help you sort easily through these listings, I've divided the rooms into three categories based on the price for a standard double room with bath:

$$$ **Higher Priced**
$$ **Moderately Priced**
$ **Lower Priced**

To give maximum information in a minimum of space, I use the following code to describe the accommodations. Prices listed are per room, not per person.

When a price range is given for a type of room (such as double rooms listing for €100-150), it means the price fluctuates with the season, size of room, or length of stay.

S = Single room (or price for one person in a double).
D = Double or twin. Double beds are usually big enough for nonromantic couples.
T = Triple (generally a double bed with a single).
Q = Quad (usually two double beds).
b = Private bathroom with toilet and shower or tub.
s = Private shower or tub only (the toilet is down the hall).

According to this code, a couple staying at a "Db-€140" hotel would pay a total of €140 (about $200) for a double room with a private bathroom. Unless otherwise noted, breakfast is included, hotel staff speaks basic English, and credit cards are accepted.

If I mention "Internet access" in a listing, there's a public terminal in the lobby for guests to use. If I say "Wi-Fi," you can generally access it in your room (usually for free), but only if you have your own laptop.

You should find most prices listed in this book to be good through 2010 (except during major holidays and festivals—see page 622). Prices can soften off-season, for stays of two nights or longer, or for payment in cash (rather than by credit card). Always mention that you found the place through this book— many of the accommodations listed offer special deals to my readers.

During these times of economic uncertainty, many hotels will likely be discounting deeply to snare what customers they can. Try to avoid paying rack rates. If you email several places and ask for their best prices, you'll find some eager to discount and others more passive. This can save you big bucks—with prices potentially far below those listed in this guidebook.

INTRODUCTION

Unless I note otherwise, the cost of a room includes breakfast (sometimes continental, but more often an all-you-can-eat buffet). The price is usually posted in the room. Before accepting, confirm your understanding of the complete price.

Germans depend heavily on expensive imported fuel and are very aware of their energy use. You'll endear yourself to your hosts if you turn off lights when you leave and avoid excessively long showers. Air-conditioning is rare (and rarely needed), but if you're here during a heat spell, ask to borrow a fan.

Types of Accommodations

B&Bs *(Pensions)*

Compared to hotels, bed-and-breakfast places *(Pensions)* give you double the cultural intimacy for half the price. While you may lose some of the conveniences of a hotel—such as lounges, in-room phones, daily bed-sheet changes, and credit-card payments—I happily make the trade-off for the lower rates and personal touches. If you have a reasonable but limited budget, skip hotels and go the *Pension* way.

Throughout Germany, people rent out rooms *(Zimmer)* in their homes to travelers. Look for *Zimmer Frei* or *Privatzimmer* signs. These are very common in areas popular with travelers (such as Germany's Rhine, Romantic Road, and southern Bavaria, and Austria's Tirol and Salzburg). In Germany, signs will clearly indicate whether they have available rooms (green) or not (orange). Booking direct saves both you and your host the cut the TI takes.

You'll get your own key to a private room that's clean, comfortable, and simple, though usually homey. Some B&Bs are like mini-hotels, with a separate entrance and several rooms, each with a private bath. Other B&Bs are family homes with spare bedrooms (the rooms sometimes lack sinks, but you have free access to the bathroom and shower in the home). Most B&Bs include a hearty breakfast.

Pensions and *Gasthofs* are similarly priced small, family-run hotels. Don't confuse B&Bs with the German *Ferienwohnung*, which is a self-catering apartment rented out by the week or fortnight.

Hostels

Germany has a wonderful network of youth hostels *(Jugendherberge)*. Established, "official" hostels that are members of Hostelling International are marked with either a triangular logo or a logo showing a tree next to a house. They tend to have a family atmosphere and attract student groups. Generally, travelers without a membership card ($28 per year, sold at hostels in most US cities or online at www.hiusa.org, US tel. 202/783-6161) are admitted for an extra $5. So-called "independent" hostels, mostly in big cities, cater more to the college and young adult crowd.

Hostels are open to members of all ages (though some Bavarian hostels place some restrictions or charge slightly higher rates for older travelers). Hostel bunks usually cost $20–30 per night (cheaper for those under 27). Some hostels include sheets, but others charge about $4 per sheet if you don't have your own. Many hostels serve good, cheap meals and/or provide kitchen facilities. While many hostels have a few doubles or family rooms available upon request for a little extra money, plan on gender-segregated dorms with 4 to 20 beds per room. Hostels can be idyllic and peaceful, but school groups can raise the rafters. These groups are most common on summer weekends and on school-year weekdays. I like small hostels best. While many hostels may say over the telephone that they're full, most hold a few beds for people who drop in, or they can direct you to budget accommodations nearby.

Phoning

To make international calls to Germany so you can line up hotel reservations, you'll need to know that the country code for Germany is 49. To call from the US or Canada to Germany, dial 011-49-local number (drop the initial 0 from the local number). For more information on telephoning, see "Communicating" in the appendix.

Making Reservations

Given the quality of the places I've found for this book, I'd recommend that you reserve your rooms in advance, particularly if you'll be traveling during peak season. Book several weeks ahead, or as soon as you've pinned down your travel dates. Note that some holidays jam things up and merit your making reservations far in advance (see "Major Holidays and Weekends" on page 10). Just like at home, holidays that fall on a Monday, Thursday, or Friday can turn the weekend into a long holiday, so book the entire weekend well in advance.

Requesting a Reservation: To make a reservation, contact hotels and B&Bs directly by email, phone, or fax. Email is the clearest and most economical way to make a reservation; many have secure online reservation forms and can instantly inform you of availability and any special deals. But be sure you use the hotel's official site and not a booking agency's site—otherwise you may pay higher rates than you should. If phoning from the US, be mindful of time zones (see page 11). Most hoteliers listed are accustomed to English-only speakers.

The hotelier wants to know these key pieces of information (also included in the sample request form on page 628):

- number and type of rooms
- number of nights
- date of arrival
- date of departure
- any special needs (e.g., bathroom in the room or down the hall, twin beds vs. double bed, air-conditioning, quiet, view, ground floor, etc.)

When you request a room, use the European style for writing dates: day/month/year. For example, for a two-night stay in July, I would request "2 nights, arrive 16/07/10, depart 18/07/10." (Consider carefully how long you'll stay; don't just assume you can tack on extra days once you arrive.)

If you don't get a reply to your email or fax, it usually means the hotel is already fully booked (but you can try sending the message again, or call to follow up).

Confirming a Reservation: If the hotel's response includes its room availability and rates, it's not a confirmation. You must tell them that you want that room at the given rate. Many hoteliers will request your credit-card number for a one-night deposit to hold the room. While you can email your credit-card information (I do), it's safer to share that personal info via phone call, fax, two successive emails, or secure online reservation form (if the hotel has one on its website).

Canceling a Reservation: If you must cancel your reservation, it's courteous to do so with as much advance notice as possible—at least three days. Simply make a quick phone call or send an email. Family-run hotels and B&Bs lose money if they turn away customers while holding a room for someone who doesn't show up. Understandably, many hotels bill no-shows for one night.

Hotels in larger cities such as Munich sometimes have strict cancellation policies. For example, you might lose a deposit if you cancel within two weeks of your reserved stay, or you might be billed for the entire visit if you leave early. Ask about cancellation policies before you book.

If canceling via email, request confirmation that your cancellation was received to avoid being accidentally billed.

Reconfirm Your Reservation: Always call to reconfirm your room reservation a day or two in advance from the road. Smaller hotels and *Pensions* appreciate knowing your time of arrival. If you'll be arriving after 17:00, be sure to let your hotelier know. On the small chance that a hotel loses track of your reservation, bring along a hard copy of your emailed or faxed confirmation. Don't have the TI reconfirm rooms for you; they'll take a commission.

Reserving Rooms as You Travel: If you enjoy having a flexible itinerary, you can make reservations as you travel, calling hotels or *Pensions* a few days to a week before your visit. If you prefer the flexibility of traveling without any reservations at all, you'll have greater success snaring rooms if you arrive at your destination early in the day. When you anticipate crowds (weekends are worst), call hotels at about 9:00 on the day you plan to arrive, when the hotel clerk knows who'll be checking out and just which rooms will be available.

Eating

Germanic cuisine is heavy, hearty, and—by European standards—inexpensive. Though it's tasty, it can get monotonous unless you

look beyond the schnitzel and wurst. Be adventurous. Each region has its specialties, which are often good values. Order house specials whenever possible.

Most German hotels and *Pensions* include breakfast in the room price, and pride themselves on laying out an attractive buffet spread. Expect fresh-baked bread and rolls, cereal, yogurt, cold cuts, cheese, fruit, and pastries. Even if you're not a big breakfast eater, take advantage of the buffet to fortify yourself for a day of sightseeing. At lunchtime, many Germans grab a sandwich (around €2–2.50) and perhaps a pastry (€1–1.50) from one of the ubiquitous bakeries, which often have tables to sit at (but not table service). Department-store cafeterias are common and handy, but not always cheap. Many restaurants offer inexpensive hot-lunch specials.

There are many options beyond restaurants. For basic, stick-to-the-ribs meals—and plenty of beer—look for a beer hall (*Bräuhaus*) or beer garden (*Biergarten*). *Gasthaus, Gasthof, Gaststätte,* and *Gaststube* all loosely describe an informal, inn-type eatery. A *Kneipe* is a bar, and a *Keller* (or *Ratskeller*) is a restaurant or tavern located in a cellar, usually serving traditional food. A *Schnell Imbiss* is a small fast-food take-away stand.

Most eateries have menus tacked onto their front doors, with an English menu inside. If you see a *Stammtisch* sign hanging over a table at a restaurant or pub, it means that it's reserved for regulars—don't sit here unless invited. Once you're seated, take your time—only a rude waiter will rush you. Good service is relaxed (slow to an American).

Note that restaurants may charge you for any bread or pretzels you eat from the basket on the table; ask the waiter to take it away if you don't want it. For smaller portions, order from the *kleine Hunger* (small hunger) section of the menu. To wish others "Happy eating!" offer a cheery *"Guten Appetit!"* When you want the bill, say, *"Zahlen* (TSAH-lenn), *bitte* (please)." For tips on tipping, see page 14.

German Cuisine

Germans are health-conscious, and quite passionate about choosing organic *(Bio)* products. Not only do they eat *Bio* fruits and vegetables, but also *Bio* bread, ice cream, and schnitzel. You'll often see footnotes on restaurant menus marking which dishes have additives or any other artificial ingredients. Despite Germans' healthy ways, many starchy, high-fat, high-calorie traditional foods remain staples of the German diet.

Traditional Fare

The classic dish is sausage—hundreds of varieties of *Bratwurst, Weisswurst,* and other types of wurst are served with sauerkraut as an excuse for a vegetable. The generic term *Bratwurst* means "grilled sausage," but there are many regional variations. For example, *Nürnberger* bratwurst are short and spicy, and usually browned and served over sauerkraut or with horseradish for lunch or dinner. The boiled *Weisswurst* (white sausage) is traditionally consumed before noon, with sweet mustard and a fresh soft pretzel; make sure you peel off the casing before eating it.

Another ubiquitous meat dish is schnitzel. It's traditionally made with veal, but you'll also find pork schnitzel, which is cheaper. If a dish ends in *-braten*, it means it has been roasted. *Sauerbraten* is a marinated and roasted cut of beef (sometimes pork), typically served with red cabbage and potato dumplings. *Geschnetzeltes* isn't schnitzel, but rather meat that's been diced and cooked in a cream sauce. Many traditional eateries serve some kind of meat on the bone, such as pork knuckle *(Schweinshaxe)* or shoulder, which has been roasted tender and goes down well with a big mug of beer. The fish and venison here are also good.

Besides bread and potatoes (boiled, fried, or grilled), typical starches include *Spätzle* (little round noodles made from egg dough scraped through a wide-holed sieve; often served with melted cheese and fried onions as a meal in itself called *Käsespätzle*); various kinds of *Knödel* (baseball-sized dumplings, usually made from potatoes but also from bread); *Schupfnudeln* (stubby, diamond-shaped potato noodles); and *Kartoffelsalat* (potato salad).

Germans make excellent salads, and most menus feature big, varied, dinner-size salad plates. If you're visiting in May or June, look for special asparagus menus, created to ensure the nation eats up the yearly crop. *Spargel* (giant white asparagus) is a must in early summer.

A good dish to try is the southwestern specialty *Maultaschen* ("mouth pockets"), a Swabian ravioli with meat smuggled inside a big piece of pasta. Some say it was invented by Catholics as a culinary trick to eat meat when it wasn't allowed. The German answer to pizza is *Flammkuchen,* with a thin, yeastless dough.

Ethnic Food

Ethnic restaurants provide a welcome break from Germanic fare. Italian, Turkish, Greek, and Asian food are generally good values, and Asian restaurants tend to serve inexpensive lunches. Originally from Turkey, *Döner Kebab* (sliced meat and vegetables served in pita bread) has become a classic takeout meal for Germans of all stripes (€3–3.50 at any time of day). Turkish cafés abound, even in small towns. Take a moment to study the menu; beyond the basic *Döner,* you can get a *Döner Teller* (on a plate instead of in bread), a *Döner Dürüm* (in a thin flatbread wrap, also called *Yufka*), falafel (chickpea croquettes), "Turkish pizzas," and much more.

Snacks and Sweets

Make sure to visit a bakery to browse the selection of fresh pastries and cakes. Pretzels (*Breze* or *Brez'n*), either plain or buttered, make for an inexpensive snack (the brown crust comes from dunking them in boiling water with baking soda). Gummi Bears are local gumdrops with a cult following (look for the Haribo brand). Ice-cream stores, often run by Italian immigrants, abound. Many Germans sit down to enjoy their ice cream, ordering fancy sundaes in big glass bowls.

Beverages

Germany has excellent wine and beer. Sampling some helps create fond memories of your trip. The best-known white wines are from the Rhine and Mosel, and there are some good reds, especially from the south. You can order wine by the glass or sometimes by the *Viertel* (quarter-liter, or 8 oz.). Just ask for "*Ein Viertel Weisswein* (white wine) or *Rotwein* (red wine), *bitte.*" Order your *Weisswein süss* (sweet), *halb trocken* (medium), or *trocken* (dry). Many hotels serve the inexpensive *Sekt,* or German champagne, at breakfast. *Weinschorle* is a spritzer—white wine pepped up with a little sparkling water.

The average German drinks 40 gallons of beer a year, and has a tremendous variety to choose from. *Dunkles* is dark, *helles* or *Lager* is light, *Flaschenbier* is bottled, and *vom Fass* is on tap. *Pils* is barley-based; *Weizen, Hefeweizen,* or *Weissbier* is yeasty and wheat-based; *Bock* (traditionally brewed by monks) has a higher alcohol content; and *Malzbier* is the malted soft drink that children learn with. When you order beer, ask for *eine Halbe* (a half-liter, not always available), or *eine Mass* (a whole liter, or about a quart). *Radler* is half beer and half lemon soda (specify *helles* or *dunkles Radler,*

> ## How Was Your Trip?
>
> Were your travels fun, smooth, and meaningful? If you'd like to share your tips, concerns, and discoveries, please fill out the survey at www.ricksteves.com/feedback. I value your feedback. Thanks in advance—it helps a lot.

depending on whether you prefer light or dark beer); *Colaweizen* is a mixture of Coke and wheat-based beer.

Waiters aren't exactly eager to bring you *Leitungswasser* (tap water), preferring that you buy *Mineralwasser* (*mit/ohne Gas*, with/ without carbonation). Popular soft drinks include *Apfelschorle* (half apple juice, half sparkling water) and *Spezi* (cola and orange soda). Menus list drink sizes by the tenth of a liter, or deciliter (dl): 0.2 liters is a small glass, and 0.4 or 0.5 is a larger one. If you buy bottled drinks from a store, you'll have to pay a deposit *(Pfand),* which gets refunded if you bring the bottle back. The deposit amount is listed in small print on the shelf's price label.

Traveling as a Temporary Local

We travel all the way to Europe to enjoy differences—to become temporary locals. You'll experience frustrations. Certain truths that we find "God-given" or "self-evident," such as cold beer, ice in drinks, bottomless cups of coffee, hot showers, and bigger being better, are suddenly not so true. One of the benefits of travel is the eye-opening realization that there are logical, civil, and even better alternatives.

Americans are enjoying a surge in popularity in Europe these days. But if there is a negative aspect to the image Germans have of Americans, it's that we are big, loud, aggressive, impolite, rich, superficially friendly, and a bit naive.

Americans tend to be noisy in public places, such as restaurants and trains. My German friends place a high value on speaking quietly in these same places. Listen while on the bus or in a restaurant—the place can be packed, but the decibel level is low. Try to remember this nuance, and soften your speaking voice as a way of respecting their culture.

While Germans look bemusedly at some of our Yankee excesses—and worriedly at others—they nearly always afford us individual travelers all the warmth we deserve. Judging from all the happy feedback I receive from travelers who have used this book, it's safe to assume you'll enjoy a great, affordable vacation— with the finesse of an independent, experienced traveler.

Thanks, and *gute Reise!*

Back Door Travel Philosophy
From *Rick Steves' Europe Through the Back Door*

Travel is intensified living—maximum thrills per minute and one of the last great sources of legal adventure. Travel is freedom. It's recess, and we need it.

Experiencing the real Europe requires catching it by surprise, going casual..."Through the Back Door."

Affording travel is a matter of priorities. (Make do with the old car.) You can travel—simply, safely, and comfortably—anywhere in Europe for $120 a day plus transportation costs (allow more for bigger cities). In many ways, spending more money only builds a thicker wall between you and what you came to see. Europe is a cultural carnival, and, time after time, you'll find that its best acts are free and the best seats are the cheap ones.

A tight budget forces you to travel close to the ground, meeting and communicating with the people, not relying on service with a purchased smile. Never sacrifice sleep, nutrition, safety, or cleanliness in the name of budget. Simply enjoy the local-style alternatives to expensive hotels and restaurants.

Connecting with people carbonates your experience. Extroverts have more fun. If your trip is low on magic moments, kick yourself and make things happen. If you don't enjoy a place, maybe you don't know enough about it. Seek the truth. Recognize tourist traps. Give a culture the benefit of your open mind. See things as different but not better or worse. Any culture has much to share.

Of course, travel, like the world, is a series of hills and valleys. Be fanatically positive and militantly optimistic. If something's not to your liking, change your liking.

Travel can make you a happier American as well as a citizen of the world. Our Earth is home to six and a half billion equally important people. It's humbling to travel and find that people don't have the "American Dream"—they have their own dreams. Europeans like us, but, with all due respect, they wouldn't trade passports.

Thoughtful travel engages us with the world. In tough economic times, it reminds us what is truly important. By broadening perspectives, travel teaches new ways to measure quality of life.

Globe-trotting destroys ethnocentricity, helping you understand and appreciate different cultures. Rather than fear the diversity on this planet, celebrate it. Among your prized souvenirs will be the strands of different cultures you choose to knit into your own character. The world is a cultural yarn shop, and Back Door travelers are weaving the ultimate tapestry. Join in!

MUNICH

München

Munich, Germany's most livable and "yuppie" city, is also one of its most historic, artistic, and entertaining. It's big and growing, with a population of 1.5 million. Until 1871, it was the capital of an independent Bavaria. Its imperial palaces, jewels, and grand boulevards constantly remind visitors that this was once a political and cultural powerhouse. Meanwhile, the concentration camp in nearby Dachau reminds us that 80 years ago it provided a springboard for Nazism. Today, Munich is a city of the 21st century, but still respects its past—in 2008, the city celebrated its 850th birthday.

Orient yourself in Munich's old center with its colorful pedestrian mall. Immerse yourself in the city's art and history—crown jewels, Baroque theater, Wittelsbach palaces, great paintings, and beautiful parks. Spend your Munich evenings in a frothy beer hall or outdoor *Biergarten*, prying big pretzels from buxom, no-nonsense beer maids amidst an oompah, bunny-hopping, and belching Bavarian atmosphere.

Planning Your Time

Munich is worth two days, including a half-day side-trip to Dachau. If necessary, its essence can be captured in a day (walk the center, tour a palace and a museum, and enjoy a beer-filled evening). Those in a hurry and without a car can see "Mad" King Ludwig's castles (covered in the Bavaria and Tirol chapter) as a day-trip tour from Munich. Even Austria's Salzburg (1.5–2 hours one-way by train) is within day-tripping distance.

Orientation to Munich

(area code: 089)

The tourist's Munich is circled by a ring road (site of the old town wall) marked by four old gates: Karlstor, also known as Stachus (near the main train station—the Hauptbahnhof); Sendlinger Tor; Isartor (near the river); and Odeonsplatz (no surviving gate, near the palace). Marienplatz marks the city's center. A great pedestrian-only zone (Kaufingerstrasse and Neuhauser Strasse) cuts this circle in half, running neatly from Karlstor and the train station through Marienplatz to Isartor. Orient yourself along this east-west axis. Ninety percent of the sights and hotels I recommend are within a 20-minute walk of Marienplatz and each other.

Despite its large population, Munich feels small. This big-city elegance is possible because of a law that no building can be taller than the church spires. Despite ongoing debate about changing this policy, there are still no skyscrapers in downtown Munich.

Tourist Information

Munich has two outlets for tourist information: the official TIs, and the handy travel agency called EurAide.

Official TIs

Munich has two helpful city-run TIs (www.muenchen.de). One is in front of the **main train station** (with your back to the tracks, walk through the central hall, step outside, and turn right; Mon–Sat 9:00–20:00, Sun 10:00–18:00, tel. 089/2339-6500). The other TI is on Munich's main square, **Marienplatz,** below the glockenspiel (Mon–Fri 10:00–20:00, Sat 10:00–16:00, Sun 10:00–14:00). If the line at the TI is bad, go to EurAide (described on next page).

At either TI, pick up brochures and a city map (€0.30, often free in hotel lobbies) and confirm your sightseeing plans. Consider the *Monatsprogramm* (€1.65, German-language list of sights and events calendar) and the free, twice-monthly magazine *In München* (in German, lists all movies and entertainment in town). The TI can book you a room (you'll pay about 10 percent here, then pay the rest at the hotel), but you'll get a better value by contacting my recommended hotels directly. If you're interested in a Gray Line tour of the city or to nearby castles, don't buy your ticket at the TI; instead, you can get discounted tickets for these same tours at EurAide.

The **City Tour Card,** which covers public transportation and gives stingy discounts at minor sights, is a bad deal (€10/1 day, €19/3 days, available at TIs or EurAide, validate before using). Two or more people traveling on a Munich "partner" all-day transit pass blow this deal out of the water (for details, see "Getting Around Munich," later).

The 14-day **Bavarian Castles Pass** covers admission to Munich's Residenz and Nymphenburg Palace Complex (includes the Amalienburg Palace), as well as other castles and palaces in Bavaria (for a partial list, see page 98; €20, €36 family/partner pass, annual pass also available, sold at participating sights, www.schloesser.bayern.de). For avid castle-goers, this is a deal: Two people will save €2 with a family/partner pass even if only visiting the two Munich sights.

EurAide

The hardworking, eager-to-help EurAide office is a godsend for Eurailers and budget travelers. Alan Wissenberg and his EurAide staff can answer your train-travel and accommodations questions in clear American English. Paid by the German rail company to

help you design your train travels, EurAide makes reservations and sells tickets, *couchettes,* and sleepers for the train at the same price you'd pay at the station ticket windows. You can find EurAide in one of two locations, both inside the main train station. In the morning, visit their office (with your back to track 24, walk straight down the hall and turn right, following the *EurAide* sign—see map on page 83; this office open March–April Mon–Fri 9:30–12:30, closed Sat–Sun; May–July Mon–Sat 8:30–12:30, closed Sun; Aug–Dec Mon–Fri 8:30–12:30, closed Sat–Sun; closed Jan–Feb). Most afternoons, they staff a desk in the travel center next door (March–Dec 15:30–18:00, closed Jan–Feb). EurAide sells a €0.50 city map and offers a free, information-packed newsletter, *The Inside Track* (described on page 33, always available in a rack at their door; tel. 089/593-889, www.euraide.com/ricksteves).

EurAide helps 500 visitors per day in the summer and can get really busy; do your homework and have a list of questions ready. Chances are that your questions are already answered in *The Inside Track* newsletter—scan it first.

EurAide also sells tickets for city walking tours and Gray Line city tours, as well as for tours to Neuschwanstein and Linderhof castles (both described later, under "Tours in Munich"). They offer a discount on these tickets with this book in 2010. They also sell discounted €30 tickets for the Munich-to-Rothenburg segment of the Romantic Road bus (for more on this bus, see the end of this chapter).

MUNICH

Arrival in Munich

By Train: Munich's main train station (München Hauptbahnhof) is a sight in itself—one of those places that can turn a homebody into a fancy-free vagabond.

Clean, high-tech **public toilets** are downstairs near track 26 (€0.80). For a quick rest stop, Burger King's toilets (upstairs, €0.50) are as pleasant and accessible as its hamburgers.

Check out the bright and modern **food court** opposite track 14. For a quick train picnic, I shop at **Yorma's,** by track 26 and outside the station, next to the TI.

You'll find two **tourist information** offices (the city TI and EurAide) and **lockers** (€3–5, by track 26). **Car-rental agencies** are up the steps opposite track 21. A quiet, non-smoking **waiting room** *(Warteraum)* is open to anybody (across from track 23 and up the escalator), but the nearby, plush **DB Lounge** is only for those with a first-class ticket issued by Deutsche Bahn (railpasses don't get you in). The **k presse + buch** shop (across from track 23) is great for English-language books, newspapers, and magazines. **Radius Tours** (at track 32) rents bikes, organizes tours, and provides confused visitors with information.

Subway lines, trams, and buses connect the station to the rest of the city (though many of my recommended hotels are within walking distance of the station). If you get lost in the underground maze of subway corridors while you're simply trying to get to the train station, follow the signs for *DB* (Deutsche Bahn) to surface successfully. Watch out for the hallways with blue ticket-stamping machines in the middle—these lead to the subway, where you could be fined if nabbed without a validated ticket.

By Plane: There are two good ways to connect Munich Airport and downtown Munich: subway and airport bus. (A **taxi** from the airport makes no budgetary sense—it's cheaper to ride public transit into the center, and catch a taxi from there.) You can take an easy 40-minute ride on the S-1 or S-8 **subway,** which each run every 20 minutes between the airport and Marienplatz and the train station (€9.20, or free with a validated and dated railpass). Or hop on the Lufthansa **airport bus,** which links the airport with the main train station (€11, 3/hr, 45 min, buses depart train station 5:10–19:50, buy tickets on bus; buses line up near taxi stands facing Arnulfstrasse—from inside the station, exit near track 26). Airport info: tel. 089/97500, www.munich-airport.de.

Helpful Hints

Museum Hours: Sights closed on Monday include the Alte Pinakothek, Munich City Museum, Jewish Museum, Pinakothek der Moderne, Museum Brandhorst, Glyptothek, Bavarian National Museum, Beer and Oktoberfest Museum, Dachau Concentration Camp, and BMW Museum and Factory. The Neue Pinakothek closes Tuesday. The art galleries are generally open late one night a week. On Sunday, the Pinakotheks, Glyptothek, Museum Brandhorst, and Bavarian National Museum cost just €1 apiece, but you'll pay extra for the usually free audioguides.

Internet Access: There's plenty of online access in Munich. Hole-in-the-wall call centers near the train station and all over town have Internet terminals. **Munich Walk**'s office, a few steps from Isartor, offers Internet access (€2/hr, 15 extra minutes free with this book, daily 9:00–23:00, Thomas-Wimmer-Ring 1—look for *Tourist info* sign, tel. 089/2423-1767).

Bookstore: The German bookstore chain **Hugendubel** runs a good English-language store at Salvatorplatz 2, between Marienplatz and Odeonsplatz (Mon–Sat 10:00–19:00, closed Sun, tel. 01801/484-484).

Pharmacy: Go out the front door of the train station, turn left, and walk a block to the corner of Elisenstrasse and Luisenstrasse (Mon–Fri 8:00–19:00, Sat 9:00–14:00, closed Sun, Elisenstrasse 5, tel. 089/595-444); another one is just below Marienplatz at Im Tal 13 (Mon–Fri 8:00–19:00, Sat 8:30–18:00, closed Sun, tel. 089/292-760).

Laundry: A handy self-service **Waschcenter** is a 10-minute walk from the train station (€7/load, €12 for larger machines, drop-off service for €10–18 depending on load size, daily 7:00–23:00, English instructions, Paul-Heyse-Strasse 21, near intersection with Landwehrstrasse—see map on page 83, tel. 089/531-311).

Bikes and Pedestrians: Signs painted on the sidewalk or blue-and-white street signs show which part of the sidewalk is designated for pedestrians and which is for cyclists. The strip of pathway closest to the street is usually reserved for bikes. Pedestrians wandering into the bike path may hear the cheery ding-ding of a cyclist's bell just before being knocked unconscious.

Taxi: Tel. 089/21610.

Private Driver: Johann Fayoumi is reliable and speaks English (€50/hr, mobile 0174-183-8473, www.firstclasslimousines.de, johannfayoumi@gmail.com).

Car Rental: Several car-rental agencies are located upstairs at the train station, opposite track 21 (open daily, hours vary).

The Inside Track **Train Travelers' Newsletter:** Anyone traveling by train should pick up this wonk-ish yet brilliant quarterly newsletter published by Alan Wissenberg at EurAide (free, always available in a rack by the EurAide door in the train station—described earlier, under "Tourist Information"). You'll find all the tedious but important details on getting to Neuschwanstein, Dachau, Nymphenburg, and Prague; the ins and outs of supplements and reservations necessary for railpass-holders; a daily schedule of various tours in Munich; and (of course) plenty of tips on how to take advantage of EurAide's services.

Need a Toilet? Munich had outdoor urinals until the 1972 Olympics and then decided to beautify the city by doing away with them. What about the people's needs? There's a law: Any place serving beer must admit the public (whether or not they're customers) to use the toilets.

What's with Monaco? People walking around with guidebooks to Monaco aren't lost. "Monaco di Baviera" means "Munich" in *Italiano*.

Getting Around Munich

Much of Munich is walkable. To reach sights away from the city center, use the efficient tram, bus, and subway systems. Taxis are honest and professional, but expensive and generally unnecessary (except perhaps to avoid the time-consuming trip by tram and foot to Nymphenburg Palace).

By Public Transit

Subways are called U-Bahns and S-Bahns (S-Bahns are actually commuter railways that run underground through the city). The U-Bahn mainly runs north–south, while the S-Bahn is generally east–west. All S-Bahn lines converge on the central axis running from the Hauptbahnhof to Marienplatz. Subway lines are numbered (for example, S-3 or U-5). Eurailpasses are good on the S-Bahn (but not the U-Bahn), but if you use a flexipass, it'll cost you a travel day. Trams and buses are more convenient than subways for some destinations, including Nymphenburg Palace.

The entire transit system (subway/bus/tram) works on the same tickets, sold at TIs, at booths in the subway, and at easy-to-use ticket machines marked *MVV* (which take coins and €5 and €10 bills).

A **regular ticket** *(Einzelfahrkarte)* costs €2.30 and is good for three hours in one direction, including changes. For short rides (4 stops max, only two can be on the subway lines), buy the €1.20 *Kurzstrecke* ("short stretch") ticket. The €5 **all-day pass** *(Single Tageskarte)* is a great deal for a single traveler.

For small groups, the €9 **partner all-day pass** *(Partner Tageskarte)* is an even better deal—it covers all public transportation for up to five adults and a dog (two kids count as one adult, so two adults, six kids, and a dog can travel with this ticket). The **XXL** version of this all-day ticket includes the inner "white zone" and the surrounding "green zone," and covers the trip to Dachau concentration camp (€6.70/person, €11.80/partner ticket). For longer stays, consider a **three-day ticket** (€12.30/person, €21/partner ticket for the gang, inner white zone only, does not include transportation to Dachau). All-day and multi-day passes are valid until 6:00 the following morning.

Partner tickets—while seemingly impossibly cheap—are for real. Read it again and do the arithmetic. Even two people traveling together save money, and for groups, it's a real steal. The only catch is you've got to stay together.

Maps of the transit system, available everywhere, help you navigate. To find the right platform, look for the name of the last station in the direction you want to travel. The name of this end-station is posted on trains and signs using the word *Richtung* ("direction" in German).

In Munich, you must stamp all tickets with the date and time prior to using them (for an all-day or multi-day pass, you only have to stamp it the first time you use it). For the subway, punch your ticket in the blue machine *before* going down to the platform. For buses and trams, stamp your ticket once on board. Plainclothes ticket-checkers enforce this honor system, rewarding freeloaders with stiff €40 fines. There's a transit customer-service center underground at Marienplatz (Mon–Fri 9:00–20:00, Sat 9:00–16:00, closed Sun, go down stairs by Beck's department store). For more transit info, call 01803/442-266 or visit www .mvv-muenchen.de.

By Bike

Level, compact, and with plenty of bike paths, Munich feels made for those on two wheels. When biking in Munich, follow these simple rules: You must walk your bike through pedestrian zones; you can take your bike on the subway, but not during rush hour and only if you have an extra ticket; and cyclists are expected to follow the rules of the road, just like drivers.

You can **rent bikes** quickly and easily from two great places: Radius Tours (in the train station) and Munich Walk (at Isartor). Both give a 10 percent discount with this book in 2010, and both have an extensive selection of bikes; provide helmets, maps, and route advice; and offer bike tours.

Radius Tours (*Rad* means "bike" in German) is in the train station in front of track 32 (city bikes-€3/hr, €14.50/day, €17/24 hrs, €25/48 hrs, mountain bikes 25 percent more, €50 cash or credit-card deposit, April–Oct Mon–Fri 9:00–18:00, Sat–Sun 9:00–20:00, closed in bad weather Nov–March, tel. 089/596-113, www.radiustours.com).

Munich Walk is at the other end of the tourist zone, right by Isartor (€3/hr, €15/24 hrs, 2-hour minimum, open daily 9:00–23:00, Thomas-Wimmer-Ring 1, storefront says *Tourist info*, tel. 089/2423-1767, www.munichwalktours.de).

For a great city ride, consider this day on a bike: English Garden to Olympic Park, then along the canal to Nymphenburg Palace, around the palace grounds, and back to the center (in 30 min) via Arnulfstrasse, which has a bike path the entire way. Or go for the Isar River bike ride described on page 76.

Tours in Munich

Munich has three major tour companies. **Gray Line** specializes in bus tours of the city and to the Bavarian castles of "Mad" King Ludwig. The two other major companies compete directly with each other, and in my experience, they're comparable. In addition to bike tours (described earlier), they offer walking tours and day trips to Dachau Concentration Camp and Neuschwanstein Castle. **Radius Tours** has a convenient office and meeting point in the main train station, in front of track 32 (see map on page 83, tel. 089/5502-9374, www.radiustours.com, run by knowledgeable Gabi Holder). **Munich Walk** has their office near Isartor at Thomas-Wimmer-Ring 1, and uses Marienplatz as its meeting point (see map on page 83, tel. 089/2423-1767, www.munichwalktours.de, tours@munich walktours.de, energetic Ralph Lünstroth). Both companies offer at least €1 off their walking tours with this book in 2010—don't forget to show this book and request your discount. (If you buy a Munich Walk or Gray Line tour at EurAide, ask for the discount there.)

Free Tours: You'll encounter brochures advertising "free" walking and biking tours. These tours aren't really free—tipping is expected, and the guides don't earn money unless you tip. The tours tend to be very light on history, and the guides work hard to promote their company's other tours (which are not free). The competition has forced some of the more established outfits (such as Radius Tours, listed below) to offer their own "free" tours. My advice is to avoid free tours by start-ups in favor of the more established companies' tours, where you pay for a hardworking guide who can make the city's history come alive.

Within Munich

Walking Tours—Munich Walk offers two daytime tours (€1 Rick Steves discount on each tour): a "City Walk" (€10, daily year-round at 10:45, May–mid-Oct also daily at 14:45, 2.25 hrs) and "Hitler's Munich" (€12, March–Oct daily at 10:00, Nov–Feb daily at 10:30, 2.5 hours, extended €21 five-hour version Mon and Sat only). Their "Beer and Brewery" tour is more mature than your typical hard-partying pub crawl. You visit Paulaner, Munich's oldest brewery, to learn, eat, and drink in the city that made beer famous. The price includes three different beers in the brewery; afterwards, the tour ends at the Hofbräuhaus (€18, May–mid-Sept daily at 18:15, fewer tours off-season, 3.5 hours). All Munich Walk tours depart from under the glockenspiel on Marienplatz. No need to reserve—just show up.

Radius Tours runs two city walking tours, both with reliably good guides (daily April–Oct, fewer tours off-season): "Munich Highlights" (no up-front charge but tip for guide requested, at

10:00, 2 hours) and "Hitler and the Third Reich" (€12, €2 Rick Steves discount, at 15:00, 2.5 hours). They also offer an educational "Bavarian Beer and Food" tour that includes a visit to the Beer and Oktoberfest Museum (see page 47), samples of four varieties of the sudsy stuff, and regional food (€25, €3 Rick Steves discount; Tue, Thu, and Sat at 18:00; also Wed and Fri at 18:00 mid-April–mid-Oct; 3 hours). All tours depart from the Radius office (in front of track 32 at the train station, no need to reserve—just show up).

Local Guides—I've had great days with two good guides, each charging the same prices (€110/2 hrs, €130/3 hrs): **Georg Reichlmayr** (tel. 08131/86800, mobile 0170-341-6384, program explained at his website, www.muenchen-stadtfuehrung.de, info @muenchen-stadtfuehrung.de) and **Monika Hank** (tel. 089/311-4819, mobile 0175-923-2339, monika.hank@web.de). They helped me with much of the historical information in this chapter, and Georg was my sidekick on the Munich episode of my public television series.

Bike Tours—Munich lends itself to bike touring, and three outfits fit the bill: the original Mike's Bike Tours, plus two companies described earlier, Munich Walk and Radius Tours. You don't need to reserve for any of these—just show up.

Mike's Bike Tours, popular with the college crowd, are four hours of entertainment on wheels. The tours are high-energy, if a bit clunky with pacing, and the guides are better comedians than historians. Still, you get a great ride through the English Garden (€24, tips encouraged, bikes provided, 1-hour break in Chinese Tower beer garden, daily mid-April–Aug at 11:30 and 16:00, March–mid-April and Sept–mid-Nov at 12:30, meet under tower of Old Town Hall on Marienplatz; tel. 089/2554-3987, mobile 0172-852-0660, www.mikesbiketours.com).

Munich Walk offers 3.5-hour bike tours around Munich on weekends (€22, April–Oct only, Sat–Sun at 11:15). They also have a five-hour mountain bike tour out into the countryside along the Isar River, including a lunch stop at a beer garden (€29, May–Oct only, Wed, Thu, Sat, and Sun at 10:00). Tours leave from under the glockenspiel on Marienplatz (confirm times at www.munichwalk tours.de).

Radius Tours has similar 3.5-hour bike tours on Tuesdays, Thursdays, and Sundays (€18, May–mid-Oct only at 10:30). Tours leave from the Radius office at track 32 in the train station (confirm times at www.radiustours.com).

Quickie Orientation City Bus Tour—**Gray Line Tours** has hop-on, hop-off bus tours that leave from in front of the Karstadt department store at Bahnhofplatz, directly across from the train station. Choose from a basic, one-hour "Express Circle" that heads past the Pinakotheks, Marienplatz, and Karlsplatz (3/hr,

9:00–17:30); or the more extensive "Grand Circle" that lasts 2.5 hours and also includes the Nymphenburg Palace, Olympia Park, and Schwabing neighborhood (1/hr, 9:00–16:00). This tour is actually well worthwhile—sitting upstairs on the topless double-decker bus, you'll see lots of things missed by the typical visitor wandering around the center. It complements the information in this book, though the live guide narrates (in German and English) as stiffly as a tape recording. Just show up and pay the driver (cash only), or get a €1–2 discount by buying your ticket in advance at EurAide (€13 Express tour, €18 Grand tour, daily in season, tel. 089/5490-7560, www.sightseeing-munich.com).

Beyond Munich

"Mad" King Ludwig's Castles—Two spectacular Bavarian castles, Neuschwanstein and Linderhof, make a logical day trip from Munich. For more on these destinations, see the Bavaria and Tirol chapter. If you're planning on visiting these sights as a day trip from Munich, you have three basic options: on your own by train, with an escorted train tour, or by guided bus tour.

Gray Line Tours offers rushed all-day bus tours of the two castles that also include 30 minutes in Oberammergau (€49, €7 Rick Steves discount if you buy your ticket at EurAide—cash only, two castle admissions-€15 extra, daily April–Oct, no tours Mon Nov–March, www.sightseeing-munich.com). In summer, it's wise to purchase tickets a day ahead. Tours meet at 8:10 and depart at 8:30 from the Karstadt department store (across from the station). While **Munich Walk** advertises a similar tour, they're simply selling tickets for this Gray Line trip.

Radius Tours runs all-day tours to Neuschwanstein Castle by train. Your guide will escort you onto public transportation, give you some general information, and help you into the castle for the standard tour that's included with any admission ticket (€32 with this book, €25 with railpass, castle admission-€9 extra; departs daily mid-April–Sept at 9:00 from in front of track 32 at train station, back by 19:00, book ahead; Oct–mid-April tours run Mon, Wed, and Sat at 9:00, smart to reconfirm times; tel. 089/5502-9374, www.radiustours.com).

Dachau Concentration Camp—While several companies do Dachau tours, both Radius Tours and Munich Walk are allowed to actually guide inside the camp. Considering how good and passionate their guides are—and that you're only paying about €10 for the guiding, once you factor in transportation costs—these tours are a great value. Allow about five hours total (including 20-min S-Bahn trip and 10-min bus trip each way, and about three hours at the site, with 20-min film in English).

Radius Tours offers English-language-only tours of the camp year-round (€21 includes the €6.70 cost of public transportation, €3 Rick Steves discount; April–mid-Oct Tue–Sun at 9:15 and 12:30; mid-Oct–March Tue–Sun at 11:00; no tours Mon, when camp is closed; depart from Radius office in Munich station—in front of track 32, smart to confirm times, but you can just show up). **Munich Walk** does a similar tour (€21 includes €6.70 transport costs, €3 Rick Steves discount, May–Oct Tue–Sun at 10:15 and 13:15, Nov–Feb Tue–Sun at 10:30, March–April Tue–Sun at 13:15, no tours Mon).

MUNICH

Sights in Munich

Central Munich

▲▲**City Views**—Downtown Munich's three best city viewpoints (all described in this section) are from the tops of St. Peter's Church (stairs only), Frauenkirche (stairs plus elevator), and New Town Hall (elevator).

▲▲**Marienplatz and the Pedestrian Zone**—Riding the escalator out of the subway into sunlit Marienplatz ("Mary's Square")

gives you a fine first look at the glory of Munich: great buildings bombed flat and rebuilt, outdoor cafés, and people bustling and lingering like the birds and breeze with which they share this square. Take in the ornate facades of the gray, pointy Old Town Hall and the Neo-Gothic New Town Hall, with its beloved glockenspiel.

The **New Town Hall** (Neues Rathaus), built from 1867 until 1908, dominates the square. Munich was a very royal city. Notice the politics of the statuary. The 40 statues—though sculpted only in 1900—decorate New Town Hall not with civic leaders, but with royals and blue-blooded nobility. Because this building survived the bombs and had a central location, it served as the US military headquarters in 1945.

The New Town Hall is famous for its **glockenspiel**—only 100 years old—which "jousts" daily at 11:00 and 12:00 all year (also at 17:00 May–Oct). The *Spiel* re-creates a royal wedding from the 16th century: The duke and his bride watch the action as the Bavarians (in white and blue) forever beat their enemies. Below, the barrel-makers—famous for being the

Munich at a Glance

In the Center

▲▲**Marienplatz** Munich's main square, at the heart of a lively pedestrian zone, watched over by New Town Hall (and its glockenspiel show). **Hours:** Always open; glockenspiel jousts daily at 11:00 and 12:00, plus 17:00 May–Oct; New Town Hall tower elevator runs May–Oct daily 10:00–19:00; Nov–April Mon–Fri 10:00–17:00, closed Sat–Sun. See page 39.

▲▲**Viktualienmarkt** Munich's "small-town" open-air market, perfect for a quick snack or meal. **Hours:** Mon–Sat, *Biergarten* open until late, closed Sun. See page 46.

▲▲**Hofbräuhaus** World-famous beer hall, worth a visit even if you're not chugging. **Hours:** Daily 9:00–24:00. See page 47.

▲▲**Munich City Museum** The city's history in five floors. **Hours:** Tue–Sun 10:00–18:00, closed Mon. See page 47.

▲▲**The Residenz** The elegant family palace of the Wittelsbachs, awash with Bavarian opulence. Complex includes the Residenz Museum (private apartments), Residenz Treasury (housing Wittelsbach family crowns and royal knickknacks), and the impressive, just-restored Cuvilliés Theater. **Hours:** Museum and treasury—daily April–mid-Oct 9:00–18:00, mid-Oct–March 10:00–17:00; theater—April–July and mid-Sept–mid-Oct Mon–Sat 14:00–18:00, Sun 9:00–18:00; Aug–mid-Sept daily 9:00–18:00; mid-Oct–March Mon–Sat 14:00–17:00, Sun 10:00–17:00. See page 50.

▲▲**Alte Pinakothek** Bavaria's best painting gallery, with a wonderful collection of European masters from the 14th through the 19th centuries. **Hours:** Wed–Sun 10:00–18:00, Tue 10:00–20:00, closed Mon. See page 59.

▲▲**Deutsches Museum** Germany's version of our Smithsonian Institution, with 10 miles of science and technology exhibits. **Hours:** Daily 9:00–17:00. See page 66.

▲**Neue Pinakothek** The Alte's twin sister, with paintings from 1800 to 1920. **Hours:** Thu–Mon 10:00–18:00, Wed 10:00–20:00, closed Tue. See page 63.

▲**Pinakothek der Moderne** Hip contemporary-art museum near the Alte and Neue Pinakotheks—housed in a building that's as interesting as the art. **Hours:** Tue–Sun 10:00–18:00, Thu until 20:00, closed Mon. See page 63.

▲**Museum Brandhorst** Munich's newest art museum, with collections from the turn of the 21st century. **Hours:** Tue–Sun 10:00–18:00, Thu until 20:00, closed Mon. See page 64.

▲**English Garden** The largest city park on the Continent, packed with locals, tourists, surfers, and nude sunbathers. (On a bike, I'd rate this ▲▲.) **Hours:** Always open. See page 65.

St. Michael's Church Renaissance church housing Baroque decor and a crypt of 40 Wittelsbachs. **Hours:** Church—daily 9:00–19:00, Thu until 20:45, Sun until 22:00; crypt—Mon–Fri 9:30–16:30, Sat 9:30–14:30, closed Sun, less off-season. See page 44.

Frauenkirche Huge, distinctive twin-domed church looming over the city center. **Hours:** Church—Sat-Wed 7:00–19:00, Thu 7:00–20:30, Fri 7:00–18:00; tower climb—April-Oct Mon–Sat 10:00–17:00, closed Sun and Nov–March. See page 44.

St. Peter's Church Munich's oldest church, packed with relics. **Hours:** Church—long hours daily; spire climb—Mon–Fri 9:00–18:30, Sat–Sun 10:00–18:30, off-season until 17:30. See page 45.

Away from the Center
▲▲**Nymphenburg Palace** The Wittelsbachs' impressive summer palace featuring a hunting lodge, coach museum, fine royal porcelain collection, and vast park. **Hours:** Daily April-mid-Oct 9:00–18:00, mid-Oct–March 10:00–16:00. See page 71.

▲▲**Dachau Concentration Camp** Notorious Nazi camp on the outskirts of Munich, now a powerful museum. **Hours:** Tue–Sun 9:00–17:00, closed Mon. See page 76.

▲**Museum of Transportation** Deutsches Museum's cross-town annex devoted to travel. **Hours:** Daily 9:00–17:00. See page 68.

▲**Olympic Park** Munich's 1972 Olympic stadium, now a lush park with a view tower and pool. **Hours:** Grounds always open; tower daily 9:00–24:00, pool daily 7:00–23:00. See page 74.

▲**Andechs Monastery** Baroque church, hearty food, and Bavaria's best brew, in the nearby countryside. **Hours:** *Biergarten* daily 10:00–20:00, church open until 18:00. See page 76.

BMW Museum and Factory The carmaker's futuristic museum, including glimpses of rare models. **Hours:** Tue–Fri 9:00–18:00, Sat–Sun 10:00–20:00, closed Mon. See page 74.

Central Munich

first to dance in the streets after a deadly plague lifted—do their popular jig. The glockenspiel's 32 life-size figures were restored in 2008, as Munich celebrated the clock's 100th year of entertaining the city.

The New Town Hall tower offers **views** of the city (€2, elevator from under glockenspiel; May–Oct daily 10:00–19:00; Nov–April Mon–Fri 10:00–17:00, closed Sat–Sun).

Marienplatz is marked by a statue of the **Virgin Mary,** moved here in 1638 from its original location in the Frauenkirche in thanks that the Swedes didn't sack the town during their occupation. It was also a rallying point for the struggle against the Protestants. The cherubs are fighting against the four great biblical enemies of civilization: the dragon of war, the lion of hunger, the snake of plague and disease, and the rooster-headed monster of heresy (Protestantism). The serpent that's being stepped upon represents the "wrong faith," a.k.a. Martin Luther.

The **Old Town Hall** (Altes Rathaus; at the right side of square as you face New Town Hall) was completely destroyed by

MUNICH

1. Marienplatz
2. New Town Hall
3. Old Town Hall
4. St. Michael's Church
5. Frauenkirche
6. St. Peter's Church
7. Viktualienmarkt
8. Alois Dallmayr Deli
9. Hofbräuhaus
10. Beer & Oktoberfest Museum
11. Munich City Museum
12. Jewish Synagogue & History Museum
13. Asamkirche
14. Damenstift Church
15. Residenz

▥ PEDESTRIAN ZONE
→ ENTRY POINT TO SIGHTS
Ⓤ U-BAHN STOP
Ⓢ S-BAHN STOP

WWII bombs and later rebuilt. Ludwig IV, an early Wittelsbach who was Holy Roman Emperor back in the 14th century, stands in the center of the facade. He donated this great square to the people. On the bell tower, find the city seal with its monk and towers. Munich flourished because, in its early days, all salt trade had to stop here on Marienplatz.

Back at Marienplatz, the **pedestrian mall** (Kaufingerstrasse and Neuhauser Strasse) leads you through a great shopping area, past carnivals of street entertainers and good old-fashioned slicers and dicers, the towering twin-domed Frauenkirche (built in the late 1400s, rebuilt after World War II), and several fountains, to Karlstor and the train station. As one of Europe's first pedestrian zones, the mall enraged shopkeepers when it was built in 1972 for the Olympics. Today, it is Munich's living room. Nearly

9,000 shoppers pass through it each hour. The shopkeepers are happy...and merchants nearby are begging for their streets to become traffic-free. Imagine this street in Hometown, USA.

Three Churches near Marienplatz—In the pedestrian zone around Marienplatz are three noteworthy churches: St. Michael's, the Frauenkirche, and St. Peter's. Each was heavily bombed in World War II, and each displays photos of that destruction near its entrance. As you face New Town Hall, St. Michael's is a few blocks down the pedestrian street to your left; the Frauenkirche is the big twin-domed church at 10 o'clock; and St. Peter's is over your right shoulder.

St. Michael's Church: While one of the first great Renaissance buildings north of the Alps, this church has a brilliantly Baroque interior. Inspired by the Gesù (the Jesuit's main church in Rome), it was built in the late 1500s as a home to the Jesuits in Bavaria. The statue of Michael fighting a Protestant demon (on the front facade) is a reminder that this leader of heaven's army invited the Jesuits to literally counter the Reformation from here. The interior is striking for its barrel vault, the largest in its day. The crypt contains 40 stark royal tombs, including the resting place of King Ludwig II. Judging by all the flowers, romantics are still mad about their "mad" king (church entry free, daily 9:00–19:00, Thu until 20:45, Sun until 22:00; crypt-€2, Mon–Fri 9:30–16:30, Sat 9:30–14:30, closed Sun, less off-season; frequent concerts—check the schedule outside; www.st-michael-muenchen.de).

Frauenkirche: These twin onion domes are the symbol of the city. Some say Crusaders, inspired by the Dome of the Rock in Jerusalem, brought home the idea. Others say these domes are the inspiration for the characteristic domed church spires marking villages throughout Bavaria.

Go inside (free, Sat–Wed 7:00–19:00, Thu 7:00–20:30, Fri 7:00–18:00, www .muenchner-dom.de). While much of the church was destroyed during World War II (see photos just inside the entrance, on the right), the towers survived, and the rest has been gloriously restored.

Built in Gothic style in the late 1400s, the Frauenkirche (Church of Our Lady) has been the city's cathedral since 1821. Construction was funded with the sale of indulgences, but money problems meant the domes weren't added until Renaissance times. Late-Gothic buildings in Munich were generally built of brick—easy to make locally and cheaper and faster to use than stone. This church was constructed in a remarkable 20 years. It's located on the grave of Ludwig IV (who died in 1347). His big black, ornate tomb-like monument (now in the back) was originally in front at the high altar. Standing in the back of the nave, notice how your eyes go right to the altar... Christ...and (until recently) Ludwig. Those Wittelsbachs—always trying to be associated with God. In fact, this alliance was instilled in people through the prayers they were forced to recite: "Virgin Mary, mother of our duke, please protect us." A plaque over the last pew on the left recalls the life story of Pope Benedict XVI, who occupied the archbishop's seat here from 1977 until 1982, when he moved into Pope John Paul II's inner circle in the Vatican.

You can ascend the tower for the city's highest public viewpoint, at 280 feet (€3, 86 steps to elevator, April–Oct Mon–Sat 10:00–17:00, closed Sun and Nov–March). On many Wednesday evenings in summer, you can catch an organ concert here (€8, 19:00, tickets available at München Ticket office inside Marienplatz TI).

St. Peter's Church: The oldest church in town overlooks Marienplatz from its perch near the Viktualienmarkt. It's built on

the hill where Munich's original monastic inhabitants probably settled. (Founded in 1158, the city celebrated its 850th birthday in 2008.) Outside, notice the old tombstones plastered onto the wall—a reminder that in the Napoleonic age, the cemeteries surrounding most city churches were (for hygienic and practical space reasons) dug up and moved.

St. Peter's was badly damaged in World War II. Inside, photos show the bomb damage (near the entrance). As part of the soul of the city (according to a popular song, "Munich is not Munich without St. Peter's"), the church was lovingly rebuilt—half with Augustiner beer money, the rest with private donations—and the altar and ceiling frescoes were marvelously restored (possible with the help of Nazi catalog photos—see "The History of Munich: Part 2," on page 54).

Apostles line the nave, leading up to St. Peter above the altar. On the ceiling, you'll see Peter crucified upside-down. The finely crafted gray iron chapel fences were donated after World War II by the local blacksmiths of the national railway. The precious and fragile sandstone Gothic chapel altar (front left) survived the war only because it was buried in sandbags.

Munich has more relics than any city outside of Rome. For more than a hundred years, it was the pope's bastion against the rising tide of Protestantism in northern Europe during the Reformation. Favors done in the defense of Catholicism earned the Wittelsbachs neat relic treats. For instance, check out the tomb of Munditia (second side chapel on left as you enter). She's a third-century martyr (note the ancient Roman tombstone with red lettering), whose remains were given to Munich by Rome as thanks and a vivid reminder that those who die for the cause of the Roman Church go directly to heaven without waiting for Judgment Day.

It's a long climb to the top of the spire (306 steps, no elevator)—much of it with two-way traffic on a one-lane staircase—but the view is dynamite (€1.50, Mon–Fri 9:00–18:30, Sat–Sun 10:00–18:30, off-season until 17:30, last exit 30 min after closing). Try to be two flights from the top when the bells ring at the top of the hour, and then, when your friends back home ask you about your trip, you'll say, "What?"

▲▲Viktualienmarkt—Early in the morning, you can still feel small-town Munich here, long a favorite with locals for fresh produce and good service (open Mon–Sat, food stalls open late, closed Sun). The most expensive real estate in town could never really support such a market, but the town charges only a percentage of the gross income, enabling these old-time shops to carry on (and keeping out fast-food chains).

The huge **maypole** is a tradition. Fifteenth-century town market squares posted a maypole decorated with various symbols to explain which crafts and merchants were doing business in the market. Munich's maypole shows the city's six great brews, and the crafts and festivities associated with brewing. (You can't have a kegger without coopers—find the merry barrel-makers.)

Notice the beer counter. Munich's breweries take turns here. Changing every day or two, a sign (Heute im Ausschank) announces which of the six brews is being served. Here, under the standard beer-garden chestnut trees, you can order just half a liter—unlike at other Biergartens (handy for shoppers who want to have a quick sip and then keep on going).

The Viktualienmarkt is ideal for a light meal (see page 89). To browse a more upscale food market, visit the...

Alois Dallmayr Delicatessen—When the king called out for dinner, he called Alois Dallmayr. This place became famous for its exotic and luxurious food items: tropical fruits, seafood, chocolates, fine wines, and coffee (there are meat and cheese counters, too). As you enter, read the black plaque with the royal seal by the door: Königlich Bayerischer Hof-Lieferant ("Deliverer for the King of Bavaria and his Court"). Catering to royal and aristocratic tastes (and budgets), it's still the choice of Munich's old rich. Today, it's most famous for its sweets, chocolates, and coffee—dispensed from fine hand-painted Nymphenburg porcelain jugs (Mon–Sat 9:30–19:00, closed Sun; two cafés inside—described later, under "Eating in Munich"; Dienerstrasse 13–15, down the street to the right of New Town Hall, www.dallmayr.de).

▲▲**Hofbräuhaus**—Whether or not you slide your lederhosen on its polished benches, it's a great experience just to walk through the world's most famous beer hall in all its rowdy glory (daily 9:00–24:00, live oompah music during lunch and dinner, €20 Bavarian folk evenings including all-you-can-stomach buffet nightly from 18:30–22:00; a 5-min walk northeast of Marienplatz at Platzl 6, www.hofbraeuhaus.de).

As you wander, look for the various *Stammtisch* signs (meaning "reserved"), hanging above tables where different clubs meet regularly; don't sit here unless you're specifically invited. Racks of locked steins, made of pottery and metal, are for regulars. You'll see locals stuffed into lederhosen and dirndls; giant gingerbread cookies that sport romantic messages; and postcards of the new German (and apparently beer-drinking) pope.

After being bombed in World War II, this venerable palace of beer was quickly rebuilt and back in business within a few years. Notice the quirky 1950s-style painted ceiling, with Bavarian colors, grapes, chestnuts, and fun "eat, drink, and be merry" themes. A slogan on the ceiling above the band reads, *Durst ist schlimmer als Heimweh* ("Being thirsty is worse than feeling homesick").

The bouncer at the door nabs 20–50 people (mostly Italians, he says) each day trying to steal mugs as souvenirs. The staircase to the left of the entrance displays historic old Hofbräuhaus photos and prints; there's a more extensive historical display on the second floor (daily 9:00–17:00).

For details on eating at the Hofbräuhaus, see page 89.

Beer and Oktoberfest Museum (Bier- und Oktober-festmuseum)—Get a low-tech and underwhelming take on history at this humble museum, where exhibits and artifacts outline the centuries-old quest for the perfect beer (apparently perfected in Munich) and the origins of the city's Oktoberfest celebration. The oldest house in the city center, the museum's home is noteworthy in itself (€4; open Tue–Sat 13:00–17:00, closed Sun–Mon; between Isartor and Viktualienmarkt at Sterneckerstrasse 2, tel. 089/2423-1607, www.bier-und-oktoberfestmuseum.de).

▲▲**Munich City Museum (Münchner Stadtmuseum)**—Five floors of exhibits in this newly renovated museum tell the story of life in Munich through the centuries, including the history of "monk culture," the development of National Socialism (i.e., Nazism), and World War II—illustrated with paintings, photos, and models. Their good new permanent exhibit, called "Typically

MUNICH

The History of Munich: Part 1
Monastic Beginnings to the Age of Kings

Born from Salt (1100–1500)

Munich began in the 12th century, when Henry the Lion (Heinrich der Löwe) muscled in on the lucrative salt trade, burning a rival's bridge over the Isar River and building his own near a monastery of "monks"—München. (The town's coat of arms features the Münchner Kindl, a boy in monk's robes.) Henry built walls and towers, opened a market, and peasants flocked in from the countryside. Marienplatz was the center of town, and the crossroads of the Salzstrasse (Salt Road) from Salzburg to Augsburg.

After Henry's death, the town was taken over by an ambitious merchant family, the Wittelsbachs (1240), and became the capital of the region (1255). Munich-born Louis (or Ludwig) IV (1282–1347) was elected king of Germany and Holy Roman Emperor, temporarily making Munich a major European capital.

By the 1400s, Munich's maypole-studded market bustled with trade. Besides salt, Munich gained a reputation for beer. More than 30 breweries pumped out the golden liquid that lubricated both trade and traders. The Bavarian Beer Purity Law assured quality control. Wealthy townspeople erected the twin-domed Frauenkirche and the Altes Rathaus on Marienplatz, and the Wittelsbachs built a stout castle that would eventually become the cushy Residenz. When the various regions of Bavaria united in 1506, Munich (pop. 14,000) was the natural capital.

Religious Wars, Plagues, Decline (1500–1800)

While Martin Luther and the Protestant Reformation raged in northern Germany, Munich became the ultra-Catholic heart of the Counter-Reformation. The devout citizens poured enormous funds into building the massive St. Michael's Church (1583) as a home for the Jesuits, and into the Residenz (early 1600s) as home of the Wittelsbachs. Both were showpieces of conservative power and the Baroque and Rococo styles.

During the Thirty Years' War, the Catholic city was surrounded by Protestants (1632). The Wittelsbachs surrendered quickly and paid a ransom, sparing the city from pillage, but it was soon hit by the bubonic plague. After that passed, the leaders erected the Virgin's column on Marienplatz to thank God for killing only 7,000 citizens. (Munich's many plagues are also remembered today when the glockenspiel's barrel-makers do their daily dance to ward off the plague.)

The double whammy of invasion and disease left Munich bankrupt and powerless, overshadowed by the more powerful Habsburgs of Austria. The Wittelsbachs took their cultural cues from France (Nymphenburg Palace is a mini-Versailles), England (the English Garden), and Italy (the Pitti Palace–inspired Residenz). While the rest of Europe modernized and headed toward democracy, Munich remained conservative and backward.

The Kings (1806–1918): Max I, Ludwig I, Max II, Ludwig II, Ludwig III

When Napoleon's army surrounded the city (1800), the Wittelsbachs again surrendered hospitably. Napoleon rewarded the Wittelsbach "duke" with more territory and a royal title: "king." Maximilian I (r. 1806–1825, see page 113), a.k.a. Max Joseph, now ruled the Kingdom of Bavaria, an independent nation bigger than Switzerland, with a constitution and parliament. When Max's popular son Ludwig got married (Sept 1810), it touched off a two-week celebration that became an annual event: Oktoberfest.

As king, Ludwig I (r. 1825–1848) set about rebuilding the capital in the Neoclassical style we see today. Medieval walls and ramshackle houses were replaced with grand buildings of columns and arches (including the Residenz and Alte Pinakothek). Connecting these were broad boulevards and plazas for horse carriages and promenading citizens (Ludwigstrasse and Königsplatz). Ludwig established the university and built the first railway line, turning Munich (pop. 90,000) into a major transportation hub, budding industrial city, and fitting capital for the new country.

In 1846, the skirt-chasing King Ludwig (see Nymphenburg's Gallery of Beauties, page 72) was beguiled by a notorious Irish dancer named Lola Montez. She became his mistress and he fawned over her in public, scandalizing Munich. The Münchners resented her spending their tax money and dominating their king (supposedly inspiring the phrase "Whatever Lola wants, Lola gets"). In 1848, as Europe was swept by a tide of revolution, the citizens rose up and forced Ludwig to abdicate. His son Maximilian II (r. 1848–1864) continued Ludwig's enlightened program of modernizing, while studiously avoiding dancers from Ireland.

In 1864, 18-year-old Ludwig II (r. 1864–1886) became king. He immediately invited the composer Richard Wagner to Munich, planning a lavish new opera house to stage Wagner's operas. Munich didn't like the idea, and Ludwig didn't like Munich. For most of his reign, Ludwig avoided the Residenz and Nymphenburg, instead building castles in the Bavarian countryside at the expense of Munich taxpayers. (For more on the king, see page 114.)

In 1871, Bavaria became part of the newly united Germany, and overnight, Berlin overtook Munich as Germany's power center. But turn-of-the-century Munich was culturally rich, birthing the abstract art of Wassily Kandinsky, Paul Klee, and the Blue Rider group. This artistic flourishing didn't last long.

World War I devastated Munich. Poor, hungry, disillusioned, unemployed Münchners roamed the streets. Extremists from the left and right battled for power. In 1918, a huge mob marched to the gates of the Residenz and drove the forgettable King Ludwig III (r. 1913–1918)—the last Bavarian king—out of the city, ending nearly 700 years of continuous Wittelsbach rule.

For "The History of Munich: Part 2," see page 54.

Munich!", examines the various stereotypes—both negative and positive—that people around the world associate with this city (€4, free on Sun, discount with Jewish History Museum, open Tue–Sun 10:00–18:00, closed Mon, few English descriptions, no crowds, bored and playful guards, 3 blocks off Marienplatz at St.-Jakobs-Platz 1, tel. 089/2332-2370, www.stadtmuseum-online.de). The museum's Stadt Café is handy for a good meal (see page 94).

Jewish Synagogue and History Museum (Jüdisches Museum München)—Thanks to Germany's acceptance of religious refugees from former USSR states, Munich's Jewish population has now reached its pre-Nazi size—10,000 people. The city's new synagogue and Jewish History Museum anchor a revitalized Jewish quarter, which includes a kindergarten and day school, children's playground, kosher restaurant, and bookstore.

While the **synagogue** is shut tight to the non-Jewish public, its architecture is striking from the outside. Lower stones of travertine evoke the Wailing Wall in Jerusalem, while an upper section represents the tent that held important religious wares during the 40 years of wandering through the desert until the Temple of Solomon was built, ending the Exodus. The synagogue's door features the first 10 letters of the Hebrew alphabet, symbolizing the Ten Commandments.

The cube-shaped **museum** is stark, windowless, and as inviting as a bomb shelter. Its small permanent exhibit in the basement is disappointing. The two floors of temporary exhibits, always Munich-specific, might justify the entry fee (€6, discount with Munich City Museum, Tue–Sun 10:00–18:00, closed Mon, across the street from the Munich City Museum at St.-Jakobs-Platz 16, tel. 089/2339-6096, www.juedisches-museum-muenchen.de).

Rococo Churches—Near the Munich City Museum, the private church of the Asam brothers **(Asamkirche)** is a gooey, drippy Baroque-concentrate masterpiece by Bavaria's top two Rococonuts. A few blocks away, the small **Damenstift Church** has an incredibly realistic sculptural rendition of the Last Supper (at intersection of Altheimer Ecke and Damenstiftstrasse, a block south of the pedestrian street).

The Residenz

For a long hike through corridors of gilded imperial Bavarian grandeur, tour the Wittelsbachs' family palace (largely rebuilt after World War II). The Wittelsbachs, who ruled Bavaria for nearly 700 years, modeled the front of their enormous palace on the Medici family's Pitti Palace in Florence. The sprawling place evolved from the 14th through the 19th centuries—as you'll see on the charts near the entrance. Whatever happened to the Wittelsbachs, the longest continuously ruling family in European history? They're still around—but since they're no longer royalty, most of them have real jobs now. If you're torn between Munich's top two palaces, I'd say the Residenz interior is best, while Nymphenburg (see page 70) has the finest garden.

MUNICH

Cost, Hours, Location: €6 each to visit the Residenz Museum (palace apartments) and the Treasury, including audioguides; €9 combo-ticket covers both; covered by Bavarian Castles Pass. The Halls of the Nibelungen are always free (and due to reopen sometime in 2010 after renovation). All parts of the palace are open daily April–mid-Oct 9:00–18:00, mid-Oct–March 10:00–17:00, last entry one hour before closing. The complex is located three blocks north of Marienplatz.

Information: Your ticket includes a free English audioguide. For more in-depth information, consider the €10 English guidebook, but don't bother with the dry €3 version. Tel. 089/290-671, www.residenz-muenchen.de.

Orientation: While impressive, the Residenz can be confusing for visitors. Enter the complex from the main entrance on Max-Joseph-Platz (at the corner of the palace nearest Marienplatz) or from the entrance on Residenzstrasse. Just inside the main entrance are the Halls of the Nibelungen (free), as well as the ticket booth for both the Residenz Museum and the Treasury (located in separate wings).

Halls of the Nibelungen (Nibelungensäle)—The mythological scenes in these fascinating halls (which will hopefully reopen sometime in 2010 after renovation) were the basis of Wagner's *Der Ring des Nibelungen*. Wagner and "Mad" King Ludwig were friends and spent time hanging out here (c. 1864). These very images could well have inspired Wagner to write his *Ring* and Ludwig to build his "fairy-tale castle," Neuschwanstein. Note that even if you're not touring the rest of the Residenz, these rooms (when open) are free to enter.

▲▲Residenz Museum (Residenzmuzeum)—This museum includes the most spectacular halls and private apartments in the Wittelsbachs' palace complex. It's the best place to get a glimpse of the opulent lifestyle of Bavaria's late, great royal family.

◑ Self-Guided Tour: Since it's so big, different sections of the Residenz Museum are open in the mornings and in the afternoons (after 13:30 in summer, 12:30 in winter). Leave the ticket office to your right (without going back outside), and follow the *Rundgang* signs. This self-guided tour is designed to coincide with the afternoon route (a little more interesting than the morning's). Due to ongoing renovations, either tour route can change without notice. To help you find the highlights, I have numbered the rooms as they appear on the official map (free at entry), though be warned the rooms themselves aren't all numbered.

Shell Grotto (Room 6, actually outside, ground floor): This artificial grotto was an exercise in man controlling nature—a cel-

ebration of humanism. Renaissance humanism was a big deal when this was built in the 1550s. Imagine the ambience here during that time, with Mercury—the pre-Christian god of trade and business—overseeing the action, and red wine spurting from the mermaid's breasts and dripping from Medusa's head in the courtyard. The strange structure is made from Bavarian freshwater shells. This palace was demolished by WWII bombs. After the war,

people had no money to contribute to the reconstruction—but they could gather shells. All the shells you see here were donated by small-town Bavarians as the grotto was rebuilt according to Nazi photos (see "The History of Munich: Part 2" sidebar). To the right of the shells, the door marked *OO* leads to public toilets.

Antiquarium (Room 7, ground floor): In the mid-16th century, Europe's royal families (such as the Wittelsbachs) collected

and displayed busts of emperors— implying a connection between themselves and the ancient Roman rulers. Given the huge demand for these Classical statues in the courts of Europe, many of the "ancient busts" are fakes cranked out by crooked Romans. Still, a third of the statuary you see here is original. This was, and still is, a festival ban-

quet hall. Two hundred dignitaries can dine here, surrounded by allegories of the goodness of just rule on the ceiling. Check out the small paintings around the room—these survived the bombs because they were painted in arches. Of great historic interest, these paintings show 120 Bavarian villages as they looked in 1550. Even today, when a Bavarian historian wants a record of how his village once looked, he comes here. Notice the town of Dachau in 1550 (above the door on the left as you enter).

Reliquary (Room 95, upper floor, often closed in the morning): Meet St. John the Baptist and his mother, Elizabeth (#47 and #48—skulls on jeweled pillows).

Private Chapel of Maximilian I (Room 98, upper floor, often closed in the morning): Duke Maximilian I, the dominant Bavarian figure in the Thirty Years' War, built one of the most precious rooms in the palace. The miniature pipe organ (from about 1600) still works. The room is sumptuous, from the gold leaf and the fancy hinges to the stucco marble. (Stucco marble is fake marble—a special mix of stucco, applied and polished. Designers liked it because it was less expensive than real marble and the color could be controlled.) Note the post-Renaissance perspective tricks decorating the walls; they were popular in the 17th century. The case (on the right as you enter) supposedly contains skeletons of three babies from the slaughter of the innocents in Bethlehem (where Herod, in an attempt to murder the baby Jesus, ordered all sons of a certain age killed).

Chapel (Room 89, ground floor, also viewable from Room 96 on the upper floor, often closed in the morning): Dedicated to Mary, this late-Renaissance/early-Baroque gem was the site of "Mad" King Ludwig's funeral after his mysterious murder—or suicide—in 1886. (He's buried in St. Michael's Church; see page 44.) Though Ludwig was not popular in the political world, he was beloved by his people, and his funeral drew huge crowds. "Mad" King Ludwig's grandfather (Ludwig I) was married here in 1810. After the wedding ceremony, carriages rolled his guests to a rollicking reception, which turned out to be such a hit that it became an annual tradition—Oktoberfest.

Red Room (Room 62, upper floor): The ultimate room is at the end of the corridor—the coral red room from 1740. (Coral red was *the* most royal of colors in Germany.) Imagine visiting the duke and having him take you here to ogle miniature copies of the most famous paintings of the day, composed with one-haired brushes. Notice the fun effect of the mirrors around you—the corner mirrors make things go forever and ever.

Precious Rooms (Rooms 55–62, upper floor): The Wittelsbachs were always trying to keep up with the Habsburgs, and this long string of ceremonial rooms was all for show. The decor and furniture are Rococo. The family art collection, now in the Alte Pinakothek, once decorated these walls. The bedroom (Room 60) was the official sleeping place, where the duke would publicly go to bed and awaken, à la Louis XIV.

Nymphenburg Porcelain (Room 5, at the end of the family gallery—described below, ground floor): In the 18th century, a royal family's status was bolstered by an in-house porcelain works (like Meissen for the Wettins in Dresden). The Wittelsbach family had their own Nymphenburg porcelain made for the palace. See

The History of Munich: Part 2
Troubled 20th Century and Today's Revitalization

This picks up where "Part 1" leaves off (see page 48).

Nazis, World War II, and Munich Bombed (1918-1945)

Germany after World War I was in chaos. In quick succession, the prime minister was gunned down, Communists took power, and the army restored the old government. In the hubbub, one fringe group emerged—the Nazi party, centered around the charismatic war veteran Adolf Hitler.

Hitler—an Austrian who'd settled in Munich—made stirring speeches in Munich's beer halls (including the Hofbräuhaus) and galvanized the city's disaffected. On November 8-9, 1923, the Nazis launched a coup d'état known as the Beer Hall Putsch. They kidnapped the mayor, and Hitler led a mob to overthrow the German government in Berlin. The march got as far as Odeonsplatz before Hitler was arrested and sent to prison in nearby Landsberg. Though the Nazis eventually gained power in Berlin, they remembered their roots, dubbing Munich "Capital of the Movement." The Nazi headquarters stood near today's obelisk on Brienner Strasse, Dachau was chosen as the regime's first concentration camp, and Odeonsplatz was designated as a place where all who passed by were required to perform the Nazi salute.

As World War II drew to a close, it was clear that Munich would be destroyed. Hitler did not allow the evacuation of much of the town's portable art treasures and heritage—a mass emptying of churches and civil buildings would have caused hysteria and been a statement of no confidence in his leadership. While museums were closed (and could be systematically emptied over the war years), public buildings were not. Rather than save the treasures, the Nazis photographed everything.

Munich was indeed pummeled mercilessly by air raids, leveling nearly half the city. What the bombs didn't get was destroyed by 10 years of rain and freezing winters.

Munich Rebuilds (1945-Present)

After the war, with generous American aid, the Münchners set to reconstructing their city. During this time, many German cities

how the mirrors and porcelain vases give the effect of infinite pedestals. If this inspires you to own some pieces of your own, head to the Nymphenburg Porcelain Store at Odeonsplatz (see "Shopping in Munich," later).

Gallery of the Wittelsbach Family (Room 4, ground floor): This room is from the 1740s (about 200 years younger than the Antiquarium). All official guests had to pass through here to meet the duke. The family tree in the center is labeled "genealogy of an imperial family." The big Wittelsbach/Habsburg rivalry was established commissions to debate their rebuilding strategy: They could restore the old towns, or bulldoze and go modern. While Frankfurt decided to start from scratch (hence its Manhattan-like feel today), Munich voted—by a close margin—to rebuild its old town.

Münchners took care to preserve the original street plan and re-create the medieval steeples, Neo-Gothic facades, and Neoclassical buildings. They blocked off the city center to cars, built the people-friendly U-Bahn system, and opened up Europe's first pedestrian-only zone (Kaufingerstrasse and Neuhauser Strasse). Only now, nearly 65 years after the last bombs fell, are the restorations—based on those Nazi photographs—finally being wrapped up. And those postwar decisions still shape the city: Buildings cannot exceed the height of the church spires.

The 1972 Olympic Games, featuring a futuristic stadium and a squeaky-clean city, were to be Munich's postwar statement that it had arrived. However, the Games turned tragic when a Palestinian terrorist group stormed a dormitory and kidnapped (and eventually killed) 11 Israeli athletes. In 1989, when Germany reunited, Berlin once again became the focal point of the country, relegating Munich to the role of sleepy Second City.

These days, Munich seems to be comfortable just being itself rather than trying to keep up with Berlin. In fact, the city seems to be on a natural high, especially since the ascension of Joseph Ratzinger (the local archbishop) to the papacy in 2005, his wildly successful homecoming visit in 2006, and Munich hosting the World Cup soccer tournament that same year.

Today's Munich is rich—home to BMW and Siemens AG, and a producer of software, books, movies, and the latest fashions. It's consistently voted one of Germany's most-livable cities—safe, clean, cultured, a university town, built on a people scale, and close to the beauties of nature. Though it's the capital of Bavaria and a major metropolis, Munich's low-key atmosphere has led Germans to dub it *Millionendorf*—the "village of a million people."

worked out through 500 years of marriages and battles—when they failed to sort out a problem through strategic weddings, they had a war. Opposite the tree are portraits of Charlemagne and Ludwig IV, each a Holy Roman Emperor and each wearing the same crown (now in Vienna). Ludwig IV was the first Wittelsbach HRE—an honor used for hundreds of years to substantiate the family's claim to power. You are surrounded by a scrapbook covering centuries of Wittelsbach family history.

Allied bombs took their toll on this hall. Above, the central

ceiling painting has been restored, but since there were no photos of the other two ceiling paintings, those spots remain empty.
Looking at the walls, you can see how each painting was hastily
cut out of its frame. Museums were closed in 1939, then gradually evacuated in anticipation of bombings. But public buildings
like this palace, which remained open to instill confidence in local
people, could not prepare for the worst. It wasn't until 1944, when
bombs were imminent, that the last-minute order was given to
slice all portraits out of their frames and hide them away.

▲▲**Residenz Treasury (Schatzkammer)**—The Treasury, next
door to the Residenz, shows off a thousand years of Wittelsbach
crowns and knickknacks. Vienna's jewels are better, but this is
Bavaria's best, with fine 13th- and 14th-century crowns and delicately carved ivory and glass (for cost and hours, see page 51).

   ❍ **Self-Guided Tour:** A long clockwise circle through the
eight rooms takes you chronologically through a thousand years
of royal treasure. (It's a one-way system—getting lost is not an
option.) Your ticket includes an English audioguide, but I've
explained the highlights below.

   The oldest jewels in the first room are 200 years older than
Munich itself. Many of these came from various prince-bishop collections when they were secularized (and their realms came under
the rule of the Bavarian king from Munich) in the Napoleonic
Era (c. 1800). The tiny mobile altar allowed a Carolingian king
(from Charlemagne's family of kings) to pack light in 890—and
still have a little Mass while on the road.

   In Room 3, study the reliquary with St. George killing the
dragon—sparkling with more than 2,000 precious stones (#58).
Get up close (it's OK to walk around the rope posts)...you can
almost hear the dragon hissing. It was made to contain the relics of St. George, who never existed (Pope John Paul II declared
him nothing more than a legend). If you could lift the miniscule
visor, you'd see that the carved ivory face of St. George is actually
the Wittelsbach duke (the dragon represents the "evil" forces of
Protestantism).

   In the next room (#4), notice the vividly carved ivory crucifixes
from 1630 (#157 and #158, on the right). These incredibly realistic
sculptures were done by local artist Georg Petel, a friend of Peter
Paul Rubens (whose painting of Christ on the cross—which you'll
see across town in the Alte Pinakothek—is Petel's obvious inspiration). Look at the flesh of Jesus' wrist pulling around the nails.

   Continue into Room 5. The freestanding glass case (#245)
holds the never-used royal crowns of Bavaria. Napoleon ended the
Holy Roman Empire and let the Wittelsbach family rule as kings
of Bavaria. As a sign of friendship, this royal coronation gear was
made in Paris by the same shop that crafted Napoleon's crown. But

before the actual coronation, Bavaria joined in an all-Europe anti-Napoleon alliance, and suddenly these were too French to be used.

Cuvilliés Theater—Attached to the Residenz is the exquisite Cuvilliés Theater. Designed by the same brilliant dwarf architect

who also did the Amalienburg Palace (see page 72), this newly restored theater is dazzling enough to send you back to the days of divine monarchs (€3, covered by Bavarian Castles Pass; April–July and mid-Sept–mid-Oct Mon–Sat 14:00–18:00, Sun 9:00–18:00; Aug–mid-Sept daily 9:00–18:00; mid-Oct–March Mon–Sat 14:00–17:00, Sun 10:00–17:00; last entry one hour before closing).

Max-Joseph-Platz—The centerpiece of this square, which faces the Residenz and National Theater, is a grand statue of King Maximilian I, a.k.a. Max Joseph, who was installed as Bavaria's first king in 1806 by Napoleon. Because Napoleon was desperate to establish his family as royal, crowning Max Joseph came with one condition: that his daughter marry Napoleon's stepson.

With the Holy Roman Empire gone and Napoleon history, modern 19th-century kings had little choice but to embrace constitutions that limited their power. Max Joseph liberalized his realm with a constitution, emancipated Protestants and Jews, and established the Viktualienmarkt (with his statue in the center). He was a particularly popular king, and both his reign and his son's reign were full of grand building projects designed to show that Bavaria was an enlightened state, Munich was a worthy capital, and the king was an equal with Europe's other royalty. The National Theater, which opened in 1818, celebrated Bavaria's strong culture, roots, and legitimacy.

Though Max Joseph was busy and had plenty of vision, his son and successor, Ludwig I, was the builder king who made Munich a grand capital. His Ludwigstrasse remains an impressive boulevard, with 60-foot-tall buildings stretching a mile from the Hall of Generals to the Arch of Victory, capped with a figure of Bavaria riding a lion-drawn chariot. And it was Ludwig I's wedding festival in 1810 that became an annual bash, giving Munich perhaps its greatest claim to fame: Oktoberfest.

Near the Residenz

Hofgarten—The elegant people's state garden (Hofgarten) is a delight on a sunny afternoon. The "Renaissance" temple centerpiece has great acoustics (and usually a musician performing for tips from lazy listeners). The lane leads to a building that houses the government of Bavaria and the Bavarian war memorial, which honors the fallen *heroes* of World War I, but only the *fallen* of World War II. The venerable old **Café Tambosi,** with a Viennese elegance inside and a relaxing garden setting outside, is a good antidote to all the beer halls (daily 8:00–24:00, Odeonsplatz 18, tel. 089/298-322). Just beyond is a lazy gravel *boules* court.

Odeonsplatz and Nearby—This square near the Hofgarten is a part of the grand imperial Munich vision. The church on Odeonsplatz (Theatinerkirche) contains about half of the Wittelsbach tombs. The loggia in the Hofgarten (honoring Bavarian generals) is modeled in the Florentine Renaissance style (in fact, after the famous loggia in Florence). A Roman-type triumphal arch hovers in the distance to the north (at the end of Ludwigstrasse). And to the west, a grand axis (Brienner Strasse) heads toward the Greek-inspired museum quarter.

    Brienner Strasse: From Odeonsplatz, look (or wander) down Brienner Strasse to get a taste of the Wittelsbachs' ambitious city

planning. At Karolinenplatz, the black obelisk commemorates the 30,000 Bavarians who marched with Napoleon to Moscow and never returned. Beyond that is the grand Königsplatz, or "King's Square," with its stern Neoclassicism, evocative of ancient Greece (and home to Munich's cluster of art museums, described next).

    On the way to this imperial splendor, Brienner Strasse goes through a square called **Platz der Opfer des Nationalsozialismus** ("Square of the Victims of Nazism"). Nearby, you'll find two former Nazi administration buildings; one is now the music academy, though it's still very much fascist in its architecture. A plaque on the street explains the buildings' history.

Munich's Cluster of Art Museums

This cluster of blockbuster museums (the Alte, Neue, and Moderne Pinakotheks, the Museum Brandhorst, the currently closed Lenbachhaus, and the Glyptothek) displays art spanning from the 14th century to the 21st. The Glyptothek and Lenbachhaus are right by the Königsplatz stop on the U-2 subway line. The three Pinakothek museums and the Brandhorst are just to the northeast.

Handy tram #27 whisks you right to the Pinakothek stop from Karlsplatz (near the train station), or you can walk 10 minutes from the Theresienstrasse or Königsplatz stops on the U-2 line.

A €12 combo-ticket covers the three Pinakotheks and the Brandhorst, and pays for itself if you visit two museums. On Sundays, these museums and the Glyptothek let you in for just a token €1, but charge for the useful audioguides (normally included).

▲▲Alte Pinakothek

Bavaria's best painting gallery (the "Old Art Gallery," pronounced ALL-tuh pee-nah-koh-TAYK) shows off a world-class collection of European masterpieces from the 14th to 19th centuries, starring the two tumultuous centuries (1450–1650) when Europe went from medieval to modern. See paintings from the Italian Renaissance (Raphael, Leonardo, Botticelli, Titian) and the German Renaissance it inspired (Albrecht Dürer). The Reformation of Martin Luther eventually split Europe into two subcultures—Protestants and Catholics—with their two distinct art styles (exemplified by Rembrandt and Rubens, respectively).

Cost, Hours, Location: €9, €1 on Sun, covered by €12 combo-ticket, open Wed–Sun 10:00–18:00, Tue 10:00–20:00, closed Mon, last entry 30 min before closing, free and excellent audioguide (€4.50 on Sun), obligatory lockers with refundable €2 deposit, no flash photos, U-2: Theresienstrasse or tram #27, Barer Strasse 27, tel. 089/2380-5216, www.pinakothek.de/alte-pinakothek.

◐ Self-Guided Tour: From the ticket counter, head toward the back wall and walk up the stairway to the left. All the paintings we'll see are on the upper floor, which is laid out like a barbell. Start at one fat end and work your way through the "handle" to the other end. Along the way you'll find the following paintings, roughly in this order.

German Renaissance—Room II: Albrecht Altdorfer's *The Battle of Issus (Schlacht bei Issus)* shows a world at war. Masses of soldiers are swept along in the currents and tides of a battle completely beyond their control, their confused motion reflected in the swirling sky. We see the battle from a great height, giving us a godlike perspective. Though the painting depicts Alexander the Great's victory over the Persians (find the

Alte Pinakothek

MUNICH

Persian king Darius turning and fleeing), it could as easily have been Germany in the 1520s. Christians were fighting Muslims, peasants battled masters, and Catholics and Protestants were squaring off for a century of conflict. The armies melt into a huge landscape, leaving the impression that the battle goes on forever.

Albrecht Dürer's larger-than-life *Four Apostles (Johannes und Petrus* and *Paulus und Marcus)* are saints of a radical new religion: Martin Luther's Protestantism. Just as Luther challenged Church authority, Dürer—a friend of Luther's—strips these saints of any rich clothes, halos, or trappings of power and gives them down-to-earth human features: receding hairlines, wrinkles, and suspicious eyes.

The inscription warns German rulers to follow the Bible rather than Catholic Church leaders. The figure of Mark—a Bible in one hand and a sword in the other—is a fitting symbol of the dangerous times.

Dürer's *Self-Portrait in Fur Coat (Selbstbildnis im Pelzrock)* looks like Jesus Christ but is actually 28-year-old Dürer himself, gazing out, with his right hand solemnly giving a blessing. This is the ultimate image of humanism: the artist as an instrument of God's continued creation. Get close and enjoy the intricately braided hair, the skin texture, and the fur collar. To the left of the head is Dürer's famous monogram—"A.D." in the form of a pyramid.

Italian Renaissance—Room IV: With the Italian Renaissance—the "rebirth" of interest in the art and learning of ancient Greece and Rome—artists captured the realism, three-dimensionality, and symmetry found in classical statues. Leonardo da Vinci's *Virgin and Child (Maria mit dem Kind)* need no halos—they radiate purity. Mary is a solid pyramid of maternal love, flanked by Renaissance-arch windows that look out on the hazy distance. Baby Jesus reaches out to play innocently with a carnation, the blood-colored symbol of his eventual death.

Raphael's *Holy Family at the Canigiani House (Die hl. Familie aus dem Hause Canigiani)* takes Leonardo's pyramid form and runs with it. Father Joseph forms the peak, with his staff as the strong central axis. Mary and Jesus (on the right) form a pyramid-within-the-pyramid, as do Elizabeth and baby John the Baptist on the left. They all exchange meaningful contact, safe within the bounds of the stable family structure.

In Botticelli's *Lamentation over Christ (Die Beweinung Christi)*, the Renaissance "pyramid" implodes, as the weight of the dead Christ drags everyone down, and the tomb grins darkly behind them.

Venetian Painting—Room V: In Titian's *Christ Crowned with Thorns (Die Dornenkronung)*, a powerfully built Christ sits silently enduring torture by prison guards. The painting is by Venice's greatest Renaissance painter, but there's no symmetry, no pyramid form, and the brushwork is intentionally messy and Impressionistic. By the way, this is the first painting we've seen done on canvas rather than wood, as artists experimented with vegetable oil–based paints.

Rubens and Baroque—Room VII: Europe's religious wars split the Continent in two—Protestants in the northern countries, Catholics in the south. (Germany itself was divided, with Bavaria remaining Catholic.) The Baroque style, popular in Catholic countries, featured large canvases, bright colors, lots of flesh, rippling motion, wild emotions, grand themes...and pudgy winged babies, the sure sign of Baroque. This room holds several canvases by the great Flemish painter Peter Paul Rubens.

In Rubens' 300-square-foot *Great Last Judgment (Das Grosse Jüngste Gericht)*, Christ raises the righteous up to heaven (left side) and damns the sinners to hell (on the right). This swirling cycle of nudes was considered risqué and kept under wraps by the very monks who'd commissioned it.

Rubens and Isabella Brant shows the artist with his first wife, both of them the very picture of health, wealth, and success. They lean together unconsciously, as people in love will do, with their hands clasped in mutual affection. When his first wife died, 53-year-old Rubens found a replacement—16-year-old Hélène Fourment, shown in an adjacent painting (just to the left) in her wedding dress. You may recognize Hélène's face in other Rubens paintings.

The Rape of the Daughters of Leucippus (Der Raub der Tochter des Leukippos) has many of Rubens' most typical elements—fleshy, emotional, rippling motion; bright colors; and a classical subject. The legendary twins Castor and Pollux crash a wedding and steal the brides as their own. The chaos of flailing limbs and rearing horses is all held together in a subtle X-shaped composition. Like the weaving counterpoint in a Baroque fugue, Rubens balances opposites.

Notice that Rubens' canvases were—to a great extent—cranked out by his students and assistants from small "cartoons" the master himself made (displayed in the next room).

Rembrandt and Dutch—Room IX: From Holland, Rembrandt van Rijn's *Six Paintings from the Life of Christ* are a down-to-earth look at supernatural events. The *Adoration (Die*

Anbetung der Hirten) of Baby Jesus takes place in a 17th-century Dutch barn with ordinary folk as models. The canvases are dark brown, lit by strong light. The *Adoration*'s light source is the Baby Jesus himself—literally the "light of the world." In the *Deposition (Kreuzabnahme),* the light bounces off Christ's pale body onto his mother Mary, showing how his death also hurts her. The drama is underplayed, with subdued emotions. Looking on is a man dressed in blue—a self-portrait of Rembrandt.

MUNICH

▲Neue Pinakothek

The Alte Pinakothek's sister is a twin building across the street, showing off paintings from 1800 to 1920: Romanticism, Realism, Impressionism, *Jugendstil,* Claude Monet, Pierre-Auguste Renoir, Vincent van Gogh, Francisco Goya, and Gustav Klimt (€7, €1 on Sun, covered by €12 combo-ticket, open Thu–Mon 10:00–18:00, Wed 10:00–20:00, closed Tue, well-done audioguide is usually free but €4.50 on Sun, classy Café Hunsinger in basement spills into park, U-2: Theresienstrasse or tram #27, Barer Strasse 29 but enter on Theresienstrasse, tel. 089/2380-5195, www.pinakothek .de/neue-pinakothek).

▲Pinakothek der Moderne

This museum picks up where the other two leave off, covering the 20th century. Four permanent displays (graphics, design, architecture, and paintings) are layered within the striking minimalist architecture. You'll find works by Pablo Picasso, Salvador Dalí, Joan Miró, René Magritte, Max Beckmann, Max Ernst, and abstract artists. The big white high-ceilinged building itself is worth a look. Even if you don't pay to visit the exhibits, step into the free entrance

hall to see the sky-high atrium and the colorful blob-column descending the staircase (€10, €1 on Sun, covered by €12 combo-ticket, open Tue–Sun 10:00–18:00, Thu until 20:00, closed Mon, U-2: Theresienstrasse or tram #27, Barer Strasse 40, tel. 089/2380-5360, www.pinakothek.de/pinakothek-der-moderne). This far-out collection offers little information in English—and there's no English audioguide. However, some temporary exhibits may have an English flier; ask at the information desk.

Green Munich

Although the capital of a very conservative part of Germany, Munich has long been a liberal stronghold. For nearly two decades, the city council has been controlled by a Social Democrat/Green Party coalition. The city policies are pedestrian-friendly—you'll find much of the town center closed to normal traffic, with plenty of bike lanes and green spaces. As you talk softly and hear birds rather than motors, it's easy to forget you're in the center of a big city. On summer Mondays, the peace and quiet make way for "blade Monday"—when streets in the center are closed to cars and as many as 30,000 inline skaters swarm around town in a giant rolling party.

▲Museum Brandhorst

Opened in 2009, the Brandhorst covers the end of the 20th century and the beginning of the 21st, with full English captions.

You can't miss the building—thousands of colored cylinders line the outside. The top floor (of three) is devoted to American artist Cy Twombly. A highlight is an ensemble of 12 Twombly paintings called *Lepanto,* after a 1571 battle in which Venice defeated the Ottoman fleet; six huge canvases of roses fill another room. On the lower floor, don't miss the giant medicine cabinet full of multicolored pills by Damien Hirst, and the sizable Andy Warhol collection (€7, €1 on Sun, covered by €12 combo-ticket, audioguide usually free but €4.50 on Sun, open Tue–Sun 10:00–18:00, Thu until 20:00, closed Mon, small café, U-2: Theresienstrasse or tram #27, Theresienstrasse 35a, tel. 089/2380-51325, www.museum-brandhorst.de).

▲Lenbachhaus

Closed for renovation until sometime in 2012, this museum is housed in a beautiful late 19th-century Tuscan-style villa (owned by painter Franz von Lenbach). It features the most complete collection of the early Modernist movement known as Blaue Reiter (Blue Rider), a branch of Expressionism that flourished from 1911 to 1914. When Wassily Kandinsky, Paul Klee, Franz Marc, Gabriele Münter, and some of their art-school cronies got fed up with being told how and what to paint, they formed the Blaue Reiter around a common ideology: to strive for new forms that expressed spiritual truth. Already controversial in their own day, their work was later targeted by the Nazis as *entartete Kunst* ("degenerate art"). The collection allows visitors to trace Kandinsky's progression from his earlier, more realistic works to the complete abstraction he's best known for. Münter, Kandinsky's lover and a great painter in her own right, donated her entire private collection (90 paintings and 330 other works) to Lenbachhaus in 1957, putting this little museum on the world art map (when open: €5–10 depending on exhibits, Tue–Sun 10:00–18:00, closed Mon, worthwhile €3 audioguide, €8 guidebook is a nice souvenir but otherwise unnecessary, small café, U-2: Königsplatz, Luisenstrasse 33, tel. 089/2333-2000, www.lenbachhaus.de).

Glyptothek

A collection of Greek and Roman sculpture started by King Ludwig I, the Glyptothek includes the famous *Barberini Faun*, statues from the Greek Classical period, funerary monuments of

wealthy Athenian families, and pediments of the Temple of Aegina. For a Who's Who of ancient celebrities, visit the Room of Ancient Portraits, where you'll come face to face with Alexander the Great and other luminaries from ancient political and philosophical spheres (€3.50, €1 on Sun, not much in English so invest in the worthwhile €1 guidebook, Tue–Sun 10:00–17:00, Thu until 20:00, closed Mon, U-2: Königsplatz, on Königsplatz, tel. 089/286-100).

In and near the English Garden

▲**English Garden (Englischer Garten)**—Munich's "Central Park," the largest one on the Continent, was laid out in 1789 by an American. More than 100,000 locals commune with nature here on sunny summer days. The park stretches three miles from the center, past the university to the trendy and bohemian Schwabing quarter. For the best quick visit, follow the river from the surfers (under the bridge just past Haus der Kunst) downstream into the garden. Just beyond the hilltop temple (walk up for a postcard view of the city), you'll find the big Chinese Tower beer garden and other places to enjoy a drink or a meal (described later, under "Eating in Munich"). A rewarding respite from the city, the park is especially fun—and worth ▲▲—on a bike under the summer sun and on warm evenings (unfortunately, there are no bike-rental agencies in or near the park; to rent some wheels, see page 35). Caution: While local law requires sun-worshippers to wear clothes on the tram, the park is sprinkled with buck-naked sunbathers—quite a shock to prudish Americans (they're the ones riding their bikes into the river and trees).

Haus der Kunst—Built by Hitler as a temple of Nazi art, this bold and fascist building is now an impressive shell for various temporary art exhibits. Ironically, the art now displayed in Hitler's "house of art" is the kind that annoyed the Führer most—modern (€5–10 per exhibit, combo-tickets save money if seeing at least two exhibits, daily 10:00–20:00, Thu until 22:00, little information in English but some exhibits may have English handouts, at south end of English Garden, tram #17 or bus #100 from station to Nationalmuseum/Haus der Kunst, Prinzregentenstrasse 1, tel. 089/211-270, www.hausderkunst.de).

Just beyond the Haus der Kunst, where Prinzregentenstrasse crosses the Eisbach canal, you can watch adventure-seekers surfing in the rapids created as the small river tumbles underground.

Bavarian National Museum (Bayerisches National-museum)—This tired but interesting collection features Tilman Riemenschneider woodcarvings, manger scenes, traditional living rooms, and old Bavarian houses (€5, €1 on Sun, open Tue–Sun 10:00–17:00, Thu until 20:00, closed Mon, tram #17 or bus #100 from station to Nationalmuseum/Haus der Kunst, Prinzregentenstrasse 3, tel. 089/211-2401, www.bayerisches-nationalmuseum.de).

Deutsches Museum

Germany's answer to our Smithsonian National Air and Space Museum, the Deutsches Museum traces the evolution of science and technology. The main branch of the Deutsches Museum is centrally located. The two branches—the Museum of Transportation and the Flight Museum—are situated outside the city center, but are worth the effort for enthusiasts. You can pay separately for each museum, or buy one €15 combo-ticket, which covers all three. Since this ticket has no time limit, you can spread out your visits to the various branches over your entire stay.

▲▲Deutsches Museum (Main Branch)

Enjoy wandering through well-described rooms of historic airplanes (Hitler's "flying bomb"—Wernher von Braun's notorious V-2 rocket—from 1944), spaceships, mining, the harnessing of wind and water power, hydraulics, musical instruments, printing, chemistry, computers, clocks, and astronomy...it's the Louvre of technical know-how. The museum is designed to be hands-on; if you see a button, push it. But with 10 miles of exhibits, from astronomy to zymurgy, even those on roller skates will need to be selective. While the museum was a big deal a generation ago, today it feels to many a bit dated, dusty, and overrated.

Cost, Hours, Information: €8.50, €15 combo-ticket includes Museum of Transportation and Flight Museum, daily 9:00–17:00, worthwhile €4 English guidebook, self-service cafeteria, tel. 089/21791, www.deutsches-museum.de. Most sections of the museum are well-described in English. The much-vaunted high-voltage demonstrations (3/day, 15 min, all in German) show the noisy creation of a five-foot bolt of lightning.

Getting There: Take the S-Bahn to Isartor, then walk 300 yards over the river, following signs.

❍ Self-Guided Tour: First head to the **mines,** which trace the history of mining since prehistoric times (mines closed during daily German-language tours at 9:45 and 13:45). As you follow the spiral stairs down to the mines, notice the 19th-century miners' chapel on the left. (Also notice the handy WC on the right.) While descriptions are only in German, the reconstructions of coal, potash, and salt mines are still impressive. It's a fun haunted house–type experience, with creepy life-like miners tucked away in dark corners. Enjoy the photo ops, like the chairlift that used to transport workers. (Hop in!) Apart from the fun and games, the museum has made great efforts to include realistic, accurate details to show what rigorous, dangerous work mining has always been. When you emerge from the mines, skip the mineral oil and natural gas section *(Erdöl und Erdgas)* and follow the signs for *Ausgang* (exit).

The fascinating, compact exhibit on **marine navigation** (on the ground floor) has models of sail, steam, and diesel vessels, from early canoes to grand sailing ships. Take the staircase down into the galley, below the main floor, to check out how life on passenger ships has changed—and don't miss the bisected U1 submarine. This first German submarine, dating from 1906, has been in the museum since 1921.

Flying high above the masts of the marine navigation exhibit is the section on **aeronautics** (first floor). Displays cover the most basic airborne flights (flying insects and seed pods), Otto Lilienthal's successful efforts in 1891 to imitate bird flight, and the development of hot-air balloons and gas-powered zeppelins. Many of the planes here are original, including the Wright brothers' Type A (1909), fighters and cargo ships from the two World Wars, and the first functioning helicopter, made in 1936. Climb into the planes whenever permitted, and try out the flight simulator.

The **astronautics** exhibit is located on the second floor. Back in the 1920s, Germany was working on rocket-propelled cars and sleds. Germany's research provided the US and Soviet space teams with much of their technical know-how. Here, you can peer at models of the V-2 (one of the first remote-controlled rockets/weapons, from World War II), an early Messerschmitt jet fighter, motors from the American Saturn rockets, and various space capsules, including Spacelab. The main focus is the walk on the moon, the Apollo missions, and the dogs-in-space program (monkeys, too)...but if you've ever been curious about space underwear, you'll find your answer here. Skip the nearby Altamira Caves exhibit, a replica of the 15,000-year-old drawings found in a cave in northern Spain; it's so dark that you can barely see anything.

The third floor traces the **history of measurement,** including time (from a 16th-century sundial and an 18th-century clock to a scary Black Forest wall clock complete with grim reaper), weights, geodesy (surveying and mapping), and computing (from 18th-century calculators to antiquated computers from the 1940s and 1950s).

On your way to the state-of-the-art **planetarium** (worth a visit if open, requires €2 extra ticket, lecture in German), poke your head out into the **sundial garden** located above the third floor. Even if you're not interested in sundials, this is a great place for a view of the surrounding landscape. On a clear day, you can see the Alps.

▲Museum of Transportation (Verkehrszentrum)

You don't need to be an engineer or race-car driver to get a kick out of this fun museum. The Deutsches Museum celebrated its 100th anniversary in 2003 by opening this annex across town that shows off all aspects of transport, from old big-wheeled bikes to Benz's first car (a three-wheeler from the 1880s) to sleek ICE super-trains. It's housed in a recently renovated early 20th-century conference hall and three giant hangar-like exhibition halls near the Oktoberfest grounds, a.k.a. Theresienwiese.

Cost, Hours, Location: €5, €15 combo-ticket includes Deutsches Museum and Flight Museum, daily 9:00–17:00, Theresienhöhe 14a, U-4 or U-5: Schwanthalerhöhe, tel. 089/5008-06762, www.deutsches-museum.de.

Tours: The free tours daily at 13:30, 14:00, 14:30, and 15:15 (each focusing on one part of the museum) are primarily in German, but English-speaking guides are happy to share.

❍ Self-Guided Tour: True to the Deutsches Museum's interactive spirit, the Museum of Transportation is totally hands-on,

Greater Munich

━━━ Ring Roads / Freeways
─── Other Roads

2 miles
3 km

TO Dachau
Dachauer Str.

TO Rothenburg & Romantic Road
A.8
Nymph. Str.

Nymphenburg Palace & Gardens

Amalienburg Palace

TO Airport & Nürnberg
A.9

BMW Museum

Tower Olympic Park

Flight Museum

Chinesischer Turm Beer Gdn.

Leopold

English Garden

Brienner-Str.

Main Train Station

Bavarian Nat'l. Museum

Landsberger Str.

TO Landsberg & Romantic Road

Museum of Transportation

Old City

East Stn.

Rosen-heimer

Lindwurm Str.

Oktoberfest Site (Theresienwiese)

River

Isar

A.96
TO Landsberg

A.95
TO Garmisch

TO Thalkirchen

A.995
A.8
TO Salzburg

DCH

MUNICH

and comes with plentiful English explanations. Without getting too academic, it traces the physiological and socioeconomic origins of motion and travel, from basic human and animal anatomy (try to identify those paw prints) to nomadic herders and camel caravans. What would our lives be like without transportation? Exhibits show how modes of transportation developed from sheer necessity into entertainment and competition, from Neolithic "bone" skates (predecessors to today's inline skates), to 19th-century Lapland skis, to today's snowboards and fast cars.

Hall 1 takes an inside-out look at Munich's public-transportation system—ride the tram and marvel at a cross-section of the intricate and multi-layered subway system.

Hall 2 gives you a look at the development of transportation for the sake of overland travel. Although it focuses primarily on trains, don't miss the chance to climb into the old carriage: The metal track simulates what it would have felt like to travel in the 18th century over different terrain (grass and cobblestones—pretty uncomfortable). Admire the Maffei S3/6, a.k.a. "The Pride of Bavaria" (in its heyday the fastest steam engine, at nearly 80 miles per hour); the clever old postal train (complete with a mail slot on the side); and the 1950s panorama bus that shuttled eager tourists to fashionable destinations such as Italy.

Hall 3 is all about fun: motorcycles, bicycles, skis, and race cars. Famous prewar models include the deluxe Mercedes-Benz 370 (1930s) and the Auto Union Type C "Grand Prix" race car. Other tiny racers—which resemble metal pickles to the uninitiated—include the 1950s Mercedes-Benz 300 SLR and the famous Messerschmitt 200. You'll also find early 18th-century bicycles based on Leonardo da Vinci's drawings. Before the invention of the pedal crank, bikes were just silly-looking scooters for adults.

Flight Museum (Flugwerft Schleissheim)

Fans of all things winged will enjoy the Deutsches Museum's Flight Museum, with more than 50 planes, helicopters, gliders, and an original Europa rocket housed in a historical aerodrome on a former military airfield. Inside the museum is the glass-walled workshop, where visitors can watch as antique planes are restored (€5, €15 combo-ticket includes Deutsches Museum and Museum of Transportation, daily 9:00–17:00; 20-min S-Bahn trip from Marienplatz, take S-1 direction: Freising Flughafen and get off at Oberschleissheim, trip covered by Munich XXL day pass, Effnerstrasse 18, tel. 089/315-7140, www.deutsches -museum.de).

Nymphenburg Palace Complex

Nymphenburg Palace and the surrounding one-square-mile park are good for a royal stroll or bike ride. Here you'll find a pair of palaces, the Royal Stables Museum, and playful extras such as a bathhouse, pagoda, and artificial ruins.

Cost and Hours: €10 for everything, less for each of the six individual parts, covered by Bavarian Castles Pass. All sights are open daily April–mid-Oct 9:00–18:00, mid-Oct–March 10:00–16:00. The park is open daily from 6:30 to dusk. Tel. 089/179-080, www.schloss-nymphenburg.de.

Getting There: The palace is three miles northwest of central Munich. Getting there from the center is easy, if a bit time-consuming: Take tram #17 from Karlstor (20 min to palace) or the train station (15 min to palace) to the Schloss Nymphenburg stop. From the bridge by the tram stop, you'll see the palace, but you'll have to walk another 10 minutes to get there. A pleasant bike path follows Arnulfstrasse from the train station all the way to Nymphenburg (a 30-min pedal).

▲▲Nymphenburg Palace

In 1662, after 10 years of trying, the Bavarian ruler Ferdinand Maria and his wife, Henriette Adelaide of Savoy, finally had a

son, Max Emanuel. In gratitude for a male heir, Ferdinand gave this land to his Italian wife, who proceeded to build an Italian-style Baroque palace. Their son expanded the palace to today's size. For 200 years, this was the Wittelsbach family's summer escape from Munich. (They still refer to themselves as princes and live in one wing of the palace.) If "Wow!" is your first impression, that's intentional.

Your visit is limited to 16 main rooms on one floor: the Great Hall (where you start), the King's Wing (to the right), and the Queen's Wing (on the left). The €2.50 audioguide is informative and easy to use (better than the €6 English guidebook). For most visitors, the following self-guided tour is all you'll need.

◑ Self-Guided Tour: The **Great Hall** in the middle was the dining hall. One of the grandest Rococo rooms in Bavaria, it was decorated by Johann Baptist Zimmermann (of Wieskirche fame) and François de Cuvilliés in about 1760. The painting on the ceiling shows Olympian gods keeping the peace (the ruler's duty).

The **King's Wing** (right of entrance) has walls filled with Wittelsbach portraits and stories. In the second room straight ahead, notice the painting showing the huge palace grounds, with Munich (and the twin onion domes of the Frauenkirche) three miles in the distance. Imagine the logistics when the royal family—with their entourage of 200—decided to move out to the summer palace. The Wittelsbachs were high rollers; from 1624 until 1806, one of the seven electors of the Holy Roman Emperor was a Wittelsbach. In 1806, Napoleon ended that institution and made the Wittelsbachs kings. (Note: For simplicity, I often refer to the Wittelsbachs as kings and queens, even though before 1806, these rulers were technically dukes, duchesses, and electors—and some were even Holy Roman Emperors.)

In the **Queen's Wing** (left of entrance), enter the first room, then head to the right to find the very red room. You'll see the founding couple, Henriette Adelaide and Ferdinand Maria (after the Counter-Reformation, Bavarian men were named Maria—but his high heels and leggings were another story altogether). The inlaid table was a wedding present. The real pay-off, this palace, didn't come until Henriette (who was 14 when she married) got pregnant. The green room is the ceremonial bedroom. The painting to the right of the bed shows Max Emanuel as a kid in a double portrait with his older sister. Both are dressed in the latest French fashions.

King Ludwig I's Gallery of Beauties, near the end of the long hall in the Queen's Wing, is decorated with portraits of 36 beautiful women—all of them painted by Joseph Stieler from 1827 to 1850. King Ludwig I was a consummate girl-watcher who prided himself on the ability to appreciate beauty regardless of social rank. He would pick the prettiest women from the general public and invite them to the palace for a portrait. The women range in status from royal princesses to a humble cobbler's daughter...but Ludwig seemed to prefer brunettes. The portraits reflect the modest Biedermeier style, as opposed to the more flamboyant Romanticism of the same period. If only these creaking floors could talk. Something about the place feels highly sexed, in a Prince Charles kind of way.

The next rooms are decorated in the Neoclassical style of the Napoleonic Era. At the rope, see the room where Ludwig II was born (August 25, 1845). Royal births were carefully witnessed. The mirror allowed for a better view. While Ludwig's death was shrouded in mystery (see page 114), his birth was well-documented.

Amalienburg Palace
Three hundred yards from the Nymphenburg Palace, hiding in the park (ahead and to the left as you go through to the back of the palace), you'll find one of the finest Rococo buildings in all of Europe. In 1734, Elector Karl Albrecht had this hunting lodge built for his wife, Maria Amalia. The palace was another Rococo jewel designed by François de Cuvilliés and decorated by Johann Baptist Zimmermann. Above the pink-and-white grand entryway, notice Diana, goddess of the chase, flanked by busts of satyrs. Look for the perch atop the roof where the queen would do her shooting. Behind a wall in the garden, dogs would scare non-flying pheasants. When they jumped up in the air above the wall, the sporting queen—as if shooting skeet—would pick the birds off.

Tourists enter this tiny getaway through the back door. The first room has doghouses under gun cupboards. Next, in the fine yellow-and-silver bedroom, see Vulcan forging arrows for amorous cupids at the foot of the bed. The bed is flanked by portraits of Karl Albrecht and Maria Amalia—decked out in hunting attire. She liked her dogs. The door under the portrait leads to stairs to the rooftop pheasant-shooting perch.

The mini–Hall of Mirrors is a blue-and-silver commotion of Rococo nymphs designed by Cuvilliés in the mid-1700s. Cuvilliés, short and hunchbacked, showed a unique talent for art and was sent to Paris to study. In the next room, paintings depict court festivities, formal hunting parties, and no-contest kills (where the animal is put at an impossible disadvantage—like shooting fish in a barrel). Finally, the kitchen is decorated with Chinese picnics on blue Dutch tiles.

Royal Stables Museum (Marstallmuseum)

This huge garage is lined with gilded Cinderella coaches. The highlight is just inside the entrance: the 1742 Karl Albrecht coro-

nation coach. When the Elector Karl Albrecht was chosen as Emperor, he rode in this coach, drawn by eight horses. Kings got only six.

Wandering through the collection, you can trace the evolution of 300 years of coaches—getting lighter and with better suspension as they were harnessed to faster horses. The carousel for the royal kids made development of dexterity fun—lop off noses and heads and toss balls through the snake. The glass case is filled with accessories.

In the room after the carousel, find the painting on the right of "Mad" King Ludwig on his sleigh at night. In his later years, Ludwig was a Howard Hughes–type recluse who stayed away from the public eye and only went out at night. (At his nearby Linderhof Palace, he actually had a hydraulic-powered dining table that would rise from the kitchen below, completely set for the meal—so he wouldn't be seen by his servants.) In the next room, you'll find Ludwig's actual sleighs. Next to them is the coach designed for his wedding, but it was never used. Ludwig's over-the-top coaches were Baroque. But this was 1870. The coaches, like the king, were in the wrong century. Notice the photos (c. 1865, in the glass case) of Ludwig with the Romantic composer Richard Wagner. Ludwig cried on the day Wagner was married. Hmmm.

Across the passage from the museum entrance, the second hall is filled with coaches for everyday use. Upstairs is a collection of **Nymphenburg porcelain** (described by an English loaner booklet at the entrance). Historically, royal families such as the Wittelsbachs liked to have their own porcelain plants to make fit-for-a-king plates, vases, and so on. The Nymphenburg Palace porcelain works is still in operation. Ludwig ordered the masterpieces of his royal collection (now at the Alte Pinakothek) to be copied in porcelain for safekeeping into the distant future. Take a close look—these are exquisite.

▲Olympic Park (Olympiapark München)

Munich's great 1972 Olympic stadium and sports complex is now a lush park. You can get a good look at the center's striking "cobweb" style of architecture while enjoying the park's picnic potential. In

addition, there are several activities on offer at the park, including a tower with a commanding but so-high-it's-boring view from 820 feet (Olympiaturm, €4.50, daily 9:00–24:00, last trip 23:30, tel. 089/3066-8585, www.olympiapark -muenchen.de) and an excellent swimming pool (Olympia-Schwimmhalle, €3.80, daily 7:00–23:00, last entry 22:00, tel. 01801-796-223, www.swm.de).

With the construction of Munich's new Allianz soccer stadium for the 2006 World Cup, Olympic Park has been left in the past. It will now melt into the neighborhood as simply a fine park and swimming pool. To reach the park, take U-3 to Olympia-Zentrum direct from Marienplatz.

BMW Museum and Factory

The museum at BMW headquarters is now open after a complete remodel. The bowl-shaped building encloses a world of floating

walkways between exhibits highlighting BMW motorcycle and car design and technology through the years. The museum also includes a good look at rare cult models (though the Deutsches Museum's Museum of Transportation—described earlier—has a much better old-car exhibit). Those without a

passion for vehicles may find themselves starting to yawn (€12, Tue–Fri 9:00–18:00, Sat–Sun 10:00–20:00, closed Mon, last entry 30 min before closing, U-3: Olympia-Zentrum, tel. 0180-211-8822, www.bmw-museum.de). From the U-Bahn, walk through the futuristic glass-and-steel BMW World building—where lucky customers go to pick up their new Beamers (free, daily 9:00–20:00)— then over the pedestrian bridge to the museum. Factory tours are available for true BMW fans and booked long in advance; register online or call, or check in the BMW World building for cancellations, released a half-hour before each tour (€6, 2.5 hrs, books up fast—especially July–Aug, tel. 0180-211-8822, www.bmw-werk-muenchen.de).

Near Munich

Near Munich

For day trips to many Bavarian destinations, including the first four listed here, consider traveling by train with the **Bayern-Ticket**. It covers up to five people from Munich to anywhere in Bavaria (plus Salzburg) and back for only €28 (€20 for one person, €2 extra if bought at ticket counters instead of machines, valid until 3:00 in the morning on the day after purchase, not valid before 9:00 Mon–Fri, valid only on slower "regional" trains). The ticket is explained in *The Inside Track* newsletter and sold at EurAide. Note that on weekdays, the Bayern-Ticket is only valid after 9:00—so if you're visiting "Mad" King Ludwig's Castles, you'll need to plan your entrance time accordingly.

▲▲▲**"Mad" King Ludwig's Castles**—The spectacular Neuschwanstein and Linderhof castles make a great day trip. Your easiest option is to take a tour (see "Tours in Munich," earlier). Without a tour, only Neuschwanstein is easy (2 hrs by train to Füssen, then 10-min bus ride to the castle). Or spend the night there. For all the details, see the next chapter.

▲▲Nürnberg—A handy express train gets you to Nürnberg in about an hour (departures several times an hour), making this very historic city a viable day trip from Munich. For information, see the Nürnberg chapter.

▲▲▲Salzburg—This Austrian city is an easy day trip, and offers some exciting sightseeing (hourly trains from Munich get you there in less than 2 hrs). For details, see the Salzburg and Berchtesgaden chapter.

▲Berchtesgaden—This resort, near Hitler's Eagle's Nest getaway, is easier as a side-trip from Salzburg (just 12 miles from there). For more, see page 190.

▲Isar River Bike Ride—Munich's river, lined by a gorgeous park, leads bikers into the pristine countryside in just a few minutes. From downtown (easy access from the English Garden or Deutsches Museum), follow the riverside bike path south (upstream) along the east (left) bank. You can't get lost. Just stay on the lovely bike path. It crosses the river after a while, passing tempting little *Biergartens* and lots of Bavarians having their brand of fun—including gangs enjoying Munich's famous river party rafts. Go as far as you like, then retrace your route to get home. The closest bike rental is at Munich Walk, near Isartor, which also offers a guided bike tour along this route (see page 35).

▲Andechs Monastery—This monastery crouches quietly with a big smile between two lakes just south of Munich. For a fine Baroque church in a rural Bavarian setting at a monastery that serves hearty cafeteria-quality food and perhaps the best beer in Germany, consider a short side-trip here. The cafeteria terrace offers first-class views and second-class prices (*Biergarten* open daily 10:00–20:00, church open until 18:00, tel. 08152/3760, www.andechs.de). Reaching Andechs from Munich without a car is frustrating but doable (buy Munich Gesamtnetz day ticket for €10, take the S-5 train to Herrsching, then catch a shuttle bus or taxi; or hike or bike 3 miles). Don't miss the stroll up to the church, where you can sit peacefully and ponder the striking contrasts a trip through Germany offers.

▲▲Dachau Concentration Camp Memorial (KZ-Gedenkstätte Dachau)—Dachau was the first Nazi concentration camp (1933). Today, it's the most accessible camp for travelers and an effective voice from our recent but grisly past, pleading "Never again." A visit here is a valuable experience and, when approached thoughtfully, well worth the trouble. After this most powerful sightseeing experience, many people gain more respect for history and the dangers of mixing fear, blind patriotism, and an evil government. You'll likely see lots of students here, as all German schoolchildren are required to visit a concentration camp. It's interesting to think that a couple of generations ago, people greeted each other with a robust "Sieg Heil!" Today, almost no Germans know the lyrics of their national anthem, and German flags are a rarity outside of major soccer matches.

Cost and Hours: Free, Tue–Sun 9:00–17:00, closed Mon except holidays, last entry 30 min before closing. Though the museum shuts down at 17:00, the grounds are open until 18:00. The museum discourages parents from bringing children under 12.

Getting There: The camp is a 45-minute trip from downtown Munich. Take S-2 (direction: Petershausen) from any of the central S-Bahn stops in Munich to Dachau (3/hr, 20-min trip from Hauptbahnhof). Then, from the Dachau station, catch bus #726 to the KZ-Gedenkstätte stop (3/hr, 7 min; on Sun only, bus #724 also runs to KZ-Gedenkstätte). The Munich XXL day pass covers the entire trip, both ways (€6.70/person, €11.80/partner ticket). Drivers follow Dachauer Strasse from downtown Munich to Dachau-Ost, then follow *KZ-Gedenkstätte* signs. You can also take a tour from Munich (described earlier, under "Tours in Munich").

The Town: The town of Dachau is more pleasant than its unfortunate association with the camp on its outskirts, and tries hard to encourage you to visit its old town and castle (www.dachau .de). With 40,000 residents and quick access to downtown Munich, Dachau is now a high-priced and in-demand place to live.

Background: While a relatively few 32,000 inmates died in Dachau between 1933 and 1945 (in comparison, more than a million were killed at Auschwitz in Poland), the camp is notorious because it was the Nazis' first. It was originally established to house political prisoners and opponents of the Nazi regime, and only later played a role in World War II. In the 1930s, the camp was located outside built-up areas, and was surrounded by a mile-wide restricted area. It was a work camp, where inmates were used for slave labor, including constructing the buildings that you see. A huge training center stood next to the camp. The people who ran the entire concentration-camp system during the war were trained here, and it was former Dachau officials who went on to manage the death camps further east, mostly in Nazi-occupied Poland.

After war broke out, the regime found more purposes for Dachau: a departure point for people shipped east to the gas chambers, a special prison for priests, a center for barbaric medical experimentation on inmates, and finally—as the Nazis retreated— a transfer destination for prisoners from other camps. Few realize

Dachau

ⓑ Bus Stop   🅿 Parking   ROBERT-BOSCH-STRASSE →

ALTE RÖMERSTRASSE

GUARD TOWER   RECONSTRUCTED BARRACK

CARMELITE CONVENT

RELIGIOUS MEMORIALS

FORMER

THEATER   → MUSEUM

SCULPTURE →

BARRACKS

"THE BUNKER"

PATH

RECONSTRUCTED BARRACK

MUSEUM ENTRY   PATH

CREMATORIUM + GAS CHAMBER   ENTRANCE "ARBEIT MACHT FREI" GATE   VISITORS CENTER   ⓑ BUS #726 (TO/FROM S-BAHN STN.)

MEMORIAL GARDEN   DCH   TO DACHAU TOWN CENTER + S-BAHN STATION ↓

that Dachau actually housed people longer *after* the war than during the war. After liberation, the fences were taken down, but numerous survivors who had nowhere else to go stayed. It later served as a prison for camp officials convicted in the Dachau trials. Still later, it housed refugees from Eastern Europe. Until the 1960s, it was like a small town, with a cinema, shops, and so on.

Visitors Center: Coming from the bus stop or parking lot, you'll first see the new visitors center, outside the camp wall. It has a café serving simple lunches, a bookstore, and a desk where you can rent an audioguide or sign up for tours, but no exhibits.

Tours: The €3 **audioguide** is informative and gives you extras like survivor stories, but isn't essential, since the camp is fully labeled in English. Two different English **guided walks** are offered: a 30-minute introduction (€1.50; May–Sept Tue–Fri at 12:30, Sat–Sun at 11:00 and 12:30; Oct–April Thu and Sat–Sun at 12:30) and a more in-depth 2.5-hour walk (€3; May–Sept Tue–Fri at 13:30, Sat–Sun at 12:00 and 13:30; Oct–April Thu and Sat–Sun at 13:30). To confirm times, call 08131/669-970 or visit www.kz -gedenkstaette-dachau.de.

❍ Self-Guided Tour: Walking past the visitors center, turn right into the main compound. You enter, like the inmates did, through the infamous **iron gate** with the taunting slogan *Arbeit macht frei* ("Work makes you free"). Inside are the key experiences of the memorial: the museum, the bunker behind the museum, the restored barracks, and a pensive walk across the huge but now-empty camp to the shrines and crematorium at the far end.

The large camp-administration building has been converted

into a gripping **museum**. Inside the entrance, a small shop sells a €0.50 information sheet, a €3 booklet dating from the 1960s, and an excellent 200-page book with CD (€15). Exhibits are thoughtfully and completely described in English. Computer touch-screens let you watch early newsreels. The **theater** shows a powerful documentary movie (shows in English usually at 11:30, 14:00, and 15:30).

The long, low **bunker** behind the museum was a cellblock for "special prisoners," such as failed Hitler assassins, German religious leaders, and politicians who challenged Nazism. Exhibits profile the inmates and the SS guards who worked at Dachau (you exit the movie by the bunker door; otherwise walk around museum past the *Arbeit macht frei* sign).

The big **square** between the museum and the reconstructed barracks was used for roll call. Twice a day, the entire camp population assembled here. They'd stand at attention until all were accounted for. If someone was missing (more likely dead than escaped), everyone would have to stand—often through the night—until the person was located.

Beyond the two reconstructed **barracks,** a long walk takes you past the foundations of the other barracks to four places of meditation and worship (Jewish, Catholic, Protestant, and Russian Orthodox). Beyond that is a Carmelite convent.

To the left of the shrines, find the memorial garden surrounding the camp **crematorium,** which was used to burn the bodies of prisoners who had died. Look at the smokestack. You're standing on ground nourished by the ashes of those who died at Dachau. Next to the crematorium is a **gas chamber,** which worked on the same principles as the much larger one at Auschwitz. It was never put to use at Dachau for mass murder, but some historians suspect that a few prisoners were killed in it experimentally.

To end your visit, retrace your steps back to the visitors center and bus stop.

Experiences in Munich

Oktoberfest

The 1810 marriage reception of King Ludwig I was such a success

that it turned into an annual bash. These days, the Oktoberfest lasts just over two weeks (Sept 18–Oct 3 in 2010), starting on the third Saturday in September and usually ending on the first Sunday in October (but never before Oct 3—the day Germany celebrates its recent reunification).

Oktoberfest kicks things off with an opening parade of more than 6,000 participants. Every night, it fills eight huge beer tents with about 6,000 people each. A million gallons of beer later, they roast the last ox.

It's best to reserve a room early, but if you arrive in the morning (except Fri or Sat) and haven't called ahead, the TI can usually help. The Theresienwiese fairground (south of the main train station), known as the "Wies'n," erupts in a frenzy of rides, dancing, and strangers strolling arm-in-arm down rows of picnic tables while the beer god stirs tons of brew, pretzels, and wursts in a bubbling cauldron of fun. The triple-loop roller coaster must be the wildest on earth (best before the beer-drinking). During the fair, the city functions even better than normal. It's a good time to sightsee, even if beer-hall rowdiness isn't your cup of tea. For details, see www.oktoberfest.de.

If you're not visiting while the party's on, don't worry: You can still dance to oompah bands, dunk huge pretzels, and show off your stein-hoisting skills any time of year at Munich's classic beer halls, including the venerable **Hofbräuhaus** (see page 89). Also in the city center, the **Beer and Oktoberfest Museum** gives a historical take on the festival (see page 47).

Shopping in Munich

You'll find beer steins to take home at shops on the pedestrian zone by St. Michael's Church and at the gift shops that surround the Hofbräuhaus. Münchners take their shoes very seriously; the pedestrian zone abounds with shoe stores featuring everything from expensive Italian models to Birkenstocks.

Here are a few areas and stores to consider:

Department Stores: You'll see lots of modern department stores. Locals rate them this way: **C&A** (which sells only clothing) is considered cheap yet respected; **Kaufhof** (which sells everything) is mid-range; and **Karstadt** is upmarket.

On Marienplatz: Beck's, an upscale department store, has been a local institution since 1861, when it began meeting the needs of the royal family, including "Mad" King Ludwig. This shop has long been to fabrics what Alois Dallmayr is to fine food (see page 93). Today, it sells stationery, cosmetics, and its own clothing label and designer duds (Mon–Sat 10:00–20:00, closed Sun). If you're facing the glockenspiel on New Town Hall, look to your right—you can't miss it on the corner. Also on Marienplatz is the **Hugendubel** bookstore, but there's a better English selection at their English-language store on Salvatorplatz, behind Fünf Höfe (see "Helpful Hints," earlier).

Weinstrasse/Theatinerstrasse: Shoppers will want to

stroll from Marienplatz down the pedestrianized Weinstrasse (it begins to the left as you face New Town Hall). As you walk down Weinstrasse, look for **Fünf Höfe** on your left, a delightful mall filled with Germany's top shops (open until 20:00, www.fuenf hoefe.de). Named for its five courtyards, this is where tradition meets modern. Note how its Swiss architects (who also designed Munich's grand new Allianz soccer stadium for the 2006 World Cup) play with light and color. Even if you're not a shopper, wander through the **Kunsthalle** to appreciate the architecture, the elegant window displays, and the sight of Bavarians living very well.

For fine-quality (and very expensive) traditional clothing, visit **Loden-Frey Verkaufshaus** (a block west of Weinstrasse). The third floor of this fine department store is dedicated to classic Bavarian wear for men and women (Mon–Sat 10:00–20:00, closed Sun, Maffeistrasse 7, tel. 089/210-390, www.loden-frey.com).

Theatinerstrasse spills out onto Odeonsplatz, where you'll find the **Nymphenburg Porcelain Store** (Mon–Fri 10:00–18:30, Sat 10:00–16:00, closed Sun, Odeonsplatz 1, tel. 089/282-428, www .nymphenburg.com).

Maximilianstrasse: For the most exclusive shops, stroll this street. Ludwig I made the grand but very impersonal Ludwigstrasse; as a reaction to that unpopular street by an unpopular king, his son Maximilian built a street designed for the people and for shopping. It leads from the National Theater, over the Isar River to the Bavarian Parliament (which you can see from the theater end).

Sleeping in Munich

Unless you hit Munich during a fair, convention, or big holiday, you can sleep reasonably here. Lots of student hotels around the station house anyone who's young at heart for €20, and it's easy to find a fine double with breakfast in a good basic hotel for €80. I've listed accommodations in two neighborhoods: within a few blocks of the central train station (Hauptbahnhof) and in the old center. Many of these places have complicated, slippery pricing schemes. I've listed the normal non-convention, non-festival prices. There are major conventions about 30 nights a year—prices increase from 20 percent to as much as 300 percent during Oktoberfest (Sept 18–Oct 3 in 2010; reserve well in advance). On the other hand, during slow times, you may be able to do better than the rates listed here—always ask. Sunday is very slow and usually comes with a huge discount if you ask.

Near the Train Station
Good budget hotels cluster in the multicultural area immediately south of the station. It feels seedy after dark (erotic cinemas and

Sleep Code

(€1 = about $1.40, country code: 49, area code: 089)
S = Single, **D** = Double/Twin, **T** = Triple, **Q** = Quad, **b** = bathroom, **s** = shower only. Unless otherwise noted, credit cards are accepted, a buffet breakfast is included, there is an elevator but no air-conditioning, and English is spoken.

To help you sort easily through these listings, I've divided the rooms into three categories based on the price for a standard double room with bath:

$$$ Higher Priced—Most rooms €100 or more.

$$ Moderately Priced—Most rooms between €70–100.

$ Lower Priced—Most rooms €70 or less.

men with moustaches loitering in the shadows), but it's dangerous only for those in search of trouble. Still, hotels in the old center (listed later) might feel more comfortable to many readers.

$$ Hotel Monaco is a delightful and welcoming little hideaway, tucked inside the fifth floor of a giant nondescript building two blocks from the station. Emerging from the elevator, you're warmly welcomed by Christine into her flowery, cherub-filled oasis. It's homey, with 24 clean and fresh rooms (Sb-€45–70, Db-€55–75, Tb-€90–120, breakfast-€8, free Wi-Fi, Schillerstrasse 9, entrance on Adolf-Kolping-Strasse, tel. 089/545-9940, fax 089/550-3709, www.hotel-monaco.de, info@hotel-monaco.de).

$$ Litty's Hotel advertises "cheap and cozy," and that's exactly what it delivers. Opened in 2008, the hotel features 37 rooms and charming managers Verena and Bernd Litty (S-€46, Sb-€58, D-€66, Ds-€74, Db-€82, T-€93, free Wi-Fi—ask for a room with strong signal, near Schillerstrasse at Landwehrstrasse 32c, tel. 089/5434-4211, fax 089/5434-4212, www.littyshotel.de, info@littyshotel.de).

$$ Hotel Royal is perhaps the best value in its price range (as long as you can look past the strip joints flanking the entry). While a bit institutional, it's clean, entirely non-smoking, and plenty comfortable. Most importantly, it's energetically run by Pasha and Changiz. Each of its 40 rooms is fresh and bright (Sb-€54–69, Db-€74–89, Tb-€94–109, Qb-€114–129, lower prices generally Nov–March, book direct for a 10 percent discount off the prevailing price with this book in 2010, ask for a room on the quiet side—especially in summer when you'll want the window open, free Internet access and Wi-Fi, Schillerstrasse 11a, tel. 089/5998-8160, fax 089/5998-81616, www.hotel-royal.de, info@hotel-royal.de).

$$ Hotel Bristol has 57 comfortable business-class rooms. While a longer walk from the station, it's bright, efficient, and

Hotels near the Train Station

- ▥ Pedestrian Zone
- **U** U-Bahn Stop
- **S** S-Bahn Stop

200 YARDS
200 METERS

- ① Hotel Monaco
- ② Litty's Hotel
- ③ Hotel Royal
- ④ Hotel Bristol
- ⑤ Hotel Uhland
- ⑥ Hotel Reinbold
- ⑦ Hotel Deutsches Theater
- ⑧ Hotel Europäischer Hof
- ⑨ Hotel Mark
- ⑩ CVJM (YMCA)
- ⑪ Wombat's Hostel, Euro Youth Hotel & Jaeger's Hostel
- ⑫ La Vecchia Masseria Rest.
- ⑬ To Augustiner Beer Garden
- ⑭ EurAide Office
- ⑮ Pharmacy
- ⑯ Launderette
- ⑰ Radius Tours
- ⑱ Gray Line Tour Bus Stop
- ⑲ Airport & Romantic Road Bus Stops

pleasantly located just across the street from the Sendlinger Tor U-Bahn stop (Sb-€89, Db-€99, hearty buffet breakfast, non-smoking rooms, free Internet access and Wi-Fi, one U-Bahn stop from station, U-1 or U-2: Sendlinger Tor, Pettenkoferstrasse 2, tel. 089/5434-8880, fax 089/5434-888111, www.bristol-munich.de, info@bristol-munich.de).

$$ Hotel Uhland is a stately mansion that rents 31 delightful rooms in a safe-feeling, less-seedy residential neighborhood a slightly longer walk from the station than the others in this section (toward the Theresienwiese Oktoberfest grounds). It's been in the same wonderful Hauzenberger family for 50 years (Sb-€70–85, small Db-€85, big Db-€95, Tb-€120, save about €10 a night by booking through their website, great family rooms and deals, non-smoking floor, free Wi-Fi, limited free parking; from station, take bus #58 to Georg-Hirth-Platz, or walk 15 minutes: go up Goethestrasse and turn right on Pettenkoferstrasse, cross Georg-Hirth-Platz to Uhlandstrasse and find #1; tel. 089/543-350, fax 089/5433-5250, www.hotel-uhland.de, info@hotel-uhland.de).

$$ Hotel Reinbold has 65 sunny rooms very close to the station (Sb-€59, Db-€79, Tb-€109, breakfast-€9, ask about Rick Steves discount when you email, free Wi-Fi, Adolf-Kolping-Strasse 11, tel. 089/5999-3902, fax 089/5999-3994, www.hotel-reinbold.de, info@hotel-reinbold.de).

$$ Hotel Deutsches Theater, with the same owners as the Hotel Reinbold, is a brass-and-marble-filled place with 27 tight, modern three-star rooms. The back rooms face the courtyard of a neighboring theater—when there's a show, there can be some street noise (Sb-€59, Db-€79, Tb-€109, pricier suites, breakfast-€9, ask about Rick Steves discount when you email, non-smoking floors, free Wi-Fi, Landwehrstrasse 18, tel. 089/545-8525, fax 089/5458-5261, www.hoteldeutschestheater.de, info@hoteldeutsches theater.de).

$$ Hotel Europäischer Hof, across from the station, is a huge impersonal business hotel with 150 decent rooms. Official rates are sky-high, but actual rates are usually lower (close to S-€50, Sb-€85, smaller "tourist class" D with head-to-toe twin beds-€57, Db-€92; 10 percent discount on prevailing rate in 2010 with this book and advance reservation, *or* if you pay cash—no double discounts; no discounts during conventions, major events, and Oktoberfest weekends; check website for other discounts, non-smoking rooms, family rooms, free Internet access, pay Wi-Fi, Bayerstrasse 31, tel. 089/551-510, fax 089/5515-11444, www.heh.de, info@heh.de). They also run **$$ Hotel Mark** around the corner, with a large lobby, dim hallways, 95 fine rooms, and a similar institutional 1970s ambience (S-€50, Sb-€75, D-€60, basic Db-€82, ask for 10 percent discount described above, free Internet access, pay Wi-Fi, Senefelderstrasse

12, tel. 089/559-820, fax 089/5598-22444, www.hotel-mark.de, mark@heh.de).

$ The **CVJM (YMCA),** open to all ages, rents 85 beds in modern rooms with sinks in the rooms and showers down the hall (S-€35, D-€59, T-€82.50, €27.50/bed in a shared triple, those over 26 pay about 10 percent more, cheaper for 3 nights or more and in winter, only €5/night per person more during Oktoberfest—reserve months ahead; includes sheets, breakfast, and Internet access, but no lockers; Landwehrstrasse 13, tel. 089/552-1410, fax 089/550-4282, www.cvjm-muenchen.org, hotel@cvjm-muenchen.org).

"Hostel Row" on Senefelderstrasse, a Block from the Station

All three of the following hostels are casual and well-run, with friendly and creative management, and all cater expertly to the needs of young beer-drinking backpackers enjoying Munich on a shoestring. There's no curfew at any of these places, and each one has a lively bar that rages until the wee hours, along with staff who speak English as the primary language. All have 24-hour receptions, laundry facilities, and include linens; none has a kitchen. Sleep cheap in big dorms, or spend a little more for a two-, three-, or four-bed room.

$ **Wombat's Hostel** rents cheap doubles and six- to eight-bed dorms with lockers. Each bedroom is fresh and modern, with its own bathroom, and there's a relaxing and peaceful winter garden (374 beds, dorm bed-€24, Db-€70, breakfast-€3.50, cheaper off-season, pay Internet access, free Wi-Fi, Senefelderstrasse 1, tel. 089/5998-9180, www.wombats-hostels.com, office@wombats -munich.de).

$ **Euro Youth Hotel** fills a rare pre-WWII building and is probably the most comfortable hostel for older travelers (200 beds, 10- to 12-bed dorms-€20.50/bed, 3- to 5-bed dorms-€23.50/bed, breakfast in dorms is €3.90 extra; D-€55, Db-€65, breakfast included for private rooms; free Wi-Fi, bike rental-€10/day, Senefelderstrasse 5, tel. 089/5990-8811, www.euro-youth-hotel.de, info@euro-youth-hotel.de, run by Alfio).

$ **Jaeger's Hostel** rounds out this trio, with 300 cheap beds and all the fun and efficiency you'd hope for in a hostel (40-bed dorm-€19/bed, 8-bed dorm-€22/bed, 3- to 6-bed rooms-€25/bed, includes breakfast, cheaper off-season, towels-€1/day, pay Internet access, free Wi-Fi, Senefelderstrasse 3, tel. 089/555-281, fax 089/592-598, www.jaegershostel.de, info@jaegershostel.de).

In the Old Center

A few good deals remain in the area south of Marienplatz, going towards Sendlinger Tor.

$$$ Mercure München Altstadt Hotel is a huge, impersonal, basic business-class hotel with all the modern comforts on a boring street very close to the Marienplatz action. If you want an American-style hotel room buried deep in Munich for a decent price, this place has 75 of them (Sb-€106, Db-€128 for most days, breakfast-€15, parking-€17/day, non-smoking floors, air-con, pay Wi-Fi, a block south of the pedestrian zone at Hotterstrasse 4, tel. 089/232-590, fax 089/2325-9127, www.mercure-muenchen -altstadt.de, h3709@accor.com).

$$$ Hotel Blauer Bock, formerly a dormitory for Benedictine monks, has been on the same corner near the Munich City Museum since 1841. It's a little pricey and feels spartan, but offers 69 clean, decent rooms and a straightforward pricing system (the same rates every day, except during fairs and Oktoberfest). Breakfast is served in its very mod and sleek restaurant next door, though most of the decor feels like the monks still run the place (S-€54, Sb-€71–85, twin D-€86, D-€90, Db-€115–126, Db suite-€165, extra bed including breakfast- €40, €10 fee if paying with Visa or MasterCard, free Wi-Fi if you book online—otherwise €5/day, parking-€17, Sebastianplatz 9, tel. 089/231-780, fax 089/2317-8200, www.hotelblauerbock.de, info@hotelblauerbock.de).

$$ Pension Lindner is clean and quiet, with nine pleasant pastel-bouquet rooms off a bare stairway (S-€39, D-€60, Ds-€70, Db-€80, these special prices promised with this book through 2010, cash preferred, pay Wi-Fi, Dultstrasse 1, tel. 089/263-413, fax 089/268-760, www.pension-lindner.com, info@pension -lindner.com, Marion Sinzinger).

$$ Hotel Atlanta is conveniently located 50 yards from the Sendlinger Tor U-Bahn stop and a 10-minute walk from Marienplatz. Its 20 rooms are split between two buildings connected by a peaceful patio. To minimize street noise, ask for a room in the older back building (S-€40, Ss-€55, Sb-€70, Ds-€70, Db-€80–90, family rooms, breakfast-€7, pay Wi-Fi, Sendlinger Strasse 58, tel. 089/263-605, fax 089/260-9027, www.hotel-atlanta .de, info@hotel-atlanta.de).

$$ Hotel Münchner Kindl is jolly, with 22 decent rooms above a friendly neighborhood bar (S-€45, D-€72, Db-€92, Tb-€115, Qb-€130, these prices through 2010 with this book except during Oktoberfest and special events, lower rates possible in summer—ask, non-smoking rooms, no elevator, night noises travel up central courtyard, no air circulation in courtyard-facing rooms so they can get hot in summer—request a fan, pay Wi-Fi in most rooms, Damenstiftstrasse 16, tel. 089/264-349, fax 089/264-526, www.hotel-muenchner-kindl.de, reservierung@hotel-muenchner -kindl.de, Gunter and Renate).

MUNICH

Central Munich Hotels and Restaurants

★ MARIENPLATZ & ⓘ
Ⅲ PEDESTRIAN ZONE
Ⓤ U-BAHN STOP
Ⓢ S-BAHN STOP

¼ MILE
400 METERS   DCH

❶ Mercure München Altstadt Hotel
❷ Hotel Blauer Bock
❸ Pension Lindner
❹ Hotel Atlanta
❺ Hotel Münchner Kindl
❻ Hofbräuhaus Beer Hall
❼ Die Münchner Suppenküche (2)
❽ Jodlerwirt Pub
❾ Nürnberger Bratwurst Glöckl am Dom & Andechser am Dom
❿ Altes Hackerhaus
⓫ Der Pschorr Beer Hall & Schrannenhalle
⓬ Spatenhaus Beer Hall
⓭ Heilig-Geist-Stüberl
⓮ To Chinesischer Turm Biergarten & Seehaus
⓯ Glockenspiel Café & Hugendubel Bookstore
⓰ Alois Dallmayr Deli
⓱ Stadt Café (in Munich City Museum)
⓲ Prinz Myshkin Veggie Rest.
⓳ Riva Bar Pizzeria
⓴ Café Tambosi
㉑ Nymphenburg Porcelain Store
㉒ Beer & Oktoberfest Museum
㉓ Munich Walk Office

Away from the Center

$ Munich's venerable **International Youth Camp Kapuzinerhölzl** (a.k.a. "The Tent") offers 400 spots on the wooden floor of a huge circus tent and never fills up. You'll get a mattress (€7.50) or bed (€10.50), or pitch your own tent (€5.50/tent plus €5.50/person). Blankets, hot showers, lockers, a kitchen, and Wi-Fi are all included; breakfast is a few euros extra. It can be a fun but noisy experience—kind of a cross between a slumber party and Woodstock. There's a cool table-tennis-and-Frisbee atmosphere throughout the day, nightly campfires, and no curfew (open early-June–mid-Oct only, prices a little higher during Oktoberfest, cash only, pay Internet access, self-service laundry, bikes-€8/day, catch tram #17 from train station for 17 minutes to Botanischer Garten, direction Amalienburgstrasse, and follow the crowd down Franz-Schrank-Strasse, tel. 089/141-4300, www.the-tent.com, cu @the-tent.com).

Eating in Munich

Munich cuisine is best seasoned with beer. You have two basic types of places to choose from: beer halls such as the Hofbräuhaus, where you'll find music and tourists; or the mellower beer gardens, where you'll find the Germans. I'm here for the beer-garden fun. But when the *Wurst und Kraut* get to be too much for you, Munich has more Michelin-star restaurants than any other German city, plus a galaxy of good, more affordable alternatives. All restaurants are now smoke-free. The only ashtrays you'll see throughout Bavaria are outside.

In beer halls, beer gardens, or at the Viktualienmarkt, try the most typical meal in town: *Weisswurst* (white-colored veal sausage—peel off the skin before eating, often available only until noon) with *süsser Senf* (sweet mustard), a salty *Brezel* (pretzel), and *Weissbier* ("white" wheat beer). Another traditional favorite is *Obatzda* (a.k.a. *Obatzter*), a mix of soft cheeses and butter with paprika and raw onions that's spread on bread. *Brotzeit*, literally "bread time," gets you a wooden platter of cold cuts, cheese, and pickles and is a good option for a light dinner. Also unique and memorable is a *Steckerlfisch*—fish on a stick (great with a pretzel and a big beer).

Beer Halls, Beer Gardens, and Bavarian Food

The Hofbräuhaus is the place that really lives up to the name "beer hall." On a warm day when you're looking for the authentic outdoor beer garden experience, your best options are the Augustiner (near the train station), the small beer garden at the Viktualienmarkt (near Marienplatz), or the thousands of tables in the Englischer Garten.

The **Hofbräuhaus** (HOFE-broy-howze) is the world's most famous beer hall. Although it's grotesquely touristy, it's a Munich

must. Even if you don't eat here, check it out; it's fun to see 200 Japanese people drinking beer in a German beer hall...across from a Hard Rock Café. Germans go for the entertainment—to sing "Country Roads," see how Texas girls party, and watch tourists try to chug beer (daily 9:00–24:00, music during lunch and dinner,

5-min walk from Marienplatz at Platzl 6, tel. 089/290-1360, www .hofbraeuhaus.de). You can drop by anytime for a large or light meal (my favorite: €6.50 for *Schweinswurst mit Kraut*—pork sausages with sauerkraut), or just order a drink. Except for Weissbier, they only sell beer by the one-liter mug, or *Mass* (€6.90). And they sell 10,000 of these liters every day. The Hofbräuhaus is the only beer hall in town offering regular live oompah music. This music-every-night atmosphere is thick, and the fat, shiny-leather bands even get church mice to stand up and conduct three-quarter time with breadsticks. They also host a gimmicky Bavarian folk evening in the upstairs *Festsaal* (second floor) nightly from 18:30 to 22:00, including an all-you-can-eat buffet, for €20 (mostly music, plus folk dancing and whip-cracking). Walk up the stairs to the left of the entrance just to see the historic old Hofbräuhaus photos and prints. For more on this Munich institution, see page 47.

Augustiner Beer Garden is a sprawling haven for well-established local beer-lovers on a balmy evening. For a true under-the-leaves beer garden packed with Münchners, this is a delight. In fact, most Münchners consider Augustiner the best beer garden in town. There's no music, it's away from the tourist hordes, and it serves up great beer, good traditional food, huge portions, reasonable prices, and the perfect conviviality. The outdoor self-service ambience is best—making this place ideal on a nice summer evening (figure €12 for a main dish and a drink). There's also indoor and outdoor seating at a more expensive restaurant with table service (€10–17 main dishes) by the entrance (daily 10:00–24:00, self-service food until 22:00, Arnulfstrasse 52, 3 loooong blocks from station going away from the center—or take tram #17 one stop, taxis always waiting at the gate, tel. 089/594-393, www .augustinerkeller.de).

The small beer garden at the center of the **Viktualienmarkt** taps you into about the best budget eating in town just steps from Marienplatz (closed Sun, see page 46). There's table service wherever you see a tablecloth; to picnic, choose a table without

MUNICH

Munich's Beer Scene

In Munich's beer halls *(Bräuhäuser)* and beer gardens *(Biergartens)*, meals are inexpensive, white radishes are salted and cut in delicate spirals, and surly beer maids pull mustard packets from their cleavage. Unlike with wine, spending more money on beer doesn't get you a better drink. Beer is truly a people's drink, and you'll get the very best here in Munich. The big question among connoisseurs (local and foreign) is, "Which brew today?"

Beer gardens go back to the days when monks brewed their beer and were allowed to sell it directly to the thirsty public. They stored their beer in cellars under courtyards kept cool by the shade of bushy chestnut trees. Eventually, tables were set up, and these convivial eateries evolved. The tradition (complete with chestnut trees) survives, and any real beer garden will keep a few tables (those without tablecloths) available for customers who buy only beer and bring in their own food.

Huge liter beers (called *ein Mass* in German, or "ein pitcher" in English) cost about €6–7. You can order your beer *helles* (light but not "lite"—which is what you'll get if you say *"ein* beer"), *dunkles* (dark), or *Radler* (half lemon-lime soda, half beer). Most beer gardens have a deposit *(Pfand)* system for their big glass steins: You pay €1 extra, and when you're finished, you can take the mug to the return man *(Pfandrückgabe)* for your refund, or leave it on the table and lose your money. (Men's rooms come with vomitoriums.)

Many beer halls have a cafeteria system. Eating outside is made more pleasant by the *Föhn* (warm winds that come over the Alps from Italy), which gives this part of Germany 30 more days of sunshine than the North—and sometimes even an Italian ambience. (Many natives attribute the city's huge increase in outdoor dining to global warming.)

Beer halls take care of their regular customers. You'll notice many *Stammtische* (tables reserved for regulars and small groups, such as the "Happy Saturday Club"). They have a long tradition of being launch pads for grassroots action. The Hofbräuhaus was the first place Hitler talked to a big crowd.

one. Buy your drinks from the counter. Countless stalls surround the beer garden and sell wurst, sandwiches, produce, and so on. This B.Y.O.F. tradition goes back to the days when monks served beer but not food. This is a good spot to grab a typical Munich *Weisswurst*—and some beer.

Die Münchner Suppenküche, a self-service soup joint at the Viktualienmarkt, is fine for a small, cozy sit-down lunch at picnic tables under a closed-in awning (€4–6 soup meals, Mon–Fri 10:00–19:00, Sat 9:00–17:00, closed Sun; near corner of Reichenbachstrasse and Frauenstrasse). There's another branch behind the New Town Hall (described later).

Jodlerwirt is tiny and cramped—a smart-alecky, yodeling kind of pub. The food is great, and the ambience is as Bavarian as you'll find. Avoid the basic ground-floor bar and climb the stairs into the action. Good food and lots of belly laughs...completely incomprehensible to the average tourist (Tue–Sat 18:00–3:00 in the morning, food until 23:00, closed Mon except Sept–Dec, always closed Sun, accordion act nightly from 20:30, between Hof-bräuhaus and Marienplatz at Altenhofstrasse 4, tel. 089/221-249).

Nürnberger Bratwurst Glöckl am Dom, popular with tourists, offers a classier, fiercely Bavarian evening. Dine outside under the trees or in the dark, medieval, cozy interior—patrolled by wenches and spiked with antlers. I come here to enjoy the explosively tasty little *Nürnberger* sausages with kraut (€8–17 main dishes, daily 10:00–24:00, at the rear of the twin-domed Frauenkirche, Frauenplatz 9, tel. 089/291-9450).

The trendier **Andechser am Dom,** on the same breezy square, serves Andechs beer and great food to appreciative regulars. Münchners favor the dark beer (ask for *dunkles*), but I love the light *(helles)*. The €11.50 *Gourmetteller* is a great sampler of their special-ties, and the *Rostbratwurst* with kraut (€6.90) gives you the virtual *Nürnberger* bratwurst experience with the better Andechs beer (€5–15 main dishes, daily 10:00–24:00, Weinstrasse 7a, reserve during peak times, tel. 089/298-481).

Altes Hackerhaus is popular with locals—especially from the adjacent newspaper building—for its traditional *Bayerischer* (Bavarian) fare served with a fancier white-tablecloth feel in one of the oldest buildings in town. It offers a small courtyard and a fun forest of characteristic nooks festooned with old-time paint-ings and posters (€10–25 main dishes, €7–10 wurst dishes, daily 10:00–24:00, Sendlinger Strasse 14, tel. 089/260-5026).

Der Pschorr, an upscale beer hall occupying a former slaugh-terhouse with a terrace overlooking the Viktualienmarkt, serves a special premium version of what many consider Munich's finest beer. With organic "slow food" and chilled glasses, this place mixes modern concepts—no candles, industrial-strength conviviality—

with traditional, quality, classic dishes (€10–22 main dishes, €8 lunch specials, daily 10:00–24:00, Viktualienmarkt 15, at end of Schrannenhalle, tel. 089/5181-8500).

Spatenhaus is the opera-goers' beer hall, serving more elegant food in a woodsy, traditional setting since 1896. You can also eat outside, on the square facing the opera and palace. It's pricey, but you won't find better-quality Bavarian cuisine (€11–25 main dishes, daily 9:30–24:00, on Max-Joseph-Platz opposite opera, Residenzstrasse 12, tel. 089/290-7060, www.kuffler.de).

Heilig-Geist-Stüberl ("Holy Ghost Pub") is a funky, retro little hole-in-the-wall where you are sure to meet locals (the German cousins of those who go to Reno because it's cheaper than Vegas, and who consider karaoke high culture). The interior, a 1980s time warp, makes you feel like you're stepping into an alcoholic cuckoo clock (just off the Viktualienmarkt at Heiliggeiststrasse 1, tel. 089/297-233).

In the English Garden

For outdoor ambience and a cheap meal, spend an evening at the English Garden's **Chinesischer Turm** (Chinese Tower) *Biergarten.* You're welcome to B.Y.O. food and grab a table, or buy from the picnic stall *(Brotzeit)* right there. Don't bother to phone ahead—they have 6,000 seats. This is a fine opportunity to try a *Steckerlfisch,* sold for €9 at a separate kiosk (daily, long hours in good weather, usually live music, tel. 089/3838-7327, www .chinaturm.de; take tram #17 from main train station or Sendlinger Tor to Tivolistrasse, or U-3 or U-6 to Universität).

Seehaus im Englischen Garten is famous among Münchners for its idyllic lakeside setting and excellent Mediterranean and traditional cooking. It's dressy and a bit snobbish, and understandably filled with locals who fit the same description. Choose from classy indoor or lakeside seating (€20–25 main dishes, daily 10:00–24:00, a pleasant 15-min hike into the English Garden—located on all the city maps—or take tram #44 or a taxi to the doorstep, Kleinhesselohe 3, tel. 089/3816-130).

Seehaus Beer Garden, adjacent to the fancy Seehaus restaurant, is a less expensive, more casual beer garden with all the normal wurst, kraut, pretzels, and fine beer at typical prices. What makes this spot special: You're buried in the English Garden, enjoying the fine lakeside setting (daily, long hours from 11:00 when the weather's fine).

Non-Beer Hall Restaurants

Man does not live by beer alone. Well, maybe some do. But for the rest of us, I recommend the following alternatives to the beer-and-wurst circuit.

On or near Marienplatz

With a Bird's-Eye Marienplatz View: **Glockenspiel Café** is good for a coffee or a meal with a view down on the Marienplatz action. There are several dining zones. Locals like the sunroof, but regardless of the weather, I grab a seat overlooking Marienplatz (Mon-Sat 10:00–24:00, Sun 10:00–19:00, ride elevator from Rosenstrasse entrance, opposite glockenspiel at Marienplatz 28, tel. 089/264-256). For a quicker and less crowded option, go to the Starbucks-style café on the top floor of **Hugendubel** bookstore (take the glass elevator, Mon-Sat 9:30–20:00, closed Sun).

An Elegant Picnic or Café: The crown in **Alois Dallmayr**'s emblem reflects that the royal family assembled its picnics at this historic and expensive delicatessen. Pretend you're a Bavarian aristocrat and put together a royal picnic to munch in the nearby Hofgarten. Or visit the classy but pricey cafés that serve light meals on the ground floor and first floor (Mon-Sat 9:30–19:00, closed Sun, behind New Town Hall, Dienerstrasse 13–15). For more information, see page 46.

Soup-Kitchen Chain: **Die Münchner Suppenküche,** famous for its location in Viktualienmarkt (described earlier), has another cheap-and-cheery locals-pleasing outlet just off the Weinstrasse shopping street at Schäfflerstrasse 7 (near the New Town Hall; €4–6 for a great selection of today's soups, open for lunch daily except Sun).

A Budget Picnic: To save money, browse at Dallmayr's but buy in the **supermarkets** that hide in the basements of department stores: the **Kaufhof** stores at Marienplatz and Karlsplatz (Mon-Sat 9:30–20:00, closed Sun), the more upmarket **Karstadt** across from the train station (same hours), or the **Minimal** at Fünf Höfe (Mon-Sat 7:00–20:00, closed Sun).

Trendy Eateries South of Marienplatz

The area south of Marienplatz is becoming a kind of SoHo, with lots of fun shops, wine bars, and bistros handy for a healthy and quick lunch. Most of these recommended restaurants are located on the map on page 87.

Schrannenhalle, an old grain hall that burned in the 1930s, was reconstructed with original pieces and reopened in 2005 as a fun little mall/food circus. In the evenings, it feels like a community center, with people grabbing a bite from whatever eatery appeals and sitting down for a free movie, sporting event, or concert on the central big screen. The basement hosts a dance club for "over-30s." Pop in, if for no other reason than to see the fine reconstruction job on the amazingly preserved old beams (Pralat-Zistl-Strasse, between Viktualienmarkt and St.-Jakobs-Platz).

Stadt Café is a lively diner/café serving healthy fare, with great daily specials (€6–9) and an inventive menu of Italian, German, salads, and vegetarian dishes. This high-energy, no-frills restaurant is packed with enthusiastic local eaters, newspaper-readers, and coffee-sippers. Dine in the quiet cobbled courtyard, inside, or outside facing the new synagogue (lunch specials-€6, blackboard has today's specials, daily 10:00–24:00, in Munich City Museum, St.-Jakobs-Platz 1, tel. 089/266-949).

Prinz Myshkin is everybody's favorite upscale vegetarian eatery in the old center. You'll find a clever, appetizing selection of €10–15 main dishes. The decor is modern, the arched ceilings are cool, the outside seating is on a quiet street, and the clientele is entirely local. Don't miss the enticing appetizer selection on display as you enter (they do a fine mixed-appetizer plate). They also have vegetarian sushi and their own baker, so they're proud of their sweets (€6 lunch specials, daily 11:30–23:00, Hackenstrasse 2, tel. 089/265-596).

Riva Bar Pizzeria is a long, skinny bar with an open oven popping out great pizzas to a crowd of young Münchners. It's very popular for its fresh, homemade-quality pizzas, "salad pizzas," pastas, and salads. There's a crowded dining area in back and a few pleasant tables outside on the busy sidewalk (€9–11 pizzas, Mon–Sat 8:00–24:00, Sun 12:00–24:00, 50 yards toward Marienplatz from Isartor at Im Tal 44, tel. 089/220-240).

La Vecchia Masseria, near the train station hotels, serves simple Italian food inside amid a cozy Tuscan farmhouse decor, or outside in a beautiful flowery courtyard. Try the €24 tasting *menu* (€6–8 pizza or pasta, €15 main courses, daily 11:30–23:00, reservations smart, cash or AmEx only, Mathildenstrasse 3—see map on page 83, tel. 089/550-9090).

Munich Connections

Munich is a super transportation hub (one reason it was the target of so many WWII bombs). For quick help at the main train station, stop by the service counter in front of track 18. For better English and more patience, drop by the EurAide office (with your back to track 24, follow signs down the hallway and to the right; see page 83). Train info: tel. 0180-599-6633 (€0.14/min). For airport information, see page 32.

From Munich by Train to: Füssen (hourly, 2 hrs, some direct but most with easy transfer in Buchloe; for a Neuschwanstein Castle day trip, leave as early as possible and no later than 9:00), **Reutte,** Austria (every 2 hrs, 2.5 hrs, change in Garmisch), **Oberammergau** (nearly hourly, 1.75 hrs, change in Murnau), **Salzburg,** Austria (2/hr, 1.5–2 hrs), **Berchtesgaden** (at least hourly, 2.5–3 hrs, change in Freilassing), **Nürnberg** (2–3/hr, 1–1.25 hrs), **Köln** (2/hr, 4.5 hrs, some with 1 change), **Würzburg** (1–2/hr, 2 hrs), **Rothenburg** (hourly, 2.5–3.5 hrs, 2–3 changes), **Frankfurt** (hourly, 3.25 hrs), **Frankfurt Airport** (2/hr, 3.5 hrs, some change in Mannheim), **Dresden** (hourly, 5.75 hrs, change in Nürnberg), **Berlin** (1–2/hr, 6–6.75 hrs, every 2 hrs direct, otherwise a change in Göttingen), **Vienna** (direct trains every 2 hrs, 4.25 hrs), **Venice** (1/day direct, 6.75 hrs, reservations required, more with change in Verona), **Paris** (4/day, 6 hrs, usually with 1 change), **Prague** (2/day direct, 6.25 hrs; 6 more/day with change in Nürnberg then express bus, 5.25 hrs; no night trains), **Zürich** (4/day direct, 4.25 hrs, more with changes). Night trains run daily to Berlin, Vienna, Venice, Florence, Rome, Paris, Amsterdam, Budapest, Copenhagen (at least 6 hrs to each city). To use a railpass for a night train to Italy, your pass must include all countries on the train route (i.e., Austria or Switzerland), or you'll have to buy the segment that's not included.

MUNICH

Romantic Road Bus: The Romantic Road bus (early May–late Oct only) connects Munich to Füssen, Dinkelsbühl, Rothenburg, Würzburg, Frankfurt, and other destinations en route. For more information, see page 287. You can go from Munich to Rothenburg for €30 one-way by purchasing tickets at EurAide. This slower but more scenic alternative to the train allows a glimpse of towns such as Augsburg, Nördlingen, and Dinkelsbühl (no advance reservations needed, daily early May–late Oct, departs Munich at 11:00, arrives Rothenburg at 16:00). To find the bus stop, exit the station by track 26 and walk 100 yards to the left along Arnulfstrasse to the bus stop labeled *Hauptbahnhof Nord;* look for small *Touring* and *Romantische Strasse* signs.

BAVARIA and TIROL

*Füssen • King's Castles • Wieskirche • Oberammergau
• Linderhof Castle • Ettal Monastery • Zugspitze
• Reutte, Austria*

Two hours south of Munich, between Germany's Bavaria and Austria's Tirol, is a timeless land of fairy-tale castles, painted buildings shared by cows and farmers, and locals who still yodel when they're happy.

In Germany's Bavaria, tour "Mad" King Ludwig II's ornate Neuschwanstein Castle, Europe's most spectacular. Stop by the Wieskirche, a textbook example of Bavarian Rococo bursting with curly curlicues, and browse through Oberammergau, Germany's woodcarving capital and home of the famous Passion Play, performed again in 2010. Then, just over the border in Austria's Tirol, explore the ruined Ehrenberg Castle and scream down the mountain on an oversized skateboard.

In this chapter, I'll cover Bavaria first, then Tirol. My favorite home base for exploring Bavaria's castles is actually in Austria, in the Tirolean town of Reutte. Reutte's hotels offer better value to those with a car. Füssen, in Germany, is more touristy, but a handier home base for train travelers.

Planning Your Time

While Germans and Austrians vacation here for a week or two at a time, the typical speedy American traveler will find two days' worth of sightseeing. With a car and more time, you could enjoy three or four days, but the basic visit ranges anywhere from a long day trip from Munich to a three-night, two-day visit. If the

Füssen and Reutte Area

VIEW

MTN. LIFT

CASTLE

ROMANTIC ROAD
TO
ROTHENBURG

N

ECHELSBACHER
BRIDGE
(GORGE)

STEINGADEN

WIES-
KIRCHE

FORGGEN-
SEE

TO
MUNICH
VIA
BUCHLOE

G E R M A N Y

TO
KEMPTEN

LINDER-
HOF

OBER-
AMMERGAU

LUGE

TO
MUNICH

TEGELBERG

FÜSSEN

NEUSCHWANSTEIN
HOHENSCHWANGAU

ETTAL

UNTER
PINS-
WANG

ALP-
SEE

GUTSHOF ZUM
SCHLUXEN

REUTTE

GARMISCH-
PARTEN-
KIRCHEN

EIB-
SEE

EHRENBERG
RUINS

PLANSEE

LERMOOS

ZUGSPITZE
2973 m

STANZACH

BLINDSEE

EHR-
WALD

REST STOP

LUGE
BIBERWIER

NAMLOS

FERNPASS

FALLERSCHEIN

A U S T R I A

5 MILES

10 KM

TO
INNSBRUCK

D.C.H

(Weather's good and you're not going to Switzerland on your trip, be sure to ride a lift to an alpine peak.)

By Car: Here's a good one-day circular drive from Reutte (or from Füssen, starting half an hour later): 7:30—Breakfast; 8:00—Depart hotel; 8:30—Arrive at Neuschwanstein to pick up tickets for the two castles (Neuschwanstein and Hohenschwangau); 9:00—Tour Hohenschwangau; 11:00—Tour Neuschwanstein; 13:00—Drive to Oberammergau, and spend an hour there to browse the carving shops (consider skipping this town during the run of the Passion Play, May 15–Oct 3, when things will be very crowded); 15:00—Drive to Ettal Monastery for a half-hour stop (if you're not otherwise seeing the Wieskirche), then on to Linderhof Castle; 16:00—Tour Linderhof; 18:00—Drive along scenic Plansee lake back into Austria (or return to Füssen); 19:00—Back at hotel; 20:00—Dinner at hotel. Off-season (Oct–March), start your day an hour later, since Neuschwanstein and Hohenschwangau don't open until 10:00; and skip Linderhof, as it closes an hour early.

The next morning, you could stroll through Reutte, hike to the Ehrenberg ruins, and ride the luge on your way to Munich, Innsbruck, Switzerland, Venice, or wherever.

By Public Transportation: Train travelers can use Füssen as a base and bus or bike the three miles to Neuschwanstein. Reutte is connected by bus with Füssen (or €30 one-way for a taxi). While Reutte is a less convenient base if you're without a car, travelers staying there can easily bike to the Ehrenberg ruins (just outside Reutte). To reach the Neuschwanstein Castle/Tegelberg luge area from Reutte, you can bike (1.5 hours), take a bus into Füssen and transfer to a Neuschwanstein-bound bus there, or hire a taxi (€35 one-way from Reutte to Neuschwanstein). Or, if you stay at the recommended Gutshof zum Schluxen hotel (in Pinswang, Austria), it's a one-hour hike through the woods to Neuschwanstein.

Helpful Hints

Sightseeing Pass: The Bavarian Palace Department offers a 14-day **Bavarian Castles Pass** that covers admission to Neuschwanstein (but not Hohenschwangau) and Linderhof; the Residenz, Nymphenburg Palace, and Amalienburg Palace in Munich; the Imperial Palace in Nürnberg; the Residenz and Marienberg Fortress in Würzburg; and many other castles and palaces not mentioned in this book. The one-person pass costs €20, and the family/partner version (up to two adults plus children) costs €36. If you are planning to visit at least three of these sights within a two-week period, the pass will likely pay for itself. (For longer stays, there's also an annual pass available—€45/single, €65/family.) The pass is sold at all covered castles. For more information, see www.schloesser .bayern.de.

Crowd Alert: The village of Oberammergau stages its world-famous Passion Play in 2010. Expect all sights in Bavaria to be jammed with tourists while the play is running (May 15–Oct 3).

Getting Around Bavaria and Tirol

By Car: This region is ideal by car. All the sights are within an easy 60-mile loop from Reutte or Füssen. Even if you're doing the rest of your trip by train, consider renting a car in Füssen or in Reutte for your time here.

By Public Transportation: Local bus service in the region is spotty for sightseeing. If you're rushed and without wheels, I'd skip Reutte, the Wieskirche, Linderhof, Ettal Monastery, and the Biberwier luge ride (speed freaks should instead consider the Tegelberg luge near Neuschwanstein, which is within walking distance of the castle and served regularly by bus). I've listed connections below for each of the possible home bases in the region: Füssen (best overall base for non-drivers, especially for Ludwig's castles, also decent for Oberammergau and Reutte); Oberammergau (good base for Linderhof, Ettal Monastery, and Garmisch/Zugspitze); and Reutte (most challenging home base for non-drivers). Note that the bus connections listed below are for summer weekdays; on weekends and out of season, frequency plummets. Confirm all bus schedules locally: Check the big board at the bus stop across from the Füssen train station, buy the indispensable bus timetable (€0.30, *OVG Fahrpläne der Linienbusse*) at the TI or train station newsstand, check online at www.rva-bus .de, or call 08362/939-0505. For longer-distance bus trips (such as side-tripping from Füssen to Oberammergau), you'll likely save money if you buy a *Tagesticket* (day pass). If you'll be taking a lot of trains in Bavaria (for example, day-tripping from Munich to the castles), consider the **Bayern-Ticket** (covers buses and slower regional trains throughout Bavaria for five people for €28/day, for one person for €20/day, not valid Mon–Fri before 9:00; for more information, see page 75 in the Munich chapter).

From Füssen: Füssen is connected by hourly train with **Munich** (2-hour trip, some with transfer in Buchloe). Füssen is three miles from Ludwig's castles (Neuschwanstein and Hohenschwangau), easily reachable by bus (or by bike).

From Füssen, handy buses connect to **Ludwig's castles,** and most continue to the **Tegelberg luge** (buses #73 and #78, 1–2/hr, 10 min). There's also a bus connection to **Oberammergau** (bus #73 to Echelsbacher Brücke, change there to bus #9622—often marked *Garmisch,* confirm with driver that bus will stop in Oberammergau; 4–6/day in summer, 1.5 hrs total); the same bus continues to **Garmisch,** where you can ascend the **Zugspitze.** (From Oberammergau, you can also connect to **Linderhof Castle** and **Ettal Monastery**—see "From Oberammergau," later—but sparse buses make these sights challenging to do in a day from Füssen; rent a car instead.) To reach **Reutte,** you can take the bus (#74, Mon–Fri almost hourly, last bus 19:00; Sat–Sun every 2 hrs, last bus 18:00; less off-season, 45 min, €3.40) or a taxi (€30). You can reach the **Wieskirche** relatively easily (various buses, 4–5/day, 40–50 min each way, more frequently with a transfer in Steingaden; or just hop on the Romantic Road bus, leaving Füssen early May–late Oct daily at 8:00); however, return connections from the Wieskirche to Füssen are infrequent, likely leaving you with more time at the church than you want.

From Oberammergau: Oberammergau is a fine home base for seeing Linderhof Castle, Ettal Monastery, and the Zugspitze. Bus #9622 heads from Oberammergau to **Linderhof** (nearly hourly, 25–40 min); some also stop at **Ettal Monastery** en route. Buses also go to **Garmisch** (nearly hourly, 40 min; also possible by train with a transfer in Murnau, 1.5 hrs), where you can head up to the **Zugspitze.** Oberammergau is also reasonably well-connected to **Füssen** (4–6/ day in summer, transfer at Echelsbacher Brücke, 1.5 hrs total). The trip between Oberammergau and **Munich** is better directly by train (nearly hourly, 1.75 hrs, change in Murnau) than via Füssen by bus.

From Reutte: Reutte is the most challenging home base for non-drivers. It's a 45-minute bus ride from Füssen (Mon–Fri almost hourly, last bus 19:00; Sat–Sun every 2 hrs, last bus 18:00; less off-season, €3.40; taxis from Reutte to Ludwig's castles are €35 one-way; to Füssen, €30). In Füssen, you can connect to **Ludwig's castles, Oberammergau,** and other sights. From Reutte, a train departs almost hourly to **Ehrwald** (30 min) and then **Garmisch** (1 hr), each of which has connections up to the **Zugspitze;** in Garmisch, you can also connect to **Oberammergau.**

By Tour: If you're interested only in Bavarian castles, consider an all-day organized bus tour of the Bavarian biggies as a side-trip from Munich (see page 38 in the Munich chapter).

By Bike: This is great biking country. Shops in or near train stations rent bikes for €8–15 per day. The ride from Reutte to Neuschwanstein and the Tegelberg luge (1.5 hrs) is a natural.

By Thumb: Hitchhiking, always risky, is a slow-but-possible way to connect the public-transportation gaps. For example, even reluctant hitchhikers can catch a ride from Linderhof back to Oberammergau, as virtually everyone leaving there is a tourist like you and heading that way.

Füssen

Dramatically situated under a renovated castle on the lively Lech River, Füssen is a handy home base for exploring the region. Füssen has been a strategic stop since ancient times. Its main street sits on the Via Claudia Augusta, which crossed the Alps (over the Brenner Pass) in Roman times. Going north, early traders could follow the Lech River downstream to the Danube, and then cross over to the Main and Rhine valleys—a route now known to modern travelers as the "Romantic Road." Today, while Füssen is overrun by tourists in the summer, few venture to the back streets... which is where you'll find the real charm. Apart from my self-guided walk and the City Museum, there's little to do here. It's just a pleasant small town with a big history and lots of hardworking people in the tourist business.

Halfway between Füssen and the border (as you drive, or a woodsy walk from the town) is the **Lechfall,** a thunderous waterfall (with a handy WC).

Orientation to Füssen

(area code: 08362)
Füssen's train station is a few blocks from the TI, the town center (a cobbled shopping mall), and all my hotel listings.

Tourist Information

The TI is in the center of town (June–mid-Sept Mon–Fri 9:00–18:00, until 17:00 off-season, Sat 10:00–14:00, Sun 10:00–12:00, one free Internet terminal, 3 blocks down Bahnhofstrasse from station, tel. 08362/93850, www.fuessen.de). If necessary, the TI can help you find a room. After hours, the little self-service info pavilion near the front of the TI features an automated room-finding service with a phone to call hotels.

Arrival in Füssen

From the train station (lockers available, €2–3), exit to the left and walk a few blocks to reach the center of town and the TI. Buses to Neuschwanstein, Reutte, and elsewhere leave from a parking lot next to the station.

Helpful Hints

Internet Access: Beans & Bytes is the best place to get online, with fast terminals and good drink service (€2.50/hr, Wi-Fi, Skype, disc-burning, Mon–Sat 10:00–22:00, closed Sun, down the pedestrian alley off the main drag at Reichenstrasse 33, tel. 08362/926-8960).

Bike Rental: Bike Station, sitting right where the train tracks end, outfits sightseers with good bikes and tips on two-wheeled fun in the area (€8–10/24 hrs, April–Sept Mon–Fri 9:00–18:00, Sat 10:00–14:00, Sun in good weather 10:00–12:00, closed Oct–March, tel. 08362/505-9155, mobile 0176-2205-3080, www.ski-sport-luggi.de). For a strenuous but enjoyable 20-mile loop trip, see page 118.

BAVARIA AND TIROL

Füssen

BAVARIA AND TIROL

1 Hotel/Rest. Kurcafe

2 Hotel Hirsch

3 Hotel Sonne

4 Altstadthotel zum Hechten & Restaurant Ritterstub'n

5 Mein Lieber Schwan Apts.

6 Gasthof Krone

7 House LA (2)

8 Allgäuer Gästehaus

9 To Youth Hostel

10 Aquila das Restaurant

11 Markthalle Food Court

12 Hohes Schloss Italian Ice Cream

13 Supermarket

14 Internet Café

15 Bike Rental

16 Schlichtling Car Rental

17 To Auto Osterried Car Rental

Car Rental: **Peter Schlichtling,** in the town center, rents cars for reasonable prices (€62/day, includes insurance, Mon–Fri 8:00–18:00, Sat 9:00–12:00, closed Sun, Kemptener Strasse 26, tel. 08362/922-122, www.schlichtling.de).

    Auto Osterried/Europcar rents at similar prices, but is an €8 taxi ride away from the train station. Their cheapest car goes for about €59 per day (daily 8:00–19:00, past waterfall on road to Austria, Tiroler Strasse 65, tel. 08362/6381).

Local Guide: **Silvia Beyer** speaks English and knows the region very well (silliby@web.de, mobile 0160-901-13431).

Self-Guided Walk

Welcome to Füssen

For most, Füssen is just a touristy home base for visiting Ludwig's famous castles. But the town has a rich history and hides some evoc-

ative corners, as you'll see when you follow this short orientation walk. Throughout the town, "City Tour" information plaques explain points of interest in English. Use them to supplement the information I've provided.

• *Begin at the square in front of the TI, three blocks from the train station.*

  ❶ Kaiser-Maximilian-Platz: The entertaining "Seven Stones" fountain on this square (in front of the TI) was built in 1995 to celebrate Füssen's 700th birthday. The stones symbolize community, groups of people gathering, conviviality...each is different, with "heads" nodding and talking. It's granite on granite. The moving heads are not connected, and nod only with water-power. While frozen in winter, it's a popular and splashy play zone for kids on hot summer days.

• *Just half a block down the busy street stands...*

  ❷ Hotel Hirsch and Medieval Wall: Hotel Hirsch, one of the first hotels in town, dates from the 19th century, when aristocratic tourists started coming to appreciate the castles and natural wonders of the Alps. Across the busy street stands one of two surviving towers from Füssen's medieval town wall (c. 1515). Farther down the street (50 yards, just before the second tower), a gate leads into the old town (read the information plaque).

• *Step through the gate (onto today's Klosterstrasse), and immediately turn left into the old cemetery.*

  ❸ Historic Cemetery of St. Sebastian (Alter Friedhof): This peaceful oasis of Füssen history, established in the 16th century,

Füssen Walk

BAVARIA AND TIROL

1 Kaiser-Maximilian-Platz

2 Hotel Hirsch & Medieval Wall

3 Historic Cemetery of St. Sebastian

4 Town View from Franciscan Monastery

5 Lech Riverbank

6 Church of the Holy Spirit, Bread Market & Lute-Makers

7 Benedictine Monastery

8 City Museum

9 St. Magnus Basilica

10 High Castle

fills a corner between the town wall and the Franciscan monastery. It's technically full, and only members of great and venerable Füssen families (who already own plots here) can join those who are buried (free, daily 7:30–19:00).

Just inside the gate (on right) is the tomb of Dominic Quaglio, who painted the Romantic scenes decorating the walls of Hohenschwangau Castle in 1835. Over on the old city wall is the World War I memorial, listing all the names of men from this small town killed in that devastating conflict (along with each one's rank and place of death). A bit to the right, also along the old wall, is a statue of the hand of God holding a fetus—a place to remember babies who died before being born. And in the corner, farther to the right, are the simple wooden crosses of Franciscans who lived just over the wall in the monastery. Note the fine tomb art from many ages collected here, and the loving care this community gives its cemetery.

• *Exit on the far side, just past the dead Franciscans, and continue toward the big church.*

❹ Town View from Franciscan Monastery (Franziskanerkloster): From the Franciscan Monastery (which still has big responsibilities, but only a handful of monks in residence), there's a fine view over the medieval town. The Church of St. Magnus and the High Castle (the summer residence of the Bishops of Augsburg) break the horizon. The chimney (c. 1886) on the left is a reminder that when Ludwig built Neuschwanstein, the textile industry (linen and flax) was very big here.

• *Go down the steps into the flood zone, and stay left, following the roar of the charging river, through the medieval "Bleachers' Gate," to the riverbank.*

❺ Lech Riverbank: This low end of town, the flood zone, was the home of those whose work depended on the river—bleachers, rafters, and fishermen. The Lech River was—in its heyday—an expressway to Augsburg (about 70 miles to the north). Around the year 1500, the rafters established the first professional guild in Füssen. As Füssen was on the Via Claudia, cargo from Italy passed here en route to big German cities farther north. Rafters would assemble rafts, and pile them high with goods—or with people needing a lift. If the water was high, they could float all the way to Augsburg in as little as one day. There they'd disassemble their raft and sell off the lumber along with the goods they'd carried, then make their way home to raft again. Today you'll see no water sports here, as there's a hydroelectric plant just downstream.

• *Walk upstream a bit, and head inland immediately after crossing under the bridge.*

❻ Church of the Holy Spirit, Bread Market, and Lute-Makers: Climbing uphill, you pass the colorful Church of the Holy Spirit (Heilig-Geist-Spitalkirche) on the left. As this was the church of the rafters, their patron, St. Christopher, is prominent on the facade. Today it's the church of Füssen's old folks' home (it's adjacent—notice the easy-access skyway).

Farther up the lane (opposite the entry to the big monastery) is Bread Market Square (Brotmarkt), with its fountain honoring the famous 16th-century lute-making family, the Tieffenbruckers. In its day, Füssen was a huge center of violin- and lute-making, with about 200 workshops. Today only two survive.

• *Backtrack and enter the courtyard in the huge monastery just across the street.*

❼ Benedictine Monastery (Kloster St. Mang): From 1717 until secularization in 1802, this was the powerful center of town. Today the courtyard is popular for concerts, and the building houses the City Hall and City Museum (and a public WC, closed until May).

❽ City Museum: Füssen's one must-see sight is scheduled to reopen in late May after undergoing renovations (€2.50, €3 includes castle gallery; April–Oct Tue–Sun 11:00–17:00, closed Mon; Nov–March Fri–Sun 13:00–16:00, closed Mon–Thu; tel. 08362/903-146, www.tourismus-fuessen .de). Pick up the loaner English translations and follow the one-way route. In the St. Anna Chapel, you'll see the famous *Dance of Death*. This was painted shortly after a plague devastated the community in 1590. It shows 20 social classes, each dancing with the Grim Reaper—starting with the pope and the emperor. The words above say, essentially, "You can say yes or you can

say no, but you must ultimately dance with death." Leaving the chapel, you walk over the metal lid of the crypt. Upstairs, exhibits illustrate the rafting trade and violin- and lute-making (with a complete workshop). The museum also includes an exquisite *Festsaal* (main festival hall), an old library, a textile factory, and a Ludwig's "castle dream room."

• *Leaving the courtyard, hook left around the monastery and uphill. The square tower marks...*

❾ St. Magnus Basilica (Basilika St. Mang): St. Mang (or Magnus) is Füssen's favorite saint. In the eighth century, he worked miracles all over the area with his holy rod. For centuries, pilgrims came from far and wide to enjoy art depicting the great works of St. Magnus. Above the altar dangles a glass cross containing his relics (including that holy stick). Just inside the door is a chapel remembering a much more modern saint—Franz Seelos (1819–1867), the local boy who went to America (Pittsburg and New Orleans) and lived such a saintly life that in 2000 he was made a saint. If you're in need of a miracle, there are cards to fill out next to the candles.

• *From the church, a lane leads high above, into the castle courtyard.*

🔟 **High Castle (Hohes Schloss):** This castle, long the summer residence of the Bishop of Augsburg, houses a painting gallery. Its courtyard is interesting for the striking perspective tricks painted onto its flat walls. From below the castle, the city's main drag (once the Roman Via Claudia, and now Reichenstrasse) leads from a grand statue of St. Magnus past lots of shops, cafés, and strolling people to Kaiser-Maximilian-Platz and the TI...where you began.

Sleeping in Füssen

(country code: 49, area code: 08362)

Though I prefer sleeping in Reutte, convenient Füssen is just three miles from Ludwig's castles and offers a cobbled, riverside retreat. It's very touristy, but it has plenty of rooms. All recommended accommodations are within a few blocks of the train station and the town center. Parking is easy at the station. Prices listed are for one-night stays. Most hotels give about 5 to 10 percent off for two-night stays—always request this discount. Competition is fierce, and off-season prices are soft. High season is mid-June through September. Rooms are generally 10–15 percent less in shoulder season and much cheaper in off-season. To locate these hotels, see the Füssen map, earlier.

$$$ Hotel Kurcafe is deluxe, with 30 spacious rooms and all of the amenities. The standard rooms are comfortable, and the newer, bigger rooms have elegant touches and fun decor—such as canopy drapes and cherubic frescoes over the bed (Sb-€85–92, standard Db-€109–129, bigger Db-€135–159 depending on size, Tb-€129–146, Qb-€142–159, 4-person suite-€195–219, high prices are for July–Aug, €10 more for weekends and holidays, you'll likely save money by booking via their website, elevator, free Wi-Fi, parking-€5/day, a block from station at Bahnhofstrasse 4, tel. 08362/930-180, fax 08362/930-1850, www.kurcafe.com, info @kurcafe.com, Norbert and the Schöll family).

$$$ Hotel Hirsch is a big romantic, well-maintained tour-class hotel with 53 rooms on the main street in the center of town. Their standard rooms are fine, and their rooms with historical and landscape themes are a fun splurge (Sb-€65–85, standard Db-€110–140, theme Db-€145–175, price depends on room size and demand, cheaper Nov–March and during slow times, family

Sleep Code

(€1 = about $1.40, Germany country code: 49, Austria country code: 43)

S = Single, **D** = Double/Twin, **T** = Triple, **Q** = Quad, **b** = bathroom, **s** = shower only. Unless otherwise noted, credit cards are accepted, English is spoken, and breakfast is included. The region's €1.60 per person, per night "tourist tax" is not included in these rates.

To help you sort easily through these listings, I've divided the rooms into three categories, based on the price for a standard double room with bath:

$$$ Higher Priced—Most rooms €100 or more.
$$ Moderately Priced—Most rooms between €60–100.
$ Lower Priced—Most rooms €60 or less.

rooms, elevator, expensive Internet access and Wi-Fi, free parking, Kaiser-Maximilian-Platz 7, tel. 08362/93980, fax 08362/939-877, www.hotelhirsch.de, info@hotelhirsch.de).

$$$ Hotel Sonne, in the heart of town, rents 50 stylish and spacious rooms (Sb-€93–109, Db-€93–159, Tb-€118–148, Qb-€164–200, higher prices are for huge rooms in the new wing, cheaper Oct–mid-May or with Web reservations, elevator, free Internet access and Wi-Fi, free sauna, parking-€4–6/day, kitty-corner from TI at Prinzregentenplatz 1, tel. 08362/9080, fax 08362/908-100, www.hotel-sonne.de, info@hotel-sonne.de).

$$ Altstadthotel zum Hechten, with 35 rooms, offers all the modern comforts in a friendly, traditional building right under Füssen Castle in the old-town pedestrian zone (Sb-€57, Db-€90–94, Tb-€117, Qb-€140, beds can be short, fun miniature bowling alley in basement, free Wi-Fi and Internet access in lounge, free parking with this book; from TI, walk down pedestrian street and take second right to Ritterstrasse 6; tel. 08362/91600, fax 08362/916-099, www.hotel-hechten.com, hotel.hechten@t-online.de, Pfeiffer and Tramp families).

$$ Mein Lieber Schwan, a block from the train station, is a former private house with four superbly outfitted apartments, each with a double bed, sofa bed, and kitchen. The catch is the three-night minimum stay (Sb-€69, Db-€75, Tb-€87, Qb-€95, slightly cheaper off-season, no breakfast, free Wi-Fi, garden, laundry facilities, free parking, from station turn left at traffic circle to Augustenstrasse 3, tel. 08362/509-980, fax 08362/509-914, www.meinlieberschwan.de, fewo@meinlieberschwan.de, Herr Bletschacher).

Füssen's Budget Beds

$ Gasthof Krone, a rare bit of pre-glitz Füssen in the pedestrian zone, has dumpy halls and stairs and 12 big worn time-warp rooms (S-€31, D-€58, extra bed-€26, extra bed for kids under 12-€20, €3 more per person for 1-night stays, closed Nov–early June; from TI, head down pedestrian street and take first left to Schrannengasse 17; tel. 08362/7824, fax 08362/37505, www.krone-fuessen.de, info@krone-fuessen.de).

$ House LA has two branches, run by energetic mason Lahdo Algül. Their backpacker house has 11 basic, clean four-bed dorm rooms at rock-bottom prices about a 10-minute walk from the station (€18/bed, D-€42, breakfast-€2, inexpensive Wi-Fi, Wachsbleichstrasse 2). A second building has five family apartments with kitchen and bath, each sleeping four to six people (apartment-€60–90, breakfast-€2, inexpensive Wi-Fi, 6-minute walk back along tracks from station to von Freybergstrasse 26; contact info for both: mobile 0170-624-8610, fax 08362/505-9181, www.housela.de, info@housela.de).

$ Allgäuer Gästehaus has six cheap and slightly run-down rooms based out of a kebab shop on a busy street near the center of town; it's a five-minute walk from the station (Db-€54, Luitpoldstrasse 10, tel. 08362/926-8425, pensionfuessen@gmx.de).

$ Füssen Youth Hostel is a fine German-run place that welcomes travelers, especially younger ones (bed in 2- to 6-bed dorm rooms-€20, D-€56, €3 more for non-members, includes breakfast and sheets, guests over age 26 pay €4 penalty for being so old, laundry, cheap dinners, office open 7:00–12:00 & 17:00–23:00, until 22:00 off-season, from station backtrack 10 min along tracks, Mariahilfer Strasse 5, tel. 08362/7754, fax 08362/2770, www.fuessen.jugendherberge.de, jhfuessen@djh-bayern.de).

Eating in Füssen

Aquila das Restaurant serves modern international dishes in a simple, traditional *Gasthaus* setting with great seating outside on the delightful little Brotmarkt square (€9–15 main dishes, serious salads, Thu–Tue 11:30–14:30 & 17:30–22:00, closed Wed, Brotmarkt 9, tel. 08362/6253).

Restaurant Ritterstub'n offers delicious, reasonably priced fish, salads, veggie plates, and a fun kids' menu. They have three eating zones: dressy in front, casual in back, and courtyard. Demure Gabi serves while her husband cooks standard Bavarian fare (€7–14 main dishes, €15 three-course fixed-price meal, Tue–Sun 11:30–14:30 & 17:30–23:00, closed Mon, Ritterstrasse 4, tel. 08362/7759).

Schenke & Wirtshaus (inside the recommended Altstadthotel zum Hechten) dishes up hearty, traditional Bavarian fare. They specialize in pike *(Hecht)* pulled from the Lech River, served with a tasty fresh herb sauce (€8–14 main dishes, salad bar, cafeteria ambience, daily 10:00–22:00, Ritterstrasse 6, tel. 0836/91600).

Hotel Kurcafe's fine restaurant, right on Füssen's main traffic circle, has good weekly specials. Choose between a traditional dining room and a pastel winter garden, and enjoy the live Bavarian zither music most Fridays and Saturdays during dinner (open daily 11:30–14:30 & 18:00–22:00, Bahnhofstrasse 4, tel. 08362/930-180).

Markthalle, just across the street from Gasthof Krone, is a fun food court offering a wide selection of reasonably priced, wurst-free food. Located in an old warehouse from 1483, it's now home to a fishmonger; Chinese, Turkish, and Italian delis; a fruit stand; a bakery; and a wine bar. Buy your food from one of the vendors, park yourself at any one of the tables, then look up and admire the Renaissance ceiling (Mon–Fri 7:30–18:30, Sat 7:30–14:00, closed Sun, corner of Schrannengasse and Brunnengasse).

Gelato: **Hohes Schloss Italian Ice Cream** is a good *gelateria* on the main drag, with cheap ice cream to go and an inviting perch for a coffee or dessert while people-watching (Reichenstrasse 14).

Picnic Supplies: Bakeries and *Metzger*s (butcher shops) abound and frequently have ready-made sandwiches. For groceries, try the **Plus** supermarket at the roundabout on your way into town from the train station (Mon–Sat 8:00–20:00, closed Sun).

Füssen Connections

From Füssen to: Neuschwanstein (bus #73 or #78, departs from train station, most continue to Tegelberg lift station after castles, 1–2/hr, 10 min, €1.80 one-way, €3.60 round-trip; taxis cost €10 one-way); **Oberammergau** (bus #73 to Echelsbacher Brücke, change there to bus #9622—often marked *Garmisch*, confirm with driver that bus will stop in Oberammergau; 4–6/day in summer, 1.5 hrs total)—from Oberammergau you can connect to **Linderhof Castle, Ettal Monastery,** or **Garmisch/Zugspitze; Reutte** (bus #74, Mon–Fri almost hourly, last bus 19:00, Sat–Sun every 2 hrs, last bus 18:00, 45 min, €3.40 one-way; taxis cost €30 one-way); **Wieskirche** (4–5/day, 40–50 min each way, more frequently with a transfer in Steingaden; or take Romantic Road bus—see next page); **Munich** (hourly trains, 2 hrs, some change in Buchloe); **Innsbruck** (5 trains/day, 4.25 hrs, change in Munich); **Rothenburg ob der Tauber** (every 2 hrs, 5 hrs, change in Augsburg, Treuchtlingen, and Steinach); **Frankfurt** (hourly, 5–6 hrs, 1–2 changes). Train info: tel. 0180-599-6633 (€0.14/min).

Romantic Road Buses: The northbound Romantic Road bus departs Füssen at 8:00; the southbound bus arrives in Füssen at 19:15 (daily, early May–late Oct only, bus stop is at train station, www .romanticroadcoach.de). A railpass gets you a 20 percent discount on the Romantic Road bus (without using up a day of a flexipass). The northbound bus arrives in Munich at 11:00 and in Rothenburg at 16:00. This is much slower than the train; the only reason to take the bus is that it gives you the briefest glimpse of the Wieskirche, Ettal, Oberammergau, and other sights along the way, and requires no changes. Note that the northbound bus stops at the **Wieskirche** for 17 minutes, but the southbound bus stops there only by request. For more details on the bus, see page 287 in the Rothenburg chapter.

The Best of Bavaria

Within a short drive of Füssen and Reutte, you'll find some of the most enjoyable—and most tourist-filled—sights in Germany. The otherworldly "King's Castles" of Neuschwanstein and Hohenschwangau capture romantics' imaginations, the ornately decorated Wieskirche puts the faithful in a heavenly mood, and the little town of Oberammergau overwhelms visitors with cuteness. Yet another impressive castle (Linderhof), another fancy church (Ettal), and a sky-high viewpoint (the Zugspitze) round out Bavaria's top attractions.

The King's Castles

The most popular tourist destinations in Bavaria are the "King's Castles" (Königsschlösser). The older Hohenschwangau, King Ludwig's boyhood home, is less touristy but more historic. The more dramatic Neuschwanstein, which inspired Walt Disney, is the one everyone visits. I'd recommend visiting both, and planning some time to hike above Neuschwanstein to Mary's Bridge—and if you enjoy romantic hikes, down through the gorge below. Reservations are a magic wand to smooth out your visit. With fairy-tale turrets in a fairy-tale alpine setting built by a fairy-tale king, these castles are understandably a huge hit.

Getting There

If arriving by **car,** note that road signs in the region refer to the sight as Königsschlösser, not Neuschwanstein. There's plenty of parking (all lots-€4.50). The first lots require more walking. Drive right through Touristville and past the ticket center, and park in lot #4 by the lake for the same price.

From **Füssen,** those without cars can catch **bus** #73 or #78 (1–2/hr, €1.80 one-way, €3.60 round-trip, 10 min, catch bus at train station, extra buses often run when crowded), take a **taxi** (€10 one-way), or ride a rental **bike** (two level miles). The bus drops you at the tourist office; it's a one-minute walk from there to the ticket office.

From **Reutte,** take bus #74 to the Füssen train station, then hop on bus #73 or #78 to the castles.

For a romantic twist, hike or mountain-bike from the trailhead at the recommended hotel **Gutshof zum Schluxen** in Pinswang, Austria (described on page 141; they rent bikes). When the dirt road forks at the top of the hill, go right (downhill), cross the Austria-Germany border (marked by a sign and deserted hut), and follow the narrow paved road to the castles. It's a 1- to 1.5-hour hike or a great circular bike trip (allow 30 min; cyclists can return to Schluxen from the castles on a different 30-min bike route via Füssen).

The King's Castles Sights

For all the logistics, see "Visiting the Castles" on page 114.

▲▲▲Hohenschwangau Castle

Standing quietly below Neuschwanstein, the big, yellow Hohenschwangau Castle was Ludwig's boyhood home. Originally built in the 12th century, it was ruined by Napoleon. Ludwig's father, King Maximilian II, rebuilt it in 1830. Hohenschwangau (hoh-en-SHVAHN-gow, loosely translated as "High Swanland") was used by the royal family as a summer hunting lodge until 1912.

The interior decor is harmonious, cohesive, and original—all done in 1835, with paintings inspired by Romantic themes. The Wittelsbach family (which ruled Bavaria for nearly seven centuries) still owns the place (and lived in the annex—today's shop—until the 1970s). As you tour the castle, imagine how the paintings must have inspired young Ludwig. For 17 years, he lived here at his dad's place and followed the construction of his dream castle across the way—you'll see the telescope still set up and directed at Neuschwanstein.

The excellent 30-minute tours give a better glimpse of Ludwig's life than the more-visited and famous Neuschwanstein Castle tour. Tours here are smaller (35 people rather than 60) and more relaxed.

▲▲▲Neuschwanstein Castle

Imagine "Mad" King Ludwig as a boy, climbing the hills above his dad's castle, Hohenschwangau, dreaming up the ultimate fairy-tale castle. Inheriting the throne at the young age of 18, he had the

The King's Castles

(MARIENBRÜCKE) **MARY'S BRIDGE**

Wunderbar View!

SCHLOSS / CASTLE **NEUSCHWANSTEIN**

TEGELBERG 5500'

UPPER BUS STOP

STEEP!

PRIVATE ROAD

HANG GLIDERS

PÖLLAT GORGE

LUGE

HORSE CART ENDS

WC

VILLAGE

LOWER BUS STOP

PICNIC SPOT

BOAT RENTAL

COLOMAN STRASSE

ROMANTISCHE

TO MUNICH & ROTHENBURG

SCHWANGAU

POST

CASTLE TICKET CENTER

HORSE CART STARTS

ALP SEE

TO PINSWANG 1 HOUR

PARK STR.

STRASSE

SCHLOSS / CASTLE **HOHENSCHWANGAU**

FORGGEN SEE

B.17

GERMANY AUSTRIA

TO KAUFBEUREN ON MUNICH-LINDAU LINE

CASTLE **FÜSSEN**

WATER-FALL

DCH

10 MILES TO REUTTE

— ROAD
--- TRAIL
!↙ VIEW

Ⓑ BUS STOP
Ⓟ PARKING

NOTE: MAP NOT TO SCALE
BORDER TO ALPSEE PARKING = 3 MILE DRIVE
ALPSEE PARKING TO NEUSCH. = 30 MIN. HIKE
TRAILS ARE SLIPPERY WHEN WET.

❶ Alpenhotel Meier
❷ Beim "Landhannes" Rooms
❸ Sonnenhof Rooms
❹ Royal Crystal Baths
❺ Festspielhaus & Bike Path Start

BAVARIA AND TIROL

power to make his dream concrete and stucco. Neuschwanstein (noy-SHVAHN-shtine, roughly "New Swanstone") was designed by a theater set designer first...then by an architect. It looks

medieval, but it's modern iron-and-brick construction with a sandstone veneer—only about as old as the Eiffel Tower. It feels like something you'd see at a home show for 19th-century royalty. Built from 1869 to 1886, it's the epitome of the Romanticism popular in 19th-century Europe. Construction stopped with Ludwig's death (only a third of the interior was finished), and within six weeks, tourists were paying to go through it.

"Mad" King Ludwig

A tragic figure, Ludwig II (a.k.a. "Mad" King Ludwig) ruled Bavaria for 22 years until his death in 1886 at the age of 40. Bavaria was weak. Politically, Ludwig's reality was to "rule" either as a pawn of Prussia or a pawn of Austria. Rather than deal with politics in Bavaria's capital, Munich, Ludwig frittered away most of his time at his family's hunting palace, Hohenschwangau. He spent much of his adult life constructing his fanciful Neuschwanstein Castle—like a kid builds a tree house—on a neighboring hill upon the scant ruins of a medieval castle. Although Ludwig spent 17 years building Neuschwanstein, he lived in it only 172 days.

Ludwig was a true romantic living in a Romantic age. His best friends were artists, poets, and composers such as Richard Wagner. His palaces are wallpapered with misty medieval themes—especially those from Wagnerian operas. Eventually he was declared mentally unfit to rule Bavaria and taken away from Neuschwanstein. Two days after this eviction, Ludwig was found dead in a lake. To this day, people debate whether the king was murdered or committed suicide.

Today, guides herd groups of 60 through the castle, giving an interesting—if rushed—30-minute tour. You'll go up and down more than 300 steps, through lavish rooms based on Wagnerian opera themes, the king's gilded-lily bedroom, and his extravagant throne room. You'll visit 15 rooms with their original furnishings and fanciful wall paintings. After the tour, before you descend to the king's kitchen, see the 20-minute video about the king's life and passions accompanied by Wagner's music (next to the café, alternates between English and German, schedule board at the entry says what's playing and what's on deck). After the kitchen (state of the art for this high-tech king in its day), you'll see a room lined with fascinating drawings (described in English) of the castle plans, construction, and drawings from 1883 of Falkenstein—a whimsical, over-the-top, never-built castle that makes Neuschwanstein look stubby. Falkenstein occupied Ludwig's fantasies the year he died.

Visiting the Castles
Cost: Each castle costs €9, a *Königsticket* for both castles costs €17, and children under 18 (accompanied by an adult) are admitted free. Neuschwanstein, but not Hohenschwangau, is covered by the Bavarian Castles Pass—see page 98.

Hours: Both castles are open April–Sept daily from 9:00 with last tour departing at 18:00, Oct–March daily from 10:00 with last tour at 16:00.

Getting Tickets for the Castles: Every tour bus in Bavaria converges on Neuschwanstein, and tourists flush in each morning from Munich. A handy reservation system (described below) sorts out the chaos for smart travelers. Tickets come with admission times. If you miss your appointed tour time, you can't get in. To tour both castles, you must do Hohenschwangau first (logical, since this gives a better introduction to Ludwig's short life). You'll get two tour times: Hohenschwangau and then, two hours later, Neuschwanstein.

A **ticket center** for both castles is located at street level between the two (daily April–Sept 8:00–17:00, Oct–March 9:00–15:00, last tickets sold for Neuschwanstein one hour before closing, for Hohenschwangau 30 min before closing). If you have a reservation, there's a short line for picking up tickets. If you don't have a reservation...welcome to the very long line. Arrive by 8:00 in summer, and you'll likely be touring by 9:00. During August, the busiest month, tickets for English tours usually run out between 16:00 and 17:00.

Reservations: It's smart to reserve in peak season (July–Sept, especially Aug). Reservations cost €1.80 per person per castle, and must be made no later than 18:00 on the previous day by phone (tel. 08362/930-830), email (info@ticket-center-hohenschwangau.de), or online (www.ticket-center-hohenschwangau.de). You must pick up reserved tickets well before the appointed entry time (30 min before your Hohenschwangau tour, one hour before your Neuschwanstein tour). Why the long wait? Sure, it takes a while to walk to the castles. But many of the businesses serving tourists are owned by the old royal family...so they require more waiting time than necessary in the hope that you'll spend more money.

Getting Up to the Castles: From the ticket booth, Hohenschwangau is an easy 10-minute climb, and Neuschwanstein is a steep 30-minute hike. To minimize hiking to Neuschwanstein, you can take a shuttle bus (leaves every few minutes from in front of Hotel Lisl, just above ticket office and to the left) or a horse-drawn carriage (in front of Hotel Müller, just above ticket office and to the right), but neither gets you to the castle doorstep. The shuttle bus drops you off near Mary's Bridge (Marienbrücke), leaving you a steep, 10-minute downhill walk to the castle—so be sure to see the view from Mary's Bridge *before* hiking down (€1.80 one-way, the €2.60 round-trip is not worth it since you have to hike uphill to the bus stop for your return trip). Carriages (€6 up, €3 down) are slower than walking and stop below Neuschwanstein, leaving you a five-minute uphill hike. Here's the most economic and least strenuous plan: Ride the bus to Mary's Bridge for the view, hike down to Neuschwanstein, and then catch the horse carriage from the castle back down to the parking lot.

Entry Procedure: For each castle, tourists jumble at the entry, waiting for their ticket number to light up on the board. When it does, power through the mob (most waiting there are holding higher numbers) and go to the turnstile. Warning: You must use your ticket while your number is still on the board. If you space out while waiting for a polite welcome, you'll miss your entry window and never get in.

Services: The helpful TI, bus stop, ATM, WC (€0.50), and telephones cluster around the main intersection (**TI** open daily June–Sept 11:00–19:00, Oct–March 11:00–17:00, April–May 11:00–18:00, tel. 08362/819-765, www.schwangau.de).

Eating: The "village" at the foot of Europe's Disney castle feeds off the droves of hungry, shop-happy tourists. The **Bräustüberl cafeteria** serves the cheapest grub (€6–7 gut-bomb grill meals, often with live folk music, from 11:00, close to end of road and lake). The Alpsee lake is ideal for a picnic, but there are no grocery shops nearby. Your best bets are to bring along a picnic, get food to go from one of the many bratwurst stands (between the ticket center and TI), or buy a sandwich at the shop adjacent the ticket booth. Enjoy a lazy lunch at the lakeside park or in one of the old-fashioned rowboats (rented by the hour in summer).

Near the Castles

Mary's Bridge (Marienbrücke)—Before or after the Neuschwanstein tour, climb up to Mary's Bridge to marvel at Ludwig's castle, just as Ludwig did. This bridge was quite an engineering accomplishment 100 years ago. From the bridge, the frisky can hike even higher to the *Beware—Danger of Death* signs and an even more glorious castle view. (Access to the bridge is closed in bad winter weather, but many travelers walk around the barriers to get there—at their own risk, of course.) For the most interesting descent from Neuschwanstein (15 min longer but worth it, especially with new steel walkways and railings that make the slippery area safer), follow signs to the Pöllat Gorge *(Pöllatschlucht)*.

▲**Tegelberg Gondola**—Just north of Neuschwanstein is a fun play zone around the mighty Tegelberg Gondola. For €17 round-trip (€10 one-way), you can ride the lift to the 5,500-foot summit

BAVARIA AND TIROL

(daily 9:00–17:00, closed Nov, 4/hr, last ride at 16:30, in bad weather call first to confirm, tel. 08362/98360, www.tegelberg bahn.de; most buses #73 and #78 from Füssen continue from the castles to Tegelberg). On a clear day, you get great views of the Alps and Bavaria and the vicarious thrill of watching hang gliders and paragliders leap into airborne ecstasy. Weather permitting, scores of adventurous Germans line up and leap from the launch ramp at the top of the lift. With someone leaving every two or three minutes, it's great for spectators. Thrill-seekers with exceptional social skills may talk themselves into a tandem ride with a paraglider. From the top of Tegelberg, it's a steep and demanding 2.5-hour hike down to Ludwig's castle. (Avoid the treacherous trail directly below the gondola.) At the base of the gondola, you'll find a playground, a cheery eatery, the stubby remains of an ancient Roman villa, and a luge ride (described next).

▲**Tegelberg Luge**—Next to the Tegelberg Gondola is a luge course. A luge is like a bobsled on wheels (for more details, see "Luge Lesson" on page 137). This stainless-steel track is heated, so it's often dry and open even when drizzly weather shuts down the concrete luges. It's not as scenic as Austria's Biberwier luge (described on page 136), but it's handy and half the price (€2.60/ride, 6-ride sharable card-€10.50, July–Sept daily 10:00–18:00, otherwise same hours as gondola, in winter sometimes opens late due to wet track, in bad weather call first to confirm, waits can be long in good weather, no children under 6, tel. 08362/98360, www.tegelbergbahn.de). A funky cable system pulls riders (in their sleds) to the top without a ski lift.

▲**Royal Crystal Baths (Königliche Kristall-Therme)**—This pool/sauna complex just outside Füssen is the perfect way to relax on a rainy day, or to cool off on a hot one. The downstairs contains two heated indoor pools and a café; outside you'll find a shallow kiddie pool, a lap pool, a heated *Kristallbad* with massage jets and a whirlpool, and a salty mineral bath. The extensive saunas upstairs are well worth the few extra euros, as long as you're OK with nudity. (Swimsuits are required in the downstairs pools, but *verboten* in the upstairs saunas.) You'll see pool and sauna rules in German all over, but don't worry—just follow the locals' lead. To enter the baths, first choose the length of your visit and your focus (big outdoor pool only, all ground-floor pools but not the saunas, or the whole enchilada—a flier explains all the prices in English). You'll get a wristband and a credit-card-sized ticket with a bar code. Insert that ticket into the entry gate, and keep it—you'll need it to get out. Enter through the yellow changing stalls—where you'll change into your bathing suit—then choose a storage locker (€1 coin deposit). When it's time to leave, reinsert your ticket in the gate—if you've gone over the time limit, feed extra euros into the machine (€8.50/2 hrs, €12.20/4 hrs, €15.80/day, saunas-€4, towel rental-€2.50, bathing suit rental-€3, Sun–Thu 9:00–22:00, Fri–Sat until 23:00, nude swimming everywhere Tue and Fri after 19:00; from Füssen, drive, bike, or walk across the river, turn left toward Schwangau, and then, about a mile later, turn left at signs for *Kristall-Therme*, Am Ehberg 16; tel. 08362/819-630, www.kristalltherme-schwangau.de).

Bike Ride Around Forggensee—On a beautiful day, nothing beats a bike ride around the bright turquoise Forggensee lake. This 20-mile ride is almost exclusively on bike paths, with just a few stretches on country roads. Locals swear that going clockwise is less work, but either way has a couple of strenuous uphill parts. Still, the amazing views of the surrounding Alps will distract you from your churning legs—so this is still a great way to spend the afternoon. Rent a bike, pack a picnic lunch, and figure about a three-hour round-trip. From Füssen, follow *Festspielhaus* signs; once you reach the theater, follow *Forggensee Rundweg* signs. From the theater, you can also take a boat ride on the Forggensee (€8/50-min cruise, 6/day; €11/2-hr cruise, 3/day; or buy a one-way ticket and bike back, fewer departures Oct–May, tel. 08362/921-363, www.schifffahrt.fuessen.de).

Sleeping near the King's Castles

(€1 = about $1.40, country code: 49, area code: 08362)
Inexpensive farmhouse *Zimmer* (B&Bs) abound in the Bavarian countryside around Neuschwanstein, offering drivers a decent value. Look for *Zimmer Frei* signs ("room free," or vacancy). The going rate is about €50–65 for a double, including breakfast. Though a bit inconvenient for those without a car, my three listings below are a quick taxi ride from the Füssen train station.

$$ Alpenhotel Meier is a small, family-run hotel with 18 rooms in a bucolic setting. It's a 15-minute walk from the castle ticket office, not far beyond the humongous parking lot (Sb-€48–58, perfectly fine older Db-€80, newer Db-€88, Tb-€110, these are book-direct prices, 5 percent discount with cash and this book in 2010, all rooms have porches or balconies—some with castle views, family rooms, elevator, free parking, just before tennis courts at Schwangauer Strasse 37, tel. 08362/81152, fax 08362/987-028, www.alpenhotel-allgaeu.de, info@alpenhotel-allgaeu.de, Frau Reiss).

BAVARIA AND TIROL

$ **Beim "Landhannes,"** a 200-year-old working dairy farm run by Connie Schon, rents six creaky but sunny rooms, and keeps flowers on the balconies, big bells and antlers in the halls, and cows in the yard (Sb-€30, Db-€60, 20 percent discount for 3 or more nights, apartment with kitchen, cash only, poorly signed in the village of Horn on the Füssen side of Schwangau, look for the farm down a tiny lane through the grass 100 yards in front of Hotel Kleiner König, Am Lechrain 22, tel. 08362/8349, www .landhannes.de, mayr@landhannes.de).

$ **Sonnenhof** is a big woody old house with four spacious, traditionally decorated rooms (all with balconies) and a cheery garden. It's a 15-minute walk through the fields to the castles (S-€35, D-€50, Db-€60, cash only; at Pension Schwansee on the Füssen-Neuschwanstein road, follow the small lane 100 yards to Sonnenweg 11; they'll pick you up from the Füssen train station if you request ahead, tel. 08362/8420, Frau Görlich).

Wieskirche

Germany's greatest Rococo-style church, this "Church in the Meadow" is newly restored and looking as brilliant as the day it floated down from heaven. It's worth ▲▲. Overripe with decoration but bright and bursting with beauty, this church is a divine droplet, a curly curlicue, the final flowering of the Baroque movement.

Cost and Hours: Donation requested, summer daily 8:00–19:00, winter daily 8:00–17:00, tel. 08862/932-930, www .wieskirche.de.

Getting There: The Wieskirche is a 30-minute drive north of Neuschwanstein. The Romantic Road bus tour stops here for 17 minutes—but only on the northbound route to Frankfurt. Southbound buses stop here to pick up and drop off only on request. For information on taking the bus from Füssen to the Wieskirche, see page 99. By car, head north from Füssen, turn right at Steingaden, and follow the signs. Take a commune-with-nature-and-smell-the-farm detour back through the meadow to the parking lot (€1/hr).

➲ **Self-Guided Tour:** This pilgrimage church is built around the much-venerated statue of a scourged (or whipped) Christ, which supposedly wept in 1738. The carving—too graphic to be accepted by that generation's Church—was the focus of worship in a peasant's barn. Miraculously, it shed tears—empathizing with all those who suffer. Pilgrims came from all around. A tiny and humble chapel was built to house the statue in 1739. (You can see it where the lane to the church leaves the parking lot.) Bigger and bigger crowds came. Two of Bavaria's top Rococo architects, the Zimmermann brothers (Johann Baptist and Dominikus), were commissioned to build the Wieskirche that stands here today.

Follow the theological sweep from the altar to the ceiling: Jesus whipped, chained, and then killed (notice the pelican above the altar—recalling a pre-Christian story of a bird that opened its breast to feed its young with its own blood); the painting of a baby Jesus posed as if on the cross; the sacrificial lamb; and finally, high on the ceiling, the resurrected Christ before the Last Judgment. This is the most positive depiction of the Last Judgment around. Jesus, rather than sitting on the throne to judge, rides high on a rainbow—a symbol of forgiveness—giving any sinner the feeling that there is still time to repent, with plenty of mercy on hand. In the back, above the pipe organ, notice the empty throne—waiting for Judgment Day—and the closed door to paradise.

Above the entrances to both side aisles are murky glass cases with 18th-century handkerchiefs. People wept, came here, were healed, and no longer needed their hankies. Walk up either aisle flanking the high altar to see votives—requests and thanks to God (for happy, healthy babies, and so on). Notice how the kneelers are positioned so that worshippers can meditate on scenes of biblical miracles painted high on the ceiling and visible through the ornate tunnel frames. A priest here once told me that faith, architecture, light, and music all combine to create the harmony of the Wieskirche.

Two paintings flank the door at the rear of the church. One shows the ceremonial parade in 1749 when the white-clad monks of Steingaden carried the carved statue of Christ from the tiny church to its new big one. The second painting, from 1757, is a votive from one of the Zimmermann brothers, the artists and architects who built this church. He is giving thanks for the successful construction of the new church.

If you can't visit the Wieskirche, visit one of the other churches that came out of the same heavenly spray can: Oberammergau's church, Munich's Asamkirche, Würzburg's Hofkirche Chapel (at the Residenz), the splendid Ettal Monastery (free and near Oberammergau), and, on a lesser scale, Füssen's basilica.

Route Tips for Drivers: If you're driving from Wieskirche to Oberammergau, you'll cross the **Echelsbacher Bridge,** which arches 230 feet over the Pöllat Gorge. Thoughtful drivers let their passengers walk across to enjoy the views, then meet them at the other side. Any kayakers? Notice the painting of the traditional village woodcarver (who used to walk from town to town with his art on his back) on the first big house on the Oberammergau side. It holds the Almdorf Ammertal shop, with a huge selection of overpriced carvings and commission-hungry tour guides.

Oberammergau

The Shirley Temple of Bavarian villages, and exploited to the hilt by the tourist trade, Oberammergau wears way too much makeup. When this year's Passion Play is running (May 15–Oct 3), the crush may be unbearable—and the prices at the hotels and restaurants may be as well. The village has about 1,200 beds for the 5,000 playgoers coming daily. If you're passing through outside of those dates, it's a ▲ sight—worth a wander among the half-timbered *Lüftlmalerei* houses frescoed (in a style popular throughout the town in the 18th century) with biblical scenes and famous fairy-tale characters. It's also a relatively convenient home base for visiting Linderhof Castle, Ettal Monastery, and the Zugspitze (via Garmisch).

Tourist Information: The TI is at Eugen-Papst-Strasse 9A (Mon–Fri 9:00–18:00, Sat 10:00–13:00, Sun 10:00–12:00; Nov–May closed Sun; tel. 08822/922-740, www.oberammergau.de).

Getting There

From Füssen to Oberammergau, four to six **buses** run daily (fewer in winter, 1.5 hrs). All buses start at the train station and stop two minutes later near the TI closer to the center. **Trains** run from Munich to Oberammergau (nearly hourly, 1.75 hrs, change in Murnau). **Drivers** entering the town from the north should cross the bridge, take the second right, and park in the free lot a block beyond the TI. Leaving town (to Linderhof or Reutte), head out past the church and turn toward Ettal on Road 23. You're 20 miles from Reutte via the scenic Plansee. If heading to Munich, Road 23 takes you to the autobahn, which gets you there in less than an hour.

Sights in Oberammergau

Oberammergau Church—Visit the town church, a poor cousin of the one at Wies. Being in a woodcarving center, it's only logical that all the statues are made of wood, and then stuccoed and gilded to look like marble or gold. Saints Peter and Paul flank the altar, where the central painting can be raised to reveal a small stage decorated to celebrate special times during the church calendar. In the central dome, a touching painting shows Peter and Paul bidding each other farewell (with the city of Rome as a backdrop) on the day of their execution—the same day in the year A.D. 67.

Oberammergau

◣ View
🅿 Parking
--- Foot Path

Passion Play Theater

To ❸ & Wieskirche via Road 23

Train Station

Post

Church

100 YARDS
100 METERS

❶ Pilatus House
❷ Oberammergau Museum
❸ To Sommerrodelbahn Steckenberg
❹ Gasthof zur Rose & Gästehaus Magold
❺ Hotel Wittelsbach
❻ Hotel Garni Fux
❼ Anton Zwink Rooms
❽ Youth Hostel
❾ Hotel Maximilian (Beer Garden)

MT. KOFEL (IN DISTANCE)

ROAD 23 TO ETTAL, LINDERHOF, REUTTE, GARMISCH & MUNICH

DCH

On the left, Peter is crucified upside-down. On the right, Paul is beheaded with a sword. (A fine little €3 booklet explains it all.) Wander through the lovingly maintained graveyard. A stone WWI and WWII memorial at the gate reads, "We honor and remember the victims of the violence that our land gave the world."

Passion Play—Back in 1633, in the midst of the bloody Thirty Years' War and with horrifying plagues devastating entire cities, the people of Oberammergau promised God that if they were spared from extinction, they'd "perform a play depicting the suffering, death, and resurrection of our Lord Jesus Christ" every decade

Woodcarving in Oberammergau

The Ammergau region is relatively poor, with no appreciable industry and no agriculture, save for some dairy farming. What they *do* have is wood. Carving religious and secular themes became a lucrative way for the locals to make some money, especially when confined to the house during the long, cold winter. Carvers from Oberammergau peddled their wares across Europe, carrying them on their back as far away as Rome. Today, the Oberammergau Carving School is a famous institution that takes only 20 students per year out of 450 applicants. Their graduates do important restorative work throughout Europe. For example, much of the work on Dresden's Frauenkirche (see page 44) was done by these artists.

thereafter. The town survived and, heading into its 41st decade, the people of Oberammergau are still making good on the deal. For 100 days every 10 years (see it this year or wait until 2020), about half of the town's population (a cast of 2,000) is involved in the production of this extravagant five-hour Passion Play—telling the story of Jesus' entry into Jerusalem, Crucifixion, and Resurrection. If you miss it, you'll have to settle for reading the book or seeing Nicodemus tool around town in his VW. Because of this year's Passion Play, there will be no backstage theater tours in 2010.

Tickets for Oberammergau's 2010 Passion Play: Starting on May 15, about 5,000 people a day will watch the five-hour play. For the first time, the play will be shown in the afternoon and evening, rather than starting in the morning. While in past decades the performances have sold out far in advance, the German National Tourist Office said sales have been slower for 2010. It's still smart to book as far in advance as you can. If any tickets are left, they sell for €50–165 (www.passionsspiele2010.de).

Local Arts and Crafts—The town's best sights are its woodcarving shops. Browse through these small art galleries filled with very expensive whittled works. The beautifully frescoed **Pilatus House** on Ludwig-Thomas-Strasse often has woodcarvers and painters at work (free; mid-May–mid-Oct Tue–Sat 13:00–18:00, closed Sun–Mon; open two weeks after Christmas 11:00–17:00; closed rest of year, tel. 08822/949-511). For folk art, see the **Oberammergau Museum** (€4, April–Oct and Dec–mid-Jan Tue–Sun 10:00–17:00, closed Mon, closed Nov and mid-Jan–March, Dorfstrasse 8, tel. 08822/94136, www.oberammergaumuseum.de).

Sommerrodelbahn Steckenberg—This stainless-steel luge track (near Oberammergau) is faster than the Tegelberg luge, but not quite as wicked as the one in Biberwier (€2.50/ride, €11/6 rides, May–Oct daily 10:00–18:00, closed when wet, Liftweg 1 in Unterammergau, clearly marked and easy 2.5-mile bike ride to Unterammergau along Bahnhofstrasse/Rottenbucherstrasse, take the first left when entering Unterammergau, tel. 08822/4027, www.steckenberg.de).

Sleeping in Oberammergau

(€1 = about $1.40, country code: 49, area code: 08822)

$$ **Gasthof zur Rose** is a big central family-run place with 21 rooms (Sb-€40, Db-€70, Tb-€81, Qb-€88, Internet access, Dedlerstrasse 9, tel. 08822/4706, fax 08822/6753, www.hotel -oberammergau.de, gasthof-rose@t-online.de, Frank family).

$$ **Hotel Wittelsbach** is a romantic tourist-class hotel. Its creaky 1970s-style public areas hide 40 deluxe, spacious rooms, many with geranium-clad balconies (Sb-€65–95, Db-€80–120, Tb-€110–150, Wi-Fi, Dorfstrasse 21, tel. 08822/92800, www .hotelwittelsbach.de, info@hotelwittelsbach.de).

$$ **Hotel Garni Fux**, quiet and romantic, rents six large rooms and eight apartments decorated in the Bavarian *Landhaus* style (Sb-€65, Db-€84, apartments €106–168, prices nearly double during Passion Play, cheaper Nov–April, free Internet access and Wi-Fi, Mannagasse 2a, tel. 08822/93093, www.firmafux.de, info@firmafux.de).

$ **Anton Zwink** offers 10 small quiet no-frills rooms in a neighborhood adjacent to the town center (Sb-€38, Db-€60, behind Gasthof zur Rose at Daisenbergerstrasse 10, tel. 08822/6334, www .pension-zwink.de, info@pension-zwink.de).

$ **Gästehaus Magold** is a homey, grandmotherly place with three bright and spacious rooms—twice as nice as the cheap hotel rooms, and for much less money (Db-€48, cash only, also has two family apartments, immediately behind Gasthof zur Rose at Kleppergasse 1, tel. 08822/4340, fax 0882/242-127, www.gaeste haus-magold.de, info@gaestehaus-magold.de, Christine).

$ The **youth hostel,** on the river, is a short walk from the center (€20 beds, €24.50 during Passion Play, includes breakfast and sheets, Malensteinweg 10, tel. 08822/4114, fax 08822/1695, www.oberammergau.jugendherberge.de, jhoberammergau@djh -bayern.de).

Eating in Oberammergau

Locals won't be caught dead inside the chic **Hotel Maximilian.** But they fill its serene beer garden to enjoy the hotel's homemade beer and summertime grill, which cooks up delicious chicken, sausage, and spareribs for around €10 (daily 9:00–21:00, right behind the church, Ettaler Strasse 5, tel. 08822/948-740).

Oberammergau Connections

From Oberammergau to: Füssen (4–6 buses/day in summer, transfer at Echelsbacher Brücke, 1.5 hrs total), **Linderhof Castle** (bus #9622, nearly hourly, 25–40 min; some of these also stop at **Ettal Monastery**), **Garmisch** (nearly hourly buses, 40 min; also possible by train with a transfer in Murnau, 1.5 hrs; from Garmisch you can ascend the **Zugspitze**), **Munich** (nearly hourly trains, 1.75 hrs, change in Murnau).

Linderhof Castle

This homiest of "Mad" King Ludwig's castles is small and comfortably exquisite—good enough for a minor god, and worth ▲▲.

Set in the woods 15 minutes from Oberammergau and surrounded by fountains and sculpted, Italian-style gardens, it's the only palace I've toured that actually had me feeling envious.

Ludwig was king for 22 of his 40 years. He lived much of his last eight years here—the only one of his castles that was finished in his lifetime. Frustrated by the limits of being a "constitutional monarch," he retreated to Linderhof, inhabiting a private fantasy world where extravagant castles glorified his otherwise weakened kingship. He lived here as a royal hermit; his dinner table—pre-set with dishes and food—rose from the kitchen below into his dining room, so he could eat alone.

Beyond the palace is Ludwig's **grotto.** Inspired by Wagner's *Tannhäuser* opera, this performance space is 300 feet long and 70 feet tall. Its rocky walls are actually made of cement poured over an iron frame. The grotto provided a private theater for the reclusive king to enjoy his beloved Wagnerian operas by himself. The first electricity in Bavaria was generated here, to change the colors of the stage lights and to power Ludwig's fountain and wave machine.

Cost and Hours: €7, covered by Bavarian Castles Pass—see page 98, daily April–mid-Oct 9:00–18:00, mid-Oct–March 10:00–16:00, last tour 30 min before closing, fountains often erupt on the half-hour, tel. 08822/92030, www.linderhof.de.

Getting There: Without a car, getting to (and back from) Linderhof is a royal headache, unless you're staying in Oberammergau. From that village, there is a bus nearly hourly in summer (less frequently off-season; see "Oberammergau Connections," earlier). If you're driving, park near the ticket office (obligatory €2.50).

Visiting the Castle: The complex sits isolated in natural splendor. Plan for lots of walking and a two-hour stop to fully enjoy this royal park. Your ticket comes with an entry time to tour the palace, which is a five-minute hike from the ticket office. At the palace entrance, wait in line for your number to take the required 30-minute English-language tour. Afterwards, hike 10 minutes uphill to the grotto (take the brief but interesting free tour in English, no reservations necessary). Then see the other royal buildings dotting the king's playground if you like.

Crowd-Beating Tips: July and August crowds can cause delays at the palace of up to two hours. During this period, you're wise to arrive after 15:00. Any other time of year, you should get your palace tour time shortly after you arrive. There are no online reservations, but you can download a ticket order form from the website and fax it back.

Ettal Monastery and Pilgrimage Church

In 1328, the Holy Roman Emperor was returning from Rome with what was considered a miraculous statue of Mary and Jesus. He was in political and financial trouble, so to please God, he founded a monastery with this statue as its centerpiece. The monastery was located here because it was suitably off the beaten path, but today Ettal is on one of the most-traveled tourist routes in Bavaria. Stopping here (free and easy for drivers) offers a convenient peek at a splendid Baroque church.

Cost and Hours: Free, daily 8:00–19:45 in summer, until 18:00 off-season, tel. 08822/740, www.kloster-ettal.de.

Getting There: The Ettal Monastery is a few minutes' **drive** (or a delightful **bike** ride) from Oberammergau. Just park for free and wander in. Some Oberammergau-to-Linderhof **buses** stop here (see "Oberammergau Connections," earlier).

◐ Self-Guided Tour: As you enter the more than 1,000-square-foot **courtyard,** imagine the 14th-century Benedictine abbey, an independent religious community. It produced everything it needed right here. In the late Middle Ages, abbeys like this had jurisdiction over the legal system, administration, and taxation of their district. Since then, the monastery has had its ups and downs. Secularized during the French Revolution and Napoleonic age, the Benedictines' property was confiscated by the state and sold. Religious life returned a century later. Today the abbey survives, with 50 or 60 monks. It remains a self-contained community, with living quarters for the monks, workshops, and guests' quarters. Along with their religious responsibilities, the

20 † C † M † B † 10

All over Germany (and much of Catholic Europe), you'll likely see written on doorways a mysterious message: "20 † C † M † B † 10." This is marked in chalk on Epiphany (Jan 6), the

Christian holiday celebrating the arrival of the Magi to adore the newborn Baby Jesus. In addition to being the initials of the three wise men (Caspar, Melchior, and Balthazar), the letters also stand for the Latin phrase *Christus mansionem benedicat*—"May Christ bless the house." The little crosses separating the letters remind all who enter that the house has been blessed in this year (20†10). Epiphany is a bigger deal in Catholic Europe than in the US. The holiday includes gift-giving, feasting, and carol-ing door to door—often collecting for a charity organization. Those who donate get their doors chalked up in thanks, and these marks are left on the door through the year.

brothers make their famous liqueur, brew beer, run a hotel, and educate 380 students in their private high school.

At the front of the church, you pass a **tympanum** over the door dating from 1350. It shows the founding couple, Emperor Louis the Bavarian and his wife Margaret, directing our attention to the crucified Lord and inviting us to enter the church contem-platively.

Stepping inside, the light draws our eyes to the **dome** (it's a double shell design 230 feet high) rather than to the high altar.

Illusions—with the dome opening right to the sky—merge heaven and earth. The dome fresco shows hun-dreds of Benedictines wor-shipping the Holy Trinity... the glory of the Benedictine Order. This is classic "south German Baroque."

Statues of the **saints** on the altars are either engaged in a holy conversation with each other or singing the praises of God. Broken shell-style patterns seem to create constant movement, with cherubs adding to the energy. Side altars and confessionals seem to grow out of the architectural structure; its decorations and furnishings become part of an organic whole. Imagine how

18th-century farmers and woodcutters, who never traveled, would step in here on Sunday and be inspired to praise their God.

The origin of the monastery is shown over the **choir arch:** An angel wearing the robe of a Benedictine monk presents the emperor with a marble Madonna and commissions him to found this monastery. (In reality, the statue was made in Pisa, circa 1300, and given to the emperor in Italy.)

Dwarfed by all the magnificence and framed by a monumental tabernacle is that tiny, most precious statue of the abbey—the miraculous **statue of Mary and the baby Jesus.**

Zugspitze

The tallest point in Germany, worth ▲▲, is also a border crossing. Lifts from both Austria and Germany meet at the 9,700-foot

summit of the Zugspitze. You can straddle the border between two great nations while enjoying an incredible view. Restaurants, shops, and telescopes await you at the summit.

German Approach: First, head to Garmisch (for details on getting there from Füssen or Oberammergau, see page 99). From Garmisch, there are two ways to ascend the Zugspitze: the whole way by cogwheel train (1.25 hrs one-way), or a faster cogwheel train-plus-cable car option (about 45 min one-way). Both cost the same (€47 round-trip). Although the train ride takes longer, many travelers enjoy the more involved cog-railway experience. The train departs from Garmisch, stops at Eibsee for the cable-car connection, and then continues up—and through—the mountain. The cable car simply zips you to the top in five minutes from the Eibsee station. Cable cars go up daily from 8:00–14:15. The last cable car down departs at about 16:30 (tel. 08821/7970, www.zugspitze.de). Allow plenty of time for afternoon descents: If bad weather hits in the late afternoon, cable cars can be delayed at the summit, causing tourists to miss their train connection from Eibsee back to Garmisch.

Drivers can park for €3 at the cable-car station at Eibsee. Hikers can enjoy the easy six-mile walk around the lovely Eibsee (start 5 min downhill from cable-car station).

Austrian Approach: The Tiroler Zugspitzbahn ascent is less crowded and cheaper. Departing from above the village of Ehrwald (a 30-min train trip from Reutte, runs almost hourly), the lift zips you to the top in 10 minutes (€34 round-trip, departures in each direction at :00, :20, and :40 past the hour, daily 8:40–16:40 except closed April–mid-May and most of mid-Oct–Nov, last ascent at 16:00, drivers follow signs for *Tiroler Zugspitzbahn*, free parking, Austrian tel. 05673/2309, www.zugspitze .com). While the German ascent from Garmisch is easier

for those without a car, buses connect the Ehrwald train station and the Austrian lift nearly every hour (or pay €8 for the 5-minute taxi ride from Ehrwald train station).

○ **Self-Guided Tour:** Whether you ascended from the Austrian or German side, you're high enough now to enjoy a little tour of the summit. The two terraces—Bavarian and Tirolean— are connected by a narrow walkway, which was the border station before Germany and Austria opened their borders. The Austrian (Tirolean) side was higher until the Germans blew its top off in World War II to make a flak tower, so let's start there.

Tirolean Terrace: Before you stretches the Zugspitzplatt gla- cier. Each summer, a 65,000-square-foot reflector is spread over the ice to try to slow the shrinking. Since metal ski lift towers col- lect heat, they, too, are wrapped to try to save the glacier. Many ski lifts fan out here, as if reaching for a ridge that defines the border between Germany and Austria. The circular metal building is the top of the cog-railway line that the Germans cut through the mountains in 1931. Just above that, find a small square building— the wedding chapel (Hochzeitskapelle) consecrated in 1981 by Cardinal Joseph Ratzinger (now Pope Benedict XVI).

Both Germany and Austria use this rocky pinnacle for com- munication purposes. The square box on the Tirolean Terrace provides the Innsbruck airport with air-traffic control, and a tower nearby is for the German *Kathastrophenfunk* (civil defense net- work).

This highest point in Germany (there are many higher points in Austria) was first climbed in 1820. The Austrians built a cable car that nearly reached the summit in 1926. (You can see it just over the ridge on the Austrian side—look for the ghostly aban- doned concrete station.) In 1964, the final leg, a new lift, was built connecting that 1926 station to the actual summit, where you stand now. Before then, people needed to hike the last 650 feet to the top. Today's lift dates from 1980, but was renovated after a 2003 fire. The Austrian station, which is much nicer than the German station, has a fine little museum—free with Austrian ticket, €2 if you came up from Germany—that shows three interesting videos

(6-min 3-D mountain show, 30-min making-of-the-lift documentary, and 45-min look at the nature, sport, and culture of the region).

Looking up the valley from the Tirolean Terrace, you can see the towns of Ehrwald and Lermoos in the distance, and the valley that leads to Reutte. Looking farther clockwise, you'll see the Eibsee lake below. Hell's Valley, stretching to the right of Eibsee, seems to merit its name.

Bavarian Terrace: The narrow passage connecting the two terraces used to be a big deal—you'd show your passport here at the little blue house, and shift from Austrian shillings to German marks. Notice the regional pride here: no German or Austrian banners, but regional ones instead—Freistaat Bayern and Land Tirol.

The German side features a golden cross marking the summit...the highest point in Germany. A priest and his friends hauled it up in 1851. The historic original was shot up by American soldiers using it for target practice in the late 1940s, so what you see today is a modern replacement. In the summer, it's easy to "summit" the Zugspitze, as there are steps and handholds all the way to the top. Or you can just stay behind and feed the birds. The yellow-beak ravens get chummy with those who share a little pretzel or bread.

The oldest building up here is the rustic tin-and-wood weather tower, erected in 1900 by the *Deutscher Wetterdienst* (German weather service). The first mountaineers' hut was built in 1897, but didn't last. The existing one—entwined with mighty cables that cinch it down—dates from 1914. In 1985, observers clocked 200-mph winds up here—those cables were necessary. Step inside the restaurant to enjoy museum-like photos and paintings on the wall (including a look at the team who hiked up with the golden cross in 1851).

Reutte, Austria

Reutte (ROY-teh, with a rolled *r*), a relaxed Austrian town of 5,700, is located 20 minutes across the border from Füssen. While overlooked by the international tourist crowd, it's popular with Germans and Austrians for its climate. Doctors recommend its "grade 1" air. I like Reutte for the opportunity to simply be in a real community. As an example of how the town is committed to its character, real estate can be sold only to those using it as a primary residence. (Many formerly vibrant alpine towns made a pile of money but lost their sense of community by becoming resorts. They allowed wealthy foreigners—who just drop in for a week or two a year—to buy up all the land, and are now shuttered up and dead most of the time.)

Reutte's one claim to fame with Americans: As Nazi Germany was falling in 1945, Hitler's top rocket scientist, Werner von Braun, joined the Americans (rather than the Russians) in Reutte. You could say that the American space program began here.

Reutte isn't featured in any other American guidebook. While its generous sidewalks are filled with smart boutiques and lazy coffeehouses, its charms are subtle. It was never rich or important. Its castle is ruined, its

buildings have painted-on "carvings," its churches are full, its men yodel for each other on birthdays, and its energy is spent soaking its Austrian and German guests in *Gemütlichkeit*. Most guests stay for a week, so the town's attractions are more time-consuming than thrilling.

Orientation to Reutte

(country code: 43, area code: 05672)

Remember, Reutte is in a different country. While Austrians use the same currency the Germans do, postage stamps and phone cards only work in the country where you buy them.

To **telephone** from Germany to Austria, dial 00-43- and then the number listed in this section (omitting the initial zero). To call from Austria to Germany, dial 00-49- and then the number (again, omitting the initial zero).

Tourist Information

Reutte's TI is a block in front of the train station (Mon–Fri 8:00–12:00 & 14:00–17:00, no midday break July–Aug, Sat 8:30–12:00, closed Sun, Untermarkt 34, tel. 05672/62336, www.reutte.com). Go over your sightseeing plans, ask about a folk evening, pick up city and biking maps and the *Sommerprogramm* events schedule (in German only), and ask about discounts with the hotel guest cards. Their free informational booklet has a good self-guided town walk.

Arrival in Reutte

If you're coming by car from Germany, skip the north *(Nord)* exit and take the south *(Süd)* exit into town. For parking in town, blue lines denote pay-and-display spots. There is a free lot (P-1) near the train station on Muhlerstrasse.

While Austria requires a **toll sticker** *(Vignette)* for driving on its highways (€8/10 days, buy at the border, gas stations, car-rental agencies, or *Tabak* shops), those just dipping into Tirol from Bavaria do not need one.

Helpful Hints

Internet Access: There's a **call shop** in the town center (Mon–Fri 9:00–21:00, closed Sat–Sun). Otherwise, rely on your hotel.

Laundry: There isn't an actual launderette in town, but the recommended **Hotel Maximilian** lets even non-guests use its self-service machines.

Bike Rental: Try **Intersport** (€15/day, Mon–Fri 9:00–18:00, Sat 9:00–17:00, closed Sun, Lindenstrasse 25, tel. 05672/62352), or check at the recommended Hotel Maximilian.

Car Rental: Autoreisen Köck rents cars at Muhlerstrasse 12 (tel. 05672/62233).

"Nightlife": Reutte is pretty quiet. For any action at all, there's a strip of bars, dance clubs, and Italian restaurants on Lindenstrasse.

Sights in and near Reutte

▲▲Ehrenberg Castle Ensemble (Festungsensemble Ehrenberg)

If Neuschwanstein was the medieval castle dream, Ehrenburg is the medieval castle reality. Just a mile outside of Reutte are the brooding ruins of four castles that once made up the largest fort in Tirol. This impressive "castle ensemble" was built to defend against the Bavarians and to bottle up the strategic Via Claudia trade route, which cut through the Alps as it

connected Italy and Germany. Today, these castles have become a European "castle museum," showing off 500 years of military architecture in one swoop. The European Union is helping fund the project (paying a third of its €9 million cost) because it promotes the heritage of a multinational region—Tirol—rather than a country.

The complex has four parts: the fortified Klause toll booth on the valley floor, the oldest castle on the first hill above (Ehrenberg), a mighty and more modern castle high above (Schlosskopf, built in the age when cannon positioned there made the original castle vulnerable), and a smaller fourth castle across the valley (Fort Claudia, an hour's hike away). All four were a fortified complex once connected by walls. Signs posted throughout the castle complex help visitors find their way and explain some background on

Reutte

P PARKING

🔎 VIEW

--- FOOT PATH

"DOWNTOWN" **REUTTE**

LECH-ASCHAU

REUTTENER BERGBAHN

HÖFEN

GLIDER AIRSTRIP

LECH R.

EHEN-BICHL

TO PFLACH, PINSWANG (OBER & UNTER), & FÜSSEN (GERMANY) ⑩

MAIN TRAIN STATION

MÜHLER STRASSE

BREITEN-WANG

Reutte-Schulzentrum TRAIN STATION

UNTER MARKT

OBERMARKT

POST PLANSEE

LECH

SÜD TIROL STR.

KAISER-LOTH.

INNSBRUCKER STR.

REUTTENER STR.

AM KANAL

KÖG

PLANSEE STRASSE

314

MÄCKELBERG STR.

TO PLANSEE & LINDERHOF (GERMANY)

HOSPITAL

CAMPING

KRANKENHAUS STR.

EHRENBERG

EHRENBERG CASTLE ENSEMBLE

NOT TO SCALE

SCHLOSSKOPF

KLAUSE VALLEY FORT MUSEUM

TO LUGES, FERNPASS & INNSBRUCK

BAVARIA AND TIROL

① Hotel/Café "Das Beck" & Museum

② Hotel/Rest. Goldener Hirsch & Internet Access

③ Alpenhotel Ernberg & Moserhof Hotel/Restaurant

④ Hosp Rooms

⑤ Hotel/Rest. Maximilian

⑥ Gasthof-Pension Waldrast

⑦ Pension Hohenrainer

⑧ Gintherhof

⑨ Gästehaus am Graben Hostel

⑩ To Gutshof zum Schluxen

⑪ Storfwirt Restaurant

⑫ Non Solo Pasta

⑬ Bike Rental

⑭ Car Rental

the region's history, geology, geography, culture, flora, and fauna. (While the castles are free and open all the time, the museum and multimedia show at the fort's parking lot charge admission.)

Getting to the Castle Ensemble: The Klause, Ehrenberg, and Schlosskopf castles are on the road to Lermoos and Innsbruck. These are a pleasant walk or a short bike ride from Reutte; bikers can use the *Radwanderweg* along the Lech River (the TI has a good map).

▲**Klause Valley Fort Museum**—Historians estimate that about 10,000 tons of precious salt passed through this valley (along the route of Rome's Via Claudia) each year in medieval times, so it's no wonder the locals built this complex of fortresses and castles. Beginning in the 14th century, the fort controlled traffic and levied tolls on all who passed. Today, these scant remains hold a museum and a theater with a multimedia show (€8 for museum, €11 combo-ticket also includes multimedia show, €18 family pass for 2 adults and any number of kids, daily 10:00–17:00, closed Nov–mid-Dec, tel. 05672/62007, www.ehrenberg.at).

While there are no real artifacts here (other than the sword used in A.D. 2008 to make me the honorary First Knight of Ehrenberg), the clever, kid-friendly **museum** takes one 14th-century decade (1360–1370) and attempts to bring it to life. It's a hands-on experience, well-described in English. You can try on a set of armor (and then weigh yourself), see the limited vision knights had to put up with when wearing their helmet, empathize with victims of the plague, and join a Crusade.

The **multimedia show** takes you on a 30-minute spin through the 2,000-year history of this valley's fortresses, with images projected on the old stone walls and modern screens (generally in German, in English at 13:00 or sometimes by request).

▲▲**Ehrenberg Ruins**—Ehrenberg, a 13th-century rock pile, provides a super opportunity to let your imagination off its leash. Hike up 30 minutes from the parking lot of the Klause Valley Fort Museum for a great view from your own private ruins. Ehrenberg (which means "Mountain of Honor") was the first castle here, built in 1296. Thirteenth-century castles were designed to stand boastfully tall. With the advent of gunpowder, castles dug in. (Notice the 18th-century **ramparts** around you.)

Approaching Ehrenberg Castle, look for the small **door** to the left. It's the night entrance (tight and awkward, and therefore safer against a surprise attack). Entering this castle, you go through two doors. Castles allowed step-by-step retreat, giving defenders time to regroup and fight back against invading forces.

Before climbing to the top of the castle, follow the path around to the right to a big, grassy courtyard with commanding views and a fat, newly restored **turret.** This stored gunpowder and held a big cannon that enjoyed a clear view of the valley below. In medieval times, all the trees approaching the castle were cleared to keep an unobstructed view.

Look out over the valley. The pointy spire marks **Breitenwang,** which was a stop on the ancient Via Claudia. In A.D. 46, there was a Roman camp there. In 1489, after the Reutte bridge crossed the Lech River, Reutte (marked by the onion-domed church) was made a market town and eclipsed Breitenwang in importance. Any gliders circling? They launch from just over the river in Höfen.

For centuries, this castle was the seat of government—ruling an area called the "judgment of Ehrenberg" (roughly the same as today's "district of Reutte"). When the emperor came by, he stayed here. In 1604, the ruler moved downtown into more comfortable quarters, and the castle was no longer a palace.

Now climb to the top of Ehrenberg Castle. Take the high ground. There was no water supply here—just kegs of wine, beer, and a cistern to collect rain.

Ehrenberg repelled 16,000 Swedish soldiers in the defense of Catholicism in 1632. Ehrenberg saw three or four other battles, but its end was not glorious. In the 1780s, a local businessman bought the castle in order to sell off its parts. Later, in the late 19th century, when vagabonds moved in, the roof was removed to make squatting miserable. With the roof gone, deterioration quickened, leaving only this evocative shell and a whiff of history.

▲**Schlosskopf**—From Ehrenberg, you can hike up another 30 minutes to the mighty Schlosskopf ("Castle Head"). When the Bavarians captured Ehrenberg in 1703, the Tiroleans climbed up to the bluff above it to rain cannonballs down on their former fortress. In 1740, a mighty new castle—designed to defend against modern artillery—was built on this sky-high strategic location. By the end of the 20th century, the castle was completely overgrown with trees—you literally couldn't see it from Reutte. But today the trees are shaved away, and the castle has been excavated. In 2008, the Castle Ensemble project, led by local architect Armin Walch, opened the site with English descriptions and view platforms. One spot gives spectacular views of the strategic valley. The other looks down on the older Ehrenberg Castle ruins, illustrating the strategic problems presented with the advent of cannon.

In the Town

Reutte Museum (Museum Grünes Haus)—Reutte's city museum, offering a quick look at the local folk culture and the story of the castles, is more cute than impressive. Perhaps someday a little English will bring more meaning to the exhibits (€2, May–Oct Tue–Sun 10:00–16:00, closed Mon and Nov–April, in the bright-green building at Untermarkt 25, around corner from Hotel Goldener Hirsch, tel. 05672/72304, www.museum-reutte.at).

▲▲**Tirolean Folk Evening**—Ask the TI or your hotel if there's a Tirolean folk evening scheduled. During the summer (July–Aug), nearby towns (such as Höfen on Tuesdays) occasionally put on an evening of yodeling, slap dancing, and Tirolean frolic. These are generally free and worth the short drive. Off-season, you'll have to do your own yodeling. There are also weekly folk concerts featuring the local choir or brass band in Reutte's Zeiller Platz (free, July–Aug only, ask at TI). For listings of these and other local events, pick up a copy of the German-only *Sommerprogramm* schedule at the TI.

▲**Flying and Gliding**—For a major thrill on a sunny day, drop by the tiny airport in Höfen across the river and fly. A small single-prop plane can buzz the Zugspitze and Ludwig's castles and give you a bird's-eye peek at Reutte's Ehrenberg ruins (2 people for 30 min-€110, 1 hr-€220, tel. 05672/63207, phone rarely answered and then not in English, so your best bet is to show up at the Höfen airport on good-weather afternoons). Or, for something more angelic, how about *Segelfliegen?* For €40, you get 30 minutes in a glider for two (you and the pilot, €65/1 hr) from Segelflugverein Ausserfern. Just watching the towrope launch the graceful glider like a giant slow-motion rubber-band gun is exhilarating (May–mid-Sept 12:00–19:00, sometimes in April and Oct if not too snowy, in good but breezy weather only, find someone in the know at the "Thermik Ranch," tel. 05672/71550, mobile 0676-557-1085, www.segelflugverein-ausserfern.at).

Reuttener Bergbahn—This mountain lift swoops you high above the tree line to a starting point for several hikes and an alpine flower park, with special paths leading you past countless varieties of local flora. Unique to this lift is a barefoot hiking trail *(Barfusswanderweg)*, designed to be walked without shoes—no joke (€10 one-way, €14 round-trip, flowers best in late July, runs usually mid-June–Sept daily 9:00–12:00 & 13:00–17:00, weekends only late May–mid-June and Oct, across the river in Höfen, tel. 05672/62420, www.reuttener-seilbahnen.at).

Near Reutte

Bird Lookout Tower—Between Reutte and Füssen is a pristine (if you get past the small local industrial park) nature preserve with an impressive wooden tower from which to appreciate the vibrant bird life in the wetlands along the Lech River. Look for *Vogel-Erlebnispfad* signs as you're driving through the village of Pflach (on the road between Reutte and Füssen). The EU gave half the money needed to enjoy the nature preserve—home to 110 different species of birds that nest here. The best action is early in the day. Be quiet, as eggs are being laid.

▲▲**Biberwier Luge Course**—Near Lermoos, on the road from Reutte toward Innsbruck, you'll find the Biberwier *Sommerrodelbahn*. At 4,250 feet, it's the longest luge in Tirol (20 min from Reutte, stay on main road, Biberwier is the first

Luge Lesson

Taking a wild ride on a luge (pronounced "loozh") is a quintessential alpine experience. It's also called a *Sommerrodelbahn*, or "summer toboggan run." To try one of Europe's great accessible thrills (€3–7), take the lift up to the top of a mountain, grab a wheeled sled-like go-cart, and scream back down the mountainside on a banked course. Then take the lift back up and start all over again.

Luge courses are highly weather-dependent, and can close at the least hint of rain. If the weather's questionable, call ahead to confirm that your preferred luge is open. Stainless-steel courses are more likely to stay open in drizzly weather than concrete ones.

Operating the sled is simple: Push the stick forward to go faster, pull back to apply brakes. Even a novice can go very, very fast. Most are cautious on their first run, speed demons on their second...and bruised and bloody on their third. A woman once showed me her travel journal illustrated with her husband's dried five-inch-long luge scab. He had disobeyed the only essential rule of luging: Keep both hands on your stick. To avoid getting into a bumper-to-bumper traffic jam, let the person in front of you get way ahead before you start. You'll emerge from the course with a windblown hairdo and a smile-creased face.

Here are a few key luge terms:

Lenkstange	lever
drücken / schneller fahren	push / go faster
ziehen / bremsen	pull / brake
Schürfwunde	scrape
Schorf	scab

exit after a long tunnel). The only drawbacks are its brief season, short hours, and a proclivity for shutting down sporadically—even at the slightest bit of rain (€6.90/ride, less for 3-, 5-, and 10-ride tickets, late May–early Oct daily 9:00–16:30, closed early Oct–late May, tel. 05673/2111, www.langes.at). If you don't have a car, this is not worth the trouble; consider the luge near Neuschwanstein instead (see "Tegelberg Luge" on page 117). Daredevils may want to rent the "Monsterroller" or "Mountainboard" to bike or skateboard down the mountain (€7 for the roller, €10/2 hrs lift usage). The ugly cube-shaped building marring the countryside near the luge course is a hotel for outdoor adventure enthusiasts. You can ride your mountain bike right into your room, or skip the elevator by using its indoor climbing wall.

▲**Fallerschein**—Easy for drivers and a special treat for those who may have been Kit Carson in a previous life, this extremely remote log-cabin village is a 4,000-foot-high flower-speckled world of serene slopes and cowbells. Thunderstorms roll down the valley like it's God's bowling alley, but the pint-size church on the high ground, blissfully simple in a land of Baroque, seems to promise that this huddle of houses will survive, and the river and breeze will just keep flowing. The couples sitting on benches are mostly Austrian vacationers who've rented cabins here. Some of them, appreciating the remoteness of Fallerschein, are having affairs.

Sleeping in Fallerschein: **$ Lottes Fallerscheiner Stube** is a family-friendly mountain-hut restaurant with a low-ceilinged attic space that has basic beds for up to 17 sleepy hikers. The accommodations aren't fancy, but if you're looking for remote, this is it (dorm bed-€9, sheets-€4, open early May–Oct only, closed Tue, wildlife viewing deck, tel. 05632/2140, www.alpe-fallerschein.at, Gapp family).

Getting to Fallerschein: From Reutte, it's a 45-minute drive. Take road 198 to Stanzach (passing Weisenbach am Loch, then Forchach), then turn left toward Namlos. Follow the L-21 Berwang road for about five miles to a parking lot. From there, it's a two-mile walk down a drivable but technically closed one-lane road. Those driving in do so at their own risk.

Sleeping in and near Reutte

(€1 = about $1.40, country code: 43, area code: 05672)

Reutte is a mellow Füssen with fewer crowds and easygoing locals with a contagious love of life. Come here for a good dose of Austrian ambience and lower prices. While it's not impossible by public transport, staying here makes most sense for those with a car. Reutte is popular with Austrians and Germans, who come here year after year for one- or two-week vacations. The hotels are big, elegant, and full of comfy carved furnishings and creative ways to spend lots of time in one spot. They take great pride in their restaurants, and the owners send their children away to hotel-management schools. All include a great breakfast, but few accept credit cards. Most hotels give about a 5 percent discount for stays of two nights or longer.

The Reutte TI has a list of 50 private homes that rent out generally good rooms *(Zimmer)* with facilities down the hall, pleasant communal living rooms, and breakfast. Most charge €20 per person per night, and the owners speak little or no English. As these are family-run places, it is especially important to cancel in advance if your plans change. I've listed a few favorites below, but the TI can always find you a room when you arrive.

Reutte is surrounded by several distinct "villages" that basically feel like suburbs—many of them, such as Breitenwang, within easy walking distance of the Reutte town center. If you want to hike through the woods to Neuschwanstein Castle, stay at Gutshof zum Schluxen (listed below). To locate the recommended accommodations, see the Reutte map. Remember, to call Reutte from Germany, dial 00-43- and then the number (minus the initial zero).

In Central Reutte

$$ Hotel "Das Beck" offers 16 clean, sunny rooms (many with balconies) filling a modern building in the heart of town close to the train station. It's a great value, and guests are personally taken care of by Hans, Inge, Tamara, and Pipi. Their small café offers tasty snacks and specializes in Austrian and Italian wines. Expect good conversation overseen by Hans (Sb-€46, Db-€70, Tb suite-€92, Qb suite-€109, these prices with this book in 2010, Internet access free for Rick Steves readers, free parking, Untermarkt 11, tel. 05672/62522, fax 05672/625-2235, www.hotel-das-beck.at, info@hotel-das-beck.at).

$$ Hotel Goldener Hirsch, also in the center of Reutte just two blocks from the station, is a grand old hotel with 56 rooms and one lonely set of antlers (Sb-€58–62, Db-€85–92, Db suite-€90–98, Tb-€125–135, Qb-€140–145, 2-night discounts, elevator, free Wi-Fi, restaurant, Mühlerstrasse 1, tel. 05672/62508, fax 05672/625-087, www.goldener-hirsch.at, info@goldener-hirsch.at; Monika, Helmut, and daughters Vanessa and Nina).

In Breitenwang

Now basically a part of Reutte, the older and quieter village of Breitenwang has good *Zimmer* and a fine bakery. It's a 20-minute walk from the Reutte train station: At the post office roundabout, follow Planseestrasse past the onion-dome church to the pointy straight-dome church near the two hotels. The Hosps—as well as other B&Bs—are along unmarked Kaiser-Lothar-Strasse, the first right past this church. If your train stops at the tiny Reutte-Schulzentrum station, hop out here—you're just a five-minute walk from Breitenwang.

$$ Alpenhotel Ernberg's 26 rooms are run with great care by friendly Hermann, who combines Old World elegance with modern touches. Nestle in for some serious coziness among the carved-wood eating nooks, tiled stoves, and family-friendly back-yard (Sb-€45, Db-€84, less for longer stays, free Wi-Fi, popular restaurant, Planseestrasse 50, tel. 05672/71912, fax 05672/719-1240, www.ernberg.at, info@ernberg.at).

$$ Moserhof Hotel has 35 new-feeling rooms plus an elegant dining room (Sb-€53, Db-€92, these special rates promised in 2010 if you ask for the Rick Steves discount when you reserve, extra bed-€35, most rooms have balconies, elevator, free Wi-Fi, restaurant, sauna, free parking, Planseestrasse 44, tel. 05672/62020, fax 05672/620-2040, www.hotel-moserhof.at, info@hotel-moserhof.at, Hosp family).

$ Walter and Emilie Hosp rent three rooms in a comfortable, quiet, and modern house two blocks from the Breitenwang church steeple. You'll feel like you're staying at Grandma's (D-€40, T-€60, Q-€80, cash only, Kaiser-Lothar-Strasse 29, tel. 05672/65377).

In Ehenbichl, near the Ehrenberg Ruins

The next listings are a bit farther from central Reutte, a couple of miles upriver in the village of Ehenbichl (under the Ehrenberg ruins). From central Reutte, go south on Obermarkt and turn right on Kög, which becomes Reuttener Strasse, following signs to Ehenbichl.

$$ Hotel Maximilian offers 30 rooms at a great value. It includes table tennis, a children's playroom, a pool table, and the friendly service of Gabi, Monika, and the rest of the Koch family. They host many special events, and their hotel has lots of wonderful extras such as a sauna and a piano (Sb-€48–55, Db-€76–90, ask for these special Rick Steves prices when you reserve, family deals, elevator, free Internet access and Wi-Fi, laundry service, good restaurant, tel. 05672/62585, fax 05672/625-8554, www.maxi hotel.com, info@hotelmaximilian.at). They rent cars to guests only (€0.72/km, book in advance) and bikes to anyone (€5/half-day, €8/day, higher if you're not a guest, those staying at the hotel have free use of older bikes).

$$ Gasthof-Pension Waldrast, separating a forest and a meadow, is run by the farming Huter family. The place feels hauntingly quiet and has no restaurant, but it's inexpensive and offers 10 nice rooms with generous sitting areas and castle-view balconies (Sb-€37, Db-€62, Tb-€75, Qb-€95; discounts with this book in 2010: 5 percent for 2 nights, 10 percent for 3 nights or more; cash only, all rooms non-smoking, free parking; about a mile from Reutte, just off main drag toward Innsbruck, past campground and under castle ruins on Ehrenbergstrasse; tel. & fax 05672/62443, www.waldrasttirol.com, info@waldrasttirol.com, Gerd).

$ Pension Hohenrainer, a big quiet no-frills place, is a good value with 12 modern rooms and some castle-view balconies (Sb-€25–30, Db-€49–55, €3 per person extra for one-night stays, cheaper for longer stays and in April–June and Sept–Oct, cash only, family rooms, non-smoking rooms, free Internet access, restaurant and reception in Gasthof Schlosswirt across the street, follow signs up the road behind Hotel Maximilian into village of Ehenbichl, tel. 05672/62544 or 05672/63262, fax 05672/62052, www.hohenrainer.at, hohenrainer@aon.at).

$ **Gintherhof** is a working farm that provides its guests with fresh milk, butter, and bacon. Annelies Paulweber offers geranium-covered balconies, six nice rooms with carved-wood ceilings, and a Madonna in every corner (Db-€46–50, Internet access, Unterried 7, just up the road behind Hotel Maximilian, tel. 05672/67697, www.gintherhof.com, gintherhof@aon.at).

A Hostel Across the River

The homey $ **Gästehaus am Graben hostel** has 2–6 beds per room and includes breakfast and sheets. It's lovingly run by the Reyman family—Frau Reyman, Rudi, and Gabi keep the 50-bed place traditional, clean, and friendly—and they serve guests a great €7.50 dinner. This is a super value less than two miles from Reutte, and the castle views are fantastic. If you've never hosteled and are curious (and have a car or don't mind a bus ride), try it. If traveling with kids, this is a great choice. The double rooms are hotel-grade, and they accept non-members of any age (dorm bed-€22, bunk-bed D-€44, hotel-style Db-€56, cash only, non-smoking, laundry service, pay Internet access, no curfew, closed April and Nov–mid-Dec; from downtown Reutte, cross bridge and follow main road left along river, or take the bus—hourly until 19:30, ask for Graben stop, no buses Sun; Graben 1, tel. 05672/626-440, fax 05672/626-444, www.hoefen.at, info@hoefen.at).

In Pinswang

The village of Pinswang is closer to Füssen (and Ludwig's castles), but still in Austria.

$$ **Gutshof zum Schluxen** gets the "Remote Old Hotel in an Idyllic Setting" award. This family-friendly farm offers rustic elegance draped in goose down and pastels. Its picturesque meadow setting will turn you into a dandelion picker, and its proximity to Neuschwanstein will turn you into a hiker—the castle is just an hour's hike away (Sb-€45–50, Db-€80–92, extra person-€28, these prices with this book in 2010, lower prices off-season, 5 percent discount for stays of 4 or more nights, self-service laundry-€7, mountain-bike rental-€10/day, restaurant, fun bar, between Reutte and Füssen in village of Pinswang, free pick-up from Reutte or Füssen, call ahead if you'll arrive after 18:00, tel. 05677/8903, fax 05677/890-323, www.schluxen.com, welcome@schluxen.com).

Eating in Reutte

The hotels here take great pride in serving local cuisine at reasonable prices to their guests and the public. Rather than go to a cheap restaurant, eat at a hotel. Most offer €8–14 dinners from 18:00 to 21:00 and are closed one night a week. Reutte itself has plenty of inviting eateries, including traditional, ethnic, fast food, grocery stores, and delis.

Since hospitality is such a big part of the local scene, **hotel restaurants** are generally your best bet for a good meal. Many of the hotels recommended earlier, under "Sleeping in and near Reutte"—including Hotel Goldener Hirsch, Alpenhotel Ernberg, Moserhof Hotel, and Hotel Maximilian—offer fine restaurants.

Storfwirt is *the* place for a quick and cheap weekday lunch. You can get the usual sausages here, as well as baked potatoes and salads (€5–7 daily meals, salad bar, always something for vegetarians, Mon–Fri 8:30–14:30, closed Sat–Sun, Schrettergasse 15, tel. 05672/62640).

Non Solo Pasta, just off the traffic circle, is a local favorite for Italian food (€7–8 pizzas, €8–12 entrées, Mon–Fri 11:30–14:00 & 18:00–23:00, Sat 18:00–23:00, closed Sun, Lindenstrasse 1, tel. 05672/72714).

Picnic Supplies: **Billa** supermarket has everything you'll need (across from TI, Mon–Fri 7:15–19:30, Sat 7:15–18:00, closed Sun).

Reutte Connections

From Reutte by Train to: Ehrwald (at base of Zugspitze lift, almost hourly, 30 min), **Garmisch** (almost hourly, 1 hr), **Innsbruck** (every 2 hrs, 2.5 hrs, change in Garmisch), **Munich** (every 2 hrs, 2.5 hrs, change in Garmisch).

By Bus to: Füssen (Mon–Fri almost hourly, Sat–Sun every 2 hrs, 45 min, €3.40, buses depart from in front of the train station, pay driver).

Taxis cost €30 one-way to Füssen, or €35 to the King's Castles.

SALZBURG (AUSTRIA) and BERCHTESGADEN

Salzburg, just over the Austrian border, makes a fun day trip from Munich (1.5–2 hours by direct train). Salzburg is forever smiling to the tunes of Mozart and *The Sound of Music.* Thanks to its charmingly preserved old town, splendid gardens, Baroque churches, and Europe's largest intact medieval fortress, Salzburg feels made for tourism. It's a museum city with class. Vagabonds wish they had nicer clothes.

Nearly next door to Salzburg is Berchtesgaden, a German alpine town that was once a favorite of Adolf Hitler's, but thrills a better class of nature-lovers today.

Planning Your Time

While Salzburg's sights are rather mediocre, the town itself is a Baroque museum of cobbled streets and elegant buildings— simply a touristy stroller's delight. Even if your time is short, consider allowing half a day for the *Sound of Music* tour. The *S.O.M.* tour kills a nest of sightseeing birds with one ticket (city overview, *S.O.M.* sights, and a fine drive by the lakes).

You'd probably enjoy at least two nights in Salzburg—nights are important for swilling beer in atmospheric local gardens and attending concerts in Baroque halls and chapels. Seriously consider one of Salzburg's many evening musical events (a few are free, some are as cheap as €12, and most average €30–40).

To get away from it all, bike down the river or hike across the Mönchsberg. Or consider swinging by Berchtesgaden, just 12 miles away in Germany. A direct bus gets you there in 45 minutes.

Salzburg

Even without Mozart and the von Trapps, Salzburg is steeped in history. In about A.D. 700, Bavaria gave Salzburg to Bishop Rupert in return for his promise to Christianize the area. Salzburg remained an independent city (belonging to no state) until Napoleon came in the early 1800s. Thanks in part to its formidable fortress, Salzburg managed to avoid the ravages of war for 1,200 years... until World War II. Much of the city was destroyed by WWII bombs (mostly around the train station), but the historic old town survived.

Eight million tourists crawl its cobbles each year. That's a lot of Mozart balls—and all that popularity has led to a glut of businesses hoping to catch the tourist dollar. Still, Salzburg is both a must and a joy.

Orientation to Salzburg

(country code: 43, area code: 0662)

Salzburg, a city of 150,000 (Austria's fourth-largest), is divided into old and new. The old town, sitting between the Salzach River and its mini-mountain (Mönchsberg), holds nearly all the charm and most of the tourists. The new town, across the river, has its own share of sights and museums, plus some good accommodations.

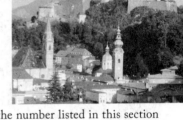

Welcome to Austria: Austria uses the same euro currency as Germany, but postage stamps and phone cards only work in the country where you buy them.

To **telephone** from Germany to Austria, dial 00-43- and then the number listed in this section (omitting the initial zero). To call from Austria to Germany, dial 00-49- and then the number (again, omitting the initial zero).

Note that **Berchtesgaden**—also covered in this chapter—is in Germany, not Austria.

Tourist Information

Salzburg has three helpful TIs (main tel. 0662/889-870, www .salzburg.info): at the **train station** (daily June–Aug 8:15–20:00, April–May and Sept–Oct 8:45–19:00, Nov–March 8:45–18:00, tel. 0662/8898-7340); on **Mozartplatz** in the old center (daily 9:00–18:00, July–mid-Sept until 19:00, closed Sun mid-Jan–Easter and Oct–mid-Nov, tel. 0662/889-870); and at the **Salzburg Süd**

Salzburg

200 YARDS
200 METERS

TO TRAIN STATION

TO AUGUSTINER BRÄUSTÜBL

MIRABELL PALACE

❸
❷

MIRABELL PLATZ

MIRABELL GDNS.

SCHWARZ

DREI-GASSE

INSTITUTE ST. SEBASTIAN

ST. SEB. CEM.

LINZERGASSE

MOZARTEUM CONCERT HALL

MOZART'S RESIDENCE

KAPUZINER-BERG

MARIONETTE THEATER

MAKART PLATZ

FRANZ JOSEF KAI

MÜLLNER HAUPTSTR.

MUSEUM OF MODERN ART

S A L Z

❽

PED. BRIDGE

HANAK

STEG

PLATZL

MONASTERY

A C H

ELEV.

GRIESGASSE

HANUSCH PLATZ

STAATS

R I V E R

IMBERGSTRASSE

MOZART'S BIRTHPLACE

❾

RUDOLFS-

PED. BRIDGE

TO HALLEIN

GETREIDEGASSE

JUDENGASSE

STADTALM CAFÉ

U-PLATZ

GOLD

❶

HOFSTALLGASSE

ALTE RESIDENZ

RES. PLATZ

❾

MOZART-PLATZ

FESTIVAL CONCERT HALLS

DOM-PLATZ

❻

NEUE RESIDENZ

TO AIRPORT, MOOS STR. B+B'S & FREEWAY

TRAIL

KAP. PL.

CATHEDRAL

ST. PETER'S

CEM.

❼

SCHANZL

MÖNCHSBERG

FUNICULAR

❺

NONNBERG ABBEY

👁 VIEW

/\ CLIFFS

HOHEN-SALZBURG FORTRESS

DCH

❶ Bob's Special Tours (Sound of Music by Minibus)

❷ Salzburg Panorama Tours (Sound of Music by Big Bus)

❸ Fräulein Maria Tours (Sound of Music by Bike)

❹ Start of Steingasse Stroll

❺ Start of Mönchsberg Walk

❻ Salzburg Museum & Panorama 1829 Exhibit

❼ Alm River Canal Exhibit

❽ City Cruise Line

❾ Bike Rentals (2)

SALZBURG

park-and-ride (generally open
daily July–Aug 10:00–16:30 but
sometimes longer hours, May–
June Thu–Sat 10:00–16:30, Sept
Mon–Sat 10:00–16:30, closed in
winter, tel. 0662/8898-7360).

At any TI, you can pick
up a free city-center map (the
€0.70 map has a broader cove-
rage and more information on sights, but probably isn't necessary),
the Salzburg Card brochure (listing sights with current hours and
prices), and a bimonthly schedule of events. Book a concert upon
arrival. The TIs also book rooms for a €2.20 fee.

Salzburg Card: The TIs sell the Salzburg Card, which covers
all your public transportation (including elevator and funicular) and
admission to all the city sights (including Hellbrunn Castle and a
river cruise). The card is pricey (€24/24 hrs, €32/48 hrs, €37/72 hrs,
€2 cheaper Oct–April), but if you'd like to pop into all the sights,
it can save money and enhance your experience. To analyze your
potential savings, here are the major sights and what you'd pay
without the card: Hohensalzburg Fortress and funicular-€10.50;
Mozart's Birthplace and Residence-€10; Hellbrunn Castle-€8.50;
Salzburg Panorama 1829-€2; Salzach River cruise-€13; 24-hour
transit pass-€4.20. Busy sightseers can save plenty. Get this card,
feel the financial pain once, and the city will be all yours.

Arrival in Salzburg

By Train: The Salzburg station is user-friendly. The TI is at track
2A. Downstairs at street level, you can store your luggage, buy

tickets, and get train information. Bike rental is nearby (see
"Getting Around Salzburg,"
later). City buses depart from
the lot facing the station
(monitors clearly show each
bus' destination—any bus
heading for *Zentrum* stops
near the main bridge in the

old town, including buses #1, #3, #5, #6, and #25; get off at the first
stop after you cross the river for most sights and city-center hotels,
or just before the bridge for Linzergasse hotels). Figure €7 for a
taxi to the center.

To walk downtown (15 min), leave the station ticket hall to
the left, and walk straight down Rainerstrasse, which leads under
the tracks past Mirabellplatz, turning into Dreifaltigkeitsgasse.
From here, you can turn left onto Linzergasse for many of my

recommended hotels, or cross the Staatsbrücke bridge for the old town (and more hotels). For a more dramatic approach, leave the station the same way but follow the tracks to the river, turn left, and walk the riverside path toward the fortress.

By Car: Coming on A-8 from Munich, cross the border into Austria. Take A-10 toward Hallein, and then take the next exit (Salzburg Süd) in the direction of Anif. First, you'll pass Hellbrunn Castle (and zoo), then the Salzburg Süd TI and a park-and-ride service—a smart place to park while visiting Salzburg. Park your car (€5), get sightseeing information and transit tickets from the TI (see above), and catch the shuttle bus into town (€1.80 for a single ticket, or covered by €4.20 *Tageskarte* day pass, both sold at the TI, more expensive if you buy tickets on board, every 5 min, bus #3, #8, or #28).

Mozart never drove in the old town, and neither should you. If you don't believe in park-and-rides, the easiest, cheapest, most central parking lot is the 1,500-car Altstadt lot in the tunnel under the Mönchsberg (€14/day, note your slot number and which of the twin lots you're in, tel. 0662/846-434). Your hotel may provide discounted parking passes.

Helpful Hints

Recommendations Skewed by Kickbacks: Salzburg is addicted to the tourist dollar, and it can never get enough. Virtually all hotels are on the take when it comes to concert and tour recommendations, influenced more by their potential kick-back than by what's best for you. Take their advice with a grain of salt.

Internet Access: The Internet kiosk a few doors down from the Mozartplatz TI is well-located, but too expensive (€2/10 min). Cheaper places around the old town aren't hard to find. Two Internet cafés at the bottom of the cliff, between Getreidegasse and the Mönchsberg lift, have good prices and hours (€2/hr, daily 10:00–22:00). Across the river, there's a big, handy Internet café on Theatergasse (near Mozart's Residence, €2/hr, daily 9:00–23:00), and plenty more near the station (including Bubblepoint, a modern launderette—see "Laundry," below). Readers of this book can get online free at the Panorama Tours terminal on Mirabellplatz (daily 8:00–18:00).

Post Office: A full-service post office is located in the heart of town, in the new Residenz (Mon–Fri 7:00–18:30, Sat 8:00–10:00, closed Sun).

Laundry: The launderette at the corner of Paris-Lodron-Strasse and Wolf-Dietrich-Strasse, near my recommended Linzergasse hotels, is handy (€10 self-service, €15 same-day full-service, Mon–Fri 7:30–18:00, Sat 8:00–12:00, closed Sun, tel. 0662/876-381). To do your laundry and email at the same time, head to **Bubblepoint** (wash and dry for €6, 6 Internet terminals, daily 7:00–23:00; with your back to the train station, take the first left for one block, then head right to Karl-Wurmb-Strasse 2; tel. 0664/471-1484).

Getting Around Salzburg

By Bus: Single-ride tickets for central Salzburg *(Einzelkarte–Kernzone)* are sold on the bus for €2. At machines and *Tabak/Trafik* shops, you can buy €1.80 single-ride tickets or a €4.20 day pass *(Tageskarte,* good for 24 hours, €5 if you buy it on the bus). To signal the driver that you want to get off, press the buzzer on the pole. Bus info: tel. 800-660-660.

By Bike: Salzburg is fun for cyclists. The following two bike-rental shops offer 20 percent off with a valid train ticket or Eurailpass—ask for it. **Top Bike** rents bikes from two outlets: at the river side of the train station (exit to the left and walk 50 yards), and on the river next to the Staatsbrücke (€6/2 hrs, €10/4 hrs, €15/24 hrs, usually daily April–June and Sept–Oct 10:00–17:00, July–Aug 9:00–19:00, closed Nov–March, tel. 06272/4656, mobile 0676-476-7259 and 0676-720-0047, www.topbike.at, Sabine). **Velo-Active** rents bikes in the old town, just outside the TI on Mozartplatz (€4.50/1 hr, €7/2 hrs, €15/24 hrs; mountain bikes-€6/hr, €18/24 hrs; daily 9:00–18:00, until 19:00 July–Aug, but hours unreliable—you may have to call or let the Panorama Tours man nearby help you, shorter hours off-season and in bad weather, passport number for security deposit, tel. 0662/435-5950, mobile 0676-435-5950). Some of my recommended hotels and pensions also rent bikes, and several of the B&Bs on Moosstrasse let guests use them for free.

By Funicular and Elevator: The old town is connected to the top of the Mönchsberg mountain (and great views) via funicular and elevator. The **funicular** *(Festungsbahn)* whisks you up to the imposing Hohensalzburg Fortress (included in castle admission, goes every few minutes—for details, see page 162). The **elevator** *(MönchsbergAufzug)* on the east side of the old town propels you to the recommended Gasthaus Stadtalm café and hostel, the Museum of Modern Art, wooded paths, and more great views (€2 one-way, €3 round-trip, daily 8:30–19:00, Wed until 21:00; July–Aug daily until 1:00 in the morning, May–Sept starts running at 8:00).

By Taxi: Meters start at about €3 (from train station to your hotel, allow about €7). As always, small groups can taxi for about the same price as riding the bus.

By Buggy: The horse buggies *(Fiaker)* that congregate at Residenzplatz charge €36 for a 25-minute trot around the old town (www.fiaker-salzburg.at).

Tours in Salzburg

Walking Tours—On any day of the week, you can take a two-language, one-hour guided walk of the old town without a reservation—just show up at the TI on Mozartplatz and pay the guide. The tours are informative, but you'll be listening to a half-hour of German (€8, daily at 12:15 and 14:00, tel. 0662/8898-7330). To save money (and avoid all that German), you can easily do it on your own using my self-guided walk (see page 152).

Private Guides—**Christiana Schneeweiss** ("Snow White"), a hardworking young guide and art historian with a passion for fitting local history into the big picture, gives spirited private tours (€80/1 hr, €129/2 hrs, €150/3 hrs, tel. 0664/340-1757, www.kultur-tourismus.com, info@kultur-tourismus.com). Check her website for bike tours, private minibus tours, and more. **Bärbel Schalber,** one of Salzburg's senior guides, offers a two-hour walk packed with information and spicy opinions (€75 per family, €108 for a group of adults, tel. 0662/632-225, mobile 0664-412-3708, schalber.salzburg@aon.at). Salzburg has many other good guides (to book, call 0662/840-406).

▲▲*Sound of Music* **Tour**—I took this tour skeptically (as part of my research)—and liked it. It includes a quick but good gene-

ral city tour, hits the *S.O.M.* spots (including the stately home, flirtatious gazebo, and grand wedding church), and shows you a lovely stretch of the Salzkammergut Lake District. This is worthwhile for *S.O.M.* fans and those who won't otherwise be going into the Salzkammergut. Warning: Many think rolling through the Austrian countryside with 30 Americans singing "Doe, a deer..." is pretty schmaltzy. Local Austrians don't understand all the commotion, and the audience is mostly native English speakers. For more on *S.O.M.*, see "*The Sound of Music* Debunked" sidebar.

Of the many companies doing the tour, consider Bob's Special Tours (usually uses a minibus) and Panorama Tours (more typical and professional, big 50-seat bus). Each one provides essentially the same tour (in English with a live guide, 4 hours) for essentially the same price: €37 for Panorama, €40 for Bob's. You'll get a €5 discount from either if you book direct, mention Rick Steves, bring this book along, and pay cash. Getting a spot is simple—just call and make a reservation (calling Bob's a week or two in advance is smart). Note: Your hotel will be eager to call to reserve for you—to get their commission—but if you let them do

Salzburg at a Glance

▲▲▲**Salzburg's Old Town Walk** Old Town's best sights in handy orientation walk. **Hours:** Always open. See page 152.

▲▲**Salzburg Cathedral** Glorious, harmonious Baroque main church of Salzburg. **Hours:** Easter–Oct Mon–Sat 9:00–18:00, Sun 13:00–18:00; Nov–Easter Mon–Sat 10:00–17:00, Sun 13:00–17:00. See page 156.

▲▲**Getreidegasse** Picturesque old shopping lane with characteristic wrought-iron signs. **Hours:** Always open. See page 160.

▲▲**Hohensalzburg Fortress** Imposing castle capping the Mönchsberg mountain overlooking town, with tourable grounds, impressive interior, commanding views, and good evening concerts. **Hours:** Daily May–Sept 9:00–19:00, Oct–April 9:30–17:00. Concerts nearly nightly. See page 163.

▲▲**Mozart's Residence** Restored house where the composer lived, with the best Mozart exhibit in town. **Hours:** Daily 9:00–17:00, July–Aug until 20:00. See page 167.

▲▲**The *Sound of Music* Tour** Cheesy but fun tour through the *S.O.M.* sights of Salzburg and the surrounding Salzkammergut Lake District, by minibus or big bus. **Hours:** Various options daily at 9:00, 9:30, 14:00, and 16:30. See page 149.

▲**Salzburg Panorama 1829** A vivid peek at the city in 1829. **Hours:** Daily 9:00–17:00, Thu until 20:00. See page 154.

▲**Mozart's Birthplace** House where Mozart was born in 1756, featuring his instruments and other exhibits. **Hours:** Daily 9:00–17:00, July–Aug until 20:00. See page 161.

it, you're unlikely to get the discount I've negotiated.

Minibus Option: Most of **Bob's Special Tours** use an eight-seat minibus and therefore have good access to old-town sights, promote a more casual feel, and spend less time waiting to load and unload. Calling well in advance increases your chances of getting a seat (€40 for adults, €5 discount with this book if you pay cash and book direct, €35 for kids and students with ID, €30 for kids in car seats, daily at 9:00 and 14:00 year-round, they'll pick you up at your hotel for the morning tour, afternoon tours leave from Bob's office along the river just east of Mozartplatz at Rudolfskai 38, tel. 0662/849-511, mobile 0664-541-7492, www.bobstours .com). Nearly all of Bob's tours stop for the luge ride when the

▲**Mönchsberg Walk** "The hills are alive" stroll you can enjoy right in downtown Salzburg. **Hours:** Doable anytime during daylight hours. See page 165.

▲**Mirabell Gardens and Palace** Beautiful palace complex with fine views, Salzburg's best concert venue, and *Sound of Music* memories. **Hours:** Gardens—always open; concerts—free in the park May–Aug Sun at 10:30 and Wed at 20:30, in the palace nearly nightly. See page 167.

▲**Steingasse Stroll** Historic cobbled lane with trendy pubs—a tranquil, tourist-free section of old Salzburg. **Hours:** Always open. See page 168.

▲**St. Sebastian Cemetery** Baroque cemetery with graves of Mozart's wife and father, and other Salzburg VIPs. **Hours:** Daily April–Oct 9:00–18:30, Nov–March 9:00–16:00. See page 169.

▲**Hellbrunn Castle** Palace on the outskirts of town featuring gardens with trick fountains. **Hours:** Daily May–Sept 9:00–17:30, July–Aug until 21:00, mid-March–April and Oct 9:00–16:30, closed Nov–mid-March. See page 170.

St. Peter's Cemetery Atmospheric old cemetery with mini-gardens overlooked by cliff face with monks' caves. **Hours:** Cemetery—daily April–Sept 6:30–19:00, Oct–March 6:30–18:00; caves—May–Sept Tue–Sun 10:30–17:00, closed Mon, shorter hours Oct–April. See page 158.

St. Peter's Church Romanesque church with Rococo decor. **Hours:** Open long hours daily. See page 159.

weather is dry (mountain bobsled–€4 extra, generally April–Oct, confirm beforehand). Some travelers looking for Bob's tours at Mozartplatz have been hijacked by other companies...have Bob's pick you up at your hotel (morning only) or meet the bus at their office. If you're unable to book with Bob's, and still want a minibus tour, try **Kultur Tourismus** (€50, tel. 0664/340-1757, www.kultur-tourismus.com, info@kultur-tourismus.com).

Big-Bus Option: Salzburg Panorama Tours depart from their smart kiosk at Mirabellplatz daily at 9:30 and 14:00 year-round (€37, €5 discount with this book if you book direct and pay cash, book by calling 0662/874-029 or online at www.panoramatours.com). Many travelers appreciate their more businesslike feel, roomier buses, and slightly higher vantage point.

Bike Option: For some exercise with your tour, you can meet **Fräulein Maria** at the Mirabell Gardens (at Mirabellplatz 4, 50 yards to the left of palace entry) for a *S.O.M.* bike tour. The main attractions that you'll pass during the seven-mile pedal include the Mirabell Gardens, the horse pond, St. Peter's Cemetery, Nonnberg Abbey, Leopoldskron Palace and, of course, the gazebo (€24 includes bike, €2 discount with this book, €15 for kids 6–15, €10 for kids under 6, daily May–Sept at 9:30, June–Aug also at 16:30, allow 3.5 hours, family-friendly, reservations required only for afternoon tours, tel. 0650/342-6297, www.mariasbicycletours.com).

More Tours—Both Bob's and Panorama Tours also offer an extensive array of other day trips from Salzburg (Berchtesgaden/ Eagle's Nest, salt mines, and Salzkammergut lakes and mountains are the most popular, with the same discount—€5 off with this book if you book direct and pay cash). The tours are explained in their brochures, which litter hotel lobbies all over town.

City Cruise Line (a.k.a. Stadt Schiff-Fahrt) runs a basic 40-minute round-trip river cruise with recorded commentary (€13, 9/day July–Aug, 7/day in June, fewer Sept–Oct and April–May, no boats Nov–March). For a longer cruise, ride to Hellbrunn and return by bus (€16, 1–2/day April–Oct). Boats leave from the old-town side of the river just downstream of the Makartsteg bridge (tel. 0662/8257-6912). While views can be cramped, passengers are treated to a fun finale just before docking, when the captain twirls a fun "waltz."

Self-Guided Walk

▲▲▲Salzburg's Old Town

I've linked the best sights in the old town into this handy self-guided orientation walk.

• *Begin in the heart of town, just up from the river, near the TI on...*

❶ Mozartplatz

All the happy tourists around you probably wouldn't be here if not for the man honored by this statue—Wolfgang Amadeus Mozart (erected in 1842). Mozart spent much of his first 25 years (1756–1777) in Salzburg, the greatest Baroque city north of the Alps. But the city itself is much older: The Mozart statue sits on bits of Roman Salzburg, and the pink Church of St. Michael that overlooks the square dates from A.D. 800. The first Salzburgers settled right around here. Near you is the TI (with a concert box office), and just around the downhill corner is a pedestrian bridge leading over the Salzach River to the quiet and most medieval street in town, Steingasse (described later).

• *Walk toward the cathedral and into the big square with the huge fountain.*

❷ Residenzplatz

Important buildings ringed this square when it was the ancient Roman forum...and they still do. Salzburg's energetic Prince-Archbishop Wolf Dietrich (who ruled 1587–1612) was raised in Rome, counted the Medicis as his buddies, and had grandiose Italian ambitions for Salzburg. After a convenient fire destroyed the cathedral, he set about building the "Rome of the North." This square, with his new cathedral and palace, was the centerpiece of his Baroque dream city. A series of interconnecting squares—like you'll see nowhere else—make a grand processional way, leading from here through the old town.

For centuries, Salzburg's leaders were both important church officials *and* princes of the Holy Roman Empire, hence the title "prince-archbishop"—mixing sacred and secular authority. But Wolf Dietrich misplayed his hand, losing power and spending his last five years imprisoned in the Salzburg castle.

The fountain is as Italian as can be, with a Triton matching Bernini's famous Triton Fountain in Rome. Situated on a busy trade route to the south, Salzburg was well-aware of the exciting things going on in Italy. Things Italian were respected (as in colonial America, when a bumpkin would "stick a feather in his cap and call it macaroni"). Local artists even Italianized their names in order to raise their rates.

• *Along the left side of Residenzplatz (as you face the cathedral) is the...*

❸ New (Neue) Residenz & Glockenspiel

This former palace, long a government administration building, now houses the central post office, the **Heimatwerk** (a fine shop showing off all the best local handicrafts, Mon–Fri 9:00–18:00, Sat 9:00–17:00, closed Sun), the fascinating **Salzburg Panorama 1829** exhibit (definitely worth the €2 and described later), and the new **Salzburg Museum.** The first floor of this museum shows off various influential Salzburgers. The second floor explores Salzburg's history, particularly its longstanding reputation as a fairy-tale "Alpine Arcadia." While it's impressively well-done and described in English, the museum is only enjoyable to the extent that you're fascinated with the city—so most will find this merely a good rainy-day option (€7, €8 combo-ticket with Salzburg Panorama, both tickets about €2 cheaper on Sun, includes audioguide, Tue–Sun 9:00–17:00, Thu until 20:00, closed Mon except July–Aug and Dec—when it's open Mon 9:00–17:00, tel. 0662/620-808-700, www.smca.at).

The famous **glockenspiel** rings atop the new Residenz. This

Salzburg's Old Town Walk

bell tower has a carillon of 35 17th-century bells (cast in Antwerp) that chimes throughout the day and plays tunes (appropriate to the month) at 7:00, 11:00, and 18:00. There was a time when Salzburg could afford to take tourists to the top of the tower to see the big barrel with adjustable tabs turn (like a giant music-box mechanism)...pulling the right bells in the right rhythm. Notice the ornamental top: an upside-down heart in flames surrounding the solar system (symbolizing that God loves all of creation).

Look back, past Mozart's statue, to the 4,220-foot-high Gaisberg—the forested hill with the television tower. A road leads to the top for a commanding view. Its summit is a favorite destination for local nature-lovers and kids learning to ski.

• *Before continuing our walk, round the corner toward the back of the cathedral and drop into the...*

❹ Salzburg Panorama 1829

In the early 19th century, 360-degree "panorama" paintings of great cities or events were popular. These creations were even

KAPUZINERBERG

1 Mozartplatz
2 Residenzplatz
3 New (Neue) Residenz & Glockenspiel
4 Salzburg Panorama 1829
5 Old (Alte) Residenz
6 Salzburg Cathedral
7 Kapitelplatz
8 St. Peter's Cemetery
9 St. Peter's Church
10 Toscanini Hof
11 Universitätsplatz
12 Getreidegasse
13 Mozart's Birthplace
14 Alter Markt

GASSE
IMBERGSTRASSE
GISELAKAI
MOZART STEG
RIVER
MOZART PLATZ
PFEIFERGASSE
KALGASSE
GASSE
NONNBERG ABBEY
NONNTALER BRÜCKE
RUDOLFS PLATZ
KAJETANER PLATZ
NONNTALER HAUPTSTR.
PETERSBRUNNSTR.

TO HALLEIN

TO HELLBRUNN PALACE

P Parking
⚑ View

SALZBURG

taken on extended road trips. Salzburg, at a stagnant stage in its development, had this circular view painted by Johann Michael Sattler: the city as seen from the top of its castle. When complete, it spent 10 years touring the great cities of Europe, showing off Salzburg's breathtaking setting. Today, the exquisitely restored painting, rated ▲, offers a fascinating look at the city in 1829. The river was slower and had beaches. The old town looks essentially as it does today, and Moosstrasse still leads into idyllic farm country. Paintings from that era of other great cities around the world are hung around the outside wall with numbers but without labels, as a kind of quiz game. A flier gives the cities names on one side, and keys them to the numbers. See how many 19th-century cities you can identify (€2, €8 combo-ticket with Salzburg Museum, combo-ticket is about €2 cheaper on Sun, open daily 9:00–17:00, Thu until 20:00, Residenzplatz 9).

• *Backtrack into Residenzplatz and head to the opposite end from the new Residenz. This building is the...*

❺ Old (Alte) Residenz

Opposite the new Residenz is Wolf Dietrich's skippable palace, the old Residenz, which is connected to the cathedral by a skyway. A series of ornately decorated rooms and an art gallery are open to visitors with time to kill (€8, €5 without gallery, Tue–Sun 10:00–17:00, closed Mon, tel. 0662/840-4510).

• *Walk under the prince-archbishop's skyway and step into Domplatz (Cathedral Square), where you'll find the...*

❻ Salzburg Cathedral (Salzburger Dom)

This cathedral, rated ▲▲, was one of the first Baroque buildings north of the Alps. It was consecrated in 1628, during the Thirty

Years' War. (Pitting Roman Catholics against Protestants, this war devastated much of Europe and brought most grand construction projects to a halt.) Experts differ on what motivated the builders: to emphasize Salzburg's commitment to the Roman Catholic cause and the power of the Church here, or to show that there could be a peaceful alternative to the religious strife that was racking Europe at the time. Salzburg's archbishop was technically the top papal official north of the Alps, but the city managed to steer clear of the war. With its rich salt production, it had enough money to stay out of the conflict and carefully maintain its independence from the warring sides.

The dates on the iron gates refer to milestones in the church's history: In 774, the previous church (long since destroyed) was founded by St. Virgil, to be replaced in 1628 by the church you see today. In 1959, a partial reconstruction was completed, made necessary by a WWII bomb that had blown through the dome.

Domplatz is surrounded by the prince-archbishop's secular administration buildings. The **statue of Mary** (1771) is looking away from the church, welcoming visitors. If you stand in the rear of the square, immediately under the middle arch, you'll see that she's positioned to be crowned by the two angels on the church facade.

Step inside the cathedral (donation requested; Easter–Oct Mon–Sat 9:00–18:00, Sun 13:00–18:00; Nov–Easter Mon–Sat 10:00–17:00, Sun 13:00–17:00). Enter the cathedral as if part of a festival procession—drawn toward the resurrected Christ by the brightly lit area under the dome, and cheered on by ceiling paintings of the Passion. The stucco, by a Milanese artist, is

SALZBURG

exceptional. Sit under the **dome**—surrounded by the tombs of 10 archbishops from the 17th century—and imagine all four organs playing, each balcony filled with musicians...glorious surround-sound. Mozart, who was the organist here for two years, would advise you that the acoustics are best in pews immediately under the dome. Study the symbolism of the decor all around you—intellectual, complex, and cohesive. Think of the altar in Baroque terms, as the center of a stage, with sun-rays as spotlights in this dramatic and sacred theater. In the left transept, stairs lead down into the **crypt** *(Krypta)*, where you can see foundations of the earlier church, more tombs, and a tourist-free chapel (reserved for prayer) directly under the dome.

Built in just 14 years (1614–1628), the church boasts harmonious architecture. When Pope John Paul II visited in 1998, some 5,000 people filled the cathedral (330 feet long and 230 feet tall). The baptismal font (dark bronze, left of the entry) is from the previous cathedral (basin from about 1320, although the lid is modern). Mozart was baptized here (Amadeus means "beloved by God"). Concert and Mass schedules are posted at the entrance; the Sunday Mass at 10:00 is famous for its music.

The **Cathedral Museum** (Dom Museum) has a rich collection of church art (entry at portico, €5, mid-May–Oct Mon–Sat 10:00–17:00, Sun 11:00–18:00, closed Nov–mid-May except during Advent, tel. 0662/8047-1870).

• *From the cathedral, exit left and walk toward the fortress into the next square.*

❼ Kapitelplatz

Head past the underground public WCs (free, but small tip expected) to the giant **chessboard.** It's just under the golden orb topped by a man gazing up at the castle, trying to decide whether to walk up or shell out €10 for the funicular. Every year since 2002, a foundation has commissioned a different artist to create a new work of public art somewhere in the city; this is the piece from 2008. A small road leads uphill to the fortress (and fortress funicular; see arrow pointing to the *Steigkeller*).

SALZBURG

Keep going across the square to the pond. This was a **horse bath**, the 18th-century equivalent of a car wash. Notice the puzzle above it—the artist wove the date of the structure into a phrase. It says, "Leopold the Prince Built Me," using the letters LLDVICMXVXI, which total 1732 (add it up...it works)—the year it was built. With your back to the cathedral, leave the square through a gate in the right corner that reads *zum Peterskeller*. It leads to a waterfall and St. Peter's Cemetery.

The **waterwheel** is part of a canal system that has brought water into Salzburg from Berchtesgaden, 16 miles away, since the 13th century. Climb uphill a few steps to feel the medieval water power. The stream, divided from here into smaller canals, was channeled through town to provide fire protection, to flush out the streets (Saturday morning was flood-the-streets day), and to power factories (there were more than 100 watermill-powered firms as late as the 19th century). Drop into the fragrant and traditional **bakery** at the waterfall. It's hard to beat their rocklike *Roggenbrot* (various fresh rolls for less than €1, Thu–Tue 7:00–17:30, Sat until 13:00, closed Wed). There's a good view of the funicular climbing up to the castle from here. For more on the canal system, check out the free **Alm River Canal exhibit** nearby (described on page 165).

• *Now find the* Katakomben *sign and step into...*

❽ St. Peter's Cemetery

This collection of lovingly tended mini-gardens abuts the Mönchberg's rock wall (free, silence is requested, daily April–Sept 6:30–19:00, Oct–March 6:30–18:00). Walk in about 50 yards to the intersection of lanes at the base of the cliff marked by a stone ball. (It's seemingly made-to-order for a little back-stretching break. Go ahead...I'll wait.) You're surrounded by three churches, each founded in the sixth century atop a pagan Celtic holy site. St. Peter's Church is closest to the stone ball. Notice the fine Romanesque stonework on the chapel nearest you, and the fancy rich guys' Renaissance-style tombs decorating its walls.

Wealthy as those guys were, they ran out of caring relatives. The graves surrounding you are tended by descendants of the deceased. In Austria, gravesites are rented, not owned. Rent bills are sent out every 10 years. If no one cares enough to make the payment, your remains are chucked. Iron crosses were much cheaper than tombstones. While the cemetery where the von Trapp family hid out in *The Sound of Music* was a Hollywood set, it was inspired by this one.

Look up the cliff. Legendary medieval hermit monks are said to have lived in the hillside—but "catacombs" they're not. For €1, you can climb lots of steps to see a few old caves, a chapel, and some fine views (May–Sept Tue–Sun 10:30–17:00, closed Mon; Oct–April Wed–Thu 10:30–15:30, Fri–Sun 10:30–16:00, closed Mon–Tue).

• *Continue downhill through the cemetery and out the opposite end. Just outside, hook right and drop into...*

❾ St. Peter's Church

Just inside, enjoy a carved Romanesque welcome. Over the inner doorway, a fine tympanum shows Jesus on a rainbow flanked by Peter and Paul over a stylized Tree of Life and under a Latin inscription reading, "I am the door to life, and only through me can you find eternal life." Enter the nave and notice how the once purely Romanesque vaulting has since been iced with a sugary Rococo finish. Salzburg's only Rococo interior feels Bavarian (because it is—the fancy stucco work was done by Bavarian artists). Up the right side aisle is the tomb of St. Rupert, with a painting showing Salzburg in 1750 (one bridge, salt ships sailing the river, and angels hoisting barrels of salt to heaven as St. Rupert prays for his city). If you're here during the town's Ruperti-Kirtag festival in late September, you'll see candles and fresh flowers, honoring the city's not-forgotten saint. On pillars farther up the aisle are faded bits of 13th-century Romanesque frescos. Similar frescoes hide under Rococo whitewash throughout the church.

Leaving the church, notice on the left the recommended Stiftskeller St. Peter restaurant—known for its Mozart Dinner Concert. Charlemagne ate here in A.D. 803—allowing locals to claim that it's the oldest restaurant in Europe. Opposite where you entered the square (look through the arch), you'll see St. Rupert waving you into the next square (early-20th-century Bauhaus-style dorms for student monks), with a modern crucifix (1926) on the far wall.

• *Walk through the archway next to the crucifix into...*

❿ Toscanini Hof

This square faces the 1925 **Festival Hall.** The hall's three theaters seat 5,000. This is where Captain von Trapp nervously waited before walking onstage (in the movie, he sang "Edelweiss"), just before he escaped with his family. On the left is the city's 1,500-space, inside-the-mountain parking lot; ahead, behind the *Felsenkeller* sign, is a tunnel (generally closed) leading to the actual concert hall; and to the right is the backstage of a smaller hall where carpenters are often building stage sets (door open on hot days). The stairway leads to the top of the cliff and eventually to the recommended Stadtalm Café and hostel.

• *Walk downhill through Max-Reinhardt-Platz, to the right of the church and past the public WC, into...*

SALZBURG

⓫ Universitätsplatz

This square hosts an **open-air produce market**—Salzburg's liveliest (mornings Mon–Sat, best on Sat). Locals are happy to pay more here for the reliably fresh and top-quality produce. (These days, half of Austria's produce is grown organically.) The market really bustles on Saturday mornings, when the farmers are in town. Public marketplaces have fountains for washing fruit and vegetables. The fountain here—a part of the medieval water system—plummets down a hole and to the river. The sundial (over the water hole) is accurate (except for the daylight savings hour) and two-dimensional, showing both the time (obvious) and the date (less obvious). The fanciest facade overlooking the square (the yellow one) is the backside of Mozart's Birthplace (we'll see the front soon).

• *Continue past the fountain to the end of the square, passing several characteristic and nicely arcaded medieval tunnels (on right) that connect the square to Getreidegasse. Cross the big road for a look at the giant horse troughs, adjacent to the prince's stables. Paintings show the various breeds and temperaments of horses in his stable. Like Vienna, Salzburg had a passion for the equestrian arts.*

Take two right turns and you're at the start of...

⓬ Getreidegasse

This street, rated ▲▲, was old Salzburg's busy, colorful main drag. It's lined with *Schmuck* (jewelry) shops. Famous for its old wrought-iron signs (best viewed from this end), the architecture on the street still looks much as it did in Mozart's day—though its former elegance is now mostly gone, replaced by chain outlets.

On the right at #39, **Sporer** serves up homemade spirits (€1.40 per shot). This has been a family-run show for a century—fun-loving, proud, and English-speaking. *Nuss* is nut, *Marille* is apricot (typical of this region), the *Kletzen* cocktail is like a super-thick Baileys with pear, and *Edle Brande* are the stronger schnapps. The many homemade firewaters are in jugs at the end of the bar.

Continue down Getreidegasse, noticing the old doorbells—one per floor. At #40, **Eisgrotte** serves good ice cream. Across from Eisgrotte, a tunnel leads to the recommended **Balkan Grill** (signed as *Bosna Grill*), the local choice for the very best sausage in town. Farther along, you'll pass McDonald's (while required to keep its arches Baroque and low-key, it just couldn't hang anything less than the biggest sign on the street).

The knot of excited tourists and salesmen hawking goofy gimmicks marks the home of Salzburg's most famous resident. **Mozart's Birthplace** (Geburtshaus, ⓭ on map)—the house where Mozart was born, and where he composed many of his early works—is worth a visit for his true fans (described next). But for most, his Residence, across the river, is more interesting (described later).

• *Continue on, past City Hall (Rathaus) and its clock tower, and turn right into...*

⓮ Alter Markt

Here in Salzburg's old marketplace you'll find a sausage stand, the recommended **Café Tomaselli**, a fun **candy shop** at #7 (Mon–Fri 9:00–18:00, Sat 10:00–18:00, closed Sun), and, next door, the beautifully old-fashioned **Alte F.E. Hofapotheke** pharmacy—duck in discreetly to peek at the Baroque shelves and containers (be polite—the people in line are here for medicine, Mon–Fri 8:00–18:00, Sat 8:00–12:00, closed Sun, no photography).

• *Our walk is finished. From here, you can head up to the Hohensalzburg Fortress on the cliffs over the old town (see page 163); or continue to some of the sights across the river. To reach those sights, head for the river, jog left (past the fast-food fish restaurant and free WCs), climb to the top of the Makartsteg pedestrian bridge, and turn to page 166.*

Sights in Salzburg

▲Mozart's Birthplace (Geburtshaus)

Mozart was born here in 1756. It was in this building—the most popular Mozart sight in town—that he composed most of his boy-genius works. For fans, it's almost a pilgrimage. American artist Robert Wilson was recently hired to spiff up the exhibit, to make it

feel more conceptual and less like a museum. But I was unimpressed. If you're tackling just one Mozart sight, skip this one. Instead, walk 10 minutes from here to Mozart's Residence (described on page 167), which provides a more informative visit. But if you want to max out on Mozart, a visit here is worthwhile.

Cost, Hours, Location: €6.50, or €10 for combo-ticket that includes Mozart's Residence, daily 9:00–17:00, July–Aug until 20:00, last entry 30 min before closing, Getreidegasse 9, tel. 0662/844-313.

◑ Self-Guided Tour: Here's what you'll see as you shuffle through with the herd:

Room 1: Around a baby crib showing an infant both old and young (Mozart's music is timeless...get it?) are walls heavy with historic etchings, portraits, and documents. Most important: an engraving of the family (lower right) and a fine "portrait with a bird's nest" of Mozart, painted from life when he was nine years old (upper left).

Room 2: The living room shows off authentic family portraits: Wolfgang's mom, dad, sister, and wife. Wolfgang composed his first pieces as a child on a clavichord (like the one in this room). A predecessor of the piano, it hit the strings with simple teeter-totter keys that played very softly...ideal for composers living in tight apartment quarters.

Room 3: The nursery is decorated like Mozart's music: light and free as a bird (hence the flying birds). Embedded in the walls are Mozart's personal possessions—his ring, silk wallet, and violin. He was born in this room, and the entire family slept here until Wolfgang was 14.

Room 4: Exactly what Mozart looked like is a bit of a mystery. Various portraits in this room give us something to go on.

Corridor: The neon phrase shows Mozart's juvenile sense of humor. It's a rhyme: *Madame Mutter, ich esse gerne Butter.* (Dear mother, I love to eat butter.) The next room is wallpapered with reproductions of circa-1840 photos of Mozart's wife and son (as an old man). More strange Wilson-designed rooms follow: Mozart loved to turn things upside-down—so the Salzburg cityscapes are that way, with stars on the floor. Downstairs, just before the shop, rooms dedicated to Mozart's operas play various video clips continuously.

Atop the Cliffs Above the Old Town

The main "sight" above town is the Hohensalzburg Fortress. But if you just want to enjoy the sweeping views over Salzburg, you have a couple of cheap options: Head up to the castle grounds on foot, take the elevator up the cliffs of Mönchsberg (explained earlier, under "Getting Around Salzburg"), or visit the castle in the evening on a night when they're hosting a concert (about 300 nights a year). This is the only time you can buy a funicular ticket without paying for the castle entrance—since the castle museum is closed, but the funicular is still running to bring up concert-goers.

▲▲Hohensalzburg Fortress (Festung)—Built on a rock (called Festungsberg) 400 feet above the Salzach River, this fortress

was never really used. That's the idea. It was a good investment—so foreboding, nobody attacked the town for a thousand years. The city was never taken by force, but when Napoleon stopped by, Salzburg wisely surrendered. After a stint as a military barracks, the fortress was opened to the public in the 1860s by Emperor Franz Josef. Today, it remains one of Europe's mightiest castles, dominating Salzburg's skyline and offering incredible views.

Cost: Your daytime funicular ticket includes admission to the fortress grounds and all the museums inside—whether you want to see them or not (€10.50, €24.50 family ticket). Save money by walking up—the climb is much easier than it looks, and the views are fantastic. From the top you can opt to see the museums for €7, but many visitors are content to simply take in the grounds and views (free if you've walked up). If you'd rather take the funicular but want to skip the museums, head up the hill in the evening (within one hour of the museum's closing time, it's €6 one-way/€7.50 round-trip for funicular and entry to castle grounds; after closing time, the funicular is €3.60 round-trip).

Hours: The complex is open daily year-round (May–Sept 9:00–19:00, Oct–April 9:30–17:00, last entry 30 min before closing, tel. 0662/8424-3011). On nights when there's a concert, the castle grounds are free and open after the museum closes until 21:30.

Concerts: The fortress also serves as a venue for evening concerts (Festungskonzerte). For details, see "Entertainment in Salzburg," later.

Café: The café between the funicular station and the castle entry is a great place to nibble on apple strudel while taking in the jaw-dropping view.

Orientation: The fortress visit has three parts: a relatively dull courtyard with some fine views from its various ramparts; the fortress itself (with a required and escorted 45-min audiotour); and the palace museum (by far the best exhibit of the lot). At the bottom of the funicular, you'll pass through an interesting little exhibit on the town's canal system (free, described on page 158).

SALZBURG

○ Self-Guided Tour: From the top of the funicular, head to your right and down the stairs to bask in the view, either from the café or the view terrace a little farther along. Once you're done snapping photos, walk through to the castle grounds and go left, following the path up and around to reach the inner courtyard (labeled *Inneres Schloß*). Immediately inside, circling to the right (clockwise), you'll encounter cannons (still poised to defend Salzburg against an Ottoman invasion), the marionette exhibit, the palace museum, the Kuenburg bastion, scant ruins of a Romanesque church, the courtyard (with path down for those walking), toilets, shops, a restaurant, and the fortress tour.

• *Begin at the...*

Marionette Exhibit: Several fun rooms show off this local tradition, with three videos playing continuously: two with peeks at Salzburg's ever-enchanting Marionette Theater performances of Mozart classics (see listing under "Entertainment in Salzburg," later), and one with a behind-the-scenes look at the action. Give the hands-on marionette a whirl.

• *Hiking through the former palace, you'll find the sight's best exhibits at the...*

Palace Museum (Festungsmuseum Carolino Augusteum): The second floor has exhibits on castle life, from music to torture. The top floor shows off fancy royal apartments, a sneak preview of the room used for the nightly fortress concerts, and the Rainier military museum, dedicated to the Salzburg regiments that fought in both World Wars.

Castle Courtyard: The courtyard was the main square of the castle residents, a community of a thousand—which could be self-sufficient when necessary. The square was ringed by the shops of craftsmen, blacksmiths, bakers, and so on. The well dipped into a rain-fed cistern. The church is dedicated to St. George, the protector of horses (logical for an army church) and decorated by fine red marble reliefs (c. 1502). Behind the church is the top of the old lift that helped supply the fortress. (From near here, steps lead back into the city, or to the mountaintop "Mönchsberg Walk," described later.) You'll also see the remains of a Romanesque chapel, which are well-described.

• *Near the chapel, turn left into the Kuenburg Bastion (once a garden) for fine city and castle views.*

Kuenburg Bastion: Notice how the castle has three parts: the original castle inside the courtyard, the vast whitewashed walls (built when the castle was a residence), and the lower, beefed-up fortifications (added for extra defense against the expected Ottoman invasion). Survey Salzburg from here and think about fortifying an important city by using nature. Mönchsberg (the cliffs to the left) and Festungsberg (the little mountain you're on) naturally cradle the old town, with just a small gate between the ridge and the river needed to bottle up the place. The new town across the river needed a bit of a wall arcing from the river to its hill. Back then, only one bridge crossed the Salzach into town, and it had a fortified gate.

• *Back inside the castle courtyard, continue your circle. The Round Tower (1497) helps you visualize the inner original castle.*

Fortress Interior: Tourists are allowed in this part of the fortified palace only with an escort. (They say that's for security, though while touring it, you wonder what they're protecting.) A crowd assembles at the turnstile, and every quarter-hour 40 people are issued their audioguides and let in for the escorted walk. You'll go one room at a time, listening to a 45-minute commentary. While the interior furnishings are mostly gone—taken by Napoleon—the rooms survived as well as they did because no one wanted to live here after 1500, so the building was never modernized. Your tour includes a room dedicated to the art of "excruciating questioning" ("softening up" prisoners, in American military jargon)—filled with tools of that gruesome trade. The highlight is the commanding city view from the top of a tower.

• *After seeing the fortress, consider hiking down to the old town, or along the top of Mönchsberg (see "Mönchsberg Walk," below). If you take the funicular down, keep an eye out for the...*

Alm River Canal Exhibit: At the base of the funicular, below the castle, is this fine little exhibit on how the river was broken into five smaller streams—powering the city until steam took up the energy-supply baton. Pretend it's the year 1200 and follow (by video) the flow of the water from the river through the canals, into the mills, and as it's finally dumped into the Salzach River (free, access from the bottom of the lift as you're leaving, or through amber shop next door if you're not riding the funicular).

▲**Mönchsberg Walk**—For a great 30-minute hike, exit the fortress by taking the steep lane down from the castle courtyard. At the first intersection, right leads into the old town, and left leads across the Mönchsberg. The lane leads 20 minutes through the woods high above the city (stick to the high lanes, or you'll end up back in town), taking you to the recommended Gasthaus Stadtalm café (light meals, cheap beds). From the Stadtalm, pass under the medieval wall and walk left along the wall to a tableau showing how it once looked. Take the switchback to the right and follow the lane downhill to the Museum of Modern Art (described

SALZBURG

next), where the elevator zips you back into town (€2 one-way, €3 round-trip, daily 8:30–19:00, Wed until 21:00, July–Aug daily until 1:00 in the morning, May–Sept starts running at 8:00). If you stay on the lane past the elevator, you eventually pass the Augustine church that marks the rollicking Augustiner Bräustübl (recommended under "Eating in Salzburg," later).

In 1669, a huge Mönchsberg landslide killed more than 200 townspeople. Since then the cliffs have been carefully checked each spring and fall. Even today, you might see crews on the cliff, monitoring its stability.

Museum of Modern Art on Mönchsberg—The modern-art museum on top of Mönchsberg, built in 2004, houses Salzburg's Rupertinum Gallery, plus special exhibitions. While the collection is not worth climbing a mountain for, the M32 restaurant has some of the best views in town (€8, €9.70 including elevator ticket, Tue–Sun 10:00–18:00, Wed until 20:00, closed Mon except during festival; restaurant open Tue–Sat 9:00–24:00, Sun 9:00–18:00, closed Mon except during festival; both at top of Mönchsberg elevator, tel. 0662/842-220, www.museumdermoderne.at).

In the New Town, North of the River

The following sights are across the river from the old town. I've connected them with walking instructions.

• *Begin at the Makartsteg pedestrian bridge, where you can survey the...*

Salzach River—Salzburg's river is called "salt river" not because it's salty, but because of the precious cargo it once carried—the salt mines of Hallein are just nine miles upstream. Salt could be transported from here all the way to the Danube, and on to the Mediterranean via the Black Sea. The riverbanks and roads were built when the river was regulated in the 1850s. Before that, the Salzach was much wider and slower-moving. Houses opposite the old town fronted the river with docks and "garages" for boats. The grand buildings just past the bridge (with their elegant promenades and cafés) were built on reclaimed land in the late 19th century, in the historicist style of Vienna's Ringstrasse.

Scan the cityscape. Notice all the churches. Salzburg, nicknamed the "Rome of the North," has 38 Catholic churches (plus two Protestant churches and a synagogue). Find the five streams gushing into the river. These date from the 13th century, when the river was split into five canals running through the town to power its mills. The Stein Hotel (upstream, just left of next bridge) has a popular roof-terrace café (see page 169). Downstream, notice the Museum of Modern Art atop Mönchsberg, with a view restaurant and a faux castle (actually a water reservoir). The Romanesque bell tower with the green copper dome in the distance is the Augustine church, site of the best beer hall in town (the recommended Augustiner Bräustübl).

• *Cross the bridge, pass the recommended Café Bazar (a fine place for a drink), walk two blocks inland, and take a left past the heroic statues into...*

▲**Mirabell Gardens and Palace (Schloss)**—The bubbly gardens laid out in 1730 for the prince-archbishop have been open

to the public since 1850 (thanks to Emperor Franz Josef, who was rattled by the popular revolutions of 1848). The gardens are free and open until dusk. The palace is open only as a concert venue (explained later). The statues and the arbor (far left) were featured in *The Sound of Music*. Walk through the gardens to the palace. Look back, enjoy the garden/cathedral/castle view, and imagine how the prince-archbishop must have reveled in a vista that reminded him of all his secular and religious power. Then go around to the river side of the palace and find the horse.

The rearing **Pegasus statue** (rare and very well-balanced) is the site of a famous *Sound of Music* scene where the kids all danced before lining up on the stairs (with Maria 30 yards farther along). The steps lead to a small mound in the park (made of rubble from a former theater, and today a rendezvous point for Salzburg's gay community).

Nearest the horse, stairs lead between two lions to a pair of tough dwarfs (early volleyball players with spiked mittens) welcoming you to Salzburg's **Dwarf Park.** Cross the elevated walk (noticing the city's fortified walls) to meet statues of a dozen dwarfs who served the prince-archbishop—modeled after real people with real fashions in about 1600. This was Mannerist art, from the hyper-realistic age that followed the Renaissance.

There's plenty of **music,** both in the park and in the palace. A brass band plays free park concerts (May–Aug Sun at 10:30 and Wed with lighted fountains at 20:30, unless it's raining). To properly enjoy the lavish Mirabell Palace—once the prince-archbishop's summer palace, and now the seat of the mayor—get a ticket to a Schlosskonzerte (my favorite venue for a classical concert—see page 173).

• *To visit Salzburg's best Mozart sight, go a long block southeast to Makartplatz, where you'll find...*

▲▲**Mozart's Residence (Wohnhaus)**—This reconstruction of Mozart's second home (his family moved here when he was 17) is the most informative Mozart sight in town. The English-language audioguide (included with admission, 1.5 hrs) provides fascinating insight into Mozart's life and music, with the usual scores, old pianos, and an interesting 30-minute film (#17 on your audioguide for soundtrack) that runs continuously (€6.50, or €10 for combo-ticket that includes Mozart's Birthplace in the old town, daily 9:00–17:00, July–Aug until 20:00, last entry 30 min before closing, allow at least one hour for visit, Makartplatz 8, tel. 0662/8742-2740).

In the main hall—used by the Mozarts to entertain Salzburg's high society—you can hear original instruments from Mozart's time. Mozart was proud to be the first in his family to compose a duet. Notice the family portrait (circa 1780) on the wall, showing Mozart with his sister Nannerl, their father, and their mother—who'd died two years earlier in Paris. Mozart also had silly crude bull's-eyes made for the pop-gun game popular at the time (licking an "arse," Wolfgang showed his disdain for the rigors of high society). Later rooms feature real artifacts that explore his loves, his intellectual pursuits, his travels, and more.

• *From here, you can walk a few blocks back to the main bridge (Staatsbrücke), where you'll find the Platzl, a square once used as a hay market. Pause to enjoy the kid-pleasing little fountain. Near the fountain (with your back to the river), Steingasse leads darkly to the right.*

▲**Steingasse Stroll**—This street, a block in from the river, was the only road in the Middle Ages going south over the Alps to Venice (this was the first stop north of the Alps). Today, it's wonderfully tranquil and free of Salzburg's touristy crush.

At #9, a plaque (of questionable veracity) shows where Joseph Mohr, who wrote the words to "Silent Night," was born—poor and illegitimate—in 1792. There is no doubt, however, that the popular Christmas carol was composed and first sung in the village of Oberndorf, just outside of Salzburg, in 1818. Stairs lead from near here up to a 17th-century Capuchin monastery.

On the next corner, the wall is gouged out. This scar was left even after the building was restored, to remind locals of the American GI who tried to get a tank down this road during a visit to the town brothel—two blocks farther up Steingasse. Inviting cocktail bars along here come alive at night (see "Steingasse Pub Crawl" on page 189).

At #19, find the carvings on the old door. Some say these are notices from beggars to the begging community (more numerous after post-Reformation religious wars, which forced many people out of their homes and towns)—a kind of "hobo code" indicating whether the residents would give or not. Trace the wires of the old-fashioned doorbells to the highest floors.

Farther on, you'll find a commanding Salzburg view across the river. Notice the red dome marking the oldest nunnery in the German-speaking world (established in 712) under the fortress and to the left. The real Maria from *The Sound of Music* taught in this nunnery's school. In 1927, she and Captain von Trapp were married in the church you see here (not the church filmed in the movie). He was 47. She was 22. Hmmmm.

From here look back, above the arch you just passed through, at part of the town's medieval fortification. The coat of arms on the arch is of the prince-archbishop who paid Bavaria a huge ransom to stay out of the Thirty Years' War (smart move). He then built this fortification (in 1634) in anticipation of rampaging armies from both sides.

Today, this street is for making love, not war. The Maison de Plaisir (a few doors down, at #24) has for centuries been a Salzburg brothel. But the climax of this walk is more touristic.

• *For a grand view, head back to the Platzl and the bridge, enter the Stein Hotel (left corner, overlooking the river), and ride the elevator to...*

Stein Terrasse—This café offers perhaps the best views in town (aside from the castle). Hidden from the tourist crush, it's a trendy, professional, local scene. You can discreetly peek at the view, or enjoy a drink or light meal (small snacks, indoor/outdoor seating, Sun–Thu 9:00–24:00, Fri–Sat 9:00–1:00 in the morning).

• *Back at the Platzl and the bridge, you can head straight up Linzergasse (away from the river) into a neighborhood packed with recommended accommodations, as well as our final new town sight...*

▲**St. Sebastian Cemetery**—Wander through this quiet place, so Baroque and so Italian (free, daily April–Oct 9:00–18:30,

Nov–March 9:00–16:00, entry at Linzergasse 43 in summer; in winter go around the corner to the right, through the arch at #37, and around the building to the doorway under the blue seal). Mozart is buried in Vienna, his mom's in Paris, and his sister is in Salzburg's old town (St. Peter's)—but Wolfgang's wife Constanze ("Constantia") and his father Leopold are buried here (from the black iron gate entrance on Linzergasse, walk 17 paces and look left). When Prince-Archbishop Wolf Dietrich had the cemetery moved from around the cathedral and put here, across the river, people didn't like it. To help popularize it, he had his own mausoleum built as its centerpiece. Continue straight past the Mozart tomb to this circular building (English description at door).

Near Salzburg

For information on Berchtesgaden—also near Salzburg—see the end of this chapter.

▲**Hellbrunn Castle**—About the year 1610, Prince-Archbishop Sittikus (after meditating on stewardship and Christ-like values)

decided he needed a lavish palace with a vast and ornate garden purely for pleasure. He built this and just loved inviting his VIP guests out for fun with his trick fountains. Today, the visit is worthwhile for the garden full of clever fountains...and the sadistic joy the tour guide gets from soaking tourists. (Hint: When you see a wet place, cover your camera.) After buying your ticket, you must wait for the English tour and laugh and scramble through the entertaining 40-minute trick-water-toy tour, and are then free to tour the forgettable palace with an included audioguide (€8.50, daily May–Sept 9:00–17:30, July–Aug until 21:00—but tours from 18:00 on don't include the castle, mid-March–April and Oct 9:00–16:30, these are last tour times, closed Nov–mid-March, tel. 0662/820-3720, www.hellbrunn.at).

Hellbrunn is nearly four miles south of Salzburg (bus #25 from station or from Staatsbrücke bridge, 2–3/hr, 20 min). While it can be fun—especially on a hot day or with kids—for many, it's a lot of trouble for a few water tricks. The Hellbrunn Baroque garden, one of the oldest in Europe, now features *S.O.M.*'s "Sixteen Going on Seventeen" gazebo.

Hellbrunn makes a good 30-minute bike excursion along the riverbank from Salzburg (described next).

▲▲**Riverside or Meadow Bike Ride**—The Salzach River has smooth, flat, and scenic bike lanes along each side (thanks to medieval tow paths—cargo boats would float downstream and be dragged back up by horses). On a sunny day, I can think of no more shout-worthy escape from the city. The nearly four-mile path upstream to Hellbrunn Castle is easy, with a worthy destination (leave Salzburg on castle side). For a nine-mile ride, continue on to Hallein (where you can tour a salt mine—see next listing; the north, or new town, side of river is most scenic). Perhaps the most pristine, meadow-filled farm-country route is the four-mile Hellbrunner Allee from Akademiestrasse. Even a quickie ride across town is a great Salzburg experience. In the evening, the riverbanks are a world of floodlit spires.

▲**Hallein Bad Dürrnberg Salt Mine (Salzbergwerke)**—This salt-mine tour (above the town of Hallein, nine miles from

Greater Salzburg

GERMANY

1 MILE
2 KM

TO VIENNA

TO MUNICH

GERMANY

SALZ. MITTE EXIT

SALZACH RIVER

SALZBURG NORD EXIT

E-14 A1

TO VIENNA & SALZKAMMERGUT LAKE DISTRICT

AUTOBAHN

3

TRAIN STN.

GRAZ. BUND. STR.

AUGUSTINER BRÄUSTÜBL

LINZER.

KAP.-BERG

GAIS-BERG

SALZ. WEST EXIT

AIRPORT

FORTRESS

2

1

MTN. LIFT

MORZGER STR.

ALPENSTR.

7

5

6

4

VON TRAPP MANSION
(LEOPOLDS-KRON)

MOOS-STRASSE

PARK + RIDE

You are 16...

AIGNERSTR.

TO MUNICH & INNSBRUCK

"The hills are alive..." –Julie

HELLBRUNN CASTLE
(GAZEBO)

E-14 A10

ANIF

MTN. LIFT

UNTERSBERG

SALZ. SÜD EXIT

N

☐ SEE DETAIL MAPS

✪ OLD TOWN CENTER

TO BERCHTESGADEN (GERMANY)

DCH

TO HALLEIN

❶ Hotel Rosenvilla
❷ Haus Arenberg
❸ Brigitte Lenglachner Rooms
❹ Pension Bloberger Hof

❺ Frau Ballwein Rooms
❻ Helga Bankhammer Rooms
❼ Haus Reichl

Salzburg) is a popular excursion from Salzburg. Wearing white overalls and sliding down the sleek wooden chutes, you'll cross underground from Austria into Germany while learning about the old-time salt-mining process. The tour entails lots of time on your feet as you walk from cavern to cavern, learning the history of the mine by watching a

series of video skits with an actor channeling Prince-Archbishop Wolf Dietrich. The visit also includes a "Celtic Village" open-air museum (€17, allow 2.5 hours for the visit, daily April–Oct 9:00–17:00, Nov–March 10:00–15:00, these are last tour times, English-speaking guides—but let your linguistic needs be known loud and clear, tel. 06132/200-2400, www.salzwelten.at). The convenient *Salz Erlebnis* ticket from Salzburg's train station covers admission, train, and shuttle bus tickets, all in one money-saving round-trip ticket (€22, buy ticket at train station, no discount with railpass; 40-min trip with hourly departures in each direction at about :15 after the hour, with synchronized train-bus connection in Hallein—schedule posted in flier). Salt mine tours cost substantial time and money. One's plenty.

Entertainment in Salzburg

▲▲**Salzburg Festival (Salzburger Festspiele)**—Each summer, from late July to the end of August, Salzburg hosts its famous Salzburg Festival, founded in 1920 to employ Vienna's musicians in the summer. This fun and festive time is crowded, but there are plenty of beds (except for a few August weekends). There are three big halls: the Opera and Orchestra venues in the Festival House, and the Landes Theater, where German-language plays are performed. Tickets for the big festival events are generally expensive (€50–600) and sell out well in advance (bookable from Jan). Most tourists think they're "going to the Salzburg Festival" by seeing smaller non-festival events that go on during the festival weeks. For these lesser events, same-day tickets are normally available (the ticket office on Mozartplatz, in the TI, prints a daily list of concerts and charges a 30 percent fee to book them). For specifics on this year's festival schedule and tickets, visit www.salzburg festival.at, or contact the Austrian National Tourist Office in the United States (tel. 212/944-6880, fax 212/730-4568, www.austria .info, travel@austria.info).

▲▲**Musical Events Year-Round**—Salzburg is busy throughout the year, with 2,000 classical performances in its palaces and churches annually. Pick up the events calendar at the TI (free, bimonthly). I've never planned in advance, and I've enjoyed great concerts with every visit. Whenever you visit, you'll have a number of concerts (generally small chamber groups) to choose from. Here are some of the more accessible events:

Concerts at Hohensalzburg Fortress (Festungskonzerte): Nearly nightly concerts—Mozart's greatest hits for beginners—are held atop Festungsberg, in the "prince's chamber" of the fortress, featuring small chamber groups (open seating after the first six more expensive rows, €31 or €38 plus €3.40 for the funicular; at 19:30, 20:00, or 20:30; doors open 30 min early, tel. 0662/825-858 to reserve, pick up tickets at the door). The medieval-feeling chamber has windows overlooking the city, and the concert gives you a chance to enjoy the grand city view and a stroll through the castle courtyard. (The funicular ticket costs €3.40 within an hour of the show—ideal for people who just want to ascend for the view.) For €51, you can combine the concert with a four-course dinner (starts 2 hours before concert).

Concerts at the Mirabell Palace (Schlosskonzerte): The nearly nightly chamber music concerts at the Mirabell Palace are performed in a lavish Baroque setting. They come with more sophisticated programs and better musicians than the fortress concerts. Baroque music flying around a Baroque hall is a happy bird in the right cage (open seating after the first five pricier rows, €29, usually at 20:00—but check flier for times, doors open one hour ahead, tel. 0662/848-586, www.salzburger-schlosskonzerte.at).

"Five O'Clock Concerts" (5-Uhr-Konzerte): These concerts—next to St. Peter's in the old town—are cheaper, since they feature young artists (€12, July–Sept Thu–Tue at 17:00, no concerts Wed or Oct–June, 45–60 min, tel. 0662/8445-7619, www.5-uhr-konzerte.com). While the series is formally named after the brother of Joseph Haydn, it offers music from various masters.

Mozart Piano Sonatas: St. Peter's Abbey hosts these concerts each weekend (€18, €9 for children, €45 for a family of four, Fri and Sat at 19:00 year-round, in the abbey's Romanesque Hall—a.k.a. Romanischer Saal, tel. 0664/423-5645). This short and inexpensive concert is ideal for families.

Marionette Theater: Salzburg's much-loved marionette theater offers operas with spellbinding marionettes and recorded music. Music-lovers are mesmerized by the little people on stage (€18–35, nearly nightly at 17:00 or 19:30 June–Sept except Sun, also 3–4/week in May, some 14:00 matinees, box office open Mon–Sat 9:00–13:00 and 2 hours before shows, near the Mirabell Gardens and Mozart's Residence at Schwarzstrasse 24, tel. 0662/872-406, www.marionetten.at). For a sneak preview, check out the videos playing at the marionette exhibit up in the fortress.

The Sound of Music Debunked

Rather than visit the real-life sights from the life of Maria von Trapp and family, most tourists want to see the places where Hollywood chose to film this fanciful story. Local guides are happy not to burst any *S.O.M.* pilgrim's bubble, but keep these points in mind:

- "Edelweiss" is not a cherished Austrian folk tune or national anthem. Like all the "Austrian" music in *The S.O.M.*, it was composed for Broadway by Rodgers and Hammerstein. It was, however, the last composition that the famed team wrote together, as Hammerstein died in 1960—nine months after the musical opened.

- *The S.O.M.* implies that Maria was devoutly religious throughout her life, but Maria's foster parents raised her as a socialist and atheist. Maria discovered her religious calling while studying to be a teacher. After completing school, she joined the convent not as a nun, but as a novitiate (that is, she hadn't taken her vows yet).

- Maria's position was not as governess to all the children, as portrayed in the musical, but specifically as governess and teacher for the Captain's second-oldest daughter, also called Maria, who was bedridden with rheumatic fever.

- The Captain didn't run a tight domestic ship. In fact, his seven children were as unruly as most. But he did use a whistle to call them—each kid was trained to respond to a certain pitch.

- Though the von Trapp family did have seven children, the show changed all their names and even their genders. Rupert, the eldest child, responded to the often-asked question, "Which one are you?" with a simple, "I'm Liesl!"

- The family didn't escape by hiking to Switzerland (which is a five-hour drive away). Rather, they pretended to go on one of their frequent mountain hikes. With only the possessions in their backpacks, they "hiked" all the way to the

Mozart Dinner Concert: For those who'd like some classical music but would rather not sit through a concert, Stiftskeller St. Peter (see page 184) offers a traditional candlelit meal with Mozart's greatest hits performed by a string quartet and singers in historic costumes gavotting among the tables. In this elegant Baroque setting, tourists clap between movements and get three courses of food (from Mozart-era recipes) mixed with three 20-minute courses of crowd-pleasing music (€48, Mozart-lovers with this guidebook pay €39 when booking direct, almost nightly at 20:00, dress is "smart casual," call to reserve at 0662/828-695, www.mozartdinnerconcert.com). When they run out of space, they book a second quartet to perform in the adjacent Haydn Zimmer. I find the ambience much nicer in the main Baroque train station (it was at the edge of their estate) and took a train to Italy. The movie scene showing them climbing into Switzerland was actually filmed near Berchtesgaden, Germany...home to Hitler's Eagle's Nest, and certainly not a smart place to flee to.

• The actual von Trapp family house exists...but it's not the one in the film. The mansion in the movie is actually two different buildings—one used for the front, the other for the back. The interiors were all filmed on Hollywood sets.

• For the film, Boris Levin designed a reproduction of the Nonnberg Abbey courtyard so faithful to the original (down to its cobblestones and stained-glass windows) that many still believe the cloister scenes were really shot at the abbey. And no matter what you hear in Salzburg, the graveyard scene (in which the von Trapps hide from the Nazis) was also filmed on the Fox lot.

• In 1956, a German film producer offered Maria $10,000 for the rights to her book. She asked for royalties, too, and a share of the profits. The agent explained that German law forbids film companies from paying royalties to foreigners (Maria had by then become a US citizen). She agreed to the contract and unknowingly signed away all film rights to her story. Only a few weeks later, he offered to pay immediately if she would accept $9,000 in cash. Because it was more money than the family had seen in all of their years of singing, she accepted the deal. Later, she discovered the agent had swindled them—no such law existed.

Rodgers, Hammerstein, and other producers gave the von Trapps a percentage of the royalties, even though they weren't required to—but it was a fraction of what they otherwise would have earned. Maria was not bitter. "The great good the film and the play are doing to individual lives is far beyond money," she said.

Hall—when making the booking, get a promise that that's where you'll be seated.

Sound of Salzburg Dinner Show: The show at the recommended Sternbräu Inn is Broadway in a dirndl with tired food. But it's a good show, and *Sound of Music* fans leave with hands red from clapping. A piano player and a hardworking quartet of singers wearing historical costumes perform an entertaining mix of *S.O.M.* hits and traditional folk songs (€46 for dinner, begins at 19:30). You can also come by at 20:30, pay €32, skip the dinner, and get the show. Those who book direct (not through a hotel) and pay cash get a 10 percent discount with this book (nightly mid-May–mid-Oct, Griesgasse 23, tel. 0662/826-617, www.soundof salzburgshow.com).

Music at Mass: Each Sunday morning, two great churches offer a Mass generally with glorious music. The Salzburg Cathedral is likely your best bet for fine music to worship by (10:00). The Franciscan church (9:00) is enthusiastic about its musical Masses, and St. Peter's Church also has music (10:30). See the Salzburg events guide for details.

Free Brass Band Concert: A traditional brass band plays in the Mirabell Gardens (May–Aug Sun at 10:30 and Wed at 20:30).

Sleeping in Salzburg

Finding a room in Salzburg, even during its music festival (mid-July–Aug), is usually easy. Rates rise significantly (20–30 percent) during the music festival, and sometimes around Easter and Christmas; these higher prices do not appear in the ranges I've listed. Many places charge 10 percent extra for a one-night stay. Remember, to call Salzburg from Germany, dial 00-43- and then the number (minus the initial zero).

In the New Town, North of the River

These listings, clustering around Linzergasse, are in a pleasant neighborhood (with easy parking) a 15-minute walk from the train station (for directions, see "Arrival in Salzburg," earlier) and a 10-minute walk to the old town. If you're coming from the old town, simply cross the main bridge (Staatsbrücke) to the mostly traffic-free Linzergasse. If driving, exit the highway at Salzburg-Nord, follow Vogelweiderstrasse straight to its end, and turn right.

$$$ Altstadthotel Wolf-Dietrich, around the corner from Linzergasse on pedestrians-only Wolf-Dietrich-Strasse, is well-located (with half its rooms overlooking St. Sebastian Cemetery). With 27 tastefully plush rooms, it's the best value I could find for a big, stylish hotel (Sb-€85–105, Db-€140–190, price depends on size, family deals, €20–40 more during festival, complex pricing but readers of this book get a 10 percent discount on prevailing price—insist on this discount deducted from whatever price is offered that day, elevator, pool with loaner swimsuits, sauna, free DVD library, Wolf-Dietrich-Strasse 7, tel. 0662/871-275, fax 0662/871-2759, www.salzburg-hotel.at, office@salzburg-hotel.at). Their annex across the street has 14 equally comfortable rooms (but no elevator, and therefore slightly cheaper prices).

Sleep Code

(€1 = about $1.40, country code: 43, area code: 0662)
S = Single, **D** = Double/Twin, **T** = Triple, **Q** = Quad, **b** = bathroom, **s** = shower only. Unless otherwise noted, credit cards are accepted and breakfast is included. All of these places speak English.

To help you sort easily through these listings, I've divided the rooms into three categories, based on the price for a standard double room with bath:

$$$ Higher Priced—Most rooms €90 or more.
$$ Moderately Priced—Most rooms between €60-90.
$ Lower Priced—Most rooms €60 or less.

$$$ Hotel Trumer Stube, three blocks from the river just off Linzergasse, has 20 clean, cozy rooms and a friendly, can-do owner (Sb-€65, Db-€105, Tb-€128, Qb-€147, about €30 more during music festival, top-floor rooms have lower ceilings and are €7 less expensive, 10 percent discount if you book direct with this book and pay cash—except during festival, non-smoking, elevator, free Wi-Fi except in top-floor rooms, free Internet access, Bergstrasse 6, tel. 0662/874-776, fax 0662/874-326, www.trumer-stube.at, info@trumer-stube.at, pleasant Silvia).

$$$ Hotel Goldene Krone, about five blocks from the river, is plain and basic, with 25 big, quiet, creaky, and well-kept rooms. Stay a while in their pleasant cliffside garden (Sb-€69, Db-€119, Tb-€159, Qb-€189, claim your 10 percent discount off these prices with this book, dim lights, elevator, parking-€12/day, Linzergasse 48, tel. 0662/872-300, fax 0662/8723-0066, www.hotel-goldene krone.com, office@hotel-goldenekrone.com, Claudia and Günther Hausknost). Günther offers tours (€10/person, 2 hours, 5 people minimum) and a "Rick Steves Two Nights in Salzburg" deal, which covers your room, a 24-hour Salzburg Card, a concert in Mirabell Palace, and a tour with Günther (Sb-€171, Db-€304, Tb-€429, Qb-€532).

$$ Institute St. Sebastian is in a somewhat sterile but very clean historic building next to St. Sebastian Cemetery. From October through June, the institute houses female students from various Salzburg colleges, and also rents 40 beds for travelers (men and women). From July through September, the students are gone and they rent all 100 beds (including 20 doubles) to travelers. The building has spacious public areas, a roof garden, a piano that guests are welcome to play, and some of the best rooms and dorm beds in town for the money. The immaculate doubles come with modern baths and head-to-toe twin beds (S-€33.50, Sb-€41.50,

Central Salzburg Hotels

SALZBURG

1. Altstadthotel Wolf-Dietrich
2. Hotel Trumer Stube
3. Hotel Goldene Krone
4. Institute St. Sebastian
5. To Bergland Hotel & Hotel-Pension Jedermann
6. Blaue Gans Arthotel
7. Gasthaus zur Goldenen Ente
8. Hotel Weisse Taube
9. Boutique Hotel am Dom
10. Hotel-Pension Chiemsee
11. Christkönig Pension
12. To Gasthaus Stadtalm
13. To Jugendgästehaus Salzburg
14. To Pension Adlerhof
15. International Youth Hotel
16. Launderettes (2)

D-€53.50, Db-€67, Tb-€81, Qb-€96, €2.50/person extra for one-night stay, includes very basic breakfast, elevator, self-service laundry-€4/load; reception open daily July–Sept 7:30–12:00 & 13:00–21:30, Oct–June 8:00–12:00 & 16:00–21:00; Linzergasse 41, enter through arch at #37, tel. 0662/871-386, fax 0662/8713-8685, www.st-sebastian-salzburg.at, office@st-sebastian-salzburg .at). Students like the €21 bunks in 4- to 10-bed dorms (€2 less if you have sheets, no lockout time, free lockers, free showers). You'll find self-service kitchens on each floor (fridge space is free; request a key). If you need parking, request it well in advance.

Pensions on Rupertgasse: These two hotels are about five blocks farther from the river on Rupertgasse, a breeze for drivers but with more street noise than the places on Linzergasse. They're both modern and well-run—good values if you don't mind being a bit away from the old town. **$$$ Bergland Hotel** is charming and classy, with comfortable neo-rustic rooms. It's a modern building, and therefore spacious and solid (Sb-€65, Db-€95, Tb-€117, Qb-€140, elevator, Internet access, English library, bike rental-€6/day, Rupertgasse 15, tel. 0662/872-318, fax 0662/872-3188, www .berglandhotel.at, kuhn@berglandhotel.at, Kuhn family). The similar, boutique-like **$$$ Hotel-Pension Jedermann,** a few doors down, is tastefully done and comfortable, with an artsy painted-concrete ambience and a backyard garden (Sb-€65–85, Db-€90–130, Tb-€120–160, Qb-€160–200, much more during festival, elevator, Internet access, Rupertgasse 25, tel. 0662/873-2410, fax 0662/873-2419, www.hotel-jedermann.com, office @hotel-jedermann.com, Herr und Frau Gmachl).

In or Above the Old Town

Most of these hotels are near Residenzplatz. While this area is car-restricted, you're allowed to drive your car in to unload, pick up a map and parking instructions, and head for the €14-per-day garage in the mountain.

$$$ Blaue Gans Arthotel is ultra-modern and in the old town, beautifully located at the far end of Getreidegasse. Its public spaces feature contemporary Austrian art, and the 40 sleek, thoughtfully designed rooms are decorated with local materials (Sb-€115–125, standard Db-€135–160, bigger superior Db-€185–195, fancier suites, extra bed-€35–40; prices €20–25 higher per person during festival, around Christmas, and on holiday weekends; elevator, free Internet access and Wi-Fi, Getreidegasse 41, tel. 0662/842-4910, fax 0662/8424-9175, www.blauegans.at, office@blauegans.at).

$$$ Gasthaus zur Goldenen Ente is in a 600-year-old building with medieval stone arches and narrow stairs. Located above a good smoke-free restaurant, it's as central as you can be on a pedestrian street in old Salzburg. The 17 rooms are modern and

SALZBURG

newly renovated, and include classy amenities. While this hotel's advertised rates are too high, travelers with this book get 10 percent off—and prices may dip lower according to demand. Ulrike, Franziska, and Anita run a tight ship for the absentee owners (most of the year: Sb-€85, Db-€140; late July–Aug and Dec: Sb-€95, Db-€160; extra person-€29, firm mattresses, non-smoking, elevator, free Internet access, Goldgasse 10, tel. 0662/845-622, fax 0662/845-6229, www.ente.at, hotel@ente.at).

$$$ Hotel Weisse Taube has 30 comfortable rooms in a quiet dark-wood 14th-century building, well-located about a block off Mozartplatz (Sb-€67–85, Db with shower-€98–138, bigger Db with bath-€119–162, 10 percent discount with this book if you reserve direct and pay cash, elevator, Internet access, tel. 0662/842-404, fax 0662/841-783, Kaigasse 9, www.weissetaube.at, hotel@weissetaube.at).

$$$ Boutique Hotel am Dom is perfectly located—on Goldgasse a few steps from the cathedral—and offers 15 recently updated rooms (twin Db-€90–140, standard Db-€140–220, comfort Db-€150–190, air-con, non-smoking, Wi-Fi, Goldgasse 17, tel. 0662/842-765, fax 0662/8427-6555, www.hotelamdom.at, office @hotelamdom.at).

$$$ Hotel-Pension Chiemsee is a stony dollhouse nestled in a quiet lane just behind the cathedral. Hardworking Frau Höllbacher rents 10 big, beautifully renovated rooms and three suites (Sb-€48–58, Db-€88–98, Tb-€110–120; suite-€110 for 2 people, €28/person extra up to 5; during festival and Dec: Sb-€68, Db-€98–116, Tb-€120–130; these special Rick Steves prices available if you book direct and pay cash, Chiemseegasse 5, tel. 0662/844-208, fax 0662/8442-0870, www.hotel-ami.de/hotel /chiemsee, hotel-chiemsee@aon.at).

$$ Christkönig Pension makes you feel like a guest of the bishop because, in a sense...you are. With 20 rooms in a 14th-century church building just under the castle and behind the cathedral, this is where the bishop's visitors stay. It's a charming, quiet, convenient, and unique way to sleep well and affordably in the old center. Heavenly Frau Anna Huemer will take excellent care of you (S-€35, Ss-€41, Sb-€46, Ds-€68, Db-€80, suite for 2–4 people roughly €45/person, twin beds only, €3/person extra for one-night stays, usually booked up during festival, cash only, Kapitelplatz 2a, tel. 0662/842-627, www.christkoenig-kolleg.at, christkoenig-pension@salzburg.co.at).

Hostels

$ Gasthaus Stadtalm (a.k.a. the *Naturfreundehaus*) is a local version of a mountaineer's hut and a great budget alternative. Snuggled in a forest on the remains of a 15th-century castle wall atop the little mountain overlooking Salzburg, it has magnificent town and mountain views. While the 26 beds are designed-for-backpackers basic, the price and view are the best in town—with the right attitude, it's a fine experience (€18.50/person in 2-, 4-, and 6-bed dorms, same price for room with double bed; includes breakfast, sheets, and shower; lockers, 2 min from top of €2 Mönchsberg elevator, Mönchsberg 19C, tel. & fax 0662/841-729, www.diestadtalm.com—German only, info@diestadtalm.com, Peter). Once you've dropped your bags here, it's a five-minute walk down the cliffside stairs into Toscanini Hof, in the middle of the old town (path always lit).

$ **Jugendgästehaus Salzburg,** just steps from the old town center, is nevertheless removed from the bustle. While its dorm rooms are the standard crammed-with-beds variety—and the hallways will bring back high-school memories—the doubles and family rooms are modern, roomy, and bright, and a recent renovation has made the public spaces quite pleasant (bed in 8-person dorm-€20–22, Db-€65–68, Qs-€98–104, higher prices are for May–Sept, non-members pay €1.50 extra, includes breakfast and sheets, pay Internet access, free Wi-Fi, *The Sound of Music* plays daily; bike rental-€10/day, €6/half-day; free parking, just around the east side of the castle hill at Josef-Preis-Allee 18; from train station take bus #5 or #25 to the Justizgebäude stop, then head left one block along the bushy wall, cross Petersbrunnstrasse, find shady Josefs-Preis-Alle, and walk a few minutes to the end—the hostel is the big orange/green building on the right; tel. 0662/842-670, fax 0662/841-101, www.jfgh.at/salzburg.php, salzburg@jfgh .at). The new hotel at the back of the hostel isn't as cheap, but does offer more standard hotel amenities, such as TVs (Db-€82–96 depending on season, includes breakfast).

For another hostel (on the other side of the river), see "International Youth Hotel," below.

Near the Train Station

$$ **Pension Adlerhof,** a plain and decent old pension, is two blocks in front of the train station (left off Kaiserschutzenstrasse), but a 15-minute walk from the sightseeing action. It has a quirky staff, a boring location, and 30 stodgy-but-spacious rooms (Sb-€49–68, Db-€69–108, Tb-€93–123, Qb-€108–156, price depends on season and size of room, cash only, elevator, free Wi-Fi, limited free parking, Elisabethstrasse 25, tel. 0662/875-236, fax 0662/873-663, www.gosalzburg.com, adlerhof@pension-adlerhof.at).

$ **International Youth Hotel,** a.k.a. the "Yo-Ho," is the most lively, handy, and American of Salzburg's hostels. This easygoing place speaks English first; has cheap meals, 180 beds, lockers, tour discounts, and no curfew; plays *The Sound of Music* free daily at 10:30;

runs a lively bar; and welcomes anyone of any age. The noisy atmosphere and lack of a curfew can make it hard to sleep (€18–19 in 4- to 8-bed dorms, €21–22 in dorms with bathrooms, D-€44, Ds-€56, Q-€76, Qs-€88, includes sheets, cheap breakfast, pay Internet access and Wi-Fi, laundry-€4 wash and dry, 6 blocks from station toward Linzergasse and 6 blocks from river at Paracelsusstrasse 9, tel. 0662/879-649, fax 0662/878-810, www.yoho.at, office@yoho.at).

Four-Star Hotels in Residential Neighborhoods away from the Center

If you want plush furnishings, spacious public spaces, generous balconies, gardens, and free parking, consider the following places. These two modern hotels in nondescript residential neighborhoods are a fine value if you don't mind the 15-minute walk from the old town. While not ideal for train travelers, drivers in need of no-stress comfort for a home base should consider these (see map on page 171).

$$$ Hotel Rosenvilla, close to the river, offers 14 rooms with bright furnishings, surrounded by a leafy garden (Sb-€79, Db-€128, bigger Db-€142, Db suite-€188, at least €30 more during festival, free Wi-Fi, Höfelgasse 4, tel. 0662/621-765, fax 0662/625-2308, www.rosenvilla.com, hotel@rosenvilla.com).

$$$ Haus Arenberg, higher up opposite the old town, rents 17 big breezy rooms—most with generous balconies—in a quiet garden setting (Sb-€79–88, Db-€125–142, Tb-€148–158, Qb-€158–165, €25 more during music festival, Blumensteinstrasse 8, tel. 0662/640-097, fax 0662/640-0973, www.arenberg-salzburg.at, info@arenberg-salzburg.at, family Leobacher).

Private Rooms

These are generally roomy and comfortable, and come with a good breakfast, easy parking, and tourist information. Off-season, competition softens prices. While they are a bus ride from town, with a €4.20 transit day pass *(Tageskarte)* and the frequent service, this shouldn't keep you away (see map page 171). In fact, most homeowners will happily pick you up at the train station if you simply telephone them and ask. Most will also do laundry for a small fee for those staying at least two nights. I've listed prices for two nights or more—if staying only one night, expect a 10 percent surcharge. Most push tours and concerts to make money on the side. As they are earning a commission, if you go through them, you'll probably lose the discount I've negotiated for my readers who go direct.

Beyond the Train Station

$ **Brigitte Lenglachner** rents eight basic, well-cared-for rooms in her home in a quiet suburban-feeling neighborhood that's a 25-minute walk, 10-minute bike ride, or easy bus ride away from the center. Frau Lenglachner serves breakfast in the garden (in good weather) and happily provides plenty of local information and advice (S-€25, D-€40, Db-€48, T-€53, Qb-€96, 5b-€113; apartment with kitchen-€56 for Db, €90 for Tb, €110 for Qb; easy and free parking, Scheibenweg 8, tel. & fax 0662/438-044, bedand breakfast4u@yahoo.de). It's a 10-minute walk from the station: Head for the river, cross the pedestrian Pioneer Bridge (Pioniersteg), turn right, and walk along the river to the third street (Scheibenweg). Turn left, and it's halfway down on the right.

On Moosstrasse

The busy street called Moosstrasse, which runs southwest of Mönchsberg (behind the mountain and away from the old town center), is lined with farmhouses offering rooms. To locate these places, see the map on page 171. Handy bus #21 connects Moosstrasse to the center frequently (Mon–Fri 4/hr until 19:00, Sat 4/hr until 17:00, evenings and Sun 2/hr, 20 min). To get to these pensions from the train station, take bus #1, #5, #6, or #25 to Makartplatz, where you'll change to #21. If you're coming from the old town, catch bus #21 from Hanuschplatz, just downstream of the Staatsbrücke bridge near the *Tabak* kiosk. Buy a €1.80 *Einzelkarte–Kernzone* ticket (for one trip) or a €4.20 *Tageskarte* (day pass, good for 24 hours) from the streetside machine and punch it when you board the bus. The bus stop you use for each place is included in the following listings. If you're driving from the center, go through the tunnel, continue straight on Neutorstrasse, and take the fourth left onto Moosstrasse. Drivers exit the autobahn at *Süd* and then head in the direction of *Grodig*.

$$ **Pension Bloberger Hof,** while more a hotel than a pension, is comfortable and friendly, with a peaceful, rural location and 20 farmer-plush, good-value rooms. It's the farthest out, but reached by the same bus #21 from the center. Inge and her daughter Sylvia offer a 10 percent discount to those who have this book, reserve direct, and pay cash (Sb-€50–60, Db-€70, big new Db with balcony-€90, Db suite-€120, extra bed-€20, family apartment with kitchen, non-smoking, free Internet access and Wi-Fi, restaurant for guests, free loaner bikes, free station pick-up if staying 3 nights, Hammerauer Strasse 4, bus stop: Hammerauer Strasse, tel. 0662/830-227, fax 0662/827-061, www.blobergerhof .at, office@blobergerhof.at).

$ **Frau Ballwein** offers four cozy, charming, and fresh rooms in two buildings, some with intoxicating view balconies (Sb-€35–37,

Db-€55–60, Tb-€78, Qb-€80–85, prices depend on season, family deals, cash only, farm-fresh breakfasts amid her hanging teapot collection, non-smoking, small pool, 2 free loaner bikes, free parking, Moosstrasse 69-A, bus stop: Gsengerweg, tel. & fax 0662/824-029, www.haus-ballwein.at, haus.ballwein@gmx.net).

$ Helga Bankhammer rents four nondescript rooms in a farmhouse, with a real dairy farm out back (D-€46, Db-€52, no surcharge for one-night stays, family deals, non-smoking, laundry about €6/load, Moosstrasse 77, bus stop: Marienbad, tel. & fax 0662/830-067, www.privatzimmer.at/helga.bankhammer, bankhammer@aon.at).

$ Haus Reichl, with three good rooms at the end of a long lane, feels the most remote. Franziska offers free loaner bikes for guests (20-min pedal to the center) and bakes fresh cakes most days (Db-€60, Tb-€75, Qb-€92–97, cash preferred, doubles and triples have balcony and view, all have tea/coffee in room, non-smoking, between Ballwein and Bankhammer B&Bs, 200 yards down Reiterweg to #52, bus stop: Gsengerweg, tel. & fax 0662/826-248, www.privatzimmer.at/haus-reichl, haus.reichl@telering.at).

Eating in Salzburg

In the Old Town

Salzburg boasts many inexpensive, fun, and atmospheric eateries. I'm a sucker for big cellars with their smoky, Old World atmosphere, heavy medieval arches, time-darkened paintings, antlers, hearty meals, and plump patrons. Most of these restaurants are centrally located in the old town, famous with visitors but also enjoyed by the locals.

Gasthaus zum Wilden Mann is *the* place if the weather's bad and you're in the mood for *Hofbräu* atmosphere and a hearty, cheap meal at a shared table in one small, smoky, well-antlered room. Notice the 1899 flood photo on the wall. For a quick lunch, get the *Bauernschmaus,* a mountain of dumplings, kraut, and peasant's meats (€10.50). Owner Robert—who runs the restaurant with Schwarzenegger-like energy—enjoys fostering a convivial ambience (you'll share tables with strangers) and serving fresh traditional cuisine at great prices. I simply love this place (€7–12 daily specials, Mon–Sat 11:00–21:00, closed Sun, 2 min from Mozart's Birthplace, enter from Getreidegasse 22 or Griesgasse 17, tel. 0662/841-787).

Stiftskeller St. Peter has been in business for more than 1,000 years—it was mentioned in the biography of Charlemagne. It's classy and central as can be, serving uninspired traditional Austrian cuisine (€10–25 meals, daily 11:30–22:30, indoor/outdoor seating, next to St. Peter's Church at foot of Mönchsberg, restaurant tel.

Central Salzburg Restaurants

SALZBURG

1. Gasthaus zum Wilden Mann
2. Stiftskeller St. Peter Rest.
3. St. Paul's Stub'n Beer Garden
4. Fisch Krieg Rest.
5. Sternbräu Inn
6. Café Tomaselli
7. Saran Essbar
8. Bar Club Café Republic
9. Afro Café
10. Demel

11. To Gasthaus Stadtalm
12. Toscana Cafeteria Mensa
13. Balkan Grill
14. To Augustiner Bräustübl
15. Spicy Spices
16. To Biergarten die Weisse
17. Café Bazar
18. Steingasse Pub Crawl
19. Sporer Schnapps Shop
20. Stein Terrasse

0662/841-268). They host the Mozart Dinner Concert described on page 174 (€48, nearly nightly at 20:00, call 0662/828-6950 to reserve, ask about a discount if you book direct with this guidebook). Through the centuries, they've learned to charge for each piece of bread and don't serve free tap water.

St. Paul's Stub'n Beer Garden is tucked secretly away under the castle with a decidedly untouristy atmosphere. The food is better than a beer hall, and a young, Bohemian-chic clientele fills its two smoky troll-like rooms and its idyllic tree-shaded garden. *Kasnock'n* is a tasty mountaineers' pasta with cheese served in an iron pan with a side salad for €9—it's enough for two (€6–12 daily specials, €7–15 plates, Mon–Sat 17:00–22:30, open later for drinks only, closed Sun, Herrengasse 16, tel. 0662/843-220).

Fisch Krieg Restaurant, on the river where the fishermen used to sell their catch, is a great value. They serve fast, fresh, and inexpensive fish in a casual dining room—where trees grow through the ceiling—as well as great riverside seating (€2 fish-wiches to go, self-serve €7 meals, salad bar, Mon–Fri 8:30–18:30, Sat 8:30–13:00 except July–Aug until 14:00, closed Sun, Hanuschplatz 4, tel. 0662/843-732).

Sternbräu Inn, a sloppy, touristy Austrian food circus, is a sprawling complex of popular eateries (traditional, Italian, self-serve, and vegetarian) in a cheery garden setting. Explore both courtyards before choosing a seat (Bürgerstube is classic, most restaurants open daily 9:00–24:00, enter from Getreidegasse 34, tel. 0662/842-140). One fancy, air-conditioned room hosts the Sound of Salzburg dinner show (described on page 175).

Café Tomaselli (with its Kiosk annex across the way) has long been Salzburg's top place to see and be seen. While overpriced and often overcrowded, it is good for lingering and people-watching. Tomaselli serves light meals and lots of drinks, keeps long hours daily, and has fine seating on the square, a view terrace upstairs, and indoor tables. Despite its fancy inlaid wood paneling, 19th-century portraits, and chandeliers, it's surprisingly low-key (€3–7 entrées, daily 7:00–21:00, until 24:00 during music festival, Alter Markt 9, tel. 0662/844-488).

Saran Essbar is the product of hardworking Mr. Saran (from the Punjab), who cooks and serves with his heart. This delightful little eatery casts a rich orange glow under medieval vaults. Its fun menu is small (Mr. Saran is committed to both freshness and value), mixing Austrian (great schnitzel and strudel), Italian, Asian vegetarian, and salads (€9–12 meals, daily 11:00–22:00, often open later, a block off Mozartplatz at Judengasse 10, tel. 0662/846-628).

Bar Club Café Republic, a hip hangout for local young people near the end of Getreidegasse, feels like a theater lobby during intermission. It serves good food with smoky indoor and outdoor seating. It's ideal if you want something mod, untouristy, and un-wursty (trendy breakfasts 8:00–18:00, Asian and international menu, €7–12 plates, lots of hard drinks, daily until late, music with a DJ Fri and Sat from 23:00, salsa music on Tue night, no cover, Anton Neumayr Platz 2, tel. 0662/841-613).

Afro Cafe, between Getreidegasse and the Mönchsberg lift, is understandably popular with its student clientele. They serve tea, coffee, cocktails, and tasty food with a dose of '70s funk and a healthy sense of humor. The menu includes pan-African specialties—try the spicy chicken couscous—as well as standard soups and salads (€9–13 main dishes, Mon–Fri 10:00–24:00, Sat 9:00–24:00, closed Sun, between Getreidegasse and cliff face at Bürgerspitalplatz 5, tel. 0662/844-888).

Demel, the only outpost of Vienna's famed chocolatier, is a wonderland of desserts that are as beautiful as they are delectable. Sink into the pink couches upstairs, or have them box up a treat for later (daily 9:00–19:00, near TI and cathedral at Mozartplatz 2, tel. 0662/840-358).

On the Cliffs Above the Old Town: **Gasthaus Stadtalm,** Salzburg's mountaineers' hut, sits high above the old town on the edge of the cliff with cheap prices, good food, and great views. If hiking across Mönchsberg, make this your goal (traditional food, salads, cliffside garden seating or cozy-mountain-hut indoor seating—one indoor view table is booked for a decade of New Year's celebrations, daily 10:00–19:00, July–Aug until 24:00, 2 min from top of €3 round-trip Mönchsberg elevator, also reachable by stairs from Toscanini Hof, Mönchsberg 19C, tel. 0662/841-729, Peter). For location, see map on page 185.

Eating Cheaply in the Old Town

Toscana Cafeteria Mensa is the students' lunch canteen, fast and cheap—with indoor seating and a great courtyard for sitting outside with students and teachers instead of tourists. They serve a

daily soup-and-main course special for €5 (Mon–Fri 9:00–15:00, hot meals served 11:00–13:30 only, closed Sat–Sun, behind the Residenz, in the courtyard opposite Sigmund-Haffnergasse 16).

Sausage stands *(Würstelstände)* serve the town's favorite "fast food." The best stands (like those on Universitätsplatz) use the same boiling water all day, which gives the weenies more flavor. The Salzburgers' favorite spicy sausage is sold at the 60-year-old **Balkan Grill,** run by chatty Frau Ebner (€2.80; survey the five spicy options—described in English—and choose a number; take-away only, steady and sturdy local crowd, Mon–Fri 11:00–19:00, Feb–Dec also Sat 11:00–17:00, May–Dec also Sun 16:00–20:00, hours vary with demand, hiding down the tunnel at Getreidegasse 33 across from Eisgrotte).

Picnickers will appreciate the bustling morning **produce market** (daily except Sun) on Universitätsplatz, behind Mozart's Birthplace.

Away from the Center

Augustiner Bräustübl, a huge 1,000-seat beer garden within a monk-run brewery in the Kloster Mülln, is rustic and raw. On busy nights, it's like a Munich beer hall with no music but the volume turned up. When it's cool outside, you'll enjoy a historic setting inside beer-sloshed and smoke-stained halls. On balmy evenings, it's like a Renoir paint-ing—but with beer breath—under chestnut trees. Local students mix with tourists eating hearty

slabs of schnitzel with their fingers or cold meals from the self-serve picnic counter, while children frolic on the playground kegs. For your beer: Pick up a half-liter or full-liter mug, pay the lady (*schank* means self-serve price, *bedienung* is the price with waiter service), wash your mug, give Mr. Keg your receipt and empty mug, and you will be made happy. Waiters only bring beer; they don't bring food—instead, go up the stairs, survey the hallway of deli counters, and assemble your own meal (or, as long as you buy a drink, you can bring in a picnic). Classic pretzels from the bakery and spiraled, salty radishes make great beer even better. For dessert—after a visit to the strudel kiosk—enjoy the incom-parable floodlit view of old Salzburg from the nearby Müllnersteg pedestrian bridge and a riverside stroll home (open daily 15:00–23:00, closed for lunch, Augustinergasse 4, tel. 0662/431-246). It's about a 15-minute walk along the river (with the river on your right) from the Staatsbrücke bridge. After passing the pedestrian Müllnersteg bridge, just after Café am Kai, follow the stairs up to a busy street, and cross it. From here, either continue up more stairs into the trees and around the small church (for a scenic approach to the monastery), or stick to the sidewalk as it curves around to Augustinergasse. Either way, your goal is the huge yel-low building. Don't be fooled by second-rate gardens serving the same beer nearby.

SALZBURG

North of the River, near Recommended Linzergasse Hotels

Spicy Spices is a trippy vegetarian-Indian restaurant where Suresh Syad serves tasty take-out curry and rice, samosas, organic salads, vegan soups, and fresh juices (€6.50 specials, Mon–Fri 10:30–21:30, Sat–Sun 12:00–21:30, Wolf-Dietrich-Strasse 1, tel. 0662/870-712).

Biergarten die Weisse, close to the hotels on Rupertgasse and away from the tourists, is a longtime hit with the natives. If a beer hall can be happening, this one—modern yet with antlers—is it. Their famously good beer is made right there; favorites include their fizzy wheat beer *(Weisse)* and their seasonal beers (on request). Enjoy the beer with their good, cheap traditional food in the great garden seating, or in the wide variety of indoor rooms—sports bar, young and noisy, or older and more elegant (daily specials, Mon–Sat 10:00–24:00, closed Sun, Rupertgasse 10, east of Bayerhamerstrasse, tel. 0662/872-246).

Café Bazar, overlooking the river between Mirabell Gardens and the Staatsbrücke bridge, is as close as you'll get to a Vienna coffee house in Salzburg. It's *the* venerable spot for a classy drink with an old-town-and-castle view (light meals, Mon–Sat 7:30–23:00, Sun 9:00–18:00, Schwarzstrasse 3, tel. 0662/874-278).

Steingasse Pub Crawl

For a fun post-concert activity, crawl through medieval Steingasse's trendy pubs (all open until the wee hours). This is a local and hip scene, but accessible to older tourists: dark bars filled with well-dressed Salzburgers lazily smoking cigarettes and talking philosophy as avant-garde Euro-pop throbs on the soundtrack. Most of the pubs are in cellar-like caves...extremely atmospheric. (For more on Steingasse, see page 168.) These four pubs are all within about 100 yards of each other. Start at the Linzergasse end of Steingasse.

Pepe Cocktail Bar, with Mexican decor and Latin music, serves Mexican snacks *con* cocktails (nightly 19:00–3:00 in the morning, live DJs Fri–Sat from 19:00, Steingasse 3, tel. 0662/873-662).

Shrimps, next door and less claustrophobic, is more a restaurant than a bar, serving creative international dishes (spicy shrimp sandwiches and salads, Tue–Sun 18:00–24:00, closed Mon, Steingasse 5, tel. 0662/874-484).

Saiten Sprung wins the "Best Atmosphere" award. The door is kept closed to keep out the crude and rowdy. Ring the bell and enter its hellish interior—lots of stone and red decor, with mountains of melted wax beneath age-old candlesticks and a classic soul music ambience. Stelios, who speaks English with Greek charm, serves cocktails, fine wine, and wine-friendly Italian antipasti (nightly 21:00–4:00 in the morning, Steingasse 11, tel. 0662/881-377).

Fridrich, a tiny place next door with lots of mirrors and a silver ceiling fan, specializes in wine. Bernd Fridrich is famous for his martinis, and passionate about Austrian wines and food (€5–12 small entrées, nightly from 18:00 in summer or 17:00 in winter, Steingasse 15, tel. 0662/876-218).

Salzburg Connections

By train, Salzburg is the first stop over the German–Austrian border. This means that if Salzburg is your only stop in Austria, and you're using a railpass that covers Germany (including the Bayern-Ticket) but not Austria, you don't have to pay extra or add Austria to your pass to get here.

From Salzburg by Train to: Berchtesgaden (hourly, 45–60 min; bus #840 is easier—hourly, 45 min, buses leave across from Salzburg train station and also stop in Mirabellplatz and near Mozartplatz), **Reutte,** Austria (hourly, 5 hrs, change either in Munich and Kempten, or in Innsbruck and Garmisch), **Munich** (2/hr, 1.5–2 hrs), **Nürnberg** (hourly with change in Munich, 3 hrs), **Innsbruck,** Austria (direct every 2 hrs, 2 hrs), **Vienna,** Austria (2/hr, 2.5–3 hrs). Train info: tel. 051-717 (to get an operator, dial 2, then 2).

Berchtesgaden

This alpine ski town in the region of the same name (just across the border in Germany's southeastern tip, 12 miles south of Salzburg) is famous for its fjord-like lake and its mountaintop Nazi retreat. Long before its association with Hitler, it was one of the classic Romantic corners of Germany. In fact, Hitler's propagandists capitalized on the Führer's love of this region to establish the notion that the native Austrian was truly German at heart.

Getting There

From Salzburg, bus #840 is more scenic and direct than the train (bus runs hourly, 45 min, €8.50 round-trip, bus station across street from Salzburg's train station, bus also stops on Mirabellplatz, and in Salzburg's old town—on Rudolfskai, near Mozartplatz). You can also visit Berchtesgaden from Munich (at least hourly, 2.5–3 hrs, train to Salzburg or Freilassing, then train or—more frequently—bus to Berchtesgaden).

Planning Your Time

Berchtesgaden's attractions include the **town** (a touristy mess); **salt mines** (similar to tours across the border in Austria); the romantic, pristine lake called **Königsee** (extremely popular with less-adventurous Germans); and Obersalzberg with **Hitler's Eagle's Nest** (fascinating if you're into Nazi history, and stunningly scenic from the top).

Orientation to Berchtesgaden

Berchtesgaden can be inundated with Germans on vacation. During peak season, you may find yourself in a traffic jam of tourists desperately trying to turn their money into fun. Still, its sights are impressive, connections from Salzburg (and Munich) are excellent, and its various attractions are quite handy by local bus from the train station. Remember that while Salzburg is in Austria, Berchtesgaden is in Germany.

Tourist Information: The TI is across from the train station, in the yellow building with green shutters (Mon–Fri 9:00–18:00, Sat 9:00–17:00, Sun 9:00–15:00, German tel. 08652/656-500, from Austria call 00-49-8652-656-500, www.berchtesgadener -land.com).

Getting Around: From the train station, bus #840 goes to the salt mines (a 20-min walk otherwise), bus #838 goes to the Nazi Documentation Center (roughly hourly, Obersalzberg stop, plus a 5-min walk), and bus #841 goes to the Königsee (roughly hourly).

Tours in Berchtesgaden

Eagle's Nest Historical Tours—For 20 years, David and Christine Harper—who rightly consider this visit more an educational opportunity than simple sightseeing—have organized thoughtful tours of the Hitler-related sites of Berchtesgaden. Their bus tours, always led by native English speakers, depart from the TI opposite the train station (€48, €1 discount with this book, English only, daily at 13:15 mid-May–Oct, 4 hours, 25 people maximum, reservation required, German tel. 08652/64971, from Austria call 00-49-8652-64971, www.eagles -nest-tours.com). While the price is €48, your actual cost for the guiding is only about €23, as the tour includes the (otherwise obligatory) bus connections and admissions. They also arrange private guides and *Sound of Music* excursions to Salzburg (see their website for details).

Sights in Berchtesgaden

▲Salt Mines

At the Berchtesgaden salt mines, you put on traditional miners' outfits, get on funny little trains, and zip deep into the mountain. For two hours, you'll cruise subterranean lakes; slide speedily down two long, slick wooden banisters; and learn how they mined salt so long ago. Call for crowd-avoidance advice. When the weather gets bad, this place is mobbed. You can buy a ticket early and browse through the town until your appointed tour time. Tours are in German, while English-speakers get audioguides (€14, daily May–Oct 9:00–17:00, Nov–April 11:30–15:00, German tel. 08652/60020, from Austria tel. 00-49-8652-60020, www.salz zeitreise.de).

▲Königsee

The idyllic Königsee stretches like a fjord through pristine mountain scenery from Berchtesgaden to the dramatically situated Church of St. Bartholomew, and beyond. Most visitors simply glide scenically for 35 minutes on the silent, electronically propelled boat to the church, enjoy that peaceful setting, then glide back. Boats, going at a sedate Bavarian speed and filled with Germans chuckling at the captain's commentary, leave with demand—usually three per hour (€12 round-trip, bus #841 runs about hourly from train station to boat dock, parking-€3). At a rock cliff midway through the journey, your captain stops, and the first mate pulls out a trumpet to demonstrate the fine echo.

The remote red-onion-domed **Church of St. Bartholomew** (once home of a monastery, then a hunting lodge of the Bavarian royal family) is surrounded by a fine beer garden, rustic fishermen's pub, and inviting lakeside trails. The family next to St. Bartholomew's lives in the middle of this national park and has a license to fish—so very fresh trout is the lunchtime favorite.

▲▲▲Obersalzberg and Hitler's Eagle's Nest (Kehlsteinhaus)

Early in his career as a wannabe tyrant, Adolf Hitler was inspired by this dramatic corner of Bavaria, so steeped in legend and close to the soul of the German people. This place, partly Austrian and partly Bavarian, held a special appeal to the Austrian-German Hitler. In the 1920s, just out of prison, he checked into an alpine hotel here to finish up work on his memoir and Nazi primer, *Mein Kampf.* Because it was here that he claimed to be inspired and laid out his vision, some call Obersalzberg the "cradle of the Third Reich."

In the 1930s, as the German Führer, Hitler chose this place for his mountain retreat (and later, had it prepared for his last stand). His handlers crafted Hitler's image here—surrounded by nature, gently receiving alpine flowers from adoring little children, lounging around with farmers in lederhosen...no modern arms industry, no big-time industrialists, no ugly extermination camps. In reality, rather than an alpine chalet, it was a huge compound of 80 buildings—closed to the public after 1936—where the major decisions leading up to World War II were hatched. It was here that Hitler hosted world leaders, wowing them with the aesthetics and engineering of his mountain palace, the adoration of his people...and National Socialism.

Orientation: Your visit has three parts—the Obersalzberg complex and its small, modern **Nazi Documentation Center museum** (a short bus ride from Berchtesgaden, with free parking; also the terminus for the shuttle bus providing the only access to the Eagle's Nest high above); the vast and tourable remains of the **bunker system** (below the museum and included in that ticket); and the actual **Eagle's Nest** (a small yet mighty stone chalet capping the mountain high above).

Between 1945 and 1952, almost everything was destroyed by the victorious Allies (wanting to leave nothing as a magnet for future neo-Nazi pilgrims). If looking for pre-1945 artifacts, you'll only see this: the foundations of the Documentation Center (now mostly a modern building); the stripped-bare yet still evocative bunkers under it; the dramatic road to the Eagle's Nest; the stonework, elevator, and fireplace of the Eagle's Nest itself; and a very

few papers and memorabilia in glass cases in the Documentation Center.

Nazi Documentation Center: This exhibit is built upon the remains of what was the second seat of Nazi administration. It's small—three floors of exhibits— with almost no actual artifacts, but evocative for the setting. This center, with only German descriptions (rent the €2 English audioguide), is designed primarily for Germans to learn and understand their recent history. Only since the late 1990s has interest in Nazi history been considered healthy rather than taboo. Non-Germans, too, can learn from a thoughtful visit (€3; April–Oct daily 9:00–17:00; Nov–March Tue–Sun 10:00–15:00, closed Mon; last entry one hour before closing, allow 1.5 hrs for visit, German tel. 08652/947-960, from Austria tel. 00-49-8652-947-960, www.obersalzberg.de). Buses depart from here to the Eagle's Nest.

Bunkers: From the Documentation Center, stairs lead into a complex and vast bunker system (same ticket and hours as Documentation Center). Construction began in 1943, after the Battle of Stalingrad ended the Nazi aura of invincibility. This is an incredibly engineered underground town with meeting rooms, offices, archives for the government, and lavish living quarters for Hitler—all connected by four miles of tunnels cut by slave labor through solid rock. It was stripped bare after the war. Today, you can wander among the concrete and marvel at megalomania gone mad.

Eagle's Nest: Many call the entire area "Hitler's Eagle's Nest," but that name actually belongs only to the mountaintop chalet, given to the Führer for his 50th birthday in 1939. While a fortune was spent to build this perch, Hitler made only 14 official visits. Today, the chalet is basically a restaurant with a scenic terrace 100 yards below the summit of a mountain. The views are magnificent. From the

bus stop, a finely crafted tunnel (which will have you humming the *Get Smart* TV theme song) leads to a polished brass elevator—one of the rare original elements of the complex. Wander into the fancy back dining room (the best-preserved from Hitler's time) where you can see the once-sleek marble fireplace chipped up by souvenir-seeking troops in 1945.

The site is open to visitors from mid-May through October (in snowy conditions, however, the shuttle bus may stop running). Catch the bus at the parking lot at the Documentation Center. It costs €15 for the round-trip bus ride up the private road and the lift to the top (a 2,000-foot altitude gain, leaves twice hourly).

BADEN-BADEN and the BLACK FOREST

Baden-Baden • Freiburg • Staufen • Best of the Black Forest

Combine Edenism and hedonism as you explore this most romantic of German regions and dip into its mineral spas. The Black Forest ("Schwarzwald" in German) is a range of hills stretching along the French border 100 miles from Switzerland north to Karlsruhe. Its highest peak is the 4,900-foot Feldberg. Because its thick forests allowed little light in, people called it black.

Until the last century, the Schwarzwald was cut off from the German mainstream. The poor farmland drove medieval locals to become foresters, glassblowers, and clockmakers. Strong traditions continue to be woven through the thick dialects and thatched roofs. On any Sunday, you'll find Germans in traditional costumes coloring the Black Forest on *Volksmärsche* (group hikes—open to anyone).

Popular with German holiday-goers and those looking for some serious R&R, the Black Forest offers clean air, cuckoo clocks, cheery villages, and countless hiking possibilities. This is where Germans come to recuperate from their hectic workaday lives, as well as from medical ailments—often compliments of Germany's generous public health system. Key words you'll see everywhere are *Bad* (or *Baden*), meaning "bath"; and *Kur*, loosely "cure." Either term is synonymous with "spa," and directs you to a place to relax, soak, and recover. The region is also known for its favorite dessert, *Schwarzwälder Kirschtorte*—Black Forest cherry cake, a mouthwatering concoction with alternating layers of schnapps-soaked chocolate cake, cherries, and whipped cream.

The Black Forest's two major (and very different) towns are Baden-Baden in the north and Freiburg in the south. Their proximity to France lends both cities a sunny elegance. Baden-Baden is Germany's grandest 19th-century spa resort. Stroll through its

The Black Forest

elegant streets and casino. Soak in its famous baths. Freiburg is the Black Forest's de facto capital and main university town. For a small-town experience, hang your hat in cozy Staufen.

A pair of worthwhile museums in the area shows off two different sides of the local culture—the Vogtsbauernhof Black Forest Open-Air Museum near Gutach, and the German Clock Museum in Furtwangen. You'll also find plenty of opportunity for lazy drives and hikes. The area's two biggest tourist traps are the tiny Titisee (a lake not quite as big as its parking lot) and Triberg, a small town filled with cuckoo-clock shops and a sprinkling of worthwhile attractions. In spite of the crowds, the drives are scenic, the hiking is *wunderbar,* and the attractions listed in this chapter are worth a visit.

Planning Your Time

By **train,** Freiburg and Baden-Baden are easy, as is a short foray into the forest from either. Save a day and two nights for Baden-Baden. Tour Freiburg by day, but consider sleeping in charming and overlooked Staufen.

With more time and a **car,** do the whole cuckoo thing: two nights and a relaxing day in Baden-Baden, a busy day doing the small-town forest medley south (with stops at the Vogtsbauernhof Black Forest Open-Air Museum and Furtwangen's German Clock Museum), a quick visit to Freiburg, and a night in Staufen.

Baden-Baden

Of all the high-class resort towns I've seen, Baden-Baden is the easiest to enjoy in jeans with a picnic. The town makes a great first stop in Germany, especially for honeymooners (1.5 hours from Frankfurt's airport, direct trains every 2 hours).

Baden-Baden was the playground of Europe's high-rolling elite 150 years ago. Royalty and aristocracy would come from all corners to take the *Kur*—a soak in the (supposedly) curative mineral waters—and enjoy the world's top casino. Wrought-iron balconies on handsome 19th-century apartment buildings give Baden-Baden an elegant, almost Parisian feel.

The town remains popular today. How popular? Hoteliers in typical convention towns expect that 85 percent of their guests will need single rooms and 15 percent will need doubles. As spouses insist on coming to conventions held in Baden-Baden, hoteliers flip-flop those figures, anticipating that 85 percent of the demand will be for doubles.

Along with conventioneers, this lush resort town attracts a middle-class crowd consisting of tourists in search of a slower pulse, and Germans enjoying the fruits of their generous health-care system.

Orientation to Baden-Baden

(area code: 07221)

Baden-Baden, with 50,000 residents, is made for strolling with a poodle. Except for the train station and a few accommodations, everything that matters is clustered within a 10-minute walk

Baden-Baden

TO OOS, TRAIN STATION, AIRPORT & ③

TO OLD CASTLE

ZÄHRINGER-STR.

LEOPOLD-STR.

LANGE STR.

NEW CASTLE (NEUES SCHLOSS)

ROMAN-IRISH BATH

ALLEY OF SIGHS

ROTENBACHTAL-STRASSE

HINDENBURG-PLATZ

POST

SCHLOSS STR.

MARKT-PLATZ

SEUFZER-ALLE

TRINK-HALLE

LIB.

CITY CENTER

SOPHIENSTRASSE

SCHEIBENSTR.

BATHS OF CARACALLA

CASINO & KURHAUS

LEOPOLDS-PLATZ

SEE DETAIL MAP

MICHAELSTUNNEL

CONCERT

AUGUSTAPLATZ

¼ MILE

400 METERS

CITY MUSEUM

LICHTENTALER

BERTHOLD-PLATZ

BERT. STR.

RUSSIAN CHURCH

STR.

ROSE GARDEN

MAXIMILIAN STRASSE

N

T E N T A L E R   A L L E E

OOSBACH

RIVER

②

❶ Hotel Schweizer Hof
❷ Hotel-Restaurant Deutscher Kaiser
❸ To Werner Dietz Hostel

LICHTENTALER ABBEY

DCH

between the baths and the casino.

Although you'll barely notice if you just stick around the center, Baden-Baden is actually a long, skinny town, strung over several miles along the narrow valley of the Oosbach River (conveniently accessed by bus #201—see "Getting Around Baden-Baden," later). The train station is at the lower (northern) end of the valley, in a suburb called Baden-Oos, three miles from downtown; the Lichtentaler Abbey marks the upper end. The casino and town center are about halfway between, at the point where a small side valley joins the Oosbach. The church, castle, baths, and oldest sections of town are a few blocks uphill on the north slope of this side valley.

Tourist Information

Baden-Baden's main TI is in the ornate Trinkhalle building. The TI has enough recommended walks and organized excursions to keep the most energetic vacationer happy. Pick up the free monthly events program, *Baden-Baden Aktuell*, which includes a good fine-print fold-out map. If you're headed into the countryside, consider two other maps: the accessible cartoon-style €1 *Outline Map*, which helps you get your bearings for the region; and the €1.50 *Panoramaweg* map, which has better details for hikers (but is in German only). They also sell a €6 Black Forest guidebook (Mon–Sat 10:00–17:00, Sun 14:00–17:00, WC-€0.50, tel. 07221/275-200, www.baden-baden.com).

The main TI shares space with a genteel-feeling café and an agency that sells tickets to performances in town (theater, opera, orchestra, and musicals; Tue–Sat 10:00–18:00, Sun 14:00–17:00, closed Mon). Another TI is at the B-500 autobahn exit (Mon–Sat 9:00–18:00, Sun 9:00–13:00, Schwarzwaldstrasse 52).

Arrival in Baden-Baden

By Train: Walk out of the train station (lockers at platform 1, €1.50–3) and catch bus #201 in front of the kiosks on your right (€2.10 single ticket; see "Getting Around Baden-Baden," later). Get off in about 15 minutes at the 11th stop, Leopoldsplatz, usually also announced as *Stadtmitte* (town center). Allow about €16 for a taxi from the train station to the center.

By Car: Because most traffic goes underneath Baden-Baden (through long underground tunnels), finding your way to your hotel can be counterintuitive. Most hotels I recommend are in the town center; to reach them, first follow the blue *Therme* signs to the baths neighborhood, from which individual hotels are well-signed in green. Ask your hotel for parking tips (you'll likely wind up at one of the big garages in the town center). For outlying accommodations, I've listed specific driving directions (see each listing under "Sleeping in Baden-Baden," later).

By Plane: Baden-Baden's airport, called Baden Airpark, is served by several budget airlines (tel. 07229/662-000, www.baden airpark.de). Bus #205 connects the airport with Baden-Baden's city center (Mon–Fri hourly 6:30–20:30, less frequent on weekends, 45 min, tel. 07221/277-650).

Helpful Hints

Shopping: The big **Wagener Galerie** shopping mall at Lange Strasse 44 has just about everything, including a modern supermarket on the top floor (Mon–Sat 9:00–19:00, closed Sun, winner of a "Germany's best" award) and a post office on the ground floor (Mon–Fri 9:00–19:00, Sat 9:00–14:00, closed Sun).

Horse Races: Book well in advance if you'll be visiting Baden-Baden during its horse races (May 29–June 6, Aug 28–Sept 5, and Oct 22–24 in 2010; www.baden-galopp.de).

Internet Access: Two good 10-terminal places sit at opposite ends of downtown—**Internet and Callshop** in the north (€2/hr, daily 10:00–22:00, Lange Strasse 54, tel. 07221/398-400) and **Medialounge** in the south (€2.40/hr, Mon–Fri 10:00–22:00, Sat 10:00–18:00, closed Sun, in passage at Kreuzstrasse 3, tel. 07221/22522).

Laundry: The unstaffed **SB-Waschcenter** is a steep hike up from downtown—only for the committed or those with a car—and you'll need to bring €9 per load in €1 coins (€5 wash, €4 dry; Mon–Sat 7:30–19:00, last load 17:00, closed Sun; walk up Sophienstrasse, go right up Stephanienstrasse, then left on steeply uphill Scheibenstrasse to #14, then down the alley; tel. 07221/24819).

Bike Rental: You can rent cheap bikes at the parking-garage office under the casino (€1/2 hours, €2.50/6 hours, €5/12 hours, leave €20 and ID as deposit, half-price with *Kurkarte* discount card you'll get from your hotel, rental daily 8:00–18:00, return until 20:00; first-come, first-served—no reservations; enter garage and find section A, space 52—easiest way down is from stairs off Kaiserallee marked *Kasse/Garage;* tel. 07221/277-203).

Train Info: The **Derpart** travel agency, between Leopoldsplatz and the casino, posts a train schedule outside. They'll charge you a €3.90 fee to answer your train questions and/or sell you a ticket—which is pricey, but saves you a trip to the station (Mon–Fri 9:00–18:00, Sat 10:00–14:00, closed Sun, Sophienstrasse 1B).

Getting Around Baden-Baden

Within town, only one bus matters: **Bus #201** runs straight through Baden-Baden, connecting the train station in Oos, the town center, and the Lichtentaler Abbey at the southeast end of town (every 10 min until 20:00, then about every 20 min until around midnight; buy tickets from machines at stops or from driver: €2.10/person, 24-hour pass for 1 adult-€4.70, 24-hour pass for up to 5 adults-€7.10, bus info at www.kvv.de). Single tickets are valid for 90 minutes in one direction. With bus #201, you don't need to mess with downtown parking.

Bus #208 can serve as a fun sightseeing bus. Hop on anywhere in the center, and you'll take a big scenic loop through the outlying regions, returning to your starting point 55 minutes later (runs once per hour, roughly Mon–Fri 9:00–17:00, Sat 9:00–12:00, leaves from Sophienstrasse at Leopoldsplatz at :07 past the hour). **Buses #204** and **#205** go to the recommended Merkur funicular; **bus #205** also goes to the airport (in the opposite direction from the funicular; see "Baden-Baden Connections," later).

Self-Guided Walk

Welcome to Baden-Baden

• *This walk starts at the casino, loops through the old town to both of the famous baths, and ends back at the river where you can stroll up to the abbey. In other words, it covers everything. Start on the steps of the...*

Casino: The impressive building called the Kurhaus is wrapped around a grand casino. Built in the 1850s in wannabe-French style, it was declared "the most beautiful casino" by Marlene Dietrich. You can tour it in the morning, and gamble away the afternoon and evening.

To get a visual overview of the town from the casino, stand on the steps between the second and third big white columns from the entrance, and survey the surroundings from left to right: Find the ruined castle near the top of the hill, then the rock-climbing cliffs, the new castle (top of town) next to the salmon-colored spire of the Catholic Church (the famous baths are just behind that), the Merkur peak (marked by a TV tower, 2,000 feet above sea level, easy to reach by bus and funicular), and the bandstand in the Kurhaus garden. The Baden-Baden orchestra plays here on most good-weather days in summer (sometimes also weekends in spring and fall, free, usually at 16:00).

• *Now walk about 100 yards to your left, to the...*

Trinkhalle: Beyond the colonnade is the old Trinkhalle—a long entrance hall decorated with nymphs and romantic legends (explained in the book *Trinkhalle Baden-Baden: Its Tales and Legends,* sold inside for €10). It's now home to the TI, a recommended café, and a ticket agency. Wander its fancy portico, studying the romantic paintings that spa-goers a century ago could easily relate to.

BADEN-BADEN

Central Baden-Baden

TO Oos &
TRAIN STATION

100 YARDS
100 METERS

LANGESTR.

HINDENBERG-
PLATZ

STRASSE

NEUES
SCHLOSS

SCHLOSS-

BURGSTR.

ROMAN-
IRISH
BATH

Fettquelle
Spigot

BATHS
OF
CARACALLA

MARKT-
PLATZ

VINCENTISTR.

TRINK-
HALLE

KAISERALLEE

LUISENSTRASSE

LANGE STRASSE

HIRSCHSTR.

STEINSTR.

GERNSBACHERSTR.

WILLY-
BRAND-
PLATZ

CASINO &
KURHAUS
START

JESUITEN-
PLATZ

SOPHIEN-

STEPHANIESTR.

SONNEN-
PLATZ

LEOPOLDS-
PLATZ

SCHEIBENSTRASSE

ADENAUER
PLATZ

KREUZSTR.

RETTIGSTRASSE

STRASSE

GOETHE-
PLATZ

WERDERSTRASSE

FRIEDRICHSTR.

LICHTENTALER STR.

MERKURSTR.

EICHSTR.

KUNST
HALLE

END

AUGUSTA-
PLATZ

STEPHANIENSTR.

LICHTENTALER ALLEE

KONGRESS
HAUS

DU-RUSSEL-STRASSE

TO
CITY MUSEUM

DCH

TO
LICHTENTALER
ABBEY

WALKING
TOUR ROUTE

VIEW

FOUNTAIN

STEPPED
STREETS

P   PARKING

① Hotel/Rest. Rathausglöckel
   & Hotel am Markt
② Hotel/Café Beeg
③ Hotel Etol
④ Weinstube im Baldreit
⑤ Peter's am Leo Café
⑥ Gasthaus Löwenbräu
⑦ Lotus Restaurant
⑧ Café König

⑨ In der Trinkhalle Café
⑩ Böckeler Café
⑪ Wagener Galerie (Grocery)
⑫ Internet Access (2)
⑬ Launderette
⑭ Bike Rental
⑮ Derpart Travel Agency
⑯ Bus to Merkur Bergbahn

• *From the Trinkhalle, walk down the steps, tip your hat to Kaiser Wilhelm (no moustache jokes), and cross the river. Walk one block inland, then go left on the pedestrian Lange Strasse. After a block, take a hard right, and climb up Hirschstrasse (under the "Bad" Hotel zum Hirsch skybridge) until you hit a big church.*

Catholic Church and Marktplatz: Baden-Baden's Catholic Church looks over the marketplace that has marked the center of town since Roman times. You're standing upon the "emperor's spa." Though it's not open to the public, every year city officials don oxygen masks and descend, through the square metal hatch in the cobbles, to clean its sumptuous marble.

Enter the church (the door on the left side is usually open). Because it sits atop the spa, the Catholic Church is muggy and warm all year. There are no heaters inside. The floor stones are designed to transmit the natural spa heat in the winter. Notice a musty smell? The air in the nave is at a steady 85 percent humidity level. That means the wooden pews have to be replaced every 50 years, and all the art consists of copies (originals are stored safely in the regional museum).

Back outside, you can see the edge of the "new castle" towering above the square. It's owned by a Kuwaiti woman who hopes to turn it into a fabulous five-star hotel at the cost of €500 million (if she can clear the hurdles that come with renovating a historic building).

• *Now we'll explore the area around Baden-Baden's namesake and claim to fame...*

The Baths Area: Walk to the back of the church, under a modern art installation holding jugs three stories high (reminders of the Roman spa that once stood here), and down the cobbled lane behind the Roman-Irish Bath complex. Because the soil is spa-warmed, the vegetation is lush—Mediterranean pines and orange trees. At the end (top of stairs), enjoy the **viewpoint;** Baden-Baden's high-rent district—nicknamed "Paradise"—climbs the hills opposite.

Take the steps down to a water spigot called **Fettquelle** ("rich water source"). Taste the spa water. It's 105 degrees—as hot as a spa open to the public can legally be. Until recently, this was a practical source of hot water. Older locals remember being sent here to fetch hot water for their father's shave.

Find the hand-less **statue** on the lawn 50 yards farther. She's got her rear to the modern fun baths (Baths of Caracalla) and is eyeing the luxurious old-school Roman-Irish Bath (both described later).

• *Return halfway to the Fettquelle spigot and take the stairs down into the parking level (signposted* Römische Badruinen*), to the small...*

Ancient Spa Museum: This spa, now in ruins, was built for Roman soldiers to use. It's just one room—most of which you can see through the big windows—and worth the €2.50 admission only if you want to use the included audioguide to learn the story of the ancient spa, including how it was engineered. As it was only for soldiers, this spa is just a simple terra-cotta structure with hollow walls and elevated floors to let the heat circulate (mid-March–mid-Nov daily 11:00–12:00 & 15:00–16:00, closed mid-Nov–mid-March).

• *Leaving the museum, jog left, then right, and head down...*

Gernsbacher Strasse: Walking down Gernsbacher Strasse, consider the 2,000-year heritage of guests who have been housed, fed, and watered here at the spa. Fyodor Dostoyevsky, Mark Twain, Johannes Brahms, and Russian princes all called this neighborhood home in its 19th-century heyday. Germany's oldest tennis and golf clubs were created here (for the English community) in the 19th century.

The late 20th-century German health-care system was very, very good for Baden-Baden. The government provided lavishly for spa treatment for its tired citizens. Now, doctors must make the case to insurance companies that their patients are more than tired...they must actually be sick to have their visit subsidized. And the insurance company then dictates where they'll go. The government will still pay for up to three weeks of recreation at a spa like this—but patients must go to the spa that is recommended and sleep in its clinic. If they want to sleep in a hotel, the jig is up—and they lose their government funding.

• *After two blocks, you hit Sonnenplatz. Jog left, and at the corner continue right down Sophienstrasse where a signpost directs you toward Lichtentaler Allee.*

Sophienstrasse: This street enjoys the reliable shade of a long row of chestnut trees. In the 1870s, when it was lined exclusively by hotels, it was the town's aristocratic promenade. Back then there were 15,000 bedrooms for rent in Baden-Baden, triple what the city has today. (Note the bus stop just before Leopoldsplatz, where buses #204 and #205 go to the Merkur funicular—described later.)

• *Sophienstrasse leads into...*

Leopoldsplatz: Until 1985, this square was a main traffic hub, with 30,000 cars muscling through it each day. Now a 1.5-mile long tunnel takes the east–west traffic under the city, and the peace and quiet you'd expect in a spa town has returned. Actually, Baden-Baden had to get rid of the noise and pollution caused by the traffic in order to maintain its top rating as a spa resort—lose that, and Baden-Baden would lose half its business. The modern art decorating this square (and streets and squares throughout the city) rotates, as many artists want the exposure that an open-air exhibit in Baden-Baden brings.

• *From Leopoldsplatz, head left on Lichtentaler Strasse. You'll pass the venerable and recommended Café König (on right), antiques shops (on left), and fine little malls. The big fountain in the distance marks Augustaplatz. Head toward it. At the fountain, go right, through the park, and over the petite bridge, where you'll come to a sweet riverside path called Lichtentaler Allee (described under "Sights in Baden-Baden," next). From here the casino is to your right. A stroll to the left—down Lichtentaler Allee—takes you to the rose garden, City Museum (a humble but well-displayed collection of artifacts and etchings showing the history of the spa town, located in an elegant old mansion), and out to Lichtentaler Abbey. You choose which way to go. My walk is done.*

Sights in Baden-Baden

▲▲**Casino and Kurhaus**—Baden-Baden's grand casino occupies a classy building called the Kurhaus. Built in the 1850s, it was

inspired by the Palace of Versailles, and is filled with rooms honoring French royalty who never set foot in the place. But many other French people did. Gambling was illegal in 19th-century France... just over the border. The casino is licensed on the condition that it pays 92 percent of its earnings to the state. The amount of revenue it generates to help the state fund social services is a secret, but insiders estimate that it's more than $30 million a year. The staff of 150 is paid by tips from happy gamblers.

You can visit the casino on a guided tour in the mornings, when it's closed to gamblers, but the casino is most interesting to see in action, after 14:00. You can gamble if you want, but a third of the visitors come only to people-watch under the chandeliers. The scene is more subdued than at an American casino; anyone showing emotion is more likely a tourist than a serious gambler. Lean against a gilded statue and listen to the graceful reshuffling of personal fortunes. Do some imaginary gambling or buy a few chips at the window near the entrance (an ATM is nearby).

The casino is open for gambling daily from 14:00 to 2:00 in the morning (Fri–Sat until 3:00; €3 entry, €1.50 entry with *Kurkarte* discount card from your hotel, €2 minimum bet, €10,000 maximum bet, no tennis shoes, tie and coat and collared shirt required for men and can be rented for €11 with an €11 deposit, nice jeans OK, passport required—driver's license isn't enough, under 21 not admitted, no photos, livelier after dinner and liveliest after

22:00, pick up English history and game rules as you enter, tel. 07221/30240, www.casino-baden-baden.de).

Lower rollers and budget travelers can try their luck downstairs at the casino's €1 slot machines, called *Automatenspiel* (€1 entry fee or included in €3 casino admission, same hours and age restrictions, passport required, no dress code).

Casino Tour: The casino gives 30-minute German tours every morning, departing every half-hour from 9:30 to 11:30 (€4, Nov–March at 10:00; some guides speak English, or call ahead and pay €15 extra per group for an English tour—tel. 07221/30240, or just pick up the paltry English brochure). Even camera-toting peasants in T-shirts, shorts, and sandals are welcome on tours.

▲▲**Strolling Lichtentaler Allee**—Imagine yourself in top hat and tails as you promenade down the famous Lichtentaler Allee, a pleasant, picnic-perfect 1.5-mile-long lane. You'll stroll through a park along the babbling brick-lined Oosbach River, past old mansions and under hardy oaks and exotic trees (street-lit all night). By the elitist tennis courts, make sure to cross the footbridge into the free Art Nouveau rose garden (Gönneranlage, 100 labeled kinds of roses, great lounge chairs, best in early summer). If you wish, continue all the way to the historic Lichtentaler Abbey, a Cistercian convent founded in 1245. Either walk round-trip, or take city bus #201 one-way (runs along the main street, parallel to the promenade, on the other side of the river). Many bridges cross the river, making it easy to shortcut to bus #201 anytime. Biking is another option (see "Bike Rental" under "Helpful Hints," earlier), but you'll have to stay on the road in the bike lane, since the footpath is only for pedestrians.

Russian Baden-Baden—Many Russians, including Dostoyevsky and Tolstoy, flocked to Baden-Baden after the czars banned gambling in their motherland. Many lost their fortunes, borrowed a pistol, and did themselves in on the "Alley of Sighs" (Seufzerallee, near the Caracalla baths). You'll find a **Russian church** just south of the center (€1 donation requested, daily 10:00–18:00, services normally Sat 17:00–20:00 and Sun 9:40–11:30, near Gönneranlage rose garden across river from Lichtentaler Allee, or take bus #201 to Bertholdplatz stop). While the church dates from about 1900 and was quiet for generations, the current boom in the Russian population here has the church livelier than ever.

Many of Baden-Baden's top hotels are now Russian-owned. Ultra-wealthy Russians have sought out safe property investments all over Europe, and Baden-Baden is a favorite destination. While more Americans visit Baden-Baden each year, Russians stay longer and account for more overnights. You'll see Russian on multilingual signs around town.

▲**Funicular to the Summit of Merkur**—This delightful trip, to a hilltop overlooking Baden-Baden, is easy, quick, and a good reason to buy a 24-hour bus card rather than single tickets. Catch bus #204 or #205 from the city center (departing 2/hr from Sophienstrasse, just off Leopoldsplatz) and ride 11 minutes through the ritzy "Paradise" neighborhood to the end of the line at the base of the Merkur Bergbahn. Take the funicular to the 2,000-foot summit (€4 round-trip, daily 10:00–22:00). At the top, you can enjoy a meal or drink (restaurant open daily 10:00–18:00), and, if the weather's good (with winds from the south or west), you can watch the paragliders leap into ecstasy. From here, an easy paved lane takes you back to the base of the Merkur Bergbahn (2.5 miles, signposted *Merkurbahn Talstation*); hiking enthusiasts can follow many other trails from here (ask for a map at the funicular station). From the bottom of the funicular, buses depart back to Baden-Baden twice hourly.

Mini-Black Forest Walks—Baden-Baden is at the northern end of the Black Forest. If you're not going south, but want a taste of Germany's favorite woods, consider one of several hikes from town. The TI has details and can suggest routes. If you're serious about hiking, invest in the TI's good (but German-only) €1.50 *Panoramaweg* map, which outlines a 26-mile trail leading all the way around Baden-Baden's perimeter (it's easy to do just part of the trail, since you're never far from the town center).

Experiences in Baden-Baden

The Baths

Baden-Baden's two much-loved but very different baths stand side-by-side in a park at the top of the old town. The Roman-Irish Bath is traditional, stately, indoors, not very social, and extremely relaxing...just you, the past, and your body. The perky, fun, and modern Baths of Caracalla are half the price, indoor and outdoor, and more social. Caracalla is better in the sunshine. Roman-Irish is fine anytime. Some hotels sell discounted tickets (10–15 percent off) to one or both of the baths—ask at your hotel.

At either bath, your admission ticket works like a subway token—you need it to get out. If you overstay your allotted time, you pay extra. You can relax while your valuables are stowed in very secure lockers. Both baths share a huge underground Bäder-Garage, which is free (for the first 2 hours, then €1/hr) if you validate your parking ticket before leaving either bath.

▲▲▲Roman-Irish Bath (Friedrichsbad)

The highlight of most visits to Baden-Baden is a sober two-hour ritual called the Roman-Irish Bath. Friedrichsbad pampered the rich and famous in its elegant surroundings when it opened 120 years ago. Today, this steamy world of marble, brass columns, tropical tiles, herons, lily pads, and graceful nudity welcomes gawky tourists as well as locals.

Cost, Hours, Location: For €31, you get up to three hours and the works (€21 without the 10-minute massage, daily 9:00–22:00, last entry 3 hours before closing if you're getting a massage, 2 hours before otherwise, kids under 14 not allowed, Römerplatz 1, tel. 07221/275-920, www .carasana.de).

Dress Code: It is always nude. On most days, men and women use parallel and nearly identical facilities—but the sexes can mingle in the pool under the grand dome in the center of the complex (yes, everyone's nude there, too). Shy bathers should avoid Sundays, Tuesdays, and holidays, when all of the rooms are mixed—including the steam and massage rooms. If you're concerned, you needn't be; there's no ogling going on. It's a very classy and respectful ritual, and a shame to miss just because you're intimidated by nudity.

Procedure: Read this carefully before stepping out naked: In your changing cabin, load all your possessions onto the fancy hanger. Then hang it in the locker across the way, slip your card into the lock, and strap the key around your wrist. (If you'll be having a massage, strap your plastic massage "coupon" to your wrist.) As you enter (in the "body crème" room), check your weight on the digital scale. Do this again as you leave to see how much you sweated off. You will lose about a kilo...all in sweat. The complex routine is written (in English) on the walls with recommended times—simply follow the room numbers from 1 to 15. Instructions are repeated everywhere. For the first couple of stops only, you will use plastic slippers (marked with European sizes) and a towel (given to you by the attendant for the hot-room lounges) for hygienic reasons and because the slats are too hot to sit on without the towel.

Take a shower. Grab a towel and put on plastic slippers before hitting the warm-air bath for 15 minutes and the hot-air bath for five minutes. Shower again. If you paid extra, take the soap-brush massage—rough, slippery, and finished with a good Teutonic spank. Play Gumby in the shower; lounge under sunbeams in one of several thermal steam baths; and glide like a swan under a divine dome in a royal pool (one of three "mixed" pools—explained earlier). Don't skip the cold plunge. Dry in warmed towels and lie on a bed for 30 minutes, thinking prenatal thoughts, in the mellow, yellow silent room. You don't appreciate how clean you are after this experience until you put your dirty socks back on. (Bring clean ones.)

All you need is money. You'll get a key, locker, and towel; hair dryers are available. If you wear glasses, consider leaving them in your locker (it's more relaxing without them). Otherwise, you'll find trays throughout for you to park your specs.

Afterward, before going downstairs, browse through the Roman artifacts upstairs in the Renaissance Hall (also accessible to non-bathers), sip just a little of the terrible but "magic" hot water *(Thermalwasser)* from the elegant fountain, and stroll down the broad royal stairway, feeling, as they say, five years younger—or, at least, 2.2 pounds lighter.

▲▲Baths of Caracalla (Caracalla Therme)

For a more modern experience, spend a few hours at the Baths of Caracalla, a huge palace of water, steam, and relaxed people. More like a mini-water park, and with everyone clothed most of the time, this is a fun and accessible experience for those intimidated by nudity.

Hours: Daily 8:00–22:00, last entry at 20:00, sometimes closed for 2 weeks in June or July for renovation, kids under 7 not allowed, those 7–14 must be with parents (it's not really a splashing and sliding kind of pool). Tel. 07221/275-940, www.carasana.de.

Cost and Procedure: Here you need to bring a towel (or pay €5 plus a €10 deposit to rent one) and a swimsuit (shorts are OK for men). Buy a card (€14/2 hours, €17/3 hours, €20/4 hours, 10 2-hour entries for repeat visits or to split among a group cost €122) and put it in the locker to get a key. Change clothes, strap the key around your wrist, and go play. Your key gets you into another poolside locker if you want to lock up glasses or money for a tan or a drink. Bring your towel to the pool (there are plenty of places to stow it). The baths are an indoor/outdoor wonderland of steamy pools, waterfalls, neck showers, Jacuzzis, hot springs, cold pools, lounge chairs, saunas, a cafeteria, and a bar. After taking a few laps around the fake river, you can join some kinky Germans for water spankings (you may have to wait a few minutes to grab a vacant waterfall). Then join the gang in the central cauldron. The steamy "inhalation" room seems like purgatory's waiting room, with a misty minimum of visibility, filled with strange, silently aging bodies.

Nudity is limited to one zone upstairs. The grand spiral staircase leads to a naked world of saunas, tanning lights, cold plunges, and sunbathing outside on lounge chairs. At the top of the stairs everyone stows their suit in a cubbyhole and wanders around with their towel (some are modest and wrapped; others just run around buck naked). There are three eucalyptus-scented saunas of varying temperatures (80, 90, and 95 degrees) and two saunas in outdoor log cabins (with mesmerizing robotic steam-makers). Follow the instructions on the wall. Towels are required, not for modesty but to separate your body from the wood benches. The highlight is the arctic bucket in the shower room. Pull the chain. Only rarely will you feel so good. And you can do it over and over.

Sleeping in Baden-Baden

(area code: 07221)
While Baden-Baden has some grand hotels, my recommended places are mostly small (20–30 rooms), family-run, and budget-friendly (though all accommodations are pricey in this resort town). Note that most hotels here don't have 24-hour reception desks; most close up for the night at 21:00 or 23:00, though they can wait up for you if they know you're arriving later. It's wise to call ahead with your specific arrival details if you'll be coming after 17:00.

The only tight times are during the horse races (May 29–June 6, Aug 28–Sept 5, and Oct 22–24 in 2010). Hotel am Markt is a great value and worth reserving in advance. While things are busy all summer long, demand—and prices—change dramatically from day to day based on conventions and other events (as reflected by the wide price ranges in my listings).

All hotels and pensions are required to extract an additional €2.80 per person, per night "spa tax," so don't get upset when this is added to the bill. This comes with a "guest card" *(Kurkarte)*, offering small discounts on tourist admissions around town (including casino entry and bike rental). If you're coming into town by car or foot, look for the helpful green signs that direct you to each hotel by name.

In the Center, near the Baths
These well-located options stick you right in the heart of Baden-Baden, in a pleasant stepped pedestrian zone a short saunter from the baths.

$$$ Hotel Rathausglöckel is a 16th-century guest house that recently underwent a tasteful 21st-century renovation. Owner Oliver (a German-American) has turned this classic little hotel into one of the town's most inviting splurges. Steep stairs lead

---

Sleep Code

(€1 = about $1.40, country code: 49)
S = Single, **D** = Double/Twin, **T** = Triple, **Q** = Quad, **b** = bathroom,
s = shower only. Unless otherwise noted, credit cards are accepted, English is spoken, and breakfast is included.

To help you sort easily through these listings, I've divided the rooms into three categories based on the price for a standard double room with bath:

$$$ Higher Priced—Most rooms €100 or more.
$$ Moderately Priced—Most rooms between €80–100.
$ Lower Priced—Most rooms €80 or less.

---

to 15 antique-furnished rooms (plus a few grand suites) and an inviting rooftop deck (Sb-€85–100, Db-€110–200, junior suite-€130–200, multi-room suite-€160–300, 10 percent discount to Rick Steves readers if you book direct, free transfer from the train station—must pre-arrange, free Wi-Fi, church bells every 15 min 6:15–22:00, parking-€8/day, Steinstrasse 7–9, tel. 07221/90610, fax 07221/906-161, www.rathausgloeckel.de, info@rathausgloeckel.de).

$$$ Hotel Beeg rents 15 attractive and comfortable rooms, run from a delectable pastry shop/café on the ground floor. It's wonderfully situated, facing the baths on a little square in a pedestrian zone. The reception (in the café) closes at 19:00, so be sure to call ahead if you'll be arriving later (Sb-€85, Db-€109, balcony-€10 extra, apartment Db-€165, extra bed-€30, planned renovation may increase rates, elevator, includes great à la carte breakfast, on Römerplatz at Gernsbacher Strasse 44, tel. 07221/36760, fax 07221/367-610, www.hotel-beeg.de, info@hotel-beeg.de, Beeg family).

$$ Hotel am Markt is Baden-Baden's best little hotel. This warm 25-room family-run hotel offers all the comforts a commoner could want in a peaceful, central, nearly traffic-free location, two cobbled blocks from the baths. For romantics, the church bells blast charmingly through each room every quarter-hour from 6:15 until 22:00; for others, they are a nuisance. Otherwise, quiet rules. The ambience and the clientele make it a joy to have breakfast or just kill time on the small terrace (S-€32–34, Sb-€44–47, D-€64–66, Db-€82–84, Tb-€105–120, extra bed-€20, free Internet access, pay Wi-Fi, Marktplatz 18, tel. 07221/27040, fax 07221/270-444, www.hotel-am-markt-baden.de, info@hotel-am-markt-baden.de, Herr und Frau Bogner-Schindler and Frau Jung).

Also in the Center, near the Casino on Merkurstrasse

$$$ Hotel Etol is in the quiet courtyard of a renovated industrial complex, which celebrates its history as a tile and bathtub factory from around the year 1900. You'll climb the stairs to reach most of the 18 rooms, but natural light, tasteful design, friendly staff (well-run by Saraya), and a central location make this a winning choice (Sb-€78–85, Db-€105–130, ask for special Rick Steves prices, all rooms non-smoking, family rooms, pay Wi-Fi, parking-€5/day, Merkurstrasse 7—for location see map on page 206, 2-min walk from Augustaplatz stop of bus #201, tel. 07221/973-470, fax 07221/9734-7111, www.hotel-etol.de, info@hotel-etol.de).

Outside the Center

The following listings are a few stops from the center by bus #201 (for locations, see map on page 198).

$$$ Hotel Schweizer Hof's 34 rooms mix classic style and modern comfort. It's about a five-minute walk beyond the edge of the main tourist zone, on a little square near the opera building (Sb-€85, Db-€112, suite-€125, cheaper in winter, elevator, free Wi-Fi, Lange Strasse 71–73, bus #201 stop: Alter Bahnhof/Festspielhaus, drivers follow *Festspielhaus/Casino* signs and find it right next to the opera, tel. 07221/30460, www.schweizerhof.de, mail@schweizerhof.de).

$ Hotel-Restaurant Deutscher Kaiser, a good choice for those on tighter budgets, is a traditional guest house with 22 simple, spacious, dated-but-clean rooms, run by no-nonsense Frau Peter. Herr Peter cooks fine local-style meals in the hotel restaurant (€8–17 main dishes, restaurant closed Mon–Tue). It's right at the Eckerlestrasse stop of bus #201 (6/hr, 10 min from center, 20 min from train station) or a 25-minute stroll from the city center down polite Lichtentaler Allee—cross the river at the green *Restaurant Deutscher Kaiser* sign, then turn right (S-€35, Sb-€47–49, D-€46–49, Db-€59–69, family rooms, often impressive discounts on their website, mostly non-smoking rooms, pay Internet access, free Wi-Fi, free and easy parking, Hauptstrasse 35, tel. 07221/72152, fax 07221/72154, www.hoteldk.de, info@hoteldk.de). Drivers: From the autobahn, skip the town center by following *Congress* signs into Michaelstunnel. Take the tunnel's first exit, then another right at the end of the exit (direction: Lichtental). Outside, the hotel is about a half-mile down on the left. From the Black Forest, follow *Zentrum* signs. Just 10 yards after the Aral gas station, turn left down the small road to Hauptstrasse.

$ Werner Dietz Hostel, between the station and the center, is big, modern, and has the cheapest beds in town (€19.10 per bed in 4- to 6-bed dorms, €3.20 less for 2 nights or more, €3 more if you're over 26, adult non-members pay €3.10 extra, S/D rooms €5 extra per person, includes sheets and breakfast, 23:30 curfew, outdoor swimming pool next door, Hardbergstrasse 34, tel. 07221/52223, www.jugendherberge-baden-baden.de, info @jugendherberge-baden-baden.de). To reach the hostel from the train station or downtown, take bus #201 to Grosse Dollenstrasse (also announced as *Jugendherberge*), six stops from the station or five from downtown; it's a steep, well-marked 10-minute climb from there. Drivers should call the hostel for careful directions.

Eating in Baden-Baden

Dining with Elegance and Atmosphere

Weinstube im Baldreit, with both a cozy cellar and a leafy back courtyard, is ideal on a hot evening. Dining here, I feel like a pampered salamander in a Monet terrarium. While her French husband Philippe cooks wonderful regional dishes, Nicole is happy to translate the daily specials chalked in German on the board. The priority here is near-gourmet food at great prices. Reservations are smart (€8–18 meals, Mon–Sat 17:00–22:00 plus Sat lunch 12:00–14:00, closed Sun; from Lange Strasse 10, walk up the narrow alley called Küferstrasse, look for *Weinstube* signs and enter under archway, Küferstrasse 3; tel. 07221/23136). Their garden theater periodically hosts trained sea otter performances (no joke).

Hotel Rathausglöckel's homey restaurant features traditional cuisine in a dining room with understated Old World elegance. As there's no outdoor seating, eat elsewhere if the weather is really hot (€12–20 main dishes, €7 weekday lunch deals, open daily 11:30–14:00 & 17:30–22:00, reservations smart, Steinstrasse 7–9, tel. 07221/90610). There's an atmospheric wine bar in their recently excavated cellar (open nightly 17:30–1:00 in the morning).

Quick and Simple Meals near Leopoldsplatz

Peter's am Leo Café is a fun self-service place offering salads, pasta, omelets, pastries, and views over Baden-Baden's central square. (Try to snare one of the outdoor tables.) This is where commoners pile their plates high. The lively staff dons lederhosen for Oktoberfest, Hawaiian shirts in sunny weather, and striped shirts for the horse races (€5–7 meals, Mon–Sat 6:30–19:00, Sun 8:00–19:00, on Leopoldsplatz at Sophienstrasse 10, tel. 07221/392-817).

On Jesuitenplatz: This thriving people zone, between Leopoldsplatz and the baths (at the bottom of Gernsbacher Strasse), has several options. The square is dominated by **Gasthaus Löwenbräu,** a sloppy, rude Bavarian-style *Biergarten* slinging good beer and basic schnitzel fare under a vine-covered trellis (€6–10 for basic grub, €11–24 main dishes, long hours daily). Across the street, several decent restaurants offer curbside tables—great for people-watching. Two blocks up Gernsbacher Strasse from here (at #17), **Lotus Restaurant** serves big, cheap portions of Chinese and some Thai specialties, and has a few outdoor tables (€6–8 meals, daily 11:00–23:00).

Prime People-Watching Cafés

Baden-Baden's many cafés are variations on a genteel theme. They serve chocolates, coffee, cakes (including the famous *Schwärzwalder Kirschtorte*—Black Forest cake), and light meals.

Figure around €5–6 to savor a slice of cake and cup of coffee, or €5–8 for light food (such as sandwiches and salads). For the treats, you'll pay about €0.50 extra to sit down rather than getting it "to go." Most cafés are closed for dinner. While you have no shortage of options in this town, I like these four.

Café König is *the* place to bring your poodle and spend too much for an elegant cup of coffee and a slice of Black Forest cake. At the counter, you can buy pastries and chocolates to go (daily 8:30–18:30, counter opens Mon–Sat at 9:30 and Sun at 10:30, fine shady patio, look for sign with squiggly script, between Leopoldsplatz and Augustaplatz at Lichtentaler Strasse 12, tel. 07221/23573).

In der Trinkhalle, a café that shares the handsome Trinkhalle building with the TI, has comfy leather sofas, international newspapers and magazines, and a casino-view terrace (daily 10:00–24:00, Kaiserallee 3, tel. 07221/302-905).

Café Beeg fills a delightful tree-shaded square just in front of the baths with relaxing café tables (daily 7:30-18:30, Gernsbacher Strasse 44–46 at Römerplatz, tel. 07221/36760). They also rent rooms (see "Sleeping in Baden-Baden," earlier).

Böckeler Café, a good low-end option, is a bit cheaper, and has a praline counter, an ice-cream sundae menu, light meals, a modern interior, and outdoor tables along a lively pedestrian street (Mon–Fri 8:00–18:30, Sat–Sun 9:30–18:00, Lange Strasse 40–42, tel. 07221/949-594).

Baden-Baden Connections

From Baden-Baden by Train to: Freiburg (direct trains every 1–2 hrs, 45 min), **Triberg** (hourly, 70 min), **Munich** (hourly, 4 hrs, some direct but most with 1–2 changes), **Frankfurt** (hourly, 1.5 hrs, direct or with a change in Mannheim or Karlsruhe),

Frankfurt Airport (hourly, 1.5 hrs, mostly with a change in Mannheim or Karlsruhe), **Bacharach** (hourly, 3 hrs, 1–3 changes), **Strasbourg,** France (almost hourly, usually 1–1.5 hrs with a change in Appenweier), **Bern** or **Zürich,** Switzerland (every 1–2 hrs, 3 hrs, change in Basel). Train info: tel. 0180-599-6633 (€0.14/min).

Freiburg

Freiburg (FRY-burg) is the capital of the Schwarzwald. This "sunniest town in Germany," with 30,000 students, lacks must-see attractions but offers the pleasures of a university town: small shops, cozy cafés, fine food, and fewer tourists than Baden-Baden. Exuding an "I could live here" appeal, Freiburg is surrounded by lush forests and filled with environmentally aware people. Bikers and hikers seem to outnumber cars, the town center is laced with cute miniature canals, and silent, efficient trams run everywhere. The city merits a visit, if only to appreciate its thriving center and very human scale. Freiburg's striking red-sandstone cathedral is worth a peek, and its own little mountain offers sunset views over the rooftops.

Orientation to Freiburg

BLACK FOREST

(area code: 0761)
With about 210,000 people, Freiburg is a happening mid-sized city. Most points of interest to visitors are concentrated in the compact Old Town (Altstadt), bounded to the west by the train station and to the east by Freiburg's mountain, Schlossberg, and circled by a ring road. You can walk from one end of this zone to the other in about 20 minutes. The town's centerpiece, always in view, is the spiny spire of its cathedral.

Tourist Information
Freiburg's helpful TI, on Rathausplatz, has free city maps and sells better maps for €1, as well as various city and regional guidebooks that aren't necessary for a short stay. The TI also offers a room-booking service (€3 per booking plus a deposit for Freiburg and Black Forest area), weekly walking tours in English (€7, 1.5 hours, usually May–Oct Sat at 11:00—but confirm details; off-season only in German), and lots of information on the Black Forest region (TI open June–Sept Mon–Fri 8:00–20:00, Sat 9:30–17:00, Sun 10:00–12:00; Oct–May Mon–Fri 8:00–18:00, Sat 9:30–14:30, Sun 10:00–12:00; tel. 0761/388-1880, www.freiburg.de).

Arrival in Freiburg

The bustling train station has lockers (€2–4 old-fashioned lockers by track 1B, or try the high-tech €4 ones in the station hall), a WC (€0.80), and a helpful *Reisezentrum* that dispenses rail info and sells tickets (Mon–Fri 7:00–20:00, Sat 8:30–19:00, Sun 8:30–20:00). The bus station is next door (to the right as you exit).

To access city **trams** from the train platform, take the escalators up to the tram stop on the bridge above the tracks. To reach the city center by **foot** (about 15 minutes), walk straight out of the train station, cross the street, and continue ahead up the tree-lined boulevard called Eisenbahnstrasse (passing the post office). Within three blocks, you'll cross the busy ring road, then continue straight (on Rathausgasse) to Rathausplatz. This is where you'll find the TI (in the bright-red building), and where my self-guided walk begins. Most of my recommended accommodations are within a 10-minute walk of here.

Helpful Hints

Laundry and Internet Access: Do your laundry while surfing the Net at **Wash Tours** (€6.50/load, self-service, Internet access–€2/hr—plus 15 free minutes if you do laundry, Mon–Sat 9:00–19:00, closed Sun, in the passage that runs from Salzstrasse 22 to Grünwälderstrasse 19, tel. 0761/288-866, www.washtours.com). Several recommended eateries (including the Martkhalle food court) are conveniently located just a few steps from here—handy for multitaskers.

Bike Rental: Mobile, across the tracks from the train station, rents bikes and has free route maps (€8/4 hrs, €15/24 hrs, subsequent days–€5, €50–200 cash and ID for deposit, daily 10:00–18:00; from station, cross tram bridge over train tracks to round building on left and go downstairs; Wentzingerstrasse 15, tel. 0761/292-7998).

Local Guide: Iris Bürklin leads good tours around Freiburg (€99/2 hrs; book through Freiburg Kultour and request Iris: tel. 0761/290-7447, info@freiburg-kultour.com; Iris' mobile 0162-595-6876).

Getting Around Freiburg and Surroundings

The city center (which includes all my recommended hotels) is completely walkable, though you might want to use a taxi or a tram to haul luggage from the station. Trams are also useful to reach outlying sights, such as the Schauinsland lift (€2/ride, €5/24-hr pass, buy tickets from machines at stops or inside cars). For local transport info in English, see www.vag-freiburg.de.

To visit **Staufen, St. Peter,** or **St. Märgen** by regional train and bus, you'll need a two-zone ticket (€3.40 each way) or a

24-hour regional pass (€10 for 1 adult, €17 for 2–5 adults, available from ticket machines). If you're staying in one of those towns, your hotel tax includes a KONUS card, giving you free access to all public transit in the region (see page 237); unfortunately, this does not apply if you're sleeping in Freiburg.

Self-Guided Walk

Welcome to Freiburg

This orientation walk, starting at Rathausplatz (and the TI), leads you through the top sights in the old center of Freiburg in about an hour.

• *Begin on the square in front of the Town Hall buildings.*

Rathausplatz: The relaxing square with the fountain used to be an enclosed courtyard—the cloister of the neighboring Franciscan Church of St. Martin. Today it's fronted by twin city administration buildings: the bright-red Old Town Hall (on the right, with the TI inside) and the white-and-pink New Town Hall (on the left).

As an avid university center since the mid-15th century (the prestigious university is still the town's biggest employer), Freiburg prizes its internationalism and celebrates its nine **sister cities** around the world. Embedded in the cobbles in front of both of the town hall buildings, you'll see mosaic coats of arms representing each of these cities. Many of them—including Padua, Italy and Madison, Wisconsin—are university towns, like Freiburg. The most unusual is Isfahan, Iran. Freiburg is the only German city paired with an Iranian one.

• *Curl around the far side of St. Martin's Church and head up Franziskanerstrasse. As you walk, you'll notice the first of many small canals lining the street.*

Bächle: These tiny streams, running down nearly every street in the pedestrianized core since the 13th century, are Freiburg's trademark. Originally they were designed to keep fires from spreading (in case of fire, the canals could be quickly dammed to flood the street). It worked—Freiburg had no major fires after it introduced its *Bächle*. The canals also provided a constantly replenishing source of water for people and cattle. These days, the canals are just fun: A sunny day turns any kid-at-heart into a puddle-jumper. Freiburg still employs two *Bächleputzer* to scrub the canals clean each day with steel brooms. Local lore says that if you fall into a *Bächle*, you are destined to marry a Freiburger.

At the end of the church, look at the facade of the red building on the left, the **House of the Whale**, featuring the first of many whimsical little statues that decorate Freiburg. Look closely at the right-hand gargoyle on the facade. The veiny growth hanging from her neck is a goiter (a result of iodine deficiency). These were so common in the Middle Ages that the local folk costume includes a tightly fitting band around the neck to disguise a goiter.

• *Continue ahead one block, until you reach the wide cross-street...*

Kaiser-Joseph-Strasse: Since the Middle Ages, this has been the center of commerce in Freiburg, lined with its biggest department stores and malls.

Look before crossing the street: Virtually silent trams glide

along here constantly. With some 220 miles of tram and bus lines, Freiburg is very proud of its reputation as a "green" city. Only 40 percent of trips taken in Freiburg are by car, and the percentage of locals who own bikes rivals that of pedal-happy Amsterdam. The city is home to a large solar-panel factory, and started the annual Intersolar trade fair (which has since outgrown the town and moved to California).

Looking down the street to the right, you can see one of the two surviving towers of Freiburg's former town wall, **St. Martin's Tower** (or as some call it, McDonald's Tower—thanks to the not-subtle-enough golden arches that try to fit into its facade). If you were to head in that direction, then cut up the street to the right just before you reached the tower, you'd wind up in the colorful student quarter called the "Bermuda Triangle" that visitors of any age enjoy exploring (described later, under "Eating in Freiburg"). The tower is dedicated to a beloved saint who famously offered half of his cape to a beggar (and is still celebrated with a parade here in Freiburg every November 10). The top of the tower once held the town prison, so those who went to jail were euphemistically said to have "put on St. Martin's cape."

• *Jog a half-block to the right and continue straight to the...*

Münsterplatz and Market: This main square of Freiburg hosts a bustling outdoor produce and crafts market six mornings a week (Mon–Sat 7:30–13:00, biggest on Wed and Sat, no market on Sun). On the north side of the cathedral (to the left), vendors sell local produce; in front of the cathedral's door, flowers and herbs; and to the south (right), imported produce. Around the left side, you'll also find stands selling Freiburg's distinctive type of bratwurst—long, red, and skinny, called a *lange Rote*. If you order one, they'll ask you *Mit oder ohne?*—"with or without" onions.

The market goes way back. On the giant pillar to the left of the cathedral's main door, look for the **engravings** with different years (e.g., ADMCCLXX—that's A.D. 1270) next to oval and circular shapes. These were the officially decreed sizes for a loaf of bread; customers could bring their purchases here to be sure they weren't being cheated. Notice that the size of the loaf shrunk between 1270 and 1317. The price stayed the same, but the bread got smaller...medieval inflation.

In the alcove in front of the cathedral entrance are more official measures. For example, to the left, you'll see the standard measures for a basket (the circle plus the line), an "elbow" (the line), and a barrel (the square with a diagonal line). On the right are even more measures, dictating home-construction supplies (the proper size of bricks, roof tiles, floor tiles, and beams). Nearby, the inscription boasts that since the 16th century, Freiburg has enjoyed the right to hold a large-scale market twice a year (a rare privilege in the Holy Roman Empire).

• *Now's a good time to visit the **cathedral** (for all the details, see my self-guided cathedral tour on page 222). When you're done, exit the cathedral out the side door (around the right side of the building) to continue this walk.*

Münsterplatz, Side View: For many visitors, the most memorable part of the cathedral is its many **gargoyles**. Find the "mooning" gargoyle (facing the entrance, walk around the right and look at the second butt-ress)...and wait for rain.

The **Historical Merchant House** (Historisches Kaufhaus, from 1532) was the trading and customs center in the 16th century, and briefly housed the state parliament after the war. You'll notice lots of red buildings in town. During the Middle Ages around here, a red paint job on a building indicated it was a place where you'd be required to pay a tax or fee.

To the left as you face the Merchant House, you'll see the gray building that houses the **City History Museum** (with a pair of interesting models in the cellar—see page 224), then the yellow building marked *Alte Wache.* A former police station, this was recently turned into a wine bar, and is a fine place to sample local wines, either indoors or out on the square (€2–4.50 glasses, Mon–Fri 10:00–19:00, Sat 10:00–16:00, closed Sun, Münsterplatz 38, tel. 0761/202-870). Most of the wine grown here uses grapes originating in Burgundy. This corner of Germany enjoys some of the country's balmiest weather, thanks to the so-called "Burgundy Gate"—a gap between the Vosges and Jura mountains, which channels in warm Mediterranean air from the south of France. Winds coming through the "gate" also carry with them Burgundian soil sediments.

• *Go up the narrow lane (called Buttergasse) to the left of the Merchant House. Then turn left and head up...*

Schusterstrasse: This pleasant street is typical of old Freiburg, lined with a *Bächle*, with historic labels on many of the houses and mosaic seals (made of Rhine River stones) in front of most doors. For example, the building at #35 (on the left) is labeled *Haus zur kleinen Meise* (House of the Little Titmouse), with a knife mosaic out front. While the house labels date from the Middle Ages, the mosaics are typically more modern, paid for by today's merchants to match the purpose of the building. This one is a knife shop. The mosaics are portable, so if the vendor moves shop, he can just lift his up and take it with him.

• *Cross Herrenstrasse and continue up the narrow lane called Münzgasse. When it dead-ends, turn right along...*

Konviktstrasse: Named not for a convict but for a convent, this is another typical Freiburg street (see photo, next page). Chain

stores and chain restaurants are forbidden along here, and in the springtime,
the street is draped with fragrant purple
wisteria.

• *Konviktstrasse plops you onto a major street
right in front of the...*

Swabian Gate (Schwabentor):
This second of Freiburg's surviving gates
is named for the Swabians, the his-

torical rivals of the
Freiburgers (the gate
leads to where you'd
head to meet them). Just below the big painting, at the apex of the arch, look for the little
figure pulling a thorn out of his foot. This is
the last thing Freiburgers would see before
leaving town, to remind them to stay on the
right path and avoid the "thorns" of sinful
living.

• *Freiburg's little mountain, Schlossberg, is
nearby. It's best at sunset, but if you want to
head up now, simply climb the stairs at the
Schwabentor, use the pedestrian overpass to cross the busy road, and take
the free elevator on up (see page 225).*

*Or, for some back-streets experiences, stick with me for a few more
minutes. Facing the Schwabentor, turn right, then veer right again onto
the downhill road, toward the little river.*

Riverside Freiburg: This is the main branch of the much bigger river that splits into all those little canals at the top of town.
Walking down this incline, you can see how the street level of town
was actually raised to create a steeper incline to power the canals.
While this was once the smelly tanners' and millers' quarter, now
it's a delightfully low-key neighborhood. Follow the pleasant river
for a while, and soon you'll reach two recommended eateries:
across the canal (on the left) is the picturesque Sichelschmiede; a
few more steps up on the left is the modern-inside, rollicking-out-
side Hausbrauerei Feierling microbrewery, with an inviting beer
garden across the street (on the right). If you keep on past these
two, you'll end up at the broad square called Augustinerplatz, with
the entrance (uphill and to the right) to the **Augustiner Museum**
(which may still be closed for renovation). Continuing along the
little street called Grünwälderstrasse (directly across from the
Augustiner Museum entrance) brings you to even more eateries,
including the wonderful Markthalle food circus on the left (all
described later, under "Eating in Freiburg").

• *Our Freiburg walk is finished. Now go splash in those canals.*

BLACK FOREST

Sights in Freiburg

▲▲Cathedral (Münster)

The lacy spire rocketing up from Freiburg's skyline marks its impressive main church. While Germany has bigger and better cathedrals, Freiburg's has some interesting details that make it worth a visit.

Cost and Hours: Cathedral interior—free, usually open Mon–Sat 10:00–16:30, Sun 13:00–16:30; tower—€1.50, Mon–Sat 9:30–17:00, Sun 13:00–17:00, enter from outside church.

◐ Self-Guided Tour: Begin out front. The exterior **scaffolding** is a semi-permanent feature of the church. The cathedral's distinctive pink color comes from a soft local sandstone that's easy to work, but also extremely fragile. Decorations need to be replaced every 30 to 60 years. Keeping the church from falling apart is a never-ending task—elderly locals who've lived here their entire lives report having never seen the church without at least some scaffolding.

The frilly **tower** *(Münsterturm)* is as tall as the church is long (127 yards)...but not worth the 329-step ascent. Up in the tower are 16 different bells, each one with a different name and purpose. Traditionally, Catholics could not eat meat on Fridays, so instead they'd eat *Spätzle* (German noodles)—giving the oldest bell, rung just before lunchtime on Fridays, its nickname, the "*Spätzle* Bell." Other bells include one that tolls each night at 20:00 (originally to remind townspeople that the city gates were closing), and a "Tax Bell" that rings twice weekly in November and December, when taxes traditionally came due.

Before heading inside, spend a few minutes looking around the ornately decorated **entryway** (outside the door itself, but inside the gated area). The 418 colorfully painted statues (recently restored

and now protected with netting from destructive pigeons) ooze with medieval church symbolism. Each has an identifying symbol. As you look back out to the square, the first figure on the right is St. Catherine, holding a wheel (her bones were broken on a wheel).

Two particularly memorable characters have become mascots of Freiburg. First is the so-called **"praying devil."** In the tympanum (over the door), look for Jesus on the cross. Just below him and a bit to the right is a pot-bellied devil, greedily rubbing his hands together as he watches the Archangel Michael weigh the goodness of a person's soul (while two other devils try to fix the results). Then, along the left wall, notice the strange little character under the third statue from the right—playing his nose like a trumpet.

Now go **inside**. Go left and look along the back wall, where you'll find photos of Freiburg after it was devastated by WWII bombs. The city made it through most of the war virtually unscathed—until November 27, 1944, when, in a space of just 20 minutes, about 80 percent of Freiburg's buildings were destroyed by an Allied bombing run. Miraculously, the cathedral was one of the few structures that survived. Some credit divine intervention, while others claim the bombers intentionally avoided it; either way, the steeple's lattice-work top and underground lead anchors probably saved it, since shockwaves from explosions all around it would have leveled a solid, less-supported tower.

The **stained-glass windows** are originals, from the 13th and 14th centuries, which were hidden away and protected during World War II. Each one is marked with the seal of a local merchant who sponsored it (go on a scavenger hunt to find the pretzel, from the baker; the barrel, from the cooper; the scissors, from the tailor; and the hammer, tongs, and snake—representing fire—from the blacksmith).

Now stroll down the **nave** toward the altar. After its thriving market and Black Forest silver mine made Freiburg rich, this cathedral was built on the site of an earlier church. Begun in about 1200, most of the structure was finished relatively quickly (it has the only Gothic steeple in Germany that was actually completed during Gothic times, in 1330), but it still demonstrates various styles. The earliest part of the church, at the **transept**, is Romanesque (notice the rounded tops to the windows); but as Gothic engineering swept neighboring France, Freiburg's cathedral builders began to incorporate that style (see the telltale pointed arches elsewhere in the church).

Many churches from this era have 12 **pillars** lining the nave, each one with the statue of an apostle. But after the primary construction on this cathedral was finished, a large choir was added beyond the altar, so two more pillars were built—bringing the total up to 14. Judas was given the heave-ho, and pillars were granted to Paul, Matthias, and Jesus himself. Look at the statues on the two pillars flanking the altar: On the right is Jesus, and on the left is Thomas—pointing two fingers because of his insistence on touching Jesus before he'd believe in the Resurrection. Thomas' privileged position in this church is based on the philosophy that non-believers should be closest to Christ.

BLACK FOREST

You can take a quick spin around the **choir** to see some ornately decorated chapels, the crypt, and a closer look at the painting over the altar (enter to the right of the altar, free, Mon–Sat 10:00–11:30 & 13:00–16:00, Sun 13:00–16:00).

When you're finished, head outside using the side door (right transept), and you'll be back out on Münsterplatz.

Other Sights

Augustiner Museum—Freiburg's top museum is nearing the end of an extensive renovation, and might be open in time for your visit. The Upper Rhine region's most significant collection of Black Forest art and culture, with an emphasis on medieval artifacts, is displayed around the reconstructed shell of an Augustinian church. The highlights are a close-up look at some of the cathedral's original medieval stained glass and statuary, as well as Wentzinger's *Immaculata*, a two-foot-tall terra-cotta statue from the 18th century. Even if the museum is not yet fully open, some parts of the collection may be free and viewable (cost and hours not yet set; likely about €5 and open Tue–Sun 10:00–17:00, closed Mon; grand entrance on Augustinerplatz, tel. 0761/201-2531, www.freiburg.de /museen).

The area around Augustinerplatz is the heart of the **Gerberau district,** popular with locals. It's quieter and filled with little galleries and restaurants that are less expensive than on Münsterplatz (several are recommended later, under "Eating in Freiburg").

City History Museum—Telling the story of Freiburg, this museum is worthwhile if only to see the two town models in the cellar. One shows medieval Freiburg circa 1590, with the city wall and all five city gates intact. Notice the little wall around the cathedral (today's Münsterplatz). This was the town cemetery, and the little house huddled next to the grand church was the *Beinhaus* (charnel house, where exhumed remains were stored). The other model, from the early 1700s, shows how the French King Louis XIV turned the city into a gigantic fortress—one of Europe's largest at the time (see next listing). Upstairs you'll find another model—this one of the cathedral while it was under construction—along with Freiburg-manufactured player pianos and other exhibits and artifacts about town history (€2, Tue–Sun 10:00–17:00, closed Mon, Münsterplatz 30, tel. 0761/201-2515).

Schlossberg (Castle Hill)—Schlossberg towers over the east end of Freiburg's Old Town. A monstrous 18th-century fort once stood here on "Castle Hill," built by the French to control the citizens of Freiburg during a period of French occupation. The giant fortress garrisoned as many as 150,000 soldiers at once. (Consider Freiburg's highly strategic position: near the Rhine River Valley, the entrance to the Black Forest, and the French border.) The French destroyed the fortress when they retreated, leaving behind virtually no traces of the fort, except for a few stony walls. Today Schlossberg is Freiburg's playground, popular for its views over the city. A modern lookout tower (100 feet high) stands where the French Fort d'Aigle (eagle tower) once stood.

To get to the top of Schlossberg, you can either hike or (easier) take a free elevator up. From Schwabentor, the half-timbered tower at the east end of the Old Town, look for the pedestrian walkway over the busy ring road. Once across, if you want to walk, bear left and hike up the steep switchbacks for 10 minutes. Or, to take the elevator *(Aufzug)*, continue straight through the cave-like tunnel to access it. At the top of the elevator and trail, you'll come to the pricey Greiffenegg Schlössle restaurant, and (in good weather) an affordable beer garden just above; both have knockout sunset views (and are described later, under "Eating in Freiburg").

For even better views, keep hiking to higher and higher perches. About a seven-minute hike above the restaurant is a broad, flat plateau with benches overlooking the town's rooftops. From there, you can hike about five more minutes up to a stubby stone bastion; or, for the highest vantage point, trek about 20 minutes up to the modern lookout tower. You can loop up to the tower and back on different paths. For the most straightforward approach to the tower, begin at the plateau with your back to the benches, walk the level path to the left, then veer right uphill at the big white cross (follow small silver signs with a picture of the tower).

Schauinsland—Freiburg's own mountain, little more than an oversized hill, is nine miles southeast of the center. The viewpoint at its 4,000-foot summit, which won't wow anyone from Colorado, offers the handiest panorama view of the Schwarzwald for those without wheels. The gondola system that takes you up—one of Germany's oldest—was designed for Freiburgers relying on public transportation (€11.50 round-trip for gondola, €26 family ticket includes 2 adults and up to 4 kids, daily July–Sept 9:00–18:00, Oct–June 9:00–17:00; catch tram #2—direction Günterstal—from town center to the end, then take bus #21 seven stops to Talstation stop for gondola; tel. 0761/451-1777, www.bergwelt-schauinsland .de). At the top, you'll find a view restaurant, pleasant circular walks, and the Schniederli Hof, a 1592 farmhouse museum. A tower on a nearby peak offers an even more commanding Black Forest view.

BLACK FOREST

Sleeping in Freiburg

(€1 = about $1.40, country code: 49, area code: 0761)

Though I prefer nights in sleepy Staufen (where you'll get better value for your money—see page 235), Freiburg is livelier and easier for non-drivers. I've concentrated my listings in the Old Town; the Alleehaus, Freiburg's best deal, is nearly as well-located, just a few steps beyond the Old Town core.

$$$ Hotel Oberkirch is pricey but ideally situated. Nine of its 26 rooms sit right on the main square (facing the cathedral and above a restaurant); the rest are in a nearby building along a pleasant pedestrian street. Each of the Old World rooms is different; some are a bit dated, but all are clean and comfortable (flexible rates, but officially Sb-€99–118, Db-€149–152 on pedestrian street; Sb-€139–168, Db-€162–186 on square; up to €20 extra during busy times, elevator, free Wi-Fi, reception and most rooms at Schusterstrasse 11, others at Münsterplatz 22, tel. 0761/202-6868, www.hotel-oberkirch.de, info@hotel-oberkirch.de).

$$$ Kreuzblume Hotel rents eight mod, themed, recently spiffed-up rooms above a restaurant on a charming wisteria-draped shopping street in the heart of the Old Town (Sb-€75, Db-€119, €10 cheaper Oct–March, elevator, free Wi-Fi, Konviktstrasse 31, tel. 0761/31194, www.hotel-kreuzblume.de, info@hotel-kreuz blume.de).

$$ Hotel Alleehaus is tops, with 19 comfy rooms and modern decor at the south edge of the Old Town. While close to the action, it's on a quiet, leafy street in a big house that feels like home, and is warmly run by Bernd, Claudia, and their team (S-€49, Sb-€63–75, small Db-€85, twin Db-€94, larger Db-€99, Tb-€135, Qb-€154, reception closed 19:30–6:00, call by 18:00 if arriving later than 19:30, free Wi-Fi, parking-€9/day, Marienstrasse 7, tel. 0761/387-600, fax 0761/387-6099, www.hotel-alleehaus.de, wohlfuehlen @hotel-alleehaus.de). From the station, walk 20 minutes or take tram #3 (direction Vauban) or #5 (direction Rieselfeld) three stops to Holzmarkt; then walk along Holzmarkt, which becomes Wallstrasse, and turn right on Marienstrasse.

$$ Schwarzwälder Hof, just a block behind the cathedral, has 45 straightforward rooms over a reasonably priced restaurant. Their budget rooms are tidy and affordable, but the rooms-to-toilets ratio can be a bit challenging (S-€45, Ss-€48, D-€75, Ds-€78). Regular rooms include some renovated ones that are modern and slick (Sb-€70, Db-€95–105, Tb-€120; all rooms include free local transport card, elevator, free Internet access and Wi-Fi, parking-€9/day, Herrenstrasse 43, from station take tram #1 in direction Littenweiler three stops to Oberlinden, tel. 0761/38030, fax 0761/380-3135, www.shof.de, info@shof.de, Engler family).

$$ Hotel zur Sichelschmiede rents six traditional, woody budget rooms above a recommended restaurant in the cutest part of town, overlooking a canal (Sb-€59–65, Db-€79–85, Insel 1, tel. 0761/35037, Gerdi Stark and family).

Hostels

$ Black Forest Hostel has 105 of the cheapest beds in Freiburg. Run by friendly Tania, with a young, bohemian attitude, it's bare-bones simple (€13–16 per person in 10- to 21-bed rooms, €17–22 per person in 3- to 8-bed rooms, S-€29, D-€48, sheets-€3, sleeping bags OK, cash only, no curfew, no smoking in rooms, lockers, pay Internet access, self-service kitchen, laundry-€5, Kartäuser Strasse 33—look for anchor sign and go down driveway; 20-min walk from station or take tram #1—direction: Littenweiler—to Oberlinden stop, then walk 5 more min; tel. 0761/881-7870, fax 0761/881-7895, www.blackforest-hostel.de, backpacker@black forest-hostel.de). If full, they might direct you to the much larger, more distant **$ Freiburg Youth Hostel** at Kartäuser Strasse 151 (dorm bed-€22, includes sheets and breakfast, €3 more for travelers over 26, tel. 0761/67656, www.jugendherberge-freiburg.de, info@jugendherberge-freiburg.de).

Eating in Freiburg

Freiburg's best eateries are conveniently concentrated within a block or two of the square called Augustinerplatz. Browse your options here and choose your favorite.

In the Gerberau District

These two places are just downhill from Augustinerplatz, along the town creek.

Hausbrauerei Feierling is a rollicking microbrewery that also serves good meals. On warm summer evenings, their *Biergarten* across the street offers cool, leafy shade and a bustling atmosphere. If you're dining inside, try the cozy upstairs seating, looking down over the big copper vats (€5–13 entrées, daily 11:00–24:00, indoor section closed in afternoons when weather is hot, Gerberau 46, tel. 0761/243-480).

Sichelschmiede is a good option rain or shine. Its timbered alcoves and cluttered interior give it a cozy living-room feel, and its creekside seating can't be beat. Come here for easygoing seasonal regional cuisine, good value, and a family-friendly ambience (€7–15 plates, daily

12:00–23:00, Insel 1, tel. 0761/35037). Don't confuse it with a neighboring, lesser-value restaurant which shares the outdoor terrace—notice the color-coded tables.

Along Grünwälderstrasse

This street, connecting Augustinerplatz to the shopping and university zone, is lined with tempting choices.

Markthalle is a wonderful food court where you can peruse a wide option of cuisines from around the world—German, French, Swiss, Italian, Indian, Brazilian, Chinese, Arabic, and more (most meals around €5–10, Mon–Thu 8:00–20:00, Fri–Sat 8:00–24:00, closed Sun, live music on weekend evenings—no cover, Grünwälderstrasse 4). At the front of the complex is a half-Portuguese, half-Italian wine bar called **Osteria**. You can bring food from the other vendors in here to sit and enjoy, but only if you order a drink. They also serve their own food (€3–4 tapas and €5–9 light Mediterranean fare). One section of the impressive interior is elaborately done up as a Lisbon café—don't miss it (Mon–Sat 10:00–24:00, closed Sun except in summer, Grünwälderstrasse 2, tel. 0761/387-0038).

Tacheles appeals to student-size appetites (big) and budgets (small). Who knew that schnitzel could be prepared in literally a dozen different ways? Here at the self-proclaimed *"Schnitzel Paradies,"* they serve up big schnitzels (€1.20 extra for *Pute*—turkey—instead of the traditional pork), a salad, and your choice of a side dish (french fries, *Spätzle,* and so on) for a mere €6.50 for lunch or €7.50 for dinner (after 18:00). Non-schnitzel lunch specials (Mon–Fri only) cost €6.50. The pub downstairs, a favorite hangout, can be crowded and smoky; instead, opt for the quiet courtyard seating upstairs (daily 11:30–24:00 or later, also vegetarian options, nightly happy hour 18:00–20:00, occasional live *Fussball* broadcasts, Grünwälderstrasse 17, tel. 0761/319-6669).

Chang Thai, two doors down from Tacheles, is where students satisfy their Asian-food cravings (€5–7 lunches, €7–10 main dishes, Mon–Sat 12:00–23:00, Sun 13:00–22:30, Grünwälderstrasse 21).

Aran, facing the Augustiner Museum entrance right on Augustinerplatz, is an upscale sandwich shop and café (also serving soup, baked potatoes, and smoothies) with a "designy" interior and relaxing outdoor seating (€4–6 sandwiches, daily May–Oct 9:00–21:00—or until 23:00 in good weather, Nov–April 9:00–19:00, tel. 0761/290-9664).

In the "Bermuda Triangle" Neighborhood

Night owls flock around St. Martin's Tower (Martinstor), in the area affectionately called Freiburg's "Bermuda Triangle." Take the street to your right just before going through the gate and get sucked in. Look at the Burger King ahead of you; mischievous Puck does a little dance and plays the pan pipes. He's a fitting mascot for a district known for its fun, colorful bars.

At **UC/Uni-Café,** join the cerebral grad-student crowd for cheap salads, sandwiches, and breakfasts—have a cappuccino outside on the square, or pop inside to drink beer and watch a *Fussball* match on the flat-screen TV (€4–8 salads and sandwiches, Mon–Sat 8:00–23:00, Sun 10:00–23:00, Niemensstrasse 7, at Universitätsstrasse, tel. 0761/383-355).

Gelato: Drop by **Incontro,** where you'll be greeted with a robust *"Buona sera!"* before choosing your favorite flavor (€0.80/scoop, daily 10:00–23:00, on Niemensstrasse).

On Freiburg's Schlossberg

For directions on getting to these scenic eateries, see page 225.

Greiffenegg Schlössle offers rooftop views over Freiburg, but the meals are expensive, and worth it only if you can get a table on

the terrace in good weather (€11–16 starters, €20–28 main dishes, daily 11:00–24:00, reservations smart, tel. 0761/32728). Consider instead their self-service open-air **Biergarten Kastaniengarten,** just above the restaurant (€6–9 entrées, open April–Oct in good weather, same hours). If the weather is iffy, before ascending look for the *Biergarten geöffnet* ("beer garden open") sign near the base of the elevator.

Cheaper yet, consider a **picnic** at the Schlossberg viewpoint. Buy supplies at the **Migros supermarket,** in the basement of the Karstadt department store on Kaiser-Joseph-Strasse, near the cathedral.

Freiburg Connections

The full name of the town—and the station—is Freiburg im Breisgau, often abbreviated as "Freiburg (Brsg)" on schedules.

By Train to: Staufen (hourly until about 19:00, 30 min, most require transfer at Bad Krozingen; for details, see "Staufen Connections" later in this chapter), **Baden-Baden** (direct trains every 1–2 hrs, 45 min), **Munich** (hourly, 4.5 hrs, 1 change), **Basel,** Switzerland (hourly, 45 min), **Bern,** Switzerland (hourly, 2 hrs, most transfer in Basel), **Frankfurt** (hourly, 2–2.5 hrs, some direct, most require change at Mannheim or Frankfurt Airport), **Frankfurt Airport** (hourly, 2 hrs, direct or with a change in Mannheim). Train info: tel. 0180-599-6633 (€0.14/min).

Staufen

Hemmed in by vineyards and watched over by the ruins of a protective castle, Staufen (SHTOW-fehn, rhymes with "cow pen")

is small and off the beaten path. Its
quiet pedestrian zone of colorful old
buildings is bounded by a happy creek
that actually babbles. The hotels in
Staufen make a peaceful and delightful home base for your exploration of
Freiburg and the southern trunk of
the Black Forest. Don't miss Staufen's
real-world back streets—you'll find
delightful pockets of calm for two
blocks in every direction from the
main drag. You can also make Staufen
a half-day outing from Freiburg (bet-
ter for lunch than for dinner, as the last public transport back from
Staufen leaves around 19:00).

Orientation to Staufen

Little Staufen im Breisgau (pop. 7,500) is simple to master. The
main square is an easy 10-minute walk from the train station, and
everything I list is along the way (or just off it).

Tourist Information

Staufen's helpful TI, on the main square in the Rathaus, has
Internet access for €4 per hour (April–Oct Mon–Fri 9:00–12:30
& 14:00–17:30, Sat 10:00–12:00, closed Sun; Nov–March Mon–Fri
9:00–12:00 plus Mon, Wed, and Fri 14:00–16:30, closed Sat–Sun;
tel. 07633/80536, www.touristik-staufen.de).

Local Guide: Marianne Pfadt, a German who speaks
English with a charming Scottish brogue, enjoys taking visitors on
a casual but insightful tour around the back streets of her hometown (€50 for 1.5-hour walk, siegfried.pfadt@t-online.de).

Arrival in Staufen

There are no lockers at the **train station,** but try Bahnhof Hotel
(see "Sleeping in Staufen," later). To get to town, exit the station
with your back to the pond and angle right up Bahnhofstrasse.
Turn right at the post office onto Hauptstrasse, which leads
through the town center to the Rathaus and TI.

If you're arriving by **car,** follow signs for *Stadtmitte* to find the town center. If your hotel is in the pedestrian zone, it's OK to drive there to park. If you're day-tripping, you'll find a handy parking lot right at the entrance to the center (and at the start of my self-guided walk).

Self-Guided Walk

Welcome to Staufen

Few small German towns are as enjoyable to explore as Staufen.

It's tourist-friendly without being a tourist trap—a real town with real shops and residents, but still accessible to visitors. This walk will help you get your bearings. It begins at the start of the cobbled pedestrian zone, near the parking lot; if you're coming from the train station, this is the first part of the old center you'll reach.

• *Begin at the Wine Cooperative building, near the big tree, fountain, and giant wine press.*

Wine Co-op Square

As evidenced by the vineyards blanketing its little castle hill, Staufen sits amid a popular wine-growing region. Wine production (along with taxes levied on silver that was mined deeper in the Black Forest) made this town rich...and it still does. People "taking the cure" at the rehab centers in nearby Bad Krozingen come to this square to take a break from their treatment and sip local wines. The building labeled *Winzergenossenschaft* is Staufen's **bottling cooperative,** where several local vintners sell their wines. They offer free tastes and sell affordable bottles (most bottles €4–7, Mon–Fri 9:00–18:00, Sat 9:00–14:00, Sun 10:00–15:00 except closed Sun Jan–Feb, Hauptstrasse 7, tel. 07633/5510). Or, if you'd just like a glass of wine in the summer, you can sit out front at the little **wine garden** (€1.50 to €3 per glass, Sun–Fri 14:00–22:00, Sat 11:00–22:00).

At the benches between the fountain and the gigantic wine press, look for the photo of a grand red-sandstone courthouse that once stood here. That building, like much of Staufen, was devastated by an Allied bombing late in World War II (February 8, 1945)—you'll see other photos of the damage scattered around town.

• *Now walk up Staufen's main street...*

BLACK FOREST

Hauptstrasse

Like its big sister Freiburg, Staufen has little canals called *Bächle* running along its main street (originally made for fire protection and now enjoyed for their own sake). The charm of this colorful drag is governed by strict building codes: Only certain colors can be used, and the shutters are uniform. But locals grumble that sometimes the rules go too far. Notice the rain gutters that empty out onto the cobbles. These used to run underground, but were brought aboveground to be more authentically medieval—and now the streets turn into an ice rink in cold weather.

But the careful restrictions aren't just for the tourists. You'll notice that most of the shops even along this main street aren't trinket boutiques, but real services. Staufen is a thriving, self-sufficient community, and along here you'll see bakers, butchers, pharmacies (such as the old-time *Apotheke* on the right, at #52), and other everyday shops. In fact, some Freiburgers prefer to do their shopping here in Staufen, where the stores are smaller and the owner-clerks are friendlier.

Just before you reach the main square, on the left (at #47), look for the red **Gasthaus zum Löwen.** In the early 16th century, a popular and successful doctor/scientist/fortune teller/alchemist named Johann Georg Faust was brought here to Staufen to produce gold for the town. He lived and worked in this very house, experimenting with chemical processes until an accidental explosion killed him around the year 1540. This being the Middle Ages, the townspeople assumed that the devil must have had a hand in his death, and legends began to swirl. Over time, these stories grabbed the attention of various writers, including Johann Wolfgang von Goethe (the "German Shakespeare"). In Goethe's seminal work *Faust,* the title character makes a pact with a demon named Mephistopheles, who then breaks Faust's neck—a scene depicted on the side of the building. You might see a costumed Mephistopheles leading tours through the streets of Staufen (in German only).

Across the street, at #56 (marked *Stubenhaus Stadtmuseum*), you can duck into one of Staufen's oldest **courtyards.** Go down the half-timbered passage (and past the cheesy Restaurant Käsestube) to get inside. Historically, the building overlooking this courtyard was used by the local guilds to host special events...and it can still be rented out today. The courtyard itself is filled with occasional concerts (usually advertised by posters nearby).

• *Continue out to Staufen's main square...*

Marktplatz (Market Square)

Looking around the square, notice the clever design: Four streets converge, but are offset, so as you approach you see not other streets—but buildings. This makes the square feel especially cozy.

The soldier atop the **fountain** holds the shield of Staufen, with its symbol: three golden goblets on a red field. The medieval word *Stuff* meant "goblet"; Staufen was named for its castle hill, which resembles an upside-down goblet.

Dominating the square is the **Town Hall** *(Rathaus)*. The left part is older (Gothic) than the right part (Renaissance), but the whole thing was restored in 2007. The coats of arms represent the various powers that have controlled Staufen over the centuries. The golden seashell at the top of the right peak indicates that this was a

stop along the Camino de Santiago, the medieval pilgrimage route that leads all the way to the northwest corner of Spain. Inside the Town Hall are the TI and a very humble town museum (Stadtmuseum, upstairs, a few town artifacts, German only, free Mon–Fri, €1 Sat–Sun, open Mon 8:00–12:00 & 14:00–18:00, Tue–Fri 8:00–12:00, Sat–Sun 14:00–17:00).

The Town Hall restoration left the building looking beautiful...but is also threatening to destroy Staufen. Notice the troubling **cracks** running along the building facade adjoining the Town Hall. Around town you'll see many similar cracks. The renovation tapped into natural deposits of hot steam in order to use geothermal power for the building's heating and cooling. Engineers dug deep into the ground behind the Town Hall, built the heating system, and for a few weeks everything worked perfectly. But then the cracks began to appear. It turns out that the drilling punctured a layer of dry gypsum, which is now soaking up groundwater like a sponge and raising the ground beneath Staufen at a rate of about a centimeter each month. While experts scramble to stop it (if they can), more and more precious old buildings show still-growing cracks—170 homes in all have been damaged so far.

• *Before moving on, put your back to the Town Hall and look out toward the busy street in the distance. The yellow building on the right with the big* CAFE *sign is* **Café Decker**, *the best place in town for cakes and chocolates (described later, under "Eating in Staufen"). Five minutes' walk beyond that is Staufen's fascinating little cemetery (explained later).*

But first, if you'd like to see a side of Staufen most tourists miss, join me on a walk through...

BLACK FOREST

Staufen's Back Streets (Hinterstädtle)

Leave Marktplatz on the little lane (called Freihofgasse) between
the Kornhaus and the Volksbank. Stick with this lane as it
curls around to the left (pass-
ing a butcher shop on the right)
and goes through a completely
untouristy neighborhood. Then
continue moseying straight along
Spitalstrasse, the oldest quarter of
town. Traditionally, the commoners lived here, and the wealthy
aristocrats (and, later, well-heeled
retirees) lived in villas on the hillside above. But in the 1980s, a
gentrification began that has turned many of the once-humble cot-
tages in this area into fancy town houses. Today it's a hodgepodge
of spiffed-up yuppie homes and ramshackle older ones. As you
stroll, you'll enjoy the constant sound of running water from little
fountains (most marked *Kein Trinkwasser*—"not drinking water").
After passing a few art galleries, you might catch a glimpse of
the former town wall (on the right). Where the street does a little
jog and hits a bigger road, the big building on the left (marked
Renoviert A.D. 1978 on the upper window, and *Re: 1830* above the
door) was a hospice *(Spital)*, which wealthy townspeople financed
to house people who were ill and too poor to care for themselves.

Turn left and head for the church. This area has some fun boutique shops: Around the right side of the church is a local **coffee
roaster** (Coffee & More Kaffeerösterei, buy a bag of coffee to go or sip
a cup here on the square, Mon–Fri 9:30–18:00, Sat 9:30–14:00, Sun
14:00–17:30 except closed Sun Nov–Feb, St. Johannesgasse 14, tel.
07633/981-824), and around the left side is a **chocolatier** who trained
under the experts at Café Decker (Chocolaterie Sixt, €4.60/100
grams—mix and match, Wed–Fri 9:00–12:30 & 15:00–18:00, Sat
9:00–14:00, closed Sun–Tue, Kirchstrasse 11, tel. 07633/801-255).
Choose your poison. The church itself is big and empty-feeling.

You could follow the paved street right back to Marktplatz. Or,
to further immerse yourself in untouristy Staufen, face the church,
look left, and notice the big doorway at #9, marked *Jägergasse*.
Go into the passage and continue through local neighborhoods.
Watch kids having fun at the playground, peek over fences into
somebody's garden patch, and soak in local life. You can turn left
at Meiergasse, or keep going straight as the path narrows—both
options lead you right back to the cobbled pedestrian zone...you've
come full-circle.

• *Our walk is finished. If you still have time and energy, consider poking
around Staufen's evocative cemetery, just across the river, or hiking up to
its hilltop castle (both described next).*

Sights in Staufen

Cemetery (Friedhof)—Staufen has one of the most atmospheric and unexpectedly pleasant little cemeteries I've seen. It's a good place for a contemplative walk, and to ponder German burial customs. Generations of ornate headstones stand in a garden of trees and plants, giving it a comforting feel. As elsewhere in Germanic lands, plots in the cemetery are not purchased, only leased. When your lease is up, someone else moves in. Notice that some headstones have several added-on plaques identifying the remains of many generations of tenants. You may see people here lovingly tending to the graves, tidying the ivy and planting flowers: Tenants' survivors are responsible for maintenance. Some graves actually have huge trees growing right up out of them, like towering headstones reminding visitors that mortality is nothing new.

Getting There: The cemetery is worth the five-minute walk just across the river from the town center. Cross the big bridge next to Café Decker (at the edge of the pedestrian zone in front of the Town Hall), turn right, and walk a short distance between the river and the busy road. When you reach the small footbridge on your right, turn left and cross that busy road, and start walking down Wettelbrunner Strasse. A few steps down the street on the left, a small onion-domed chapel marks the cemetery.

Castle—Staufen's own little vineyard-covered mountain is topped by the remains of a castle (once the residence of the Lords of Staufen) that was destroyed by Swedish troops in 1632. The most direct route to visit these ruins is to charge right on up, but you can also take one of the less-steep roundabout trails.

Sleeping in Staufen

(€1 = about $1.40, country code: 49, area code: 07633)
In Staufen—and several other small Black Forest towns—your €1.40 per person, per night tourist tax (sometimes included in rates) comes with a big return for those relying on public transportation: the **KONUS card** *(KONUS Gästekarte),* which covers all transit for the entire Black Forest region (south to Switzerland, west to France, and north to Baden-Baden). This includes unlimited use of all trains, buses, and local transit (such as buses or trams in Freiburg or Baden-Baden), but doesn't cover express ICE or IC

trains. Unfortunately, hotel guests in Freiburg or Baden-Baden don't get the KONUS card. For more details, see www.konus -schwarzwald.info.

$$$ Hotel-Gasthof Kreuz-Post, in the pedestrian zone directly ahead of the Town Hall (on the left), is the town splurge. It rents five colorful, tidy rooms over a well-regarded restaurant (Sb-€85–90, Db-€98–110, price depends on size, free Wi-Fi, Hauptstrasse 65, tel. 07633/95320, www.kreuz-post-staufen.de, kreuz-post-staufen@t-online.de).

$$ Gasthaus Krone, the town's top value, sits in the middle of Staufen's main pedestrian drag like it owns it. Charming, friendly, and with nine comfortable rooms, it's a winner. Try here first (Sb-€65, Db-€85, Tb-€105, non-smoking, some rooms with balconies, free parking, Hauptstrasse 30, tel. 07633/5840, fax 07633/82903, www.die-krone.de, info@die-krone.de, Lahn family—father Kurt reminds me of Dan Rather).

$$ Zum Hirschen, also family-run and with a storybook location on the main pedestrian street, has 15 dated rooms and a roof deck (Sb-€65, Db-€85, Tb-€110, cheaper for 3 nights or more, some rooms with balconies, elevator, free and easy parking, Hauptstrasse 19, tel. 07633/5297, fax 07633/5295, www.hirschen-staufen.de, Dieter and Isabelle). Their top floor is a two-bedroom apartment (no kitchen) sleeping up to six people (€168 for 4 people).

$ Hotel Sonne, on a side street, is a budget alternative offering eight uninspired rooms above an Italian restaurant (Sb-€50, Db-€70, Tb-€95; restaurant serves €7–10 pastas, closed Tue; Albert-Hugard-Strasse 1, tel. 07633/95300, fax 07633/953-014). With your back to the Rathaus, walk straight for 50 yards and turn left on Mühlegasse.

$ Bahnhof Hotel is the closest thing Staufen has to a hostel. Its seven basic but cozy rooms (which share two bathrooms) are the cheapest in town. The rooms are situated over an antique restaurant/bar that delicately mingles budget travelers and grizzled locals. Packed full of old furniture, this place makes you feel like you're staying with an eccentric great-aunt. There's a dynamite castle view from the upstairs terrace, a self-service kitchen, and a tiny washing machine for guests (S-€21, D-€41, no breakfast, across from the train station, tel. 07633/6190, no English spoken).

Eating in Staufen

Many of the hotels listed above also have their own good restaurants. For a splurge option, head for **Gasthaus Krone** (appreciates vegetables and offers good meals, €19–25 main dishes, closed Fri lunch and all day Sat, Hauptstrasse 30, tel. 07633/5840) or **Hotel-Gasthof Kreuz-Post** (classic and classy dining room, German and Mediterranean cuisine, €13–18 starters, €19–30 main dishes, Thu–Tue 12:00–14:00 & 18:00–22:00, closed Wed, Hauptstrasse 65, tel. 07633/95320). For a mid-range option, try **Gasthaus zum Löwen** (tables right on the main square next to Town Hall, €6 starters, €9–13 lunches, €14–24 dinners, daily 10:00–22:00, Rathausgasse 8, tel. 07633/908-9390) or **Zum Hirschen** (cozy restaurant with €9–19 main dishes and take-your-time service, open Wed–Sun, closed Mon–Tue, Hauptstrasse 19, tel. 07633/5297). To dine cheaply, drop by **Bahnhof Hotel,** where you can eat on the tree-shaded patio or in the antler-filled restaurant. If you want to chomp red meat under a tree at a table made out of a wine barrel, this is the place. It can get raucous (€7.50 dinners, daily, across from train station, tel. 07633/6190).

Dessert: Every sweet-tooth in Staufen adores **Café Decker** for its 50 different types of chocolates (€5.10/100 grams) and long display case showing off a wide array of cakes (around €2.50/slice to go, or €3.50 to eat there). The dining room is genteel, but don't miss the inviting rooftop terrace, with views over Staufen's babbling brook (also €2–4 breakfasts and €3–7 light meals, Mon–Sat 6:30–18:00, Sun 13:30–18:00, Hauptstrasse 70, tel. 07633/5316).

Staufen Connections

By Train: Staufen is on a tiny branch line (called the Münstertalbahn) that connects to the main line at Bad Krozingen, a few stops south of Freiburg by slow milk-run train. From Freiburg, it's a 30-minute ride to Staufen (hourly, covered by a single €3.40 two-zone local transport ticket, available from ticket machines; if you're staying in Staufen, the trip is covered by your KONUS Card). Three times a day, a handy direct train connects Freiburg straight to Staufen. Otherwise, you'll transfer to another train in Bad Krozingen. Occasionally—especially late in the day—you might have to take bus #113 from Bad Krozingen to Staufen instead of the train (same ticket valid, bus stop is next to train station). Plan ahead by checking schedules online, asking at the Freiburg train or bus station (pick up a printed schedule), calling the bus station at 0761/368-0388 during business hours, or calling the regional schedule helpline at 01805-779-966 (€0.14/min, recording in German).

If you're staying in Staufen, be aware of the last through connection from Freiburg (leaves Mon–Fri at 20:15, Sat–Sun at 19:15). If you're visiting Staufen but sleeping elsewhere, note that the last through connection back to Freiburg leaves Staufen around 19:00 daily. If you really need to stay later in Staufen, a shared, subsidized taxi leaves from Staufen station for Bad Krozingen station at appointed times, but only when riders reserve a seat at least 30 minutes in advance by calling 07633/5386 (service called *Anrufsammeltaxi* or AST, regular ticket required, taxi also charges small "comfort supplement"). You can also call a regular taxi (same number).

The Best of the Black Forest

Baden-Baden, Freiburg, and Staufen are the most appealing destinations in the Black Forest. With more time, delve into the countryside in this land of cuckoo clocks and healthy hikes. Choose between two great ways to see the most representative parts of the Black Forest: a short excursion from Freiburg and back (by public transport or car); or, if you have a day to connect Baden-Baden and Freiburg by car, a longer drive that takes in some fun museums and activities. Fair warning: the Black Forest is what I'd call "gently scenic." Do it before you delve into the bigger, better Alps in Switzerland or Bavaria; otherwise, you might be underwhelmed.

Short and Scenic Black Forest Joyride from Freiburg

This pleasant loop takes you through the most representative chunk of the area, focusing on a pair of charming towns nestled in idyllic Black Forest landscape: St. Märgen and St. Peter. While designed to be done by car, this trip can also be done by public transportation.

Getting Around

By Car: Leave Freiburg on Schwarzwaldstrasse (signs to *Donaueschingen*), which becomes scenic road B-31 down the dark Höllental ("Hell's Valley"). From this road, all major tourist towns are clearly signposted. After the moody, narrow stretch of the valley, you'll hit a straightaway, then the road begins to bend back on itself as you twist up and out of the valley. At Hinterzarten (not far before Titisee), turn onto B-500 toward Furtwangen and St. Märgen. Soon you'll come to a fork, where you can choose between heading straight to Furtwangen (and its German Clock

Museum—a detour from this route but worth a visit if you have a car and plenty of time, described on page 246); or turning off for St. Märgen, then St. Peter. After St. Peter, stick with the main B-31 road (at Kirchzarten) to head right back into Freiburg. Or, for a longer drive, continue on from St. Peter, winding through idyllic Black Forest scenery up to Mount Kandel. Then the road winds steeply through a dense forest to Waldkirch, where a fast road takes you down to the Freiburg Nord autobahn entrance. From here you can return to Freiburg, or drive on to Baden-Baden.

By Train and Bus: Trains run regularly (2/hr Mon–Fri, hourly Sat–Sun) from Freiburg to Kirchzarten Bahnhof, where you can take hourly bus #7216 to St. Peter (45-min trip from Freiburg) and St. Märgen (55 min). Get off at St. Peter, hike four miles to St. Märgen, and bus/train back to Freiburg (through ticket €3.40 one-way, buy from machines). The Freiburg bus station has timetable booklets and more details on getting around the area (turn right out of Freiburg train station and walk 100 yards, tel. 0761/368-0388 during business hours; after hours, call 01805-779-966 for €0.12/min, or call Freiburg TI, tel. 0761/388-1880, www.rvf.de).

Black Forest Sights near Freiburg

These are the attractions you'll reach if following the plan outlined above. St. Märgen and St. Peter (and the walk connecting them) hold some of the best and most accessible bits of Black Forest charm. These stops are good for a very low-key, low-impact Black Forest meander.

En route, you're sure to see signs to overrated, overcrowded **Titisee.** This famous lake, with a giggle-inducing name, is improbably popular among Germans. One glance and you'll be wondering why they even bothered to develop this dull spot into a tourist attraction—and yet it's a huge hit. Don't let morbid curiosity take you to Titisee...or you'll squander valuable Black Forest time. (After all, you can't spell "tourist trap" without "T. T.")

Höllental ("Hell's Valley")

As road B-31 heads east out of Freiburg, the cliffs on either side begin to close in. Just before you enter the narrowest part of the valley, you'll pass an area known as Himmelreich ("Heaven"). The valley you're about to traverse was made to order for bandits, so those surviving "Hell's Valley" felt like they'd reached "heaven" when they got here. As you enter the narrowest part of the valley, watch for the *Hirschensprung* sign; look up to the cliff on the right to see a bronze statue of a deer *(Hirsch)* getting psyched up to make a leap *(Sprung)* over the chasm to escape a hunter, as told in a local legend.

BLACK FOREST

St. Märgen

St. Märgen is a pleasant, sleepy town dominated by its Augustinian abbey (nice, but less impressive than the abbey in St. Peter, described later; St. Märgen **TI** tel. 07669/911-817).

The only real sightseeing in town is the **Kloster Museum St. Märgen**, attached to (and named for) the Augustinian cloister. This small but delightful collection is worth a peek if it's open. While there's not a word of English, the highlights include Black Forest clocks (from ancient clocks using stones as counterweights, to more familiar cuckoo clocks, all displayed chronologically) and the *Reise ins Uhrenland* exhibit, which describes how Black Forest clock vendors spread far and wide around the world to sell these affordable timepieces. You'll see Black Forest clocks decorated for customers in many different countries. If you're not going to Furtwangen's German Clock Museum, this is a decent substitute. Rounding out the collection is ecclesiastical art, including folk pieces and paintings on glass (€3, English tour possible for €25; May–Oct Wed–Thu 10:00–13:00 & 14:00–17:00, closed Fri–Sat and Mon–Tue; year-round Sun 10:00–13:00; Rathausplatz 1, tel. 07669/911-817).

For a walk in the wilderness that combines convenience and fine vistas, consider the four-mile, 2.5-hour **"Panoramic Trail"** *(Panoramaweg)* connecting St. Märgen and St. Peter. From St. Märgen, two different trails lead uphill to the chapel called Kapfenkapelle; follow the signs to *St. Peter (Höhenweg)*. From the chapel, the path is mostly level (along a ridge overlooking the valley) before descending back into St. Peter. Hourly buses conveniently connect St. Peter and St. Märgen along the main road; when you're done with the hike, use the bus to zip back to your starting point. The TIs in St. Märgen and St. Peter have details.

St. Peter

St. Peter is one of the healthy, go-take-a-walk-in-the-clean-air places that doctors actually prescribe for people from all over Germany. The well-organized little **TI,** across from the Benedictine Abbey, can give you details on the region or recommend a countryside walk (TI open April–Oct Mon–Fri 9:00–12:00 & 15:00–17:00, Sat in July–Aug 10:00–12:00; Nov–March Mon–Fri 9:00–12:00; closed Sun year-round and Sat Sept–June; Klosterhof 11, tel. 07660/910-224).

The town of St. Peter is dominated by its giant namesake **Benedictine abbey**—red sandstone outside, with an interior dripping with white Rococo curlicues. Duck into the church for a glimpse at a classic Rococo interior. While it's not the finest in Germany—you'll see bigger and better in Bavaria—it's the best in the Black Forest (free, daily 8:00–19:00). The most interesting feature, the attached library, can be entered only with a German-language tour (€6, Tue at 11:00, Thu at 14:30, Sun at 11:30).

You can take the "**Panoramic Trail**" described above to reach St. Märgen, then come back on the hourly bus. From St. Peter, follow *St. Märgen (ü. Kapfenkapelle)* signs.

About 15 minutes by car from St. Peter is the pass over **Mount Kandel** (head for Glottertal, then just outside St. Peter turn right at Elmehof to follow brown signs to *Kandel*). At the summit is the Berghotel Kandel, with parking and fine views on either side of the ridge. For even better views, take a short hike to the 4,000-foot peak (Kandelgipfel). On a nice day, watch paragliders psych up and take off.

Sleeping in St. Peter: **$$ Gasthof Hirschen** is a traditional old 15-room guest house conveniently situated on the main square (Sb-€39–44, Db-€66–82, Tb-€87–97, Qb-€103, parking-€4/day, St. Peter/Hochschwarzwald, Bertholdsplatz 1, tel. 07660/204, fax 07660/1557, www.gasthof-hirschen.de, info@gasthof-hirschen .de). **$ Pension Kandelblick,** your budget option, has five basic rooms a 10-minute walk from the abbey and main square (D/Ds-€50–60, cash only, Seelgutweg 5, a block off the main drag at the St. Märgen end of town, tel. 07660/1259). Note that St. Peter's accommodations come with the same KONUS card public-transit deal as Staufen (see page 235).

Extended Black Forest Drive Between Baden-Baden and Freiburg

For a more thorough (and more interesting) look at the Black Forest, try this drive. Some of these sights are accessible to a point by public transportation, as noted, but can't be done as efficiently as by car. The two major museums of this area—both worth visiting—focus on different characteristics of the Black Forest: farming (the Vogtsbauernhof Black Forest Open-Air Museum) and clockmaking (Furtwangen's German Clock Museum).

Getting Around

Here are the directions for taking in all of the attractions listed here, whether you're heading from Baden-Baden to Freiburg, or vice-versa.

By Car from Baden-Baden to Freiburg: Head south from Baden-Baden on B-500, a.k.a. the Schwarzwald-Hochstrasse, which takes you along a ridge through 30 miles of pine forests (and becomes B-28—take it east, signs to Freudenstadt). Eventually you'll reach Freudenstadt, the workaday capital of the northern Black Forest. Wind your way through the sprawl of Freudenstadt, and hop on B-294 southbound toward Triberg. Just after Wolfach and before Hausach, turn south onto B-33/E-531 to Gutach, where you'll visit the Vogtsbauernhof Black Forest Open-Air Museum. Next, continue south on B-33/E-531, turning off to visit Triberg. Leaving Triberg, head south on B-500 to Furtwangen and its impressive German Clock Museum. From Furtwangen, continue south on B-500. From this road, you have two options for joining up with different scenic areas (both described earlier, under "Short and Scenic Black Forest Joyride from Freiburg"): Turn off for St. Märgen, then St. Peter. From here, you could take the slower and higher-altitude route to Freiburg via Mount Kandel and Waldkirch. For a more direct, but still scenic approach, continue a bit farther south on B-500 to Hinterzarten, where you can turn right onto B-31 and follow the claustrophobic Höllental ("Hell's Valley"). Either option brings you to Freiburg's backyard.

By Car from Freiburg to Baden-Baden: Begin by following the "Short and Scenic" joyride, described earlier, but continue north on B-500 to Furtwangen for a visit to its German Clock Museum, then Triberg. From Triberg, head north on B-33/E-531 (toward Hausach) to the open-air museum in Gutach, then continue north and pick up E-294 to Freuendstadt, and on to the Schwarzwald-Hochstrasse (B-28, then B-500), which dumps you right on Baden-Baden's back porch.

Sights Between Baden-Baden and Freiburg

▲Vogtsbauernhof Black Forest Open-Air Museum

This museum, the Schwarzwälder Freilichtmuseum Vogtsbauernhof, offers the best look at this region's traditional folk archi-

tecture. Built around one grand old farmhouse, the museum is a collection of several old farm buildings, some of which house exhibits on the local dress and lifestyles. While English information is sparse, the place gives you a good sense of traditional rural life in the Black Forest.

Cost and Hours: €6, April–Oct daily 9:00–18:00, until 19:00 in Aug, last entry one hour before closing, closed Nov–March, €8 guidebook, just outside the town of Gutach, tel. 07831/93560, www.vogtsbauernhof.org.

Getting There: Drivers will find it just south of the town of Hausach (not to be confused with nearby Halsach) on B-33/E-531; while technically in Gutach, the museum is actually in the country-side. Parking costs €4, or just €1 if you're visiting the museum (be sure to get your parking ticket validated when you buy your museum ticket). Without a car, take the **train** to Hausach (reached by train from Offenburg, on the main Baden-Baden-to-Freiburg line). From the Hausach station, take bus #7150 to the museum (7/day Mon–Fri, 4/day Sat, 6/day Sun, generally coordinated to meet the train, 5 min); otherwise, it's about a 30-minute walk to the museum.

Demonstrations and Tours: In July and August, you might see costumed docents posted at certain parts of the museum. At other times, it can be pretty sleepy, but occasional live presenta-tions give it some zip; look for a schedule of today's handicraft demonstrations on the chalkboard at the entry hall, or ask when you buy your ticket. There are no regularly scheduled English tours; if you'd like to arrange one, you'll pay €35 and must call well in advance.

❂ **Self-Guided Tour:** From the parking lot, it's a five-minute walk past eateries (described later) and under the railroad tracks to reach the ticket windows and main building. Pick up the map of the complex when you buy your ticket. The various buildings are identified out front (find English on the spinning language board), but the explanations inside are in German only. The following light commentary will bring some meaning to your visit.

The museum is named for its biggest building, the *Vogtsbauernhof,* or "farmhouse of the district governor"—the first, and only original, building on the premises, around which the rest of the complex grew. (As with all open-air folk museums, the other structures were transplanted from around the region and rebuilt here.) Built in 1612 and occupied until 1965, this giant farmhouse has distinctive Black Forest features that you'll also see (on a smaller scale) in the surrounding buildings. The charac-teristic "semi-hipped" roof is wider than the frame of the house, which creates ample dry storage space under the eaves all around the perimeter of the building. In case of a storm, the farmer and livestock could rush in quickly for shelter.

The house is built into the side of a hill, allowing easy ramp access to any of its levels—including the vast "attic." From here, hay would be unloaded into the middle level, and then could easily be dropped down as needed to where the livestock lived below.

People and animals lived under one roof. Explore the people's quarters. In that age of poor nutrition, people didn't grow as tall—you'll see short beds and short doorways made for short people. The kitchen is in the center of the building, to radiate heat to the

BLACK FOREST

living areas that flanked it. Notice the lack of a chimney, and the blackened walls in the kitchen—the stove was open to the roof to allow smoke to flow through the house, dry out the air (which was otherwise made uncomfortably humid by the animals), and sift out through the thatch. The two-story kitchen allowed farmers to smoke meat above while they cooked meals below. The soot also helped to coat and preserve the wood frame. Windows were a sure sign of wealth and status—the bigger the windows, the more prosperous the family.

Surrounding the main *Vogtsbauernhof* building are several smaller ones to explore. The **farm mill** is popular during its live grain-grinding demonstrations, when water power sets the giant gears in motion (daily at 11:15, 12:15, and 14:15, in German only). The **day laborer's cottage,** moved here only in 2001, once housed a family with 14 kids; two brothers lived here right up until 1993. Even though it has electricity, it's undeniably simple. The **bakery and distillery** has a communal oven where families from the community would bake their bread all at once—an efficient use of limited resources. The "knock-and-drop" **saw mill,** which runs only sporadically (on special request for groups), systematically—little by little—saws planks of wood from huge trunks.

Eating: The shops and restaurants scattered between the parking lot and museum entrance are awfully touristy, but are a fair source for local specialties. Skip the indoor restaurants and instead try your *Frikadelle* (a spiced pork-and-beef patty) or *Schupfnudeln* (potato-based noodles, served fried up with sauerkraut) at the outdoor stands. Don't be shy to try a little of everything; the friendly ladies ladling the portions will fill up your plate with whatever you point to and charge about €7. Be sure to indulge in a creamy slice of *Schwarzwälder Kirschtorte* (€2.50). Closer to the museum, in the main building, is the pricey but convenient Hofengel ("House Angel") restaurant (€5–10 salads, €7–9 light dishes, €12–15 main dishes).

Triberg

Deep in the Black Forest, Triberg is a mid-size town that exploits its cuckoo-clock heritage to the hilt. Despite the kitsch, it's a pleasant place to stretch your legs under giant cuckoo-clock facades. Convenient eateries cluster around the lowest reaches of the town's waterfall, near the two main attractions (described below). Touristy as Triberg is, it offers an easy way for travelers without cars to enjoy the Black Forest. The **TI** is located in Black Forest Museum (tel. 07722/866-490, www.triberg.de).

Triberg's **Black Forest Museum** (Schwarzwaldmuseum; not to be confused with the nearby Vogtsbauernhof Black Forest Open-Air Museum, described earlier) gives a fine look at the local culture.

The museum, worth ▲, is well-explained and offers a thorough look at the local culture of the town and region. As you explore its three floors, you'll find insightful exhibits on various aspects of Black Forest cultural heritage, with a special emphasis on engineering (clockmaking, railways, locally built SABA radios) and crafts (woodcarving, glassmaking). The main hall contains dozens of dolls wearing traditional dress from the region, including the distinctive maidens' hats, piled with gigantic cranberries (married women's hats have black puffballs). Player pianos, barrel organs, orchestrions ("orchestras-in-a-box"), and other music-making machines—which were built here alongside cuckoo clocks—were extremely popular in the days before radio or gramophones, when it was the only cheap way to listen to music. Rounding out the museum are exhibits on farming (a replica of a farmer's traditional quarters), mineral mining, winter sports, and creepy masks used to celebrate Germanic Mardi Gras, called Fasnacht (€4.50, pick up the free one-page English "Short Tour" at the entrance, a few additional posted explanations in English, daily May–Sept 10:00–18:00, Oct–April 10:00–17:00 except closed Mon Nov–Easter, Wallfahrtstrasse 4, tel. 07722/4434, www.schwarz waldmuseum.de).

Triberg's other claim to fame is Germany's highest **waterfall** (Triberger Wasserfall), where the Gutach River tumbles 500 feet in several bounces (€3, daily May–Sept 10:00–18:00, Oct–April 10:00–17:00, otherwise free entry). Although it seems odd to pay to see a waterfall, this one really is impressive—especially if you have time to walk through its steep, misty gorge. Three entrances lead to the waterfall, at different altitudes (scattered along the twisty main road toward Furtwangen). While the lowest entrance—"Haupteingang," in the town center, across from the Black Forest Museum—is most convenient, drivers might want to stop by the middle entrance ("Scheffelplatz," a 5-min downhill walk to the middle of the falls). If you're traveling in a group, it's handy to drop the gang off at Scheffelplatz to hike down, while the driver loops down into town to meet them at the lower entrance. If you don't want to pay, you can get a partial glimpse of the falls through the trees near the lower entrance.

The Black Forest Clockmaker Diaspora

Black Forest clockmakers specialized in affordable, every-day timepieces. Because they could be produced and sold cheaply, Black Forest clocks became popular around the world. Between 1800 and 1850 alone, 15 million Black Forest clocks were sold worldwide. This demand—combined with a need for steady employment among a growing population—persuaded many Black Forest natives to leave home and sell clocks in foreign lands.

From the 1770s through the early 1900s, roving Black Forest clockmakers (called *Uhrenhändler*) traveled far. They'd load their wares onto a wood-frame rucksack and cry, *Ins Uhrenland!*—"To clock country!"...that is, wherever people were buying clocks. Once they found a good market abroad, they'd settle in, set up shop, and create a lucrative little business. Many clockmakers were away from home for months, or even years—and quite a few married into their adopted local communities. (Emigrants from this part of Germany likely started out as clock-sellers.)

Most of these *Uhrenhändler* sold simple "shield clocks" (*Schilduhr*), with a simple face that hid the mechanical workings. The face of the clock could be painted to match the local tastes of the buyer, whether in England, France, Italy, Spain, Russia, Turkey, China, Australia...or the US. But no matter how far from home the clockmakers wandered, and no matter how different the clocks looked, they were still Black Forest at heart.

BLACK FOREST

Getting to Triberg: Drivers on B-500 will go right through the center of town. Triberg is also on the scenic Offenburg-Hausach **train** line; transfer in Offenburg to reach **Freiburg** (hourly, 1.5–1.75 hrs) or **Baden-Baden** (hourly, 1.75 hrs).

▲▲Furtwangen's German Clock Museum (Deutsches Uhrenmuseum)

The unremarkable town of Furtwangen hosts the most interesting museum in the Black Forest: the excellent German Clock Museum. More than a chorus of cuckoo clocks, this museum is practically evangelical in tracing the development of clocks from the Dark Ages to the Space Age. Because it's modern and well-presented in English, this exhibit makes the history of timekeeping more fascinating than it has any right to be.

Cost and Hours: €4, €10 family ticket, daily April–Oct 9:00–18:00, Nov–March 10:00–17:00, Robert-Gerwig-Platz 1, tel. 07723/920-2800, www.deutsches-uhrenmuseum.de.

Getting There: It's hiding out in the town center of Furtwangen; as you approach the town, closely track the low-profile signs to *Deutsches Uhrenmuseum* or simply *Uhrenmuseum*. It's related—and attached—to the local technical university.

Tours: In summer (April–Oct), you can pay €1 to join an English tour. There's no official schedule, so call ahead to ask if a tour is planned, or just show up and take your chances. If it's quiet, someone might be able to demonstrate one or two of the interactive pieces for you.

◐ Self-Guided Tour: As you enter, borrow the thorough English translations of the descriptions, then match them to the pictures on the posted information to find the right text. Appropriately enough, the collection is displayed chronologically, starting on the first floor (upstairs), then working its way down through the split-level building—follow the *Rundgang* (tour) signs.

Floor 1: Starting with Stonehenge (speculated to be a celestial calendar) and early sundials, the exhibit takes in the full breadth of timepiece history. In the display case of celestial clocks, find the highly detailed **astronomical-geographical clock** from 1787, which used just 24 gears to tell not only the time, but also the position of the stars in the night sky, which saint's day it was, and the phase of the moon.

Black Forest clockmakers achieved a breakthrough when they simplified the timekeeping mechanism so that it could be built almost entirely of wood, allowing the clocks to be sold at a much lower price (leading to a worldwide boom in clock sales). In this collection, you can watch **Black Forest clocks** evolve from rough-hewn wood to delicately painted white lacquer faces. You'll see that locals also figured out how to make musical clocks with wooden flutes and bellows—much more affordable than bells or other metal instruments.

The vast collection of **cuckoo clocks** (*Kuckucksuhren* in German) explains the evolution of the Black Forest's most iconic product. The cuckoo clock as we know it was created for a contest in 1850 by Friedrich Eisenlohr, a railway architect who modeled his *Bahnhäusleuhr* clock after a railroad house. While the clocks strike us as quaint and kitschy now, consider how Eisenlohr's idea of shaping a clock like a little house revolutionized the cuckoo-clockmaking industry. Cuckoo clocks became very popular—especially among tourists during the late-19th-century heyday of the romantic "Grand Tour" era—and were eventually copied by clockmakers in Switzerland. (If you even hint that cuckoo clocks are Swiss, proud Black Forest natives will quickly set you straight.)

On the way downstairs, ogle the gigantic **"Astronomical World Clock"** by August Noll. In addition to the giant clock dial,

notice the smaller dials to show different time zones—a new concept in the slow-travel era when this was created. The clock has many details to examine—and even more if its mechanical gears are whirring. If a tour is going on, you might get to see this giant clock in action, with Jesus blessing the 12 apostles as they shuffle past. (If it's not too busy, you can try asking the front desk to turn it on for you.) Next, head downstairs to...

Floor -1: Now in the 20th century, the exhibit shows off pocket watches with precious details (including, at #19, a French watch with decimalized time—one branch of the metric system that never took off). Wristwatches became popular first among women, who didn't have pockets, but were later adopted by men in World War I for easy access while using a rifle. The exhibit on Black Forest clockmaking in the 20th century demonstrates that, even as technology advanced, local clockmakers specialized in straightforward, affordable, everyday timepieces. Quartz technology allowed for far greater accuracy at a much lower price, which made clocks cheap and effectively crippled the industry. Furtwangen no longer makes clocks today, but it's still a respected industrial town.

Ponder this: If Germany is known for its engineering prowess, you can thank clocks. As technology evolved, technical know-how came to be applied to more and more complicated machines. And so, in a way, precision BMWs are the direct descendant of the rough wooden cuckoo clocks that have been made in the Black Forest for centuries.

Floor -2: The bottom level brings the story up to the modern day, from punch-clocks to atomic clocks that strive for ever more precise timekeeping. One fascinating exhibit explains how faster and faster transportation in the late 19th century brought about the need for standardized time across locales. In the past, each town used its own, local solar time. As the railroad advanced, this made a wreck of train schedules and connections (since different towns and countries were a few minutes off from each other). The innovation of the telegraph sealed it: The world's clocks needed to be in sync. Only in the 1870s did scientists begin to pursue standardization, leading in 1884 to the creation of the prime meridian (to use as a starting point for calculating world time zones). Germany didn't adopt a standardized time zone until 1893.

The grand finale is an upbeat combo of mechanical musical instruments, from player pianos to giant wind-up carnival organs. Notice it's in a soundproof room; to hear some of the thunderous music, you can ask at the desk for someone to turn one on for you. Hearing the amazing variety of sounds, it's fun to imagine how the simple "cuck-oo" of a clock with a little wooden bird evolved into a self-playing musical band in a box.

BLACK FOREST

ROTHENBURG and the ROMANTIC ROAD

The Romantic Road takes you through Bavaria's medieval heartland, a route strewn with picturesque villages, farmhouses, onion-domed churches, Baroque palaces, and walled cities. The Romantic Road is the most scenic way to connect Frankfurt with Munich. Clearly marked for drivers, and well-described in a free brochure available at any TI, the route technically runs from Würzburg south to Füssen. Car travelers can follow the signposts, meandering from one medieval town to the next. No trains run along the entire Romantic Road, but rail travelers can linger for a night or two in Rothenburg (ROE-tehn-burg), the most interesting town along the route. A tour bus also travels the Romantic Road once daily in each direction.

Countless travelers have searched for the elusive "untouristy Rothenburg." There are many contenders (such as Michelstadt, Miltenberg, Bamberg, Bad Windsheim, and Dinkelsbühl), but none holds a candle to the king of medieval German cuteness. Even with crowds, over-priced souvenirs, Japanese-speaking night watchmen, and, yes, even *Schneeballen*,

Rothenburg is best. Save time and mileage and be satisfied with the winner.

Rothenburg ob der Tauber

In the Middle Ages, when Frankfurt and Munich were just wide spots on the road, Rothenburg ob der Tauber was a free imperial city. With a whopping population of 6,000, it was one of Germany's largest. Today, it's the country's best-preserved medieval walled town, enjoying tremendous tourist popularity without losing its charm.

During Rothenburg's heyday, from 1150 to 1400, it was a strategic stop on the trade routes between northern and southern Europe. Today, the great trade is tourism: Two-thirds of the townspeople are employed to serve you. While 2.5 million people visit each year, a mere 500,000 spend the night. Rothenburg is yours after dark, when the groups vacate and the town's floodlit cobbles wring some romance out of any travel partner.

Too often, Rothenburg brings out the shopper in visitors before they've had a chance to see the historic town. True, this is a fine place to do your German shopping, but appreciate Rothenburg's great history and sights, too.

Planning Your Time

If time is short, you can make just a two- to three-hour midday stop in Rothenburg, but the town is really best appreciated after

the day-trippers have gone home. Spend at least one night in Rothenburg (hotels are cheap). With two nights and a day, you'll be able to see more than the essentials and actually relax a little.

Rothenburg in one day is easy, with four essential experiences: the Medieval Crime and Punishment Museum, Tilman Riemenschneider's wood carving in St. Jakob's Church, a walk along the city wall, and the entertaining Night Watchman's Tour. With more time, there are several mediocre but entertaining museums, scenic hikes and bike rides in the nearby countryside, and lots of cafés and shops.

Rothenburg is very busy through the summer and in the Christmas Market month of December. Spring and fall are a joy, but it's pretty bleak from January through March—when most locals are hibernating or on vacation. Many shops stay open on Sundays during the tourist season, but close on Sundays in November and from Christmas to Easter.

There are several Rothenburgs in Germany, so make sure you

Rothenburg

TO WÜRZBURG &
ROMANTIC ROAD

NOTE: MAP NOT TO SCALE
CASTLE GARDEN TO RÖDERTOR
IS A 15-MIN. WALK

TO
DETWANG

St. WOLFGANG'S

KLINGENTOR

P P-5

TO AUTOBAHN A-7
& BAD WINDSHEIM

BEZOLDWEG

WALL

P P-5

GALGEN-
TOR

IMPERIAL
CITY
MUSEUM

St.
JAKOB'S

SCHRANNEN-
PLATZ

HIRTENGASSE

TAUBER

KLOST.-WETH'

JUDEN-
GASSE

HEU GASSE

WHITE
TOWER

GALGENGASSE

P P-4

KLOST.-HOF

PARADIES

STOLLENGASSE

TO
TOPPLER
CASTLE

BURG-
TOR

PUPPET
THEATER

RÖDER-
TOR

POST

HERRN-
GASSE

FRAN.
CHURCH

HAFEN

RODERGASSE

TRADES-
MAN'S
House

TO
TRAIN
STATION

BURG GASSE

ALT KELLER

BIKE
RENTAL

CASTLE
GARDEN

WENGGASSE

RIVER

MEDIEVAL
CRIME &
PUNISHMENT
MUSEUM

SCHMIED

NEUGASSE

TOPPLERWEG

PLÖNLEIN

DOUBLE
BRIDGE

BURGSTR.

SPITTALGASSE

P P-1

BENSENSTR.

WC

★ MARKET SQUARE
TOURIST INFO, CLOCK
& TOWN HALL TOWER

☐ SEE DETAIL MAP

◢ ACCESS STAIRS
TO WALL

P PARKING

⋰ PATH

TO
DINKELSBÜHL
& FÜSSEN VIA
ROMANTIC ROAD
& SWIMMING POOL

DCH

are going to **Rothenburg ob der Tauber** (not "ob der" any other river); people really do sometimes drive or ride the train to other, nondescript Rothenburgs by accident.

Orientation to Rothenburg

(area code: 09861)

To orient yourself in Rothenburg, think of the town map as a human head. Its nose—the castle garden—sticks out to the left, and the skinny lower part forms a wide-open mouth, with the youth hostel and a recommended hotel in the chin. The town is a delight on foot. No sights or hotels are more than a 15-minute walk from the train station or each other.

Most of the buildings you'll see were in place by 1400. The city was born around its long-gone castle—built in 1142, destroyed in 1356—which was located where the castle garden is now. You can see the shadow of the first town wall, which defines the oldest part of Rothenburg, in its contemporary street plan. A few gates from this wall still survive. The richest and biggest houses were in this central part. The commoners built higgledy-piggledy (read: picturesque) houses farther from the center, but still inside the present walls.

Tourist Information

The TI is on Market Square (May–Oct and Dec Mon–Fri 9:00–19:00, Sat–Sun 10:00–17:00; Nov and Jan–April Mon–Fri 9:00–17:00, Sat 10:00–13:00, closed Sun; Marktplatz 2, tel. 09861/404800, www.rothenburg.de). If there's a long line, just raid the rack where they keep all the free pamphlets. The free *Map & Guide* comes with a walking guide to the town. The free *RoTour* monthly magazine lists all the events and entertainment (mostly in German; also look for current concert listing posters here and at your hotel). Ask about the daily English walking tour at 14:00 (€6, April–Oct and Dec; see "Tours in Rothenburg," later). The TI has one free Internet terminal (15-min maximum). Visitors who arrive after closing can check the handy map highlighting which hotels have rooms available, with a free direct phone connection to them; it's just outside the door. A pictorial town map is available free with this book at the Friese shop, two doors west from the TI (toward St. Jakob's Church; see "Shopping in Rothenburg," later).

Arrival in Rothenburg

By Train: It's a 10-minute walk from the station to Rothenburg's Market Square (following the brown *Altstadt* signs, exit left from station, turn right on Ansbacher Strasse, and head straight into the Middle Ages). Day-trippers can leave luggage in station lockers (€1–2, on platform) or at a local shop (try the Friese shop on Market Square, or Passage 12—both listed later, under "Shopping in Rothenburg"). Arrange train and *couchette*/sleeper reservations at the combined ticket office and travel agency in the station (€0.50 charge for questions without ticket purchase, Mon–Fri 9:00–18:00, Sat 9:00–13:00, closed Sun, tel. 09861/7711). Free WCs are behind the snack bar next door to the station. Taxis wait at the station (€5–6 to any hotel).

By Car: For tips on getting here from Frankfurt, see "Route Tips for Drivers" on page 280. While much of the town is closed to traffic, anyone with a hotel reservation can drive in and through pedestrian zones to get to their hotel. But driving in town can be a nightmare, with many narrow, one-way streets. If you're packing light, just park outside the walls and walk five minutes to the center. Parking lots line the town walls: P1 costs €5 per day; P5 and the south half of P4 are free. Only those with a hotel reservation can park within the walls after hours (but not during festivals). The easiest way to enter and leave Rothenburg is generally via Spitalgasse and the Spitaltor (south end).

Helpful Hints

Festivals: *Biergartens* spill out into the street and Rothenburgers dress up in medieval costumes to celebrate Mayor Nusch's Meistertrunk victory (May 21–24 in 2010; the story of the draught that saved the town is described under "Meistertrunk Show" on page 257, more info at www.meistertrunk.de). The Reichsstadt festival every September celebrates Rothenburg's history (September 3–5 in 2010).

Christmas Market: Rothenburg is dead in November, January, and February, but December is its busiest month—the entire town cranks up the medieval cuteness with concerts and costumes, shops with schnapps, stalls filling squares, hot spiced wine, giddy nutcrackers, and mobs of earmuffed Germans. Christmas markets are big all over Germany, and Rothenburg's is considered one of the best. The market takes place each year during Advent (Nov 28–Dec 23 in 2010). Virtually all sights listed in this chapter are open longer hours during these four weeks. Try to avoid Saturdays and Sundays, when big-city day-trippers really clog the grog.

Internet Access: When it comes to getting online, Rothenburg is still pretty medieval. Only some hotels have Internet access, and many have no phones in the rooms. **Inter@Play** has eight fast terminals (€3/hr, daily 8:00–24:00, 18 and older only, 2 blocks down Hafengasse from Market Square and around the corner to the left at Milchmarkt 3, tel. 09861/935-599). The **Nuschhaus Café** just below Market Square also has terminals

(€3/hr, Mon–Fri 10:00–19:00, Sat–Sun 10:00–20:00, Obere Schmiedgasse 23, tel. 09861/976-838). The **TI** has one free terminal for brief use (maximum 15 min). The **Passage 12** souvenir shop at Obere Schmiedgasse 12 offers limited free use of the computer at their desk upstairs (see "Shopping in Rothenburg," later).

Laundry: A handy launderette is near the station, off Ansbacher Strasse (€5.50/load, includes soap, English instructions, opens at 8:00, last load Mon–Fri at 18:00, Sat at 14:00, closed Sun, Johannitergasse 9, tel. 09861/2775).

Haircuts: At **Salon Wack** (pronounced vack, not wack), Horst and his team speak English and welcome both men and women (€18.50 for men, €28.50–33.50 for women, Tue–Fri 8:00–12:00 & 13:30–18:00, Sat 8:30–14:00, closed Sun–Mon, in the old center just off Wenggasse at Goldene Ringgasse 8, tel. 09861/7834).

Swimming: Rothenburg has a fine swimming complex, with a heated outdoor pool *(Freibad)* from mid-May to mid-September, and an indoor pool and sauna the rest of the year. It's about 15 minutes' walk south of Spitaltor along the main road toward Dinkelsbühl (adults-€4, kids-€2, swimsuit and towel rental-€2.50 each; outdoor pool Fri–Tue 9:00–20:00, Wed 6:30–20:00, Thu 10:00–20:00; indoor pool Mon 14:00–21:00, Tue–Thu 9:00–21:00, Fri–Sun 9:00–18:00; Nördlinger Strasse 20, tel. 09861/4565).

Bike Rental: You can rent a bike and follow the suggested route on page 267. **Fahrradhaus Krauss** is a big bike shop that rents eight-gear bikes. It's cheap, reliable, and right in the old town (€5/6 hrs, €10/24 hrs, no helmets, Mon–Fri 9:00–18:00, Sat 9:00–13:00, closed Sun, Wenggasse 42, tel. 09861/3495, www.fahrradhaus-krauss.de).

Taxi: For a taxi, call 09861/2000 or 09861/7227.

Tours in Rothenburg

▲▲**Night Watchman's Tour**—This tour is flat-out the most entertaining hour of medieval wonder anywhere in Germany. The Night Watchman (a.k.a. Hans-Georg Baumgartner) jokes like a medieval Jerry Seinfeld as he lights his lamp and takes tourists on his rounds, telling slice-of-gritty-life tales of medieval

Rothenburg (€6, Easter–Dec nightly at 20:00, in English, meet at Market Square, www.nightwatchman.de). This is the best evening activity in town.

Old Town Historic Walk—The TI offers 1.5-hour guided walking tours in English (€6, April–Oct and Dec daily at 14:00, Jan–March Sat only at 11:00, no tours in Nov, departs from Market Square). While the Night Watchman's Tour is fun, take this tour for the serious side of Rothenburg's history, and to make sense of the town's architecture. The tours are completely different, and it would be a shame not to take advantage of this informative tour just because you took the other.

Local Guides—A local historian can really bring the ramparts alive. Prices are standardized (€60/1.5 hrs, €78/2 hrs). Reserve a guide by emailing the TI (info@rothenburg.de; more info under "Guided Tours" at www.rothenburg.de). I've had good experiences with **Martin Kamphans,** who also works as a potter (tel. 09861/7941, www.stadtfuehrungen-rothenburg.de, post@stadt fuehrungen-rothenburg.de).

Horse-and-Buggy Rides—These farm boys, who are generally about as charming as their horses, give a relaxing 30-minute clip-clop through the old town, starting from Market Square or Schrannenplatz. Good luck negotiating a fair price (private buggy for €30–50, or wait for one to fill up for €10 per person).

Self-Guided Walk

Welcome to Rothenburg

This one-hour circular walk weaves Rothenburg's top sights together.
• *Start the walk on Market Square.*

Market Square Spin-Tour

Stand at the bottom of Market Square (10 feet below the wooden post on the corner) and spin 360 degrees clockwise, starting with the Town Hall tower. Now do it again, this time more slowly, following these notes:

Town Hall and Tower: Rothenburg's tallest spire is the Town Hall tower (Rathausturm). At 200 feet, it stands atop the old Town Hall, a white Gothic 13th-century building. Notice the tourists enjoying the best view in town from the black top of the tower (€2 and a rigorous but interesting climb, 214 steps, narrow and steep near the top—watch your head, April–Oct daily 9:30–12:30 & 13:00–17:00, closed Nov–March, enter on Market Square through middle arch of new Town Hall). After a fire burned down part of the original building, a new Town Hall was built alongside what survived of the old one (fronting the square). This half of the rebuilt complex is in the Renaissance style from 1570.

Meistertrunk Show: At the top of Market Square stands the proud Councilors' Tavern (clock tower from 1466). In its day, the city council—the rich guys who ran the town government—drank here. Today, it's the TI and the focus of most tourists' attention when the little doors on either side of the clock flip open and the wooden figures (from 1910) do their thing. Be on Market Square at 11:00, 12:00, 13:00, 14:00, 15:00, 20:00, 21:00, or 22:00 for the ritual gathering of the tourists to see the less-than-breathtaking reenactment of the Meistertrunk ("Master Draught") story:

In 1631, the Catholic army took the Protestant town and was about to do its rape, pillage, and plunder thing. As was the etiquette, the mayor had to give the conquering general a welcoming drink. The general enjoyed a huge tankard of local wine. Feeling really good, he told the mayor, "Hey, if you can drink this entire three-liter tankard of wine in one gulp, I'll spare your town." The mayor amazed everyone by drinking the entire thing, and Rothenburg was saved.

While this is a nice story, it was dreamed up in the late 1800s for a theatrical play designed (effectively) to promote a romantic image of the town. In actuality, if Rothenburg was spared, it happened because it bribed its way out of a jam. It was occupied and ransacked several times in the Thirty Years' War, and it never recovered—which is why it's such a well-preserved time capsule today.

For the best show, don't watch the clock; watch the open-mouthed tourists gasp as the old windows flip open. At the late shows, the square flickers with camera flashes.

Bottom of Market Square: On the bottom end of the square, the cream-colored building on the corner has a fine **print shop** upstairs (described later, under "Shopping in Rothenburg"). Adjoining that is the **Baumeister Haus,** featuring a famous Renaissance facade with statues of the seven virtues and the seven vices—the former supporting the latter. The statues are copies; the originals are in the Imperial City Museum (described later on this walk). The green house below that is the former home of the 15th-century Mayor Toppler (it's now the recommended Gasthof Goldener Greifen).

Keep circling to the big 17th-century **St. George's fountain.** The long metal gutters slid, routing the water into the villagers' buckets. Rothenburg had an ingenious water system. Built on a rock, it had one real source above the town, which was plumbed to serve a series of fountains; water flowed from high to low through Rothenburg. Its many fountains had practical functions beyond providing drinking water (some were stocked with fish on market days and during times of siege). Water was used for fighting fires,

Rothenburg Self-Guided Walk

1. Market Square Spin-Tour
2. Town Hall & Tower
3. Councilors' Tavern & TI
4. Geissendörfer Print Shop
5. Baumeister Haus
6. St. George's Fountain
7. Historical Town Hall Vaults
8. Green Market & Friese Shop
9. St. Jakob's Church
10. Imperial City Museum
11. Convent Garden
12. Original Barn
13. Town Wall
14. Castle Garden
15. Herrngasse
16. Eisenhut Hotel/Restaurant
17. Käthe Wohlfahrt Christmas Village & Museum
18. Doll & Toy Museum
19. Internet Cafés (2)

TO DETWANG

IMPERIAL CITY MUSEUM

TAUBER

TRAIL

BURGTOR

CASTLE GARDEN

↗ VIEW   DCH

100 YARDS
100 METERS

ROTHENBURG

and because of its plentiful water supply—and its policy of requiring relatively wide lanes as fire breaks—the town never burned entirely, as so many neighboring villages did.

Two fine buildings behind the fountain show the old-time lofts with warehouse doors and pulleys on top for hoisting. All over town, lofts were filled with grain and corn. A year's supply was required by the city so they could survive any siege. The building behind the fountain is an art gallery showing off work by members of the local artists' association (free, Tue–Sun 14:00–18:00, closed Mon). To the right is Marien Apotheke, an old-time pharmacy mixing old and new in typical Rothenburg style.

The broad street running under the Town Hall tower is **Herrngasse.** The town originated with its castle (built in 1142 but now long gone; only the castle garden remains). Herrngasse connected the castle to Market Square. The last leg of this circular walking tour will take you from the castle garden up Herrngasse to where you now stand. For now, walk a few steps down Herrngasse and stand by the arch under the Town Hall tower (between the new and old town halls). On the left wall are the town's measuring rods—a reminder that medieval Germany was made of 300 independent little countries, each with its own weights and measures. Merchants and shoppers knew that these were the local standards: the rod (4.3 yards), the *Schuh* (or shoe, roughly a foot), and the *Ell* (from elbow to fingertip—four inches longer than mine...try it). Notice the protruding cornerstone. These are all over town—originally to protect buildings from reckless horse carts (and vice versa).

• *Under the arch, you'll find the...*

▲Historical Town Hall Vaults (Historiengewölbe)

This grade-schoolish little museum gives a waxy but interesting look at Rothenburg during the Catholics-vs.-Protestants Thirty Years' War. With helpful English descriptions, it offers a look at "the fateful year 1631," a replica of the mythical Meistertrunk tankard, and a dungeon complete with three dank cells and some torture lore (€2, daily May–Oct 9:30–17:30, shorter hours April and Dec, closed Nov and Jan–March, tel. 09861/86751).

• *Leaving the museum, turn left (past a much-sketched and photographed venerable door), and walk through the courtyard to a square called...*

Green Market (Grüner Markt)

Once a produce market, this is now a parking lot that fills with Christmas shops during December. Notice the clay-tile roofs. These "beaver tail" tiles became standard after thatched roofs were outlawed to prevent fires. Today, all of the town's roofs are made of these. The little fences keep the snow from falling, and catch tiles that blow off during storms. The free public WC is on your left, the recommended Friese shop is on your right, and straight ahead is St. Jakob's Church.

Outside the church, you'll see 14th-century statues (mostly original) showing Jesus praying at Gethsemane, a common feature of Gothic churches. The artist is anonymous, because in the Gothic age (pre–Albrecht Dürer) artists were just nameless craftspeople working only for the glory of God. Five yards to the left (on the wall), notice the nub of a sandstone statue—a rare original, looking pretty bad after 500 years of weather and, more recently, pollution. Most original statues are now in the city museum. The better-preserved statues you see on the church are copies.

• *If it's your wedding day, take the first entrance. Otherwise, use the second (downhill) door to enter...*

▲▲St. Jakob's Church (St. Jakobskirche)

Built in the 14th century, this church has been Lutheran since 1544. The interior was "purified" by Romantics in the 19th century—cleaned of everything Baroque or not original, and refitted in the Neo-Gothic style. (For example, the baptismal font and the pulpit above the second pew *look* Gothic, but are actually Neo-Gothic.) The stained-glass windows behind the altar (most colorful in the morning light) are originals from the 1330s. Entrance costs €2 (daily April–Oct 9:00–17:15, Dec 10:00–16:45, Nov and Christmas–March 10:00–12:00 & 14:00–16:00, on Sun wait to enter until services end at 10:45, free helpful English info sheet, concerts and tour schedule posted on the door). There are guided tours in English for no extra charge on Saturdays at 15:00.

At the back of the church, take the stairs that lead up behind the pipe organ. In the loft, you'll find the artistic highlight of Rothenburg and perhaps the most wonderful wood carving in all of Germany: the glorious 500-year-old, 35-foot-high *Altar of the Holy Blood.* Tilman Riemenschneider, the Michelangelo of German woodcarvers, carved this from 1499 to 1504 to hold a precious rock-crystal capsule, set in a cross that contains a scrap of tablecloth mirac-ulously stained in the shape of a cross by a drop of communion wine. It's a realistic commotion, showing that Riemenschneider—while a High Gothic artist—was ahead of his time. Below, in the scene of the Last Supper, Jesus gives Judas a piece of bread, marking him as the traitor, while John lays his head on Christ's lap. Everything is portrayed exactly as described in the Bible. On the left: Jesus enters Jericho, with the shy tax collector Zacchaeus looking on from his tree. Notice the fun attention to detail—down to the nails on the horseshoe. On the right: Jesus prays in the Garden of Gethsemane. Notice how Judas, with his big bag of cash, could be removed from the scene—illustrated by photos on the wall nearby—as was the tradition for the four days leading up to Easter.

Head back down the stairs to the church's main hall. Go up front to take a close look at the **main altar** (from 1466, by Friedrich Herlin). Below Christ are statues of six saints. St. James (Jakob in German) is the one with the shell. He's the saint of pilgrims, and this church was a stop on the medieval pilgrimage route to Santiago ("St. James" in Spanish) de Compostela in Spain. Study the painted panels—ever see Peter with spectacles? Around the back of the altarpiece (upper left) is a painting of Rothenburg's Market Square in the 15th century—looking much like it does today, with the exception of the full-Gothic Town Hall (as it was before the big fire of 1501). Notice Christ's face on the veil of Veronica (center of back side). It follows you as you walk from side to side—it must have given the faithful the religious heebie-jeebies four centuries ago.

The **small altar** to the left is also worth a look. It's a century

older than the main altar. Notice the unusual Trinity: the Father and Son are literally bridged by a dove, which represents the Holy Spirit. Stepping back, you can see that Jesus is stand-ing on a skull—clearly "overcoming death."

Before leaving the front of the church, notice the old **medallions** above the carved choir stalls. They feature the coats of arms of Rothenburg's leading families and portraits of city and church leaders.

• *Leave the church and, from its outside steps, walk around the corner to the right and under the chapel (built over the road). Go two blocks down*

Klingengasse and stop at the corner of Klosterhof Street. Looking down Klingengasse, you see the...

Klingentor

This cliff tower was Rothenburg's water reservoir. From 1595 until 1910, a copper tank high in the tower provided clean spring water (pumped up by river power) to the privileged. To the right of Klingentor is a good stretch of wall rampart to walk. To the left, the wall is low and simple, lacking a rampart because it guards only a cliff. Now find the shell decorating a building on the street corner next to you. That's the symbol of St. James (pilgrims commemorated their visit to Santiago de Compostela with a shell), indicating that this building is associated with the church.

• *Turn left down Klosterhof, passing the shell and, on your right, the colorful, recommended Altfränkische Weinstube am Klosterhof pub, to reach the...*

▲▲Imperial City Museum (Reichsstadt-Museum)

You'll get a scholarly sweep through Rothenburg's history at this museum, housed in the former Dominican convent. Cloistered nuns used the lazy Susan embedded in the wall (to the right of the museum door) to give food to the poor without being seen.

Highlights include *The Rothenburg Passion*, a 12-panel series of paintings from 1492 showing scenes leading up to Christ's crucifixion (in the *Konventsaal*); an exhibit of Jewish culture in Rothenburg through the ages *(Judaika)*; a 14th-century convent kitchen *(Klosterküche)* with a working model of the lazy Susan and a massive chimney; romantic paintings of the town *(Gemäldegalerie)*; the fine Baumann collection of weapons and armor; and sandstone statues from the church and Baumeister Haus (the seven vices and seven virtues). Follow the *Rundgang/Tour* signs (€3.50, daily April–Oct 9:30–17:30, Nov–March 13:00–16:00, English info sheet and descriptions, Klosterhof 5, tel. 09861/939-043, www.reichsstadtmuseum.rothenburg.de).

• *Leaving the museum, go around to the right and into the Convent Garden (when locked at night, continue straight to the T-intersection and see the barn three doors to the right).*

Convent Garden

This spot is a peaceful place to work on your tan...or mix a poisoned potion (free, same hours as museum). Enjoy the herb garden. Monks and nuns, who were responsible for concocting herbal cures in the olden days, often tended herb gardens. Smell (but don't pick) the *Pfefferminze, Juniper* (gin), *Chamomilla* (disinfectant), and *Origanum*. Don't smell the plants in the poison corner (potency indicated by the number of crosses...like spiciness stars in a Chinese restaurant).

• *Exit opposite from where you entered, angling left through the nuns' garden (site of the now-gone Dominican church), eventually leaving via an arch at the far end. Looking to your left, you'll see the back end of an...*

Original Barn

This is the back side of a complex that fronts Herrngasse. Medieval Germans often lived in large structures like this that were like small villages in themselves, with a grouping of buildings and open spaces. The typical design included a house, a courtyard, a stable, a garden, and, finally, a barn. Notice how the bulging wall is corseted by a brace with iron washers. Crank on its nuts and the building will stand up straight.

• *Now go downhill to the...*

Town Wall

This part of the wall (view through bars, look to far right) takes advantage of the natural fortification provided by the cliff, and is therefore much smaller than the ramparts. Angle left along the wall to the big street (Herrngasse), then right under the Burgtor tower. Notice the tiny "eye of the needle" door cut into the big door. If trying to get into town after curfew, you could bribe the guard to let you through this door (which was small enough to keep out any fully armed attackers).

• *Step through the gate and outside the wall. Look around and imagine being locked out in the year 1400. This was a wooden drawbridge (see the chain slits above). Notice the "pitch nose" mask—designed to pour boiling Nutella on anyone attacking. High above is the town coat of arms: a red castle (roten Burg).*

Castle Garden (Burggarten)

The garden before you was once that red castle (destroyed in the 14th century). Today, it's a picnic-friendly park. The chapel (50 yards into the park on the left) is the only bit of the original castle to survive. It's now a memorial to local Jews killed in a 1298 slaughter. A few steps beyond that is a grapevine trellis that provides a fine picnic spot. If you walk all the way out to the garden's far end, you'll find a great viewpoint (well past the tourists, and considered the best place to kiss by romantic local teenagers). But the views of the lush Tauber River Valley below are just as good from the top end of the park. Facing the town, on the left, a path leads down to the village of Detwang (you can see the church spire below)—a town even older than Rothenburg (for a walk to Detwang, see "A Walk in the Countryside," page 266). To the right is a fine view of the fortified Rothenburg and the "Tauber Riviera" later.

• *Return to the tower, cross carefully under the pitch nose, and hike back up Herrngasse to your starting point.*

Herrngasse

Many towns have a Herrngasse, where the richest patricians and merchants (the *Herren*) lived. Predictably, it's your best chance to see the town's finest old mansions. Strolling back to Market Square, you'll pass the old-time puppet theater (German only, on left), and the Franciscan church (from 1285, oldest in town, on right). The house at #18 is the biggest patrician house on the street. The family, which has lived here for three centuries, disconnected the four old-time doorbells. Their door—big enough to allow a carriage in (with a human-sized door cut into it)—is typical of the age. To see the traditional house-courtyard-stables-garden-barn layout, pop into either #14 (now an apartment block) or—if that's closed—the shop across the street, at #11. The recommended Eisenhut Hotel, Rothenburg's fanciest, is worth a peek inside. The Käthe Wohlfahrt Christmas shops (at Herrngasse 1 and 2, described later under "Shopping in Rothenburg") are your last, and perhaps greatest, temptations before reaching your starting and ending point: Market Square.

Sights in Rothenburg

Museums Within a Block of Market Square

▲▲Medieval Crime and Punishment Museum (Mittelalterliches Kriminalmuseum)—This museum is the best of its kind, specializing in everything connected to medieval criminal justice. Learn about medieval police, medieval criminal law, and above all, instruments of punishment and torture—even a special cage complete with a metal gag for nags. The museum is more eclectic than its name, and includes exhibits on general history, superstition, biblical art, and temporary displays in a sec-

ond building. Follow the yellow arrows—the one-way traffic system makes it hard to double back. Exhibits are tenderly described in English (€3.80, daily May–Oct 10:00–18:00, Nov and Jan–Feb 14:00–16:00, Dec and March 13:00–16:00, April 11:00–17:00, last entry 45 min before closing, fun cards and posters, Burggasse 3–5, tel. 09861/5359, www.kriminalmuseum.rothenburg.de).

▲Doll and Toy Museum (Puppen- und Spielzeugmuseum)—These two floors of historic *Kinder* cuteness are a hit with many. Pick up the free English binder (just past the entry curtain) for an extensive description of the exhibits (€4, family ticket-€10, daily March–Dec 9:30–18:00, Jan–Feb 11:00–17:00, just off Market Square, downhill from the fountain at Hofbronnengasse 11–13, tel. 09861/7330, www.spielzeugmuseum.rothenburg.de).

▲German Christmas Museum (Deutsches Weihnachts-museum)—This excellent museum, upstairs in the giant Käthe Wohlfahrt Christmas Village shop, tells the history of Christmas decorations. There's a unique and thoughtfully described collection of Christmas-tree stands, mini-trees sent in boxes to WWI soldiers at the front, early Advent calendars, old-time Christmas cards, and a look at tree decorations through the ages—including the Nazi era and when you were a kid. The museum is not just a ploy to get shoppers to spend more money, but a serious collection managed by professional curator Felicitas Höptner (€4, April–Dec daily 10:00–17:30, Jan–March Sat–Sun 10:00–17:30 and irregularly on weekdays, Herrngasse 1, tel. 09861/409-365, www.germanchristmasmuseum.com). You can visit the museum at the €2.50 student rate with this book in 2010—if you promise to learn something.

More Sights in Rothenburg

▲▲Walk the Wall—Just longer than a mile and a half around, providing great views and a good orientation, this walk can be done by those under six feet tall and without a camera in less than an hour. The hike requires no special sense of balance. This walk is covered and is a great option in the rain. Photographers will stay very busy, especially before breakfast or at sunset, when the lighting is best and the crowds are fewest. You can enter or exit the ramparts at nearly every tower. The best fortifications are in the Spitaltor (south end). Climb the Rödertor en route (described next).

The names you see along the way are people who donated money to rebuild the wall after World War II, and those who've recently donated €1,000 per meter for the maintenance of Rothenburg's heritage.

▲Rödertor—The wall tower nearest the train station is the only one you can climb. It's worth the 135 steps for the view and a short but fascinating rundown on the bombing of Rothenburg in the last weeks of World War II, when the east part of the city was destroyed (€1.50, pay at top, unreliable hours, usually open daily

April–Oct 10:00–16:00, closed Nov–March, WWII photos have English translations). If you climb this, you can skip the more claustrophobic Town Hall tower climb.

▲▲The Allergic-to-Tourists Wall and Moat Walk—For a quiet and scenic break from the tourist crowds and a chance to appreciate the marvelous fortifications of Rothenburg, consider this hike: From the Castle Garden, go right and walk outside the wall to Klingentor. At Klingentor, climb up to the ramparts and walk on the wall past Galgentor to Rödertor. Then descend, leave the old town, and hike through the park (once the moat) down to Spitaltor. Explore the fortifications here before hiking a block up Spitalgasse, turning left to pass the youth hostel, popping back outside the wall, and heading along the upper scenic reaches of the "Tauber Riviera" and above the vineyards back to the Castle Garden.

▲Tradesman's House (Alt-Rothenburger Handwerker-haus)—See the everyday life of a Rothenburger in the town's heyday in this restored 700-year-old home (€2.50; Easter–Oct Mon–Fri 11:00–17:00, Sat–Sun 10:00–17:00; Dec daily 14:00–16:00; closed Nov and Jan–Easter; Alter Stadtgraben 26, near Markus Tower, tel. 09861/5810).

St. Wolfgang's Church—This fortified Gothic church is built into the medieval wall at Klingentor. Its dungeon-like passages and shepherd's-dance exhibit are pretty lame (€1.50, Wed–Mon April–Sept 10:00–13:00 & 14:30–17:00, Oct 10:00–16:00, closed Tue and Nov–March).

Near Rothenburg

▲A Walk in the Countryside—From the *Burggarten* (castle garden), head into the Tauber Valley. With your back to town, go down the hill, exiting the castle garden on your left. Once outside of the wall, walk around, keeping the castle and town on your right. The trail becomes really steep, taking you down to the wooden covered bridge on the valley floor. Across the bridge, the road goes left to Toppler Castle and right (downstream, with a pleasant parallel footpath) to Detwang.

Toppler Castle (Topplerschlösschen) is cute, skinny, sky-blue, and 600 years old. It was the castle/summer home of the medieval Mayor Toppler. The tower's top looks like a house—a sort of tree fort for grownups. It's in a farmer's garden, and it's open whenever he's around and willing to let you in (€1.50, normally Fri–Sun 13:00–16:00, closed Mon–Thu and Nov, one mile from town center at Taubertalweg 100, tel. 09861/7358). People say the mayor had this valley-floor escape built to get people to relax about leaving the fortified town...or to hide a mistress.

To extend your stroll, walk back to the bridge and follow the river downstream to the peaceful village of **Detwang**. One of the oldest villages in Franconia, Detwang dates from 968. Like Rothenburg, it has a Riemenschneider altarpiece in its church.

Franconian Bike Ride—To get a fun, breezy look at the countryside around Rothenburg, rent a bike from Fahrradhaus Krauss (listed earlier, under "Helpful Hints"). For a pleasant half-day pedal, escape the old town through Rödertor, bike along Topplerweg to Spitaltor, and follow the curvy road down into the Tauber Riviera. Turn right at the yellow *Leutzenbronn* sign to cross the double-arcaded bridge. From here a peaceful road follows the river downstream to **Detwang,** passing the cute Topplerschlösschen castle (described earlier). From Detwang, follow the main road to the old mill, and turn left to follow the *Liebliches Taubertal* bike path signs as far up the Tauber River (direction: Bettwar) as you like. After 2.5 miles, you'll arrive in the sleepy farming town of **Bettwar;** claim a spot among the chickens and the apple trees for a picnic or have a drink at one of the two restaurants in town.

Franconian Open-Air Museum (Fränkisches Freiland-museum)—A 20-minute drive from Rothenburg—in the undiscovered "Rothenburgy" town of Bad Windsheim—is an open-air folk museum that, compared with others in Europe, is a bit humble. But it tries very hard and gives you the best look around at traditional rural Franconia (€5, daily mid-March–Sept 9:00–18:00, Oct–mid-Dec 10:00–16:00, closed mid-Dec–mid-March, last entry one hour before closing, tel. 09841/66800, www .freilandmuseum.de).

Shopping in Rothenburg

Be warned...Rothenburg is one of Germany's best shopping towns. Do it here and be done with it. Lovely prints, carvings, wine glasses, Christmas-tree ornaments, and beer steins are popular. Rödergasse is the old town's everyday shopping street. There is also a modern shopping center across the street from the train station.

Christmas Souvenirs

Rothenburg is the headquarters of the **Käthe Wohlfahrt** Christmas trinkets empire, which is spreading across the half-timbered reaches of Europe. In Rothenburg, tourists flock to two Käthe Wohlfahrt stores (at Herrngasse 1 and 2, just off Market Square). Start with the **Christmas Village** (Weihnachtsdorf) at Herrngasse 1. This Christmas wonderland is filled with enough twinkling lights to require a special electrical hookup. You're greeted by instant Christmas mood music (best appreciated on a hot day in July) and American and Japanese tourists hungrily filling little woven shopping baskets with €5–8 goodies to hang on their trees. Let the spinning flocked tree whisk you in, but pause at the wall of Steiffs, jerking uncontrollably and mesmerizing little kids. (OK, I admit it, my Christmas tree sports a few KW ornaments.) The **Christmas Museum** upstairs is described earlier, under "Sights in Rothenburg." The smaller **Christmas Market** (Weihnachtsmarkt), across the street at Herrngasse 2, specializes in finely crafted wooden ornaments. A third, much smaller store is at Untere Schmiedgasse 19 (all stores open Mon–Sat 9:00–18:00, May–Dec also most Sun 10:00–18:00, Jan–April generally closed Sun, 10 percent discount on official KW products with this book in 2010, tel. 09861/4090, www.wohlfahrt.com or www.bestofchristmas.com). Käthe started the business in Stuttgart in 1964, and it's now run by her son Harald Wohlfahrt, who lives in Rothenburg.

Traditional German Souvenirs

The **Friese shop** has been welcoming readers of this book for more than 20 years (on the smaller square just off Market Square, west of TI, on corner across from free public WC). Cuckoo with friendliness, trinkets, and souvenirs, they give shoppers with this book tremendous service: a 10 percent discount and a free pictorial map (normally €1.50). Anneliese Friese, who runs the place with her sons Frankie and Berni and grandson Rene, charges only her cost for shipping, and lets tired travelers leave their bags in her back room for free. If he's not busy, ask Rene to show you pictures of the local American football team he played on (Mon–Sat 9:00–17:00, Sun 10:00–16:00, Grüner Markt 8, tel. 09861/7166, fax 09861/936-619, friese-kabalo@gmx.de).

Passage 12, a huge, more commercial souvenir shop with a vast selection of steins, knives, and noisy clocks, is locked in tooth-gnashing competition with the Friese shop. It's just a block below Market Square at Obere Schmiedgasse 12. Martina, the manager, promises a 10 percent discount on prices with this book in 2010. Customers can check their email for free upstairs, use the WC, and stash their bags in lockers in the storage room (April–Dec Mon–Sat 9:00–19:00, Sun 10:00–19:00; Jan–March Mon–Sat 10:00–18:00, usually closed Sun; tel. 09861/8196).

Werkstattladen Lebenshilfe sells tasteful, original, unconventional toys and souvenirs made in sheltered workshops by Germans with disabilities. It's a tiny shop down the side street behind Herrngasse 10 (daily April–Dec 10:30–18:00 except may close Sun in April, closed Jan–March, Kirchgasse 1, tel. 09861/ 938-401).

Romantic Prints: The Ernst Geissendörfer print shop has sold fine prints, etchings, and paintings on the corner of Market Square since 1908. To find the shop, walk a few steps down Hafengasse (it's on your right, just before the Bosporus Café). If you're interested in more expensive prints and etchings than those on display, ask Frau Geissendörfer to take you upstairs—she'll offer you a free shot of German brandy while you browse. In 2010, show this book for a 10 percent discount off marked prices on all cash purchases, or minimum €50 credit-card purchases (May–Dec daily 11:00–18:00; Jan–April Mon–Sat 11:00–18:00, closed Sun; Obere Schmiedgasse 1 at corner of Hafengasse, tel. 09861/2005, www.geissendoerfer.de).

Wine Stuff: For characteristic wine glasses, winemaking gear, and the real thing from the town's oldest winemakers, drop by the **Weinladen am Plönlein** (daily 10:00–18:00, Untere Schmiedgasse 27—see page 278 for info on wine-tasting). Although Rothenburg is technically in Bavaria, the region around Rothenburg is called *Franken* (Franconia). You'll recognize Franconian wines by the shape of the bottle—short, stubby, and round.

Books: A good bookstore is **Rothenburger Büchermarkt** at Rödergasse 3, on the corner of Alter Stadtgraben (Mon–Sat 9:00–18:30, Sun 11:00–18:00, Jan–April closed Sun).

Mailing Your Goodies Home: You can get handy yellow €2.50 boxes at the old town **post office** (Mon–Fri 9:00–13:00 & 14:00–17:30, Sat 9:00–12:00, closed Sun, inside photo shop at Rödergasse 11). The main post office is in the shopping center across from the train station.

Pastries: Those who prefer to eat their souvenirs browse the *Bäckereien* (bakeries). Their succulent pastries, pies, and cakes are pleasantly distracting...but skip the bad-tasting Rothenburger *Schneeballen.* Unworthy of the heavy promotion they receive, *Schneeballen* are bland pie crusts crumpled into a ball and dusted with powdered sugar or frosted with sticky-sweet glop. There's little reason to waste your appetite on a *Schneeball* when you can enjoy a curvy *Mandelhörnchen* (almond crescent), a triangular

Nussecke (nut "corner"), a round *Florentiner* cookie, a couple of fresh *Krapfen* (like jelly doughnuts), or even just a soft, warm German pretzel.

ROTHENBURG

Sleeping in Rothenburg

Rothenburg is crowded with visitors, but most are day-trippers. Except for the rare Saturday night and during festivals (see page 254), finding a room is easy throughout the year. If you want to splurge, you'll snare the best value by paying extra for the biggest and best rooms at the hotels I recommend.

Many hotels and guest houses will pick up tired heavy-packers at the station. If you're driving and unable to find where you're sleeping, stop and give them a call. They will likely come rescue you. Keep your key when out late. Rothenburg's hotels are small, and often lock the front entrance at about 22:00, asking you to let yourself in through a side door.

You may be greeted at the station by *Zimmer* skimmers who have rooms to rent. If you have reservations, resist them and honor your reservation. But if you haven't booked ahead, you could try talking one of these eager beavers into giving you a bed-and-breakfast room for a youth-hostel price. Be warned: These people are notorious for taking you to distant hotels and then charging you for the ride back if you decline a room. The automated hotel vacancy board at the TI is another option for those without reservations.

In the Old Town

$$$ Hotel Kloster-Stüble, deep in the old town near the castle garden, is my classiest listing. Rudolf does the cooking, while Erika—his fun and energetic first mate—welcomes guests. Twenty-one rooms fill two medieval buildings, connected by a modern atrium. The hotel is just off Herrngasse on a tiny side street (Sb-€56–76, traditional Db-€86, bigger and more modern Db-€106–126, Tb-€108–146, see website for suites and fam-

---

Sleep Code

(€1 = about $1.40, country code: 49, area code: 09861)
S = Single, **D** = Double/Twin, **T** = Triple, **Q** = Quad, **b** = bathroom, **s** = shower only. Unless otherwise noted, credit cards are accepted, English is spoken, and breakfast is included.

To help you sort easily through these listings, I've divided the rooms into three categories, based on the price for a standard double room with bath:

   $$$ Higher Priced—Most rooms €85 or more.
    $$ Moderately Priced—Most rooms between €55–85.
     $ Lower Priced—Most rooms €55 or less.

Rothenburg Accommodations

NOTE: MAP NOT TO SCALE
CASTLE GARDEN TO RÖDERTOR
IS A 15-MIN. WALK

TO WÜRZBURG &
ROMANTIC ROAD

TO DETWANG

ST. WOLFGANG'S

KLINGENTOR

TO AUTOBAHN A-7
& BAD WINDSHEIM

BEZOLDWEG

IMPERIAL CITY MUSEUM

P-5

P-5

WALL

GALGEN-TOR

TAUBER

ST. JAKOB'S

SCHRANNEN-PLATZ

HIRTENGASSE

GALGENGASSE

P-4

WHITE TOWER

STOLLENGASSE

TO TOPPLER CASTLE

BURG-TOR

PUPPET THEATER

HERRN-GASSE

FRAN.-CHURCH

RÖDER-TOR
Post

RÖDERGASSE

HAFEN

TRADES-MAN'S HOUSE

TO TRAIN STATION

CASTLE GARDEN

RIVER

MEDIEVAL CRIME & PUNISHMENT MUSEUM

WENGGASSE

NEUGASSE

PLÖNLEIN

SPITTALGASSE

TOPPLERWEG

DOUBLE BRIDGE

BURGERSTR.

★ MARKET SQUARE
TOURIST INFO, CLOCK & TOWN HALL TOWER

ACCESS STAIRS TO WALL

P PARKING

PATH

P-1

WC

BENSENSTR.

TO DINKELSBÜHL & FÜSSEN VIA ROMANTIC ROAD & SWIMMING POOL

DCH

1 Hotel Kloster-Stüble
2 Hotel Spitzweg
3 Hotel Gerberhaus
4 Gasthof Goldener Greifen
5 Hotel Altfränkische Weinstube am Klosterhof
6 Pension Elke
7 Hotel Café Uhl
8 Gästehaus Flemming

9 Gästehaus am Klosterhof
10 Gästehaus Raidel
11 Pension Gerlinger
12 Pension Pöschel
13 Frau Liebler Rooms
14 Rossmühle Youth Hostel
15 Hotel Hornburg
16 To Pension Fuchsmühle
17 Bike Rental

ROTHENBURG

ily rooms, kids 5 and under free, free Internet access and Wi-Fi, Heringsbronnengasse 5, tel. 09861/938-890, fax 09861/6474, www .klosterstueble.de, hotel@klosterstueble.de).

$$$ Hotel Spitzweg is a rustic-yet-elegant 1536 mansion (never bombed or burned) with 10 big rooms, open beams, and endearing hand-painted antique furniture. It's run by gentle Herr Hocher, whom I suspect is the former Wizard of Oz—now retired and in a very good mood (Db-€85, family rooms, non-smoking, elegant breakfast room, free parking, Internet access at a nearby hotel, Paradeisgasse 2, tel. 09861/94290, fax 09861/1412, www .hotel-spitzweg.de, info@hotel-spitzweg.de).

$$$ Hotel Gerberhaus is warmly run by Inge and Kurt and daughter Deborah, who mix modern comforts into 20 bright and airy rooms while maintaining a sense of half-timbered elegance. Enjoy the pleasant garden in back (Sb-€65–75, Db-€79–120, Tb-€139–150, Qb-€145–165, prices depend on room size; 2-room apartment with kitchen-€130/2 people, €170/4 people; 10 percent off the second and subsequent nights and a free *Schneeball* if you pay cash, non-smoking, 4 rooms have canopied 4-poster *Himmel* beds, free Internet access, free Wi-Fi with this book, laundry-€7, Spitalgasse 25, tel. 09861/94900, fax 09861/86555, www.gerber haus.rothenburg.de, gerberhaus@t-online.de). The downstairs café and *Biergarten* serve good soups, salads, and light lunches.

$$ Gasthof Goldener Greifen, once Mayor Toppler's home, is a big, traditional, 600-year-old place with 15 large rooms and all the comforts. It's run by a helpful family staff and creaks with rustic splendor (small Sb-€43, Sb-€48, small Db-€65, big Db-€77–85, Tb-€97–105, Qb-€125, 10 percent off for 3-night stays, non-smoking, full-service laundry-€8, free and easy parking, half a block downhill from Market Square at Obere Schmiedgasse 5, tel. 09861/2281, fax 09861/86374, www.gasthof-greifen-rothenburg .de, info@gasthof-greifen-rothenburg.de, Brigitte and Klingler family). The family also has a couple of loaner bikes free for guests, and runs a good restaurant, serving meals in the back garden or dining room.

$$ Hotel Altfränkische Weinstube am Klosterhof is *the* place for well-heeled bohemians. Mario, Hanne, and their lovely daughter Viktoria rent six cozy rooms above their dark and evocative pub in a 600-year-old building. It's an upscale *Lord of the Rings* atmosphere, with TVs, modern showers, open-beam ceilings, and canopied four-poster beds (Sb-€55, Db-€59, bigger Db-€74, Db suite-€82, Tb-€79, prefer cash, kid- and dog-friendly, free Wi-Fi, off Klingengasse at Klosterhof 7, tel. 09861/6404, fax 09861/6410, www.romanticroad.com/altfraenkische-weinstube, email through website). Their pub is a candlelit classic—and a favorite with locals, serving hot food to Hobbits until 22:30, and closing at 1:00 in the morning. Drop by on Wednesday evening (19:00–24:00) for the English Conversation Club (see "Meet the Locals" on page 279).

$$ Pension Elke, run by spry Erich Endress and his son Klaus, rents 12 bright, airy, and comfy rooms above the family grocery store. Guests who jog are welcome to join Klaus on his half-hour run around the city every evening at 19:30 (S-€28, Sb-€38, D-€42–48, Db-€60–65, price depends on room size, extra bed-€15, 10 percent discount with this book through 2010 when you stay at least 2 nights, cash only, free Internet access and Wi-Fi; reception in grocery store until 19:00, otherwise go around corner to back of building and ring bell at top of stairs; near Markus Tower at Rödergasse 6, tel. 09861/2331, fax 09861/935-355, www.pension-elke-rothenburg.de, info@pension-elke-rothenburg.de).

$$ Hotel Café Uhl offers 12 fine rooms over a bakery (Sb-€35–58, Db-€59–79, Tb-€79–95, Qb-€95–125, price depends on room size, 10 percent discount with this book and cash in 2010, reception in café, free Wi-Fi, parking-€6/day, closed Jan, Plönlein 8, tel. 09861/4895, fax 09861/92820, www.hotel-uhl.de, info @hotel-uhl.de, Paul and Robert the baker).

$$ Gästehaus Flemming has seven tastefully modern, fresh, and comfortable rooms and a peaceful garden behind St. Jakob's Church (Sb-€47, Db-€62, Tb-€84, cash only, non-smoking, Klingengasse 21, tel. 09861/92380, fax 09861/976-384, www.gaestehaus-flemming.de, gaestehaus-flemming@t-online.de, Regina).

$$ Gästehaus am Klosterhof offers two warmly decorated rooms and an apartment in a 16th-century house near the Klingentor (Db-€69, Tb-€79, discount for one-week stay, apartment has kitchen, Wi-Fi, breakfast nearby at Altfränkische Weinstube, Klingengasse 8, tel. 09861/87682, www.casa-nova1.de, casa-nova1@gmx.de).

$$ Gästehaus Raidel rents 12 rooms in a 500-year-old house filled with beds and furniture, all handmade by friendly Norry

Raidel himself. The ramshackle ambience makes me want to sing the *Addams Family* theme song—but the place has a rare, time-passed family charm (S-€24, Sb-€39, D-€49, Db-€59, Tb-€70, Qb-€80, Qb suite-€100, cash only, Wenggasse 3, tel. 09861/3115, Norry asks you to use the reservations form at www.romanticroad.com/raidel). Norry, who plays in a Dixieland band, has invented a fascinating hybrid saxophone/trombone called the Norryphone...and loves to jam.

ROTHENBURG

$ Pension Gerlinger, a fine value, has four comfortable rooms in a pretty 16th-century house with a small terrace for guests (Db-€55, or €53/night with 2-night stay, cash only, non-smoking, easy parking, Schlegeleinsweth 10, tel. 09861/87979, mobile 0175-672-4596, www.pension-gerlinger.de, info@pension-gerlinger.de, Hermann).

$ Pension Pöschel is simple and friendly, with six plain rooms in a concrete but pleasant building, and an inviting garden out back. Only one room has a private shower and toilet (S-€25, D-€45, Db-€50, T-€60, Tb-€65, small kids free, cash only, non-smoking, Wenggasse 22, tel. 09861/3430, www.pensionpoeschel .de, pension.poeschel@t-online.de, Bettina).

$ Frau Liebler rents two large modern ground-floor rooms with kitchenettes. They're great for those looking for real privacy—you'll have your own room fronting a quiet cobbled lane just below Market Square. She also rents a two-bedroom apartment (Db-€40, apartment-€50, extra bed-€10, 10 percent discount for 2 or more nights with this book in 2010, breakfast-€5, cash only, non-smoking, laundry-€5, behind Christmas shop at Pfäffleinsgässchen 10, tel. 09861/709-215, fax 09861/709-216, www.gaestehaus-liebler.de).

$ Rossmühle Youth Hostel, run since 1981 by Eduard Schmitz, rents 186 beds in two buildings. While it's mostly four- to six-bed dorms, this charming hostel also has 15 doubles. Reception is in the droopy-eyed building—formerly a horse mill, it was used when the old town was under siege and the river-powered mill was inaccessible (dorm bed-€20, bunk-bed Db-€46, those over 26 pay €4 extra unless traveling with a family, includes breakfast and sheets, all-you-can-eat dinner-€4.50, pay Wi-Fi, self-serve laundry including soap-€5, entrance on Rossmühlgasse, tel. 09861/94160, fax 09861/941-620, www.rothenburg.jugend herberge.de, jhrothenburg@djh-bayern.de).

Outside the Wall

$$$ Hotel Hornburg, a grand 1903 mansion, is close to the train station, a two-minute walk outside the wall. With groomed grounds, gracious sitting areas, and 10 spacious, tastefully deco-rated rooms, it's a super value (Sb-€58–78, Db-€78–108, Tb-€100–130, ground-floor rooms, non-smoking, family-friendly, dogs welcome—ask for pet-free room if you're allergic, free Internet access, expensive Wi-Fi, easy parking; if walking, exit station and go straight on Ludwig-Siebert-Strasse, then turn left on Mannstrasse until you're 100 yards from town wall; if driving, the hotel is across from parking lot P4; Hornburgweg 28, at intersec-tion with Mannstrasse, tel. 09861/8480, fax 09861/5570, www .hotel-hornburg.de, info@hotel-hornburg.de, friendly Gabriele and Martin).

$$ Pension Fuchsmühle is a guest house in a renovated old mill on the river below the castle end of Rothenburg, across from the Toppler Castle. It feels rural, but is a pleasant (though steep) 15-minute hike to Market Square, and a €10 taxi ride from the train station. Alex and Heidi Molitor, a young couple, run a book-lined café on summer weekends and offer a free look at the mill (in use until 1989). Eight bright, modern light-wood rooms fill the building's three floors (Sb-€45, Db-€68, Tb-€90, Qb-€120, 5-bed room-€150, 6-bed apartment-€180, extra bed-€25, less for longer stays at some times of year, includes healthy farm-fresh breakfasts—or €9 less per person if you don't want breakfast, non-smoking, inexpensive Wi-Fi, parking, flashlights provided for your walk back after dark, Taubertalweg 103, tel. 09861/92633, fax 09861/933895, www.fuchsmuehle.de, fuchsmuehle@t-online.de).

Eating in Rothenburg

Many restaurants take a mid-afternoon break, and stop serving lunch at 14:00 and dinner as early as 20:00. My recommendations are all within a five-minute walk of Market Square. While all survive on tourism, many still feel like local hangouts. Your choices are typical German or ethnic. Any bakery will sell you a sandwich for a couple euros.

Traditional German Restaurants

Gasthof Goldener Greifen is in a historic building just off the main square. The Klingler family serves quality Franconian food at a good price...and with a smile. The wood is ancient and polished from generations of happy use, and the ambience is practical rather than posh—and that's just fine with me (€8–16 entrées, €12 three-course daily specials, super-cheap kids' meals, Mon–Sat 11:30–21:30, may open Sun 11:30–14:00, Obere Schmiedgasse 5, tel. 09861/2281).

Hotel Restaurant Klosterstüble, on a small street off Herrngasse near the castle garden, is a classy place for delicious and beautifully presented traditional cuisine, including homemade *Maultaschen* (similar to ravioli). Chef Rudy's food is better than his English, so head waitress Erika makes sure communication goes smoothly. The shady terrace is nice on a warm summer evening. I prefer their traditional dining room to the stony, sleek, modern room (€8–17 main dishes, daily 11:00–14:00 & 18:00–21:00, Heringsbronnengasse 5, tel. 09861/938-890).

Bürgerkeller is a typical European cellar restaurant with a quiet, calming atmosphere, medieval murals, pointy pikes, and a few sidewalk tables for good weather. Without a burger in sight (*Bürger* means "townsman"), English-speaking Harry Terian and

ROTHENBURG

his family pride themselves on quality local cuisine, offering a small but inviting menu and reasonable prices. Harry likes oldies, and you're welcome to look over his impressive playlist and request your favorite music (€7–14 entrées, cash only, Thu–Tue 11:30–14:00 & 18:00–21:00, closed Wed, near bottom of Herrngasse at #24, tel. 09861/2126).

Altfränkische Weinstube am Klosterhof seems designed for gnomes to celebrate their anniversaries. At this very dark pub, classically candlelit in a 600-year-old building, Mario whips up gourmet pub grub (€7–14 entrées, hot food served 18:00–22:30, closes at 1:00 in the morning, off Klingengasse at Klosterhof 7, tel. 09861/6404). If you'd like dinner company, drop by on Wednesday evening, when the English Conversation Club has a big table reserved from 19:00 on (see "Meet the Locals," page 279). You'll eat well and with new friends—both travelers and locals.

Gasthof Rödertor, just outside the wall through the Rödertor gate, is a lively place where Rothenburgers go for a hearty meal at a good price. Their passion is potatoes—the menu is dedicated to spud cuisine. Try a €6.80 plate of *Schupfnudeln,* potato noodles with sauerkraut and bacon (€6–12 entrées, daily 11:30–14:00 & 17:30–22:30, Ansbacher Strasse 7, tel. 09861/2022). They also run a popular *Biergarten* (described later).

Eisenhut Restaurant, in Hotel Eisenhut, is a fine place for a dress-up splurge with surprisingly reasonable prices. You'll enjoy elegantly presented dishes, both traditional and international, with formal service. Sit in their royal dining room or on their garden sun terrace (€18–25 main dishes, fixed-price meals from €27, daily 12:00–14:30 & 18:30–21:30, Herrngasse 3, tel. 09861/7050).

Reichs-Küchenmeister is a forgettable big-hotel restaurant, but on a balmy evening, its pleasant tree-shaded terrace overlooking St. Jakob's Church is hard to beat. Their €13 *Vesperbrett* plate is a fine selection of cold cuts (€7–9 light meals, €10–20 main dishes, daily 11:00–22:00, Kirchplatz 8, tel. 09861/9700).

Breaks from Pork and Potatoes

Pizzeria Roma is the locals' favorite for €6.50 pizza and pastas with good Italian wine. The Magrini family moved here from Tuscany in 1970 (many Italians immigrated to Germany in those years), and they've been cooking pasta for Rothenburg ever since (Thu–Tue 11:00–24:00, closed Wed and mid-Aug–mid-Sept, Galgengasse 19, tel. 09861/4540, Ricardo).

China-Restaurant Peking, at the Plönlein, has two-course lunch specials (€5–7, Mon–Sat only), and its noisy streetside tables have a fine tower view (open daily 11:00–15:00 & 17:00–23:00, Plönlein 4, tel. 09861/938-738).

Rothenburg Restaurants

NOTE: MAP NOT TO SCALE
CASTLE GARDEN TO RÖDERTOR
IS A 15-MIN. WALK

TO WÜRZBURG &
ROMANTIC ROAD

TO
DETWANG &

ST. WOLFGANG'S

KLINGENTOR

TO AUTOBAHN A-7
& BAD WINDSHEIM

BEZOLDWEG

WALL

GALGEN-
TOR

IMPERIAL
CITY
MUSEUM

SCHRANNEN-
PLATZ

HIRTENGASSE

ST.
JAKOB'S

WHITE
TOWER

GALGENGASSE

TAUBER

JUDEN-GASSE

KLOST-HOF

STOLLENGASSE

TOPPLER
CASTLE

BURG-
TOR

PUPPET
THEATER

HERRN-
GASSE

FRAN.
CHURCH

BURG-
GASSE

RÖDER-
TOR
Post

RÖDERGASSE

HAFEN

TRADES-
MAN'S
HOUSE

CASTLE
GARDEN

RIVER

MEDIEVAL
CRIME &
PUNISHMENT
MUSEUM

PLÖNLEIN

TO
TRAIN
STATION

WENGGASSE

ALT KELLER

NEUGASSE

TOPPLERWEG

DOUBLE
BRIDGE

BURGENSTR.

SPITALGASSE

★ MARKET SQUARE
TOURIST INFO, CLOCK
& TOWN HALL TOWER

⬛ ACCESS STAIRS
TO WALL

🅿 PARKING

⋯ PATH

BENSENSTR.

WC

TO
DINKELSBÜHL
& FÜSSEN VIA
ROMANTIC ROAD
& SWIMMING POOL

DCH

ROTHENBURG

❶ Gasthof Goldener Greifen

❷ Hotel Restaurant
Klosterstüble

❸ Bürgerkeller

❹ Altfränkische Weinstube
am Klosterhof

❺ Gasthof Rödertor &
Beer Garden

❻ Eisenhut Restaurant &
Beer Garden

❼ Reichs-Küchenmeister

❽ Pizzeria Roma

❾ China-Restaurant Peking

❿ Bosporus Café

⓫ To Unter den Linden
Beer Garden

⓬ Eis Café D' Isep (Ice Cream)

⓭ Trinkstube zur Hölle

⓮ Restaurant Glocke

The **Bosporus Café** at Hafengasse 2, just off Market Square, serves cheap and tasty Turkish food to go or eat in. Their *Döner kebabs* must be the best €3 hot meal in Rothenburg (daily 9:00–21:00).

Picnic Goodies: A small **grocery store** is in the center of town at Rödergasse 6 (Mon–Fri 7:30–19:00, Sat 7:30–18:00, April–Dec also Sun 10:00–18:00, closed Sun Jan–March). **Supermarkets** are outside the wall: Exit the town through Rödertor, turn left through the cobbled gate, and cross the parking lot to reach the Edeka supermarket (Mon–Fri 8:00–20:00, Sat 8:00–18:00, closed Sun); or head to the even bigger Kaufland in the shopping center across from the train station (Mon–Sat 7:00–20:00, closed Sun).

Beer Gardens *(Biergartens)*

Rothenburg's *Biergartens* can be great fun, but they're open only when the weather is balmy.

Unter den Linden, a bohemian yet family-friendly *Biergarten* in the valley along the river, is worth the 20-minute hike on a pleasant evening (daily 10:00–21:00 in season with decent weather, sometimes later, self-service food and good beer, call first to confirm it's open, tel. 09861/5909). As it's in the valley on the river, it's cooler than Rothenburg; bring a sweater. Take a right outside the Burgtor, then a left on the footpath toward Detwang; it's at the bottom of the hill on the left.

Gasthof Rödertor, just outside the wall through the Rödertor gate, runs a backyard *Biergarten* that's great for a rowdy crowd, cheap food, and good beer (May–Sept daily 17:00–24:00, look for wooden gate, tel. 09861/2022). If the *Biergarten* is closed, their indoor restaurant (described earlier) is a good value.

Eisenhut Restaurant, behind the fancy hotel of the same name on Herrngasse (described earlier), is a good bet for gentle and casual *Biergarten* ambience within the old center.

Dessert

Eis Café D' Isep, with a pleasant "Venetian minimal" interior, is the town's ice-cream parlor, serving up cakes, drinks, fresh-fruit ice cream, and fancy sundaes. Their sidewalk tables are great for lazy people-watching (daily 9:30–22:00, closed early Oct–mid-Feb, one block off Market Square at Hafengasse 17, run by Paolo and Paola D'Isep).

Wine-Drinking in the Old Center

Trinkstube zur Hölle ("Hell") is dark and foreboding, offering a thick wine-drinking atmosphere, pub food, and a few main dishes. It's small and can get painfully touristy in summer (daily 17:00–24:00, closed Sun Jan–March, a block past Medieval Crime and Punishment Museum on Burggasse, with the devil hanging out front, tel. 09861/4229).

Mario's **Altfränkische Weinstube am Klosterhof** (listed earlier) is the liveliest place, and a clear favorite with locals for an atmospheric drink or late meal. When every other place is asleep, you're likely to find good food, drink, and energy here.

Restaurant Glocke, a *Weinstube* (wine bar) popular with locals, is run by Rothenburg's oldest winemakers, the Thürauf family. The menu, which has a very extensive wine list, is in German only because the friendly staff wants to explain your options in person. Their €4.40 deal, which lets you sample five Franconian wines, is popular (€8–18 entrées, Mon–Sat 11:00–23:00, Sun 11:00–14:00, Plönlein 1, tel. 09861/958-990).

Meet the Locals—English Conversation Club

For a rare chance to mix it up with locals who aren't selling anything, bring your favorite slang and tongue twisters to the English Conversation Club at Mario's Altfränkische Weinstube am Klosterhof (Wed 19:00–24:00; see restaurant listing earlier, under "Traditional German Restaurants"). This group of intrepid linguists has met more than 1,000 times. Hermann the German and his sidekick Wolfgang are regulars. Consider arriving early for dinner, or after 21:00, when the beer starts to sink in, the crowd grows, and everyone seems to speak that second language a bit more easily.

Rothenburg Connections

Reaching Rothenburg ob der Tauber by Train: A tiny branch train line connects Rothenburg to the outside world via **Steinach** in 14 minutes (generally 1/hr from Rothenburg at :06 and from Steinach at :35). If you plan to arrive in Rothenburg in the evening, note that the last train from Steinach to Rothenburg departs at about 22:30. All is not lost if you arrive in Steinach after the last train—there's a subsidized taxi service to Rothenburg (cheaper for the government than running an almost-empty train). To use this handy service, called AST *(Anrufsammeltaxi),* make an appointment with a participating taxi service (call 09861/2000 or 09861/7227) at least an hour in advance (2 hours ahead is better), and they'll drive you from Steinach to Rothenburg for the train fare (about €3.80/person) rather than the regular €25 taxi fare.

Train connections in Steinach are usually quick and efficient (trains to and from Rothenburg generally use track 5). The station at Steinach is not staffed, but has touch-screen terminals for fare and schedule information and ticket sales. Visit the ticket office in Rothenburg, or as a last resort call for train info at tel. 0180-599-6633 (€0.14/min).

From Rothenburg by Train to: Würzburg (hourly, 1.25 hrs), **Nürnberg** (hourly, 1.25 hrs, change in Ansbach), **Munich** (hourly, 2.5–3.5 hrs, 2–3 changes), **Füssen** (every 2 hrs, 5 hrs, change in Steinach, Treuchtlingen, and Augsburg), **Frankfurt** (hourly, 2.5–3 hrs, change in Würzburg), **Frankfurt Airport** (hourly, 3–3.25 hrs, change in Würzburg), **Berlin** (hourly, 5–6 hrs, 2 changes). Remember, all destinations also require a change in Steinach.

From Rothenburg by Bus: The Romantic Road bus stops in Rothenburg once a day (early May–late Oct) on its way from Frankfurt to Munich and Füssen (and vice versa). The bus stop is at Schrannenplatz, a short walk north of Market Square. See the schedule and tour description at the end of this chapter.

Route Tips for Drivers
From Frankfurt Airport (and Other Points North) to Rothenburg: The three-hour autobahn drive from Frankfurt Airport to Rothenburg is something even a jet-lagged zombie can handle. It's a 75-mile straight shot to Würzburg on the A-3 autobahn; just follow the blue autobahn signs towards *Würzburg*. Then turn south on A-7 and take the *Rothenburg o.d.T.* exit (#108).

The Romantic Road

The countryside between Frankfurt and Munich is Germany's medieval heartland. Walls and towers ring half-timbered towns, and flowers spill over the windowsills of well-kept houses. Glockenspiels dance from town halls by day, while night watchmen still call the hours after dark. Many travelers bypass these small towns by fast train or autobahn. But consider an extra day or two to take in the slow pace of small-town German life. With a car,

you can wander through quaint hills and rolling villages, and stop wherever the cows look friendly or a town fountain beckons.

In the 1950s, towns in this region joined together to work out a scenic driving route for visitors that they called the Romantic Road (Romantische Strasse, www.romanticroad.de). Because local train service was poor, they also organized a bus tour along the route, from Würzburg in the north to Füssen in the south.

The Romantic Road is the oldest and most famous of Germany's two dozen signposted scenic routes. Others celebrate

The Romantic Road

NOT ALL ROADS & RAIL LINES ARE SHOWN

toys, porcelain, architecture (Swabian Baroque or brick Gothic), clocks, and baths—and there are now two separate *Spargelstrassen* (asparagus roads). The "Castle Road" that runs between Rothenburg and Mannheim sounds intriguing, but it's nowhere near as interesting.

Now that the A-7 autobahn parallels the old two-lane route, the Romantic Road itself has become less important, but its destinations are still worthwhile. For drivers, the Romantic Road is basically a set of scenic stepping stones to Rothenburg, which is the most exciting town along the way. You can make a day out of the drive between Würzburg (or Frankfurt) and Rothenburg, stopping in the small towns along the Tauber River Valley. If linking Rothenburg and Munich, stop in Dinkelsbühl or Nördlingen. The drive from Rothenburg to Füssen on two-lane roads makes for a full day, but it's possible to squeeze in a quick visit to Dinkelsbühl, Nördlingen, the Wieskirche, or Landsberg am Lech, hopping on the autobahn to speed up parts of the trip. If you're driving with limited time, just zero in on Rothenburg by autobahn.

For those without a car, the tour bus that still runs along the Romantic Road route once a day during the summer is a way to connect Rothenburg with Frankfurt, Würzburg, and Munich, or to go between Munich and Füssen, while seeing more scenery than you'd get on the train.

Sights Along the Romantic Road

I've divided the Romantic Road into three sections. The stretch from Würzburg (or Frankfurt) to Rothenburg runs up the Tauber River Valley, offering views that are pleasant, though not dramatic. Rothenburg to Augsburg is fairly flat and dull. From Augsburg south to Füssen, the route follows the Lech River up to where the Alps begin, and the scenery gets more exciting at every turn. To help you find your way, I've included some driving directions. While I've listed public transit connections for major stops, most of these out-of-the-way destinations aren't worth the hassle if you lack a car.

From Würzburg (or Frankfurt) to Rothenburg

To take this scenic back-road approach from Frankfurt, take A-3, then turn south on A-81, get off at the Tauberbischofsheim exit, and follow signs for *Bad Mergentheim*. Or stay on A-3 to the Heidingsfeld–Würzburg exit and follow *Stuttgart/Ulm/Road 19* signs south to Bad Mergentheim. From Würzburg, follow *Ulm/ Road 19* signs to Bad Mergentheim.

Bad Mergentheim—In 1525, when the Teutonic Knights lost their lands in East Prussia and the Baltic states, the order's leadership retreated to their castle at Bad Mergentheim, which became their headquarters for the next three centuries. The order's properties were dissolved in 1806, but European history fans will enjoy the castle, which houses an extensive museum on the history of the order that was key in Christianizing northeastern Europe (Deutschordensmuseum, €4.20;

April–Oct Tue–Sun 10:30–17:00, closed Mon; Nov–March Tue–Sat 14:00–17:00, Sun 10:30–17:00, closed Mon; tel. 07931/52212, www.deutschordensmuseum.de). The castle park has benches for your picnic, and cafés line the street by the castle entrance and the old town square. Don't try to park in the old town; follow the *Altstadt/ Schloss* parking signs to the inexpensive covered garage, then the signs and painted footprints to the castle.

Leaving Bad Mergentheim, continue east on road 19, then L-2251. Turn into Weikersheim off the main road, following *Stadtmitte* and *Schloss* signs, then bear right to park in the large free lot. From there it's a couple minutes' walk to the town square.

Weikersheim—The town's **palace** (Schloss Weikersheim), right on the picturesque town square, has an orangerie and fine Baroque

gardens that make for a luxurious picnic spot. Admission to the gardens and a few museum exhibits is €2.50, while another €3 gets you a one-hour guided tour of the palace itself (German only—ask for English text, hourly tours, daily April–Oct 9:00–18:00, Nov–March 10:00–12:00 & 13:00–17:00, tel. 07934/992-950, www.schloss-weikersheim.de). The castle rose garden, to the right before you enter, is free; a gate off the rose garden leads to a spooky "alchemy garden" with plants used by medieval witches. The city park (Stadtpark, enter off town square) is also a fine and free picnic spot, and from it you can peer over the hedge into the palace gardens.

▲**Creglingen**—While Creglingen itself isn't worth much fuss (TI tel. 07933/631, www.creglingen.de), two quick and rewarding sights sit across the road from each other a mile south of town.

The peaceful 14th-century **Herr-gottskirche** church is graced with Tilman Riemenschneider's greatest carved altarpiece, completed sometime between 1505 and 1510. The impressive altar is nearly 30 feet high, and you can get right up close to it (€2; Easter–Oct daily 9:15–18:00; Nov–Dec and Feb–Easter Tue–Sun 13:00–16:00, closed Mon; closed Jan, tel. 07933/508, www.herrgottskirche.de).

The **Fingerhut Museum** shows off thimbles—literally, "finger hats," with descriptions in German. It's actually interesting to look at the collection, which numbers about 4,000 (but still fits in a single room) and comes from all over the world; some are centuries old. Owner Thorvald Greif got a head start from his father, who owned a thimble factory (€2, Tue–Sun April–Oct 10:00–12:30 & 14:00–17:00, Nov–March 13:00–16:00, closed Mon, tel. 07933/370, www.fingerhutmuseum.de).

From Rothenburg to Augsburg

The A-7 and A-8 autobahns parallel the Romantic Road here, and can speed up your trip. But if you stick to the Romantic Road, consider stops at Dinkelsbühl and Nördlingen.

▲**Dinkelsbühl**—Rothenburg's little sister is cute enough to merit a short stop. A moat, towers, gates, and beautifully preserved medieval wall surround this town. Dinkelsbühl is pretty, and less touristy than Rothenburg, but also less exciting.

Park at the free lots outside the town walls (there's a one-hour limit inside). To orient yourself, head for the tower of **St. Georg's Church,** at the center of town. This 15th-century church has fine carved altarpieces and a surprisingly light, airy interior. Follow the signs around the corner (first into Ledermarkt, then Altrathausplatz) to the **TI,** which sells a "Tour of the Town" brochure with a map and short walking tour; they can also help find rooms (May–Oct Mon–Fri 9:00–18:00, Sat–Sun 10:00–17:00; Nov–April daily 10:00–17:00; tel. 09851/90240, www.dinkels buehl.de). In the TI, take a minute to watch the TV monitor showing the stork nest on the top of the old town hall (also visible at www.storch24.de).

The TI doubles as the ticket office for the fine **City History Museum** (Haus der Geschichte) in the same building (€4, ask for English audioguide, same hours as TI, kids' play area). This shiny, up-to-date museum shows how Dinkelsbühl sat along important north–south travel routes in early times, and explains how the tug-of-war between Catholics and Protestants ended in a power-sharing agreement and the loss of the town's medieval prosperity. On the top floor is a self-service movie theater showing short film clips about Dinkelsbühl (in English, plus old silent clips).

You can accompany Dinkelsbühl's **Night Watchman** on his one-hour rounds every evening at 21:00 (in German only, free, April–Oct daily, Nov–March Sat only, meet at St. Georg's Church). The Kinderzeche children's festival turns Dinkelsbühl wonderfully on end for a week at the end of July, celebrating the success of the local children who pleaded with the Swedish army during the Thirty Years' War, convincing them to spare the town (www.kinderzeche.de).

Maypoles

Along the Romantic Road, and throughout Bavaria, you'll see colorfully ornamented maypoles *(Maibaum)* decorating town squares. Many are painted in Bavaria's colors, white and blue. The decorations that line each side of the pole symbolize the craftspeople and businesses of that community (similar to the Chamber of Commerce billboards you'll pass as you enter small American towns today). Originally these allowed passing traders to quickly determine whether their services were needed in that town. The decorations are festively replaced each May Day (May 1). Traditionally, rival communities try to steal each other's maypole. Locals guard their new pole night and day as May Day approaches. Stolen poles are ransomed only with lots of beer for the clever thieves.

Sleeping in Dinkelsbühl: Dinkelsbühl has a good selection of hotels. **$$ Hotel Palmengarten,** run by the Danner-Bohl family, is on a quiet side street, with small, modern rooms (Sb-€35–48, Db-€68–78, Tb-€85–90, parking garage-€5/day, free Wi-Fi, Untere Schmiedgasse 14, tel. 09851/57670, fax 09851/7548, www.sonne-palmengarten.de, info@sonne-palmengarten.de). Dinkelsbühl's **$ youth hostel** is in a handsome medieval building (€22/bed in 6- to 8-bed dorms, Koppengasse 10, tel. 09851/9509, www.dinkelsbuehl.jugendherberge.de). Both the Palmengarten and the hostel are just steps from the Schweinemarkt, where Romantic Road buses stop once a day in each direction.

No trains run to Dinkelsbühl, but there are hourly buses from the train station at Ansbach, an hour away.

Nördlingen—Though less cute than Dinkelsbühl, Nördlingen nevertheless merits a short stop if you're interested in city walls or meteorites. The town's almost perfectly circular wall is better preserved than Rothenburg's or Dinkelsbühl's and you can walk the whole way around. For centuries, Nördlingen's residents puzzled over the local terrain, a flattish plain called the Ries, which rises to a low circular

THE ROMANTIC ROAD

ridge that surrounds the town in the distance. In the 1960s, geologists figured out that Nördlingen lies in the middle of an impact crater blasted out 15 million years ago by a meteor, which hit Earth with the force of 250,000 Hiroshima bombs.

Weekday and Saturday morning parking at the entrances to the old town (and inside) is limited to 1.5 hours, which isn't really enough time to see the town. Unless visiting on Saturday afternoon or Sunday, drivers should use the big, free lots at Delninger Tor and Baldinger Tor or the free parking garage at Berger Tor.

After parking, head through one of the gates in the wall and into the center of town by zeroing in on the tower of **St. Georg's Church** (yes, the same saint as in Dinkelsbühl). The rickety 350-step climb up the church tower (which locals call "the Daniel") rewards you with the very best view of the city walls and the rim of the meteorite crater (open daily year-round, €2). The small square next to the church is called Marktplatz, and just behind the step-gabled Rathaus (town hall) is the TI, which gives out free town maps (Mon–Thu 10:00–18:00, Fri 10:00–16:30, Sat 10:00–14:00, closed Sun, Marktplatz 2, tel. 09081/84116, www.noerdlingen.de).

Now walk out the bottom of Marktplatz and down Baldinger Strasse. At the traffic light, turn right and then left, past the Stadtmuseum, to the **Ries Crater Museum** (Rieskrater-Museum). Ask them to play the two 10-minute English films, which explain meteors and the formation of the solar system. The exhibits themselves are only described in German, but for €3 they'll let you borrow a rather dry and detailed English guide (€4, Tue–Sun May–Oct 10:00–16:30, Nov–April 10:00–12:00 & 13:30–16:30, closed Mon, Eugene-Shoemaker-Platz 1, tel. 09081/273-8220, www.rieskrater-museum.de).

Circle back to Baldinger Strasse and continue to Baldinger Tor (tower). Climb the stairs to the walkway along the **town wall,** which you can follow back to the lot where your car is parked. The city started building the wall in 1327 and financed it with a tax on wine and beer; it's more than a mile and a half long, has 16 towers and five gates, and offers great views of backyards and garden furniture.

For those with extra time, there's a **City Wall Museum** (Stadtmauermuseum) in the tower at Löpsinger Tor, which lets you climb up to the tower's top level (closed Mon, no English descriptions). If you have energy for only one climb, the view from the church tower is better.

Sleeping in Nördlingen: Several small hotels surrounding St. Georg's Church vie for your business with mediocre but reasonably priced rooms. Of these, try **$$ Hotel Altreuter,** over an inviting bakery/café (Sb-€35–45, Db-€48–64, prices depend on room size, free Wi-Fi, lots of stairs, Marktplatz 11, tel. 09081/4319, fax

09081/9797, www.hotel-altreuter.de, mail@hotel-altreuter.de).

Nördlingen is reachable by train (change in Donauwörth).

Augsburg—Founded more than 2,000 years ago by Emperor Augustus, Augsburg enjoyed its heyday in the 15th and 16th centuries. Today, it's Bavaria's third-largest city (population 264,000). It lacks must-see sights, but the old town is pleasant, especially the small streets below the main square, where streams diverted from the River Lech run alongside pedestrians (www.augsburg.de).

From Augsburg to Füssen

From Augsburg, you can either continue south to Füssen on the two-lane road, or you can hop on A-8, which brings you quickly into Munich (in about an hour).

Landsberg am Lech—Like many towns in this area, Landsberg (on the River Lech) has its roots in the salt trade. Every four years, the town returns to its medieval roots and hosts the Ruethenfest. The town was shaped by the architect Dominikus Zimmerman (of Wieskirche fame). Adolf Hitler wrote *Mein Kampf* while serving his prison sentence here after the Beer Hall Putsch of 1923 (when Hitler and his followers unsuccessfully attempted to take over the government of Bavaria).

Rottenbuch—This nondescript village, near the Wieskirche, has an impressive church in a lovely setting.

Wieskirche—This is Germany's most glorious Baroque-Rococo church, beautifully restored and set in a sweet meadow. Heavenly! Romantic Road buses (described below) stop here for 17 minutes—but only on the northbound Munich-to-Frankfurt run. Southbound buses will pick up and drop off here, but only on request. (See the full Wieskirche description on page 119 of the Bavaria and Tirol chapter, which also covers Füssen.)

The Romantic Road Bus

From early May to late October, the Deutsche Touring company runs daily tour buses that roughly follow the Romantic Road. One bus per day goes from Frankfurt to Munich to Füssen, and another goes from Füssen to Munich to Frankfurt (tel. 069/4609-7280 or 069/790-3261, www.romantic roadcoach.de). While this bus tour used to be a traveler's dream, it's gone downhill in recent years—with higher prices and fewer (and shorter) sightseeing stops than before. I'd use the bus only if you're without a car and determined to ride the Romantic Road. If a specific town (such as Rothenburg) is your main interest, it's more foolproof to go there by train.

You won't see any small towns on the Frankfurt–Rothenburg leg, which follows the autobahn. The Rothenburg–Munich leg

Romantic Road Bus Schedule

The Romantic Road bus runs daily from early May to late October. Every day, one bus goes north to south (Frankfurt to Munich to Füssen), and another follows almost the same route south to north (Füssen to Munich to Frankfurt). Only the northbound bus stops at the Wieskirche. You can begin or end your journey at any of these stops. The following times include only the main stops, based on the 2009 schedule. Check the full schedule at www.romanticroadcoach.de for any changes.

North to South
Depart Frankfurt.............................8:00
Arrive Würzburg 9:45
Depart Würzburg 9:45
Arrive Rothenburg 10:40
Depart Rothenburg 11:15
Arrive Dinkelsbühl 12:05
Depart Dinkelsbühl.......................12:40
Arrive Munich 16:25
Depart Munich................................16:25
Arrive Füssen.................................19:00

South to North
Depart Füssen.................................8:00
Arrive Wieskirche 8:53
Depart Wieskirche 9:10
Arrive Munich 11:00
Depart Munich..................................11:00
Arrive Dinkelsbühl............................14:40
Depart Dinkelsbühl.......................15:10
Arrive Rothenburg 16:00
Depart Rothenburg 16:35
Arrive Würzburg 17:30
Depart Würzburg 17:30
Arrive Frankfurt..............................19:15

THE ROMANTIC ROAD

includes half-hour stops in Dinkelsbühl and Augsburg—just enough for a glimpse of each. Between Munich and Füssen, the bus stops in Oberammergau and at Ettal Monastery, and the northbound buses (Füssen–Munich) also make a 17-minute rest stop at the Wieskirche—just long enough to peek into the church. Be warned that in case of delays, these stops can be shortened or skipped altogether.

Besides the scenery, the Romantic Road bus gives you the advantage of a connection-free trip—unlike the train, where you usually have to change. The downside is that the buses run only once a day in each direction (there are hourly train connections on these same routes). The only ticket offices are in Frankfurt (see page 327) and online.

Frankfurt to Rothenburg costs €38, Rothenburg to Munich is €43, and Munich to Füssen is €28 (each about the same as the train). The entire ride (Frankfurt to Füssen) costs €99. Pay cash on the bus. Students and seniors—without a railpass—get a 10 percent discount. You can get a 20 percent discount on your bus ticket if you have a German railpass, Eurail Global Pass, or Eurail Selectpass (if Germany is one of your selected countries). You don't have to use a travel day of a flexipass to get this discount; if bus drivers say it takes a travel day, set them straight.

You can ride from Munich to Rothenburg for €30 if you purchase your ticket at the Munich EurAide office (see page 30).

Bus reservations are almost never necessary. But they are free and easy, and, technically, without one you can lose your seat to someone who has one (reserve online at www.romanticroadcoach .de, or call 069/790-3261).

Bus stops are not well-signed, but their location in each town is listed on the bus brochure and website. Look for a small *Touring* or *Romantische Strasse* sign. For schedule details, see the sidebar.

THE ROMANTIC ROAD

WÜRZBURG

A historic city—though freshly rebuilt since World War II—Würzburg is worth a stop to see its impressive prince-bishop's Residenz and the palace's sculpted gardens. Surrounded by vineyards and filled with atmospheric *Weinstuben* (wine bars), this tourist-friendly town is easy to navigate by foot or streetcar. Today, 25,000 of its 130,000 residents are students—making the town feel young and very alive.

Planning Your Time

Würzburg has a few hours' worth of sightseeing. Begin at the Residenz (prince-bishop's palace), then take my self-guided walk through town to the Old Main Bridge. With more time, hike up to the hilltop Marienberg Fortress across the bridge.

Orientation to Würzburg

(area code: 0931)

Tourist Information

Würzburg's helpful TI is in the Rococo-style Falken Haus on Market Square (May–Oct Mon–Fri 10:00–18:00, Sat–Sun 10:00–14:00; April and Nov–Dec same hours but closed Sun; Jan–March Mon–Fri 10:00–16:00, Sat 10:00–14:00, closed Sun; Market Square, tel. 0931/372-398, www.wuerzburg.de). Their free *Visitor's Guide* pamphlet and map covers the tourist's Würzburg well. The TI books rooms for free (in person only, not by phone), sells detailed maps for biking through the local wine country, and offers a one-hour walking tour in English (€6, Fri at 13:00, May–Oct also Sat at 13:00). If you'll be continuing on the Romantic Road (see previous chapter), the TI has the *Romantische Strasse* brochure and a list of car-rental options.

Sightseeing Passes: The TI sells the **Würzburg Welcome Card,** offering minimal discounts on a few sights and restaurants (€3/7 days). Würzburg's Residenz and Marienberg Fortress are covered by the **Bavarian Castles Pass** (€20, family/partner version-€36 for two adults plus children, valid for two weeks, sold at all participating sights, details on page 98).

Arrival in Würzburg

By Train: Würzburg's train station is user-friendly and filled with handy services (coin-op lockers in main hall, WCs between main hall and tunnel to platforms). Walk out of the train station to the small square in front. A big **city map** board provides a

WÜRZBURG

Würzburg's Beginnings

The city was born centuries before Christ at an easy-to-ford part of the Main River under an easy-to-defend hill. A Celtic fort stood where the fortress stands today. Later, three Irish missionary monks came here to Christianize the local barbarians. In A.D. 686, they were beheaded, and their relics put Würzburg on the pilgrimage map. About 500 years later, when the town was the seat of a bishop, Holy Roman Emperor Frederick Barbarossa came here to get the bishop's OK to divorce his wife. The bishop said, "No problem," and the emperor thanked him by giving him secular rule of the entire region of Franconia. From then on, the bishop was also a prince, and the prince-bishop of Würzburg answered only to the Holy Roman Emperor.

---

quick orientation (on small building to the right). Farther right is the **post office** and the **Romantic Road bus stop** (track 13, curb closest and parallel to station building, look for *Touring* sign and schedule).

From the cul-de-sac in front of the station, **tram #1, #2, #3, or #5** takes you one stop to the Juliuspromenade stop, near the recommended hotels (except Hotel-Pension Spehnkuch, which is near the station). Another stop (to Dom or Ulmer Hof) brings you close to Market Square and the TI. By **foot,** cross over the busy Röntgenring and head up the shop-lined Kaiserstrasse. To reach the **Residenz,** it's simplest to walk (15 min), but you can get part of the way by taking tram #1, #3, or #5 to the Dom stop.

By Car: Drivers entering Würzburg can keep it simple by following signs to the *Residenz,* and parking in the vast cobbled square that faces the palace.

Helpful Hints

Festivals: Würzburg—always clever when it comes to trade—schedules its three annual festivals (wine, Mozart, and the Kiliani-Volksfest) in rapid succession, and keeps things busy from the beginning of June through late July.

Internet Access: Log Inn Internet Café is near Market Square, down the street behind the Marienkapelle (€3/hr, Mon–Sat 9:00–23:00, Sun 10:00–23:00, Häfnergasse 5).

Supermarket: Kupsch, at Domstrasse 10, is just a few doors from City Hall (Mon–Sat 8:00–20:00, closed Sun). Another branch is on Kaiserstrasse, near the station.

Bike Rental: Fahrrad Körner rents bikes right in the old town, a five-minute walk north of Market Square (€10/24 hrs, Bronnbachergasse 3, tel. 0931/52340).

Local Guide: Maureen Aldenhoff, who grew up in Liverpool but has been married to a German for 30 years, gives good private walking tours (€90/2 hrs, €130/3 hrs, €190/full day, tel. 0931/52135, maureen.aldenhoff@web.de).

Getting Around Würzburg

You can easily walk to everything but the hilltop Marienberg Fortress. For public transit, the same tickets work on all city bus and tram lines (including the bus up to the fortress). Your options include a single ticket (*Einzelfahrschein*, €2.10, good for 90 min in one direction with transfers) or a day pass (*Tageskarte Solo*—€4.30 for one person; or *Tageskarte Familie*—€8.60 for two adults and kids under age 15). You can buy either type of ticket from the bus driver or at a streetside machine (marked *Fahrausweise*). Single tickets are only valid if you stamp them, using the little box inside the tram or bus (day passes come pre-stamped). For transit info, call tel. 0931/362-320 or visit www.wvv.de.

Sights in Würzburg

Würzburg's Residenz

Würzburg's opulent palace and its associated sights—the Chapel (Hofkirche) and garden—are the town's main attraction. Unfortunately, the Chapel is closed for restoration until 2012.

▲▲**Residenz Palace**—This Franconian Versailles features grand rooms, 3-D art, and a massive (and recently restored) fresco by Giovanni Battista Tiepolo.

Cost, Hours, Location: €7, covered by Bavarian Castles Pass, daily April–Oct 9:00–18:00, Nov–March 10:00–16:30, last entry 30 min before closing, no photos, tel. 0931/355-170 or 0931/355-1712, www.residenz-wuerzburg.de. Don't confuse the Residenz (a 15-min walk southeast of the train station) with Marienberg Fortress (on the hilltop across the river). The Residenz is the far more important sight to visit. Easy parking is available in front of the Residenz (€1.50/hr for first 2 hrs, €1 each additional hr, pay at the machine marked *Kasse* before you drive out of the lot).

Tours, Information, Services: English tours, offered daily year-round at 11:00 and 15:00, include the normally closed South Wing, which has the five best rooms (45 min, call ahead or tell the cashier you want to join the English tour, covered in entry price, but tips are welcome if the guide is good). The only other way to see the South Wing is to be trapped on a German tour (at least 3/hr). The €5 English guidebook is dry and lengthy. Few English descriptions are provided in the Residenz; follow my self-guided tour for an overview. On the right as you exit the ticket office, you'll find free WCs and storage lockers (€1 deposit is returned).

Residenz Grounds: The elaborate Chapel (Hofkirche) is next door (as you exit the palace, go left); the entrance to the picnic-worthy garden is just beyond (both described later).

⊙ **Self-Guided Tour:** The following self-guided tour gives you the basics to appreciate this fine palace.

• *Begin at the entrance.*

1. Vestibule: This area functioned as a grand circular drive-way—just right for six-horse carriages to drop off their guests at the base of the stairs. The elegant stairway comes with low steps, enabling high-class ladies to glide up gracefully, heads tilted back to enjoy Europe's largest and grandest fresco opening up above them. Hold your lady's hand high and get into the ascending rhythm. Enjoy the climb.

• *Ascend the stairs and look up at the...*

2. Tiepolo Fresco: In 1752, the Venetian master Giovanni Battista Tiepolo was instructed to make a grand fresco illustrat-ing the greatness of Europe, Würzburg, and the prince-bishop. And he did—in only 13 months. Find the four continents, each symbolized by a woman on an animal and pointing to the prince-bishop in the medallion above Europe. America—desperately uncivilized—sits naked with feathers in her hair on an alligator among severed heads. She's being served hot chocolate, a favorite import and nearly a drug for Europeans back then. Africa sits on a camel in a land of trade and fantasy animals (based on secondhand reports, and therefore inaccurate). Asia rides her elephant (with the backward ear) in the birthplace of Christianity and the alphabet. And Europe is shown as the center of high culture—Lady Culture points her brush not at Rome, but at Würzburg. The prince-bishop had a healthy ego. The ceiling features Apollo and a host of Greek gods, all paying homage to the PB.

3. The White Hall: This hall, actually gray, was kept plain to punctuate the colorful rooms on either side. It's a Rococo-stucco fantasy. (The word "Rococo" comes from the Portuguese word for the frilly rocaille shell.)

• *Straight ahead is the palace gift shop. Continue to your left, following signs for* Rundgang.

4. The Imperial Hall: This glorious hall—which was recently restored—is the ultimate example of Baroque: harmony, symmetry, illusion, and the bizarre; lots of light and mirrors facing windows; and all with a foundation of absolutism (a divine monarch, inspired by Louis XIV). Take a moment to marvel at all the 3-D tricks in the ceiling. Here's another trick: As you enter the room, look left and check out the dog in the fresco. When you get to the window, have another look...notice that he has gotten older and fatter while you were crossing the hall.

The room features three scenes: On the ceiling, find Father Main (the local river) amusing himself with a nymph. The two walls tell more history. On one, the bishop presides over the marriage of a happy Barbarossa (whose bride was actually 12 years old, unlike the woman in the painting, who looks considerably older; for more on Barbarossa, see the "Würzburg's Beginnings" sidebar). The bishop's power is demonstrated through his oversized fingers (giving the benediction) and through the details of his miter, which—unlike his face—is not shown in profile to allow you to see his coat of arms. Opposite that is the pay-off: Barbarossa, now the Holy Roman Emperor, gives the bishop Franconia and the secular title of prince. From this point onward, the prince-bishop rules. Also in the Imperial Hall, the balcony offers a great vantage point for surveying the Italian section of the garden (explained later).

5. The North Wing: This wing is a string of lavish rooms—evolving from fancy Baroque to fancier Rococo—used for the prince-bishop's VIP guests. It's a straight shot, with short English descriptions in each room, to the Green Room in the corner.

6. The Green Lacquer Room: This room is named for its silver-leaf walls, painted green. The Escher-esque inlaid floor was painstakingly restored after WWII bombings. Have fun multiplying in the mirrors before leaving. The nearby hall (look for the exit sign) shows photos of the city in rubble in 1945—and craftsmen bringing the palace back to its original splendor soon after. The little four-foot-tall doors were used by tiny servants who stoked the stoves, unseen from this hallway.

▲▲**Chapel (Hofkirche)**—This sumptuous chapel is closed for restoration until 2012. The chapel was for the exclusive use of the prince-bishop (private altar upstairs with direct entrance to his residence) and his court (ground floor). If it happens to be open, take a look around: The decor and design are textbook Baroque. Architect Johann Balthasar Neumann was stuck with the existing walls. His challenge was to bring in light and create symmetry—essential to any Baroque work. He did it with mirrors and hidden windows. All the gold is real—if paper-thin—gold leaf. The columns are "manufactured marble," which isn't marble at all but marbled plaster. This method was popular because it was uniform, economical, and the color could be controlled. Pigment was mixed into plaster, which was rolled onto the stone or timber core of the column. This half-inch veneer was then polished. You can tell if a "marble" column is real or fake by resting your hand on it. If it warms up, it's not marble. The faded painting high above the altar shows three guys in gold robes losing their heads (for more on these martyred Irish monks, see the "Würzburg's Beginnings" sidebar). The two side paintings are by the great fresco artist Tiepolo. Since the plaster wouldn't dry in the winter, Tiepolo spent his downtime painting with oil.

Residenz Garden—One of Germany's finest Baroque gardens is a delightful park (free, open daily until dusk—at latest 20:00, enter through gate at right of Residenz building). By definition, Baroque gardens have three sections: English, French, and Italian. The French section, just inside the gate, features statues of Greek gods (with lots of kidnapping action), carefully trimmed 18th-century yew trees, and an orangerie. The English section (to the right) is like a rough park. The Italian section, directly behind the palace around to the left, is grand—à la Versailles—but uses terraces to create the illusion of spaciousness (since it was originally hemmed in by the town wall). Behind the orangerie is the replanted palace kitchen garden. A modern feature has been added to the garden: WCs (to the right as you come in the main entrance, next to the orangerie).

Self-Guided Walk

Welcome to Würzburg

This brief walk gets you from the Residenz, which you may want to tour first (described above), to the Old Main Bridge (Alte Mainbrücke) via the key old-town sights.

• *Begin at the fountain in front of the Residenz palace.*

Fountain of Franconia: In 1814, the prince-bishop got the boot, and the region of Franconia was secularized and given to the Bavarian Wittelsbach dynasty. Technically, Franconia is a part of Bavaria, but that status is like Scotland being part of Great Britain. (Never call a Franconian a Bavarian.) This statue—a gift from the townspeople to their then-new royal family—turns its back to the palace and faces the town. It celebrates the artistic and intellectual genius of Franconia with statues of three great hometown boys (a medieval bard, the woodcarver Tilman Riemenschneider, and the Renaissance painter Matthias Grünewald).

• *If Franconia hopped down and ran 300 yards ahead down Hofstrasse, she'd hit the twin-spired cathedral. Meet her there.*

Central Würzburg

➡ WALKING TOUR ROUTE
🕊 VIEW
🅿 PARKING

200 YARDS
200 METERS

❶ Hotel Barbarossa
❷ City Hotel Schönleber
❸ Sankt Josef Hotel
❹ Hotel-Pension Spehnkuch
❺ Babelfish Hostel
❻ To Youth Hostel
❼ Weinstube Bürgerspital & Hockerle Pub
❽ Juliusspital
❾ Zum Stachel Weinhaus
❿ Backöfele
⓫ Alte Mainmühle
⓬ Café Michel
⓭ Weinstube Maulaffenbäck
⓮ Pasta e Olio
⓯ Internet Café
⓰ Bike Rental

St. Kilian's Cathedral (Dom): This building's core is Romanesque (1040–1188), with Gothic spires and Baroque additions to the transepts. Enter through the back (the end nearest you, on the right-hand side; open daily 8:00–19:00).

Destroyed in World War II, the cathedral was rebuilt in the 1960s. Before 1945, the entire church was slathered in Baroque stucco decor, as the apse is today. The nave has a cohesive design, progressing from the menorah (representing the Old Testament) in the back, past tombstones of centuries of prince-bishops and a crucified Jesus (above the high altar), to the apse, where a resurrected Christ welcomes you into a hopeful future. The skulls of Würzburg's three favorite saints—those Irish monks martyred in the seventh century—lie in a box on the altar (see "Würzburg's Beginnings" sidebar).

Halfway along the nave (on the left side, as you face the altar) is a fine memorial to the 15th-century Prince-Bishop

Rudolf von Scherenberg, whose name means "scissors man" (see his coat of arms). Scherenberg ruled until he was 94 years old. Carved by Tilman Riemenschneider, this tombstone is an example of late-Gothic realism. Back then, it was outrageous to portray an old bishop as...an old bishop (looking at the tombstone, you can tell he needs dentures). The next prince-bishop, whose tomb is to the right of Scherenberg's, saw how realistic his predecessor's was, and insisted on having an idealized portrait (also by Riemenschneider) done to his satisfaction before he died. (He's looking unbelievably good.)

• *Leave the church through the side door, behind Mr. Scissors. Riemenschneider's tomb is on the church wall just outside the door. Stepping outside, look up at the three martyrs (before they were beheaded), turn left, and go into the museum.*

Cathedral Museum (Museum am Dom): This museum features a poignant combination of old and new religious art. It pairs 11th- to 18th-century works with modern interpretations, sprinkles it all with a Christian theme, and wraps it in a shiny new building (€3.50, €4.50 combo-ticket includes Cathedral Treasury, Tue–Sun April–Oct 10:00–18:00, Nov–March 10:00–17:00, closed Mon year-round, tel. 0931/3866-5600, www.museum-am-dom.de).

• *Upon leaving, hook right through a tunnel, which emerges on a delightful urban scene. Domstrasse leads down to the spire of the City Hall and the Old Main Bridge (where this walk will end). On your left you'll see a sign for the* **Cathedral Treasury** *(Domschatz, €2, €4.50 combo-ticket includes Cathedral Museum, Tue–Sun 14:00–17:00, closed Mon, tel. 0931/3866-5600). But we're looping right. Go a block up Kurschner Hof. On your right, you'll pass the entrance to the...*

Neumünster Basilica: Like the cathedral, this church has a Romanesque body with a Baroque face. Go up the stairs to take a look inside, then continue up the street, noticing the vineyards in the distance. Appreciate this quiet pedestrian zone. Locals wouldn't have it any other way—electric trolleys, bikes, and pedestrians.

• *Enter the square on the left with the lacy, two-tone church.*

Market Square (Marktplatz): Imagine this square during the wine fest in June, with 75 vintners showing off their best wines, or during the Christmas market, when the square is full of quaint stalls selling holiday goodies. The fancy yellow-and-white Rococo-designed Falken Haus (House of the Falcon) once had three different facades. To fix it, the landlady gave a wandering band of stucco artists a chance to show their stuff...and ended up with this (inside are the TI and a prizewinning library with Internet access).

• *Set your eyes on the church.*

Marienkapelle: The two-tone late-Gothic church was the merchants' answer to the prince-bishop's cathedral. Since Rome didn't bankroll the place, it's ringed with "swallow shops" (like swallows' nests cuddled up against a house)—enabling the church to run little businesses. The sandstone statues (replicas of Riemenschneider originals) depict the 12 apostles and Jesus. Walk downhill along the church to the lower marketplace, where the city's produce market bustles daily except Sunday (May–Oct 8:00–16:00). The famous Adam and Eve statues (flanking the side entrance to the church) show off Riemenschneider's mastery of the human body. Continue around the church to the west portal, where the carved Last Judgment (above the main doors) shows kings, ladies, and bishops—some going to heaven, others making up the chain gang bound for hell, via the monster's mouth. (This was commissioned by those feisty town merchants tired of snooty bluebloods.) Continue around to the next entry to see the Annunciation, with a cute angel Gabriel telling Mary (who is a virgin, symbolized by the lilies) the good news. Notice how God whispers through a speaking tube as baby Jesus slips down and into her ear.

• *Go back around to the lower market (Adam-and-Eve side) and leave—passing the obelisk—in the direction of the yellow building.*

Follow Schustergasse, a pedestrian lane lined with shops that leads back to Domstrasse. The cathedral is on your left, while the City Hall and bridge are to the right. Head right to the City Hall's tower.

City Hall (Rathaus): Würzburg's City Hall is relatively humble because of the power of the prince-bishop. A side room (facing the building, around the left side, free, always open) holds the *Gedenkraum 16, März 1945.* This commemorates the 20-minute Allied bombing on March 16, 1945, that created a firestorm that destroyed (and demoralized) Würzburg six weeks before the end of World War II. Check out the sobering model, and ponder the names (lining the ceiling) of those killed. As you leave, notice the horizontal lines cut into the archway on your right. These mark the floodwaters *(Hochstand des Maines)* of the years 1342, 1682, and 1784.

• *Now, find the bridge.*

Old Main Bridge (Alte Mainbrücke): This isn't the town's "main" (as in primary) bridge; rather, it spans the Main (pronounced "mine") River, which also flows through Frankfurt.

The bridge, from 1133, is the second-oldest in Germany. The 12 statues lining the bridge are Würzburg saints and prince-bishops. Walk to the St. Kilian statue (with the golden sword)—one of the three monks who are shown being beheaded in the Residenz palace's Chapel (Hofkirche). Stand so that you can't see the white power-plant tower and enjoy the best view in town. Marienberg Fortress caps the hill. Squint up at Kilian pointing to God...with his head on.

The hillside is blanketed with grapevines destined to become the fine Stein Franconian wine. Johann Wolfgang von Goethe, the German Shakespeare, ordered 900 liters of this vintage annually. A friend once asked Goethe what he thought were the three most important things in life. He said, "Wine, women, and song." The friend then asked, "If you had to give one up, which would it be?" Without hesitating, Goethe answered "Song." Then, when asked what he would choose if he had to give up a second, Goethe paused and said, "It depends on the vintage."

• *Your walking tour is over. From here, consider paying a visit to the fortress on the hill above you (described next), or have lunch at the recommended Alte Mainmühle restaurant, with a terrace overlooking the bridge.*

Marienberg Fortress (Festung Marienberg)

This 13th-century fortified retreat was the original residence of Würzburg's prince-bishops. After being stormed by the Swedish army during the 17th-century Thirty Years' War, the fortress was rebuilt in Baroque style. The **fortress grounds** (free) provide fine city views and a good place for a picnic. There's a restaurant inside (weekends only in the winter), and a summer *Biergarten* by the entrance (both described below).

The fortress houses two museums (both covered by a €5 combo-ticket): The **City History Museum and Prince's Mansion** (Stadtgeschichtliches Museum und Fürstenbaumuseum) is in the inner courtyard (€4, covered by Bavarian Castles Pass, mid-March–Oct Tue–Sun 10:00–17:00, closed Mon and Nov–mid-March, tel. 0931/355-1750, www.schloesser.bayern .de). The **Mainfränkisches Museum,** which highlights the work of Riemenschneider, Germany's top woodcarver and onetime mayor of Würzburg, is in the red-and-white building at the back of the fortress, near the bus stop (€4, few English explanations, €3 audioguide, Tue–Sun April–Oct 10:00–17:00, Nov–March 10:00–16:00, closed Mon year-round, good €2.60 guide, tel. 0931/205-940, www.main fraenkisches-museum.de). Riemenschneider fans will also find his work throughout Würzburg's many churches.

Eating at Marienberg Fortress: If you're up here at lunchtime, the **Burggaststätte,** in the inner courtyard next to the City History Museum, is forgettable but handy (€6–12 meals; May–Sept Tue–Sun 10:00–18:00, closed Mon; Oct–April Sat–Sun only 10:00–18:00; tel. 0931/47012). There's also a self-service **beer garden** next to the Mainfränkisches Museum by the fortress entrance, with typical sausage-and-pretzel fare and a great vineyard view (weather permitting).

Getting There: Take bus #9 (€2.10 one-way, covered by *Tageskarte* passes, runs daily 10:00–18:00 every 45 min, departs from Residenzplatz and Juliuspromenade). To walk there, cross the Old Main Bridge and follow small *Festung Marienberg* signs to the right uphill for a heart-thumping 20 minutes (signs pointing left indicate a longer, more gradual 40-min path through vineyards).

Sleeping in Würzburg

Würzburg's good-value hotels and hostels provide a stress-free first or last night when flying into or out of Frankfurt. Hourly trains connect Würzburg and Frankfurt's airport in 1.5 hours.

The following listings (except the last one) are less than a 10-minute walk from the train station. To reach the two hotels on Theatergasse, head from the station up Kaiserstrasse to the circular awning at Barbarossaplatz and angle left, toward KFC, for Theaterstrasse. For the Sankt Josef Hotel, follow Theaterstrasse

Sleep Code

(€1 = about $1.40, country code: 49, area code: 0931)

S = Single, **D** = Double/Twin, **T** = Triple, **Q** = Quad, **b** = bathroom, **s** = shower only. Credit cards are accepted, English is spoken, and breakfast is included.

To help you sort easily through these listings, I've divided the rooms into two categories, based on the price for a standard double room with bath:

$$ Higher Priced—Most rooms €80 or more.
$ Lower Priced—Most rooms less than €80.

and take your first left onto Semmelstrasse. In these hotels, quieter rooms are in back, front rooms have street noise, and all rooms are entertained by church bells.

$$ Hotel Barbarossa, tucked peacefully away on the fourth floor of an older building of doctors' and lawyers' offices, rents 18 simple, comfortable rooms (S-€33, Ss-€43, Sb-€54, Db-€86, Tb-€96, a little cheaper if you pay cash, elevator, expensive Wi-Fi, across from KFC at Theaterstrasse 2, tel. 0931/321-370, fax 0931/321-3737, www.hotel-barbarossa-wuerzburg.de, info@hotel-barbarossa-wuerzburg.de, Martina Marchiorello).

$$ City Hotel Schönleber has 33 up-to-date rooms (S-€45, Sb-€69, D-€66, Ds-€72, Db-€89–99 depending on size, Tb-€118, elevator, pay Wi-Fi, Theaterstrasse 5, tel. 0931/304-8900, fax 0931/3048-9030, www.cityhotel-schoenleber.de, reservierung @cityhotel-schoenleber.de, Ulrich Kölbel).

$$ Sankt Josef Hotel's 33 rooms are small but sufficient (Sb-€55–60, Db-€80–100 depending on size, non-smoking rooms, no elevator, free Wi-Fi, reserve ahead for parking-€8/ day, Semmelstrasse 28–30, tel. 0931/308-680, fax 0931/308-6860, www.hotel-st-josef.de, hotel.st.josef@t-online.de, Herr and Frau Casagrande speak some English). The hotel restaurant serves dinner only (€8–14 main dishes, Thu–Tue from 17:00, closed Wed).

$ Hotel-Pension Spehnkuch, the best budget option near the station, has seven rooms that share two sets of bathroom facilities. It overlooks a busy and uninviting street, but inside, it's quiet (behind double-paned windows), friendly, simple, clean, and comfortable, with a cheery breakfast room (S-€33, D-€58, T-€78–81, cash only, call 72 hours in advance to cancel, free Wi-Fi; 3-min walk from station: exit station and take a right onto the first street, walk 500 feet to Röntgenring 7, ring bell, go up one floor; tel. 0931/54752, fax 0931/54760, www.pension-spehnkuch.de, info @pension-spehnkuch.de, Markus).

$ **Babelfish Hostel,** across the street from the station, welcomes travelers of all ages. This laid-back place is clean and feels safe (dorm beds-€16–20, Sb-€40, Db-€58, sheets-€2, breakfast-€5, free Internet access and Wi-Fi, laundry-€4.50; free coffee, tea, and lockers; kitchen, roof deck, wheelchair-accessible, reception on second floor, Haugering 2, tel. 0931/304-0430, fax 0931/304-3632, www.babelfish-hostel.de, info@babelfish-hostel.de).

$ Würzburg's official **youth hostel,** across the river, has 236 beds (€21.60 per bed in 4- to 8-bed rooms, a few S-€25.60, D-€47.20, includes sheets and breakfast, non-members-€3.10 extra, over 26 years old-€4 extra, slightly cheaper mid-Nov–March, family rooms, coin-op Internet access, pay Wi-Fi, no curfew—get night code; 20-min walk from station, cross Old Main Bridge and turn left on Saalgasse to Burkarderstrasse 44; or take tram #3 or #5 to Löwenbrücke stop, then follow signs; tel. 0931/42590, www.wuerzburg.jugendherberge.de, jhwuerzburg @djh-bayern.de).

Eating in Würzburg

Restaurants and Wine Bars That Support the Needy

In medieval times, rich Würzburgers founded charitable foundations to support the city's elderly and poor. They began making and selling wine to fund their charity work, and this tradition continues today. Still occupying grand Baroque complexes, the foundations have restaurants, wine shops (selling wine in the area's distinctive, bulbous *Bocksbeutel* bottles), and extensive wine cellars (for serious buyers only).

The oldest and best-known of these foundations is the **Bürgerspital,** which now cares for about a hundred local seniors. Its characteristic restaurant, pub, and wine store are right downtown, near recommended hotels. The restaurant, **Weinstube Bürgerspital,** is candlelit but informal, with a cloistered feel and gorgeous courtyard seating (€5–17 main dishes, daily 10:00–24:00, Theaterstrasse 19, tel. 0931/352-880). The funky little **Hockerle** pub, adjacent to the wine store, is a time warp, filled with locals munching B.Y.O. sandwiches while sipping wine sold by the glass—as explained on its blackboard (both pub and store open Mon–Fri 9:00–18:00, Sat 9:00–15:00, closed Sun, corner of Theaterstrasse and Semmelstrasse at Theaterstrasse 19, tel. 0931/350-3403).

Nearby, the **Juliusspital** has updated its traditional *Weinstube* with a slightly modern, Mediterranean feel. Its courtyard is especially popular (€10–16 main dishes, daily 10:00–24:00, kitchen closes at 22:00, Juliuspromenade 19 at Barbarossaplatz, tel. 0931/54080).

More Restaurants in the Center

Zum Stachel, Würzburg's oldest *Weinhaus,* originated as the town's tithe barn—where people deposited 10 percent of their produce as tax. In 1413, it began preparing the produce and selling wine. Today, it's a worthy splurge, serving gourmet Franconian meals in an elegant stone-and-ivy courtyard and woody dining room. The ceiling depicts a medieval *Stachel* (mace) in deadly action (€19–24 main dishes, €31 three-course fixed-price meals, Mon–Sat 11:00–24:00, closed Sun, reservations smart for this dressy place; from Market Square head toward river, turn right on Gressengasse to intersection with Marktgasse; Gressengasse 1, tel. 0931/52770).

Backöfele is a fun hole-in-the-wall (literally). Named "The Oven" for its entryway, this place is a hit with Germans, offering a rustic menu full of local specialties (€7–20 main dishes, daily 12:00–24:00, reservations smart; with your back to the City Hall, go straight on Augustinerstrasse, take the first left onto Wolfhartsgasse, then the first right to Ursulinergasse 2; tel. 0931/59059).

Alte Mainmühle, on the bridge in a converted mill, is a great place to end your walking tour. On a warm day, nothing beats a cold beer on their deck, which overlooks the river and the fortress—choose from their sunny top-floor terrace or the shade below. They have fresh fish specials (try their *Forelle* or *Zanderfilet*) and traditional fare with a Franconian twist. Their homemade sourdough bread *(Natursauerteigbrot)* is a delicious nod to their milling history (€7–8 wurst plates, €13–23 main dishes, daily 10:00–24:00, kitchen open 11:00–22:30, Mainkai 1, tel. 0931/16777).

Café Michel, right on Market Square and next to the TI, is a family-oriented bakery and tea house with quiet indoor seating and tables on the square. The selection of cakes and strudels is outstanding, even for Germany. It serves soups, small sandwiches, cakes, tea, coffee, and—until 16:00—inexpensive egg breakfasts. This place has been around since 1911 (€5–7 light meals, Mon–Sat 8:00–18:00, Sun 10:00–18:00, Marktplatz 11, tel. 0931/53776).

Weinstube Maulaffenbäck, tucked away in an alley near Market Square and the cathedral with a few outdoor tables, is a characteristic place for cheap Franconian meals and good wine. If you order wine, you're welcome to bring your own food—they'll provide the plate and fork. This is an old tradition unique to Würzburg. If you choose to follow this custom, consider stopping at the butcher shop next door (conveniently owned by the same family, Mon–Fri 7:30–18:00, Sat 8:00–14:00, closed Sun) to pick up great cold cuts before finding a table (€5–8 main dishes, Mon–Thu 10:00–22:00, Fri–Sat 10:00–23:00, closed Sun, Maulhardgasse 9, tel. 0931/52351).

Pasta e Olio, a couple of blocks east of Market Square, is a fun and popular stand-up pasta lunch counter. Because Signora Aucone makes pasta fresh daily, the menu is limited, but usually includes a pasta dish, lasagna, a vegetarian option, and mixed antipasti. Place your order, then eat standing at one of the tables (€4.50–5 plates, Mon–Fri 11:00–17:00, Sat 11:00–15:00, closed Sun, no WC, Eichhornstrasse 6, tel. 0931/16699).

Würzburg Connections

From Würzburg by Train to: Rothenburg (hourly, 1.25 hrs, transfer in Steinach; 50 min to Steinach, then 15 min to Rothenburg; tiny Steinach–Rothenburg train leaves usually from track 5 shortly after the Würzburg train arrives), **Frankfurt Airport** (1–2/hr, 1.5 hrs), **Frankfurt** (1–2/hr, 70 min, or 2 hrs on cheaper RE trains), **Nürnberg** (2–3/hr, 1–1.25 hrs), **Munich** (1–2/hr, 2 hrs), **Köln** (at least hourly, 2.5 hrs, usually 1 change), **Berlin** (hourly, 4 hrs, change in Göttingen or Hannover). Train info: tel. 0180-599-6633 (€0.14/min).

FRANKFURT

Frankfurt, while low on Old World charm, offers a good look at today's no-nonsense, modern Germany. There's so much more to this country than castles and old cobbled squares. Cosmopolitan Frankfurt is a business hub of the united Europe and home to the European Central Bank. Especially in the area around the train station, you'll notice the fascinating multiethnic flavor of the city. A third of its 650,000 residents carry foreign passports. For years, Frankfurt was a city to avoid...but today, its energy makes it worth a look.

Planning Your Time

You might fly into or out of Frankfurt am Main, or at least pass through—this glossy city links the best wine-and-castles stretch of the Rhine to the north with the fairy-tale Romantic Road to the south. Even two or three hours in Frankfurt leaves you with some powerful impressions. The city's great sights are a 20-minute walk from its train station, which is a 12-minute train ride from its airport. At a minimum, head up to the top of the Main Tower for commanding city views and wander through the pedestrian zone to the old town area (Römerberg). With more time or an overnight, Frankfurt has plenty of museums and other attractions to choose from.

Orientation to Frankfurt

(area code: 069)
Frankfurt, with its forest of skyscrapers perched on the banks of the Main (pronounced "mine") River, has been dubbed Germany's

"Mainhattan." The city is Germany's trade and banking capital, leading the country in high-rises (mostly bank headquarters)...and

yet, a third of Frankfurt is green space.

The convention center (Messe) and the red light district are near the train station. Just to the east is the skyscraper banking district and the shopping and pedestrian area around Hauptwache. Beyond that is what remains of Frankfurt's old town, around the Römerberg, or central market square. A short walk across the river takes you to a different part of town: Frankfurt's top museums line the south bank of the Main, and nearby is Sachsenhausen, a residential neighborhood and schmaltzy restaurant zone.

Tourist Information

Frankfurt has several TIs. The handiest (though it's small) is inside the **train station**'s main entrance, offering an abundance of brochures and a free hotel-booking service (Mon–Fri 8:00–21:00, Sat–Sun 9:00–18:00, tel. 069/2123-8800, www.infofrankfurt.de). Another TI is on **Römerberg square** (Mon–Fri 9:30–17:30, Sat–Sun 9:30–16:00); there's also one at the **airport.** At any TI, buy the city/subway map (the basic €0.50 version is fine—skip the detailed €1 map). The TI also offers bus tours of the city (see "Tours in Frankfurt," later).

Discount Deals: Two discount passes compete for your attention, both sold at local TIs. The **Museum Ticket** gets you free entry into 26 museums (€15, valid 2 days). The **Frankfurt Card** gives you a transit pass (including connections to and from the airport), 50 percent off all major museums, and 25 percent off the city bus tour, which virtually pays for the pass (1 person: €8.70/1 day, €12.50/2 days; 2–5 people: €15/1 day, €24/2 days). If you're sightseeing like mad for a day, the Frankfurt Card can be worthwhile.

Arrival in Frankfurt

By Train: The Frankfurt main train station (Hauptbahnhof) bustles with travelers. The TI is in the main hall just inside the front door. The least expensive lockers are along track 24; there are more lockers at the end of the hall that starts by track 18, and in the main hall across from the TI, where there's also a staffed baggage storage office (€5/day, Mon–Fri 6:30–19:30, closed Sat–Sun). The post office is across from track 24 (Mon–Fri 7:00–19:30, Sat 8:00–16:00, closed Sun). WCs (€0.70) are down the stairway by tracks 9 and 10. Inquire about train tickets in the *Reisezentrum* across from track 9 (Mon–Fri 6:00–22:00, Sat–Sun 7:00–22:00). Above the *Reisezentrum* is a peaceful lounge with a snack bar, clean WCs, telephones, and a children's play area (free entry with train ticket or railpass, free coffee and juice in first-class lounge). Pick up a snack at the good food court across from tracks 4 and 5. The station is a five-minute walk from the convention center (Messe), a three-minute subway ride or 20-minute walk from Römerberg, and a 12-minute shuttle train from the airport.

By Plane: See "Frankfurt Connections," at the end of this chapter.

By Car: Follow signs for *Frankfurt,* then *Messe,* and finally *Hauptbahnhof* (train station). The Hauptbahnhof garage (€25/day) is under the station, near most recommended hotels.

Helpful Hints

Closed Day: Most museums are closed Monday, and most are open until 20:00 on Wednesday.

Internet Access: There are terminals underneath the train station—take the escalators down from track 19 to the shopping level, and look left (€2/hr, daily 5:30–24:00, must be over 18).

Laundry: Miele Wash World is near the station (Mon–Sat 6:00–23:00, closed Sun, Moselstrasse 17, by the corner of Münchener Strasse). In Sachsenhausen, by the recommended Fichtekränzi restaurant, is an **SB-Waschsalon** (daily 6:00–23:00, Wallstrasse 8, instructions in German only).

Supermarket: Tengelmann, near the station, is small but well-stocked (Mon–Fri 7:00–21:00, Sat 8:00–21:00, closed Sun, Karlstrasse 4, use Kaiserstrasse exit from underground passageway). On Sundays, the smaller, expensive **Supermarket im Bahnhof** in the underground passageway station is open until 22:00. There are larger supermarkets around the Hauptwache.

Getting Around Frankfurt

By Subway: Frankfurt's subway is easy to use, but a 10-minute wait for a train is common. From the train station, follow signs for *U-Bahn* (blue *U*) or *S-Bahn* (green *S*). Buy your tickets *(Fahrkarten)* from an RMV machine. Tickets are issued with a validating stamp already on them, and are valid only immediately after they're bought. Find your destination on the chart, key in the number, choose your ticket type, then pay. Choose *Einzelfahrt* for a regular single ticket (€2.20), *Kurzstrecke* for a short ride (€1.50—valid destinations listed on machines), *Tageskarte Frankfurt* for an all-day pass (€5.80 without the airport, €9.10 with), or *Gruppentageskarte* for an all-day group ticket for up to 5 adults (€8.70 without the airport, €14 with). An individual one-way ticket to the airport costs

€3.70 (no group rate for airport-only trips). Some hotels sell guests a two-day *Tageskarte* that includes the airport for €7.90. For more information in English, see www.rmv.de.

By Taxi: A taxi stand is just outside the main entrance of the train station to your left. A typical ride, such as to Römerberg square, should cost you €7 (or up to €10 in slow traffic). To get to the airport from any of my recommended hotels, count on at least €25.

Tours in Frankfurt

City Bus Tour—The basic city bus tour gives a 2.5-hour orientation to Frankfurt, including Römerberg and a visit to either the Goethe House or (summer only) the observation deck of the Main Tower (€26, 25 percent discount with Frankfurt Card, recorded narration; April–Oct daily at 10:00 and 14:00; Nov–March daily at 14:00, Sat–Sun also at 10:00). The bus picks up at the scheduled times at the Römerberg TI, then stops 15 minutes later at the Frankfurt train station TI.

Walking Tour—Insider Tour's three-hour walks, led by Ohioan Jodean Ator and her husband David, hit the major sights and explain Frankfurt's history (€12, basic walk leaves daily at 10:30, walk following route of former city walls leaves June–Aug only at 15:00, walks depart from Römer/Paulskirche tram stop next to Römerberg TI—just show up, mobile 01520-846-4200, www .insidertour.com).

Local Guide—Elisabeth Lücke loves her city and shares it very well (€60/hr, cash only, reserve in advance, tel. 06196/45787, mobile 0173-913-3157, www.elisabeth-luecke.de, elisabeth.luecke@t -online.de).

Self-Guided Walk

Welcome to Frankfurt

This sightseeing walk shows you both the new Frankfurt and the old—starting at its train station, taking you past junkies and brothels, up the Main Tower, through the modern shopping and eating districts, into the lively square at the center of the old town, and finishing on a bridge overlooking the city and its river.

Train Station

Frankfurt has Germany's busiest train station: 350,000 travelers make their way to 25 platforms to catch 1,800 trains every day. Hop a train and you can be in either Paris or Berlin in less than four hours. While it was big news when it opened in the 1890s, it's a dead-end station, which, with today's high-speed trains, makes it

Frankfurt

S S-Bahn Stop → SELF-GUIDED WALK
U U-Bahn Stop

To A-66

OPERA

BOCK.

Alte Oper **U** FRESS
GOETHE

MESSETURM SKYSCRAPER

Taunusanlage **S**

MAIN TOWER

To A-648

U Festhalle/Messe

GR.

MESSE (FAIR)

DÜSS.

MAINZERLANDSTR.

MOSEL

ELBE

WESER

NIDDA

TAUNUSANLAGE

TAUNUS STR.

13

18

9

KAISERSTRASSE

MAINZERLANDSTR.

POST STR.

STR.

11

12

14

MÜNCHENER

15

GUTLEUT STR.

LEVSCH STR.

WIL.

START

TRAIN STATION

U **S** ℹ

10

MANNHEIMERSTR.

BASELERSTR.

17

UNTERMAIN KAI

MAIN

7

16

SPEICHERSTR.

FRIEDENS-

BRÜCKE

MUSEUMSUFER

STÄDEL COLLECTION

To A-3

Sights & Services

1 Römerberg (Market Square)
2 History Museum
3 St. Bartholomew's Cathedral
4 Schirn Art Center
5 Museum Embankment
6 Eiserner Steg Pedestrian Bridge
7 Holbein Pedestrian Bridge
8 Fressgass'
9 Red Light District
10 Romantic Road Bus Stop

FRANKFURT

Hotels & Restaurants
- ⑪ Bristol Hotel
- ⑫ Hotel Hamburger Hof
- ⑬ Manhattan Hotel
- ⑭ Victoria Hotel
- ⑮ Memphis Hotel
- ⑯ Ibis Hotel Frankfurt Friedensbrücke
- ⑰ Hotel Paris
- ⑱ Five Elements Hostel
- ⑲ Hotel Neue Kräme
- ⑳ Hotel Zentrum
- ㉑ Maingau Hotel/Rest.
- ㉒ Haus der Jugend Hostel
- ㉓ Zum Gemalten Haus
- ㉔ Adolf Wagner Rest.
- ㉕ Klaane Sachsehäuser
- ㉖ Fichtekränzi Rest.

FRANKFURT

outdated. Complaining that it takes an extra 20 minutes to stop at a dead-end station, railway officials threatened to have the speedy ICE and TGV trains bypass Frankfurt altogether unless it dug a tunnel to allow for a faster pass-through stop. But this proved too expensive, and—while some trains stop only at the pass-through airport station—most fast trains still serve downtown Frankfurt.

Leaving through the station's front door, walk directly away from the station to the traffic island facing the pedestrian Kaiserstrasse, and turn to look back at the building's Neo-Renaissance facade—a style popular with Industrial Revolution–era architects. This classic late-19th-century glass-and-iron construction survived World War II. High above, a statue of Apollo carries the world—but only with some heavy-duty help: Green copper figures representing steam power and electricity pitch in. The 1890s was the start of a confident age, when people believed that technology would solve the world's problems.

• *With your back to the station, look down...*

Kaiserstrasse

This grand 19th-century boulevard features appropriately elegant facades that were designed to dress up the approach to what was a fine new station. Towering above and beyond the 100-year-old buildings are the skyscrapers of Frankfurt's banking district. But look at street level and notice the human riffraff and cheap eateries lining this once-genteel street. As we'll see on this walk, Frankfurt is a city of contrasts. The gap between rich and poor opens wider and more visibly here than anywhere else in Germany.

Warning: This walk now goes into a neighborhood of hard-drug users and prostitutes. It can be creepy any time of day. If you use common sense, it's not dangerous, but it unnerves many. You can skip all that by hiking directly to the Main Tower via Kaiserstrasse, and flipping down to "Frankfurt's Banking District."

• *OK, if you're game, turn left (note the pyramid-topped skyscraper in the distance marking the huge Frankfurt Trade Center) and walk a block to Taunusstrasse. Turn right and walk a block to the corner of Taunusstrasse and Moselstrasse. Taunusstrasse is lined half with brothels and half with bank towers.*

▲▲Brothels and Junkies

A half-block down Moselstrasse, on the left you'll see a gang congregating in front of Café Fix (at #47), one of several such "junkie cafés" in Frankfurt. In 1992, Frankfurt began offering "pump rooms" to its hard-drug users. These centers provide clean needles and a safe and caring place for addicts to go to maintain their habit and get counseling and medical help. Two decades later, locals consider the program a success, and are accustomed to wasted people congregating in neighborhoods like this one. While unsightly, the compassionate "harm reduction" approach much of Europe uses to deal with this problem saves lives. On average, the US suffers 18,000 heroin-related deaths a year, while all of Europe—with a bigger population—has less than half the fatalities annually (8,000).

Walk a block farther down Taunusstrasse to Elbestrasse. Look or turn left down Elbestrasse, where you'll find a row of high-rise brothels, or **"eros towers."** There are about 20 of these five-story brothels within a block of here—each filled with prostitutes (charging around €25). These women rent their rooms and essentially run their own little businesses. Since they are legal and pay taxes, they are organizing to get the same benefits that other taxed workers receive. Climbing through a few of these towers may be one of the more memorable experiences of your European trip. While hiking through the towers feels safe, the aggressive women at the neighboring strip shows can be unsettling.

Ever since the Middle Ages, Frankfurt's thriving prostitution industry has gone hand-in-hand with its trade fairs. Today, prostitution thrives with the Messe (convention center). Both hotels and prostitutes double their prices during big trade fairs. Prostitutes note that business varies with the theme of the trade show—while the auto show is boom time, they complain that Frankfurt's massive book fair is a bust.

On the other side of Taunusstrasse, at 29 Elbestrasse, is a strip joint called **Pik-Dame**. Old-timers are nostalgic about this lone remnant from "the good old days" just after World War II, when 30,000 US soldiers stationed in Frankfurt provided a stimulus for this neighborhood's economy. Later, the troops left and the Russian mob moved in, replacing any old-time gentility with a criminal and thuggish edge.

• *Continue down Taunusstrasse out of the red light district and into the banking district. Look up and see why this city is nicknamed "Mainhattan." Walk to the park and go to the statue of the poet Schiller (a Romantic poet and friend of Goethe).*

▲Frankfurt's Banking District

This park is part of a circular greenbelt that circles the old center and marks the site of Frankfurt's medieval fortifications. These walls (along with many castles on the Rhine) were destroyed by the French in 1806. Napoleon was on his way to Russia, and, since he had the upper hand, he figured it was wise to preemptively destroy any German fortifications that might haunt him if the Germans turned against France in the future.

The park is the center of Frankfurt's banking district. The

post-WWII Marshall Plan was administered from here—requiring fancy money-handling. And the mighty Deutsche Mark was born in a 1930s-era building facing this square (in the low Art Deco building on the left of the square as you entered, behind the greenery from where you now stand). After World War II, Germany's economy was in chaos. In 1948, the US gave it a complete currency transfer—like a blood transfusion, literally printing up the new Deutsche Marks and shipping them across the Atlantic to inject them from here directly into the German economy. As if catching water from a fountain, banks naturally grew up around this square.

But Frankfurt was "Bankfurt" long before World War II. This was the Rothschilds' hometown. Born in the Frankfurt ghetto in 1744, Mayer Rothschild went from being a pauper to the richest banker in the world in one lifetime. His five sons set up business in Rome, London, Paris, and Vienna, and in two generations the Rothschild banking dynasty was established. (Their former palace now houses Frankfurt's Jewish Museum, described later.) Today, locals call Frankfurt's legion of bankers "penguins," as they all dress the same. Tour guides here talk of banks as part of the cultural soil (the way French Riviera guides talk of the big yachts).

Beyond the statue of Schiller stand the twin towers of the DB, or Deutsche Bundesbank. This country's #1 bank, its assets are greater than the annual budget of the German government. If money makes the world go round, decisions that spin Germany may be made in Frankfurt. But, with the recent economic crisis, a third of these skyscraper offices are empty. No one knows what the future holds for this European money capital.

• *Find the skyscraper with the red-and-white candy cane on top. Go there. Head straight a block, then turn left on Neue Mainzer Strasse to reach the...*

▲▲Main Tower

Finished in 2000, this tower houses the Helaba Bank and offers the best (and only public) viewpoint from the top of a Frankfurt skyscraper. A 45-second, ear-popping elevator ride to the 54th floor (watch the meter on the wall as you ascend) and then 50 stairs take you to the rooftop, 650 feet above the city.

Cost, Hours, Location: €5; April–Sept Sun–Thu 10:00–21:00, Fri–Sat 10:00–23:00; Oct–March Sun–Thu 10:00–19:00, Fri–Sat 10:00–21:00; last entry 30 min before closing, enter at Neue Mainzer

Strasse 52, between Taunustor and Junghofstrasse, tel. 069/3650-4777, www.maintower.de.

❍ **Self-Guided Spin-Tour:** Here, from Frankfurt's ultimate viewpoint, survey the city circling clockwise, starting with the biggest skyscraper (with the yellow emblem).

1. Commerzbank Building: Designed by Norman Foster (of Berlin Reichstag and London City Hall fame), the Commerzbank building was finished in 1997. It's 985 feet high, with nine winter gardens spiraling up its core and windows that actually open. It's considered the first ecological skyscraper...radically "green" in its day. Just to the left is Römerberg—the old town center (the half-timbered houses huddled around the red-and-white church; we'll visit there soon).

2. European Central Bank: The blue-and-gold euro symbol (€) decorates the front yard of the Euro Tower, home of the European Central Bank (a.k.a. "City of the Euro"). The all-Europe currency is administered from here. Typical of skyscrapers from the 1970s, it's slim—to allow maximum natural light into all workplaces inside. The euro symbol in the park was unveiled on January 1, 2002, the day the euro went into circulation in the first 12 Eurozone countries. Today 16 countries officially use the euro, and the euro club continues to grow.

The **Museum Embankment** (see page 321) lines Schaumainkai on the far side of the Main River, just beyond the Euro Tower.

3. Airport: The Rhine–Main airport, off in the distance in the forest, is the largest employment complex in Germany (62,000 workers). Frankfurt's massive train station dominates the foreground. From the station, the grand Kaiserstrasse cuts through the city to Römerberg.

4. Messe: The Frankfurt fair (Messe), marked by the sky-scraper with the pointy top, is a huge convention center—the size of 40 soccer fields. It sprawls behind the skyscraper that looks like a classical column sporting a visor-like capital. (The protruding lip of the capital is heated so that icicles don't form, break off, and impale people on the street below.) Frankfurt's fair originated in 1240, when the emperor promised all participating merchants safe passage. The black twin towers of the Deutsche Bank in the fore-ground are typical of mid-1980s mirrored architecture.

5. The West End: With vast green spaces and the telecommunications tower, this is Frankfurt's priciest residential quarter. The city's most enjoyable zone cuts from the West End to the right. Stretching from the classic-looking Opera House below are broad and people-filled boulevards made to order for eating and shopping. Find the "Beach Club" filling the rooftop of a parking garage with white tents and two pools. This is a popular family zone by

• *To the right, at the south side of the square, the Protestant Katharinenkirche was destroyed in the bombing raids of March 1944 and rebuilt after the war. Straight ahead of you is a boulevard called the...*

Zeil: This tree-lined pedestrian drag is Frankfurt's main shopping street. Crowds swirl through the Galeria Kaufhof department store, the Zeil Galerie, and the new MyZeil shopping center along the left side of the street. For good views or a quick lunch, the Kaufhof has a rooftop cafeteria. The Zeil Galerie has a café.

• *Instead of walking all the way down the Zeil, turn right (across from the last Kaufhof entrance doorway and the column of porthole-like windows) down Liebfraustrasse, another pedestrian street. After two blocks, you'll cross Berliner Strasse and come to Paulsplatz.*

▲St. Paul's Church (Paulskirche)

To your right, the church dominating the square is known as the "cradle of German democracy." It was here, during the political upheaval of 1848, that the first freely elected National Assembly met and the first German Constitution was drafted, paving the way for a united Germany in 1871. Following its destruction by Allied bombs in 1944, the church became the first historic building in the city to be rebuilt. This was a symbolic statement from the German people that they wanted to be free (as they had demonstrated here in 1848), democratic...and no longer fascist. Around the outside of the building, you'll see reliefs honoring people who contributed to the German nation, including Theodor Heuss, the first president, and John F. Kennedy, who spoke here on June 25, 1963.

Step inside (free, daily 10:00–17:00) to check out a circular mural from the 1980s. *The March of Members of Parliament* was controversial when unveiled. Commissioned to honor the political heroes of 1848, the portraits are cartoonish figures with faces of contemporary politicians. Political leaders seem to sneer at the working class, and two naked men who look like they're having sex represent forces of democracy and monarchy fighting within Germany. Displays described in English tell the story of 1848. This is no longer a church. Upstairs is a 900-seat assembly hall with no decor except the flags of the 16 states of the Federal Republic of Germany.

• *Crossing the street on the far side of the square brings you into what's left of...*

Frankfurt's Old Town

Römerberg: Frankfurt's market square, worth ▲, was the birthplace of the city. This is where the first trade fairs were held in the

12th century. The Town Hall *(Römer)* houses the *Kaisersaal,* or Imperial Hall, where Holy Roman Emperors celebrated their coronations. Today, the *Römer* houses the city council and mayor's office. The cute row of half-timbered homes (rebuilt in 1983) opposite the *Römer* is typical of Frankfurt's quaint old center before the square was completely destroyed in World War II.

From Christmas markets to violent demonstrations, this square is Frankfurt's ground zero.

• *Facing the Town Hall, the river and the bridge where this walk ends are just two blocks to the left. But first, we'll take a short detour. Circle around the red-and-white church (heading left from the skippable History Museum) to Saalgasse.*

Saalgasse and Roman Ruins: Literally "Hall Street," Saalgasse is lined by postmodern buildings echoing the higgledy-

piggledy houses that stood here until World War II. In the 1990s, famous architects from around the world were each given a ruined house of the same width and told to design a new structure to reflect the one that stood there before the war. As you continue down the street, guess which one is an upside-down half-timbered house with the stars down below. (Hint: Animals are on the "ground floor.")

Saalgasse leads to some ancient Roman ruins in front of St. Bartholomew's Cathedral (turn left when you first see the

cathedral). The grid of stubs was the subfloor of a Roman bath (allowing the floor to be heated). Romans had settled Frankfurt by A.D. 100, although the town wasn't mentioned in records until 794, when Charlemagne (king of the Franks and the first Holy Roman Emperor) held a meeting here with the local bishop. In the center is a small model of the church that stood upon this Roman site in the early Middle Ages. All around you is the architectural hodgepodge of postwar Frankfurt. The skyscraper with the yellow emblem in the distance is the Commerzbank building, the tallest office block in Western Europe (985 feet). The shorter, glassy building next to it, also with a red-and-white antenna, is the Main Tower we visited earlier.

• *Behind the Roman ruins is...*

St. Bartholomew's Cathedral (Kaiserdom): Walk around the front of the church and enter on the side opposite the river (free, daily 9:00–20:00). Rebuilt in the 1950s, the church—still bright and airy like the original—is made of modern concrete with paint to imitate mortar and medieval bricks. Holy Roman Emperors were elected here starting in 1152, and crowned here from 1562 to 1792. The cathedral was destroyed by fire in 1867 and had to be rebuilt. It was seriously damaged in World War II (as the photos in the entranceway testify), but repaired and reopened in 1953. Frescoes from the 13th century survive (flanking the high altar and ringing the choir). They show 27 scenes from the life of St. Bartholomew. Everything of value that could be moved was taken out of the church before the WWII bombs came. The delightful red-sandstone chapel of Sleeping Mary (to the left of the high altar), carved and painted in the 15th century, was too big to move—so it was fortified with sandbags. The altarpiece and fine stained glass next to it survived the bombing. The Dom Museum (€3 entry, enter from church vestibule) is not particularly interesting.

• *Retrace your steps back to Römerberg. Finish this tour by walking down to the river and out onto the fine old iron Eiserner Bridge. From the middle of the bridge, survey the skyline and enjoy the lively scene along the riverbanks of Frankfurt.*

Either the U-Bahn or trams #11 and #12, from the stop across the street from the square, will bring you back to your starting point at the train station.

Sights in Frankfurt

In or near the Old Town (Römerberg)

▲**Goethe House (Goethehaus)**—Johann Wolfgang von Goethe (1749–1832), a scientist, minister, poet, lawyer, politician, and playwright, was a towering figure in the early Romantic Age. His birthplace, now a fine museum, is a five-minute walk northwest of Römerberg. It's furnished as it was in the mid-18th century, when the boy destined to become the "German Shakespeare" grew up here (€5, €2 high-tech but easy-to-use and informative audioguide, €1.50 English booklet has same info as free laminated cards—worthwhile only as a souvenir, Mon–Sat 10:00–18:00, Sun 10:00–17:30; 15-min walk from Hauptbahnhof up Kaiserstrasse, turn right on Am Salzhaus to Grosser Hirschgraben 23; tel. 069/138-800, www.goethehaus-frankfurt.de).

Borrow a laminated card at the bottom of the stairs for a refreshingly brief commentary on each of the 16 rooms. Since nothing's roped off and there are no posted signs, it's easy to picture real people living here. Goethe's father dedicated his life and wealth to cultural pursuits, and his mother told young Johann Wolfgang fairy tales every night, stopping just before the ending so that the boy could exercise his own creativity. Goethe's family gave him all the money he needed to travel and learn. His collection of 2,000 books was sold off in 1795. Recently, 800 of these have been located and repurchased by the museum (you'll see them in the library). This building honors the man who inspired the Goethe-Institut, dedicated to keeping the German language strong.

Schirn Art Center (Schirn Kunsthalle)—Opened in 1986, this facility has quickly become one of Europe's most respected homes to modern and contemporary art. Rotating exhibits pay homage to everything and everyone from Kandinsky and Kahlo to contemporary artists, movements, and topics (€6–9 depending on exhibits, Tue–Sun 10:00–19:00, Wed–Thu until 22:00, closed Mon, Römerberg, tel. 069/299-8820, www.schirn.de).

Jewish Sights—Housed in the former Rothschild Palace (of the famous banking family), the worthwhile **Jewish Museum** (Jüdisches Museum) traces the history of Frankfurt's Jews since the 12th century. Rather than simply presenting artifacts, it tries to engage visitors in a dialogue about culture and society as a whole. The €7.80 English guidebook is unnecessary, since detailed English handouts are available on each floor (€4, €5 combo-ticket with Museum Judengasse—see below, Tue–Sun 10:00–17:00, Wed until 20:00, closed Mon, Untermainkai 14/15, tel. 069/2123-5000, www.juedischesmuseum.de). The museum is along the river between Römerberg and the train station, just across the road from the lovely riverside promenade—a perfect place to rest your feet and watch people and planes go by.

The museum also runs the smaller and less interesting **Museum Judengasse,** centering on the foundations of the buildings (built in 1462) in the old Jewish ghetto (€2, €5 combo-ticket with Jewish Museum, same hours as Jewish Museum; Kurt-Schumacher-Strasse 10 at corner of Battonstrasse, a few blocks or one tram stop east of Römerberg, tel. 069/297-7419).

Behind the Museum Judengasse and more worth seeing is Frankfurt's old **Jewish cemetery.** You can look through the locked gate into the cemetery grounds—only a few gravestones survive. But the real draw is the cemetery wall, where 11,000 tiny metal memorials bear the names of Frankfurt Jews killed in the Holocaust, including Anne Frank (who was born in Frankfurt in 1929, though her family later moved to Amsterdam).

Across the River, on the South Bank

Schaumainkai and Frankfurt's Museum Embankment (Museumsufer)—The Schaumainkai riverside promenade (across the river from Römerberg over the Eiserner Steg pedestrian bridge, and then to the right) is great for an evening stroll or people-watching on any sunny day. Keep your eyes peeled for nude sunbathers. Every other Saturday, the museum strip street is closed off for a sprawling flea market.

Nine museums in striking buildings line the Main River along Schaumainkai. In the 1980s, Frankfurt decided that it wanted to buck its "Bankfurt" and "Krankfurt" (*krank* means "sick") image. It went on a culture kick and devoted 11 percent of the city budget to the arts and culture. The result: Frankfurt has become a city of art. These nine museums (including architecture, film, world cultures, and great European masters—the Städel Collection) and a dozen others are all well described in the TI's *Museumsufer* brochure (all museums here are covered by the 2-day €15 Museum Ticket sold at TIs and participating museums—see page 307; most museums open Tue–Sun 10:00–17:00, Wed until 20:00, closed Mon; www.kultur.frankfurt.de).

Sleeping in Frankfurt

Planning to sleep in Frankfurt is a gamble, since the city's numerous trade fairs *(Messe)* send hotel prices skyrocketing—a €70 double can suddenly shoot up to €300. Visit www.messefrankfurt.com (and select "The Company," then "Publications," then "Calendar of Trade Fairs") for an exact schedule.

Keep overnights in Frankfurt to a minimum—pleasant Rhine and Romantic Road towns are just a quick drive or train ride away, offering a mom-and-pop welcome that you won't find here in the big city. Especially during trade fairs, skip Frankfurt altogether and stay in Würzburg, Bacharach, or St. Goar.

Even when trade fairs aren't in town, room prices in most Frankfurt hotels fluctuate €20 or more with demand and the day of the week. The lower prices listed are usually for weekends, with the higher prices for weekdays. The ranges listed here are only approximate, and may skew higher or lower. If you'll be overnighting in Frankfurt during a non-convention summer weekend, you can land a great place relatively cheaply. Since Frankfurt hotels are business-oriented, many are empty and desperate for guests these days. I'd try emailing several to see who's willing to cut you a discount.

Near the Train Station

The following places are within a few blocks of the train station and its fast and handy train to the airport (to sleep even nearer to the

FRANKFURT

Sleep Code

(€1 = about $1.40, country code: 49, area code: 069)
S = Single, **D** = Double/Twin, **T** = Triple, **Q** = Quad, **b** = bathroom, **s** = shower only. Unless otherwise noted, credit cards are accepted, English is spoken, and breakfast is included. All listed hotels have non-smoking rooms.

To help you sort easily through these listings, I've divided the rooms into three categories, based on the price for a standard double room with bath:

$$$ Higher Priced—Most rooms €100 or more.
$$ Moderately Priced—Most rooms between €75–100.
$ Lower Priced—Most rooms €75 or less.

airport, see "Sleeping at or near Frankfurt Airport," page 329). This isn't the safest part of town; don't wander into seedy-feeling streets, and be careful after dark. The first three hotels are on the north (and most sedate) side of the station. The Victoria and the Memphis are in a more middlebrow, mostly Turkish-immigrant neighborhood to the east of the station. The last three hotels are south of the station, where there are many Eastern European shops and services.

For a rough idea of directions to hotels, stand with your back to the main entrance of the station: Manhattan Hotel is across the street at 10 o'clock, Five Elements at 11 o'clock, Victoria Hotel at 1 o'clock, Memphis Hotel at 2 o'clock, Hotel Paris at 5 o'clock, and Bristol Hotel and Hotel Hamburger Hof at 7 o'clock. The Ibis Hotel is on a nicer street two blocks beyond Hotel Paris.

$$$ Bristol Hotel is a swanky 145-room place, part of a new generation of train-station hotels. It serves up style and flair, from its nod to Pacific Rim architecture to its teak-furnished breakfast room and patio café. Although it's just two blocks from the station, it enjoys quiet and respectable surroundings. If you're looking to splurge on your first or last night in Europe, this is the place (Sb-€70–95, larger Sb-€80–120, Db-€95–160, larger Db-€115–180, huge breakfast buffet, elevator, Wi-Fi, Ludwigstrasse 15, tel. 069/242-390, fax 069/251-539, www.bristol-hotel.de, info @bristol-hotel.de). Exit the station by track 24, cross the street, turn left, then right on Ottostrasse, then left on Niddastrasse to Ludwigstrasse.

$$ Hotel Hamburger Hof, right next to the train station but in a quiet and safe-feeling location, has a shiny lobby and 66 elegantly simple rooms. The side facing the station is cheerfully sunny, while rooms on the other side are quieter (Sb-€55–75, Db-€75–95, Tb-€90–105, non-smoking floors, elevator, free Internet access and cable Internet in lobby, expensive Wi-Fi, Poststrasse 10–12, tel. 069/2713-9690, fax 069/235-802, www.hamburgerhof.com, hamburgerhof@t-online.de). Exit the station by track 24, cross the street, turn left, and walk to the end of the block.

$$ Manhattan Hotel, with 60 fine rooms, fronts a high-traffic street very close to the station (Sb-€55–99, Db-€65–125, mention this book when reserving to get a 10 percent discount during non-convention times in 2010, kids under 12 free, elevator, free Wi-Fi, Düsseldorfer Strasse 10, tel. 069/269-5970, fax 069/2695-97777, www.manhattan-hotel.com, manhattan-hotel@t-online .de). Exit the station by track 24, cross the street, and go right until you see the hotel; to cross Düsseldorfer Strasse safely, walk up to the tram stop.

$$ Victoria Hotel, midway between the station and Römerberg on the grand Kaiserstrasse, is friendly, has 75 newly redone rooms (with lots of pillows), and feels a world apart from the red light district a block away (Sb-€55–65, Db-€75–90, Db suite-€105–130, free Internet access and cable Internet in lobby, expensive Wi-Fi, Kaiserstrasse 59, entrance on Elbestrasse, tel. 069/273-060, fax 069/2730-6100, www.victoriahotel.de, victoria -hotel@t-online.de). To reach the hotel, go down the escalators to the underground passageway below the station and follow the *Kaiserstrasse* signs.

$$ Memphis Hotel, three long blocks or one tram stop from the station on a colorful street in the Turkish district, has 42 rooms and is another stylish business hotel that's affordable when there's no convention in town (Sb-€55–85, Db-€70–95, prices soft—call for exact rates, ask for a room on the quiet side—*ruhige Seite*, Internet access, pay Wi-Fi, Münchener Strasse 15, tel. 069/242-6090, fax 069/2426-0999, www.memphis-hotel.de, memphis -hotel@t-online.de). To get here, use the same directions as for the Hotel Victoria, then cut one street right to the parallel Münchener Strasse.

$ Ibis Hotel Frankfurt Friedensbrücke, a reliable chain hotel, is a good value, with 233 rooms on a quiet riverside street away from the station (Sb/Db-€59–79, Tb-€109, breakfast-€10/ person, elevator, free Internet access, pay Wi-Fi, parking-€10/day; exit station by track 1 and follow busy Baseler Strasse 3 blocks, before river turn right on Speicherstrasse to #4; tel. 069/273-030, fax 069/237-024, www.ibishotel.com, h1445@accor.com).

$ Hotel Paris, on a street with Eastern European restaurants, has 20 small but fine rooms and a nice staff, making this a great value (Sb-€40–60, Db-€50–80, Tb-€65–95, no elevator, free Wi-Fi, Karlsruher Strasse 8, tel. 069/273-9963, fax 069/2739-9651, www.hotelparis.de, info@hotelparis.de). Exit the station by track 1, cross the street, turn right and go one block, and then turn left on Karlsruher Strasse.

Hostel: **$ Five Elements** has 150 beds a block from the train station. It's clean and new and feels very safe. But since it's smack in the middle of the red light district, families might feel more comfortable elsewhere (€18 per bed in 6- and 8-bed dorms, €22 in 4-bed dorms, Sb-€60, D-€50, Db-€70, breakfast-€4; includes sheets, lockers, and free Wi-Fi; laundry-€4.50, Moselstrasse 40, tel. 069/2400-5885, fax 069/2424-6955, www.5elementshostel.de, welcome@5elementshostel.de). From the station, exit the underground hall onto Taunusstrasse and go one block to the corner of Moselstrasse; the hostel is across the intersection to your left.

Away from the Station

If you're in Frankfurt for one night, stay near the station—but if you're in town for a few days and want to feel like you belong, choose one of the following listings. Hotel Neue Kräme and Hotel Zentrum are near Römerberg, and the Maingau Hotel and the hostel are in the Sachsenhausen district (see "Eating in Frankfurt," later).

$$ Hotel Neue Kräme is a quiet little 21-room oasis tucked away above the center of Frankfurt's downtown action, just steps from Römerberg. Friendly Hermann, who lived in the US and loves to revive his English, welcomes guests in this bright and cheerful little blue-and-white place (Sb-€69–77, Db-€79–88, mention this book when reserving to get these prices, elevator, expensive Wi-Fi, parking-€27/day, Neue Kräme 23, tel. 069/284-046, fax 069/296-288, www.hotel-neuekraeme.de, info@hotel-neuekraeme.de).

$$ Hotel Zentrum, on the upper floors of a downtown building, has good rooms in a great location just steps from the Hauptwache (Sb-€66–77, Db-€77–88, Tb-€99–110, Qb-€140–170, 5b-€160–180, mention this book when reserving to get these prices, elevator, free Internet access and Wi-Fi, Rossmarkt 7, tel. 069/5050-0190, fax 069/5050-01977, www.hotel-zentrum.de, info@hotel-zentrum.de).

$$ Maingau Hotel, located across the river in the Sachsenhausen district, is in a quiet, residential neighborhood facing a park. The hotel hallways are dark, but the 90 rooms are bright. If you're looking for a little tranquility in an authentic residential neighborhood, stay here (Sb-€62–75, Db-€87–96, prices soft, expensive Wi-Fi, fancy dinners at adjacent Maingau Stuben restaurant—see "Eating in Frankfurt," Schifferstrasse 38–40, tel. 069/609-140, fax 069/620-790, www.maingau.de, info@maingau.de).

Hostel: The **$ Haus der Jugend** hostel, with 434 beds, is right along the river (€17 per bed in 8- and 10-bed dorms, €20 in 3- to 4-bed dorms, Sb-€35.50, Db-€61; €3.50 more for guests age 27 or older, families excepted; €3.10 more per day for non-members, includes sheets and breakfast, €5 for lunch or dinner, pay Internet access, laundry, 2:00 curfew, Deutschherrnufer 12, tel.

069/610-0150, fax 069/6100-1599, www.jugendherberge-frankfurt
.de, jugendherberge-frankfurt@t-online.de). To reach the hostel, take bus #46 (3/hr, direction: Mühlberg) from the station to
Frankensteiner Platz.

Eating in Frankfurt

Near the Station and Downtown

Expect to eat ethnic around Frankfurt's train station—there
are dozens of hole-in-the-wall Asian and Turkish restaurants
on Kaiserstrasse, Münchener Strasse, and surrounding streets.
Downtown, your options include the café-lined Fressgass'
(described on my "Self-Guided Walk," earlier); the top-floor cafeterias in the department stores near Hauptwache; and the few,
somewhat overpriced but handy restaurants right around the
Römerberg.

In the Sachsenhausen District

Instead of beer-garden ambience, Frankfurt entices visitors
and locals to its apple-wine pub district. The cobbled and cozy
Sachsenhausen neighborhood is both a well-heeled residential area
and a traditional eating-and-drinking zone. There are more than a
hundred characteristic apple-wine pubs here (and plenty of other
options). *Apfelwein,* drunk around here since Charlemagne's time
1,200 years ago, became more popular in the 16th century, when
local grapes were diseased. It enjoyed another boost two centuries
later, when a climate change made grape-growing harder. Apple
wine is about the strength of beer (5.5 percent alcohol), and is
served spiced and warm in winter, cold in summer. To complement
your traditional drink with a traditional meal, order Frankfurt
sausage or pork chops and kraut.

All the places I've listed have both indoor and outdoor seating in a woodsy, rustic setting (except Maingau Stuben). Not
just for tourists, these characteristic places are truly popular with
Frankfurters, too. If you are craving *Leiterchen* ("mini-ladders," or
spare ribs—surprisingly meaty and salty), these are your best bet.
Two more widely available local specialties for the adventurous to
try are boiled eggs (or beef) and potatoes topped with a green sauce
of seven herbs, called *Grüne Sosse;* and an aged, cylindrical ricotta-
like cheese served with onions and vinegar, called *Handkäse mit
Musik* ("hand cheese with music").

In West Sachsenhausen, near Schweizer Strasse

These are in the handsome residential neighborhood along
Schweizer Strasse, in the west of Sachsenhausen. To get there from
Römerberg, cross the river on the pedestrian-only Eiserner Steg

and walk right. From the train station, take tram #16 (direction: Offenbach) to the Schwantalerstrasse stop, or take the U-Bahn (changing at Willy-Brandt-Platz) to Schweizer Platz.

Zum Gemalten Haus, named for the wall murals that adorn its facade, serves German cuisine and is deceptively mellow—it's rumored to get a little wild on the weekends (€5–12 entrées, Tue–Sun 10:00–24:00, closed Mon, Schweizer Strasse 67, tel. 069/614-559).

Adolf Wagner, two buildings away, is a traditional joint that serves pork knuckles and ribs, as well as less meaty fare, to a local constituency (€7–13 entrées, daily 11:00–24:00, Schweizer Strasse 71, tel. 069/612-565).

In East Sachsenhausen

These listings are in the core of the apple-wine area in the east of Sachsenhausen. To get here from Römerberg, cross the river on the pedestrian-only Eiserner Steg or the Alte Brücke, and walk left. From the train station, take tram #16 (direction: Offenbach) to the Textorstrasse stop and walk left up Darmstädter Landstrasse, or take bus #46 (direction: Mühlberg) to Frankensteiner Platz.

Klaane Sachsehäuser, owned by the same family for five generations, is popular with German tour groups and locals alike, and prides itself on its *Leiterchen* (€9–15 entrées, €5–8 Wurst plates, Mon–Sat 12:00–24:00, closed Sun, Neuer Wall 11, tel. 069/615-983).

Fichtekränzi offers the typical specialties (and some lighter fare), both in its cozy, bench-filled beer hall and outside under the trees. The staff is friendly and the atmosphere relaxed—expect to share a table and make some new friends (€9–14 entrées, daily from 17:00, Wall Strasse 5, tel. 069/612-778).

International Splurge: **Maingau Stuben** is often hailed as one of the best restaurants in Frankfurt. It boasts an extensive wine list, fancy "tasting *menus,*" recommended wine pairings, and an international lineup, including filet of venison and vegetarian options such as thyme-infused risotto. For less of an investment, come for lunch. Don't be fooled by its modest exterior—this place is elegant inside. Reservations are a must (most main dishes around €25; fixed-price meals are €33–67, more with wine pairings, vegetarian dinner–€34; Tue–Fri 11:30–15:00 & 17:00–22:30, Sat 18:00–22:30, Sun 11:30–15:00, closed Mon, tel. 069/610-752, Schifferstrasse 38, www.maingau.de).

Pub Crawl: Irish pubs and salsa bars clutter the pedestrian zone around Rittergasse and Klappergasse, close to Frankensteiner Platz. The cobblestone streets and medieval buildings feel like Epcot Center, rather than historic Frankfurt. But if you're looking for a place to do a pub crawl, this is it.

Frankfurt Connections

By Train

From Frankfurt am Main by Train to German Destinations: **Rothenburg** (hourly, 2.5–3 hrs, changes in Würzburg and Steinach; the tiny Steinach–Rothenburg train often leaves from track 5, shortly after the Würzburg train arrives), **Würzburg** (1–2/hr, 70 min, or 2 hrs on cheaper RE trains), **Nürnberg** (1–2/hr, 2 hrs), **Munich** (hourly, 3.25 hrs, some with change), **Baden-Baden** (hourly, 1.5 hrs, direct or transfer in Mannheim or Karlsruhe), **Bacharach** (hourly, 1.5–2 hrs, change in Mainz or Bingen), **Freiburg** (hourly, 2–2.5 hrs, most with 1 change), **Bonn** (2/hr, 2 hrs, most with change in Mainz or Köln), **Cochem** (1–2/hr, 2.25–3 hrs), **Köln** (direct trains hourly, 80 min; slower, cheaper, less frequent trains show you more of the Rhine), **Berlin** (hourly, 4 hrs). Train info: tel. 0180-599-6633 (€0.14/min).

By Train to International Destinations: **Amsterdam** (every 2 hrs, 4 hrs direct), **Bern** (every 1–2 hrs, 4 hrs, many with changes in Basel), **Zürich** (1–2/hr, 4–4.5 hrs), **Brussels** (every 2 hrs, 3.5 hrs direct or 4.5 with change in Köln), **Copenhagen** (4/day, 9–11 hrs, most change in Hamburg), **Paris** (every 1–2 hrs, 4–6 hrs, most with 1 change), **Vienna** (7/day direct, 7 hrs), **Prague** (almost hourly, 7–8.25 hrs, change in Dresden or Nürnberg).

By Romantic Road Bus

The bus departs promptly at 8:00 (early May–late Oct) from the Deutsche Touring bus stop on the south side of the Frankfurt train station. Exit the station by track 1; the bus stop is to the right under the white canopy marked with a turquoise *Touring* sign (the Deutsche Touring/Eurolines office is across the street). You can either pay cash when you board, or buy your ticket at the Deutsche Touring office (Mon–Fri 7:30–19:30, Sat 7:30–14:00, Sun 7:30–13:00; entrance at Mannheimer Strasse 15—tel. 069/4609-7280 or 069/790-3261, www.romanticroadcoach.de). Book a seat for free on the website, or by calling ahead. Frankfurt to Rothenburg costs €38, to Munich €81, and all the way to Füssen €99. For more information, see page 287.

By Plane

Frankfurt's airport *(Flughafen)* is just a few stops by S-Bahn from the city center, and has its own long-distance train station, which makes it a snap to connect from a flight to other German cities. There are two separate terminals (know your terminal—check your ticket or the airport website, www.airportcity-frankfurt .com). **Terminal 1,** a multi-level maze of check-in counters and shops, is linked to the train station. **Terminal 2** is small and quiet, with few services. A Skytrain and buses connect the two terminals. Pick up the free brochure *Your Airport Guide* for a map and detailed information (available at the airport and at most Frankfurt hotels). For flight information in English, visit www.airportcity-frankfurt .com, call 01805-372-4636, or contact your airline.

Services: The airport has three **baggage-storage** desks (*Gepäckaufbewahrung*, €5/day per bag; the branch in Terminal 1A, Level 1 is open 24 hours, others daily 6:00–22:00). There is a **post office** (in Terminal 1B, Level 2, daily 7:00–22:00), a **pharmacy** (in Terminal 1B, Level 2, and also in Terminal 2, daily 7:00–22:00), a 24-hour **medical clinic** (Terminal 1C, Level 1), public **showers** (Terminal 1B, Level 2, near the pharmacy, €6, shampoo and towel included, open 24 hours), and expensive **Wi-Fi.** A good-sized, fairly priced **supermarket** is handy for last-minute shopping for European treats (Terminal 1C, Level 0, daily 6:00–22:00; tricky to find: go down the escalators from the underpass on Level 1 between Terminals 1B and 1C, or up the escalators from train platforms 1–3). Take advantage of the **luggage carts,** ingeniously designed to ride on the airport's escalators (and even all the way up to, but not into, the Skytrain). But heed the instructions on the carts and at the escalator entrances. If you're meeting someone, each terminal has a hard-to-miss **"meeting point"** near where those arriving pop out. There are **customs desks** in both terminals for VAT refunds (daily 7:00–21:00; after hours, ask the information desk to page a customs officer for you). There's even McBeer at three McDonald's, one allegedly Europe's largest. McWelcome to Germany.

Frankfurt Airport Train Station

The airport's train station has two parts, both reachable from Terminal 1. Regional S-Bahn trains to downtown Frankfurt and nearby towns and suburbs depart from platforms 1–3. Long-distance trains to other German cities leave from the slightly more distant *Fernbahnhof*, platforms 4–7.

Getting Between the Airport and Downtown Frankfurt: The airport is a 12-minute train ride on the **S-Bahn** from Frankfurt's main train station, or Hauptbahnhof (€3.70, 4/hr, ride included in €8.70 Frankfurt Card and €9.10 version of all-day *Tageskarte Frankfurt* transit pass, but not in €5.80 version of *Tageskarte Frankfurt*). Figure about €25 for a **taxi** from the airport to any of my recommended hotels.

From Frankfurt Airport by Long-Distance Train: Train travelers can validate railpasses or buy tickets at the counters on the level above the long-distance train platforms. Destinations include **Rothenburg** (hourly, 3–3.25 hrs, change in Würzburg and Steinach), **Würzburg** (1–2/hr, 1.5 hrs), **Nürnberg** (1–2/hr, 2.5

hrs), **Munich** (2/hr, 3.5 hrs), **Baden-Baden** (roughly hourly, 1.5 hrs, change in Karlsruhe and/or Mannheim), **Köln** (1–2/hr, 1 hr; trains along Rhine go less often and take 2.25 hrs), **Koblenz** (1–2/hr, 1.25–1.5 hrs, some transfer in Mainz), **Bacharach** (hourly, 1.5 hrs, most change in Mainz, some depart from regional platforms), **Berlin** (1–2/hr, 4.5–5 hrs, most with 1 change). There are also many **international connections** from here (such as Paris, London, Brussels, Amsterdam, Zürich, Bern, and Prague).

Sleeping at or near Frankfurt Airport

Because train connections to Frankfurt Airport are so good, if your flight doesn't leave too early, you can sleep in another city and still make it to the airport for your flight. If you wake up in Köln, Baden-Baden, Würzburg, or Bacharach, you can still catch a late-morning or midday flight; you can often make it from Nürnberg, Rothenburg, Freiburg, the Mosel, and even Munich for an early-afternoon flight. But plan ahead and leave room for delays; don't take the last possible connection.

Because of these easy connections—and since downtown Frankfurt is just 12 minutes away by frequent train—it makes little sense for train travelers to sleep at the airport. Drivers who want to stay near the airport the night before returning a rental car can try two hotels in Kelsterbach, just across the expressway from the airport: **$$ Airport Hotel Tanne** (Db-€82–90, Tannenstrasse 2, tel. 06107/9340, www.airporthoteltanne.de, Laun family) or **$$ Ibis Frankfurt Hotel** (Sb/Db without breakfast-€69–79, Langer Kornweg 9a–11, tel. 06107/9870, www.ibishotel.com). If you're desperate, **$$$ Sheraton Frankfurt** is conveniently connected to Terminal 1 and has 1,008 international business-class rooms (Db-about €200–250, check website or the hotel desk in the airport for lower rates, tel. 069/69770, www.sheraton.com/frankfurt, reservationsfrankfurt@sheraton.com).

"Frankfurt" Hahn Airport

This smaller airport, misleadingly dubbed "Frankfurt" for marketing purposes, is actually almost two hours' drive away in the Mosel region. Regular buses connect Frankfurt Hahn Airport to Bullay (for trains to Cochem), Trier, Mainz, Köln, and Frankfurt (more info at www.hahn-airport.de). Hahn Airport is popular with low-cost carriers (such as Ryanair). To avoid any confusion, double-check the three-letter airport code on your ticket (FRA for Frankfurt Airport, HHN for Frankfurt Hahn).

RHINE VALLEY

Best of the Rhine • Bacharach • St. Goar

The Rhine Valley is storybook Germany, a fairy-tale world of legends and robber-baron castles. Cruise the most castle-studded stretch of the romantic Rhine as you listen for the song of the treacherous Loreley. For hands-on thrills, climb through the Rhineland's greatest castle, Rheinfels, above the town of St. Goar. Castle connoisseurs will also enjoy the fine interior of Marksburg Castle. Spend your nights in a castle-crowned village, either Bacharach or St. Goar.

Planning Your Time

The Rhineland is magical, but doesn't take much time to see. Both Bacharach and St. Goar are an easy 1.5-hour train ride (€10) or drive from Frankfurt Airport, and make a good first or last stop for travelers flying in or out.

The blitziest tour of the area is an hour looking at the castles from your train window. The super-express ICE trains between Köln and Frankfurt bypass the Rhine entirely; to see the river, take the slower IC express trains or regional trains (with stops in Koblenz and Mainz). For a better look, cruise in, tour a castle or two, sleep in a medieval town, and take the train out.

Ideally, if you have two nights to spend here, sleep in Bacharach, cruise the best hour of the river (from Bacharach to St. Goar), and tour Rheinfels Castle. If rushed, focus on Rheinfels Castle and cruise less. With more time, ride the riverside bike path. With another day, mosey through the neighboring Mosel Valley or day-trip to Köln (both covered in different chapters).

There are countless castles in this region, so you'll need to be selective in your castle-going. Aside from Rheinfels Castle, my favorites are Burg Eltz (see page 379 in next chapter; well-preserved with medieval interior, set evocatively in a romantic forest the next valley over), Marksburg Castle (page 342; rebuilt medieval interior, with commanding Rhine perch), and Rheinstein Castle (page 346; 19th-century duke's hunting palace overlooking the Rhine). Of these, Marksburg is the easiest to reach by train. Though only in German, www.burgen-am-rhein .de is a handy website with photos and opening times of the main Rhine castles.

The Best of the Rhine

Ever since Roman times, when this was the empire's northern boundary, the Rhine has been one of the world's busiest shipping rivers. You'll see a steady flow of barges with 1,000- to 2,000-ton loads. Tourist-packed buses, hot train tracks, and highways line both banks.

Many of the castles were "robber-baron" castles, put there by petty rulers (there were 300 independent little countries in medieval Germany, a region about the size of Montana) to levy tolls on passing river traffic. A robber baron would put his castle on, or even in, the river. Then, often with the help of chains and a tower on the opposite bank, he'd stop each ship and get his toll. There were 10 customs stops in the 60-mile stretch between Mainz and Koblenz alone (no wonder merchants were early proponents of the creation of larger nation-states).

Some castles were built to control and protect settlements, and others were the residences of kings. As times changed, so did the lifestyles of the rich and feudal. Many castles were abandoned for more comfortable mansions in the towns.

Most Rhine castles date from the 11th, 12th, and 13th centuries. When the pope successfully asserted his power over the German emperor in 1076, local princes ran wild over the rule of their emperor. The castles saw military action in the 1300s and 1400s, as emperors began reasserting their control over Germany's many silly kingdoms.

The castles were also involved in the Reformation wars, in which Europe's Catholic and Protestant dynasties fought it out using a fragmented Germany as their battleground. The Thirty Years' War (1618–1648) devastated Germany. The outcome: Each ruler got the freedom to decide if his people would be Catholic or Protestant, and one-third of Germany was dead. (Production of Gummi Bears ceased entirely.)

The French—who feared a strong Germany and felt the Rhine

Rhine Overview

was the logical border between them and Germany—destroyed most of the castles prophylactically (Louis XIV in the 1680s, the Revolutionary army in the 1790s, and Napoleon in 1806). Many were rebuilt in Neo-Gothic style in the Romantic Age—the late 1800s—and today are enjoyed as restaurants, hotels, hostels, and museums.

Getting Around the Rhine

The Rhine flows north from Switzerland to Holland, but the scenic stretch from Mainz to Koblenz hoards all the touristic charm. Studded with the crenellated cream of Germany's castles, it bustles with boats, trains, and highway traffic. Have fun exploring with a mix of big steamers, tiny ferries *(Fähre)*, trains, and bikes.

By Boat: While some travelers do the whole Mainz–Koblenz trip by boat (5.5 hours downstream, 8.5 hours up), I'd just focus on the most scenic hour—from St. Goar to Bacharach. Sit on the top deck with your handy Rhine map-guide (or the kilometer-keyed

K-D Line Rhine Cruise Schedule

Boats run May through September and on a reduced schedule for parts of April and October; no boats run November through March. These times are based on the 2009 schedule. Check www.k-d.com for the latest.

Koblenz	Boppard	St. Goar	Bacharach
–	9:00	10:20	11:30
*9:00	*11:00	*12:20	*13:30
11:00	13:00	14:20	15:30
—	14:00	15:20	16:30
14:00	16:00	17:20	18:30
13:10	11:50	10:55	10:15
14:10	12:50	11:55	11:15
—	13:50	12:55	12:15
18:10	16:50	15:55	15:15
*20:10	*18:50	*17:55	*17:15

*These sailings are on the 1913 paddle-wheeler Goethe.

tour in this chapter) and enjoy the parade of castles, towns, boats, and vineyards.

Two boat companies take travelers along this stretch of the Rhine. Boats run daily in both directions from early April through October, with no boats off-season.

Most travelers sail on the bigger, more expensive, and romantic **Köln–Düsseldorfer (K-D) Line** (free with a German railpass or any Eurailpass that covers Germany, but uses up a day of any flexipass; recommended Bacharach–St. Goar trip: €10.50 one-way, €12.80 round-trip, bikes–€2.50, €2 extra if paying with credit card; discounts: on Mon and Fri—half-price for seniors over 60, on Tue—2 bicyclists travel for the price of 1; tel. 06741/1634 in St. Goar, tel. 06743/1322 in Bacharach, www.k-d.com). You'll see K-D's abridged schedule above. Complete, up-to-date schedules are posted at any Rhineland station, hotel, TI, and www.k-d.com. Purchase tickets at the dock up to five minutes before departure. (Confirm times at your hotel the night before.) The boat is never full. Romantics will enjoy the old-time paddle-wheeler *Goethe*, which sails each direction once a day (noted on schedule, confirm time locally).

The smaller **Bingen–Rüdesheimer Line** is slightly cheaper

than the K-D, isn't covered by railpasses, and makes three two-hour round-trip St. Goar–Bacharach trips daily (€10 one-way, €12 round-trip, buy tickets on boat; departs St. Goar at 11:00, 14:10, and 16:10; departs Bacharach at 10:10, 12:00, and 15:00; tel. 06721/14140, www.bingen-ruedesheimer.com).

By Car: Drivers have these options: 1) skip the boat; 2) take a round-trip cruise from St. Goar or Bacharach; 3) draw pretzels and let the loser drive, prepare the picnic, and meet the boat; 4) rent a bike, bring it on the boat for free, and bike back; or 5) take the boat one-way and return by train. When exploring by car, don't hesitate to pop onto one of the many little ferries that shuttle across the bridgeless-around-here river (see below).

By Ferry: While there are no bridges between Koblenz and Mainz, you'll see car-and-passenger ferries (usually family-run for generations) about every three miles. Bingen–Rüdesheim, Lorch–Niederheimbach, Engelsburg–Kaub, and St. Goar–St. Goarshausen are some of the most useful routes (times vary; St. Goar–St. Goarshausen ferry departs each side every 15–20 min, Mon–Sat 6:00–21:00, Sun 8:00–21:00, May–Sept until 23:00; one-way fares: adult-€1.30, car and driver-€3.50, pay on the boat; www.faehre-loreley.de). For a fun little jaunt, take a quick round-trip with some time to explore the other side.

By Bike: You can bike on either side of the Rhine, but for a designated bike path, stay on the west side, where a 35-mile path runs between Koblenz and Bingen. The six-mile stretch between St. Goar and Bacharach is smooth and scenic, but mostly along the highway. The bit from Bacharach to Bingen hugs the riverside and is road-free. Either way, biking is a great way to explore the valley. Many hotels provide free or cheap bikes to guests; in Bacharach, anyone can rent bikes at Hotel Hillen (see page 349, €12/day for non-guests).

Consider biking one-way and taking the bike back on the riverboat, or designing a circular trip using the fun and frequent shuttle ferries. A good target might be Kaub (where a tiny boat shuttles sightseers to the better-from-a-distance castle on the island) or Rheinstein Castle.

By Train: Hourly milk-run trains down the Rhine hit every town (St. Goar–Bacharach, 10 min; Bacharach–Mainz, 1 hr; Mainz–Koblenz, 1.5 hr). Some train schedules list St. Goar but not Bacharach as a stop, but any schedule listing St. Goar also stops at Bacharach. Tiny stations are not staffed—buy tickets at the platform machines (user-friendly, take paper money). Prices are cheap (for example, €3.10 between St. Goar and Bacharach); consider the **Rhineland-Pfalz-Ticket**, which covers travel on milk-run trains to anywhere in this chapter—and the Mosel and Trier chapters (€19, €27 for up to five people, not good before 9:00 on weekdays).

Express trains speed past the small towns, taking only 50 minutes between Koblenz and Mainz.

Self-Guided Tour

▲▲▲Rhine Blitz Tour by Train or Boat

One of Europe's great train thrills is zipping along the Rhine enjoying this blitz tour. Or, even better, do it relaxing on the deck of a Rhine steamer, surrounded by the wonders of this romantic and historic gorge. This quick and easy tour (you can cut in anywhere) skips most of the syrupy myths filling normal Rhine guides. You can follow along on a train, boat, bike, or car. By train or boat, sit on the left (river) side going south from Koblenz. While nearly all the castles listed are viewed from this side, train travelers need to clear a path to the right window for the times I yell, "Cross over!"

You'll notice large black-and-white kilometer markers along the riverbank. I erected these years ago to make this tour easier to follow. They tell the distance from the Rhinefalls, where the Rhine leaves Switzerland and becomes navigable. Now the river-barge pilots have accepted these as navigational aids as well. We're tackling just 36 miles (58 km) of the 820-mile-long (1,320-km) Rhine. Your Rhine Blitz Tour starts at Koblenz and heads upstream to Bingen. If you're going the other direction, it still works. Just hold the book upside-down.

Km 590—Koblenz: This Rhine blitz starts with Romantic Rhine thrills—at Koblenz. Koblenz is not a nice city (it was hit hard in World War II), but its place as the historic *Deutsche Eck* (German corner)—the tip of land where the Mosel joins the Rhine—gives it a certain historic charm. Koblenz, from the Latin for "confluence," has Roman origins. If you stop here, take a walk through the park, noticing the reconstructed memorial to the *Kaiser*. Across the river, the yellow Ehrenbreitstein Castle now houses a hostel. It's a 30-minute hike from the station to the Koblenz boat dock.

Km 585—Lahneck Castle (Burg Lahneck): Above the modern autobahn bridge over the Lahn River, this castle *(Burg)* was built in 1240 to defend local silver mines; the castle was ruined by the French in 1688 and rebuilt in the 1850s in Neo-Gothic style. Burg Lahneck faces another Romantic rebuild, the yellow Schloss Stolzenfels (out of view above the train, a 10-min climb from tiny parking lot, open for touring, closed Mon). Note that a *Burg* is a defensive fortress, while a *Schloss* is mainly a showy palace.

Km 580—Marksburg Castle: This castle (black and white, with the three modern chimneys behind it, just before the town of Spay) is the best-looking of all the Rhine castles and the only surviving medieval castle on the Rhine. Because of its commanding

The Best of the Rhine

TO BONN & KÖLN

TO COCHEM & BURG ELTZ

NOTE:
NUMBERS REFER TO RIVERSIDE SIGNS INDICATING KILOMETERS NORTH OF THE RHINEFALLS

EHRENBREITSTEIN

KOBLENZ 590

5 MILES
8 KM

LAHNECK 585

STOLZENFELS

MARKSBURG 580

N

BOPPARD 570

STERRENBERG & LIEBENSTEIN 567

MAUS 559

ST. GOARSHAUSEN

RHEINFELS

KATZ 556

ST. GOAR 557

LORELEY 554

KAUB

GUTENFELS 546

OBERWESEL 550

PFALZ

SCHÖNBURG

NIEDERWALD MONUMENT 528

LORCH 540

ASSMANNS-HAUSEN

STAHLECK

RÜDES-HEIM

BACHARACH 543

SOONECK 538

REICHENSTEIN 534

TO MAINZ

BINGEN

MÄUSETURM

RHEINSTEIN 533

EHRENFELS 530

🏰 CASTLE
■ OTHER MONUMENT
● TOWN
⋯ CAR FERRIES

DCH

position, it was never attacked in the Middle Ages (though it was captured by the US Army in March of 1945). It's now open as a museum with a medieval interior second only to the Mosel's Burg Eltz. (A self-guided tour for Marksburg appears later in this chapter; Burg Eltz is covered in the next chapter.) The three modern smokestacks vent Europe's biggest car-battery recycling plant just up the valley.

If you haven't read the sidebar on river traffic in this chapter, now's a good time.

Km 570—Boppard: Once a Roman town, Boppard has some impressive remains of fourth-century walls. Notice the Roman towers and the substantial chunk of Roman wall near the train station, just above the main square.

If you visit Boppard, head to the fascinating church below the main square. Find the carved Romanesque crazies at the doorway. Inside, to the right of the entrance, you'll see Christian symbols from Roman times. Also notice the painted arches and vaults (originally, most Romanesque churches were painted this way). Down by the river, look for the high-water *(Hochwasser)* marks on the arches from various flood years. (You'll find these flood marks throughout the Rhine and Mosel valleys.)

Km 567—Sterrenberg Castle and Liebenstein Castle: These are the "Hostile Brothers" castles across from Bad Salzig. Take the wall between the castles (actually designed to improve the defenses of both castles), add two greedy and jealous brothers and a fair maiden, and create your own legend. Burg Liebenstein is now a fun, friendly, and affordable family-run hotel (9 rooms, Db-€120, suite-€145, giant king-and-the-family room-€220, easy parking, tel. 06773/308 or 06773/251, www.castle-liebenstein.com, hotel -burg-liebenstein@rhinecastles.com, Nickenig family).

Km 560: While you can see nothing from here, a 19th-century lead mine functioned on both sides of the river, with a shaft actually tunneling completely under the Rhine.

Km 559—Maus Castle (Burg Maus): The Maus (mouse) got its name because the next castle was owned by the Katzenelnbogen family. (*Katz* means "cat.") In the 1300s, it was considered a state-of-the-art fortification...until Napoleon had it blown up in 1806 with state-of-the-art explosives. It was rebuilt true to its original plans in about 1900. Today, the castle hosts a falconry show (€8, late-March–mid-Oct Tue–Sun at 11:00 and 14:30, also at 16:30 on Sun, closed Mon and off-season, 20-min walk up, tel. 06771/7669, www.burg-maus.de).

Km 557—St. Goar and Rheinfels Castle: Cross to the other side of the train. The pleasant town of St. Goar was named for a sixth-century hometown monk. It originated in Celtic times (really old) as a place where sailors would stop, catch their breath, send home a postcard, and give thanks after surviving the seductive and treacherous Loreley crossing. St. Goar is worth a stop to explore its mighty Rheinfels Castle. (For information, a self-guided castle tour, and accommodations, see page 361.)

Km 556—Katz Castle (Burg Katz): Burg Katz (Katzen-elnbogen) faces St. Goar from across the river. Together, Burg Katz (built in 1371) and Rheinfels Castle had a clear view up and down the river, effectively controlling traffic (there was absolutely no duty-free shopping on the medieval Rhine). Katz got Napoleoned in 1806 and rebuilt in about 1900.

Today, the castle is shrouded by intrigue and controversy. In

Rhine River Trade and Barge-Watching

The Rhine is great for barge-watching. There's a constant parade of action, and each boat is different. Since ancient times, this has been a highway for trade. Today, Europe's biggest port (Rotterdam) waits at the mouth of the river.

Barge workers are almost a subculture. Many own their own ships. The captain lives in the stern, with family. The family car is often parked on the stern. Workers live in the bow.

In the Rhine town of Kaub, there was once a boarding school for the children of the Rhine merchant marine—but today it's closed, since most captains are Dutch, Belgian, or Swiss. The flag of the boat's home country flies in the stern (Dutch—horizontal red, white, and blue; Belgian: vertical black, yellow, and red; Swiss—white cross on a red field; German—horizontal black, red, and yellow; French—vertical red, white, and blue). Logically, imports go upstream (Japanese cars, coal, and oil) and exports go downstream (German cars, chemicals, and pharmaceuticals). A clever captain manages to ship goods in each direction. Recently, giant Dutch container ships (which transport five times the cargo) have been driving many of the traditional barges out of business, presenting the German economy with another challenge.

Going downstream, tugs can push a floating train of up to five barges at once, but upstream, as the slope gets steeper (the stream gradient gets higher), they can push only one at a time. Before modern shipping, horses dragged boats upstream (the faint remains of towpaths survive at points along the river). From 1873 to 1900, workers laid a chain from Bonn to Bingen, and boats with cogwheels and steam engines hoisted themselves

1995, a wealthy and eccentric Japanese man bought it for about $4 million. His vision: to make the castle—so close to the Loreley that Japanese tourists are wild about—an exotic escape for his countrymen. But the town wouldn't allow his planned renovation of the historic (and therefore protected) building. Stymied, the frustrated investor just abandoned his plans. Today, Burg Katz sits empty...the Japanese ghost castle.

Below the castle, notice the derelict grape terraces—worked since the eighth century, but abandoned only in the last generation. The Rhine wine is particularly good because the local slate absorbs the heat of the sun and stays warm all night, resulting in sweeter grapes. Wine from the flat fields above the Rhine gorge is cheaper, and good only as table wine. The wine from the steep side of the Rhine gorge—harder to grow and harvest—is tastier and more expensive.

About Km 555: A statue of the Loreley, the beautiful-but-deadly nymph (see next listing for legend), combs her hair at the upstream. Today, 265 million tons travel each year along the 530 miles from Basel on the German-Swiss border to the Dutch city of Rotterdam on the Atlantic.

Riverside navigational aids are of vital interest to captains who don't wish to meet the Loreley (see below). Boats pass on the right unless they clearly signal otherwise with a large blue sign. Since downstream ships can't stop or maneuver as freely, upstream boats are expected to do the tricky do-si-do work. Cameras monitor traffic all along and relay warnings of oncoming ships by posting large triangular signals before narrow and troublesome bends in the river. There may be two or three triangles per signpost, depending upon how many "sectors," or segments, of the river are covered. The lowest triangle indicates the nearest stretch of river. Each triangle tells whether there's a ship in that sector. When the bottom side of a triangle is lit, that sector is empty. When the left side is lit, an oncoming ship is in that sector.

The **Signal and River Pilots Museum** (Wahrschauer- und Lotsenmuseum), located at the signal triangles at the upstream edge of St. Goar, explains how barges are safer, cleaner, and more fuel-efficient than trains or trucks (free, May–Sept Wed and Sat 14:00–17:00, outdoor exhibits always open).

end of a long spit—built to give barges protection from vicious ice floes that until recent years raged down the river in the winter. The actual Loreley, a cliff (marked by the flags), is just ahead.

Km 554—The Loreley: Steep a big slate rock in centuries of legend and it becomes a tourist attraction—the ultimate Rhinestone. The Loreley (flags and visitors center on top, name painted near shoreline), rising 450 feet over the narrowest and deepest point of the Rhine, has long been important. It was a holy site in pre-Roman days. The fine echoes here—thought to be ghostly voices—fertilized legend-tellers' imaginations.

Because of the reefs just upstream (at kilometer 552), many ships never made it to St. Goar. Sailors (after days on the river) blamed their misfortune on a *wunderbares Fräulein* whose long blond hair almost covered her body. Heinrich Heine's *Song of Loreley* (the CliffsNotes version is on local postcards) tells the story of a count sending his men to kill or capture this siren after she distracted his horny son, who forgot to watch where he was sailing and drowned. When the soldiers cornered the nymph in her cave, she called her father (Father Rhine) for help. Huge waves, the likes of which you'll never see today, rose from the river and carried Loreley to safety. And she has never been seen since.

But alas, when the moon shines brightly and the tour buses are parked, a soft, playful Rhine whine can still be heard from the Loreley. As you pass, listen carefully ("Sailors...sailors...over my bounding mane").

Km 552—The Seven Maidens: Killer reefs, marked by red-and-green buoys, are called the "Seven Maidens." Okay, one more goofy legend: The prince of Schönburg Castle (*über* Oberwesel—described next) had seven spoiled daughters who always dumped men because of their shortcomings. Fed up, he invited seven of his knights to the castle and demanded that his daughters each choose one to marry. But they complained that each man had too big a nose, was too fat, too stupid, and so on. The rude and teasing girls escaped into a riverboat. Just downstream, God turned them into the seven rocks that form this reef. While this story probably isn't entirely true, there was a lesson in it for medieval children: Don't be hard-hearted.

Km 550—Oberwesel: Cross to the other side of the train. Oberwesel was a Celtic town in 400 B.C., then a Roman military station. It now boasts some of the best Roman-wall and medieval-tower remains on the Rhine, and the commanding Schönburg Castle. Notice how many of the train tunnels have entrances designed like medieval turrets—they were actually built in the Romantic 19th century. Okay, back to the river side.

Km 546—Gutenfels Castle and Pfalz Castle, the Classic Rhine View: Burg Gutenfels (see white-painted *Hotel* sign) and the shipshape Pfalz Castle (built in the river in the 1300s) worked very effectively to tax medieval river traffic. The town of Kaub grew rich as Pfalz raised its chains when boats came, and lowered them only when the merchants had paid their duty. Those who didn't pay spent time touring its prison, on a raft at the bottom of its well. In 1504, a pope called for the destruction of Pfalz, but the locals withstood a six-week siege, and the castle still stands. Notice the overhanging outhouse (tiny white room—with faded medieval stains—between two wooden ones). Pfalz (also known as Pfalzgrafenstein) is tourable but bare and dull (€3 ferry from Kaub, €3 entry; March–Oct Tue–Sun 10:00–18:00, until 17:00 in March, closed Mon; Nov and Jan–Feb Sat–Sun 10:00–17:00, closed Mon–Fri; closed Dec; last entry one hour before closing, tel. 0172/262-2800).

In Kaub, on the riverfront directly below the castles, a green statue honors the German general Gebhard von Blücher. He was Napoleon's nemesis. In 1813, as Napoleon fought his way back to Paris after his disastrous Russian campaign, he stopped at Mainz—hoping to fend off the Germans and Russians pursuing him by controlling that strategic bridge. Blücher tricked Napoleon. By building the first major pontoon bridge of its kind here at the Pfalz Castle, he crossed the Rhine and outflanked the French. Two years later, Blücher and Wellington teamed up to defeat Napoleon once and for all at Waterloo.

Km 544—"The Raft Busters": Immediately before Bacharach, at the top of the island, buoys mark a gang of rocks notorious for busting up rafts. The Black Forest, upstream from here, was once poor, and wood was its best export. Black Foresters would ride log booms down the Rhine to the Ruhr (where their timber fortified coal-mine shafts) or to Holland (where logs were sold to shipbuilders). If they could navigate the sweeping bend just before Bacharach and then survive these "raft busters," they'd come home reckless and likely horny—the German folkloric equivalent of American cowboys after payday.

Km 543—Bacharach and Stahleck Castle (Burg Stahleck): Cross to the other side of the train. The town of Bacharach is a great stop (see details and accommodations on page 347). Some of the Rhine's best wine is from this town, whose name likely derives from "altar to Bacchus." Local vintners brag that the medieval Pope Pius II ordered Bacharach wine by the cartload. Perched above the town, the 13th-century Burg Stahleck is now a hostel.

Km 540—Lorch: This pathetic stub of a castle is barely visible from the road. Check out the hillside vineyards. These vineyards once blanketed four times as much land as they do today, but modern economics have driven most of them out of business. The vineyards that do survive require government subsidies. Notice the small car ferry (3/hr, 10 min), one of several along the bridgeless stretch between Mainz and Koblenz.

Km 538—Sooneck Castle: Cross back to the other side of the train. Built in the 11th century, this castle was twice destroyed by people sick and tired of robber barons.

Km 534—Reichenstein Castle and **Km 533—Rheinstein Castle:** Stay on the other side of the train to see two of the first castles to be rebuilt in the Romantic era. Both are privately owned, tourable, and connected by a pleasant trail. See my listing for Rheinstein Castle on page 346.

Km 530—Ehrenfels Castle: Opposite Bingerbrück and the Bingen station, you'll see the ghostly Ehrenfels Castle (clobbered by the Swedes in 1636 and by the French in 1689). Since it had no view of the river traffic to the north, the owner built the cute little *Mäuseturm* (mouse tower) on an island (the yellow tower you'll see near the train station today). Rebuilt in the 1800s in Neo-Gothic style, it's now used as a Rhine navigation signal station.

Km 528—Niederwald Monument: Across from the Bingen station on a hilltop is the 120-foot-high Niederwald monument, a memorial built with 32 tons of bronze in 1877 to commemorate "the reestablishment of the German Empire." A lift takes tourists to this statue from the famous and extremely touristy wine town of Rüdesheim.

From here, the Romantic Rhine becomes the industrial Rhine, and our tour is over.

Sights Along the Rhine

The following sights—Marksburg Castle, the Loreley Visitors Center, and Rheinstein Castle—are listed in the order you'd see them on the Rhine Blitz Tour, described earlier.

▲▲Marksburg Castle

Medieval invaders decided to give Marksburg a miss thanks to its formidable defenses. This best-preserved castle on the Rhine can be toured only with a guide. Tours are in German (4/hr in summer, 1/hr in winter). There are no explanations in English in the castle itself, but your ticket includes an English handout. It's an awesome castle, and between the handout and my self-guided tour, you'll feel fully informed.

Cost, Hours, Location: €5, family card-€13, daily Easter–Oct 10:00–18:00, Nov–Easter 11:00–17:00, last tour departs one hour before closing, tel. 02627/206, www.marksburg.de. Marksburg caps a hill above the village of Braubach on the east bank of the Rhine.

Getting There: By **train,** it's a 10-minute trip from Koblenz to Braubach (1–2/hr); from Bacharach or St. Goar, it takes 1.5–2 hours, depending on the length of the layover in Koblenz (€10.30 one-way). The train is quicker than the **boat** (downstream from Bacharach to Braubach-2.25 hours, upstream return-3.5 hours; €20.80 one-way, €26.80 round-trip). Consider taking the downstream boat to Braubach, and the train back. If traveling with luggage, store it in the convenient lockers in the underground passage at the Koblenz train station (Braubach has no station—and no lockers).

Once you reach Braubach, **walk** into the old town (follow *Altstadt* signs—coming out of tunnel from train platforms, it's to your right); then follow the *Zur Burg* signs to the path up to the castle. Allow 20–30 minutes for the climb up. Scarce **taxis** charge about €10 from the station to the castle. A green **tourist train** circles up to the castle, but there's no fixed schedule, so don't count on it (Easter–Oct only, €2.50 one-way, €4.50 round-trip, leaves from Barbarastrasse, tel. 06773/587, www.ruckes-reisen.de). Even if you take the train, you'll still have to climb the last five minutes up to the castle from the parking lot (cars-€2).

❷ **Self-Guided Tour:** The tour starts inside the castle's first gate.

1. Inside the First Gate: While the dramatic castles lining the Rhine are generally Romantic rebuilds, Marksburg is the real McCoy—nearly all original construction. It's littered with bits of its medieval past, like the big stone ball that was swung on a rope to be used as a battering ram. Ahead, notice how the inner gate—originally tall enough for knights on horseback to gallop through—was made smaller, and therefore safer from enemies on horseback. Climb the Knights' Stairway carved out of slate and pass under the murder hole—handy for pouring boiling pitch on invaders. (Germans still say someone with bad luck "has pitch on his head.")

2. Coats of Arms: Colorful coats of arms line the wall just inside the gate. These are from the noble families who have owned the castle since 1283. In that year, financial troubles drove the first family to sell to the powerful and wealthy Katzenelnbogen family (who made the castle into what you see today). When Napoleon took this region in 1803, an Austrian family who sided with the French got the keys. When Prussia took the region in 1866, control passed to a friend of the Prussians who had a passion for medieval things—typical of this Romantic period. Then it was sold to the German Castles Association in 1900. Its offices are in the main palace at the top of the stairs.

3. Romanesque Palace: White outlines mark where the larger original windows were located, before they were replaced by easier-to-defend smaller ones. On the far right, a bit of the original plaster survives. Slate, which is vulnerable to the elements, needs to be covered—in this case, by plaster. Because this is a protected historic building, restorers can use only the traditional plaster methods...but no one knows how to make plaster that works as well as the 800-year-old surviving bits.

4. Cannons: The oldest cannon here—from 1500—was back-loaded. This was advantageous because many cartridges could be pre-loaded. But since the seal was leaky, it wasn't very powerful. The bigger, more modern cannons—from 1640—were one piece and therefore airtight, but had to be front-loaded. They could easily hit targets across the river from here. Stone balls were rough, so they let the explosive force leak out. The best cannonballs were stones covered in smooth lead—airtight and therefore more powerful and more accurate.

5. Gothic Garden: Walking along an outer wall, you'll see 160 plants from the Middle Ages—used for cooking, medicine, and witchcraft. *Schierling* (hemlock, in the first corner) is the same poison that killed Socrates.

6. Inland Rampart: This most vulnerable part of the castle had a triangular construction to better deflect attacks. Notice the factory in the valley. In the 14th century, this was a lead, copper, and silver mine. Today's factory—Europe's largest car-battery recycling plant—uses the old mine shafts as vents (see the three modern smokestacks).

7. Wine Cellar: Since Roman times, wine has been the traditional Rhineland drink. Because castle water was impure, wine— less alcoholic than today's beer—was the way knights got their fluids. The pitchers on the wall were their daily allotment. The bellows were part of the barrel's filtering system.

Stairs lead to the...

8. Gothic Hall: This hall is set up as a kitchen, with an oven designed to roast an ox whole. The arms holding the pots have notches to control the heat. To this day, when Germans want someone to hurry up, they say, "give it one tooth more." Medieval windows were made of thin sheets of translucent alabaster or animal skins. A nearby wall is peeled away to show the wattle-and-daub construction (sticks, straw, clay, mud, then plaster) of a castle's inner walls. The iron plate to the left of the next door enabled servants to stoke the heater without being seen by the noble family.

9. Bedroom: This was the only heated room in the castle. The canopy kept in heat and kept out critters. In medieval times, it was impolite for a lady to argue with her lord in public. She would wait for him in bed to give him what Germans still call "a curtain lecture." The deep window seat caught maximum light for needlework and reading. Women would sit here and chat (or "spin a yarn") while working the spinning wheel.

10. Hall of the Knights: This was the dining hall. The long table is an unattached plank. After each course, servants could replace it with another pre-set plank. Even today, when a meal is over and Germans are ready for the action to begin, they say, "Let's lift up the table." The action back then consisted of traveling minstrels who sang and told of news gleaned from their travels.

Notice the outhouse—made of wood—hanging over thin air. When not in use, its door was locked from the outside (the castle side) to prevent any invaders from entering this weak point in the castle's defenses.

11. Chapel: This chapel is still painted in Gothic style with the castle's namesake, St. Mark, and his lion. Even the chapel was designed with defense in mind. The small doorway kept out heavily armed attackers. The staircase spirals clockwise, favoring the sword-wielding defender (assuming he was right-handed).

12. Linen Room: About the year 1800, the castle—with diminished military value—housed disabled soldiers. They'd earn a little extra money working raw flax into linen.

13. Two Thousand Years of Armor: Follow the evolution of armor since Celtic times. Because helmets covered the entire head, soldiers identified themselves as friendly by tipping their visor up with their right hand. This evolved into the military salute that is still used around the world today. Armor and the close-range weapons along the back were made obsolete by the invention of the rifle. Armor was replaced with breastplates—pointed (like the castle itself) to deflect enemy fire. This design was used as late as the start of World War I. A medieval lady's armor hangs over the door. While popular fiction has men locking up their women before heading off to battle, chastity belts were actually used by women as protection against rape when traveling.

14. The Keep: This served as an observation tower, a dungeon (with a 22-square-foot cell in the bottom), and a place of last refuge. When all was nearly lost, the defenders would bundle into the keep and burn the wooden bridge, hoping to outwait their enemies.

15. Horse Stable: The stable shows off bits of medieval crime and punishment. Cheaters were attached to stones or pillories. Shame masks punished gossipmongers. A mask with a heavy ball had its victim crawling around with his nose in the mud. The handcuffs with a neck hole were for the transport of prisoners. The pictures on the wall show various medieval capital punishments. Many times the accused was simply taken into a torture dungeon to see all these tools and, guilty or not, confessions spilled out of him. On that cheery note, your tour is over.

The Loreley Visitors Center (Besucherzentrum Loreley)

Easily reached from St. Goar, this lightweight exhibit reflects a little on Loreley, but focuses mainly on the landscape, culture, and people of the Rhine Valley. Though English explanations accompany most of the geological and cultural displays, the information about the famous mythical *Mädchen* is given in German only—making this place not worth its admission price. The 3-D movie is essentially a tourist brochure for the region, with scenes of the grape harvest over Bacharach that are as beautiful as the sword-fighting is lame (€2.50, daily March 10:00–17:00, April–mid-Nov 10:00–18:00, closed mid-Nov–Feb, tel. 06771/599-093, www.loreley-besucherzentrum.de). Far more exciting than the exhibit is the view from the cliffs themselves. A five-minute walk from the bus stop and visitors center takes you to the impressive viewpoint overlooking the Rhine Valley from atop the famous rock. From there, it's a steep 15-minute hike down to the riverbank.

Getting There: For a good two-hour **hike** from St. Goar up to the Loreley, catch the ferry across to the village of St. Goarshausen (€2.60 round-trip, every 15–20 min, Mon–Sat 6:00–21:00, Sun 8:00–21:00, May–Sept until 23:00). Then follow green *Burg Katz* (Katz Castle) signs up Burgstrasse under the train tracks to find steps on right *(Loreley über Burg Katz)* leading to the Katz Castle (privately owned) and beyond. Traverse the hillside, always bearing right toward the river. You'll pass through a residential area, hike down a 50-yard path through trees, then cross a wheat field until you reach the Loreley Visitors Center (with shops and restaurants) and rock-capping viewpoint. From here, it's a steep 15-minute hike back down to the river, where the riverfront road takes you back to St. Goarshausen and the St. Goar ferry.

If you're not up for a hike, you can catch the hourly **bus** from St. Goarshausen up to the visitors center, and hike or bus back down again. From the St. Goarshausen ferry ramp, walk to your left along the river about 40 yards to get the bus (€2.20 each way; first bus at 10:15, then at :30 past each hour 11:30–16:30; last bus down leaves at 16:42).

▲▲Rheinstein Castle (Schloss Burg Rheinstein)

This castle seems to rule its chunk of the Rhine from a commanding position. While its 13th-century exterior is medieval as can be, the interior is mostly a 19th-century duke's hunting palace. Visitors wander freely (with an English flier) among trophies, armor, and Romantic Age decor.

Cost and Hours: €4, mid-March–mid-Nov daily 9:30–17:30, mid-Nov–mid-Dec and Feb–mid-March Sat–Sun only 10:00–16:30, closed mid-Dec–Jan, tel. 06721/6348, www.burg-rheinstein.de.

Getting There: This castle (at river kilometer marker #533, 2 kilometers upstream from Trechtingshausen on the main highway, B-9) is easy by **car** (small, free parking lot on B-9, steep 5-min hike from there), or **bike** (35 min upstream from Bacharach, stick to the great riverside path, after kilometer marker #534 look for small *Burg Rheinstein* sign and Rösler–Linie dock). It's less convenient by **boat** (no K-D stop nearby) or **train** (nearest stop in Trechtingshausen, 30-min walk away).

Bacharach

Once prosperous from the wine and wood trade, charming Bacharach (BAHKH-ah-rahkh, with a guttural *kh* sound) is now just a pleasant half-timbered village of a thousand people working hard to keep its tourists happy.

Orientation to Bacharach

Tourist Information

The TI, on the main street in the Posthof courtyard next to the church, will store bags for day-trippers. Note that the TI might

move to the train station, so check there first if you arrive by train (April–Oct Mon–Fri 9:00–17:00, Sat–Sun 10:00–15:00; Nov–March Mon–Fri 9:00–12:00, closed Sat–Sun; Oberstrasse 45, from train station turn right and walk 5 blocks down main street with castle high on your left, tel. 06743/919-303, www.bacharach

.de or www.rhein-nahe-touristik.de, Herr Kuhn and his team).

Helpful Hints

Shopping: The **Jost** German gift store, across the main square from the church, carries most everything a souvenir-shopper could want—from beer steins to cuckoo clocks—and can ship purchases to the US. The Josts offer discounts to my readers: 10 percent if paying with cash, 5 percent discount with credit card (March–Oct Mon–Fri 8:30–18:00, Sat 8:30–17:00, Sun 10:00–16:00; Nov–Feb shorter hours and closed Sun; Blücherstrasse 4, tel. 06743/1224, www.phil-jost-germany .com, phil.jost@t-online.de).

Internet Access: The Rhine's cheapest Internet café is in the basement of the Lutheran-church-run kindergarten at Koblenzer Strasse 10, a few doors past the Altes Haus (€1/hr, Mon–Tue and Thu–Fri 16:00–21:00, closed Sat–Sun and Wed). The TI has a coin-op terminal (€0.50/15 min).

Bacharach

TO STEEG &
A-31 FREEWAY

NOT TO SCALE-
K-D DOCK TO
CASTLE IS A
15-20 MIN. WALK

↗ VIEW
P PARKING
--- PATH

BURG
STAHLECK
CASTLE

OLD
TOWN
WALLS

BLÜCHERSTRASSE

BANK

ROSENSTRASSE

TOWER

VINEYARDS

WERNER
KAPELLE

STEEP
TRAIL

JOST
OUTLET

BAHN-
HOF

OBERSTRASSE

ALTES
HAUS

SPUR.

KRAN.

BAUER

MARKT

BANK

POST

PHONE

PHONE

LANG- STRASSE

BAHN.

MARKT
TOWER

HIGHWAY 9

PED. UNDERPASS

←TO
BINGEN,
CAMPGROUND
& FRANKFURT

PLAY-
GROUND

MEM.

PARK

WC

P

TO →
ST GOAR
&
KOBLENZ

B-R
DOCK

K-D
DOCK
EURAIL
VALID

RHINE   RIVER   DCH

1 Rhein Hotel & Stüber Rest.
2 Hotel/Rest. Kranenturm
3 Pension im Malerwinkel
4 Pension Binz
5 Hotel Hillen & Bike Rental
6 Pension Lettie
7 Pension Winzerhaus
8 Ursula Orth B & B
9 Irmgard Orth B & B
10 Jugendherberge Stahleck Hostel
11 Altes Haus Restaurant
12 Kurpfälzische Münze Restaurant
13 Eis Café Italia
14 Bastian's Weingut zum
    Grüner Baum
15 Weingut Karl Heidrich
16 Old Posthof
17 Internet Café

Post Office: It's inside a news agents' shop, across from the church and Altes Haus, at Oberstrasse 56 (Mon–Fri 9:00–12:00 & 14:00–18:00, Sat 9:00–12:00, closed Sun).

Grocery Store: There are none in Bacharach, a small grocery in nearby St. Goar, and supermarkets in Oberwesel.

Bike Rental: While many hotels loan bikes to guests, the only real bike-rental business in the town center is run by Erich at the recommended **Hotel Hillen** (€12/day for non-guests, €7/day for guests, 25 bikes available, daily 9:00 until dark, Langstrasse 18, tel. 06743/1287).

Local Guides: Get acquainted with Bacharach by taking a walking tour with guides who enjoy sharing their town with visitors: **Birgit Wessels** (tel. 06743/937-514, wessels.birgit @t-online.de) or Aussie **Joanne Augustin** (tel. 06743/919-300, mobile 0179-231-1389, jopetit90@yahoo.com). Or take my self-guided walk below.

Self-Guided Walks

Welcome to Bacharach

• *Start at the Köln–Düsseldorfer ferry dock (next to a fine picnic park).*

Riverfront: View the town from the parking lot—a modern landfill. The Rhine used to lap against Bacharach's town wall, just over the present-day highway. Every few years the river floods, covering the highway with several feet of water. The **castle** on the hill is now a youth hostel. Two of the town's original 16 towers are visible from here (up to five if you look really hard). The huge roadside wine keg declares that this town was built on the wine trade.

Reefs farther upstream forced boats to unload upriver and reload here. Consequently, in the Middle Ages, Bacharach became the biggest wine-trading town on the Rhine. A riverfront crane hoisted huge kegs of prestigious "Bacharach" wine (which, in practice, was from anywhere in the region). The tour buses next to the dock and the flags of the biggest spenders along the highway remind you that today's economy is basically founded on tourism.

• *Before entering the town, walk upstream through the riverside park.*

Park: This park was laid out in 1910 in the English style: Notice how the trees were planted to frame fine town views, highlighting the most picturesque bits of architecture. Until recently, stepping on the grass was verboten. The dark, sad-looking monument—its "eternal" flame long snuffed out—is a war memorial. The German psyche is permanently scarred by war memories. Today, many Germans would rather avoid monuments like this, which revisit the dark periods before Germany became a nation of pacifists.

Take a close look at the monument. Each panel honors sons of Bacharach who died for the Kaiser: in 1864 against Denmark, in 1870 against France, in 1914 during World War I. The military Maltese cross—flanked by classic German helmets—has a W at its center, for Kaiser Wilhelm.

• *Continue to where the park meets the playground, and then cross the highway to the fortified riverside wall of the Catholic church—decorated with high-water marks recalling various floods.*

Check out the metal ring on the medieval slate wall. Before the 1910 reclamation project, the river extended out to here, and boats would use the ring to tie up. Upstream from here, there's a trailer park, and beyond that there's a campground. In Germany, trailer vacationers and campers are two distinct subcultures. Folks who travel in trailers, like many retirees in the US, are a nomadic bunch, hauling around the countryside in their mobile homes and paying a few euros a night to park. Campers, on the other hand, tend to set up camp—complete with comfortable lounge chairs and even TVs—and stay put for weeks, even months. They often come back to the same plot year after year, treating it like their own private estate. These camping devotees have made a science out of relaxing.

• *At the church, go under the 1858 train tracks and hook right past the yellow floodwater yardstick and up the stairs onto the town wall. Atop the wall, turn left and walk under the long arcade. After a few steps, notice a well on your left. This is one of 40 such wells that, until 1900, provided water to the townsfolk. You'll pass the recommended Rhein Hotel (hotel is before the Markt tower, which marks one of the town's 15 original 14th-century gates), descend, pass another well, and follow Marktstrasse toward the town center, the two-tone church, and the town's main intersection.*

Town Center: From here, Bacharach's main street (Oberstrasse) goes right to the half-timbered red-and-white Altes Haus (from 1368, the oldest house in town) and left 400 yards to the train station. To the left (south) of the church, a golden horn hangs over the old **Posthof** (home to the TI, free WC upstairs in courtyard). The post horn symbolizes the postal service throughout Europe. In olden days, when the postman blew this, traffic stopped and the mail sped through. This post station dates from 1724, when stagecoaches ran from Köln to Frankfurt and would change horses here, Pony Express–style.

Step past the old oak doors into the courtyard—once a carriage house and inn that accommodated Bacharach's first VIP visitors. Notice the fascist eagle (from 1936, on the left as you enter; a swastika once filled its center) and the fine view of the church and a ruined chapel above. The Posthof is on a charming square. Spin around to enjoy the higgledy-piggledy building style.

Two hundred years ago, Bacharach's main drag was the only road along the Rhine. Napoleon widened it to fit his cannon wagons. The steps alongside the church lead to the castle. Return to the church, passing the recommended Italian ice-cream café (Eis Café Italia), where friendly Mimo serves his special invention: Riesling wine–flavored gelato.

Inside the **Protestant church** (April–Oct daily 9:30–18:00, closed Nov–March, English info on table near door), you'll find Grotesque capitals, brightly painted in medieval style, and a mix of round Romanesque and pointed Gothic arches. To the left of the altar, some medieval frescoes survive where an older Romanesque arch was cut by a pointed Gothic one.

• *Continue down Oberstrasse to the Altes Haus.*

Notice the 14th-century building style—the first floor is made of stone, while upper floors are half-timbered (in the ornate style common in the Rhine Valley). Some of its windows still look medieval, with small, flattened circles as panes (small because that's all that glass-blowing technology of the time would allow), pieced together with molten lead. Frau Weber welcomes visitors to enjoy the fascinating ground floor of the recommended Altes Haus, with its evocative old photos and etchings (consider eating here later).

• *Keep going down Oberstrasse to the old mint (Münze), marked by a crude coin in its sign.*

Across from the mint, the recommended Bastian family's wine garden is the liveliest place in town after dark. Above you in the vineyards stands a lonely white-and-red tower—your destination.

At the next street, look right and see the mint tower, painted in the medieval style (illustrating that the Dark Ages weren't really that dark), and then turn left. Wander 30 yards up Rosenstrasse to the **well.** Notice the sundial and the wall painting of 1632 Bacharach with its walls intact. (You can walk along the route of the old town walls by following the *Stadtmauer-Rundweg* signs in town; see next description.) Climb the tiny-stepped lane behind the well up into the vineyard and to the tall tower. The slate steps lead to a small path through the vineyard that deposits you at a viewpoint atop the stubby remains of the old town wall. If the

tower's open, hike to its top floor for the best view.

Town View: A grand medieval town spreads before you. For 300 years (1300–1600), Bacharach was big (population 4,000), rich, and politically powerful.

From this perch you can see the chapel ruins and six surviving **city towers.** Visually trace the wall to the castle. The castle was actually the capitol of Germany for a couple of years in the 1200s. When Holy Roman Emperor Frederick Barbarossa went away to fight the Crusades, he left his brother (who lived here) in charge of his vast realm. Bacharach was home of one of seven electors who voted for the Holy Roman Emperor in 1275. To protect their own power, these elector-princes did their best to choose the weakest guy on the ballot. The elector from Bacharach helped select a two-bit prince named Rudolf von Habsburg (from a no-name castle in Switzerland). However, the underestimated Rudolf brutally silenced the robber barons along the Rhine and established the mightiest dynasty in European history. His family line, the Habsburgs, ruled much of Central and Eastern Europe until 1918.

Plagues, fires, and the Thirty Years' War (1618–1648) finally did in Bacharach. The town, with a population of about a thousand, has slumbered for several centuries. Today, the castle houses commoners—40,000 overnights annually by youth hostelers.

In the mid-19th century, painters such as J. M. W. Turner and writers such as Victor Hugo were charmed by the Rhineland's romantic mix of past glory, present poverty, and rich legend. They put this part of the Rhine on the old Grand Tour map as the "Romantic Rhine." Victor Hugo pondered the ruined 15th-century chapel that you see under the castle. In his 1842 travel book, *Rhein Reise (Rhine Travels),* he wrote, "No doors, no roof or windows, a magnificent skeleton puts its silhouette against the sky. Above it, the ivy-covered castle ruins provide a fitting crown. This is Bacharach, land of fairy tales, covered with legends and sagas." If you're enjoying the Romantic Rhine, thank Victor Hugo and company.

• *To get back into town, take the level path away from the river that leads along the once-mighty wall up the valley past the next tower. Then cross the street into the parking lot. Pass Pension Malerwinkel on your right, being careful not to damage the old arch with your head. Follow the creek past a delightful little series of half-timbered homes and cheery gardens known as "Painters' Corner" (Malerwinkel). Resist looking into some pervert's peep show (on the right) and continue downhill back to the village center. Nice work.*

Walk Along the Old Town Walls

A well-maintained and clearly marked walking path follows the remains of Bacharach's old town walls and makes for a good hour's workout. The TI has maps that show the entire route. The path starts near the train station, then climbs up to the youth hostel, descends into the side valley, and then continues up the other side to the tower in the vineyards before returning to town. To start the walk at the train station, find the house at Oberstrasse 2 and climb up the stairway to its left. Now follow the Stadtmauer-Rundweg signs. Good bilingual signposts tell the history of each of the towers along the wall—some are intact, one is a private residence, and others are now only stubs.

Sleeping in Bacharach

(area code: 06743)

Ignore guest houses and restaurants posting *Recommended by Rick Steves* signs. If they're not listed in the current edition of this book, I do not recommend them. Parking in Bacharach is simple along the highway next to the tracks (3-hour daytime limit is generally not enforced) or in the boat parking lot. For locations, see the map on page 348.

$$$ Rhein Hotel, with 14 spacious and comfortable rooms, is classy, well-run and decorated with modern flair, and overlooks the river. Since it's right on the train tracks, its river- and train-side rooms come with four-paned windows and air-conditioning. This place has been in the Stüber family for six generations (Sb-€55, Db-€90 with this book and direct reservation in 2010, cheaper for longer stays, half-board €16–20 per person, non-smoking, free loaner bikes for guests, pay Wi-Fi, directly inland from the K-D boat dock at Langstrasse 50, tel. 06743/1243, fax 06743/1413, www .rhein-hotel-bacharach.de, info@rhein-hotel-bacharach.de). For a culinary splurge, consider dining here.

$$ Hotel Kranenturm, offering castle ambience without the climb, combines hotel comfort with *Zimmer* coziness right down-town. Run by hardworking Kurt Engel and his intense but friendly wife, Fatima, this hotel is part of the medieval fortification. Its former *Kran* (crane) towers are now round rooms. When the riverbank was higher, cranes on this tower loaded barrels of wine onto Rhine boats. While just 15 feet from the train tracks, a combination of medieval sturdiness, triple-paned windows, and included earplugs makes the riverside rooms sleepable (Sb-€39–45, small Db-€56–62, regular Db-€58–65, Db in huge tower rooms with castle and river views-€72–80, Tb-€85–95, Qb great for families with small kids-€100–115, honeymoon special-€85–105, lower prices April–Oct with 3-night stay and Nov–March with 2-night stay, family deals, cash preferred, Rhine views come with train noise, back rooms are quiet, non-smoking, showers can be temperamental,

Sleep Code

(€1 = about $1.40, country code: 49)
S = Single, **D** = Double/Twin, **T** = Triple, **Q** = Quad, **b** = bathroom, **s** = shower only. All hotels speak some English. Breakfast is included and credit cards are accepted unless otherwise noted.

To help you sort easily through these listings, I've divided the rooms into three categories, based on the price for a standard double room with bath:

$$$ Higher Priced—Most rooms €80 or more.
$$ Moderately Priced—Most rooms between €55–80.
$ Lower Priced—Most rooms €55 or less.

The Rhine is an easy place for cheap sleeps. B&Bs and *Gasthäuser* with €25–30 beds abound (and normally discount their prices for longer stays). Rhine-area hostels offer €15–18 beds to travelers of any age. Each town's TI is eager to set you up, and finding a room should be easy any time of year (except for winefest weekends in Sept and Oct). Bacharach and St. Goar, the best towns for an overnight stop, are 10 miles apart, connected by milk-run trains, riverboats, and a riverside bike path. Bacharach is a much more interesting town, but St. Goar has the famous castle (for St. Goar recommendations, see that section).

kid-friendly, good breakfast, free Internet access and Wi-Fi, laundry service-€13, Langstrasse 30, tel. 06743/1308, fax 06743/1021, www.kranenturm.com, hotel-kranenturm@t-online.de). Kurt, a good cook, serves €8–14 dinners.

$$ Pension im Malerwinkel sits like a grand gingerbread house that straddles the town wall in a quiet little neighborhood

so charming it's called "Painters' Corner" *(Malerwinkel)*. The Vollmer family's 20-room place is super-quiet and comes with a sunny garden on a brook, views of the vineyards, and easy parking (Sb-€38, Db-€62 for 1 night, €56 for 2 nights, €53 for 3 nights or more, cash only, some rooms have balconies, no train noise, non-smoking, free Wi-Fi, bike rental-€6/day; from Oberstrasse, turn left at the church, and stay to the left of the babbling brook until you reach Blücherstrasse 41–45; tel. 06743/1239, fax 06743/93407, www.im-malerwinkel.de, pension@im-malerwinkel.de, Armin and Daniela).

$$ Pension Binz offers four large, bright, plainly furnished rooms in a good location with no train noise (Sb-€37, Db-€60, third person-€18, slightly cheaper for 3 nights or more, apartment with kitchen but no breakfast and 2-night minimum-€65, Koblenzer Strasse 1, tel. 06743/1604, fax 06743/937-9916, pension .binz@freenet.de, warm Carla speaks a little English).

$ Hotel Hillen, a block south of the Hotel Kranenturm, has a little less charm and similar train noise (with the same ultra-thick windows). It offers spacious rooms, good food, and friendly owners (S-€30, Sb-€35, D-€40, Ds-€45, Db-€50, Tb-€65, Qb-€80, these special prices with a 2-night stay when you reserve directly with this book in 2010, €5 more for 1-night stays, closed mid-Nov–mid-March, family rooms, Langstrasse 18, tel. 06743/1287, fax 06743/1037, hotel-hillen@web.de, kind Iris speaks some English). The hotel also rents bikes (see page 349).

$ At Pension Lettie, effervescent and eager-to-please Lettie offers four bright rooms. Lettie speaks English (she worked for the US Army before they withdrew) and does laundry for €12/load (Sb-€38, Db-€53, Tb-€75, Qb-€90, 5b-€105, these prices with this book in 2010 if you reserve direct rather than through TI, €3–5 discount for 2-night stays, 10 percent more if paying with credit card, strictly non-smoking, buffet breakfast with waffles and eggs, no train noise, inexpensive Wi-Fi, a few doors inland from Hotel Kranenturm, Kranenstrasse 6, tel. 06743/2115, pension.lettie @t-online.de).

$ Pension Winzerhaus, a 10-room place run by friendly Sybille and Stefan, is outside the town walls, 200 yards up the side-valley road from the town gate, directly under the vineyards. Though you can't hear the train, there is slight noise from passing cars. The rooms are simple, clean, and modern, and parking is easy (Sb-€30, Db-€49, Tb-€65, Qb-€75, 10 percent off in 2010 when you show this book at check-in, cash only, non-smoking, free loaner bikes for guests, Blücherstrasse 60, tel. 06743/1294, www .pension-winzerhaus.de, winzerhaus@gmx.de).

$ Orth *Zimmer*: Delightful sisters-in-law run two fine little B&Bs across the lane from each other (from station, walk down Oberstrasse, turn right on Spurgasse, and look for *Orth* sign). **Ursula Orth** rents five rooms, speaks a smidge of English, and is proud of her homemade jam (Sb-€22, Db-€37, Tb-€45, cash only, rooms 4 and 5 on ground floor, Spurgasse 3, tel. 06743/1557). **Irmgard Orth** rents three fresh rooms, two of which share a bathroom on the hall. She speaks even less English but is exuberantly cheery and serves homemade honey with breakfast (S-€22, D-€34–35, Db-€37, cash only, Spurgasse 2, look for beehive signs, tel. 06743/1553). Their excellent prices assume you're booking direct, instead of through the TI.

$ Jugendherberge Stahleck hostel is a 12th-century castle on the hilltop—500 steps above Bacharach—with a royal Rhine view. Open to travelers of any age, this is a gem with 168 beds and a private modern shower and WC in most rooms. The steep 20-minute climb on the trail from the town church is worth it for the view, even if you're not sleeping there. The hostel serves hearty €6.50 all-you-can-eat buffet dinners, and its pub serves cheap local wine and snacks until midnight. To reach the hostel with luggage from the train station, call an €8.50 taxi at 06743/1653 or 0674-4488 (€17.40 dorm beds with breakfast and sheets, non-members-€3.10 extra, couples can share one of five €48 Db, no smoking in rooms, expensive Internet access and Wi-Fi, laundry-€6, reception open 7:30–20:00, last arrival at 21:30, curfew at 22:00, tel. 06743/1266, fax 06743/2684, www.diejugendherbergen .de, bacharach@diejugendherbergen.de). If driving, don't go in the driveway; park on the street and walk 200 yards.

Eating in Bacharach

Restaurants

You can easily find inexpensive (€10–15), atmospheric restaurants offering indoor and outdoor dining. Two of the recommended hotels—Rhein and Kranenturm—have good restaurants. Non-German options on the main street include a pizzeria and *Döner Kebab* joint (open daily until late) and an Irish pub.

The Rhein Hotel's **Stüber Restaurant** is Bacharach's best top-end choice. Chef Andreas Stüber is the sixth generation to prepare regional, seasonal plates, served on river- and track-side seating or indoors with a spacious wood-and-white-tablecloth elegance. Consider their €14.50 William Turner pâté sampler plate, named after the British painter who liked Bacharach (€10–19 main dishes, March–mid-Dec Wed–Mon 12:00–14:00 & 17:30–21:00, closed Tue and mid-Dec–Feb, call to reserve on weekends or for an outdoor table, facing the K-D boat dock just below the center of town, Langstrasse 50, tel. 06743/1243).

Altes Haus, the oldest building in town (see page 351), serves reliably good food with Bacharach's most romantic atmosphere. Find the cozy little dining room with photos of the opera singer who sang about Bacharach, adding to its fame (€9–15 main dishes,

Easter–Nov Thu–Tue 12:00–15:30 & 18:00–23:00, closed Wed and Dec–Easter, dead center by the church, tel. 06743/1209).

Kurpfälzische Münze, while more expensive than Altes Haus, is a popular standby for lunch or a drink on its sunny terrace or in its pubby candlelit interior (main dishes–€7–20, daily 10:00–22:00, in the old mint, a half-block down from Altes Haus; tel. 06743/1375).

Hotel Kranenturm is another good value, with hearty dinners (Kurt prides himself on his *Sauerbraten*—marinated beef with potato dumplings and red cabbage) and good main-course salads. If you're a train-spotter, sit on their track-side terrace and trade travel stories with new friends over dinner, letting screaming trains punctuate your conversation. If you prefer charming old German decor, sit inside (€8–14 dinners, open 6 days a week 17:00–21:00—closed day varies, restaurant closed Dec–Feb). Kurt and Fatima are your hosts.

Eis Café Italia, on the main street and run by friendly Mimo Calabrese, is known for its refreshing, not-too-sweet Riesling-flavored gelato. Notice the big sundae bowls on the shelves. To enjoy your *Eis* German-style, sit down and order ice cream off the menu, or just stop by for a cone before an evening stroll (€0.70/scoop, no tastes offered, April–mid-Oct daily 10:00–22:00, closed off-season, opposite Posthof at Oberstrasse 48).

Wine-Tasting

Bacharach is proud of its wine. Two places in town—Bastian's rowdy and rustic Grüner Baum, and sophisticated Weingut Karl Heidrich—offer visitors an inexpensive chance to join in on the fun. Each creates carousels of local wines that small groups of travelers (who don't mind sharing a glass) can sample and compare.

At **Bastian's Weingut zum Grüner Baum,** groups of 2–6 people pay €14 for a wine carousel of 15 glasses—14 different white wines and one lonely rosé—and a basket of bread. Your mission: Team up with others who have this book to rendezvous here after dinner. Spin the Lazy Susan, share a common cup, and discuss the taste. Doris Bastian insists: "After each wine, you must talk to each other." They offer soup and cold cuts, and good ambience indoors and out (Mon–Wed and Fri from 13:00, Sat–Sun from 12:00, closed Thu and Feb–mid-March, just past Altes Haus, tel. 06743/1208). To make a meal of a carousel, consider the *Käse Teller* (seven different cheeses, including *Spundekäse*, the local soft cheese).

Weingut Karl Heidrich is a fun family-run wine shop and *Stube* in the town center (at Oberstrasse 18, near Hotel Kranenturm), where Markus proudly shares his family's wine while passionately explaining its fine points to travelers. They offer a variety of carousels with six wines and bread (€10), which are ideal for the more sophisticated wine-taster (Easter–Oct Thu–Tue 11:00–22:00, closed Wed and Nov–Easter, tel. 06743/93060).

Bacharach Connections

Train Connections from the Rhine

Milk-run trains stop at Rhine towns each hour starting as early as 6:00, connecting at Mainz and Koblenz to trains farther afield. Trains between St. Goar and Bacharach depart at about :20 after the hour in each direction (€3.10, buy tickets from the machine in the unstaffed stations). The ride times listed below are calculated from Bacharach; for St. Goar, the difference is only 10 minutes. Train info: tel. 0180-599-6633 (€0.14/min).

From Bacharach by Train to: St. Goar (hourly, 10 min), **Moselkern** near Burg Eltz (hourly, 1.75 hrs, change in Koblenz), **Cochem** (hourly, 1.5 hrs, change in Koblenz), **Trier** (hourly, 2.5 hrs, change in Koblenz), **Köln** (hourly, 1.75 hrs with change in Koblenz, 2.5 hrs direct), **Frankfurt Airport** (hourly, 1.5 hrs, most change in Mainz or Bingen), **Frankfurt** (hourly, 1.5–2 hrs, change in Mainz or Bingen), **Rothenburg ob der Tauber** (every 2 hrs, 4–5 hrs, 3–4 changes), **Munich** (hourly, 5 hrs, 2 changes), **Berlin** (hourly, 6–7 hrs, 1–3 changes), **Amsterdam** (6/day, 6 hrs, change in Köln).

Route Tips for Drivers

This area is a logical first (or last) stop in Germany. If you're using Frankfurt Airport, here are some tips.

Frankfurt Airport to the Rhine: Driving from Frankfurt to the Rhine or Mosel takes 1.5 hours (follow blue autobahn signs from airport, major cities are signposted).

The Rhine to Frankfurt: From St. Goar or Bacharach, follow the river to Bingen, then autobahn signs to *Mainz,* then *Frankfurt.* From there, head for the airport *(Flughafen)* or downtown (signs to *Messe,* then *Hauptbahnhof,* to find the parking under Frankfurt's main train station—see "Arrival in Frankfurt—By Car," page 308).

St. Goar

St. Goar is a classic Rhine town. Its hulk of a castle overlooks a half-timbered shopping street and leafy riverside park, busy with

sightseeing ships and contented strollers. Rheinfels Castle, once the mightiest on the Rhine, is the single best Rhineland ruin to explore. From the riverboat docks, the main drag—a dull pedestrian mall without history—cuts through town before ending at the road up to the castle.

While the town of St. Goar itself isn't much more than a few hotels and restaurants—and is less interesting than Bacharach—it still makes a good base for hiking or biking the region. A tiny car ferry will shuttle you back and forth across the busy Rhine from here. (One of my favorite pastimes in St. Goar is chatting with friendly Heike at the K-D boat kiosk.) For train connections, see "Bacharach Connections," earlier.

Orientation to St. Goar

Tourist Information

The helpful St. Goar TI, which books rooms and stores bags for free, is on the pedestrian street, three blocks from the K-D boat dock and train station (May–Sept Mon–Fri 9:00–12:30 & 13:30–18:00, Sat 10:00–12:00, closed Sun; April and Oct Mon–Fri until 17:00, closed Sat–Sun; Nov–March Mon–Thu until 17:00, Fri 9:00–14:00, closed Sat–Sun; from train station, go downhill around church and turn left, Heerstrasse 86, tel. 06741/383, www.st-goar.de).

Helpful Hints

Picnics: St. Goar's waterfront park is hungry for picnickers. You can buy picnic fixings at the tiny **St. Goarer Stadtladen** grocery store on the pedestrian street (Mon–Fri 8:00–18:00, Sat 8:00–13:00, closed Sun, Heerstrasse 106).

Shopping: The helpful Montag family runs two shops (one specializes in steins and the other in cuckoo clocks) and a hotel, all at the base of the castle hill road. The stein shop under the hotel has Rhine guides and fine steins (daily March–Oct 8:30–18:00, Nov–Feb 10:00–16:00). Both shops offer 10

St. Goar

NOT TO SCALE:
K-D DOCK TO
CASTLE = 15 MIN. WALK

P PARKING

BURG RHEINFELS CASTLE

TRAIL TO BACHARACH

NATURE TRAIL

SCHLOSSBERG

TRAIN STATION

TOWER

ULMENHOF

BISMARCKWEG

VINEYARD TRAIL

TO BACHARACH & FRANKFURT

PHONE

OBERSTRASSE

POST

HEERSTRASSE

PHONE

HEERSTRASSE

TO BOPPARD & KOBLENZ

HIGHWAY 9

WC

HARBOR

PARK

BUS (ONLY) PARKING

K-D DOCK (EURAIL VALID)

RHINE RIVER

B-R DOCK

FERRY

ST. GOARSHAUSEN

TO LORELEY

DCH

① Schlosshotel Rheinfels
② Hotel am Markt
③ Rhein Hotel & Hotel Hauser
④ Frau Kurz Rooms
⑤ St. Goar Hostel
⑥ Grocery Store
⑦ Stein Shop
⑧ Bike Rental

percent off any of their souvenirs (including Hummels) for travelers with this book (€5 minimum purchase). They'll ship, or if you're carrying purchases home, they'll give you a VAT form to claim your refund at the airport. Another good souvenir shop is across from the K-D boat dock.

Internet Access: The **TI** is your best bet (€3/hr), but if it's crowded or closed, the backup option is **Hotel Montag**'s expensive coin-op access (€6/hr, 6 terminals, Heerstrasse 128).

Bike Rental: Goar Bike, run by Richard and Gabriele Langhans, is five doors from the train station (€6/6 hours, €11.50/day, must show ID and leave €50 deposit, April–Oct daily 9:00–13:00 & 15:00–19:00, closed Nov–March, go right as you exit station, Oberstrasse 44, tel. 06741/1735). Ask the TI for maps and suggested routes.

Parking: A free lot is at the downstream end of town.

Sights in St. Goar

▲▲▲Rheinfels Castle

Sitting like a dead pit bull above St. Goar, this mightiest of Rhine castles rumbles with ghosts from its hard-fought past. Burg Rheinfels *was* huge—once the biggest castle on the Rhine (built in 1245). It withstood a siege of 28,000 French troops in 1692. But in 1797, the French Revolutionary army destroyed it. For years, the castle was used as a source of building stone, and today—while still mighty—it's only a small fraction of its original size. This hollow but interesting shell offers your single best hands-on ruined-castle experience on the river.

Cost and Hours: €4, family card-€10; mid-March–Oct daily 9:00–18:00, last entry at 17:00; Nov–mid-March Sat–Sun only 11:00–17:00, last entry at 16:00—weather permitting; tel. 06741/7753, in winter 06741/383, www.st-goar.de.

Tours and Information: Call in advance or gather 10 English-speaking tourists and beg to get an English tour—perhaps from Günther, the "last knight of Rheinfels" (tel. 06741/7753). Otherwise, follow my self-guided tour (later). The castle map is helpful, and the €2 English booklet is good, with history and illustrations. If it's damp, be careful of slippery stones. A handy WC is immediately across from the ticket booth (check out the guillotine urinals—stand back when you pull to flush).

Let There Be Light: If planning to explore the mine tunnels, bring a flashlight, or do it by candlelight (museum sells candles with matches, €0.50).

Getting to the Castle by Taxi or Mini-Train: A taxi up from town costs €5 (tel. 06741/7011). Or take the kitschy "tschu-tschu" tourist train (€2 one-way, €3 round-trip, 7 min to the top, April–Oct daily 10:00–17:00 but sometimes unpredictable, 2/hr, runs from square between station and dock, also stops by beer-stein shop, complete with lusty music, mobile 0171-496-3762).

Hiking Up to the Castle: Two steep but scenic paths take you up to the castle from the town (allow 15–20 minutes up). You can also simply follow the main road up through the railroad underpass at the top end of the pedestrian street, but it's not as much fun.

To take the **vineyard trail,** start at the beer-stein shop at the end of the pedestrian street, walk uphill through the underpass, make an immediate right on Bismarcksweg along the railroad tracks following the *Fussweg Burg Rheinfels* and yellow *Zur Burg*

St. Goar's Rheinfels Castle

CLIFFS

DETOUR THAT INCLUDES TUNNELS

STAIRS

TUNNELS

1ST STEEL RAILING

2ND STEEL RAILING

START ❶

❷

WELL

CATAPULT BALLS

❸

POSTS

❶❶

MOAT

P

2 ARCHES

BRIDGE

SHUTTLE STOP

ROAD

BRIDGE

HOTEL/REST.

❾ ❹

❶❶

❶⓿

CLIFFS

❼

❻

❺

CLIFFS

WC TICKETS

ROAD

RHINE RIVER →

TO ST. GOAR

- – ▸ – ROUTE FROM PARKING LOT TO MUSEUM
- ➡ WALKING TOUR ROUTE
- ·· ▸ WALKING TOUR ROUTE (TUNNEL OPTION)
- ···· PORTION OF TOUR ROUTE IN LOW TUNNELS
- **P** PARKING

❶ Museum & Castle Model (Start of Tour)

❷ Medieval Castle Courtyard

❸ Castle Garden

❹ Highest Castle Tower Lookout

❺ Covered Defense Galleries

❻ "Minutemen" Holes

❼ Corner of Castle

❽ Thoop . . . You're Dead

❾ Prison

❿ Slaughterhouse (Below)

⓫ Big Cellar (Below)

signs, pass the youth hostel, and then follow the yellow *Zur Burg* signs up the hill through the vineyard. The last couple hundred yards are along the road.

To take the **nature trail,** start at the St. Goar train station. Take the underpass under the tracks at the north end of the station, climb the steep stairs uphill, and turn right (following *Burg Rheinfels* signs) along the path just above the old city wall, which takes you to the castle in 10 minutes.

❍ **Self-Guided Tour:** Rather than wander aimlessly, visit the castle by following this tour. The route I suggest is basically the same as the one marked on the castle map, but my numbering differs a little from the red signposts that you'll see.

• *From the ticket gate, walk straight. Pass* Grosser Keller *on the left (where we'll end this tour) and walk through an internal gate past the* zu den Wehrgängen *sign on the right (where we'll pass later) uphill to the...*

❶ **Museum and Castle Model:** The pleasant museum, located in the only finished room of the castle, has good English descriptions, but it's not as important as seeing the castle itself. Skip the museum if you're short on time (museum open mid-March–Oct daily 10:00–12:30 & 13:00–17:30, closed Nov–mid-March, included in castle entry).

The seven-foot-tall carved stone immediately inside the door (marked *Flammensäule*)—a tombstone from a nearby Celtic grave—is from 400 years before Christ. There were people here long before the Romans...and this castle. Find the old wooden library chair near the tombstone. If you smile sweetly, the man behind the desk may demonstrate—pull the chair's back forward and it becomes stairs for accessing the highest shelves.

The sweeping castle history exhibit in the center of the room is well-described in English. The massive fortification was the only Rhineland castle to withstand Louis XIV's assault during the 17th century. At the far end of the room is a model reconstruction of the castle (not the one with the toy soldiers) showing how much bigger it was before French Revolutionary troops destroyed it in the 18th century. Study this. Find where you are. (Hint: Look for the tall tower.) This was the living quarters of the original castle, which was only the smallest ring of buildings around the tiny central courtyard (13th century). The ramparts were added in the 14th century. By 1650, the fortress was largely complete. Ever since its destruction by the French in the late 18th century, it's had no military value. While no WWII bombs were wasted on this ruin, it served St. Goar as a stone quarry for generations. The basement of the museum shows the castle pharmacy and an exhibit of Rhine-region odds and ends, including tools and an 1830 loom. Don't miss the photos of ice-breaking on the Rhine. While once routine, ice-breaking hasn't been necessary here since 1963.

• *Exit the museum and walk 30 yards directly out, slightly uphill into the castle courtyard.*

❷ **Medieval Castle Courtyard:** Five hundred years ago, the entire castle encircled this courtyard. The place was self-sufficient and ready for a siege, with a bakery, pharmacy, herb garden, brewery, well (top of yard), and livestock. During peacetime, 300–600 people lived here; during a siege, there would be as many as 4,000. The walls were plastered and painted white. Bits of the original 13th-century plaster survive.

• *Continue through the courtyard and out Erste Schildmauer, turn left into the next courtyard, and walk straight to the two old wooden upright posts. Find the pyramid of stone catapult balls on your left.*

❸ **Castle Garden:** Catapult balls like these were too expensive not to recycle—they'd be retrieved after any battle. Across from the balls is a well—essential for any castle during the age of sieges. Look in. Spit. The old posts are for the ceremonial baptizing of new members of the local trading league. While this guild goes back centuries, it's now a social club that fills this court with a huge wine party the third weekend of each September.

• *If weary, skip to #5; otherwise, climb the cobbled path up to the castle's best viewpoint—up where the German flag waves.*

❹ **Highest Castle Tower Lookout:** Enjoy a great view of the river, the castle, and the forest. Remember, the fortress once covered five times the land it does today. Notice how the other castles (across the river) don't poke above the top of the Rhine canyon. That would make them easy for invading armies to see.

• *Return to the catapult balls, walk down the road, go through the tunnel, veer left through the arch marked* zu den Wehrgängen *("to the defense galleries"), go down two flights of stairs, and turn left into the dark, covered passageway. From here, we will begin a rectangular walk taking us completely around (counterclockwise) the perimeter of the castle.*

❺ & ❻ **Covered Defense Galleries with "Minutemen" Holes:** Soldiers—the castle's "minutemen"—had a short commute: defensive positions on the outside, home in the holes below on the left. Even though these living quarters were padded with straw, life was unpleasant.

• *Continue straight through the dark gallery and to the corner of the castle, where you'll see a white painted arrow at eye level. Stand with your back to the arrow on the wall.*

❼ Corner of Castle: Look up. A three-story, half-timbered building originally rose beyond the highest stone fortification. The two stone tongues near the top just around the corner supported the toilet. (Insert your own joke here.) Turn around and face the wall. The crossbow slits below the white arrow were once steeper. The bigger hole on the riverside was for hot pitch.

• *Follow that white arrow along the outside to the next corner. Midway you'll pass stairs on the right leading down* zu den Minengängen *(sign on upper left). Adventurers with flashlights can detour here (described later, under "Optional Detour—Into the Mine Tunnels"). You may come out around the next corner. Otherwise, stay with me, walking level to the corner. At the corner, turn left.*

❽ Thoop...You're Dead: Look ahead at the smartly placed crossbow slit. While you're lying there, notice the stonework. The little round holes were for scaffolds used as they built up. They indicate this stonework is original. Notice also the fine stonework on the chutes. More boiling pitch...now you're toast, too.

• *Continue along the castle wall around the corner. At the gray railing, look up the valley and uphill where the sprawling fort stretched. Below, just outside the wall, is land where attackers would gather. The mine tunnels are under there, waiting to blow up any attackers.*

Keep going along the perimeter, jog left, go down five steps and into an open field, and walk toward the wooden bridge. You may detour here into the passageway (on right) marked 13 Halsgraben. *The "old" wooden bridge is actually modern. Angle left through two arches (before the bridge) and through the rough entry to the* Verliess *(prison) on the left.*

❾ Prison: This is one of six dungeons. You just walked through an entrance prisoners only dreamed of 400 years ago. They came and went through the little square hole in the ceiling. The holes in the walls supported timbers that thoughtfully gave as many as 15 residents something to sit on to keep them out of the filthy slop that gathered on the floor. Twice a day, they were given bread and water. Some prisoners actually survived longer than two years in here. While the town could torture and execute, the castle had permission only to imprison criminals in these dungeons. Consider this: According to town records, the two men who spent the most time down here—2.5 years each—died within three weeks of regaining their freedom. Perhaps after a diet of bread and water, feasting on meat and wine was simply too much.

• *Continue through the next arch, under the white arrow, then turn left and walk 30 yards to the* Schlachthaus.

❿ Slaughterhouse: Any proper castle was prepared to survive a six-month siege. With 4,000 people, that's a lot of provisions. The cattle that lived within the walls were slaughtered in this room. The castle's mortar was congealed here (by packing all the organic waste from the kitchen into kegs and sealing it). Notice the drainage gutters. "Running water" came through from drains built into the walls (to keep the mortar dry and therefore strong... and less smelly).

• Back outside, climb the modern stairs to the left (zum Ausgang sign). A skinny, dark passage (yes, that's the one) leads you into the...

⓫ **Big Cellar:** This *Grosser Keller* was a big pantry. When the castle was smaller, this was the original moat—you can see the rough lower parts of the wall. The original floor was 13 feet deeper. The drawbridge rested upon the stone nubs on the left. When the castle expanded, the moat became this cellar. Halfway up the walls on the entrance side of the room, square holes mark spots where timbers made a storage loft, perhaps filled with grain. In the back, an arch leads to the wine cellar (sometimes blocked off) where finer wine was kept. Part of a soldier's pay was wine...table wine. This wine was kept in a single 180,000-liter stone barrel (that's 47,550 gallons), which generally lasted about 18 months.

The count owned the surrounding farmland. Farmers got to keep 20 percent of their production. Later, in more liberal feudal times, the nobility let them keep 40 percent. Today, the German government leaves the workers with 60 percent...and provides a few more services.

• You're free. Climb out, turn right, and leave. For coffee on a terrace with a great view, visit Schlosshotel Rheinfels, opposite the entrance.

Optional Detour—Into the Mine Tunnels: In about 1600, to protect their castle, the Rheinfellers cleverly booby-trapped the land just outside their walls by building tunnels topped with thin slate roofs and packed with explosives. By detonating the explosives when under attack, they could kill hundreds of invaders. In 1626, a handful of underground Protestant Germans blew 300 Catholic Spaniards to—they figured—hell. You're welcome to wander through a set of never-blown-up tunnels. But be warned: It's 600 feet long, assuming you make no wrong turns; it's pitch-dark, muddy, and claustrophobic, with confusing dead-ends; and you'll never get higher than a deep crouch. It cannot be done without a light (candles available at entrance).

After stop #7 of the above tour, follow the stairs on the right leading down *zu den Minengängen* (sign on upper left). The *Fuchsloch* (foxhole) sign welcomes you to a covered passageway. Walk level (take no stairs) past the first steel railing (where you hope to emerge later) around a few bends to the second steel railing. Climb down.

The "highway" in this foxhole is three feet high. The ceiling may be painted with a white line indicating the correct path.

Don't venture into the narrower side aisles. These were once filled with the gunpowder. After a small decline, take the second right. At the T-intersection, go right (uphill). After about 10 feet, go left. Take the next right and look for a light at the end of the tunnel. Head up a rocky incline under the narrowest part of the tunnel and you'll emerge at that first steel railing. The stairs on the right lead to freedom. Cross the field, walk under the bigger archway, and continue uphill toward the old wooden bridge. Angle left through two arches (before the bridge) and through the rough entry to the *Verliess* (prison) on the left. Rejoin the tour here at stop #9.

Sleeping in St. Goar

(€1 = about $1.40, country code: 49, area code: 06741)
Parking in St. Goar is tight; ask at your hotel.

$$$ Schlosshotel Rheinfels ("Rheinfels Castle Hotel") is the town splurge. Part of the castle, but in a purpose-built new building, this luxurious 64-room place is good for those with money and a car (Db-€165–225, higher prices are for weekends, river views, and balconies, extra adult bed-€70, extra bed for kids ages 12–18-€45, extra bed for kids ages 7–11-€30, kids under age 7 free, elevator, non-smoking rooms, free Internet access and Wi-Fi, indoor pool and sauna, dressy restaurant, free parking, Schlossberg 47, tel. 06741/8020, fax 06741/802-802, www.schloss-rheinfels.de, info@schloss-rheinfels.de).

$$ Hotel am Markt, well-run by Herr and Frau Velich, is rustic and a good deal, with all the modern comforts. It features a hint of antler with a pastel flair, 18 bright rooms, and a good restaurant. It's a good value and a stone's throw from the boat dock and train station (S-€40, Sb-€50, standard Db-€65, bigger riverview Db-€80, cheaper March–mid-April and Oct, closed Nov–Feb, Markt 1, tel. 06741/1689, fax 06741/1721, www.hotel-am-markt-sankt-goar.de, hotel.am.markt@gmx.de).

$$ Rhein Hotel, two doors away and run by the Velichs' energetic son Gil (a trained chef), has 10 rooms of similar quality and its own restaurant (Sb-€50, Db-€65–85, higher price is for Rhine-view rooms with balcony, non-smoking, free Wi-Fi at reception, closed mid-Nov–Feb, Heerstrasse 71, tel. 06741/981-240, fax 06741/981-267, www.rheinhotel-st-goar.de, info@rheinhotel-st-goar.de).

$ Hotel Hauser, across the square from Hotel am Markt, is another good deal, warmly run by another Frau Velich. Its 12 simple rooms sit over a fine restaurant (S-€23, D-€46, Db-€54, great Db with Rhine-view balconies-€58, these prices promised with this book and cash through 2010, cash preferred, à la carte half-pension–€14, free Wi-Fi in lounge, Heerstrasse 77, tel. 06741/333, fax 06741/1464, www.hotelhauser.de, hotelhauser@t-online.de).

$ Frau Kurz offers St. Goar's best B&B, renting three delightful rooms (sharing 2.5 bathrooms) with bathrobes, a break-

fast terrace, garden, fine view, and homemade marmalade (S–€28, D–€48, 2-night minimum, D–€46 if you stay at least 4 nights, cash only, non-smoking, free and easy parking, honor your reservation or call to cancel, Ulmenhof 11, tel. & fax 06741/459, www .gaestehaus-kurz.de, jeanette .kurz@superkabel.de). It's a memorably steep five-minute hike from the train station: Exit left from the station, take an immediate left at the yellow phone booth, pass under the tracks, go up the stairs, and follow the zigzag path, turning right through an archway onto Ulmenhof; #11 is just past tower.

$ St. Goar Hostel, the big beige building down the hill from the castle, rents 18 doubles and piles of beds in 4- to 10-bed dorms. It has a well-run, strong, institutional atmosphere with a 22:30 curfew (but you can borrow the key) and hearty €6 dinners (dorm beds–€15, D–€36, includes breakfast, non-members–€3.10 extra, non-smoking, expensive Wi-Fi, all ages welcome, open all day, Bismarckweg 17, tel. 06741/388, fax 06741/2869, st-goar @diejugendherbergen.de). It's a fairly level 10-minute walk from the train station: Veer left and go all the way down narrow red-brick Oberstrasse, then turn left through the underpass and make an immediate right on Bismarcksweg, following the red *Jugendherberge* signs.

Eating in St. Goar

Hotel am Markt serves tasty traditional meals with plenty of game and fish (specialties include marinated roast beef and homemade cheesecake) at fair prices with good atmosphere and service (€9–16 main dishes, March–Oct daily 8:00–21:00, closed Nov–Feb, Markt 1, tel. 06741/1689).

Schlosshotel Rheinfels is your Rhine splurge, with an incredible view terrace in an elegant, dressy setting. As it's at the hilltop castle, you'll have to hike, taxi, or drive up (€19–24 main dishes, €36 three-course fixed-price meals, daily 12:00–14:00 & 18:30–21:00, call to reserve a window table, tel. 06741/8020; see also hotel listing). Their downstairs **Burgschänke** has no view, but is family-friendly and cheaper (€9–12 main dishes, Sun–Thu 11:00–18:00, Fri–Sat 11:00–21:00, tel. 06741/802-806).

Other Options: St. Goar has a couple of Italian eateries, and the grocery has plenty for a picnic to enjoy on the riverside park. For more restaurants, take the quick train to Bacharach, which leaves and returns hourly (last train at 22:00).

MOSEL VALLEY

Cochem • Burg Eltz • Beilstein

The misty Mosel is what some visitors hope the Rhine will be—peaceful, sleepy, romantic villages slipped between impossibly steep vineyards and the river; fine wine; a sprinkling of castles (Burg Eltz is tops); and lots of friendly small pensions. Boat, train, and car traffic here is a trickle compared to the roaring Rhine. While the swan-speckled Mosel moseys 300 miles from France's Vosges mountain range to Koblenz (where it dumps into the Rhine), the most scenic piece of the valley lies between the towns of Bernkastel-Kues and Cochem. I'd savor only this section. Cochem and Trier (see next chapter) are easy day trips from each other (45–60 minutes by train, 55 miles by car). Cochem is the handiest home base, unless you have a car and want the peace of Beilstein.

Getting Around the Mosel Valley

By Train and Bus: Fast trains zip you between Koblenz, Cochem, Bullay, and Trier in a snap. Other destinations require changing to a slow train or bus. Beilstein is a 20-minute ride on bus #716 from Cochem (about hourly Mon–Fri, 3–4/day on weekends, last bus leaves between 18:00 and 19:00, €3.05). Burg Eltz is a scenic 1.5-hour hike or €20 taxi ride from the tiny Moselkern train station (or a €40 taxi ride from Cochem). For bus times, pick up printed schedules at train stations and TIs, or check the regional transit website (http://vrminfo.de) or Germany's train timetable (http://bahn.hafas.de/bin/query.exe/en).

By Boat: Thanks to its many locks, Mosel cruises feel more like a canal-boat ride than the cruises on the mighty Rhine. The Kolb Line has the most frequent departures and allows you to cruise the most scenic stretch of the Mosel (tel. 02673/1515, www.moselfahrplan.de). A simple and fun outing is the one-hour cruise between **Cochem** and **Beilstein,** passing through the Fankel lock (4–5/day in each direction May–Oct, weekends only in April, no boats off-season, first departure from Cochem at about 10:30, last departure from Beilstein at about 17:30, €11 one-way, €14 round-trip). Another option is the boat in the other direction (downstream) from **Cochem** to **Treis-Karden** (3/day daily July–Oct, Wed and Sat–Sun only May–June, 45 min, €9 one-way, €11 round-trip). From Treis-Karden, you can get to Burg Eltz via a long hike (2 hours, steep in places), train-and-hike combination, or a taxi ride, though it's much easier to reach Burg Eltz from the Moselkern train station. Kolb also runs one-hour **sightseeing cruises** and two-hour **dancing cruises** from Cochem (€9 sightseeing cruises 5/day April–Oct; €15 dancing cruises with live music daily at 20:15 mid-July–Aug, Tue and Sat only May–mid-July and Sept–Oct).

The KD (Köln–Düsseldorfer) line sails the lower Mosel, between **Cochem** and **Koblenz,** but only once a day in each direction (€24.90 one-way, daily mid-June–Sept, Fri–Mon only May–mid-June, none in winter, Koblenz to Cochem 9:45–15:00, Cochem to Koblenz 15:40–20:00; free with a German railpass or any Eurailpass that covers Germany, but uses up a day of a flexipass; tel. in Cochem 02671/980-023, www.k-d.com).

In early to mid-June, the Mosel locks close for 10 days of annual maintenance, and none of the boats listed here runs.

By Car: The easygoing Mosel Wine Route turns anyone into a relaxed Sunday driver. Pick up a local map at a TI or service station. Two-lane roads run along both riverbanks. While riverside roads are a delight, the river valley is very windy. Shortcuts overland can "cut the corners" and save you serious time—especially between Burg Eltz and Beilstein (see page 384) and if you're driving between the Mosel and the Rhine (note the Brodenbach–Boppard shortcut). Both Koblenz and Trier have car-rental agencies.

By Bike: Biking along the Mosel is the rage among Germans. You can rent bikes in most Mosel towns (I've listed options in both Cochem and Beilstein). A fine bike path follows the river from Koblenz to Zell (with some bits sharing the road with cars). Allow one hour between Cochem and Beilstein. Many pedal one-way, then relax on a return cruise or train ride.

By Ferry: About a dozen car-and-passenger ferries *(Fähre)*

Mosel Valley

cross the Mosel between Koblenz and Trier. These are marked *AF* for auto and *PF* for pedestrian on the *Moselle Wine Road/Mosellauf* brochure.

By Air: The confusingly named Frankfurt Hahn Airport, a popular hub for low-fare airlines such as Ryanair, is actually near the Mosel (www.hahn-airport.de). You can ride a bus from the airport to Bullay (€6.55, 2–4/day, 45 min; then 10-min train ride from Bullay to Cochem) or use the subsidized taxi service (Cochem to airport-€9.50/person, arrange 24 hours in advance, www.vuag.de /airporthahn or www.5c5.de, email them at fax@5c5.de).

Helpful Hints

Wine Festivals: Throughout the Mosel region on summer weekends and during the fall harvest, wine festivals with oompah bands, dancing, and colorful costumes are powered by good food and wine. You'll find a wine festival in some nearby village any weekend, June through September. The tourist season lasts from April through October. Things close down tight through the winter.

Carry Cash: Be prepared to pay cash for nearly everything in the Mosel Valley, including food, hotels, and transportation.

Helpful Guidebook: Look for the booklet *The Castles of the Moselle* (€3.80, at local TIs), with information on castles from Koblenz to Trier (including Burg Eltz, Cochem, and Metternich in Beilstein). The booklet not only has historical and structural information, but also some drawings of what the now-ruined castles looked like originally.

Cochem

With a majestic castle and picturesque medieval streets, Cochem is the hub of the middle Mosel. With 6,000 inhabitants, it's a larger, more bustling town than Beilstein, Bacharach, or St. Goar. Duck into a damp wine cellar to sample the local white wine (*Weinprobe* means "wine-tasting"). Stroll pleasant paths along the idyllic riverbank, play life-size chess, or just grab a bench and watch Germany at play. River-cruise passengers clog the old town during the day, but evenings are peaceful.

Orientation to Cochem

(area code: 02671)

MOSEL VALLEY

Tourist Information

The information-packed TI is by the bridge at the main bus stop. Most of the pamphlets (free map with town walk, town history flier) are kept behind the desk—ask. Their thorough 24-hour room listing in the window comes with a free phone connection. The TI also has information on special events, wine-tastings held by local vintners, public transportation to Burg Eltz, and area hikes. You can also pick up the informative €3 *Mosellauf* brochure or the cartoony €1 *Moselle Wine Road* map (July–Oct Mon–Sat 9:00–17:00, Sun 10:00–12:00; May–June Mon–Fri 9:00–17:00, Sat 9:00–15:00, closed Sun; Nov–April Mon–Fri 9:00–13:00 & 14:00–17:00, closed Sat–Sun; tel. 02671/60040, www.cochem.de).

Arrival in Cochem

By Train: Cochem's train station has no lockers, but you can leave your bags at the Taxi-Zentrale storefront (€2/day, daily 9:00–18:00, to the right as you exit the station at Bahnhofsvorplatz 3). Make a hard right out of the station and walk about 10 minutes along cobbled Ravenéstrasse to the TI and bus station (both on your left, before the bridge). To get to the main square (Markt) and colorful medieval town center, continue under the bridge (€0.30 WC), then angle right and follow Bernstrasse.

By Car: Drivers can park in the multi-story garage just up Endertstrasse from the bridge, or in a lot behind the train station (€1.50/day, reach it by circling around on Ravenéstrasse and Pinnerstrasse).

Helpful Hints

Internet Access: The very pleasant **Espresso I-O** café has two terminals (€1/15 min, €3.50/hr, also has Wi-Fi, Mon–Fri 7:00–18:00, Sat 8:00–18:00, Sun 10:00–18:00, between TI and train station at Ravenéstrasse 18–20). After 18:00, head for the **Log-In Netzwerk Café** at Brückenstrasse 4, just before the railroad underpass (€4/hr, daily 10:00–24:00, ages 16 and over only).

Bike Rental: Radsport Schrauth, between the station and TI, is run by serious cyclists, with a good selection and helpful service (€5/half-day, €7/day, €10/day for mountain bikes, Mon–Fri 9:30–18:00, Sat 9:00–13:00, Sun only May–Oct 10:00–12:00, arrange weekend drop-off time, leave driver's license for deposit, Ravenéstrasse 20, tel. 02671/7974). Consider taking a bike on the boat or train and riding back.

Festival: Cochem's biggest wine festival is held the last weekend in August (Aug 26–30 in 2010). High season for wine aficionados lasts from August through October.

Sights in Cochem

Cochem Castle (Reichsburg Cochem)—This pretty, pointy castle on a hill above town is the work of overly imaginative

19th-century restorers. It can only be visited on a tour (€4.50; follow one of the frequent 40-min German tours while reading English explanation sheets, or gather 12 English speakers and call a day ahead to schedule an English tour; mid-March–mid-Nov daily from 9:00, last tour at 17:00, fewer tours mid-Nov–Dec, closed Jan–mid-March, tel. 02671/255, www.reichsburg-cochem .de). Below the entrance, the resident falconer frequently shows off his flock; check the notice at the gate to see if the birds are in fine feather (€3.50, 40-min show, Tue–Sun at 11:00, 13:00, 14:30, and 16:00, no shows Mon, look for *Falknerei* sign, mobile 0160-9912-7380).

Getting There: From the old town's main square (Markt), the castle is a very scenic 25-minute walk up a mostly gentle slope: Look for the red "A" hanging over Herrenstrasse, and head down it until it veers left to meet Burgfrieden Street, marked by the helpful man pointing to the castle; from there, the path is easy to follow. If you've already *probed* a little *Wein* and would rather ride up, consider the shuttle bus that runs to the castle from the bus station (next to the TI)—though you still have to walk the last 10 minutes uphill (€2 one-way, 1–3/hr, May–Oct only, first bus up at 10:30, last bus down at 17:48, look for *Reichsburg Shuttle-Bus* sign at bus station).

Chairlift and Hikes—For great views, ride the *Sesselbahn* chairlift, which ascends the hill on the opposite side of town from the castle (€4.30 one-way, €5.80 round-trip, late March–mid-Nov 10:00–18:00, closed off-season, tel. 02671/989-065, www .cochemer-sesselbahn.de). There's a reasonably priced restaurant at the top, along with a short, rocky path that leads to the Pinnerkreuz overlook. Instead of riding to the top, you can scramble up the narrow path under the lift for 20 minutes of heart-pounding, aerobic excitement. Or take the trail up to the same point from behind the train station (find trailhead behind station parking lot). For the best of all worlds, ride the lift up, take in the view from the restaurant, then follow the path to the station *(Bahnhof)*, down through the forest and then the vineyards to a wine-tasting at Weingut Rademacher.

Wine-Tasting—At **Weingut Rademacher,** behind the train station, you can taste four local wines for €2.90. There's no charge for tasting if you buy at least three bottles or are staying in their rooms (normally open Mon–Sat 9:00–20:00, Sun 9:00–13:00, different hours during festivals, call ahead to confirm, Pinnerstrasse 10, tel. 02671/4164, www.weingut-rademacher.de; they also rent rooms—see "Sleeping in Cochem," later). Other wine cellars in town also offer tastings. For a unique treat, look for the Roter-Weinbergs-Pfirsich Likör—a local cordial made from the small, tart "red peaches" that are unique to the Mosel Valley.

If you have a car, consider going upriver to **Zell,** famous for its Schwarze Katze ("Black Cat") wine. English-speaking Peter Weis runs **F. J. Weis** winery and gives a clever, entertaining, and free tour of his 40,000-bottle-per-year wine cellar. The tour usually runs daily at 17:00, but it's important to call ahead to reserve a spot. Buying a bottle or two helps keep this fine tour going (open April–mid-Nov daily 10:30–18:00, usually closed at lunchtime, closed mid-Nov–March except with advance notice, tel. 06542/41398, mobile 0172-780-7153, www.weingut-fjweis.de, f.j.weis@t-online.de). A blue flag marks his *Weinkeller,* south of the town of Zell. It's 200 yards past the bridge toward Bernkastel, riverside at Notenau 30. Peter also rents two luxurious apartments with kitchen facilities (Db-€60, less for 2 or more nights, extra person-€12, breakfast-€7).

Swimming, Tennis, and Golf—Cochem's Moselbad and Freizeit Zentrum offers an array of family-friendly activities: an indoor wave pool, an outdoor pool, a sauna, tennis courts, and mini-golf. The downside: It's 30 minutes on foot from the center of town (indoor pool-€7.70/3 hrs, Tue–Fri 10:00–22:00, Sat–Sun 10:00–19:00, closed Mon; other activities have different hours and prices; 10 min beyond youth hostel at Moritzburger Strasse 1, tel. 02671/97990, www.moselbad.de).

Cruise—The Kolb Line offers one-hour sightseeing cruises and schmaltzy two-hour "Tanz Party" dancing cruises with live music (see "Getting Around the Mosel Valley," page 370).

Sightseeing Train—A little yellow **tourist train** leaves from under the bridge at the TI and does a 25-minute sightseeing loop through town. Since the commentary is only in German (ask for English flier), and Cochem is such a pedestrian-friendly town anyway, this is worth it only if you're bored and lazy (€4.80, includes a glass of wine, 1–2/hr, May–Oct daily 10:00–17:00, doesn't run Nov–April).

Sleeping in Cochem

(area code: 02671)

Cochem is a good base for train travelers. Weingut Rademacher is a five-minute walk from the train station; all the other listings are within a 10- to 15-minute walk. August is very tight, with various festivals and generally inflated prices. Cochem has no launderette.

$$$ Hotel Lohspeicher, an upscale-rustic hotel just off the main square on a street with tiny steps, is for those willing to pay a bit extra for quality lodgings in the thick of things. Its nine high-ceilinged rooms have modern comforts (Sb-€60, Db-€90–114, prices depend on room size, includes big breakfast in a fine stone-and-timber room, elevator, free Wi-Fi, fancy restaurant, parking-€6/day, closed Feb, Obergasse 1, tel. 02671/3976, fax 02671/1772, www.lohspeicher.de, service@lohspeicher.de, Ingo).

$$$ Hotel am Hafen, across the bridge from the TI, offers views over the river to Cochem amidst a mellow atmosphere. Some of the 20 rooms have balconies (Sb-€70–85, Db-€85, slightly nicer Db-€108, deluxe Db-€120, €10 less Nov–June or for 2 nights, free Internet access and Wi-Fi, Uferstrasse 3, tel. 02671/97720, fax 02671/977-227, www.hotel-am-hafen.de, hotel-am-hafen .cochem@t-online.de).

$$ Weingut Rademacher rents six beautiful ground-floor rooms, which share a TV room with a fridge and microwave. Wedged between vineyards and train tracks, with a pleasant garden, it's a great value. Charming hostess Andrea and her husband Hermann own the vineyards behind the house and will happily show you the wine cellar (Sb-€32, Db on train side-€53, Db on vineyard side-€59, cheaper for 3 nights, family deals, non-smoking, free parking; exit station at rear and walk diagonally across the municipal parking lot to Pinnerstrasse 10—see map on website;

Sleep Code

(€1 = about $1.40, country code: 49)

S = Single, **D** = Double/Twin, **T** = Triple, **Q** = Quad, **b** = bathroom, **s** = shower only. Unless otherwise noted, credit cards are accepted, English is spoken, and breakfast is included.

To help you sort easily through these listings, I've divided the rooms into three categories based on the price for a standard double room with bath:

$$$ Higher Priced—Most rooms €75 or more.
$$ Moderately Priced—Most rooms between €50-75.
$ Lower Priced—Most rooms €50 or less.

tel. 02671/4164, fax 02671/91341, www.weingut-rademacher.de, info@weingut-rademacher.de). This place also offers wine-tastings to guests and non-guests alike (described earlier, under "Sights in Cochem").

$ Haus Andreas has 10 clean rooms at fair prices in the old town (Sb-€25–30, Db-€38–42, Tb-€57–63, prices vary by length of stay, cash only, free parking, Schlossstrasse 9, reception is often across the street in shop at #16, tel. 02671/1370 or 02671/5155, fax 02671/603-808, www.hausandreas.de, best to reserve by fax, kind Frau Pellny speaks a little English). From the main square, take Herrenstrasse (go straight if coming from the station); after a block, angle right up the steep hill on Schlossstrasse.

$ Gasthaus zum Fröhlichen Weinberg, also in the old town, is a relaxed jumble of nine inexpensive rooms, some with low ceilings and tiny bathrooms. It's run by a mother-and-daughter team (Sb-€23.50, Db-€47, ask about family rooms, lower prices for longer stays, cash only, lots of stairs, Schlaufstrasse 11, tel. 02671/4193, fax 02671/917-559, www.zum-froehlichen-weinberg .de, weinberg-cochem@t-online.de). From the main square, go up Oberbachstrasse and then go left up tiny Schlaufstrasse.

Hostel: Cochem's **$ hostel** is a huge, family-friendly complex just across the river from the train station, with 146 beds, picnic tables, grill pit, playground, game room, bar, restaurant, and a sundeck over the Mosel (dorm bed-€20, Db-€51, €3 more for non-members, includes sheets and breakfast, half- and full-board options available, fills up—reserve in advance, Klottener Strasse 9, tel. 02671/8633, fax 02671/8568, www.diejugendherbergen.de /cochem, cochem@diejugendherbergen.de). From the train station, walk straight down to the river, turn left, and use the stairway to cross the modern bridge to the hostel.

Eating in Cochem

Zum Stüffje, in the old town, is a traditional half-timbered *Weinstube* with €10–24 main dishes and €9 veggie options (Wed–Mon 11:30–14:00 & 17:30–21:00, closed Tue, Oberbachstrasse 14, enter on side street, tel. 02671/7260).

Gaststätte Noss is one of several restaurants along the riverside promenade. It's open later than most and supplies meat from its own butcher shop—a plus in Germany. Don't confuse it with the hotel of the same name (€10–14 main dishes; Easter–Oct Fri–Wed 10:00–22:00, also open Thu July–Oct only; Nov–Easter Fri–Wed 10:00–15:00 & 17:30–22:00, closed Thu; Moselpromenade 4, tel. 02671/7067).

Alte Gutschänke, better known as "Arthur's place," is where locals go for a glass of wine in a cozy cellar. Seating is at long, wooden, get-to-know-your-neighbor tables (extensive wine list and basic pub food, Easter–Oct Tue–Fri from 18:00, Sat–Sun from 14:00, closed Mon and in winter, just uphill from the old town's Markt square at Schlossstrasse 6, tel. 02671/8950).

Picnics: The **Diewald supermarket** is at Ravenéstrasse 33, between the train station and TI; enter from the side lane (Mon–Fri 7:30–20:00, Sat 8:00–18:00, closed Sun).

Cochem Connections

From Cochem by Train to: Moselkern (for hike to Burg Eltz; hourly, 20 min), **Trier** (2/hr, 45–60 min), **Frankfurt Airport** (hourly, 2–2.5 hrs, change in Koblenz and sometimes Mainz), **Köln** (hourly, 1.75–2.25 hrs, most change in Koblenz), **Bacharach** (hourly, 1.5 hrs, change in Koblenz), **Rothenburg** (every 1–2 hrs, 5 hrs, 3–4 changes), **Berlin** (roughly hourly, 6–7 hrs, 1–3 changes), **Paris** (hourly, 4–5 hrs, best to transfer once in Saarbrücken or Luxembourg).

Train info: tel. 0180-599-6633 (€0.14/min). Bus info: tel. 02671/8976.

Burg Eltz

My favorite castle in all of Europe—worth ▲▲▲—lurks in a mysterious forest. It's been left intact for 700 years, and is decorated and furnished throughout much as it was 500 years ago. Thanks

to smart diplomacy, clever marriages, and lots of luck, Burg Eltz was never destroyed (it survived one five-year siege). It's been in the Eltz family for 850 years. The scenic 1.5-hour walk up the Elz Valley to the castle makes a great half-day outing if you're staying anywhere along the Mosel—and a worthwhile day trip if you're staying on the Rhine.

Elz is the name of a stream that runs past the castle through a deep valley before emptying into the Mosel. The first record of a *Burg* (castle) on the Elz is from 1157. By about 1490, the castle looked like it does today, with the homes of three big landlord families gathered around a tiny courtyard within one formidable fortification. Today, the excellent 45-minute tour winds you through two of those homes, while the third is still the residence of the castellan (the man who maintains the castle). This is where members of the Eltz family stay when they're not at one of their other feudal holdings. The elderly countess of Eltz—whose family goes back 33 generations here (you'll see a photo of her family)—enjoys flowers. Each week for 40 years, she's had grand arrangements adorn the public castle rooms.

It was a comfortable castle for its day: 80 rooms made cozy by 40 fireplaces and wall-hanging tapestries. Many of its 20 toilets were automatically flushed by a rain drain. The delightful **chapel** is on a lower floor. Even though "no one should live above God," this chapel's placement was acceptable because it filled a bay window, which flooded the delicate Gothic space with light. The three families met—working out common problems as if sharing a condo—in the large "conference room." A carved jester and a rose look down on the big table, reminding those who gathered that they were free to discuss anything ("fool's freedom"—jesters could say anything to the king), but nothing discussed could leave the room (the "rose of silence"). In the **bedroom,** have fun with the suggestive decor: the jousting relief carved into the canopy, and the fertile and phallic figures hiding in the lusty green wall paintings.

Near the exit, the **treasury** fills the four higgledy-piggledy floors of a cellar with the precious, eccentric, and historic mementos of this family that once helped elect the Holy Roman Emperor and, later, owned a sizable chunk of Croatia (Habsburg favors). The silver and gold work—some of Germany's best—is worth a close look with the help of an English flier.

The castle is undergoing a much-needed renovation over the next few years, which will leave it with iron corseting to help it stand strong, and climate control to better preserve its many treasures. Although scaffolding mars the majesty of its exterior, the tour is as good as ever.

Cost, Hours, Information: €8 castle entry (includes guided tour and treasury, credit cards accepted), April–Oct daily from 9:30, last tour departs at 17:30, closed Nov–March. Pick up the free English descriptions at entry. Tel. 02672/950-500, www.burg -eltz.de, burg@eltz.org.

Tours: The only way to see the castle is with a 45-minute tour (included in entry price). Guides speak English and thoughtfully collect English-speakers into their own tours—well worth waiting for (30-minute wait at most; visit treasury in the meantime). In early spring and late fall, call ahead to see when an English tour is expected. In a pinch, you can also join a German tour (with helpful English fact sheets, €0.60).

Eating: The café serves soups and bratwurst-and-fries cuisine for €4–5 (April–Oct daily 9:30–17:30, cash only, no nearby ATM).

Burg Eltz Area

N

1 MILE
1 KM
P PARKING

TO E-44
AUTOBAHN

MÜNSTERMAIFELD

METTERNICH

TO
KOBLENZ

HATZEN-
PORT

WIERSCHEIM

LASSERG

ELZBACH
CREEK

BURG
ELTZ

SHUTTLE
VANS OR
10-MIN
WALK

RIVER

BURGEN

1.5 HOUR TRAIL
THRU WOODS

TREIS-
KARDEN
STATION

KARDEN

MOSELKERN

TO
COCHEM
+ TRIER

B-416

MOSEL

B-49

TREIS

DCH

TO
BURG
ELTZ

THIS INSET
NOT TO SCALE

DIRT
PATH

ELZBACH
CREEK

HOTEL
RINGELSTEINER
MÜHLE

TO
KOBLENZ &
BURG ELTZ
VIA ROAD

PAVED
ROAD

MOSELKERN
TRAIN
STATION

MAIN ROAD
B-416

CHURCH

RIVER

TO
COCHEM
& TRIER

MOSEL

DCH

MOSEL VALLEY

Getting to Burg Eltz

While the castle isn't served by public transportation, it's a pleasant 1.5-hour walk from the nearest train station. The footpath to Burg Eltz from the little village of Moselkern is not difficult, and it's the most fun and scenic way to visit the castle. If the weather is poor or you'd prefer not to walk, take a taxi. Cars (and taxis) park in a lot near, but not quite at, Burg Eltz. From the lot, hike 10 minutes downhill to the castle or wait (10 minutes at most) for the red castle shuttle bus (€1.50 each way).

Hiking from Moselkern

The hike between Moselkern train station and Burg Eltz runs through a magical pine forest, where sparrows carry crossbows, and maidens, disguised as falling leaves, whisper "watch out." You can do the hike in 70 minutes at a steady clip, but allow an extra 20 minutes or so to enjoy the scenery. The trail is mostly gentle, except for a few uneven parts that are slippery when wet and the steep flight of stairs leading up to the castle at the end. But the overall rise from the river to the castle is less than 400 feet.

To start the hike, take the slow milk-run train (hourly) to Moselkern from Cochem (20 min, €3.70) or Koblenz (30 min). The Moselkern train station is unstaffed, and has no lockers, phones, or taxis. The path up to the castle begins at the other end of Moselkern village. To reach this path, turn right from the station along Oberstrasse. Cross the intersection with Weinbergsstrasse and continue straight along narrow Oberstrasse, passing the village church on your right after about five minutes. Keep going straight a few houses past the church; then, as the street ends, turn right through the underpass. On your left is the Elzbach stream that you'll follow all the way up to the castle. Follow the road straight along the stream through a mostly residential neighborhood. Where the road crosses the stream on a stone bridge, take either the footpath (stay right) or the bridge—they join up again later.

After about a 30-minute walk from the train station, the road ends at the parking lot of the Hotel Ringelsteiner Mühle. Stay to the right of the hotel and continue upstream along the easy-to-follow trail, which starts out paved but soon changes to dirt—from here, it's another 45 minutes to the castle.

Hiking from Karden (with Optional Boat Trip)

If you don't mind a longer hike, consider a boat ride to the village of Karden, then walk to Burg Eltz from there. (Karden is also on the train line between Cochem and Moselkern.) This two-hour hike is steep in places, and harder to follow and less shady than the hike from Moselkern.

Kolb Line riverboat cruises run between Cochem and Karden three times a day (described on page 371). Make sure to disembark the boat in Karden (not in Treis, across the river). If you come by train, get off at the Treis-Karden stop, which also serves the village of Treis. The path from Karden to Burg Eltz starts at the far end of Karden village, beyond the white-towered St. Castor's church (follow *Burg Eltz* signs). Get a trail map (available locally), and be prepared for full sun when the hike travels through open fields.

If you need to **store luggage** before the hike, the elegant Schloss-Hotel Petry, across from the Treis-Karden station, is happy to guard your bags if you eat at their restaurant (€10–22 main dishes, lunch daily 11:30–14:15, St. Castorstrasse 80, tel. 02672/9340, www.schloss-hotel-petry.de).

To ride the boat but avoid the lengthy hike to Burg Eltz, you can either hop the hourly train from Treis-Karden to Moselkern, and hike from there (described earlier); or take a taxi from Karden to the castle (described next).

By Taxi

You can taxi to the castle from **Cochem** (30 min, about €40 one-way for up to 4 people, Cochem taxi tel. 02671/8080), **Moselkern** (€20, taxi tel. 02672/1407), or **Karden** (€25, taxi tel. 02672/1407). Even with a taxi, you still have a 10-minute walk from the parking lot to the castle. If you're planning to taxi from Moselkern, call ahead and ask the taxi to meet your train at Moselkern station. Consider taxiing up to Burg Eltz and then enjoying the hike downhill back to the train station in Moselkern.

By Car

Be careful: Signs direct drivers to two different "Burg Eltz" parking lots—some deceptively lodge drivers far from the castle, while others take you right there. From Koblenz, leave the river at Hatzenport, following the white *Burg Eltz* signs through the towns of Münstermaifeld and Wierschem. From Cochem, follow the *Münstermaifeld* signs from Moselkern. The castle parking lot (€1.50/day, daily 9:00–18:30) is just over a mile past Wierschem. (Note that the *Eltz* signs at Moselkern lead to Hotel Ringelsteiner Mühle and the trailhead for the 45-minute hike to the castle. To drive directly to the castle, ignore the *Eltz* signs until you reach Münstermaifeld.)

Drive/Hike Combo: If you're traveling by car but would enjoy the path up to the castle, you can drive to Moselkern, follow the *Burg Eltz* signs up the Elz Valley, park at the Hotel Ringelsteiner Mühle (€2, buy ticket from machine), and enjoy the 45-minute hike up to the castle from there (described earlier).

Shortcut to Beilstein: If driving from Burg Eltz to Beilstein, you'll save 30 minutes with this shortcut: Cross the river at Treis-Karden, go through town, and bear right at the swimming pool (direction: Bruttig–Fankel). This overland route deposits you in Bruttig, a scenic three-mile riverside drive from Beilstein.

Beilstein

Just upstream from Cochem is the quaintest of all Mosel towns. Cozy Beilstein (BILE-shtine) is Cinderella-land—touristy but tranquil, except for its territo-rial swans. Beilstein has zero food shops, zero ATMs (make sure to bring cash), one bus stop, one mailbox, and 180 residents who run about 30 guest houses and eateries. It's nicknamed the "Sleeping Beauty of the Mosel" because until about 1900, it was inaccessible except by boat.

Planning Your Time

Car travelers use Beilstein as a base, day-tripping from here to Cochem, Trier, Burg Eltz, and the Rhine. If you're staying in Cochem and using public transportation, you can day-trip to Beilstein: Take the bus to Beilstein, follow my self-guided walk up to the castle, have lunch, and then return by boat. While the town is peaceful and a delight in the evening, midday crowds in peak sea-son can trample all its charm and turn it into a human traffic jam.

Getting to Beilstein

Beilstein has no train station, but it's easy to reach from Cochem—either by **bus** (#716, about hourly Mon–Fri, 3–4/day on weekends, last bus leaves between 18:00 and 19:00, 20 min, €3, http://vrminfo. de), by **taxi** (€25), or by **river cruise** (4–5/day in each direction May–Oct, weekends only in April, no boats off-season, first depar-ture from Cochem at about 10:30, last departure from Beilstein at about 17:30, €11 one-way, €14 round-trip). If **driving,** you can park for free in any space you find along the riverside road.

Orientation to Beilstein

Beilstein has no TI, but there is an **information board** by the bus stop, and cafés and guest houses can give you town info.

Self-Guided Walk

Welcome to Beilstein

Explore the narrow lanes, ancient wine cellar, resident swans, and ruined castle by following this short walk.

• *Stand where the village hits the river.*

Beilstein's Riverfront: In 1963, the big road and the Mosel locks were built, making the river peaceful today. Before then, access to Beilstein was limited to a tiny one-way lane and the small ferry. The cables that tether the ferry once allowed the motorless craft to go back and forth, powered only by the current and an angled rudder. Since the river was tamed by locks, it has no current, and the ferry needs its motor. Today, the funky little ferry shuttles people (€1.30), bikes, and cars constantly (Easter–Oct daily 9:00–12:00 & 13:00–18:00, no ferries off-season).

The campground across the river is typical of German campgrounds—nearly all of its residents set up their trailers and tents at Easter and use them as summer homes until October, when the regular floods chase them away for the winter.

If you stood where you are now through the winter, you'd have cold water up to your crotch five times.

Look inland. The town was given market rights in 1310, and was essentially an independent city-state for centuries (back when there were 300 such petty kingdoms and dukedoms in what we now call "Germany"). The Earl of Beilstein ruled from his castle above town. He built the Altes Zollhaus in 1634 to levy tolls from river traffic. Today, the castle is a ruin, the last monk at the once-mighty monastery (see the big church high on the left) retired in 2009, and the town's economy is based only on wine and tourists.

Beilstein is so well-preserved because it was essentially inaccessible by road until about 1900. And its tranquility is a result of Germany's WWI loss, which cost the country the region of Alsace (now part of France). Before World War I, the Koblenz–Trier train line—which connects Alsace to Germany—was the busiest in the country, tunneling through the grape-laden hill across the river in what was the longest train tunnel in Germany. The construction of a supplemental line designed to follow the riverbank (like the lines that crank up the volume on the Rhine) was stopped in 1914, and since Alsace went to France in 1918, the new line no longer made any sense, and the plans were scuttled.

MOSEL VALLEY

• *Follow Bachstrasse into town. You'll notice blue plaques on the left marking the high-water* (Hochwasser) *points of historic floods. At the first corner (Weingasse), detour left to a picturesque corner.*

Town Center: In 1840, a quarter of the town's 300 inhabitants were Jewish. The synagogue (which dates from 1310) and the adjacent rabbi's home were at #13. The medallion above the door shows the Star of David embedded in the double-headed eagle of the Holy Roman Emperor, indicating that the Jews would be protected by the emperor. This was perhaps of some comfort, but not reliable. Of the town's many Jews, a majority left for the US in the late 1800s. By 1933, only one Jewish family was left in Beilstein to deal with the Nazis. There are no practicing Jews in town today.

• *Continue on this lane uphill, heading right, and then right again, with the church high above. You'll reach a long flight of stairs (marked* Klostertreppe*) that leads to the monastery.*

Although the last Carmelite monk just retired, Rome maintains a handsome but oversized-for-this-little-town Catholic church that runs a restaurant with a great view. It's a screwy situation that no one in the town was comfortable explaining to me.

Continue back to the main street. Bachstrasse ("Creek Street") continues straight inland through Beilstein, covering up the brook that once flowed through town, providing a handy disposal service 24/7. Today, Bachstrasse is lined by wine cellars. The only way for a small local vintner to make any decent money these days is to sell his wine directly to customers in inviting little places like these.

• *On the other side of Bachstrasse is the...*

Market Square (Marktplatz): For centuries, neighboring farmers sold their goods on Marktplatz. The *Zehnthaus* (tithe house) was the village IRS, where locals would pay one-tenth *(Zehnte)* of their produce to their landlord (either the Church or the earl). Pop into the Zehnthauskeller. Stuffed with peasants' offerings 400 years ago, it's now packed with vaulted medieval ambience. It's fun at night for candlelit wine-tasting, soup and cold cuts, and schmaltzy music (often live Fri and Sat). The adjacent Bürgerhaus (above the fountain) had nothing to do with medieval fast food. First the village church, then the residence of the *Bürger* (like a mayor), and later the communal oven and the village grade school, today it's *the* place for a town party or wedding (upstairs) and a venue for local craftspeople to show their goodies (below). Haus Lipmann (on the riverside, now a recommended hotel and restaurant) dates from 1727. It was built by the earl's family as a residence after the French destroyed his castle. Haus Lipmann's main dining hall was once the knights' hall.

• *The stepped lane leads uphill (past the Zehnthaus, follow signs for* Burgruine Metternich*) to...*

Beilstein's Castle: Beilstein once rivaled Cochem as the most powerful town on this part of the Mosel. Like so much around here, it was destroyed by the French in 1688. Its castle (officially named Burg Metternich) is a sorry ruin today, but those who make the steep 10-minute climb are rewarded with a postcard Mosel view and a chance to hike even higher to the top of its lone surviving tower (€2.50, Easter–Oct daily 9:00–18:00, closed Nov–Easter, view café/restaurant, tel. 02673/93639, www .burgmetternich.de). Every Easter weekend (Sat–Mon), the castle hosts a fun fair and medieval market.

MOSEL VALLEY

For more exercise and an even better view, exit through the turnstile at the rear of the castle and continue uphill 100 yards, where you'll find the ultimate "castle/river bend/carpets of vineyards" photo op. The derelict roadside vineyard is a sign of recent times—the younger generation is abandoning the family plots, opting out of all that hard winemaking work.

From this viewpoint, a surprising sight is 200 yards farther up the road: a small but evocative **Jewish cemetery** (*Jüdische Friedhof*). A small Jewish community in Koblenz maintains this lovely cemetery.

To reach the viewpoint and the cemetery without going through the castle, continue up the road past the castle entrance, then follow the signs for *Jüdische Friedhof.*

• *From here, you can return to the castle gate, ring the bell* (Klingel), *and show your ticket to get back in and retrace your steps; or continue on the road, which curves and leads downhill (a gravel path at the next bend on the left leads back into town).*

Activities in Beilstein

Biking and Boating—Boats come and go all day for extremely relaxing river trips (for details, see page 371). While scenic, these rides can take longer than you'd like because of the locks. I prefer a riverside bike ride (perhaps combined with a boat trip). Biking is very popular along the Mosel, and roads are accompanied by smooth and perfectly flat bike lanes. The lanes are separate from the car traffic, letting you really relax as you pedal through gorgeous riverside scenery. To rent a quality bike in Beilstein, visit **Herr Nahlen** (€7/day, daily 9:00–12:00, return bikes between 16:00 and 19:00, reservations smart for groups, Bachstrasse 47, tel. 02673/1840, www.fahrradverleih-in-beilstein.de).

Five-Hour Trip to Zell and Back: You could rent a bike in Beilstein, catch the 9:30 boat to Zell (2.5-hour ride), enjoy that pretty town, and cycle 15 miles back to Beilstein along the sleepy and windy riverside bike path.

Ninety-Minute Loop: For a shorter bike trip, ride the little ferry across the river from Beilstein, explore the campground, continue left past Poltersdorf, cycle under vineyards to Senhals, cross the bridge to Senheim, and return to Beilstein on the other side of the river. At the edge of Mesenich, leave the road and take the peaceful bike lane along the river, explore another campground, and head for Beilstein, with its castle in the distance encouraging you home.

Sleeping in Beilstein

(€1 = about $1.40, country code: 49, area code: 02673)
Many of Beilstein's hotels shut down from mid-November through March.

$$$ Hotel Haus Lipmann is your chance to live in a medieval mansion with hot showers and TVs. A prizewinner for atmosphere, it's been in the Lipmann family for 200 years. The creaky wooden staircase and the elegant dining hall, with long wooden tables surrounded by antlers, chandeliers, and feudal weapons, will get you in the mood for your castle sightseeing, but the riverside terrace may mace your momentum. There are six guest rooms in the main building and six larger rooms in an equally old building next door (Sb-€75–90, Db-€85–100, Tb-€105–125, Qb-€125–150, price depends on length of stay and day of week, usually €20 higher Fri–Sat, cash only, €15 half-board deals, free Internet access and Wi-Fi, closed Nov–April, Marktplatz 3, tel. 02673/1573, fax 02673/1521, www.hotel-haus-lipmann.com, hotel.haus.lipmann@t-online.de). The entire family—Marion (née Lipmann) and her husband Jonas Thölén, their hardworking son David, and his wife Anja—hustle for their guests.

$$$ Hotel Lipmann Am Klosterberg, run by Marion's brother Joachim and his wife Malene, is a big, modern place with 17 comfortable rooms at the extremely quiet top of town (Sb-€50, Db-€75–90, closed mid-Nov–Easter, elevator, no Internet access, Auf dem Teich 8, up the main street 200 yards inland, tel. 02673/1850, fax 02673/1287, www.hotel-lipmann.de, lipmann@t-online.de).

$$$ Hotel Lipmann Altes Zollhaus, run by Joachim Lipmann's daughter Julia, packs all the comforts into eight tight, bright riverfront rooms (same prices and contact details as Hotel Lipmann Am Klosterberg; adjoining restaurant Alte Stadtmauer, run by Joachim's daughter Kristina, is open daily 11:00–23:00, closed mid-Nov–Easter).

$$ Hotel Gute Quelle offers half-timbers, a good restaurant, and 13 inviting rooms, plus seven more in an annex across the street (Sb-€40, Db-€64, closed Dec–March, free Wi-Fi, Marktplatz 34, tel. 02673/1437, fax 02673/1399, www.hotel-gute-quelle.de, info @hotel-gute-quelle.de, helpful Susan speaks Irish).

The welcoming **$ Gasthaus Winzerschenke an der Kloster-treppe** is a great value, with five rooms right in the tiny heart of town at the bottom of the stairs to the cloister (Db-€50, bigger Db-€60, cash only, discount for 4-night stays, open weekends only Nov–Easter, free Internet access, go up main street and take second left onto Fürst-Metternich-Strasse, reception in restaurant, tel. 02673/1354, fax 02673/962-371, www.winzerschenke-beilstein.de, winzerschenke-beilstein@t-online.de, young and eager Stefanie and Christian Sausen).

Eating in Beilstein

You'll have no problem in Beilstein finding a characteristic dining room or a relaxing riverview terrace.

Restaurant Haus Lipmann serves good, fresh food with daily specials on a glorious, leafy riverside terrace. For a wonderful trip memory, enjoy a slow meal here while watching the lazy riverside action and the changing light on the distant vineyards (€8–19 main dishes, May–Oct daily 10:00–23:00, last meal order at 20:00, closed Nov–April).

The **Zehnthauskeller** on the Marktplatz is *the* place for wine-tasting, a light meal, and lively *Schlager* music (kitschy German folk-pop). Hang with old locals on holiday, sitting under a dark medieval vault (soup, *Flammkuchen*—German version of white pizza, €8–9 cold plates, Easter–Oct Tue–Sun 11:00–23:00, closed Mon and Nov–Easter, run by Joachim Lipmann's daughter Sabine).

The recommended **Hotel Gute Quelle** runs a popular restaurant (€10–20 main dishes, daily 11:00–21:00, closed Dec–March, Marktplatz 34).

TRIER

Germany's oldest city lies at the head of the scenic Mosel Valley, near the border with Luxembourg. An ancient Roman capital, Trier brags that it was inhabited by Celts for 1,300 years before Rome even existed. Today, Trier is thriving and feels very young. A short stop here offers you a look at Germany's oldest Christian church, one of its most enjoyable market squares, and its best Roman ruins.

Founded by Augustus in 16 B.C., Trier was a Roman town called Augusta Treverorum for 400 years. When Emperor Diocletian (who ruled A.D. 285–305) divided his overextended Roman Empire into four sectors, he made Trier the capital of the west: roughly modern-day Germany, France, Spain, and England. For most of the fourth century, this city of 80,000—with a four-mile wall, four great gates, and 47 round towers—was a favored residence of Roman emperors. Emperor Constantine lived here, spending lavishly on urban projects. As a military town in a godforsaken corner of the empire, Trier received lots of perks from Rome to make it livable for those assigned here. But when the last emperor checked out in A.D. 395, the money pretty much dried up, and that was the end of Trier's ancient glory days. In the late 400s, when Rome fell to the barbarians, so did Trier.

Roman Trier was much bigger than medieval Trier. The pedestrian center of town—containing nearly all of your sightseeing and browsing—is defined by the medieval wall (which encloses half the area the Roman wall did). Trier's Roman sights include the huge city gate (Porta Nigra), basilica, baths, and amphitheater. Trier's main draw is the chance to experience Germany's

Roman and early Christian history. If you're more interested in wine-tasting and scenery, stay elsewhere on the Mosel River (see previous chapter).

Orientation to Trier

(area code: 0651)

Tourist Information

Trier's cramped and busy TI is just through the Porta Nigra. The TI sells an easily readable map for €1.50, but cheapskates can squint at the free and sufficient small-print map. The TI also sells a useful little guide to the city called *Trier: History and Monuments* (€4). Also consider the booklet *Walking Tours Through Trier* (€3), which has little information on sights but a great map and proposed walking routes (Roman, medieval, Jewish, rainy day). The TI also offers tours (see "Tours in Trier," later) and a free room-booking service (May–Oct Mon–Sat 9:00–18:00, Sun 10:00–17:00; Nov–Dec and March–April Mon–Sat 9:00–18:00, Sun 10:00–15:00; Jan–Feb Mon–Sat 9:00–17:00, Sun 10:00–13:00; tel. 0651/978-080, www.trier.de).

Discount Deals: The **Trier Card** allows free use of city buses and roughly 25 percent discounts on city tours, museums, and Roman sights (€9, family-€19, valid for 3 days, sold at TI). Since the town is small and walkable, this is only a good deal if you'll be here for two or three days and plan to visit lots of sights. If you're visiting at least three Roman sights (including the Porta Nigra, Imperial Baths, Viehmarkt Baths, and amphitheater, but not the Archaeological Museum), buy the **Roman sights combo-ticket** instead (€6.20, family ticket-€14.80, each sight costs €2.10 individually or €5.10 for families—do the math and decide, available at participating sights).

Arrival in Trier

By Train: The *Reisezentrum* at the train station can answer your train-schedule questions and book tickets (Mon–Fri 6:50–19:15, Sat 8:30–17:15, Sun 10:30–18:15). The station also has lockers (€1.50–2.50), a WC (€0.50—coin needed), and bike rental (see "Helpful Hints," next). To reach the town center from the train station, walk 10 boring minutes and four blocks up Theodor-Heuss-Allee to the big black Roman gate (Porta Nigra), and turn left under the gate to find the TI. From here, the main pedestrian mall (Simeonstrasse) leads right to the sights: Market Square and the cathedral (a five-minute walk), and the basilica (five more minutes).

By Car: Drivers get off at Trier Verteilerkreis and follow signs to *Zentrum.* There's parking near the gate and TI.

Helpful Hints

Laundry: A well-maintained self-service launderette is just beyond Karl Marx's House (€7.50/load, daily 8:00–22:00, instructions in English, Brückenstrasse 19).

Internet Access: Arcor/ITS-Trier, across the busy intersection from the Porta Nigra, charges a low hourly rate (€1.50/hr, Mon–Fri 10:00–22:00, Sat–Sun 12:00–22:00, Porta Nigra Platz 4).

Bike Rental: A local citizens' group called **Bürgerservice** rents bikes for reasonable daily rates. Find them just off track 11 at the train station (€9/24 hrs, spiffy 27-gear bikes-€2 extra, show ID and leave €30 as deposit; mid-April–Oct daily 9:00–13:00 & 15:00–19:00; Nov–mid-April Mon–Fri 10:00–13:00 & 15:00–18:00, closed Sat–Sun; tel. 0651/148-856).

Tours in Trier

Walking Tours—The TI offers a €7 two-hour walking tour in English on Saturdays at 13:30 (May–Oct only), and can put you in touch with local guides who do private tours (€80/2 hrs, tel. 0651/978-0821).

Bus Tours—For a live guide and a big air-conditioned bus, take the one-hour tour offered by the TI (€7, May–Oct daily at 13:00 in English, at 11:00 and 12:00 in German, no tours Nov–April).

Tourist Train—If you're tired and want a city overview, consider riding the hokey little red-and-yellow tourist train, the Römer-Express, for its 35-minute loop of Trier's major old-town sights (€7, daily April–Oct 2/hr 10:00–18:00, daily March and Nov–Dec hourly 10:00–17:00, Jan–Feb may run Sat–Sun hourly 11:00–16:00—weather permitting, recorded narration in English, departs from TI, buy tickets from driver or at TI, tel. 0651/9935-9525, www.roemer-express.de).

Self-Guided Walk

Welcome to Trier

This fascinating walk, offering a taste of Trier old, new, and in-between, laces together the historic city's top sights.

• *Start at the...*

everyone knew it. Understandably paranoid, they needed fortified houses like this one. Look for the floating door a story above the present-day entrance. A wooden staircase to this door—once the only way in or out—could be pulled up when necessary.

• *Continue down the pedestrian street. As you walk, ignore street-level storefronts—instead, look up to appreciate the variety and richness of the town's architecture. Eventually you'll reach the...*

▲▲Market Square (Hauptmarkt)

Trier's Hauptmarkt is a people-filled swirl of fruit stands, flowers,

painted facades, and fountains (with a handy public WC). This is one of Germany's most in-love-with-life market squares.

For an orientation to the sights, go to the square's center-piece, a market cross, and stand on the side of the cross closest to the big gray-stone **cathedral** a block away. This cathedral (described later in more detail) was the seat of the archbishop. In medieval times, the cathedral was its own walled city, and the archbishop of Trier was one of the seven German electors who chose the Holy Roman Emperor. This gave the archbishop tremendous political, as well as spiritual, power.

The pink-and-white building (now an H&M clothing store) on the corner of the lane leading to the cathedral was a **palace** for the archbishop. Notice the seal above the door: a crown flanked by a crosier (representing the bishop's ecclesiastical power) and a sword (demonstrating his political might). This did not sit well with the townspeople of Trier. The square you're standing in was the symbolic battlefield of a centuries-long conflict between Trier's citizens and its archbishop.

The stone market **cross** (a replica of the A.D. 958 original, now in the City Museum) was the archbishop's way of bragging about the trading rights granted to him by King Otto the Great. This was a slap in the face to Trier's townspeople. They'd wanted Trier to be designated a "free imperial city," with full trading rights and beholden only to the Holy Roman Emperor, not a local prince or archbishop.

Look across the square. Facing the cathedral is the 15th-century **Town Hall** (Steipe). The people of Trier wanted a town hall, but the archbishop wouldn't allow it—so they built this "assembly hall" instead, with a knight on each second-story corner. The knight on the left, facing Market Square, has his mask up, watching over his people. The other knight, facing the cathedral and the archbishop, has his mask down and his hand on his sword, ready for battle.

Just below the knights are four brightly painted 16th-century statues of Christian figures nestled between the arches (right to left): St. Paul, with his sword, was patron saint of Trier's university in the 15th century. St. Peter, with his bushy beard and key, is the patron saint of Trier. St. Helena, Emperor Constantine's mom and a devout Christian, lived in Trier and brought many super relics here from the Holy Land, giving the town lasting importance. And St. James, with his staff and scallop shell, is the patron saint of pilgrims—a reminder that Trier was the staging point for northern European pilgrims heading south on the spiritual trek to Santiago de Compostela (in northwest Spain).

Elsewhere on the square are more indications of tension between the archbishop and the townsfolk. Look to the left, at the tall white steeple with yellow trim. This is the Gothic tower of the **Church of St. Gangolf,** the medieval townspeople's church and fire watchman's post. (From medieval times until the present day, a bell has rung nightly at 22:00, reminding local drunks to go home. When the automatic bell-ringer broke a few years back, concerned locals flooded the mayor with calls.) In 1507, Trier's mayor built this new Gothic tower to make the people's church higher than the cathedral. A Bible verse in Latin adorns the top in gold letters: "Stay awake and pray." In retaliation, the archbishop raised one tower of his cathedral (all he could afford). He topped it with a threatening message of his own, continuing the Town Hall's verse: "For you never know the hour when the Lord will come."

Look farther to the left, to the Renaissance **St. Peter's Fountain** (1595). This fountain symbolizes thoughtful city government, with allegorical statues of justice (sword and scale), fortitude (broken column), temperance (wine and water), and prudence (a snake and, formerly, a mirror—but since the mirror was stolen long ago, she's now empty-handed). The ladies represent idealized cardinal virtues—but notice the rude monkeys hiding on the column behind them, showing the naughty way things are really done. The recommended **Zum Domstein** restaurant is next to the fountain (described later, under "Eating in Trier").

The rest of the square is a textbook of architectural styles. Look for the Art Deco hotel that now houses a McDonald's (forced to keep its advertising low-key). The half-timbered houses at the north end of the square (toward the Porta Nigra) mark Trier's 14th-century Jewish ghetto. Judengasse ("Jews' Alley") led under these facades into a gated ghetto where 60 families earned enough from moneylending to buy protection from the archbishop. But the protection only went so far—in 1418 Trier's Jews were expelled. (They tried to collect interest owed them by the prince, but rather than pay up, he sent them packing.) The buildings lining Judengasse today, while quaint, date only from the 18th century.

• *When you're finished on the square, head down Sternstrasse to the...*

▲▲Cathedral (Dom)

This is the oldest Christian church in Germany. After Emperor Constantine legalized Christianity in the Roman Empire in A.D.

312, his mother, Helena (now a saint), allowed part of her palace in Trier to be used as the first church on this spot. In A.D. 326, to celebrate the 20th anniversary of his reign, Constantine began the construction of two great churches: St. Peter's in Rome and this huge cathedral in Trier—also called St. Peter's.

The cathedral itself is free (daily April–Oct 6:30–18:00, Nov–March 6:30–17:30, www.trierer-dom.de). The Dom Information Office (on the square facing the church) books German-language tours, provides services for Santiago de Compostela–bound pilgrims, and runs a gift shop (Mon–Sat 9:30–17:30, Sun 12:00–17:30, tel. 0651/979-9790, handy public WC).

Begin your visit in the large front **courtyard** of the cathedral. As you face the cathedral, look in the corner behind you and to your left (near the pink palace); you'll see a large patch of light-colored bricks in an L shape in the ground. The original Roman cathedral was more than four times its present size; these light-colored bricks mark one corner of this massive "double cathedral." (The opposite corner was at the back of the smaller Liebfrau church, waaay across the courtyard.) The plaque by the corner shows the floor plan of the original Roman cathedral (from A.D. 380).

The cathedral's mighty facade is 12th-century Romanesque. To the right is the more delicate 13th-century Gothic facade of the Liebfrau church (which dates from 1235 and claims to be the oldest Gothic church in Germany; closed for renovation through 2010).

As you walk toward the cathedral entrance, you'll pass an evocative bit of Roman scrap stone (just outside the door on the left). This was part of a 60-ton ancient granite column quarried near Frankfurt—one of four columns used in the fourth-century Roman church.

Enter the cathedral (€0.50 English info brochure in racks on right). The many altars lining the nave are dedicated not to saints, but to bishops. These ornate funeral altars were a

fashionable way for the powerful archbishop-electors to memo-
rialize themselves. Even the elaborate black-and-white altar at
the back of the church (above where you entered) is not a religious shrine, but a memorial for a single rich archbishop. (His
black 1354 tomb dominates the center of that chapel.)

The "pilgrim's walk" (the stairway to the right of the altar)
leads to the chapel at the far east end of the church that holds
the cathedral's most important relic: the supposed Holy Robe of
Christ, thought to have been found by St. Helena on a pilgrimage to Jerusalem (rarely on view, but you can see its reliquary;
look for photos of the robe itself as you approach, after the first
flight of stairs).

Midway along the "pilgrim's walk," you'll find the entrance
to the treasury (Schatzkammer), displaying huge bishops' rings,
medieval Bibles, St. Andrew's sandal (in a box topped with a
golden foot), and a holy nail supposedly from the Crucifixion
(€1.50, April–Oct Mon–Sat 10:00–17:00, Sun 12:30–17:00,
shorter hours in winter). At the base of the steps below the treasury, pause and look back up at the statues of St. Helena and
Emperor Constantine.

Down the stairs, the door on your immediate left marked
Kreuzgang leads to the peaceful 12th-century Domkreuzgang
cloister between the Dom and the Liebfrau church.

As you walk back toward the main door, notice the controversial modern (1972) paintings at the back of the church,
representing the Alpha (Paradise/Creation, to the left) and
the Omega (the Last Judgment, to the right). The archbishop
pushed this artwork through, arguing that a living church needs
contemporary art, and overriding objections from the congregation's conservative old guard.

Leaving the cathedral, go right, then turn down the first
street on your right (Windstrasse). As you walk with the
cathedral on your right, you'll be able to see the different eras
of its construction. The big red cube that makes up the back half
of the present-day cathedral is all that remains of the enormous,
original fourth-century Roman construction (at one time twice
as tall as what you see here). Arched bricks in the facade show
the original position of Roman windows and doors. Around
this Roman nucleus, chunks were grafted on over a millennium
and a half of architectural styles: the front half of the cathedral
facing the big courtyard, added in the 11th century; the choir
on the back, from the 12th century; and the transept and round
Baroque shrine on the far back, from the 18th century.

If you look at the original Roman construction squarely,
you'll see that it's not perfectly vertical. Locks were built along the
Mosel River in the 1960s, depleting groundwater—which was the

only thing preserving the church's original wooden foundation. When dry, the foundation disintegrated, and the walls began to settle. Architects competed to find a way to prevent the cathedral from collapsing. The winning solution: a huge steel bracket above the main nave, holding the walls up with cables.

• *Just past the cathedral on Windstrasse to the left is the...*

▲Bishop's Museum (Bischöfliches Diözesanmuseum)

This potentially wonderful cathedral museum suffers from a lack of English information. Its highlight is the pieced-together remains of exquisite ceiling frescoes from St. Helena's palace. The vivid reds, greens, and blues of the restored works depict frolicking cupids, bejeweled women, and a philosopher clutching his scroll. The panels are displayed in such a way that you feel mysteriously transported back to when they were made, in A.D. 320. The 50,000 pieces of the frescoes were discovered while cleaning up from WWII bombs. Incredibly, with the help of computers (and using patterns from the wattle-and-daub work on the back sides of the pieces), the jigsaw puzzle was put back together. Just as incredibly, there's not a word to describe this treasure for visitors who don't speak German. (They do sell a book in English that explains the frescoes and their restoration.) Elsewhere in the museum, you'll see an interesting model of the original Roman church, stone capitals, gold chalices, vestments, and icons (€3.50, Mon–Sat 9:00–17:00 except closed Mon Nov–March, Sun 13:00–17:00, Windstrasse 6, tel. 0651/710-5255, www.museum.bistum-trier.de).

• *Return to the front of the cathedral and head two blocks south (passing the Liebfrau church, under an arch capped by a crucifixion scene indicating you're leaving the archbishop's walled ecclesiastical city). Bear left on An der Meerkatz, to the 200-foot-by-100-foot...*

▲▲Basilica/Imperial Throne Room (Konstantin Basilica)

This building is the largest intact Roman structure outside of Rome. It's best known as a basilica, but it actually started out as a throne room. Go inside (free, good €1 English booklet brings the near-empty shell to life; April–Oct Mon–Sat 10:00–18:00, Sun 12:00–18:00; Nov–March Tue–Sat 11:00–12:00 & 15:00–16:00, Sun 12:00–13:00, closed Mon; tel. 0651/72468, www.konstantin-basilika.de).

Standing inside the vast structure, you see the genius of Roman engineering. Notice the 65-foot-wide round arch over the apse. The small rectangular holes between the windows were chimneys, which vented the hot air that circulated below the floor, heating the place. It's a huge expanse to span without columns. Each of the squares in the ceiling above you measures 10 feet by 10 feet—as big as your hotel room. While today's roof cheats, using concrete girders, the Roman original was all wood, relying on triangular trusses above the flat ceiling. Today's windows match the Roman originals—small frosted panes held in place by a wooden frame. The place is enormous. (A little model in the back near the entry shows the Porta Nigra fitting comfortably inside this building.)

Picture this throne room in ancient times, decorated with golden mosaics, rich marble, colorful stucco, and busts of Constantine and his family filling the seven niches. The emperor sat in majesty under a canopy on his altar-like throne. The windows in the apse around him were smaller than the ones along the side walls, making his throne seem even bigger.

The last emperor moved out in A.D. 395, and petty kings set up camp in the building throughout the Middle Ages. By the 12th century, the archbishops had taken it over, using the nave as a courtyard and converting the apse into a five-story palace. The building became a Lutheran church in 1856, and it remains the leading Protestant church in Trier. It was badly damaged by WWII bombs (as illustrated by photographs at the cashier's desk), and later restored. For a rundown on the history, including artist reconstructions that help you envision how the basilica was used through the ages, follow the exhibit along the far wall (described in English).

A pink Rococo wing, the Elector's Palace, was added to the basilica in the 18th century to house the archbishop-elector; today, it houses local government offices (closed to the public).

• The Rococo wing faces a fragrant picnic-riffic garden. Beyond the garden are three more sights: an interesting archaeological museum, the remains of a Roman bath, and a 16,000-seat Roman amphitheater. Cut across the garden toward Weimarer Strasse (the main street in the distance) and veer right, passing through the medieval city wall to the entrance of the...

▲▲Archaeological Museum (Rheinisches Landesmuseum)

Beautifully described in English and with arguably the best collection of Roman art in Germany, this is clearly Trier's top museum. Your visit begins on the ground floor (walk through the courtyard with its big painted model, and see funeral reliefs and mosaics), then continues upstairs, where you'll see coins, other artifacts, and a fine model of Roman Trier (€5, Tue–Sun 9:30–17:30, closed Mon, tel. 0651/97740, www.landesmuseum-trier.de).

Start at the gaudy copy of a **Roman funerary monument** in the courtyard. (The original still stands in a nearby Mosel River Valley village.) Most of the ground floor is devoted to funerary monuments like this. For pagan Roman big shots, the closest thing to eternal life was to be remembered after they died. Consequently, those who could afford it erected big memorials to their own lives and accomplishments along the road leading into Trier. When Roman Trier went Christian in A.D. 320, these pagan ideals were no longer respected. The memorials were scavenged for their stones, which were then used as a foundation for a nearby fortress and forgotten. In 1890, a resident of the modern village sitting on the ruins of that Roman fortress dug up one of these stones, the museum paid a handsome price for it, and everyone in the village went wild digging up old Roman stones to cash in.

Enter the big room facing the courtyard to see the museum's rich collection of **funerary art;** originally these were all painted like the courtyard replica. Browse around, finding glimpses of everyday Roman life: the tax collector at work, the boys with their Latin teacher, a woman visiting a beauty salon, and a ship laden with barrels of Mosel wine. Behind the wine ship, a wall painting shows how the mausoleum-lined road into Roman Trier might have looked. Archeologists have learned a lot about life in this corner of the Roman Empire by studying these artifacts.

The **Roman mosaics** (just beyond the wine ship) are another highlight. On the wall is a mosaic of four horses surrounding the superstar charioteer Polydus, discovered intact at the Imperial Baths. Mosaic floors were the *Sports Illustrated* covers of the Roman world.

Upstairs, a small exhibit shows **coins** through the centuries of Roman rule. In 1993, some Trier construction workers dug up a bag holding 2,600 golden Roman coins. Experts used the emperor's face on each coin to date the finds. Follow the steady progression of emperors and their coins from Nero (54 B.C.) to Septimius Severus (A.D. 211). It's impressive that 250 years of coinage were in circulation when this bag was lost.

Don't miss the huge **model** of Roman Trier—a thriving city of 80,000. Pick out the sights you're visiting today: Porta Nigra, the grid street plan, the cathedral, basilica, baths, and amphitheater.

• *Exit the Archaeological Museum, walk right (paralleling the main Weimarer Strasse through the trees), then follow the* Tourist Route *signs through the archway in the wall to the modern, red-brick entry arcade of the...*

Imperial Baths (Kaiserthermen)

Built by Constantine, these were destined to be the biggest of Trier's three Roman baths, and the most intricate baths of the Roman world. Trier's cold northern cli-

mate, the size of the complex, and the enormity of Constantine's ego meant that these Imperial Baths required a two-story subterranean complex of pipes, furnaces, and slave galleys to keep the water at a perfect 47 degrees Celsius (120 degrees Fahrenheit). But the grandiose vision was never finished. When Constantine left Trier in A.D. 316, the huge and already costly project was scuttled. Later the site was used as a military barracks. The giant courtyard—originally for exercising and lounging—became a parade ground for the Pretorian Guard. Stepping into the unfinished building section, you can imagine the intended pools (cold, tepid, and hot) and the heated floor. Thirty years of construction left nearly a mile of underground tunnels and foundation work, which are fun to explore. Imagine the engineering, slave labor, and wood that would have been necessary to make all this work, if it had ever been completed. A literal river of water was planned to flow into the baths via an aqueduct. And the surrounding land would ultimately have been deforested as it supplied enough wood to keep the ovens going to heat the water (€2.10, daily April–Sept 9:00–18:00, March and Oct 9:00–17:00, Nov–Feb 9:00–16:00, good €2.50 English booklet, tel. 0651/436-2550, www.burgen-rlp.de).

• *To finish your tour of Trier's Roman sights, hike from the baths about 10 minutes farther to the amphitheater. If you're beat, you can skip it (just look at amphitheater photos in shop postcard racks), head back to Market Square, and enjoy the town.*

To reach the amphitheater, follow the signs through the pedestrian underpass, then follow Hermesstrasse as it curves up the hill, and then turn left on Olewigerstrasse.

Amphitheater

Roman Trier's amphitheater, built around A.D. 200, seated at least 16,000. The city was largely inhabited by Celts who learned Latin and wanted to adopt to the Roman lifestyle. And any self-respecting Roman town needed an amphitheater. While Trier's amphitheater had some gore, the scene here wasn't Roman degenerates egging on gladiators—it was more often used for less-bloody spectacles, assemblies, and religous festivals.

You'll enter where grand processions did. To tour the site, follow the crude little map you'll get with your ticket, which sends you left up the hill to a handy illustrated diagram of ancient Trier that helps put the amphitheater into context with the city. After enjoying this best high vantage point, walk away from the amphitheater around back, circling down and left. Enter the amphitheater through one of its grand entries (called vomitoria, these were named for the way crowds could spew out quickly after events). Then descend a staircase in the center of the amphitheater into the cellar, where gear for the spectacles was kept (and which is below the water table—so it's always wet). After Rome fell, the amphitheater was used as a refuge from barbarian attacks, a quarry, and a vineyard (€2.10, daily April–Sept 9:00–18:00, March and Oct 9:00–17:00, Nov–Feb 9:00–16:00, tel. 0651/73010).

More Sights in Trier

Karl Marx's House—Communists can lick their wounds at Karl Marx's birthplace, a 1727 house with two floors of exhibits. While the influential economist/philosopher is a fascinating and important figure, this place has almost no historic artifacts. Visiting this "museum" is like reading a book in a foreign language, while standing up. The included audio-guide gives more meaning to the displays, but even that is pretty tedious (€3, includes free brochure, daily April–Oct 10:00–18:00, Nov–March 11:00–17:00, from Market Square

follow signs for 10 min to Brückenstrasse 10, tel. 0651/970-680, www.fes.de/Karl-Marx-Haus).

Viehmarkt Baths Museum—A beautiful modern glass building covers the ruins of a Roman bath, mixed with stone monastery foundations and medieval waste-wells. It's certainly historic, but almost meaningless unless you have a freakish interest in Roman stones and a good guide. You can see nearly everything without paying just by looking in from the entry and through the many windows (€2.10, Tue–Sun 9:00–18:00, closed Mon, Viehmarktplatz). The best thing about going here is walking down Fahrstrasse to the museum—a block away, you'll pass a cool fountain showing Trier craftsmen at work.

Sleeping in Trier

Near the Porta Nigra

$$$ **Hotel zum Christophel** offers top comfort in its 11 classy rooms next to the Porta Nigra, above a fine restaurant and with a kind owner. It's an easy roll from the train station with your luggage (Sb-€65, Db-€90–95, elevator, free Wi-Fi, Am Porta Nigra Platz 1, tel. 0651/979-4200, fax 0651/74732, www.zumchristophel .de, info@zumchristophel.de).

$$$ **Hotel Römischer Kaiser,** next door, is also nice, but a lesser value—charging more for a polished lobby and 43 comparable rooms (Sb-€75–85, Db-€105–125, more during festivals, elevator, free Wi-Fi in lobby, free parking, Am Porta Nigra Platz 6, tel. 0651/977-0100, fax 0651/9770-1999, www.friedrich-hotels .de, rezeption@friedrich-hotels.de).

$$ **Astoria Hotel,** three blocks beyond the Porta Nigra when coming from the train station, is a 15-room family-run place with a frilly pink breakfast room, rosy outside terrace, and colorfully decorated rooms (Sb-€58–62, Db-€82–88, lower prices are for weekdays, cheaper Nov–March, no elevator, parking-€5/day, Bruchhausenstrasse 4, tel. 0651/978-350, fax 0651/41121, www .astoria-hotel.de, info@astoria-hotel.de, half-American Paula and her husband Sudhir).

Near Market Square

$$ **Hotel Frankenturm,** decked out in modern style with track lighting and cheery color schemes, has 12 rooms above a lively saloon and next to a medieval keep of the same name. The six rooms with private baths are on the first floor up; the other six rooms are two floors up, with a shared bath (S-€45, Sb-€65, D-€55, Db-€85, T-€65, Tb-€95, no elevator, Dietrichstrasse 3, tel. 0651/978-240, fax 0651/978-2449, www.hotel-frankenturm.de, frankenturm @t-online.de).

$ **Warsberger Hof,** run by a local citizens' league, is a clean, simple hostel and budget hotel two blocks from Market Square, with 168 beds and an inexpensive restaurant. This is your best value for cheap sleeps in town (€21.50 per bed in 3- to 6-bed dorms, includes sheets, S-€26–28, D-€47–51, T-€71, Q-€86–92, showers down the hall, breakfast-€5.80, pay Internet access, Dietrichstrasse 42, tel. 0651/975-250, fax 0651/975-2540, www.warsberger-hof.de, info@warsberger-hof.de).

Near the Train Station

$$ **Hotel Pieper,** a good value, is run by the friendly Becker family (he cooks and she keeps the books). They rent 20 comfortable rooms furnished with dark wood over a pleasant neighbor-

---

Sleep Code

(€1 = about $1.40, country code: 49, area code: 0651)
S = Single, **D** = Double/Twin, **T** = Triple, **Q** = Quad, **b** = bathroom,
s = shower only. Unless otherwise noted, credit cards are
accepted, English is spoken, and breakfast is included.

To help you sort easily through these listings, I've divided
the rooms into three categories, based on the price for a
standard double room with bath:

$$$ Higher Priced—Most rooms €90 or more.
$$ Moderately Priced—Most rooms between €55–90.
$ Lower Priced—Most rooms €55 or less.

---

hood restaurant (Sb-€48, Db-€78, Tb-€115, pay Wi-Fi, 8-min
walk from station, 2 blocks off main drag, Thebäerstrasse 39,
tel. 0651/23008, fax 0651/12839, www.hotel-pieper-trier.de, info
@hotel-pieper-trier.de). From the station, follow Theodor-Heuss-
Allee (toward Porta Nigra) to the second big intersection, angle
right onto Göbenstrasse, and continue as the road curves and
becomes Thebäerstrasse.

Outside the Center

$$$ Hotel Petrisberg Trier, up a steep road behind the amphi-
theater, is top-quality and ideal if you have a car. It's on a hill-
side overlooking the city, exuding old-school elegance without
being stuffy. The Pantenburg family takes great care to spoil all
their guests; Helmut whips up tasty egg breakfasts, while his
niece Christina—the 2001 Trier Wine Queen—works reception.
A pleasant footpath brings you downhill to the cathedral in 20
minutes (35 rooms, Sb-€70, Db-€98, family rooms, non-smoking,
free Internet access, Wi-Fi in breakfast room, taxi from train sta-
tion-€7.50, Sickingenstrasse 11–13, tel. 0651/4640, fax 0651/46450,
www.hotel-petrisberg.de, info@hotel-petrisberg.de).

Eating in Trier

Good eateries abound on the side streets leading away from the
pedestrian drag (Simeonstrasse) and from Market Square. Most of
the recommended hotels have good-value restaurants.

Zum Domstein, right on Market Square, serves standard
German fare at decent prices and also has a special, pricier menu
of entrées based on ancient Roman recipes. The Roman menu was
inspired during renovations, when the owner discovered a Roman
column in her cellar. (In Trier, you can't put a rec room in your

basement without tripping over Roman ruins.) The finished cellar dining room incorporates the column, plus a mini-museum of Roman crockery (€10–20 main dishes, cheaper lunch specials, open daily 8:30–22:30, Roman dishes served in cellar 18:00–21:00, Am Hauptmarkt 5, tel. 0651/74490).

At **Krim,** just off Market Square, young locals enjoy trendy Mediterranean cuisine (€9–17 main dishes, cheaper lunch specials, Mon–Sat 9:00–24:00, Sun 10:00–24:00, Glockenstrasse 7, tel. 0651/73943).

Hotel Frankenturm, a few doors down Dietrichstrasse from Market Square, offers German cuisine with a twist of Asian and Mediterranean in a modern pub-style atmosphere (€9–15 main dishes, €5–8 weekday lunch specials, Mon–Sat 8:00–24:00, closed Sun, Dietrichstrasse 3, tel. 0651/978-240).

Warsberger Hof Eateries: A few doors farther down Dietrichstrasse, in the big yellow pastel building on the right, the recommended **Warsberger Hof hostel** runs three inexpensive eateries: the **Leonardy** pub and café (Mon–Sat 11:30–15:00 & 17:00–24:00, closed Sun), the **Rautenstrauch** restaurant (€11–17 main dishes, daily 11:30–14:30 & 18:00–22:00, nice enclosed terrace, kid-friendly), and the **Kasino** self-service cafeteria, serving cheap lunches (Mon–Fri 11:30–14:15, closed Sat–Sun).

The recommended **Hotel zum Christophel** also has a reasonably priced restaurant with a view of the Porta Nigra (daily 11:00–23:00, Am Porta Nigra Platz).

Picnics: One of several supermarkets in the center is in the basement of the Karstadt department store on Simeonstrasse (open Mon–Sat 9:00–20:00, closed Sun).

Trier Connections

From Trier by Train to: Cochem (2/hr, 45 min–1 hour), **Koblenz** (hourly fast train, 1.5 hrs), **Köln** (at least hourly, 2.5–3 hrs, some change in Koblenz), **St. Goar/Bacharach** (hourly, 2.5 hrs, change in Koblenz), **Frankfurt Airport** (hourly, 3 hrs, change in Koblenz and sometimes Mainz), **Paris** (roughly hourly, 3–3.5 hrs, best routings with change in Saarbrücken or Luxembourg). Train info: tel. 0180-599-6633 (€0.14/min).

KÖLN and the
UNROMANTIC RHINE

Romance isn't everything. Köln is an urban Jacuzzi that keeps the Rhine churning. It's home to Germany's greatest Gothic cathedral and its best collection of Roman artifacts, a world-class art museum, and a healthy dose of German urban playfulness.

Peaceful Bonn, which offers good people-watching and fun pedestrian streets, used to be the capital of West Germany. The small town of Remagen had a bridge that helped defeat Hitler in World War II, and unassuming Aachen, near the Belgian border, was once the capital of Europe.

Köln

Germany's fourth-largest city, Köln ("Cologne" in English), has a compact, lively center. The Rhine was the northern boundary

of the Roman Empire and, 1,700 years ago, Constantine—the first Christian emperor—made Colonia the seat of a bishopric. Five hundred years later, under Charlemagne, Köln became the seat of an archbishopric. With 40,000 people within its walls, it was the largest German city and an important cultural and religious center throughout the Middle Ages. Today, the city is most famous for its toilet water: Eau de Cologne was first made here by an Italian chemist in 1709.

During World War II, bombs destroyed 95 percent of Köln—driving its population from 800,000 down to an estimated 30,000 at its lowest ebb. But with the end of the war, the city immediately began putting itself back together (the population rebounded to about 400,000 by Christmas of 1945). Today, it's a bustling commercial and cultural center that still respects its rich past.

Planning Your Time

Köln makes an ideal on-the-way stop; it's a major rail junction, and its top sights are clustered near the train station. With a couple of hours, you can toss your bag in a locker, take my self-guided town walk, zip through the cathedral, and make it back to the station for your train. If you're planning that short of a stop, make sure you'll be here when the whole church is open (times are listed on page 414). More time (or an overnight) allows you to delve into a few of the city's fine museums and take in an old-time beer pub.

Orientation to Köln

(area code: 0221)

Köln's core was bombed out, then rebuilt in mostly modern styles with a sprinkling of quaint. There are two areas that matter to visitors. One is the section right around the train station and cathedral. Here you'll find most sights, all my recommended hotels, plus the TI and plenty of eateries and services. Hohe Strasse, Köln's pedestrian shopping street, begins near the cathedral. The other area—called the "old town"—is between the river and the Alter Markt, a few blocks to the south. After the war, this section was chosen to be restored in the old style. It's known for its pubs, small streets, and waterfront park.

Tourist Information

Köln's energetic TI, opposite the cathedral entrance, has a basic €0.20 city map and can find you a room (Mon–Sat 9:00–20:00, Sun 10:00–17:00, Kardinal-Höffner-Platz 1, tel. 0221/2213-0400, www.koelntourismus.de).

Arrival in Köln

Köln couldn't be easier to visit—its three important sights cluster within two blocks of the TI and train station. This super pedestrian zone is a constant carnival of people.

By Train: Köln's busy train station has everything you need: drugstore, bookstore, food court, juice bar, grocery store, pricey "McClean" WC (€1), travel center (*Reisezentrum*, Mon–Fri 6:00–22:00, Sat–Sun 7:00–21:00), and high-tech lockers (€4/24 hrs, accepts coins and €5 and €10 bills, put money in and wait 30 sec-

Köln

RHINE RIVER

CATHEDRAL

MUSEUM LUDWIG

HOHENZOLLERN BRIDGE

ROMAN-GERMANIC MUSEUM

200 YARDS
200 METERS

K-D BOAT DOCK

WALLRAF-RICHARTZ MUSEUM

DEUTZER BRIDGE

TO CHOCOLATE MUSEUM

→ SELF-GUIDED WALK

- ❶ Classic Hotel Harmonie & Hotel Cristall
- ❷ Hotel Ibis Koeln am Dom
- ❸ Hotel Engelbertz
- ❹ Central Hotel am Dom
- ❺ Hotel Müller
- ❻ Station Hostel
- ❼ Gaffel Haus Restaurant
- ❽ Papa Joe's Klimperkasten Pub
- ❾ Papa Joe's Jazzlokal
- ❿ Früh am Dom Restaurant
- ⓫ Holtmann's im MAK
- ⓬ Café Eigel
- ⓭ Schreckenskammer Rest.
- ⓮ To Päffgen Restaurant
- ⓯ Frankenwerft Bars & Eateries
- ⓰ Internet Café
- ⓱ Bike Rentals (2)
- ⓲ To Kolumba Diocesan Museum

KÖLN

onds for door to open, your luggage—up to four pieces—is transferred to storage via an underground conveyor belt and retrieved when you re-insert your ticket; next to *Reisezentrum*). Exiting the front of the station (the end near track 1), you'll find yourself smack-dab in the shadow of the cathedral. Up the steps and to the right is the main entrance to the cathedral (TI across street). For the recommended Hotel Müller, leave the station from the back (near track 11).

By Car: If you drive to Köln, follow signs to *Zentrum*, then continue to the huge Parkhaus am Dom pay lot under the cathedral (€1.80/hr, €18/day).

By Boat: If you're arriving on a K-D Line boat, exit the boat to the right, then walk along the waterside park until just before the train bridge, when the cathedral comes into view on the left.

Helpful Hints

Closed Day: Note that most museums are closed on Monday, though the cathedral remains open. The cathedral has limited public hours on Sunday due to frequent services. For information on Köln's museums, visit www.museenkoeln.de.

Sightseeing Discount Cards: Köln has two different cards, one of which is worth considering. The **MuseumCard** is valid for two consecutive days. It covers all local public transportation on the first day (including local trains to Bonn—but not the slick InterCity and ICE trains), and also includes the Roman-Germanic Museum, Museum Ludwig, Wallraf-Richartz Museum, and quite a few lesser museums (but not the cathedral sights). If you're visiting all three of these museums, this card will save you money (€12.20/person, or €20.40 for a family pass—includes 2 adults and 2 kids up to 18, available at participating museums, www.museenkoeln.de). The **WelcomeCard,** offering small discounts on some museums, is a waste of money; though it covers the city's transit system, you can easily reach the top sights on foot (€9/24 hrs, €14/48 hrs, €19/72 hrs; family and group cards available, www.koelntourismus.de).

Internet Access: Consider **Via Phone Internet Café,** a block from the station at Marzellenstrasse 3–5 (€2/hr, also sells cheap phone cards, Mon–Sat 9:00–24:00, Sun 10:00–24:00, tel. 0221/1399-6200).

Baggage Storage: The train station's baggage service is the most convenient (see "Arrival in Köln," earlier), but cheapskates can save a few euros by using Museum Ludwig's €0.50 lockers. From the station's underground passage, take the escalator to Platform 1, do a U-turn at the top, and walk past Section A, all the way down to where the platform joins the street—look straight ahead for the museum's large sign.

Bike Rental: Convenient rental is available at friendly **Radstation,** tucked under the train-track arcade (€5/3 hrs, €10/day, Mon–Fri 5:30–22:30, Sat 6:30–20:00, Sun 8:00–20:00, exit station by track 11 to Breslauer Platz, turn right and cross street, tel. 0221/139-7190). You can also rent bikes from the riverside **Kölner Fahrradverleih,** a 10-minute walk from the station (€2/hr, €10/day, April–Oct daily 10:00–18:00, on Markmannsgasse, 100 yards upstream from K-D Line docks, mobile 0171-629-8796). Consider biking the path along the Rhine River up past the convention center *(Messe)* to the Rheinpark for a picnic. Or consider a guided bike tour (described under "Tours in Köln," below).

Gadget Supply: You can pick up a new memory card or whatever high-tech gizmo you're lacking for a fair price at **Media Markt,** Germany's version of Best Buy, conveniently located two blocks from the cathedral (Mon–Thu 10:00–20:00, Fri–Sat 10:00–21:00, closed Sun, corner of Hohe Strasse and Minoritenstrasse).

Festival: Köln's Lichter Festival lights up the sky on July 17 in 2010, with fireworks, music, and lots of boats on the river (get details from TI or at www.koelner-lichter.de).

Tours in Köln

Bus Tours—The TI sells tickets and is the departure point for hop-on, hop-off city bus tours and standard 1.5-hour bus tours offered by three competing companies (€10–12, departures at least hourly in summer; most have recorded commentary in both German and English, but one company, Stadtrundfahrten, has live guides every 2 hours—see www.cityfahrten.de).

Bike Tours—Kölner Fahrradverleih (listed earlier, under "Bike Rental") offers German/English guided bike tours of the city (€15, 3–3.5 hours, daily April–Oct at 13:30, rain poncho provided just in case, max 10 people per guide, reservations recommended, mobile 0171-629-8796, www.koelnerfahrradverleih.de).

Self-Guided Walk

▲▲Welcome to Köln

Köln lends itself to a fine orientation walk. The old town, towering cathedral, and most of the sights cluster near the train station. Starting at the train station, this walk takes less than an hour and provides a good introduction.

Bahnhofplatz: Stepping out of the train station, you're confronted with a modern hodgepodge of post-WWII architecture and the towering icon of Köln, its cathedral. The city feels rebuilt—because it was. The Allies bombed Köln hard in retaliation for Germany's bombing of London. Your gaze is grabbed by the cathedral. While it was built according to the original 13th-century plans, and the left (east) part was completed in the 13th century, the right half wasn't built until after German unification, in the 1880s.

• *Climb the steps and circle right, to the people-filled square facing the cathedral.*

Cathedral Plaza (Roncalli Platz): In centuries past, a clutter of half-timbered huts crowded around the cathedral. They were all cleared out in the late 1800s so the great building would have a suitable approach. This has been a busy commercial zone since ancient times. The Roman arch was discovered nearby and set up here as a reminder of the town's Roman roots. This north gate of the Roman city, from A.D. 50, marks the start of Köln's nearly 2,000-year-old main shopping street, Hohe Strasse.

Look for the life-size replica tip of a spire. The real thing is 515 feet above you. The cathedral facade, while finished in the 1880s, is exactly what was envisioned by the original church planners in 1280. (For more on the cathedral, see page 414.)

• *Continue around the right side of the church, passing modern buildings and public spaces. Step up to the window of the Roman-Germanic Museum to see a...*

Roman Mosaic: Through the Roman-Germanic Museum's generous window, budget travelers can get a free look at the museum's prize piece—a fine mosaic floor. Once the dining-room floor of a rich Roman merchant, this is actually in its original position (the museum was built around it). It shows scenes from the life of Dionysus...wine, women, and song, Roman-style. The mosaic is quite sexy, with several scenes showing a satyr seducing and ultimately disrobing a half-goddess, half-human maenad. First he offers her grapes, then he turns on the music. After further wining and dining—all with an agenda—the horny satry finally scores. The cupid on a lion's back symbolizes the triumph of physical love.

The mosaic is at the original Roman street level. The tall monument above and left of the mosaic is the mausoleum of a first-century Roman army officer. Directly across from you (at eye level, beyond the mosaic) are beautifully carved stone reliefs—an indication of what a fine city Roman Köln must have been. If you'd like to visit the Roman-Germanic Museum's good collection, see page 420.

KÖLN

• *Walk 20 steps beyond the mosaic farther along the cathedral and look down to see the...*

Cathedral Workshop: Any church of this size is a work in progress. There is constant renovation, repairs, and care. Sandstone blocks are stacked and waiting to be shaped and plugged in wherever needed. The buttresses above are the church's showiest, because they face the bishop's palace, city center, and original entrance (south transept). For 500 years, the church was left unfinished, simply capped off midway. You're facing the functional part of church, where services were held from the 1300s until the late 1800s.

• *From the cathedral, walk past the Museum Ludwig (described on page 420, and with a convenient WC in the lobby) and toward the river.*

Riverfront: The statue (to your left) honors Kaiser Wilhelm II, who paid for the Hohenzollernbrücke (named after his family)—the busiest railway bridge in the world (30 trains an hour all day long). A classic Industrial Age design from around 1900, the bridge was destroyed in World War II and rebuilt in its original style. Stairs lead down to a people-friendly riverside park. This is urban planning from 1970s: Real and forward-looking. The riverside, once a noisy highway, is now a peaceful park. All that traffic still courses through the city, but flows unnoticed, below you in a tunnel. A bike-and-pedestrian path follows the riverside in each direction, and families let their children frolic in the fountain.

Turn right, walking away from the bridge, to a small square in front of the Romanesque church tower. (Köln's famous chocolate museum, described on page 421, is a five-minute walk farther downstream.) Notice a strip of sockets for a metal flood wall (on the inland side of the grassy stretch). The eight-foot-high flood wall can be erected when needed. Locals see a change in climate here: They say that "floods of the century" now happen every decade, thunderstorms are ten times more prevalent, and for the first time, this part of Europe has witnessed little tornadoes.

Fish Market Square and "Old Town": At the foot of Great St. Martin Church, this tiny square—once the fish market—faces the river. Fish Market Square is ringed by medieval-looking buildings from the 1930s. In the early 20th century, Köln's entire old town was a scruffy, half-timbered, prostitute-ridden slum. To the disgusted Nazis, prostitutes were human dirt. Their vision for old towns all over Germany: Clear out the clutter, boot the riffraff, and rebuild in the clean, tidy, stone-and-stucco style you see here. After World War II, Köln decided to rebuild in the same faux-medieval style. This square and the streets around the church are from that period.

• *From the church door, a passageway leads away from the river directly to Alter Markt (Old Market) Square.*

Alter Markt Square and City Hall: The ornate City Hall tower symbolized civic spirit standing strong against the power of the bishops in the 15th century. (The square's a mess today because of subway construction.) Circle around the tower to see the City Hall's fine Renaissance porch—the only historic facade left standing after the 1945 bombings. Its carvings stress civic independence. The busts of emperors bring to mind Köln's strong Roman past. Lions symbolize the evil aspect of church authority. Above the door, the mayor kills the lion (thus establishing independence from church government for his city). This scene is flanked by Biblical parallels: the angel saving Daniel from the lions (on right), and Samson fighting lions (on left). Beware of flying rice—the City Hall is often busy with civil wedding parties (Mon–Sat).

• *From the City Hall, pass through Laurenzplatz and walk two blocks farther away from the river to Hohe Strasse.*

Shopping, Church Art, and Eau de Cologne: Jog left onto the town's busy pedestrian shopping street, then take your first right on Brückenstrasse to the modern white building, set atop the ruins of a bombed-out Gothic church. This is the Kolumba Diocesan Museum (described on page 420). Inside, from the corner, you can grab a free peek at what was the church interior.

Across the busy Tunisstrasse stands Köln's circa-1960s Opera House (a big deal in Germany when built). And across the street from that, on the right, is a historic building—4711 Glockengasse, which claims to be the birthplace of the original Eau de Cologne. In 1810, the local toilet water switched from being a medicine to a perfume, putting Köln on the map. Locals claim Cologne was the first perfume based on alcohol (86 percent alcohol; the rest is herbal fragrances). The original Cologne water runs in a fountain by the door, and this year's new fragrances are free to try at the counter. There's a small, free exhibit just up the stairs.

Sights in Köln

▲▲▲Köln's Cathedral (Dom)

The Gothic Dom—Germany's most exciting church—looms immediately up from the train station in one of Germany's starkest juxtapositions of the modern and the medieval. The church is so big and so important that it has own information office, the Domforum, in a separate building across the street (described later, under "More Cathedral Sights").

Cost and Hours: Free, open daily May–Oct 6:00–22:00, Nov–April 6:00–

Köln Cathedral

19:30—but no tourist visits during services (generally Mon–Sat at 6:30, 7:15, 8:00, 9:00, 12:00, and 18:30; Sun at 7:00, 8:00, 9:00, 10:00, 12:00, 17:00, and 19:00; get the day's schedule at Domforum office or www.koelner-dom.de).

Tours: The one-hour English-only tours are reliably excellent (€6, Mon–Sat at 10:30 and 14:30, Sun at 14:30, meet inside front door of Dom, tel. 0221/9258-4730). Your tour ticket also gives you free entry to the 20-minute English video in the Domforum directly following the tour.

❷ Self-Guided Tour: If you don't take the guided tour, follow this seven-stop walk (note that stops 3–7 are closed off during confession Sat 14:00–18:00, and any time services are underway).

❶ Cathedral Exterior: The cathedral—the most ambitious Gothic building project north of France in the 13th century—was stalled in the Middle Ages and not finished until 1880. Even though most of it was built in the 19th century, it's still technically a Gothic church (not "Neo-Gothic") because it was finished according to its original plans.

• *Step inside the church. Grab a pew in the center of the nave.*

❷ **Nave:** If you feel small, you're supposed to. The 140-foot-tall ceiling reminds us of our place in the vast scheme of things.

Lots of stained glass—enough to cover three football fields—fills the church with light, representing God.

The church was begun in 1248. The choir—the lofty area from the center altar to the far end ahead of you—was inaugurated in 1322. Later, during the tumultuous wars of religious reformation, Catholic pilgrims stopped coming. This dried up funds, and eventually construction stopped. For 300 years, the finished end of the church was walled off and functioned as a church, while the unfinished nave (where you now sit) waited. For centuries, the symbol of Köln's skyline was a huge crane that sat atop the unfinished west spire.

With the rise of German patriotism in the early 1800s, Köln became a symbol of German unity. And the Prussians—the movers and shakers behind German unity—mistakenly considered Gothic (which was French) a German style. They paid for the speedy completion of this gloriously Gothic German church. With nearly 700 workers going at full speed, the church was finished in just 38 years (1842–1880). The great train station was built in the shadow of the cathedral's towering spire.

The glass windows at the east end of the church (in the chapels and high above) are medieval. The glass surrounding you in the nave

is not as old, but it's precious nevertheless. The glass on the left is early Renaissance. Notice the many coats of arms, which depict the lineage of the donors. One of these windows would have cost as much as two large townhouses. The glass on the right—a gift from Ludwig I, grandfather of the "Mad" King Ludwig who built the fairy-tale castles—is 19th-century Bavarian. Compare both the colors and the realism of the faces between the windows to see how techniques advanced and tastes changed over the centuries.

While 95 percent of Köln was destroyed by WWII bombs, the cathedral held up fairly well. (It was hit by 15 bombs, but the skeletal Gothic structure flexed, and it remained standing.) In anticipation of the bombing, the glass and art treasures were taken to shelters and saved.

The new "swallow's nest" organ above you was installed to celebrate the cathedral's 750th birthday in 1998. Attaching it to the wall would have compromised the cathedral's architectural integrity, so the organ is actually suspended from precarious-looking steel wires.

The guys in the red robes are cathedral cops, called *Schweizer* (after the Swiss guard at the Vatican); if a service is getting ready to start, they hustle tourists out (but you can stay for the service if you like).

• *Leave the nave by stepping through the gate on the left, into the oldest part of the church. As you enter, look down.*

This 19th-century mosaic shows a saint holding the Carolingian Cathedral, which stood on this spot for several centuries before this one was built.

❸ **Gero-Crucifix:** Ahead of you on the left, the Chapel of the Cross features the oldest surviving monumental crucifix from north of the Alps. Carved in the 970s with a sensitivity that was 300 years ahead of its time, it shows Jesus not suffering and not triumphant—but with eyes closed...dead. He paid the price for our sins. It's quite a two-fer: great art and powerful theology in one. The cathedral has three big pilgrim stops: this crucifix, the Shrine of the Magi, and the *Madonna of Milan*.

• *Continue to the front end of the church, stopping to look at the big golden reliquary in the glass case behind the high altar.*

❹ **Shrine of the Magi:** Relics were a big deal in the Middle Ages. Köln's acquisition of the bones of the Three Kings in the 12th century put it on the pilgrimage map and brought in enough money to justify the construction of this magnificent place. By some stretch of medieval Christian logic, these relics also justified the secular power of the German king. This reliquary, made in about 1200 of gilded silver, jewels, and enamel, is the biggest and most splendid I've seen. On the long sides, Old Testament prophets line the bottom, and 12 New Testament apostles—with a wingless angel in the center—line the top. The front looks like three stacked coffins, showing scenes of Christ's flagellation, Crucifixion, and Resurrection.

Inside sit the bones of the Magi...three skulls with golden crowns. So what's the big deal about these three kings (of Christmas-carol fame)? They were the first to recognize Jesus as the Savior and the first to come as pilgrims to worship him. They inspired medieval pilgrims and countless pilgrims since. For a thousand years, a theme of this cathedral has been that life is a pilgrimage...a search for God.

• *Opposite the shrine, at the far east end of the church, is the...*

❺ **Chapel of the Three Magi:** The center chapel, at the church's far end, is the oldest. It also features the church's old-est window (center, from 1265). The design is typical: a strip of Old Testament scenes on the left with a theologically and visually parallel strip of New Testament scenes on the right (such as, on bottom panels: to the left, the birth of Eve; to the right, the birth of Mary with her mother Anne on the bed).

Later glass windows (which you saw lining the nave) were made from panes of clear glass that were painted and glazed. This medieval window, however, is actually colored glass, which is assembled like a mosaic. It was very expensive. The size was lim-ited to what pilgrim donations could support. Notice the plain, budget design higher up.

• *Peek into the center zone between the high altar and the carved wooden central stalls. (You can usually get inside only if you take the tour.)*

❻ **Choir:** The choir is surrounded by 13th- and 14th-century art with carved oak stalls, frescoed walls, statues painted as they would have been, and original stained glass high above. Study the fanciful oak carvings. The woman cutting the man's hair is a Samson-and-Delilah warning to the sexist men of the early Church.

• *The nearby chapel holds one of the most precious paintings of the impor-tant Gothic School of Köln.*

❼ **Chapel of the Virgin:** *The Patron Saints of Köln* was painted around 1440, probably by Stefan Lochner. Notice the photographic

realism and believable depth. There are literally dozens of identifiable herbs in the grassy foreground. During the 19th century, the city fought to move the painting to a museum. The Church went to court to keep it. The judge ruled that it could stay in the cathedral—as long as a Mass was said before it every day. For more than a hundred years, that happened at 18:30. Now, 21st-century comfort has trumped 19th-century law: In winter, services take place in the warmer Sacraments Chapel instead. (If you like this painting, you'll enjoy the many other fine works from the School of Köln at the Wallraf-Richartz Museum—see page 421.)

Overlooking the same chapel (between the windows), the

delicate *Madonna of Milan* sculpture (1290), associated with miracles, was a focus of pilgrims for centuries. Its colors, scepter, and crown were likely added during a restoration in 1900. The reclining medieval knight in the cage at the back of the chapel (just before the gate) was a wealthy but childless patron who donated his entire county to the cathedral.

As you head for the exit, look into the transept on your left. The stained-glass windows above you are a random and abstract pattern of 80 colors, "sampled" from the church's more-historic windows. The local artist Gerhard Richter designed these windows to create a "harmony of colors" in 2007.

Before leaving, look above the tomb with the cage and find the statue of St. Christopher (with Jesus on his shoulder and the pilgrim's staff). He's facing the original south transept entry to the church. Since 1470, pilgrims and travelers have looked up at him and taken solace in the hope that their patron saint is looking out for them.

• *Go in peace.*

More Cathedral Sights

Church Spire Climb (Dom-Turm)—An exterior entry (to the right of the church as you face the west facade) takes you into a modern excavation site, where you can see an arch and the foundations from the cathedral's predecessor (free), and climb the cathedral's dizzying south tower. For 509 steps and €2.50, you can enjoy a fine city view (€5 combo-ticket also includes treasury, daily May–Sept 9:00–18:00, March–April and Oct until 17:00, Nov–Feb until 16:00). From the *Glockenstube* (only 400 steps up), you can see the Dom's nine huge bells, including *Dicke Peter* (24-ton Fat Peter), claimed to be the largest free-swinging church bell in the world.

Treasury—The treasury sits outside the cathedral's left transept (when you exit through the front door, turn right and continue right around the building to the gold pillar marked *Schatzkammer*). The six dim, hushed rooms are housed in the cathedral's 13th-century stone cellar vaults (€4, €5 combo-ticket also includes spire climb, daily 10:00–18:00, last entry 30 min before closing, lockers at entry with €1 coin deposit, tel. 0221/1794-0530).

Spotlights shine on black cases filled with gilded chalices and crosses, medieval reliquaries (bits of chain, bone, cross, and cloth in gold-crusted glass capsules), and plenty of fancy bishop garb: intricately embroidered miters and vestments, rings with fat gemstones, and six-foot gold crosiers. Displays come with brief English descriptions, but the little €4 book sold inside the cathedral shop provides extra information.

Domforum—This helpful visitors center, across from the entrance of the cathedral, is a good place to support the Vatican Bank (notice the Pax Bank ATM just outside the entrance), or just to take a break (Mon–Fri 10:00–18:30, Sat 10:00–17:00, Sun 13:00–17:00, may close for special events, plenty of cathedral info, welcoming lounge with €1 coffee and juice, clean WC downstairs—€0.50, tel. 0221/9258-4720, www.domforum.de). They offer an English "multi-vision" video on the history of the church (Mon–Sat at 11:30 and 15:30, Sun at 15:30 only, starts slow but gets a little better, 20 min, €2 or included with church tour).

Kolumba Diocesan Museum—This museum contains some of the cathedral's finest art. A stop on my self-guided walk, it's on Kolumbastrasse, which runs between Minoritenstrasse and Brückenstrasse a few blocks southwest of the cathedral. Built around the Madonna in the Ruins church, the museum is conceived as a place of reflection. There are no tours or information or noise. It's just you and the art in a modern building built upon the rubble of war. The daring modernist rebuild is a statement: We lost the war. Just accept it (€5, Wed–Mon 12:00–17:00, closed Tue, tel. 0221/933-1930, www.kolumba.de).

Near the Cathedral

▲▲Roman-Germanic Museum (Römisch-Germanisches Museum)—One of Germany's top Roman museums offers minimal English among its elegant and fascinating display of Roman artifacts: glassware, jewelry, and mosaics. All these pieces are evidence of Köln's status as an important site of civilization long before the cathedral was ever imagined. The permanent collection is downstairs and upstairs; temporary exhibits are on the ground floor. Upstairs, you'll see a reassembled arched original gate to the Roman city with the Roman initials for the town, CCAA, still legible, and incredible glassware that Roman Köln was famous for producing. The museum's main attraction, described on page 412 of my self-guided walk, is its in situ Roman mosaic floor— which you can see from the street for free through the large window (€5, Tue–Sun 10:00–17:00, closed Mon, Roncalliplatz 4, tel. 0221/2212-4590, www.museenkoeln.de/rgm). The gift shop's €0.50 brochure provides too little information on the collection, and the €20 *Roman-Germanic Cologne* book too much.

▲▲Museum Ludwig—Next door and more enjoyable, this museum—in a slick and modern building—offers a stimulating trip through the art of the last century, including American Pop and post-WWII art. The ground floor shows special exhibits. Upstairs (on the right) is the Haubrich collection. Josef Haubrich managed to keep his impressive collection of German Expressionist art out of Nazi hands (they considered it "decadent art") and eventually gave it to the city. The collection includes works by the great German Expressionists Max Beckmann, Otto Dix, and Ludwig Kirchner, all of whom fled Germany during Nazi times and did much of their best work outside their homeland. Their paintings capture the loss of idealism and innocence following World War I, and helped take art into the no-holds-barred modern world. The first floor also has a fine Picasso collection. The top floor is mostly contemporary and abstract paintings (€9, often more because of special exhibitions, Tue–Sun 10:00–18:00, closed Mon, audioguide-€3, €0.50 lockers mandatory for big bags, free WC in entry hall, exhibits are fairly well-described in English; pricey cafeteria; Heinrich-Böll-Platz, tel. 0221/2212-6165, www.museum-ludwig.de).

Hohe Strasse—In the Middle Ages, when Köln was a major player in the heavyweight Hanseatic League of northern European merchant towns, two major trading routes crossed here. This high street thrived. Following its complete destruction in World War II, Hohe Strasse has emerged once again as an active trading street. Today this first pedestrian shopping mall in Germany is a rather soulless string of chain stores, most interesting for its seas of shoppers.

Farther from the Cathedral

These museums are several blocks south of the cathedral.

▲▲**Wallraf-Richartz Museum**—Housed in a cinderblock of a building near the City Hall, this minimalist museum features a world-class collection of old masters, from medieval to northern Baroque and Impressionist. You'll see the best collection anywhere of Gothic School of Köln paintings (1300–1550), offering an intimate peek into those times. Included are German, Dutch, Flemish, and French works by masters such as Albrecht Dürer, Peter Paul Rubens, Rembrandt, Frans Hals, Jan Steen, Vincent van Gogh, Pierre-Auguste Renoir, Claude Monet, Edvard Munch, and Paul Cézanne (€6–10, price depends on special exhibitions, Tue–Fri 10:00–18:00, Thu until 22:00, Sat–Sun 11:00–18:00, closed Mon, on Obenmarspforten, tel. 0221/2212-1119, www.museenkoeln.de/wrm).

▲**Imhoff Chocolate Museum (Schokoladenmuseum)**—

Chocoholics love this place, cleverly billed as the "MMMuseum." Three levels of displays—well-described in English—follow the cocoa bean from its origin to the finished product. Local historians, noting the "dumbing-down" of this generation of tourists, complain that this museum gets more visitors than all of Köln's other museums combined. You'll see displays on the history and culture of chocolate, step into a hot and muggy

KÖLN

greenhouse to watch the beans grow, and follow sweet little treats as they trundle down the conveyor belt in the functioning chocolate factory, the museum's highlight. The top-floor exhibit of chocolate advertising is fun. Some find that the museum takes chocolate too seriously, and wish the free samples weren't so meager—you'll have to do your indulging in the fragrant, choc-full gift shop (€7.50, Tue–Fri 10:00–18:00, Sat–Sun 11:00–19:00, closed Mon, last entry one hour before closing, Am Schokoladenmuseum 1a, tel. 0221/931-8880, www.schokoladenmuseum.de). The museum is a pleasant 10-minute walk south on the riverfront, between the Deutzer and Severins bridges.

Käthe Kollwitz Museum—This contains the largest collection of the artist's powerful Expressionist art, welling from her experiences living in Berlin during the tumultuous first half of the 20th century (€3, Tue–Fri 10:00–18:00, Sat–Sun 11:00–18:00, closed Mon, Neumarkt 18–24, tel. 0221/227-2899, www.kollwitz.de). From Hohe Strasse, go west on Schildergasse for about 10 minutes to Neumarkt; go past the Neumarkt Gallerie shopping center to Neumarkt Passage, enter Neumarkt Passage, and walk to the glass-domed center courtyard. Take the glass elevator to the fifth floor.

Sleeping in Köln

Köln is *the* convention town in Germany. Consequently, hotels are either jam-packed, with their rooms going for €180–200, or empty and hungry for guests. Unless otherwise noted, prices listed are the non-convention weekday rates. Prices are soft on weekends (always ask) and for slow-time drop-ins. During conventions, rates double or even triple. Outside of convention times, the TI can always get you a discounted room in a business-class hotel (free by phone or Internet, walk-ins pay a €3 booking fee).

An updated list of dates for conventions in 2010 is posted in German at www.koelnmesse.de (click on "Messen und Veranstaltungen," then look for the link to "Messen in Köln"). Unlisted smaller conventions can lead to small price increases. Big conventions in nearby Düsseldorf can also fill rooms and raise rates in Köln.

All the options listed here are an easy roll from the train station with your luggage.

Classy Hotels on Ursulaplatz

Two good business-class splurge hotels stand side-by-side a five-minute walk northwest of the station (exit straight out, near track 1, then turn right on Marzellenstrasse, up to Ursulaplatz). These can be pricey but are an excellent value on non-convention weekends.

Sleep Code

(€1 = about $1.40, country code: 49, area code: 0221)
S = Single, **D** = Double/Twin, **T** = Triple, **Q** = Quad, **b** = bathroom,
s = shower only. Unless otherwise noted, credit cards are
accepted, English is spoken, and breakfast is included.

To help you sort easily through these listings, I've divided
the rooms into three categories, based on the price for a
standard double room with bath:

$$$ Higher Priced—Most rooms €95 or more.
$$ Moderately Priced—Most rooms between €70–95.
$ Lower Priced—Most rooms €70 or less.

$$$ Classic Hotel Harmonie is a lesson in elegance, striking a perfect balance between modern and classic. Its 72 rooms include some luxurious "superior" rooms (with hardwoods and swanky bathrooms, including a foot-warming floor). Rates are plenty pricey during conventions, but become affordable on weekends and a downright steal when business is slow (it's important to check—call ahead and ask the helpful staff for prices). So *this* is how the other half lives (Sb-€60–90, Db-€80–110, price depends on room category, non-smoking rooms, most doubles have air-con, elevator, pay Wi-Fi, Ursulaplatz 13–19, tel. 0221/16570, fax 0221/165-7200, www.classic-hotel-harmonie.de, harmonie @classic-hotels.com).

$$$ Hotel Cristall is a modern "designer hotel" with 97 cleverly appointed rooms (enjoy the big easel paintings). The deeply hued breakfast room and lounge are so hip that German rock stars have photo shoots here (Sb-€69, Db-€89, prices can drop—especially in summer, request quiet room to escape street and train noise, non-smoking rooms, elevator, free Wi-Fi in lobby, pricey pay Wi-Fi in rooms, limited parking-€9/day—can't reserve in advance, Ursulaplatz 9–11, tel. 0221/16300, fax 0221/163-0333, www.hotelcristall.de, info@hotelcristall.de).

Mid-Range Hotels near the Station

The first three of these moderately priced hotels, centrally located along the pedestrian zone, are more convenient than charming. Hotel Müller is on the other side of the station, in a quieter neighborhood.

$$ Hotel Ibis Koeln am Dom, a 71-room chain hotel, offers predictability, tidiness, and an extremely short walk from the train station—but no personality (Sb-€79, Db-€94; convention rate: Sb-€139–199, Db-€159–219; breakfast-€10, non-smoking rooms, air-con, elevator, free Internet access, pay Wi-Fi, Hauptbahnhof, entry across from station's *Reisezentrum,* tel. 0221/912-8580, fax 0221/9128-58199, www.ibishotel.com, h0739@accor.com).

$$ Hotel Engelbertz is a fine family-run 40-room enterprise. It's an eight-minute walk from the station and cathedral at the end of the pedestrian mall (specials in 2010 for readers with this book who request a discount during non-convention times: last-minute Sb-€55 and Db-€79 if you reserve on same day or day before, Sb-€65 and Db-€89 with advance reservation; regular rate Sb-€75 and Db-€108, convention rate Db-€195, elevator, inexpensive Internet access and Wi-Fi, just off Hohe Strasse at Obenmarspforten 1–3, coming from station turn left at Hohe Strasse 96, tel. 0221/257-8994, fax 0221/257-8924, www.hotel-engelbertz.de, info@hotel-engelbertz.de).

$$ Central Hotel am Dom's proximity to the station (one block away) and cathedral (two blocks away) make it a decent value. It's on a busy, noisy street corner (Sb-€59, Db-€80–90, can be cheaper in summer, non-smoking rooms, pricey Wi-Fi, An den Dominikanern 3, tel. 0221/135-088, fax 0221/135-080, www.centralamdom.de, info@centralamdom.de).

$$ Hotel Müller, run with great pride by enthusiastic Frau Müller, has 16 recently renovated rooms on a quiet street and offers three-star quality at two-star prices (because it doesn't have an elevator). Enjoy the grotto-like basement breakfast room/bar and the courtyard terrace (Sb-€60, Db-€75, Tb-€95, non-smoking, pay Wi-Fi; exit station by track 11 to Breslauer Platz, walk 2 short blocks up Johannisstrasse, then left on Brandenburger Strasse to #20; tel. 0221/912-8350, fax 0221/9128-3517, www.hotel-mueller-koeln.de, info@hotel-mueller.net). If it's full, there are other affordable, family-run hotels on Brandenburger Strasse and the nearby Domstrasse.

Budget Rooms

$ Station Hostel, with 200 beds, is a five-minute walk from the train station and full of young travelers (dorm bed-€17–22, S-€32, Sb-€39, twin-bed D-€48, Db-€55, Tb-€75, includes sheets, key deposit-€1, does not include breakfast—café on premises, kitchen, no elevator, no curfew, free Internet access and Wi-Fi, laundry-€4, tel. 0221/912-5301, fax 0221/912-5303; exit station on cathedral side, walk straight 1 block, turn right on Marzellenstrasse to #44–56; www.hostel-cologne.de, station@hostel-cologne.de).

Eating in Köln

The city's distinct type of beer, called *Kölsch,* is pale, hoppy, and highly fermented. Most of Köln's breweries (such as Gaffel and Päffgen) run their own restaurants, which you'll find in districts like Alter Markt and Friesenplatz.

Near Alter Markt

Gaffel Haus, run by the Gaffel Kölsch brewery, serves meaty local food, including nearly two-foot-long bratwursts. Look for the wall filled with coats of arms of Köln's old guilds *(Gaffeln)*—see how many crafts you can guess by their pictures (€10–17 main dishes, daily 11:00–24:00, near Lintgasse at Alter Markt 20–22, tel. 0221/257-7692).

Papa Joe's Klimperkasten is a dark pub packed with memorabilia and live jazz daily (€5–10 pub meals, daily 11:00–24:00, live piano jazz Sept–May Sun–Thu from 20:00, Alter Markt 50–52, tel. 0221/258-2132). A couple minutes' walk away is its rowdier sibling, **Papa Joe's Jazzlokal** (live bands nightly from 20:00, Buttermarkt 37, tel. 0221/257-7931, www.papajoes.de for jazz schedule). Both of these win the "atmosphere award."

Near the Train Station and Cathedral

Früh am Dom, close to the cathedral, offers three floors of touristy, traditional German drinking and dining options. Head to the back wall to check out a painting of what the city looked like in 1534 (€10–15 main dishes, daily 8:00–24:00, Am Hof 12–14, tel. 0221/261-3211).

Holtmann's im MAK, a museum café with sophisticated locals enjoying light fare, is a good option for a non-*Bräuhaus* lunch. If you eat here on a Sunday morning, be sure to sit outside and enjoy a free organ concert al fresco—the courtyard abuts a church (€8–10 main dishes, Tue–Fri 11:00–17:00, Sat–Sun 10:00–18:00, closed Mon, on other side of Hohe Strasse from the cathedral in Museum of Applied Arts—Museum für Angewandte Kunst—at An der Rechtschule 1, inside front door and down the stairs, no museum ticket needed, tel. 0221/2779-8860).

Café Eigel, just off Hohe Strasse near the recommended Hotel Engelbertz, is a good option for *Kaffee und Küchen* (afternoon cake and coffee) or for a light lunch of salads or omelets. It's been in the same location for 50 years, but was recently remodeled in a fresh, sleek, modern style. Enjoy delicious pastries in the airy atrium, and be sure to pick up some homemade chocolates (€7–10 main dishes, €3–4 slices of cake, Mon–Fri 9:00–19:00, Sat 9:00–18:00, Sun 14:00–18:00, Brückenstrasse 1–3, tel. 0221/257-5858).

Schreckenskammer is a down-home joint and the least touristy brewery in Köln. It's located just behind the St. Ursula church, near the recommended Harmonie and Cristall hotels and the Station Hostel. The sand on the floor, swept out and replaced each morning, buffs the hardwood and also keeps it clean. The *kammer* is small and cozy, so be prepared to share a table and make new friends over a *Kölsch* or two. Most meals (choose from the *Tageskarte*, or daily specials) start with a complimentary cup of

Brühe (broth). Don't mistake this as an act of hospitality—it only serves to make you thirstier. This eatery is really popular with locals, so arrive early or make a reservation (€7–14 main dishes, €6–10 lunch specials, Mon–Sat 11:00–13:45 & 16:30–22:30, closed Sun, cash only, Ursulagartenstrasse 11–15, tel. 0221/132-581).

Near Friesenplatz

This neighborhood, a 20-minute walk west along busy streets (or two stops on the U-5 subway) from the cathedral and train station, is thick with restaurants, clubs, and pubs—some run by breweries. **Päffgen** is one brewery outlet where the *Köbes* (Köln's traditionally grumpy waiters) really live up to their reputation as they dish out traditional *Kölsch* food. Beers are served in delicate glasses (by Bavarian standards) and shuttled around in small wreath-like trays *(Bierkranz)*. This is the place to satisfy your cravings for blood sausage *(Blutwurst)* and kidneys *(Nierchen)*...or, for something a little more mainstream, try the tasty *Rheinischer Sauerbraten* with *Klössen* (dumplings) and applesauce (€8–15 main dishes, daily 10:00–24:00, food served 11:00–23:00, Friesenstrasse 64–66, tel. 0911/135-461).

Köln Connections

From Köln by Train to: Bonn (5/hr, 20–30 min), **Remagen** (2–3/hr, 30–50 min), **Aachen** (2/hr, 50–60 min), **Frankfurt** (direct trains hourly, 80 min; also slower, cheaper trains along Rhine, 2.25 hrs), **Frankfurt Airport** (1–2/hr, 1 hr; trains along Rhine go less often and take 2.25 hrs), **Bacharach** or **St. Goar** (hourly; 1.75 hrs with change in Koblenz, 2.5 hrs direct), **Cochem** (hourly, 1.75–2.25 hrs; most change in Koblenz), **Trier** (at least hourly, 2.5–3 hrs, some change in Koblenz), **Würzburg** (at least hourly, 2.5 hrs, usually 1 change), **Munich** (2/hr, 4.5 hrs, some with 1 change), **Berlin** (hourly, 4.75 hrs), **Paris** (6/day direct, 4 hrs, Thalys train—requires seat reservation, slower options also available), **Amsterdam** (6/day direct, 2.5 hrs). Train info: tel. 0180-599-6633 (€0.14/min).

The Unromantic Rhine

Highlights

▲Bonn—Bonn was chosen for its sleepy, cultured, and peaceful nature as a good place to plant West Germany's first post-Hitler government. Since the two Germanys became one again in 1989, Berlin has taken back its position as capital.

Today, Bonn is sleek, modern, and, by big-city standards, remarkably pleasant and easygoing. The pedestrian-only old town stretching out from the station will make you wonder why the US

can't trade in its malls for real, people-friendly cities. The market square and Münsterplatz—filled with street musicians—are a joy. People-watching doesn't get much better, though the actual sights are disappointing. There's a sparse exhibit at Beethoven's House (€5; April–Oct Mon–Sat 10:00–18:00, Sun 11:00–18:00; Nov–March Mon–Sat 10:00–17:00, Sun 11:00–17:00; last entry 25 min before closing, free English brochure, tel. 0228/981-7525, www.beethoven-haus-bonn .de). The **TI** is a five-minute walk from the station (Mon–Fri 9:00–18:30, Sat 9:00–16:00, Sun 10:00–14:00, go straight on Windeckstrasse, next to Karstadt department store, tel. 0228/775-000, www.bonn.de).

▲Remagen—Midway between Koblenz and Köln are the scant remains of the Bridge at Remagen, of WWII (and movie) fame. But the memorial and the bridge stubs are enough to stir the emotions of Americans who remember when it was the only bridge that remained, allowing the Allies to cross the Rhine and race to Berlin in 1945. A small museum tells the bridge's fascinating story in English. It was built during World War I to help supply the German forces on the Western Front. Ironically, one war later, Eisenhower said the bridge was worth its weight in gold for its service *against* Germany. Hitler executed four generals for their failure to blow it up. Ten days after US forces arrived, the bridge did collapse, killing 28 American soldiers. Today you can pay your respects at the bridge and visit its "Peace Museum" (€3.50, early March–mid-Nov daily 10:00–17:00, May–Oct until 18:00, closed mid-Nov–early March; it's on the Rhine's west bank, south side of Remagen town, follow *Brücke von Remagen* signs; www.bruecke-remagen.de). Remagen **TI:** tel. 02642/20187.

▲**Aachen (Charlemagne's Capital)**—This city was the capital of Europe in A.D. 800, when Charles the Great (Charlemagne) called it Aix-la-Chapelle. The remains of his rule include an impressive Byzantine- and Ravenna-inspired church, with his sarcophagus and throne. Enjoy the town's charming historic pedestrian center and festive Christmas market. See the head-liner newspaper museum and great fountains, including a clever arrange-'em-yourself version.

Lowlights

Heidelberg—This famous old university town attracts hordes of Americans. Any surviving charm is stained almost beyond recognition by commercialism. It doesn't make it into Germany's top three weeks.

Mainz, Wiesbaden, and Rüdesheim—These towns are all too big or too famous. They're not worth your time. Mainz's Gutenberg Museum is also a disappointment.

NÜRNBERG

Nürnberg (sometimes spelled "Nuremberg" in English), Bavaria's second city, is known for its glorious medieval architecture, its important Germanic history museum, its haunting Nazi past, its famous Christmas market (Germany's biggest), and its little bratwurst (Germany's tiniest). Nürnberg was one of Europe's leading cities in about 1500, and its large imperial castle marks it as a stronghold of the Holy Roman Empire. Today, though Nürnberg has half a million residents, the charming Old Town with its red-sandstone Gothic buildings makes visitors feel like they are in a far smaller city.

Planning Your Time

Nürnberg is an easy add-on to any itinerary that includes Munich, Würzburg, or Rothenburg (each about an hour away by frequent trains), and a handy stop on the way to Frankfurt, Berlin, or Dresden. If you are staying one night or day-tripping from elsewhere, visit the Nazi sites, stroll through the Old Town from the train station up to the castle (following my self-guided walk), and—on the way back to the station (or your hotel)—dip into the wonderful Germanic National Museum. If you have two days (only worthwhile if you have a serious interest in Nazi history), spend one on Nazi sites and the other in the Old Town. For the quickest visit to Nürnberg, toss your bag in a locker at the station and head directly to the former Nazi Rally Grounds.

Orientation to Nürnberg

(area code: 0911)

Nürnberg's Old Town (containing all the non-Nazi sights) is surrounded by its three-mile-long wall and moat, and, beyond that, a ring road. At the southeast corner of the ring is the train station; across the street, just inside the ring, is the medieval Frauentor gate. From the Frauentor, sights cluster along a straight line (Königstrasse) downhill to the small Pegnitz River, then back uphill through the main market square (Hauptmarkt) to the castle (Kaiserburg). The former Nazi Rally Grounds are southeast of the center (easily accessible by tram or bus).

Tourist Information

Nürnberg's handy and helpful TI is across the ring road from the station, in the modern building just opposite the Frauentor (Mon–Sat 9:00–19:00, Sun 10:00–16:00, Königstrasse 93, tel. 0911/233-6132, www.tourismus.nuernberg.de). Pick up the free city guidebooklet (with updated sight hours and prices) and get information about bus and walking tours. The TI also offers free Internet access (15-min maximum), books rooms (no fee), and sells transit passes and the Nürnberg Card (see below). The TI has a small branch office at #18 on the Hauptmarkt (Mon–Sat 9:00–18:00, also open Sun May–Oct and during the Christmas market 10:00–16:00).

Discount Deals: Buy a €5 ticket for any of Nürnberg's city-run museums—including the Nazi Documentation Center, Albrecht Dürer House, Toy Museum, and the City Museum—and you can visit all the others as well for no extra charge on the same day (see www.museen.nuernberg.de). Because this is such a great value, I'd skip the two other available deals: the **"Take Five" Ticket** (€19, covers five entrances into your choice of seven different museums, shareable by multiple people, sold at participating sights and at Frauentor TI) and the **Nürnberg Card** (€19/2 days, free for kids 12 and under, sold at the TI and most hotels, covers all of your local transportation and admission to all of Nürnberg's museums, plus small discounts off bus and walking tours, only available to those spending at least one night in Nürnberg). Finally, another €12 combo-ticket offers admission to the National Germanic Museum and Albrecht Dürer House (otherwise €11) and includes a handheld computer guide to the museums and the walking route connecting them (€20 deposit for computer).

Arrival in Nürnberg

By Train: Nürnberg's stately old Hauptbahnhof—with a shiny new interior—is conveniently located just outside the old city walls and ring road. The station has WCs, lockers, ATMs, and lots of shops. You can get train information and buy tickets at the *Reisezentrum* in the main hall (center of building, Mon–Fri 6:00–21:00, Sat–Sun 8:00–21:00).

To reach the **Frauentor** (the medieval city's southern gate)— which is near most recommended hotels and is also the starting point for exploring the Old Town—follow signs for *Ausgang/City* down the escalator, then signs to *Königstor/Frauentor* and *Altstadt* in the underpass. When you emerge, the TI is on your right and the Frauentor tower is on your left.

To go directly to the **former Nazi Rally Grounds** from the station, follow the pink *Tram* signs in the underpass to the stop in front of the Postbank Center, and catch tram #9 in the direction of Doku-Zentrum (leaves every 10 min).

Getting Around Nürnberg

Most of Nürnberg's sights are in the strollable Old Town, but the Nazi sites are far beyond walking distance. Nürnberg has the typical German lineup of trams, buses, U-Bahns (subways), and S-Bahns (faster suburban trains). All work on the same tickets, which you can buy at vending machines (marked *VAG Fahrausweise*) on the tram platform or before entering the U- or S-Bahns, or on board (buses only). A **single ticket** *(Einzelfahrkarte)* costs €1.90 (good for 90 min of travel in one direction, including transfers). A **day ticket** is €3.80 (*TagesTicket Solo*, good for one calendar day or both Sat and Sun; the €6.60 *TagesTicket Plus* covers 2 adults and up to 4 children; day tickets also sold at TI). Everything in this book is within zone *(Preisstufe)* 2. Vending machines time-stamp single and day tickets, so you don't need to validate them separately. Some other kinds of tickets, less useful for visitors, have to be punched on board (for the bus or tram) or before going down to the platform (for the subway). For more information, see www.vgn.de.

Helpful Hints

Internet Access: While there are several Internet cafés in the city center, save some euros and take advantage of free Internet access in the **TI** (15-min time limit).

Laundry: An **SB-Waschsalon** coin launderette with instructions in English is at Pirckheimerstrasse 121, right at the Wurzelbauerstrasse stop of tram #9 (5 stops from train station, direction Thon, same tram as Nazi Rally Grounds but in the other direction; daily 6:00–23:00).

Tours in Nürnberg

Walking Tours—Tours in English of Nürnberg's Old Town leave from the branch TI at Hauptmarkt 18 daily in the tourist season at 13:00 (May–Oct and Dec, €9 plus castle admission, kids under 14 free, 2.5 hrs, no reservation needed, buy ticket from TI or guide, www.nuernberg-tours.de). This is the only way to see the sights in the castle interior with an English-speaking guide.

Bus Tours—These tours, which include some walking, leave daily at 9:30 (May–Oct and Dec) from the Old Granary (Mauthalle) at Hallplatz, two blocks up from the Frauentor TI (€14, buy ticket on bus or at TI, 2.5 hrs, in German and English, tel. 0911/202-290, www.neukam.de).

Tourist Train—A goofy little tourist train makes the rounds in the Old Town (€6, 40 min, live narration in German only, written information in English, schedule posted at fountain, leaves Hauptmarkt about hourly 10:30–16:00, www.nuernberg-tourist.de).

Private Guide—For a good and charming local guide, call **Doris Ritter** (€95/3 hrs, tel. 0911/518-1719, mobile 0176-2421-5863, doris.ritter@nuernberg-tours.de). Guides can also be booked through the TI (tel. 0911/233-6123, fuehrung@ctz-nuernberg.de).

Self-Guided Walk

▲▲Nürnberg's Old Town

Nürnberg's best sights are conveniently clustered along a straight-line thoroughfare connecting the train station (Hauptbahnhof) with the main market square (Hauptmarkt) and the castle (Kaiserburg). For a good orientation, take the following self-guided stroll. Plan on an hour, not including stops.

• *Begin at the Frauentor (where you emerge from the Hauptbahnhof underpass). Review the lay of the land on the 10-foot-tall city map posted in front of the tunnel (find the four towers). This tour will take you from the red dot at the bottom to the* Burg *(castle) at the top.*

Frauentor

This tower guards one of the four medieval entrances to Nürnberg's Old Town. Of the three miles of wall that once surrounded the city, 90 percent survives. Many Central European cities (such as Vienna) tore down their walls to make way for expansion in the 1800s, and Nürnberg nearly did the same. Now they're glad they didn't—it's better for tourism.

• *Between the walls just next to the gate, you'll see the entrance to the...*

Central Nürnberg

200 YARDS
200 METERS

— OLD CITY WALLS
← SELF-GUIDED WALK
S S-BAHN
U U-BAHN
↙ VIEW

IMPERIAL CASTLE

CITY MUSEUM

ALBRECHT DÜRER HOUSE

Toy Museum

MARKET SQUARE (HAUPTMARKT) & FRAUENKIRCHE

PEGNITZ RIVER

SCHÜTT-INSEL

HOLY GHOST HOSPITAL

ST. LAWRENCE CHURCH

OLD GRANARY

GERMANIC NATIONAL MUSEUM

TRAM #9 TO NAZI SITES

START

INNER RING ROAD

FRAUENTOR & CRAFTSMEN'S COURTYARD

GERMAN RAILWAY MUSEUM

TRAIN STATION

POST

NÜRNBERG

1 Hotel Victoria
2 Hotel Drei Raben & Aldi Supermarket
3 Ibis Altstadt Hotel
4 City Hotel
5 Hotels Probst & Keiml
6 Hotel Elch
7 Hotel/Café Lucas
8 Nürnberg Youth Hostel

9 Barfüsser Beer Cellar
10 Nassauer Keller Restaurant
11 Goldenes Posthorn Rest.
12 Literaturhaus Nürnberg Rest.
13 Burgwächter Restaurant
14 Bratwursthäusle Rest.
15 Kettensteg Biergarten
16 Karstadt Supermarket

Craftsmen's Courtyard (Handwerkerhof)

This hokey collection of half-timbered houses was built in 1971 to celebrate craftsmanship and to honor the 500th birthday of Nürnberg's famous resident Albrecht Dürer. Nürnberg did not have abundant natural resources or a navigable waterway, so its citizens made their living through trade and crafts (such as making scientific instruments, weapons, and armor). Dürer, arguably Germany's best painter, was considered the ultimate craftsman. The proud medieval tradition of craftsmanship continues today, as the city is home to some of Germany's top goldsmiths and glassblowers.

While a bit kitschy, this courtyard is good for picking up a medieval vibe as you enter the Old Town. It's packed with replicas of medieval shops, where artisans actually make—and, of course, sell—leather, pottery, and brass goods. In the Middle Ages, this area between the walls was not a medieval mall but *Passkontrolle*—a customs and security checkpoint zone where all visitors had to register before they could enter the town.

At the back of the courtyard, step through the old gate and out onto a bridge over what was the moat. The bridge marks one of four entries into the medieval town. Look up at the mighty round Frauentor tower. It was originally square, but was made round after the development of better cannons (so balls would glance off rather than hit it head-on). Imagine cannons lined up under the eaves of the tower, set to defend the city. When local kids look at the mighty train station (across the street), they remember that the first train in Germany choo-chooed from here in 1835.

• *When you're finished poking around the courtyard, head into town (with the train station at your back) on...*

Königstrasse

Though it had always been one of the four primary entrances to Nürnberg, this street became the city's main drag only after the train station was built in the early 20th century. It's lined with key sights, several recommended hotels and restaurants, and some wonderful Gothic and Neo-Gothic architecture.

Nürnberg hit its peak in the 14th century, and a 1356 conference held here issued a decree called the Golden Bull, which regularized the election of the Holy Roman Emperor. From then throughout the Middle Ages, German emperors were elected in Frankfurt, crowned in Aachen, and were supposed to hold their first Imperial Diet (a gathering of German nobles and VIPs) right here in Nürnberg...though not all bothered to follow through on such democratic notions.

Nürnberg's low point came during World War II. By the end of the war, 90 percent of the Old Town was destroyed—the only German city hit worse was Dresden. If a building was only damaged, it was repaired in the original Gothic style—check out the building with the Peschke Optik shop at Königstrasse 81. But some buildings were completely destroyed. Instead of rebuilding these exactly as they were, or replacing them with modern-style buildings, postwar German architects compromised, creating styles that were at once modern and traditional. In Nürnberg, they often rebuilt in local sandstone. Look 50 yards down the street at #71. The design is modern, but it replicates some of the Gothic lines and uses the same distinctive red stone as older buildings.

Ahead, on the left, is the small **Clara Church** (Klarakirche). In the Middle Ages, Nürnberg had nine monasteries like this one. When the Reformation hit, Nürnberg turned Lutheran, and most of the monasteries were torn down. As they fell, so did Nürnberg's importance; the city was now Lutheran, but the emperors were still Catholic. They moved the increasingly frequent Imperial Diet—once Nürnberg's claim to fame—to more Catholic-friendly Regensburg. (Today, this church is an "ecumenical free church"— meaning it's neither Lutheran nor Catholic and welcomes all stripes.)

Across the street from Clara Church, look for Mary on the second-story corner. Statues like this bless houses all over Nürnberg.

• *Continue down Königstrasse to Hallplatz and the Old Granary (where the pedestrian stretch begins). The minimalist metal arch (left) remembers the German refugees of World War II, and the hospitality of the Bavarians who took them in. If you want to visit the excellent Germanic National Museum (described on page 443) now, detour left at Hallplatz and walk 200 yards. Otherwise, check out the...*

Old Granary (Mauthalle)

Medieval Nürnberg had 11 of these huge granaries to ensure that

they'd have enough food in case of famine or siege. The grain was stored up above in the attic (behind all those little dormer windows). Today, the cellar is home to a lively and recommended beer hall, Barfüsser.

Go around the right side of the building and find the fun little **Vom Fass shop,** which sells liquor, wine, vinegar, and oils "from the tap" (as the name indicates). You bring or buy a container of any size, fill it with what you like (tastes allowed), and they'll even write a gifty message right on the bottle (An der

NÜRNBERG

Mauthalle 2, Mon–Fri 10:00–19:00, Sat 10:00–18:00, closed Sun, Herr Eduard Stöber).

Continue down pedestrians-only Königstrasse. This drag used to have more cars and trams than any other street in town. But when the U-Bahn came in the 1970s, this part of the street became traffic-free.

• *After another two blocks, you'll see...*

▲▲St. Lawrence Church (Lorenzkirche)

This once-Catholic, now Protestant church is a massive house of worship. It was never a cathedral—because Nürnberg never had a bishop (a fact locals were very proud of...a bishop would have

threatened their prized independence). The name of Königstrasse ("King's Street")—where you've been walking—is misleading. When most royals came to town, they actually preferred to come through the west gate, so they could approach this masterful facade head-on. Stand in front of the church's main door. Flip around and imagine the Holy Roman Emperor parading—right past Starbucks—toward this magnificent Oz-like church.

Study the 260-foot-tall **facade** (completed c. 1360). Adam and Eve flank the doors (looking for a sweater). In the first row above the left door, you'll see two scenes: an intimate take on Jesus' birth on top, and the visit from the Magi on the bottom (with the starfish of Bethlehem shining from above). Over the right door, you'll see the slaughter of the innocents (with a baby skewered by a Roman sword—classic medieval subtlety), and below that the presentation of Jesus in the temple and the flight to Egypt. Above those scenes is the Passion story (from lowest to highest: trial, scourging, carrying the cross, Crucifixion, deposition, entombment, Resurrection, and people coming out of their graves for Judgment Day). The saved (Peter—with his huge key—and company) are on the left, and the sorry chain gang of the damned (including kings and bishops) is shuttled off literally into the jaws of hell on the right. Above it all stands the triumphant resurrected Christ, with the sun and moon at his feet, flanked by angels tooting alphorns.

Step inside (enter around right side, €1 donation requested, €5 for a pass to take photos, Mon–Sat 9:00–17:00, Sun 12:30–16:00, www.lorenzkirche.de).

The **interior** wasn't completely furnished until more than a century after the church was built—just in time for the Reformation (so the Catholic decor adorned a now-Lutheran church). Most of the decorations inside were donated by wealthy Nürnbergers trying to cut down on their time in purgatory. Through the centuries, this art survived three separate threats: the iconoclasm of the Reformation, the whitewashing of the Baroque age, and the bombing of World War II. While Nürnberg was the first "Free Imperial City" to break with the Catholic Church and become Lutheran, locals didn't go wild (like Swiss Protestants did) in tearing down the rich, Mary-oriented decor of their fine churches. Luther told the iconoclasts, "Tear the idols out of your heart, and you'll understand that these statues are only pieces of wood."

Suspended over the altar, the woodcarving called *The Annunciation* is by a Nürnberg citizen who was one of Central Europe's best woodcarvers, Veit Stoss. Carved in 1517, it shows the angel Gabriel telling Mary that she'll be giving birth to the Messiah. Startled, she drops her prayer book. This is quite Catholic (notice the rosary frame with beads, and a circle of roses—one for each Hail Mary, and with a medallion depicting the "Joys of Mary"). The dove sits on Mary's head, and God the Father—looking as powerful as a Holy Roman Emperor—looks down. The figures are carved from linden trees. This survived the Reformation covered in a sack, revealed only on special occasions. Around back, enjoy more details—Mary's cascading hair, and the sun and the moon. Nearby, the altar painting at the very front of the church (behind the altar) shows the city of Nürnberg in 1483 (before the city's square towers were made round).

To the left of the altar, the frilly **tabernacle** tower is the "house of sacraments" that stored the consecrated Communion wafer. After the Mass, leftovers needed a worthy—even heavenly—home...and this was it. The cupboard behind the gold grate was the appropriate receptacle for "the body of Christ." The theme of the carving is the Passion. The scenes ascend in chronological order: Last Supper, Judas' kiss, arrest, Crucifixion, and so on. Everything is carved of stone except for the risen Christ (way up high). He was living, and so was this...it's made of wood. The man holding the tabernacle on his shoulders is the artist who created

it, Adam Kraft. In the Middle Ages, artists were faceless artisans, no more important than a blacksmith or a stonemason. But in the 1490s, when this was made, the Renaissance was in the air, and artists like Kraft began putting themselves into their works. Kraft's contemporary, the painter Albrecht Dürer, actually signed his works—an incredible act in Germany at that time (for more on Dürer, see page 442). In anticipation of the Allied bombs of World War II, this precious work was encased in protective concrete except for the top 22 feet—which was the only part destroyed when the church was hit.

Adam Kraft is looking up at a **plaque** honoring American philanthropist brothers Samuel and Rush Kress, who donated nearly a million Deutschmarks in 1950 to help rebuild the church. The plaque is in English, but it's hard to read, as it's written in an old-style black-letter font. Though the church was devastated by WWII bombs, everything movable had been hidden away in bunkers, including the stained glass you see today. Back at the rear of the church, a silent **video** (with dates in the upper corner) shows the preparations in anticipation of WWII bombs, the destruction, and the reconstruction.

As you leave, notice that the church has many **side chapels**—employing an innovative trick of expanding the nave out so the buttresses are actually inside the church.

From St. Lawrence Church to the River: Back outside, find the castle-like building on the corner across from the church facade. This is the only remaining **tower house** in Nürnberg. It was built in 1200, when there was no city wall, and the locals had to defend their own homes. It's basically a one-family castle. (In the basement, you'll find a recommended, appropriately medieval restaurant—complete with suits of armor—called the Nassauer Keller.)

Continue downhill to the river. American moralists might shield their eyes from the kinky **Fountain of the Seven Virtues.** Otherwise, play a game: Circle the sprightly fountain and try to identify the classic virtues by the symbolism: justice (on top), faith, love, hope (anchor), courage (lion), temperance (moderation), patience. Are any birds sipping?

• *Continue down the street. Caution: You'll pass Kaiserstrasse on your left—the most expensive shopping street in town (with a little shop filled with insanely expensive Steiff teddy bears). When you get to the bridge, look to the right.*

Holy Ghost Hospital (Heilig-Geist-Spital)

This river-spanning hospital was donated to Nürnberg in the 14th century by the city's richest resident, eager to do his part to help the poor... and hopefully skip purgatory altogether. (A statue of him hangs out on the second-story corner of the Spital Apotheke, the first building after the bridge.) He funded this very scenic hospital to care for ill, disabled, and elderly Nürnbergers. The wing over the river dates from the 16th century. The dove beneath the middle window under the turret represents the Holy Ghost, the hospital's namesake.

If you look in the distance to the right—beyond the hospital and the next two bridges—you'll see a half-timbered fragment of the town wall. The big white building to the right of that is Germany's biggest multiplex cinema, with 21 screens (most underground).

Cross to the other side of the bridge, and look at the next bridge over (the **"Meat Bridge"**). This is the narrowest point of the river, and flooding was a big concern. Since this bridge doesn't have any piers, there's less chance of a collapse. When this was built in 1596, it was considered an engineering feat—the most high-tech bridge in Central Europe, inspired by Venice's single-span Rialto Bridge. The river once powered the town's medieval water mills.

Continue across the bridge and study the monument depicting characters from a 15th-century satire called *The Ship of Fools (Das Narrenschiff)*. It's adapted to follies that plague modern society: violence, technology, and apathy. Hey, how about the quiet, people-friendly ambience created by making this big city traffic-free in the center? Do a slow 360-degree spin and imagine this back home.

• *Now enter the...*

▲▲Market Square (Hauptmarkt)

When Nürnberg boomed in the 13th century, it consisted of two distinct walled towns separated by the river. As the towns grew and it became obvious that the two should merge, the middle wall came down. This square, built by the Holy Roman Emperor Charles IV, became the center of the newly united city. Though Charles is more often associated with Prague (he's the namesake for the Charles Bridge and Charles University), he also loved Nürnberg—and visited 60 times during his reign.

The **Frauenkirche** church on the square is located on the site of a former synagogue (inside, there's a Star of David on the floor). When Nürnberg's towns were separate, Jewish residents were required to live in this swampy area close to the river and outside the walls. When the towns merged and the land occupied by the Jewish quarter became valuable, Charles IV allowed his subjects to force out the Jews—and 600 were killed in the process...a somber reminder that anti-Semitism predated the Nazis. Charles IV, the most powerful man in Europe in his time, oversees the square from a perch high on the church facade. He's waiting for noon, when the electors dance around him.

Year-round, the Hauptmarkt is lively with fruit, flower, and souvenir stands. For a few weeks before Christmas, it hosts Germany's largest **Christmas market** (*Christkindlmarkt,* more than 2 million visitors annually, starts the Friday before the first Sunday in Advent).

Walk across the square to the pointy gold **Beautiful Fountain** (Schöner Brunnen). Medieval tanneries, slaughterhouses, and the

hospital you just saw dumped their byproducts into the river. So this fountain brought clean drinking water into the square. Of course, it's packed with allegorical meaning. Step up to the iron railing. The outermost figures ringing the bottom represent the arts (such as philosophy, music, and astronomy). On the pillars just above them are the four church fathers and the four Evangelists, showing that religion is higher than the arts. On the column itself, the lowest figures are the seven electors of the Holy Roman Emperor and nine heroes: three Christian (including King Arthur and Charlemagne); three Jewish (such as King David); and three heathen (such as Julius Caesar). At the very top are eight prophets, hovering above—but granting legitimacy to—worldly power. On the side of the fountain facing the McDonald's, you'll probably see tourists fussing over a gold ring. If you believe in such silly tour-guide tales, spinning this ring three times brings good luck...OK, go ahead and spin it. The black ring opposite (nearest the stork bearing a baby—look for the rice on the ground) brings fertility. Civic marriage ceremonies that take place at the adjacent City Hall often end up here for photos.

• *Leave the square straight uphill from the fountain, heading for the castle. Along the way, you'll pass St. Sebald (Sebaldkirche), Nürnberg's second great Gothic church. About 100 yards farther up the hill, you'll see the...*

City Museum (Stadtmuseum Fembohaus)

This museum is packed with fine artifacts, but you'll need the English audioguide to give them meaning (included in admission). Check out the top-floor model of Nürnberg. The museum's *Noricama Nürnberg Film* is a fascinating 50-minute video shown on the hour (in English with headphones) that gives a fun and thoughtful overview of the city, its history, and its great sights in a comfortable little theater (museum-€5, film-€4, €7 combo-ticket includes both, Tue–Fri 10:00–17:00, Sat–Sun 10:00–18:00, closed Mon, Burgstrasse 15, tel. 0911/231-2595, www.museen .nuernberg.de).

• *Now huff the rest of the way up to the Imperial Castle. The cobbled path forks at the castle's base. The right fork leads to the Castle Garden and youth hostel. The left fork leads to the castle courtyard (see big, round tower high above) and over the recommended Burgwächter restaurant. For now, take the left fork and visit the...*

▲Imperial Castle (Kaiserburg)

In the Middle Ages, Holy Roman Emperors stayed here when they were in town. This huge complex has 45 buildings. The part on the right, which housed the stables and stored grain, is now a youth hostel.

The castle interior and museum are standard fare. The most interesting bits are the so-called Deep Well (which, at 165 feet, is...well, deep) and the Romanesque double-decker chapel (higher nobility in the upper chapel, lower nobility down below, plus a special balcony for the emperor). The tower climb offers only a higher city view and lots of exercise.

The castle grounds are free, but unfortunately you can only see the interior sights with a German-language tour (€6 for one-hour

tour of museum, palace, chapel, well, and then the chance to visit the museum and climb the tower on your own; €3 to visit just the well and then climb tower on your own; covered by Bavarian Castles Pass—see page 98; tickets sold in office at top end of courtyard; daily April–Sept 9:00–18:00, Oct– March 10:00–16:00, tel. 0911/244-

6590, www.schloesser.bayern.de). There is one alternative: Go with the TI's English tour of the entire Old Town, which includes the castle (departs at 13:00; see "Tours in Nürnberg," earlier).

Deep Well visits (about 4/hr), even with the German guide, are simple, quick, and fun: You'll see water poured way, waaay down— into an incredible hole dug in the 14th century. Then a small candle is lowered until it almost disappears into the water table.

• *Now you get to walk downhill again. The quick way down is to retrace your steps to the Burgwächter restaurant, then turn right and walk beneath the castle along Am Ölberg and Obere Schmiedgasse to Tiergärtnertorplatz (described below). The scenic route, which takes an extra 15 minutes, leads you around the back of the castle through the...*

NÜRNBERG

Castle Garden (Burggarten)

Find the entrance to the castle garden. It's at the back of the hill, between the main complex and the youth hostel, and signposted *Burggarten*, but a bit hidden (you may have to ask). The garden, wrapped around the back of the castle, offers great views of the town's 16th-century fortifications and former moat (free, April–Oct daily 8:00–20:00, closes at dusk if earlier, closed Nov–March).

• *Follow the path around the castle. Either make a quick return through the first archway on your left, or continue another five minutes through landscaped gardens along the old city walls. Eventually you'll be spit out in between two archways in front of a round tower (Neutor). Go through the archway on your left, then turn left, and walk two slightly uphill blocks along Neutormauer to the square with the giant rabbit statue. This is...*

Tiergärtnertorplatz

Near the top of the square, inspect the giant rabbit. While it looks like roadkill with mice gnawing at it, it's actually a modern interpretation of one of the best-known paintings by medieval Nürnberg artist Albrecht Dürer, *The Hare*. (The original painting is in Vienna.)

• *The rabbit faces a half-timbered building at the bottom of the square. That's the...*

▲Albrecht Dürer House (Albrecht-Dürer-Haus)

Nürnberg's most famous local lived in this house for the last 20 years of his life. Albrecht Dürer (1471–1528), a contemporary of

Michelangelo, studied in Venice and brought the Renaissance to stodgy medieval Germany. He did things that were unthinkable to other northern European artists of his time— such as signing his works, or painting things like hares simply for study (not on commission).

Nothing in the museum is original (all of the paintings are replicas—the only Dürer originals in Nürnberg are in the Germanic National Museum, described later). But the museum does a fine job of capturing the way that Dürer actually lived, and includes a replica of the workshop where he printed his woodcuts with a working printing press. In one room, a 17-minute movie plays continuously (in English on your headphones). The top floor is a gallery with copies of Dürer's most famous paintings and woodcuts. On Saturdays at 14:00, you can meet Dürer's wife, Agnes, who speaks English and takes you through their house (€5, includes Agnes-led audioguide, live Agnes tour–€2.50 extra, €1.50 English brochure also available, Tue–Sun 10:00–17:00, Thu until 20:00, closed Mon except July–Sept and Dec 10:00–17:00, Albrecht-Dürer-Strasse 39, tel. 0911/231-2568, www.museen.nuernberg.de/duererhaus).

Serious Dürer fans can buy a €12 combo-ticket that includes entrance to both the Albrecht Dürer House and the Germanic National Museum, as well as a handheld computer tour focusing on Dürer sights at both museums and along the route between them (available at either museum, €20 deposit for computer).

• *You've walked from the southern gate of Nürnberg to the northern gate, and your tour is over. If heading from here to the Nazi sites, bus #36 from Hauptmarkt or a taxi are your best bets. Or, for more sightseeing on your way back to the Frauentor, three more Old Town museums are listed in the next section.*

More Sights in Nürnberg

In and near the Old Town

Toy Museum (Spielzeugmuseum)—Nürnberg is famous for woodworking. You can see some examples of this local craft—and lots more—at this entertaining, interactive collection of toys from across the ages. The chronological display starts on the ground floor and heads up through four more floors. Highlights are: for history buffs—the section on the militarization of the 1930s and the rubble years through the 1950s; for Nebraskans—a miniature replica of the Omaha train station; and for kids—the top-floor play zone. Get an English audioguide (€1), or consider the good little €3 booklet (€5/adult, €10.50/family, Tue–Fri 10:00–17:00, Sat–Sun 10:00–18:00, closed Mon, Karlstrasse 13–15, near Albrecht Dürer House, tel. 0911/231-3164, www.museen.nuernberg.de).

▲▲Germanic National Museum (Germanisches Nationalmuseum)—This sprawling, sweeping museum is dedicated to

the cultural history of the German-speaking world. It occupies an interconnected maze of buildings, old and new, in the southern part of the Old Town, near the station and recommended hotels.

The museum is huge, and covers a vast spectrum of German culture from fine arts to prehistory to science to musical instruments. There are also regular temporary exhibits. You could spend days here, but the best approach is to pick up the bilingual "Floor Plan" brochure *(Orientierungsplan)*, which lists the different collections. Pick out a few things you are really interested in. Note the room numbers and the color codes of the wings you're headed for. Few labels or signposts are in English, but free English brochures on some of the exhibitions are available in a rack by the entrance.

Highlights of the museum's medieval art collection are works by Dürer (the only originals in town), Rembrandt, and Tilman Riemenschneider, often arranged into temporary exhibitions. Other "must-sees" generally on display include an early globe (since it dates from 1492, the Americas are conspicuously missing) and the delicate wooden *Nürnberg Madonna* (1515). This intimate, anonymous carving of the favorite hometown girl was the symbol of the city during the Romantic Age (19th century).

Coming in the entrance, you'll stand before a wall displaying a few street signs from East Germany, dating from the time when the Soviets had renamed the main drag in many towns *Strasse der Befreiung* ("Street of the Liberation"—from the Nazis and capitalism).

Entering the museum along Kartäusergasse, you walk along the "Way of Human Rights." Designed by an Israeli artist, its pillars trumpet each of the provisions of the United Nations' Universal Declaration of Human Rights.

Cost and Hours: €6, free Wed 18:00–21:00, worthwhile €1.50 audioguide, covered by €12 Dürer combo-ticket described earlier; Tue–Sun 10:00–18:00 (upper floor closes at 17:00), Wed all floors until 21:00, closed Mon; €2 English tours every other Sun at 14:00, mandatory bag check (lockers with €1 refundable deposit), Kartäusergasse 1, 2 blocks west of Königstrasse (enter on far side of building), tel. 0911/13310, www.gnm.de.

German Railway Museum (DB Museum)—Germany's first railway was built in Nürnberg in 1835, and the German Railway (Deutsche Bahn) now runs a huge museum just outside the Old Town telling the story of German trains from 1835 to 1989. There's only a little English (plus a free booklet you can pick up at the entrance), but rail fans won't mind. A big hands-on kids section is full of games and model railroads, while the petting zoo of real engines and carriages appeals to all ages (€4, €3 with valid train ticket, Tue–Fri 9:00–17:00, Sat–Sun 10:00–18:00, closed Mon except in Dec, Lessingstrasse 6; from Germanic National Museum take the footbridge over the old moat, cross the ring road and walk a block down Lessingstrasse; tel. 0911/231-3164, www.dbmuseum.de).

Nazi Sites

Though the city tries to recast itself as the "City of Human Rights," its reputation as Hitler's favorite place for a really big party is hard to shake. To understand Nürnberg's role in the Nazi movement, visit Hitler's vast Nazi Party Rally Grounds (Reichsparteitagsgelände), and the excellent museum—the Nazi Documentation Center—set amid the mute remains of the Third Reich.

Planning Your Time: World War II buffs might want to make this an all-day visit (a café in the museum serves lunch). With half a day, spend two hours in the museum and then another hour following the path around the lake. On a lightning visit, see the museum, peek into the courtyard of the Congress Hall, and if time allows, walk to Zeppelin Field and back. Only part of the outdoor circuit is shaded, so bring a hat and sunscreen on a hot day. Make sure to pick up the free map and the €1 English guidebook from the museum counter before doing the walk around the lake.

Getting to the Nazi Documentation Center and Rally Grounds: The sprawling complex is wrapped around a pond called Dutzendteich, southeast of the Old Town. Take handy tram #9, which leaves from the front of the Postbank Center at the train station (Hauptbahnhof) every 10 minutes (direction: Doku-Zentrum, 15-min trip). Get off at the Doku-Zentrum stop (check return times before going to the sites). From the Hauptmarkt or Rathaus (City Hall), you can also hop on bus #36, which ends at the Doku-Zentrum stop. Both options cost the same (€1.90 one-way, it's better to purchase the €3.80 day ticket). As you get off the tram or bus, you'll see the...

▲▲▲Nazi Documentation Center (Dokumentationszentrum)

Visitors to Europe's Nazi and Holocaust sites inevitably ask the same haunting question: How could this happen? This superb museum does its best to provide an answer. It meticulously traces the evolution of the National Socialist (Nazi) movement, focusing on how it both energized and terrified the German people (the exhibit's title is "Fascination and Terror"). Special attention is paid to Nürnberg's role in the Nazi movement, including the construction and use of the Rally Grounds, where Hitler's largest demonstrations took place. This is not a World War II or Holocaust museum; those events are almost an afterthought. Instead, the center frankly analyzes the Nazi phenomenon, to understand how it happened—and to prevent it from happening again.

The museum is housed in one small wing of Hitler's cavernous, unfinished Congress Hall—the largest surviving example of Nazi architecture. The building was planned to host the mammoth annual Nazi Party gatherings. Today, it's symbolically sliced open by its modern entryway to show the guts and brains of the Nazi movement.

The exhibit is a one-way walk. Allow two hours just for the fine videos you can see along the way. WWII history buffs should allow an extra hour for the two movies that play continuously in the *Kino* at the start of the exhibit, offering excellent insights into the mass hypnosis of the German nation (interviews and old footage with English subtitles). Exhibit captions are in German only, so the English audioguide is a must (turns on automatically at video presentations, you dial room numbers for overviews and specific numbers for details of displays—if rushed, listen to the overviews only). You'll see parts of Leni Riefenstahl's 1934 propaganda classic *Triumph of the Will*, and just before the end, footage of the Nürnberg Trials. The last stop (before the long ramp back to the start) is a catwalk giving you a look into the core of the Congress Hall (an artist's sketch of the hall filled with 50,000 cheering Nazis is on a nearby wall).

Cost, Hours, Location: €5, includes audioguide, Mon–Fri 9:00–18:00, Sat–Sun 10:00–18:00, Bayernstrasse 110, tel. 0911/231-5666, www.museen.nuernberg.de.

▲Rally Grounds (Reichsparteitagsgelände)

The Rally Grounds occupy four square miles behind the museum. Albert Speer, Hitler's favorite architect, designed this immense complex of buildings for the Nazi rallies. Not many of Hitler's ambitious plans were completed, but you can visit the courtyard of the Congress Hall, Zeppelin Field (where Hitler addressed his followers), and a few other remains. The easiest way to see them is to follow the circular route around the lake that's shown in the map above and on the museum's free bilingual area plan *(Geländeplan).* The numbers on the plan correspond to the information pillars that you'll find on-site (this information also appears at www.reichsparteitagsgelaende.de).

Figure an hour round-trip from the Documentation Center to do the full circuit. If you have less time, you can visit the courtyard of the Congress Hall, or walk to Zeppelin Field and back, without doing the full loop. If you're really short on time, remember that you'll get the best sense of the Rally Grounds simply from the exhibits inside the Documentation Center.

NÜRNBERG

Nazi Documentation Center and Rally Grounds

TRAM #9 TO TRAIN STATION

¼ MILE / .5 KM

S S-BAHN

➡ RALLY GROUNDS TOUR (ON FOOT)

MÜNCHENER

DOCUMENTATION CENTER

TRAM #9 STOP

BAYERNSTR.

S DUTZENDTEICH

HERZOG STR.

REGENSBURGER STRASSE

FRANKEN-STADION

S

CONGRESS HALL

START

GROSS DUTZEND-TEICH (LAKE)

ZEPPELIN FIELD

GROSSE STRASSE

ARENA

FRANKEN STADIUM

STRASSE

SILBERSEE (PLANNED SITE OF GERMAN STADIUM)

SCHÖLEBENSTRASSE

DCH

I've listed the main sites here in the order you reach them while circling the lake.

Congress Hall (Kongresshalle): This huge building—big enough for an audience of 50,000—was originally intended to

be topped with a roof and skylight. The Nazi Documentation Center occupies part of the hall. To see the vast, Colosseum-like courtyard, turn right as you leave the Documentation Center, and walk along the side of the building. Dip through the archway into the courtyard to appreciate its dimensions. Part of the hall is now used by the Nürnberg Symphony Orchestra. Turn around and return to the main path. When you get to the end,

Nazis in Nürnberg

It's no coincidence that Nürnberg appealed to Hitler. For one thing, it was convenient: Nürnberg is centrally located in Germany, making it a handy meeting point for Nazi supporters. Hitler also had a friend here, Julius Streicher (a.k.a. the "Franconian Führer"), who fanned the flames of Nazism and anti-Semitism though his inflammatory newspaper *Der Stürmer (The Storm Trooper)*.

But of far greater importance, Nürnberg was steeped in German history. Long before the rise of Nazism, the city—one-time home of Albrecht Dürer and the Holy Roman Emperor, and packed with buildings in the quintessential German Gothic style—was nicknamed the "most German of German cities." As one of the most important cities of medieval Europe, Nürnberg appealed to Hitler as a way to legitimize his Third Reich by invoking Germany's glorious past. Hitler loved the idea of staging his rallies within sight of the Kaiserburg castle, a symbol of the "First Reich" (the Holy Roman Empire).

When Hitler took power in 1933, he made Nürnberg the site of his *Reichsparteitage*—**Nazi Party Rallies.** Increasingly elaborate celebrations of Nazi culture, ideology, and power took place here annually for the next six years. The chilling images from Leni Riefenstahl's documentary *Triumph of the Will* were filmed at the

turn right again and continue walking with the Congress Hall on your right. Continue past the end of the building, and then turn left (under the *Kommen Sie gut nach Hause* sign) onto the...

Great Road (Grosse Strasse): At 200 feet wide, the Great Road was big enough to be used as a runway by the Allies after the war. Now it's a parking lot for trucks serving the nearby conference center. The road points toward Nürnberg's imperial palace, Kaiserburg—Hitler's symbolic connection to the Holy Roman Empire (the "First Reich"). The lights you see in the distance hover above the Franken Stadium (a soccer field before Hitler, then used for Nazi rallies, and most recently, during the 2006 World Cup soccer tournament).

Ahead and to the right was to be the site of the **German Stadium (Deutsches Stadion)**—the biggest in the world (with 400,000 seats). They got as far as digging a foundation before funding was redirected to the war effort. Today, the site of the stadium is a park surrounding the big lake, Silbersee—which was the hole for the never-built stadium's foundation. If you like, you can detour across the road to an information sign about the stadium. Otherwise, follow the Dutzenteich lakeshore to the left for about 15 minutes until you hit a parking lot. To your right is the huge...

1934 rallies. At the 1935 rallies, the Nazis devised the first laws—which came to be known as the **Nürnberg Laws**—that legally defined Jews as second-class citizens.

Hitler and his favorite architect, Albert Speer, designed staggeringly massive buildings (such as a stadium seating 400,000 spectators) to host the proceedings. Only a few of the plans were completed before World War II broke out in 1939, forcing the construction budget to be reassigned to the war effort. Today, it's possible to walk around the still-unfinished remains of Hitler's megalomaniacal super-structures. The Rally Grounds were the ultimate example of Hitler's preferred architecture style: stark, huge, and Neoclassical.

As the war drew to a close, the world puzzled over what to do with the Nazi officers who had overseen some of the most gruesome atrocities in the history of humankind. It was finally decided that they should be tried as war criminals by an international tribunal (spearheaded by the US and based on the Anglo-American code of law). These trials took place right here, in the **Nürnberg Trials Courtroom** (below). The Nürnberg Trials—the first ever international war-crimes tribunal—brought about a new concept of international law, which continues today in The Hague, Netherlands.

Zeppelin Field (Zeppelinwiese): This was the site of the Nazis' biggest rallies, including those famously filmed by Leni Riefenstahl. You can climb up on the grandstand and stand on the platform in front of the Zeppelin Tribune, where Hitler stood to survey the masses (up to 250,000 people at a time). The Tribune is based on the design of the ancient Greek Pergamon Altar (now in Berlin's Pergamon Museum); it was originally topped by a towering swastika, which was blown up by the Allies soon after the end of the war. Warning: Clowning around on the speaking platform with any Nazi gestures is illegal and taken seriously by the police.

From Zeppelin Field, continue the rest of the way around the lake back to the Documentation Center.

Nürnberg Trials Courtroom (Nürnberger Prozesse)

In 1945, in courtroom *(Saal)* #600 of Nürnberg's Palace of Justice (Justizgebäude), 21 Nazi war criminals stood trial before an international tribunal of judges appointed by the four victorious countries. After a year of trials and deliberations, 12 Nazis were sentenced to death by hanging, three were acquitted, and the rest were sent to prison. One of the death sentences was for Hitler's right-hand man, Hermann Göring. He wanted to be shot by firing squad—a proper military execution—but his request was denied. Instead, two hours before his scheduled hanging, Göring committed suicide with poison he had smuggled into his cell, infuriating many who thought that this death was too easy for him.

This historic courtroom is closed until sometime in summer 2010, as the city builds a new exhibit about the trials. For the latest on the opening date and entry details, visit www.museen.nuernberg.de. The building is a four-stop subway ride from the Hauptbahnhof (Fürther Strasse 110, enter on Bärenschanzstrasse, take U-1 subway line to Bärenschanze, it's just behind *Pit Stop* sign, tel. 0911/231-5666).

Sleeping in Nürnberg

Prices spike up during major conventions in the spring and fall, and in December—when the Christmas market brings visitors from around the world. July and August are generally low season and come with the lowest prices.

Near the Frauentor, on Königstrasse

These hotels cluster along Königstrasse, just inside the Frauentor and the city walls, and are convenient to both the train station and city sightseeing. From the station, you can roll your luggage here in five minutes without a single stair.

$$$ Hotel Victoria offers friendly staff and 64 fresh, new-feeling rooms behind its historic 1896 facade just inside the Frauentor. The standard rooms are a better value than the slightly bigger business rooms (standard rooms: S-€50–60, Sb-€80–90, Db-€100–110; business rooms €10 extra, discounts on slow summer weekends, 3 of 4 floors non-smoking, elevator, cable Internet in business rooms, Wi-Fi in common areas, parking garage-€11/day, Königstrasse 80, tel. 0911/24050, fax 0911/227-432, www.hotelvictoria.de, book@hotelvictoria.de).

$$$ Hotel Drei Raben is an artsy and fun splurge, with a super-stylish lobby, 22 comfortable rooms, a huge breakfast buffet (ask for eggs or a cappuccino), and lots of elegant touches. In this "theme hotel" you might get the Dürer room, the soccer room, the toys room, or even the graffiti room (Sb/Db-€100, €120, or €150 depending on size; spacious suites with freestanding bathtubs: Db-€185; ask for special summer discounts—especially on weekends; non-smoking, air-con, elevator, Wi-Fi, parking garage-€15/day, Königstrasse 63, tel. 0911/274-380, fax

Sleep Code

(€1 = about $1.40, country code: 49, area code: 0911)
S = Single, **D** = Double/Twin, **T** = Triple, **Q** = Quad, **b** = bathroom, **s** = shower only. Unless otherwise noted, credit cards are accepted, English is spoken, and breakfast is included.

To help you sort easily through these listings, I've divided the rooms into three categories, based on the price for a standard double room with bath:

$$$ **Higher Priced**—Most rooms €100 or more.
$$ **Moderately Priced**—Most rooms between €70–100.
$ **Lower Priced**—Most rooms €70 or less.

0911/232-611, www.hoteldreiraben.de, info@hoteldreiraben.de).

$ Ibis Altstadt Hotel, sandwiched between a bunch of fast-food joints, offers 61 good-value cookie-cutter rooms in a convenient location (Sb/Db-€59, €75 during Christmas market, €109 during conventions; breakfast-€10, elevator, free Internet access in lobby, pay Wi-Fi in rooms, Königstrasse 74, tel. 0911/232-000, fax 0911/209-684, www.ibishotel.com, h1069@accor.com).

$ City Hotel, with 20 old, very basic rooms, has decent prices for the location and amenities (Sb-€40, Db-€55, elevator, reception on third floor, Königstrasse 25–27, tel. 0911/232-645, fax 0911/203-999, Widtmann family).

Near the Frauentor, on Luitpoldstrasse

These two affordable hotels are next door to each other, around the corner from the ones just described, set amidst a harmless sprinkling of strip clubs and sex shops. Either will do if you're watching your budget, but some guests complain about noise, so ask for a room on the back side (especially if staying on Friday or Saturday night).

$$ Hotel Probst is run by the hardworking Probst family. They rent 37 clean, cheap rooms on floors 2–4 of an older apartment building (Ss-€40, Sb-€56, Db-€67–75, Tb-€87–93, ask about lower prices in summer and on weekends, non-smoking rooms, elevator to 3rd floor, pay cable Internet, Luitpoldstrasse 9, tel. 0911/203-433, fax 0911/205-9336, www.hotel-garni-probst.de, info@hotel-garni-probst.de).

$ Hotel Keiml is run by gracious Frau Keiml, who has been welcoming guests here since 1975. She rents 22 spacious, bright, and homey rooms up several flights of stairs (no elevator) in another former apartment building (Sb-€45, Db-€65–70, these prices with this book and cash in 2010, non-smoking rooms, free

Wi-Fi, Luitpoldstrasse 7, tel. 0911/226-240, fax 0911/241-760, reservations by fax preferred).

Closer to the Castle

These accommodations are closer to the castle at the far side of Old Town. Getting here is an €8 taxi ride or a long hike from the station. You can get partway by taking the U-Bahn (line #1) to Lorenzkirche and exiting toward Kaiserstrasse.

$$ Hotel Elch, the oldest hotel in town (with 500-year-old exposed beams adding to its classic elk-friendly woodiness), is buried deep in the Old Town near the castle. It rents 12 charming and well-equipped rooms and has a small restaurant specializing in schnitzel (Mon–Thu: Sb-€70, Db-€95; Fri–Sun and in summer: Sb-€59, Db-€70; extra bed free for kids under age 14, non-smoking, free Wi-Fi, nearby parking garage-€10/day, behind St. Sebald Church at Irrerstrasse 9, tel. 0911/249-2980, fax 0911/2492-9844, www.hotel-elch.com, info@hotel-elch.com).

$$ Hotel Lucas occupies three floors above a busy, similarly named café a short walk from the Hauptmarkt (market square). The 11 rooms are modern and cheerful, making this a great non-smoking home base if you don't mind that there's no elevator (Sb-€50–65, Db-€75–90, lower prices are for Fri–Sun; free Wi-Fi, Kaiserstrasse 22, tel. 0911/227-845, fax 0911/244-9158, www.hotel-lucas.de, info@hotel-lucas.de). Coming from the train station with luggage, I'd hop on the U-1 subway line for one stop to Lorenzkirche. Exit following the *Kaiserstrasse* signs to emerge a couple doors from the hotel.

Hostel: The 382-bed **$ Nürnberg Youth Hostel** is romantically situated at the top of the Old Town inside the castle complex (at the far right as you face it). It's scenic, but can be crowded with school-age groups in the summer. Those over age 26 pay €4 extra, unless traveling as a family (bed in 3- to 6-bed dorm-€21.90; limited singles and doubles: S-€30, D-€52; dorm dwellers pay less for longer stays, €3.10 more for non-members; includes breakfast and sheets, curfew at 1:00 in the morning, pay Internet access, pay Wi-Fi in common areas, reception tel. 0911/230-9360, reservations tel. 0911/2309-3612, fax 0911/2309-3611, www.nuernberg.jugendherberge.de, jhnuernberg@djh-bayern.de).

Eating in Nürnberg

Nürnberg is famous for its pinkie-sized bratwurst (called, like local residents, *Nürnberger*). Nürnbergers—the people—insist that size doesn't matter; they maintain that *in der Kürze liegt die Würze* (in the shortness lies the tastiness). All over town, signs read *3 im Weckle,* meaning "three *Nürnberger* bratwurst in a little bun" (a good snack for about €2). Old-timers go for mustard, while children like ketchup. Restaurant menus often offer them in 6-, 8-, or 10-weenie servings with *Beilagen* (side dishes, generally potato salad and/or kraut). Nürnberg's butchers churn out 1.3 billion of the little buggers every year.

For convenience, I've listed restaurants that are on (or near) Königstrasse, the main drag connecting the station to the castle. Only the last place is away from this tourist zone—buried in the west end of the Old Town, and known only to locals.

Barfüsser Beer Cellar serves its own popular microbrew and fills the basement of the old grain storehouse *(Mauthalle)* with jovial Germans munching meat-on-the-bone (from pork knuckle to duck) and swilling beer. This is good German fun. On hot nights, the cellar's empty and tables spill out onto Königstrasse. Locals love the *Schäufele,* oven-roasted pork shoulder in home-brewed dark beer sauce, and the *Frankenschmaus,* a "greatest hits" platter of sausages, pork shoulder, kraut, and dumplings (€7–13 meals, daily 11:00–24:00, Hallplatz 2, tel. 0911/204-242).

Nassauer Keller is a snug and classy 13th-century vaulted cellar filled with suits of armor and diners enjoying the romantic atmosphere and traditional food. A small door leads down steep steps (watch your head) into a dressy dining room—popular for roast shoulder of pork and venison dishes. It's a little pricey and worth the extra euros in wintertime—but avoid this place on hot days (€10–16 meals, Mon–Sat 12:00–15:00 & 18:00–24:00, kitchen closes at 14:00 and at 22:00, closed Sun, reservations smart, across from Lorenzkirche at Karolinenstrasse 2–4, tel. 0911/225-967).

Goldenes Posthorn is a venerable institution and—while no longer in its original historic location—was once Albrecht Dürer's favorite hangout. Come here to enjoy everything from Franconian specialties and bratwurst to daily fish and vegetarian plates, either in the light-wood chalet-chic interior or on the patio in the shadow of St. Sebald Church (€6–12 meals, daily 11:00–23:00, daily specials, cash only, Glöckleingasse 2, tel. 0911/225-153).

Literaturhaus Nürnberg is a Parisian-style café run by the local book club and popular for readings. It serves theme breakfasts (daily until 15:00) and creative international dishes for €8–14. Locals like to order several varied plates tapas-style, or just enjoy its bookish café ambience for drinks and desserts (Mon–Sat 9:00–24:00, Sun 9:00–22:00, 2 blocks from Frauentor just off Königstrasse at Luitpoldstrasse 6, tel. 0911/234-2658).

Burgwächter is just under the castle, and therefore both touristy and practical. It serves up German cuisine—in its cozy restaurant and on a covered patio with big, rustic picnic tables (€6–15 main dishes, good salads, daily 12:00–23:00, Am Ölberg 10, tel. 0911/222-126).

Bratwursthäusle is a high-energy, woody-yet-mod place with a leafy terrace (and enjoyable people-watching). Its cozy interior feels like a big farmhouse with tables gathered around an open grill. The menu is very limited, with little more than bratwurst and some nasty pickled animal parts. You come here for the best bratwurst in town—all made in-house by the *Häusle*'s own butcher, and dished up with efficient service. Chat up the owner, friendly Herr Behringer, and he'll be happy to tell you about Bratwurst Saints (Mon–Sat 10:00–22:00, closed Sun, midway between Hauptmarkt and the castle on the main drag, Rathausplatz 1, tel. 0911/227-695). For bratwurst to go, head inside, pay €2 at the half-door on your right, take your receipt to the grill...and in seconds, you'll be on your way with Nürnberg's "Little Mac" (three *Nürnberger* in a fresh roll).

Cafe Lucas, a couple blocks west of Königstrasse, has tables both indoors and out, some overlooking the river. There's a full, bratwurst-free menu of light German, Mediterranean, and Asian dishes for €9–13 and good salads for €8–9 (daily 8:00–24:00, Kaiserstrasse 22, tel. 0911/227-845).

Kettensteg Biergarten, the usual Bavarian jumble of picnic tables under trees, enjoys an above-average setting overlooking the city's river and medieval wall. It's named after, and is next to, Germany's first iron suspension bridge (built in 1824). Its youthful energy and big flames give it a tribal vibe after dark. This is ideal on a balmy evening for leafy outdoor dining surrounded by happy locals and in-the-know foreign students (€8–14 meals, modern German cuisine and decent salads, daily 11:00–23:00, west of Hauptmarkt where the river hits the wall, Maxplatz 35, tel. 0911/221-081).

Picnic: There's an Aldi discount **supermarket** near recommended hotels at Königstrasse 83 (limited selection, Mon–Sat 8:00–20:00, closed Sun), and a more upscale supermarket in the sub-basement of the Karstadt department store at the Lorenzkirche U-Bahn entrance (enter across from Karolinenstrasse 15 and take the escalators down two flights, Mon–Sat 9:30–20:00, closed Sun).

Nürnberg Connections

From Nürnberg by Train to: Rothenburg (hourly, 1.25 hrs, change in Ansbach and then Steinach), **Würzburg** (2–3/hr, 1–1.25 hrs), **Munich** (2–3/hr, 1–1.25 hrs), **Frankfurt** (1–2/hr, 2 hrs), **Frankfurt Airport** (1–2/hr, 2.5 hrs), **Dresden** (hourly, 4.5 hrs), **Berlin** (hourly, 4.5 hrs), **Salzburg** (hourly with change in Munich, 3 hrs), **Prague** (every 2 hrs, 3.75 hrs, via express bus, covered by railpasses). Train info: tel. 0180-599-6633 (€0.14/min).

DRESDEN

Dresden, the capital of Saxony, surprises visitors with fanciful Baroque architecture and excellent museums. It's historic, intriguing, and fun. While the city is packed with tourists, 90 percent of them are German or Russian. Since so few Americans have rediscovered Dresden's Baroque glory, you'll feel like you're in on a secret.

At the peak of its power in the 18th century, this capital of Saxony ruled most of present-day Poland and eastern Germany from the banks of the Elbe River. Dresden's "Louis XIV" was Augustus the Strong. As both prince elector of Saxony and king of Poland, he imported artists from all over Europe, peppering his city with stunning Baroque buildings and filling his treasury with lavish jewels and artwork. Dresden's grand architecture and dedication to the arts—along with the gently rolling hills surrounding the city—earned it the nickname "Florence on the Elbe."

Sadly, these days Dresden is better known for its destruction in World War II. American and British pilots firebombed the city on the night of February 13, 1945. More than 25,000 people were killed, and 75 percent of the historical center was destroyed. American Kurt Vonnegut, who was a POW in Dresden during the firebombing, later memorialized the event in his novel *Slaughterhouse-Five*.

When Germany was divvied up at the end of World War II, Dresden wound up in the Soviet sector. Forty years of communist rule left the city in an economic hole, from which it is just emerging. Some older Dresdeners feel nostalgia for the Red old days, when "everyone had a job." During the Cold War, Dresden was known as the "Valley of the Clueless," since it was one of the only spots in East

Germany where you couldn't get Western television. But in the two decades since the Berlin Wall fell, Dresden has made real progress in getting back on its feet—and most locals are enjoying capitalism with gusto. Today's Dresden is a young and vibrant city, crawling with happy-go-lucky students who barely remember communism.

Under the communists, Dresden patched up some of its damaged buildings, left many others in ruins, and replaced even more with huge, modern, ugly sprawl. But today, Dresden seems all about rebuilding. Circa-1946 photos are displayed everywhere, and the city's most important and beautiful historic buildings in the Old Town have been restored. Across the river, the New Town was missed by the bombs. While well-worn, it retains its prewar character and has emerged as the city's fun and lively people zone. Most tourists never cross the bridge away from the famous Old Town museums...but a visit to Dresden isn't complete without a wander through the New Town.

Planning Your Time

Dresden, conveniently located about halfway between Prague and Berlin, is well worth even a quick stop. If you're short on time, Dresden's top sights can be seen in a midday break from your Berlin–Prague train ride (each one is less than a 2.5-hour ride away). Catch the early train, throw your bag in a locker at the station (€4), follow my self-guided walk, and visit some museums before taking an evening train out. If possible, reserve far ahead to visit one of Dresden's top sights, the Historic Green Vault (for reservations details, see page 469).

If you have more time, Dresden merits an overnight stay. The city is a handy home base for a quick bike ride to the "Blue Wonder" bridge, getting back to nature at Saxon Switzerland National Park, or side-tripping to the town of Görlitz for its intriguing mix of rich architecture and culture (see next chapter).

Orientation to Dresden

(area code: 0351)

Dresden is big, with half a million residents. Its city center hugs a curve on the Elbe River. Despite the city's size, most of its sights are within easy strolling distance along the south bank of the Elbe in the Old Town (Altstadt). South of the Old Town (a 5-min tram ride or 15-min walk away) is the main train station (Hauptbahnhof). North of the Old Town, across the river, you'll find the residential-feeling New Town (Neustadt). While the New Town boasts virtually no sights, it's lively, colorful, and fun to explore—especially at night—and has some recommended hotels and restaurants.

Dresden

- **1** Münzgasse Hotels & Eateries
- **2** Hotel Kipping
- **3** Ibis Hotels Bastei, Königstein & Lilienstein
- **4** Hotel Bayerischer Hof Dresden
- **5** AHA Hotel
- **6** Hotel Martha Hospiz
- **7** To Guest House Mezcalero
- **8** Hostel Louise 20
- **9** Hostel Mondpalast Dresden
- **10** Altmarkt Keller Restaurant
- **11** Grand Café Rest. Cosel Palais
- **12** Sophienkeller Restaurant
- **13** Radeberger Spezial-ausschank Café
- **14** Augustus Garten Rest.
- **15** Wenzel Prager Bierstuben
- **16** Good Friends Restaurant
- **17** To Brauhaus am Waldschlösschen
- **18** To Ball und Brauhaus Watzke
- **19** To Feldschlösschen Stammhaus
- **20** Brauereiausschank am Goldenen Reiter
- **21** To Hygiene Museum & VW Transparent Factory
- **22** Innere Neustadt Nightlife
- **23** Roll-On Bike Rental

Tourist Information

Dresden's TI is located in the Palace of Culture on Altmarkt square (Mon–Fri 10:00–19:00, Sat 10:00–18:00, Sun 10:00–15:00, Schlossstrasse 2, tel. 0351/5016-0160, info@dresden.travel). Unfortunately, the unhelpful staff here only seems interested in booking hotel rooms (€3/person). They do, however, provide a handy, free one-page city map with a listing of key sights, hours, and prices on the back. If you'll be hitting several sights, pick up the Dresden City Card (explained next). To find out about live entertainment and cultural events, skim the monthly *Theater Konzert Kunst* (free, in German only); note that the TI shares an office with an agency that sells concert and theater tickets.

Discount Deals: The **Dresden City Card** offers you entry into all of Dresden's top museums (except the Historic Green Vault), discounts on some lesser museums, and unlimited use of the city's transit system (€21/48 hours, €32/72-hour regional pass that includes outlying areas, €42/48-hour Family City Card covers two adults and up to four children, all sold at TI).

Arrival in Dresden

Dresden has two major train stations: Hauptbahnhof and Neustadt. (Note that express trains from Berlin stop first at Neustadt, then at the Hauptbahnhof; from Prague, it's the other way around.)

If you're coming for the day and want the easiest access to the sights, use the **Hauptbahnhof** (main train station), which owes its chic new look to Sir Norman Foster of Reichstag Dome fame. Exit the station following signs for the city, taxis, and trams. To take a **tram** into the center, cross the tram tracks at Wiener Platz. Veer right (through the five-story rounded glass building) to find tram #8 or #11 (departing to your left), which zips you to the historical center (Theaterplatz or Postplatz). The 15-minute **walk** to the Old Town offers an insightful glimpse of the communist era as you stroll down Prager Strasse (described on page 473; from the station, continue straight through Wiener Platz, under and past the towering Mercure Hotel).

The **Neustadt** station serves the New Town north of the river, near some recommended hotels. From this station, tram #11 runs to Am Zwingerteich, a park in the center of the Old Town right next to the sights.

Trains run between the Hauptbahnhof and Neustadt stations every 10 minutes (€1.80, 10-min ride, most trains stop at each station—ask; the stations are also connected by slower tram #3).

Helpful Hints

Sightseeing Strategies: Note that many of Dresden's top museums are closed either Monday or Tuesday. The incredible treasury—the Historic Green Vault—requires a reservation well in advance; if you don't get one, try to line up early to buy a same-day ticket, sold at 10:00 (for all the details, see page 470). Once you have your appointed Historic Green Vault visit time, plan the rest of your day around it (it's conveniently located right in the center of the Old Town). The Hofkirche hosts free pipe-organ concerts twice a week (Wed and Sat at 11:30).

Internet Access: To check your email in the main train station, find the Sidewalk Express computers in the **Point Shop To Go** (€2/hr, one-hour minimum, open long hours daily).

Local Guides: Genteel **Maren Koban** (tel. 0351/311-1315, mobile 0176-2922-6374) and **Liane Lowe** (lianeloewe@gmx.de) each enjoy sharing the story of their hometown with visitors (€100/half-day).

Getting Around Dresden

Dresden's efficient **trams** and **buses** work well for the visitor. The tram network is so slick, you might just spend the hour your €1.80 ticket gets you joyriding—marveling at the huge investment this city is making as it rebuilds. Buy tickets at the machines on the platforms or in the trams (€1.80 for a single ticket, or *Einzelfahrkarte;* €5 for a 4-pack of *Kurzstrecke*—short-ride tickets; machines accept coins only). A day ticket (*Tageskarte,* €4.50 for one calendar day) works for sightseeing within the city. Validate your ticket by date-stamping it in the little boxes on train platforms and on board buses and trams (for the day ticket, stamp it only the first time you ride). Free use of public transit is included with the Dresden City Card (described earlier).

Taxis are reasonable, plentiful, and generally honest (€2.50 to start, then €1.20/kilometer).

DRESDEN

Self-Guided Walk

▲▲▲Do-It-Yourself
Dresden Baroque Blitz Tour

Dresden's major sights are conveniently clustered along a delightfully strollable promenade next to the Elbe River. Get to know this sightseeing zone by taking this walk. Though the city has a long and colorful history, we'll focus on the four eras that have shaped it the most: Dresden's Golden Age in the mid-18th century under Augustus the Strong; the city's destruction by firebombs in World War II; the communist regime (1945–1989); and the current "reconstruction after reunification" era.

The following walk laces together Dresden's top sights in about an hour, not counting museum stops. It includes the three major sights (Zwinger, Royal Palace with Historic Green Vault treasuries,

Central Dresden

Walking Tour Route

View

DCH

1. Theaterplatz
2. Rampart Pavilion
3. Crown Gate
4. Glockenspielpavillon (Porcelain Collection)
5. Semper Gallery (Old Masters Gallery and Royal Armory)
6. Green Vault Entrance
7. Palace Square
8. Watchman's Tower
9. Parade of Nobles Mural
10. Münzgasse
11. Goldene Reiter Statue
12. Academy of Fine Arts

and Frauenkirche), each of which is described later in the chapter. Incorporating these visits into the walk will fill your day.

• Begin at Theaterplatz (a convenient drop-off point for tram #8 from the Hauptbahnhof; tram #11 lets you off not far away, at Postplatz).

Theaterplatz

Face the equestrian statue (King John, an unimportant mid-19th-century ruler) in the middle of the square. In front of you, behind the statue, is the Saxon State Opera House—nicknamed the **Semperoper** after its architect, Gottfried Semper (visits only with a tour, see page 472).

As you face the Opera House, the nearest building on your left is the Neoclassical guardhouse called the Schinkelwache

(housing the opera box office). The big building behind it is the vast Zwinger palace complex (your next stop). Across the square from the Opera House is the Hofkirche, with its distinctive green-copper steeple, and to its right is the sprawling Royal Palace (with shiny new clock; both described later). All the buildings you see here—Dresden's Baroque treasures—are thoroughly reconstructed. The originals were destroyed in a single night by American and British bombs. For more than 60 years, Dresden has been rebuilding—and there's more work to do.

Note the building along the river with a facade that looks a bit like a Florentine villa. It's a remnant from the time of Augustus the Strong, whose son set about building the Hofkirche to gain the pope's favor. Since Protestant locals refused to build the church, he had to import Catholic workers from Italy. Knowing that the workers wouldn't exactly be welcomed here, Frederick Augustus II built them their own lodgings, in the Italian Renaissance style. Today the Italienisches Dörfchen ("Italian Hamlet") is overlooked by most visitors. Inside the main building is, no surprise, an Italian restaurant.

• *Walk through the passageway into the Zwinger courtyard, noticing the Crown Gate on the opposite side lowering majestically into view. Stop in the middle of the courtyard, where we'll survey all four wings.*

▲▲The Zwinger

This palace complex is a Baroque masterpiece—once the pride and joy of the Wettin dynasty, and today filled with fine museums. The Wettins ruled Saxony for more than 800 years, right up until the end of the First World War (like so many of Europe's royal families). Saxony wasn't ruled by a king, but by a prince elector—one of a handful of nobles who elected the Holy Roman Emperor. The prince elector of Saxony was one of Germany's most powerful people. In the 18th century, the larger-than-life Augustus the Strong—who was both prince elector of Saxony and king of Poland—kicked off Saxony's Golden Age.

"Zwinger" means the no-man's-land running along the city wall. This empty space gradually evolved into the complex of buildings you see today. By Augustus' time, the Zwinger was used for celebrations of Saxon royalty. Imagine an over-the-top royal wedding in this complex. The courtyard served as an open-air palace, complete with orange trees in huge Chinese porcelain pots.

Let's get oriented. Face the north wing (with the Crown Gate on your left). You're looking at the **Rampart Pavilion** (Wallpavillon), the first wing of the palace—an orangerie capped with a sun pavilion built for Augustus' fruit trees and parties. Up top is Atlas (who happens to have Augustus' features) with the Earth on his back—a fitting symbol for Augustus the Strong. Stairs lead to a fine view from the terrace above. This wing of the Zwinger houses the fun **Mathematics-Physics Salon** (closed until 2011).

Turn to the left, facing the **Crown Gate** (Kronentor). The gate's golden crown is topped by four golden eagles supporting a smaller crown—symbolizing Polish royalty (since Augustus was also king of Poland).

Turn again to the left to see the **Glockenspielpavillon.** The glockenspiel near the top of the gate has 40 bells made of Meissen porcelain (bells chime every 15 minutes, and play a sweet three-minute melody at 10:15, 14:15, and 17:15). This wing of the Zwinger also houses Augustus the Strong's **Porcelain Collection** (see page 469).

Turn once more to the left (with the Crown Gate behind you) to see the **Semper Gallery.** This Zwinger wing was added to the original courtyard a hundred years later by Gottfried Semper (of Opera House fame). It houses Dresden's best painting collection, the **Old Masters Gallery,** as well as the **Royal Armory** (see page 469).

Throughout the city, you'll see the local sandstone looking really sooty. Locals claim that it's not pollution, but natural oxidation that turns the stone black in about 30 years. Once restored, the statues are given a silicon treatment that lets the stone breathe but keeps it from going black.

Take time to enjoy some of the Zwinger's excellent museums. Anticipating WWII bombs, Dresdeners preserved their town's art treasures by storing them in underground mines and cellars in the countryside. This saved these great works from Allied bombs... but not from the Russians. Nearly all of the city's artwork ended up in Moscow until after Stalin's death in 1953, when the art was returned by the communist regime to win over their East German subjects. Today, Russians invade only as tourists.

Augustus the Strong
(1670-1733)

Friedrich Augustus I of the Wettin family exemplified royal excess, and made Dresden one of Europe's most important cities of culture. Legends paint Augustus as a macho, womanizing, powerful, ambitious, properly Baroque man—a real Saxon superstar. A hundred years after his death, historians dubbed Augustus "the Strong." Today, tour guides love to impart silly legends about Augustus, who supposedly fathered 365 children and could break a horseshoe in half with his bare hands.

As prince elector of Saxony, Augustus wheeled and dealed—and converted from his Saxon Protestantism to a more Polish-friendly Catholicism—to eventually become King Augustus II of Poland. Like most Wettins, Augustus the Strong was unlucky at war, but a clever diplomat and a lover of the arts.

The Polish people blame Augustus and his successors—who were far more concerned with wealth and opulence than with sensible governance—for Poland's precipitous decline after its own medieval Golden Age. According to Poles, the Saxon kings did nothing but "eat, drink, and loosen their belts" (it rhymes in Polish).

Whether you consider them the heroes of history, or the villains, Augustus and the rest of the Wettins—and the nobles who paid them taxes—are to thank for Dresden's rich architectural and artistic heritage.

When you're finished with the museums, exit the Zwinger through the Glockenspielpavillon (south gate). Halfway through the corridor, look for the **timelines** telling the history of the Zwinger in German: to the right, its construction, and to the left, its destruction and reconstruction. Notice the Soviet spin: On February 13, 1945, gangs of Anglo-American bombers obliterated *(vernichtet)* the city. On May 8, 1945, the Soviet army liberated *(befreite)* Dresden from "fascist tyranny" *(faschistischen Tyrannei)*, and from 1945 to 1964, the Zwinger was rebuilt with the "power of the workers and peasants" *(Arbeiter- und Bauern-Macht)*.

• *As you exit the corridor, cross the street and the tram tracks and jog left, walking down the perpendicular Taschenberg Strasse with the yellow Taschenberg Palace on your right (ruined until 1990, today the city's finest five-star hotel). The yellow-windowed sky bridge ahead connects the Taschenberg, which was the crown prince's palace, with the prince electors'* **Royal Palace.** *This is where you can enter the spectacular* **Green Vault** *treasuries (described later; entrance is before*

DRESDEN

crossing under the sky bridge, through fancy gate on left). But if your Historic Green Vault reservation is for later today, you can continue this walk for now.

Exiting the Royal Palace, go under the sky bridge. Ahead of you and to the right, the blocky modern building is the...

Palace of Culture (Kulturpalast)

Built by the communist government in 1969, today this hall is still used for concerts (and houses Dresden's TI). Notice the mural depicting communist themes: workers; strong women; care for the elderly; teachers and students; and, of course, the red star and the seal of former East Germany. The bronze doors on the street side give a Marxist interpretation of the history of Dresden. Little of this propaganda, which once inundated the lives of locals, survives in post-communist Germany.

• *Now turn left (with the Palace of Culture behind you). Walk along the palace wall toward the two copper spires, through a tunnel with (mostly Russian) musicians, until you emerge into the **Palace Square**. Ahead of you and to the left is the...*

Hofkirche (Cathedral)

Why does Dresden, a stronghold of local-boy Martin Luther's Protestant Reformation, boast such a beautiful Catholic cathedral? When Augustus the Strong died, his son wanted to continue as king of Poland, like his father. The pope would allow it only if Augustus Junior built a Catholic church in Dresden. Now, thanks to Junior's historical kissing-up, the mere 5 percent of locals who are Catholic get to enjoy this fine church. The elevated passageway connecting the church with the palace allowed the royal family to avoid walking in the street with commoners.

Step inside the cathedral (free, enter through side door facing palace, Mon–Thu 9:00–17:00, Fri 13:00–17:00, Sat 10:00–18:00, Sun 12:00–16:00, tel. 0351/484-4712, www.kathedrale-dresden .de). The fine Baroque pulpit—hidden in the countryside during World War II—is carved out of linden wood. The glorious 3,000-pipe organ filling the back of the nave is played for the public on Wednesdays and Saturdays at 11:30 (free).

The **Memorial Chapel** (facing the rear of the church, on the left) is dedicated to those who died in the WWII firebombing and to all victims of violence. Its evocative *pietà* altarpiece was made in 1973 of Meissen porcelain. Mary offers the faithful the crown of thorns made from Dresden's rubble, as if to remind us that Jesus—on her lap, head hanging lifeless on the left—died to save humankind. Jesus' open heart shows us his love, offers us atonement for our sins, and proves that reconciliation is more powerful than hatred. The altar (freestanding, in front) shows five flaming heads. It seems to symbolize how Dresdeners suffered...in the presence of their suffering savior. The dates on the high altar (30-1-33 and 13-2-45) mark the dark period between Hitler's rise to power and the night Dresden was destroyed.

The basement houses the **royal crypt,** including the heart of the still-virile Augustus the Strong—which, according to legend, still beats when a pretty woman comes near (crypt open only for one 45-min German tour each day).

• *As you leave the Hofkirche, you're facing the palace complex entry (with the **Watchman's Tower** above on the right—see page 470). To the left, next to the palace's main entrance, you'll see a long, yellow mural called the...*

▲▲Parade of Nobles (Fürstenzug)

This mural is painted on 24,000 tiles of Meissen porcelain. Longer than a football field, it illustrates 700 years of Saxon royalty. It was built to commemorate Saxon history and heritage after Saxony became a part of Germany in 1871. The artist carefully studied armor and clothing through the ages, allowing you to accurately trace the evolution of weaponry and fashions for seven centuries. (This is great for couples—try this for a switch: As you stroll, men watch the fashions, women the weaponry.)

The very last figure (or the first one you see, coming from this direction) is the artist himself, Wilhelm Walther. Then come

commoners (miners, farmers, carpenters, teachers, students, artists), and then the royals, with 35 names and dates marking more than 700 years of Wettin rule. Stop at 1694. That's August II (Augustus the Strong), the most important of the Saxon kings. His horse stomps on the rose (symbol of Martin Luther, the Protestant movement, and the Lutheran church today) to gain the Polish crown. The first Saxon royal is Konrad der Grosse ("the Great"). And waaay up at the very front of the parade, an announcer with a band and 12th-century cheerleaders excitedly herald the arrival of this wondrous procession. The porcelain tiles, originals from 1907, survived the bombing. When created, they were fired three times at 2,400 degrees Fahrenheit...and then fired again during the 1945 firestorm, at only 1,800 degrees.

• *When you're finished looking at the mural, dogleg right and walk into the big square. Find a statue of Martin Luther.*

Neumarkt Square

This "New Market Square," once a town center ringed by rich merchants' homes, is being rebuilt and will soon be a lively people-and-café center. The statue of Martin Luther holds not just any Bible, but the Word of God he translated into German so that regular people could get their minds on it without Church control—basically what the Reformation was all about. Toppled in 1945, he's cleaned up and back on his feet again.

• *The big church looming over the square is the...*

▲▲▲Frauenkirche (Church of Our Lady)

This church is the heart and soul of Dresden. The people of Dresden mobilized their Protestant pride to raise the money, and built this impressive Lutheran church on the ruins of a much smaller Romanesque building. When completed in 1743, this was Germany's biggest Protestant church (310 feet high). Its unique central-stone-cupola design gave it the nickname "the stone bell." While it's a great church, this building garners the world's attention primarily because of its tragic history and phoenix-like resurrection: On the night of February 13, 1945, the firebombs came. When the smoke cleared the next morning, the Frauenkirche was smoldering but still standing. It burned for two days before finally collapsing. After the war, the Frauenkirche was kept in rubble as a peace monument. It was the site of many memorial vigils. In 2005, completely rebuilt, it reopened to the public. (For touring details and more information, see page 471.)

A big hunk of the bombed **rubble** stands in the square (near door E, river side of church) as a memorial. Notice the small relief of the dome that shows where this piece came from.

• *From here, stroll downhill through a busy little restaurant-lined street, Münzgasse, and up the stairs to Dresden's grand river-view balcony. Find a bulge in the promenade 30 yards to the right. Belly up to that banister.*

▲▲Brühlsche Terrasse

This so-called "Balcony of Europe," a delightful promenade, was once Dresden's defensive rampart. Look along the side of the terrace facing the Elbe River to see openings for cannons. By Baroque times, fortresses were no longer necessary, and this became one of Europe's most charming promenades, with a leafy canopy of linden trees.

Dresden claims to have the world's largest and oldest fleet of historic paddleboat steamers: nine riverboats from the 19th century. The hills in the distance (to the left) are home to Saxon vineyards, producing some of Germany's northernmost wine. Because only a small amount of the land is suitable for vineyards, Saxony's respected, expensive wine (mostly white) is consumed almost entirely by Saxons.

Below you to the left is the **Augustus Bridge** (Augustus-brücke), connecting Dresden's old and new towns. During the

massive floods of August 2002, the water reached two-thirds of the way up the arches. At the far end of the Augustus Bridge, look for the golden equestrian statue, a symbol of Dresden. It's Augustus the Strong, the **Goldene Reiter** (Golden Rider), facing east to his kingdom of Poland.

The area across the bridge is the **New Town** (Neustadt). While three-quarters of Dresden's Old Town was decimated by Allied firebombs, much of the New Town survived. The 18th-century apartment buildings here were restored—giving the area a Baroque look instead of the blocky Soviet style predominant on the Old Town side of the river. Today, the New Town is a trendy district, and well worth exploring. The **Three Kings Church** (Dreikönigskirche, steeple visible above the Goldene Reiter) marks a neighborhood with some recommended restaurants.

The interesting **mosque-shaped building** in the distance to the far left (marked *Yenidze*), originally a tobacco factory designed to advertise Turkish cigarettes, is now an office building with restaurants and nightclubs. A few steps to your left is the recommended **Radeberger Spezialausschank Café**—the best place for a drink or meal with a river view.

Behind you on the right, you'll see the glass domes of the **Academy of Fine Arts,** capped by a trumpeting gold angel. (Locals call the big dome on the right "the lemon juicer.")

• *Your tour is over. Stairs at the end of the promenade lead back to the Palace Square; just beyond the Hofkirche is Theaterplatz, where you began.*

Sights in Dresden

The Zwinger Museums

The museums around the Zwinger courtyard all have the same hours (Tue–Sun 10:00–18:00, closed Mon—except Old Masters Gallery may be open Mon late June–Sept, tel. 0351/4914-2000, www.skd-dresden.de). Entrance to all of the museums (except the

Porcelain Collection) costs €7, and all are covered by the Dresden City Card (which also includes transit).

▲▲▲Old Masters Gallery (Gemäldegalerie Alte Meister)— Dresden's best museum features works by Raphael, Titian,

Rembrandt, Peter Paul Rubens, Jan Vermeer, and more. While it hangs 750 paintings at a time, it feels particularly enjoyable for its "quality, not quantity" approach to showing off great art. Locals remember the Old Masters Gallery as the first big public building reopened after the war, in 1956 (€7, includes Royal Armory entry, €3 audioguide, consider the good €13 English guidebook, in Zwinger's Semper Gallery).

Entering, you'll pass a small room with portraits of the Wettin kings who patronized the arts and founded this collection. The next room shows five cityscapes of Dresden, painted by Canaletto during the city's Golden Age. These paintings of mid-18th-century Dresden—showing the Hofkirche (still under construction) and the newly completed Frauenkirche—offer a great study of the city. Next, you enter a world of Rubens and Belgian Baroque. This high-powered Catholic art is followed by the humbler, quieter Protestant art of the Dutch Masters, including a fine collection of Rembrandts (don't miss his jaunty self-portrait—with Saskia on his lap and a glass of ale held aloft) and a pristine Vermeer *(Girl at a Window Reading a Letter)*. The German late-Gothic/early-Renaissance rooms include exquisite canvases by Lucas Cranach and Albrecht Dürer. Farther on, the Venetian masters include a sumptuous *Sleeping Venus* by Giorgione (1510). He died while still working on this, so Titian stepped in to finish it. Giorgione's idealized Venus sleeps soundly, at peace with the plush nature.

The collection's highlight: Raphael's masterful *Sistine Madonna*. The portrait features the Madonna and Child, two early Christian martyrs (Saints Sixtus and Barbara), and wispy angel faces in the clouds. Mary is in motion, offering the Savior to a needy world. Note the look of worry and despair on Mary's face, which makes this piece different from most *Madonna* paintings, which show her smiling and filled with joy. That's because this *Madonna* was originally part of a larger altarpiece, and Mary's mournful gaze was directed at another painting—one of the Crucifixion. These days, the gaze of most visitors is directed at the pair of whimsical angels in the foreground—which Raphael added after the painting was completed, just to fill the empty space. These lovable tykes—of T-shirt and poster fame—are bored...just hanging out, oblivious to the exciting arrival of the Messiah just behind them. They connect the heavenly world of the painting with you and me.

Royal Armory (Rüstkammer)—One big room packed with swords and suits of armor, the armory is especially interesting for its tiny children's armor and the jousting exhibit in the back (included with €7 ticket to Old Masters Gallery, across the entry passage from gallery).

Sculpture Collection (Skulpture im Zwinger)—With the Albertinum closed until 2011, some pieces from its sculpture collection are on loan to the Zwinger. Look for Degas' *Fourteen-Year-Old Dancer* (included in the €7 ticket to the Old Masters Gallery and in the €6 ticket to the Porcelain Collection, entrance on the courtyard).

Mathematics-Physics Salon (Mathematisch-Physikalischer Salon)—This fun collection features globes, lenses, and clocks from the 16th to the 19th centuries (north end of Zwinger courtyard, closed until 2011).

▲▲Porcelain Collection (Porzellansammlung)—Every self-respecting European king had a porcelain works, and the Wettins had the most famous: Meissen. The Saxon prince electors were pioneers in European porcelain production. They inspired other royal courts to get into the art form. They also collected other types—from France to Japan and China. Augustus the Strong was obsessed with the precious stuff...he liked to say he had "porcelain sickness." Here you can enjoy some of his symptoms, under chandeliers in elegant galleries (€6, good English descriptions, south end of Zwinger courtyard).

Royal Palace (Residenzschloss)

This Renaissance palace was once the residence of the Saxon prince elector. Formerly one of the finest Renaissance buildings in Germany, it's been rebuilt since its destruction in World War II. The grand state rooms of Augustus the Strong are scheduled to open sometime in 2010. Until then, the prince's treasures are the big draw here: The New Green Vault is remarkable enough, but the Historic Green Vault (reservation required) is arguably the most impressive treasury in Europe. The entire complex has the same hours (Wed–Mon 10:00–18:00, Historic Green Vault until 19:00, closed Tue), and—except for the Historic Green Vault—one entry fee (€10 for New Green Vault, Watchman's Tower, and special exhibitions). The Historic Green Vault requires a separate ticket (€10, €2 surcharge to book in advance).

▲▲▲Historic Green Vault (Historisches Grünes Gewölbe)—The famed glittering Baroque treasury collection was begun by Augustus the Strong in the early 1700s. It evolved as the royal family's extravagant treasure trove of ivory, silver, and gold knick-knacks. Your visit is thrilling in the Baroque style of wowing visitors—starting easy and crescendoing to a climax, taking a quick break, and finishing again with a flurry. Following the included (and essential) audioguide, you'll spend one hour progressing: the amber room, the ivory room, the silver room, the sumptuous crown jewels room, the soothing bronze room, and another jewels room. The incredible pieces in the crown jewels room (especially the Obeliscus Augustalis) are fine examples of *Gesamtkunstwerk*—a symphony of artistic creations. Your audioguide also describes treasures in the "pre-vault" (where you pick up and drop off the audioguide). In this room, don't miss photos of vaults before the war and Luther's signature ring.

Reservations: To protect this priceless collection and the extravagant rooms in which it's displayed, the number of visitors each day is carefully controlled. This means you have to reserve in advance (you'll be given a 15-minute entry window for your visit—once inside, you can stay as long as you like). You'll pass through a "dust sluice" as you enter to be sure you're free of irritants—a good feeling. To be assured entry, make a reservation far in advance (reserve at www.skd-dresden.de, email museum@dresden-tourist .de, or call 0351/4919-2285). If the Internet booking system shows your preferred dates as sold out, keep checking back, since tour groups often cancel at short notice. While advance entry times can be booked six months out, 270 tickets are saved for each day (the number of spots still available and entry times—*Freie Plätze*—are indicated at the ticket desk). These are sold starting at 10:00—line up early. If all else fails, you can try walking up to the ticket office to see if a tour group canceled. Once I got in this way, with a wait of only 20 minutes, even after being told that the vault was sold out for months. When planning your visit, remember that the Historic Green Vault is closed Tuesday.

▲▲**New Green Vault (Neues Grünes Gewölbe)**—This collection shows off more of the treasure in a modern setting. Don't miss the 6.2-carat one-of-a-kind green diamond that "mysteriously" appeared here from India. Invest in the €3 audioguide, which beautifully describes the best 65 objects in 1.5 hours.

Watchman's Tower (Hausmannsturm)—This palace tower is completely rebuilt (and feels entirely modern, included in €10 palace ticket). You can climb past an underwhelming coin collection, see the rebuilt medieval clock mechanism from behind, peruse an extensive series of dome-damage photos, and earn a good city view after a long climb. In bad weather, the view terrace is closed, and you'll peer through small windows—a big disappointment. If climbing the Frauenkirche tower (which affords the best view in town but costs €8), skip this.

▲▲▲Frauenkirche (Church of Our Lady)

This landmark church was originally built by local donations—Protestant people-pride. Destroyed by the Allied firebombing in

World War II, the church sat in ruins for decades. Finally, in 1992, the reconstruction of the church began. The restorers used these guidelines: rebuild true to the original design; use as much of the original material as possible; maximize modern technology in the procedure; use no concrete or rebar; and make it a lively venue for 21st-century-style worship. The church was fitted together like a giant jigsaw puzzle, with about a third made of original stones (notice the dark ones, placed in their original spots). The reconstruction cost more than €100 million, 90 percent of which came from donors around the world.

Now open, the church is as worthwhile for its glorious **interior** as for its tragic, then uplifting recent history. Stepping inside, you're struck by the shape—not so wide (150 feet) but very tall (inner dome 120 feet, under a 225-foot main dome). The color scheme is pastel, in an effort to underline the joy of faith and enhance the festive ambience of the services and ceremonies held here. The curves create a community feeling. The seven entrances are perfectly equal (as people are, in the eyes of God). When the congregation exits, the seven exits point to all quarters—a reminder of "go ye," the Great Commission to spread the Word everywhere.

The Baroque sandstone **altar** shows Jesus praying in the Garden of Gethsemane the night before his crucifixion. Soldiers, led by Judas, are on their way, but Christ is firmly in the presence of God and his angels. Eighty percent of today's altar is from original material—in the form of 2,000 individual fragments that were salvaged and pieced back together by restorers.

The **Cross of Nails** at the high altar is from Coventry, England—Dresden's sister city. Two fire-blackened nails found in the smoldering rubble of Coventry's bombed church are used as a symbol of peace and reconciliation. Coventry was bombed as thoroughly as Dresden (so thoroughly, it gave the giddy Luftwaffe a new word for "to bomb to

DRESDEN

smithereens"—to "coventrate"). From the destroyed town of Coventry was born the Community of the Cross of Nails, a worldwide network promoting peace and reconciliation through international understanding.

Near the exit stands the church's **twisted old cross,** which fell 300 feet and burned in the rubble. Lost until 1993, it was

found relatively intact and stands exactly on the place in the rubble where it was found. A copy—a gift from British people in 2000 on the 55th anniversary of the bombing—crowns the new church. It was crafted by an English coppersmith whose father dropped bombs on the church on that fateful night. As they leave, visitors are invited to light a candle before this cross and enter a wish for peace in the guest book.

Cost, Hours, Location: Free but donation requested, enter through door D, Mon–Fri 10:00–12:00 & 13:00–18:00, open between services and concerts on Sat–Sun, €2.50 for 45-min audioguide, www.frauenkirche-dresden.de.

Climbing the Dome: Those feeling energetic can get a great view over the city by climbing the stairs to the top of the dome. After an elevator takes you a third of the way, you still have a long climb (€8—consider it a donation to the church, enter through door G, follow signs to *Kuppelaufstieg,* Mon–Sat 10:00–18:00, Sun 12:00–19:00).

Gift Shop: Located behind the Albertinum, the church's shop has all of your tasteful-refrigerator-magnet needs covered. Interesting books, videos, and jewelry help fund the work and upkeep of the church (Mon–Sat 10:00–18:00, Sun 11:00–17:00, Georg-Treu-Platz 3, tel. 0351/656-0683).

More Sights in Dresden

▲**Semperoper**—This elegant opera house watches over Theaterplatz in the heart of town. Three opera houses have stood in this spot: The first was destroyed by a fire in 1869, the second by firebombs in 1945. The rebuilt Semperoper continues to be a world-class venue, and tickets for the

Saxon State Orchestra (the world's oldest) are hard to come by (on sale a year in advance, box office in Schinkelwache across the square, Mon–Fri 10:00–18:00, Sat–Sun 10:00–16:00, tel. 0351/491-1705, fax 0351/491-1700, www.semperoper.de).

The opulent interior can only be visited with a tour. German-language tours (with an English handout) go regularly throughout the day. There is one daily English tour at 14:00 (€7, €2 extra to take photos, 1 hour, tour schedule depends on rehearsal schedule, enter on right side, tel. 0351/491-1496).

Albertinum—This historic building, at the end of the Brühlsche Terrasse, is closed for renovation until 2011. When it reopens, it may once again house two good museums: the Sculpture Collection (Skulpturensammlung) and the New Masters Gallery (Gemäldegalerie Neue Meister). In the meantime, its collections have been lent to other museums (in other cities) or put in storage. Art-lovers can ask at the TI if any works from the New Masters Gallery are on display in Dresden. This collection includes paintings and sculptures by 19th- and 20th-century greats such as Pierre-Auguste Renoir, Auguste Rodin, Vincent van Gogh, Edgar Degas, and Gustav Klimt. I especially enjoy Otto Dix's moving triptych *War* (painted between the world wars), Klimt's *Buchenwald,* and one of Rodin's *Thinker*s.

Prager Strasse—This communist-built pedestrian mall, connecting the train station and the historic center, was in ruins until the 1960s. Even today, "Prague Street" reflects Soviet ideals: big, blocky, functional buildings without extraneous ornamentation. As you stroll down Prager Strasse, imagine these buildings without much color or advertising (which were unnecessary back in the no-choices days of communism). Today, the street is filled with corporate logos, shoppers with lots of choices, and a fun summertime food circus. When all the construction is finished, this will be an impressive people zone.

▲New Town (Neustadt)—A big sign across the river from the old center declares, "Dresden continues here." This seems directed at tourists who visit the city and stay exclusively in the Old Town. Don't be one of them—make a point to explore Dresden's New Town, too. While there are no famous sights in the New Town, it's the only part of Dresden that predates World War II. Today, it's thriving with cafés, shops, clubs, and—most important—regular people. I've listed several hotels and restaurants worth considering in the neighborhood (see "Sleeping in Dresden" and "Eating in Dresden," later).

Hygiene Museum (Deutsches Hygiene Museum)—Many Germans are fanatical about hygiene and public health. This museum is a highly conceptual compilation of vaguely health-related exhibits. The building has the dubious honor of once

DRESDEN

being the headquarters of the Nazi eugenics (genetic engineering through "proper" breeding) and racial studies administration. The exterior fresco—by German Expressionist painter Otto Dix—sets the tone for the unsettling interior. The museum was founded in 1911, and the current location opened its doors in 1930. Since then, the museum has produced and collected models from the 16th century to the present, including little wooden anatomical figures with removable parts (complete with strategically placed fig leaves), X-ray machines from the 1930s, and graphic wax models of venereal diseases. The exhibit is divided into weirdly themed sections (Life and Death, Disease, Physiology, Reproduction, and Grooming). You'll find some English explanations, and you can rent the €2 audioguide, but most of the exhibits speak (or shriek) for themselves. Perhaps a reflection of the typically German pragmatism toward sexuality, this place is usually filled with school groups or families with young kids. People with strong stomachs will get a kick out of this highly interactive museum, but those easily disturbed should stay away—or at least plan meal times accordingly (€6, Tue–Sun 10:00–18:00, closed Mon; Lingnerplatz 1, take tram #1, #2, or #4 from Postplatz to the Deutsches Hygiene Museum stop; tel. 0351/484-6670, www.dhmd.de).

Volkswagen Transparent Factory (Gläserne Manufaktur)— Car buffs will want to make a pilgrimage to this new VW factory on the southeastern edge of town. Two floors of this fascinating, transparent building are open to visitors interested in the assembly of one of VW's high-end cars. You don't have to custom-order a luxury-model Phaeton to see how they're manufactured. (But if you do buy a car, you can bring a folding chair, park yourself on the platform, and follow it through every moment of the 36-hour "birth" process.) The parts are delivered to the logistics plant just on the edge of town, then transported to this manufacturing plant by "cargo trams" (which are used to avoid adding to traffic congestion in town). While you're basically paying to experience a VW ad, it is interesting to see the wild building, peek at the assembly line, and play with the informative, high-tech English touch-screen displays (€4, daily 8:00–20:00, Lennestrasse 1, toll tel. 01805-896-268—costs €0.14/min, www.glaesernemanufaktur .de). Take tram #1, #2, or #4 from Theaterplatz or Prager Strasse, or tram #10 from the Hauptbahnhof, to Strassburgerplatz, from which it's a 100-yard walk.

Near Dresden

Dresden is the starting point for two pleasant excursions described below—a peaceful half-day's walk or bike ride up the Elbe River, and a day of hiking in dramatic "Saxon Switzerland."

Elbe River Valley to the Blue Wonder Bridge

The Elbe River Valley makes for a wonderful excursion from Dresden. For a great slice-of-life glimpse at Germans at play, walk or bike along the 3.5-mile path that hugs the banks of the Elbe River all the way from central Dresden to the Blue Wonder bridge. If the weather's warm, pack a swimsuit.

The path starts underneath and to the right of the Brühlsche Terrasse, and makes its scenic way—past several tempting beer gardens—to the **Blue Wonder** (a.k.a. Loschwitz Bridge), a cantilever truss bridge that connects the Dresden suburbs of Loschwitz and Blasewitz. When the bridge was completed in 1893, Blasewitz and Loschwitz were the most expensive pieces of real estate in Europe—note the ultra-posh villas near the bridge. The bridge is indeed a wonder in that it survived World War II completely untouched, and it is, in fact, blue—but its name is a pun on the German expression, "to witness a blue wonder" *(ein Blaues Wunder erleben)*, which means to experience a nasty surprise. The real surprise is how relaxing the whole trip is, as the closer you get to the bridge the more opportunities you'll find for swimming and boating (several places rent kayaks, jet skis, and so on).

Underneath the bridge, a delightful beer garden awaits: **Schiller Garten,** a vast, 300-year-old complex of gastronomic delights and cold suds. The garden area serves good grilled food, has a self-service buffet (in the building marked *Lichtspiel*), and pours a beer brewed specially for this garden by Feldschlösschen (Dresden's best brewery). The garden includes a playground and a digital departure board for the nearby Schillerplatz tram stop (€3–6 plates and snacks, daily 11:00–24:00). If you're looking for something fancier, try the sit-down restaurant in the half-timbered house, which serves excellent pheasant (€9–14 plates, daily 11:00–22:00). Both the garden and restaurant have been supplied by their own butcher and pastry kitchen since 1764 (www.schillergarten.de, tel. 0351/811-990).

Getting to the Blue Wonder: If you have enough time and sunny weather, slow down and do this outing on foot (about one hour each way), or by bike (about 30 min each way). **Roll-On** rents bikes for €9–10 per day, and will gladly deliver and pick up the bike at your hotel (in the New Town, near Albertplatz at Königsbrücker Strasse 4a, tel. 0152/2267-3460). You can also rent bikes through the German Railway at Dresden's two stations. They charge less for bikes than Roll-On does, but have a smaller selection, and

DRESDEN

the staff speaks little English (€7 per day; Hauptbahnhof: daily 7:00–21:00, tel. 0351/461-3262; Neustadt station: daily 8:00–20:00, tel. 0351/461-5601).

You can also make the trip by boat or tram: The **Saxon Steamboat Service** (Sächische Dampfschifffahrt) runs steam-powered paddle boats along the Elbe (€8 one-way, about hourly in summer, 40 min, board at Brühlsche Terrasse, get off at Blasewitz dock; to return to Dresden, board at Loschwitz). **Trams** #4 and #6 take you to Schillerplatz, about 50 yards from the Blue Wonder. The tram ride is particularly interesting as it starts in beautiful downtown Dresden and travels a path of destruction through communist prefabricated housing, then to post-unification strip-mall urban sprawl, before taking you to a delightful collection of villas and large single-family 19th-century dwellings. On the way, keep your eyes peeled at the Trinitatis Platz stop for a beautiful bombed church, which sits amid a sea of dreary prefab architecture. You can take your bike on the tram for €1.30 (choose the *Einzelfahrt-Ermäßigt* button for your bike fare).

Saxon Switzerland National Park

Consider a break from big-city sightseeing to spend a half-day taking a *wunderbar* hike through this scenic national park.

Twenty miles southeast of Dresden (an easy 45-min S-Bahn ride away), the Elbe River cuts a scenic swath through the beech forests and steep cliffs of Saxon Switzerland (Sächsische Schweiz) National Park. You'll share the trails with serious rock climbers and equally serious Saxon grandmothers. Allow five hours (including lunch) to enjoy this day trip.

Take the S-Bahn line 1 from either the Hauptbahnhof or the Neustadt station (direction Bad Schandau, departs hourly; round-trip-€5.50, family day ticket-€14.50, day ticket for a group of up to five adults-€22.50). Get off at the Kurort Rathen stop, follow the road downhill five minutes through town to the dock, and take the ferry across the Elbe (€1.70 round-trip, pay on board, crossing takes 2 min, runs continuously). When the ferry docks on the far (north) side of the river, turn your back on the river and walk 100 yards through town, with the little creek on your right. Turn left after the Sonniges Eck Restaurant (tasty lunch option, check out the 2002 flood photos in their front dining room) and walk up the lane. The trail begins with stairs on your left just past Hotel Amselgrundschlösschen (follow *Bastei* signs).

A 45-minute walk uphill through the woods leads you to the Bastei Bridge and stunning views of gray sandstone sentries rising several hundred feet above forest ridges. Elbe Valley sandstone was used to build Dresden's finest buildings (including the Frauenkirche and Zwinger), as well as Berlin's famous Brandenburg Gate. The multiple-arch bridge looks straight out of Oz—built in 1851 specifically for Romantic Age tourists, and scenic enough to be the subject of the first landscape photos ever taken in Germany. Take the time to explore the short 50-yard spur trails that reward you with classic views down on the Elbe 900 feet below. Watch the slow-motion paddleboat steamers leave V-shaped wakes as they chug upstream toward the Czech Republic, just around the next river bend. If you're not afraid of heights, explore the maze of catwalks through the scant remains of the Felsenberg Neurathen, a 13th-century Saxon fort perched precariously on the bald stony spires (€1.50, entrance 50 yards before Bastei Bridge).

Just a five-minute uphill hike beyond the bridge is the Berg Hotel Panorama Bastei, with a fine restaurant, a snack bar, and memorable views. Return back down to the Elbe ferry via the same trail.

Nightlife in Dresden

To really connect with Dresden as it unfolds, you need to go to the **Innere Neustadt** ("Inner New Town," a 10-min walk from Neustadt train station). This area was not bombed in World War II, and after 1989 it sprouted the first entrepreneurial cafés and bistros. While eateries are open long hours, the action picks up after 22:00. The clientele is young, hip, pierced, and tattooed.

Rather than seek out particular places in this continuously evolving scene, I'd just get to the epicenter (corner of Görlitzer Strasse and Louisenstrasse) and wander. Pop through the Kunsthofpassage, a Hundertwasser-type apartment block with some fun spots (Görlitzer Strasse 23). At Böhmischestrasse 34 (a half-block off Lutherplatz), the Russian-flavored Kneipe Raskolnikoff has an imported beach, giving it a Moscow/Maui ambience. The Carte Blanche Transvestite Bar is a hoot for some (€25, most nights from 20:00, Priessnitzstrasse 10, tel. 0351/204-720).

For more sedate entertainment, stroll along the New Town's riverbank after dark for fine floodlit views of the Old Town.

Sleeping in Dresden

Dresden is packed with big conference-style hotels. Characteristic, family-run places are harder to come by. (The communists didn't do "quaint" very well.) Peak season for the big business-class hotels

DRESDEN

is May, June, September, and October. Peak season for hostels is July and August (especially weekends). For locations, see the map on page 457.

In or near the Old Town

$$$ Hilton Dresden has 330 luxurious rooms (some with views of the Frauenkirche) in the heart of the Old Town, one block from the river. Complete with porters, fitness club, pool, and several restaurants, it's everything you'd expect from a soulless four-star chain hotel (Sb/Db-€120–195, breakfast-€15, parking-€19/day, An der Frauenkirche 5, tel. 0351/86420, fax 0351/864-2725, www .hilton.de, info.dresden@hilton.com).

$$ Hotel Kipping, with 20 tidy rooms 100 yards behind the Hauptbahnhof, is professionally run by the friendly and proper Kipping brothers (Rainer and Peter). The building was one of few in this area to survive the firebombing—in fact, people took shelter here during the attack (Sb-€65–105, Db-€80–120, 1-person suite-€115–130, 2-person suite-€130–145, child's bed-€25; higher prices are for weekends, May–June, and Sept–Oct; elevator, free parking, exit the station following signs to *Bayerische Strasse* near track 6, it's at Winckelmannstrasse 6, tram #8 whisks you to the Old Town, tel. 0351/478-500, fax 0351/478-5090, www.hotel-kipping .de, reception@hotel-kipping.de). Their restaurant serves international cuisine and Saxon specialties (€9–12 main dishes, Mon–Sat 18:00–22:30, closed Sun).

$$ Hotels Bastei, Königstein, and **Lilienstein** are cookie-cutter members of the Ibis chain, goose-stepping single-file up Prager Strasse (listed in order from the station to the center). Each is practically identical, with 360 rooms. Though utterly lacking in charm, they are a good value in a convenient location between the Hauptbahnhof and the Old Town (Sb-€65–70, Db-€75–80, apartment-€100 for a family of 4, prices vary with demand—book online for best deal, breakfast-€10, parking-€6/day, reservations for all: tel. 0351/4856-2000; individual receptions: tel. 0351/4856-5445, tel. 0351/4856-6445, and tel. 0351/4856-7445, respectively; www.ibis-dresden.de).

$ Aparthotels an der Frauenkirche rents 50 new units just above all the restaurant action on Münzgasse. Designed for longer stays but also welcoming two-nighters (minimum), these modern, comfortable apartments come with kitchens and the lived-in works. The Drescher family also owns two other apartment-hotels in the immediate area (studio Db-€50, two-room Db-€55, two-

DRESDEN

Sleep Code

(€1 = about $1.40, country code: 49, area code: 0351)
S = Single, **D** = Double/Twin, **T** = Triple, **Q** = Quad, **b** = bathroom, **s** = shower only. All of these places speak English and accept credit cards. Unless otherwise noted, breakfast is included.

To help you sort easily through these listings, I've divided the rooms into three categories, based on the price for a standard double room with bath:

$$$ **Higher Priced**—Most rooms €120 or more.
$$ **Moderately Priced**—Most rooms between €70–120.
$ **Lower Priced**—Most rooms €70 or less.

room Qb-€150, extra bed-€15–20, breakfast-€12, cheaper for longer stays and off-season, parking at nearby garage-€12/day, Münzgasse 10, tel. 0351/438-1111, www.aparthotels-frauenkirche .de, info@aparthotels-frauenkirche.de).

In the New Town

The first two hotels are fancy splurges in a tidy residential neighborhood surrounding the Neustadt train station. The rest are cheap and funky, buried in the trendy, newly happening café-and-club zone called the Innere Neustadt ("Inner New Town," about a 10-min walk from Neustadt station—see "Nightlife in Dresden," earlier).

$$$ Hotel Bayerischer Hof Dresden, 100 yards toward the river from the Neustadt train station, offers 50 rooms and elegant, inviting public spaces in a grand old building (Sb-€99, Db-€138, pricier suites, non-smoking rooms, elevator, free parking, Antonstrasse 33–35, yellow building across from station, tel. 0351/829-370, fax 0351/801-4860, www.bayerischer-hof-dresden .de, info@bayerischer-hof-dresden.de).

$$ Hotel Martha Hospiz, with 50 rooms near the recommended restaurants on Königstrasse, is bright and cheery. The two old buildings that make up the hotel have been smartly renovated and connected in back with a glassed-in winter garden and an outdoor breakfast terrace. It's a 10-minute walk to the historical center, and a five-minute walk to the Neustadt station (S-€55, Sb-€79–86, Db-€113, "superior" Db-€121, extra bed-€27, elevator; leaving Neustadt station, turn right on Hainstrasse, left on Theresenstrasse, and then right on Nieritzstrasse to #11; tel. 0351/81760, fax 0351/8176-222, www.hotel-martha-hospiz.de, rezeption@marthahospiz-dresden.de).

$$ AHA Hotel may have an unassuming facade on a big, noisy street, but inside you'll find a homey and welcoming ambience. The 30 simple-but-neat apartments all come with kitchens; most (except the top floor) have balconies. It's a bit farther from the center—10 minutes by foot east of Albertplatz, a 20-minute walk or a quick ride on tram #11 from the Old Town—but its friendliness, coziness, and good value make it a winner (Sb-€58, Db-€69–73, breakfast-€9, request quieter back side, non-smoking rooms, elevator, Bautzner Strasse 53, tel. 0351/800-850, fax 0351/8008-5114, www.ahahotel-dresden.de, kontakt@ahahotel -dresden.de).

$ Guest House Mezcalero, decorated Mexican from top to bottom, is a 22-room enterprise that's a 10-minute walk from the Neustadt station at the edge of the lively Innere Neustadt zone. It feels smart yet comfy, with an adobe ambience (S-€33, D-€52, Db-€65, dorm bed-€18 plus a one-time €2.50 fee for sheets and towels, breakfast-€6, Königsbrücker Strasse 64, from either station catch tram #7 to Bischofsweg, tel. 0351/810-770, fax 0351/810-7711, www.mezcalero.de, info@mezcalero.de).

$ Hostel Louise 20 rents 83 beds in the heart of the Innere Neustadt. Though located in the wild-and-edgy nightlife district, it feels safe, solid, clean, and comfy. The newly furnished rooms, guests' kitchen, cozy common room, and friendly staff make it a good place for cheap beds (S-€32, D-€42, small dorm-€17/bed, sheets-€2.50, breakfast extra, no lockers, generally booked on summer weekends, Louisenstrasse 20, tel. 0351/8894-894, www .louise20.de, info@louise20.de).

$ Hostel Mondpalast Dresden is young and hip, in the heart of the Innere Neustadt above a hip bar. Its super-groovy vibe makes it one of the coolest hostels in Europe—it's good for backpackers with little money and an appetite for late-night fun. Fortunately, breakfast is served until 14:00 (S-€34, Sb-€44, D-€44, Db-€52, dorm bed-€13–17, sheets-€2, breakfast-€6, free Wi-Fi, lockers, kitchen, lots of facilities, bike rental-€7/day, near Kamenzer Strasse at Louisenstrasse 77, tram #7 from Hauptbahnhof or #11 from Neustadt station, tel. 0351/563-4050, fax 0351/563-4055, www.mondpalast.de, info@mondpalast.de).

Eating in Dresden

As the city comes back to life, nearly every restaurant seems bright, shiny, and modern. While Old Town restaurants are touristy, the prices are reasonable, and it's easy to eat for €10–15 just about anywhere. For cheaper prices and authentic local character, leave the famous center, cross the river, and wander through the New Town.

The special local dessert sold all over town is *Dresdner Eierschecke,* an eggy cheesecake with vanilla pudding, raisins, and almond shavings.

In the Old Town

Münzgasse, the busy and touristy lane that connects the Brühlsche Terrasse promenade and the Frauenkirche, is the liveliest street in the Old Town, with a fun selection of eateries. Choose from tapas, Aussie, goulash, crêpes, and even antiques (Kunst Café Antik scatters its tables among a royal estate sale of fancy furniture and objets d'art—around the corner, riverside). Service is a necessary evil, the clientele is international, and the action spills out onto the cobbled pedestrian lane on balmy evenings.

Altmarkt Keller (a.k.a. Sächsische-Böhmische Bierhaus), a few blocks farther from the river on Altmarkt square, is a festive beer cellar that serves nicely presented Saxon and Bohemian food (from separate menus) and has good Czech beer on tap. The lively crowd, cheesy music (live Sat only), and jolly murals add to the fun. While the on-square seating is fine, the vast-but-stout air-conditioned cellar offers the most memorable seating. The giant mural inside the entryway—representing the friendship between Dresden and Prague—reads, "The sunshine of life is drinking and being happy" (€8–13 main dishes, daily 11:00–24:00, Altmarkt 4, to the right of McDonald's, tel. 0351/481-8130).

Grand Café Restaurant Cosel Palais serves Saxon and French cuisine in the shadow of the newly rebuilt Frauenkirche. This is a Baroque chandeliered dining experience with fine, if touristy, courtyard seating—great for an elegant meal or tea and pastries (€10–19 meals, daily specials, daily 10:00–24:00, An der Frauenkirche 12, tel. 0351/496-2444).

Erlebnisgastronomie *("Experience Gastronomy"):* All the rage among Dresdeners (and German tourists in Dresden) is *Erlebnisgastronomie.* Elaborately decorated theme restaurants have sprouted next to the biggest-name sights around town, with over-the-top theme-park decor and historically costumed wait-staff. These can offer a fun change of pace and aren't the bad value you might suspect. The best is **Sophienkeller,** which does its best to take you to the 18th century and the world of Augustus the Strong. The king himself, along with his countess, musicians, and magicians, stroll and entertain, while court maidens serve traditional Saxon food from a "ye olde" menu. Read their colorful brochure to better understand the place. It's big (470 seats), and it even has a rotating carousel table with suspended swing-chairs that you sit in while you eat. Before choosing a seat, survey the two big and distinct zones—one bright and wide open, the other more intimate and cellar-like (€10–15 main dishes, daily 11:00–24:00, under the five-star Taschenberg Palace Hotel, Taschenberg 3, tel. 0351/497-260).

With a River View: **Radeberger Spezialausschank Café** is dramatically situated on the Brühlsche Terrasse promenade, with a rampart-hanging view terrace and three levels taking you down to the river. For river views from the "Balcony of Europe," this is your spot. The inviting-yet-simple menu includes daily Saxon specials and cheap wurst and kraut. This is the only place in town that serves Radeberger's unfiltered beer. The cool river-level bar comes with big copper brewery vats (daily 11:00–24:00, reservations smart for view terrace, Terrassenufer 1, tel. 0351/484-8660).

In the Main Train Station: For a quick bite at the Hauptbahnhof, the healthy market-style **Marché Cafeteria** is fast and reasonable (daily 5:30–21:00).

In the New Town

Venture to these eateries—across Augustus Bridge from the Old Town—for lower prices and a more local scene. I've listed them nearest to farthest from the Old Town.

Just Across Augustus Bridge

Augustus Garten is a lazy, crude-yet-inviting beer garden with super-cheap self-service food (pork knuckle, kraut, cheap beer, and lots of mustard). You'll eat among big bellies—and no tourists—with a fun city-skyline-over-the-river view. While enjoyable in balmy weather, this place is dead when it's cool (€3–8.50 main dishes, €2–5 beers, €2 refundable deposit on beer glasses, daily 11:00–24:00, closed in bad weather, Wiesentorstrasse 2, tel. 0351/404-5854). As you walk across the bridge from the Old Town, it's on your immediate right.

On Königstrasse

For trendy elegance without tourists, have dinner on Königstrasse. After crossing the Augustus Bridge, hike five minutes up the communist-built main drag of the New Town, then turn left to find this charming Baroque street. As this is a fast-changing area, you might survey the other options on and near Königstrasse (be sure to tuck into a few courtyards) before settling down.

Wenzel Prager Bierstuben serves country Bohemian cuisine in a woodsy bar that spills out into an airy, glassed-in gallery—made doubly big by its vast mirror. Stepping inside, you immediately feel this is a winner. They offer a fun Bohemian menu with great Czech beer on tap (€7 dinner-with-beer specials on Tue–Thu, €8–13 main dishes, open daily 11:00–24:00, Königstrasse 1, tel. 0315/804-2010).

Good Friends is a favorite for Thai and Vietnamese food, and a welcome relief from pork and potatoes (€6–12 main dishes, Mon–Fri 11:30–15:00 & 17:30–23:00, Sat–Sun 12:00–23:00, An der Dreifaltigkeitskirche 9, tel. 0351/646-5814). Walk down Königstrasse to the towering Three Kings Church. It's under the steeple.

Beer Halls

All of Dresden's famous beer halls were destroyed in the war, and the communists refused to rebuild them. But after unification, ambitious Dresdeners began re-creating this tradition. Beer halls usually serve their own brew and hearty Saxon cuisine. Saxons love to eat and talk, so a beer hall is a great place to meet locals and get a taste of life outside of tourist areas. All of these places are far from the city center, but are easily reached by public transportation.

Brauhaus am Waldschlösschen is fun and lively, with nightly music that really gets going after 21:00. The restaurant serves traditional Saxon cuisine with some fine salads (main dishes under €15). The view of Dresden's Old Town from the self-service beer garden can't be beat (snacks under €6.50, €9 daily specials include a large beer, daily 11:00–24:00, Am Brauhaus 8b, tram #11 to Waldschlösschen, tel. 0351/652-3900). They offer brewery tours daily at 16:00—in German only, but still enjoyable. Their *Hefeweizen* tastes like bananas.

Ball und Brauhaus Watzke, the oldest of the beer halls, started life as a ballroom (it still holds public balls once a month). It sits pleasantly on the banks of the Elbe, with nice views of the Old Town. Watzke serves traditional beer-hall food in huge portions, and features €8 dinner-with-beer specials nightly except Sunday (€9 main dishes, open daily 11:00–24:00, Kötzschenbroderstrasse 1, tram #4 or #9 to Altpieschen, tel. 0351/852-920). The brewery also operates the **Brauereiausschank am Goldenen Reiter** pub in the New Town. It has the same beer and menu, with a good view of the Frauenkirche, but with little of the original's ambience (daily 11:00–24:00, Hauptstrasse 1—in front of the Golden Rider statue, tel. 0351/810-6820). Their *Hefeweizen* tastes like pineapple.

Feldschlösschen Stammhaus was the original brewery and hop warehouse for Feldschlösschen beer, but the company moved to another part of Dresden in the 1970s. Although significantly farther afield than the other beer halls, the Stammhaus is a cozy, energy-filled spot in a sea of East German prefab apartments. Traditional fare dominates the menu, but Stammhaus sneaks in large portions of fresh vegetables and fresh homemade bread (€11 main dishes, €9 dinner specials with a beer, daily 11:00–24:00, Budapester Strasse 32, bus #82 from the Prager Strasse Transit Center to the Arbeitsamt stop, tel. 0351/471-8855). Sadly, they don't brew *Hefeweizen* here.

Dresden Connections

From Dresden by Train to: Görlitz (hourly, 1.5 hrs), **Bautzen** (about hourly, 30–45 min; Bautzen-bound trains continue on to Görlitz), **Zittau** (better from Neustadt, hourly, 1.5–2 hrs), **Berlin** (every 2 hrs, more with a transfer in Leipzig, 2.25 hrs), **Prague** (every 2 hrs, 2.25–2.5 hrs), **Frankfurt** (hourly, 4.75 hrs), **Nürnberg** (hourly, 4.5 hrs), **Munich** (hourly, 5.75 hrs, transfer in Nürnberg), **Vienna** (2/day, 7 hrs; plus 1 night train/day, 9 hrs), **Budapest** (1/day, 9 hrs). There are overnight trains from Dresden to Zürich, the Rhineland, and Munich. Train info: tel. 0180-599-6633 (€0.14/min).

GÖRLITZ

Tucked away in Germany's easternmost corner, the surprisingly beautiful town of Görlitz is a treasure trove of architecture and one of this country's best-kept secrets.

During the Middle Ages, Görlitz was a major European crossroads, at the intersection of trade routes from Moscow to Barcelona and from the Baltic Sea to Venice. Trade in cloth and beer made the city flourish. Görlitz's rich cultural tapestry was gradually enhanced as the centuries passed, leaving it a delightful collage of architectural styles. The town escaped most of World War II's bombs, but soon after was split down the middle along its river—with half of the town in Germany, the other half in Poland. Görlitz's historic buildings were preserved by the East German government, saving it from the unsightly communist-era blemishes that mark most former East German towns.

Since the Wall fell, Görlitz has sprung back to life and is busily polishing its gorgeous facades. The town offers a unique opportunity to venture to the eastern fringes of Germany, sample Silesian culture and cuisine, and appreciate some breathtaking architecture and stay-a-while squares. Best of all, although German tourists fill Görlitz on weekends during the summer, it's still virtually undiscovered by foreign tourists—making it a real Back Door experience.

Planning Your Time

Although Görlitz is an ideal day trip from Dresden (hourly trains, 1.5 hrs), the city's subtle charm warrants an overnight stay. Görlitz opens up on long summer nights, as pubs and cafés spill out into the cobbles. Get lost and wander the back streets and alleys.

Orientation to Görlitz

(area code: 03581)

With a population of about 56,000, Görlitz is the largest city in what's left of German Silesia. While Görlitz lost a third of its population to Poland in 1945, the historic center and most sights of interest to travelers remain in Germany. The compact Old Town (Altstadt), containing almost everything to see and do, is an easy stroll, roughly between Marienplatz and the western bank of the Neisse River. The focal point of the Old Town is its twin market squares, Upper (Obermarkt) and Lower (Untermarkt).

Tourist Information

The TI, called Görlitzinformation, sells €1 maps (download for free from their website), and can book you a room for free. Information in English is sparse, but there are a few English guidebooks available, and people seem genuinely helpful and welcoming (Mon–Fri 9:00–19:00, Sat–Sun 9:00–18:00, between Obermarkt and Untermarkt at Obermarkt 32, tel. 03581/475-723, www.goerlitz .de). Pick up the €6.90 *Görlitz Town Guide*, a small but informative do-it-yourself walking tour, but skip the €3 map. The *Architectural Guide Through the Old Town of Görlitz* (€7) is overkill for most visitors but indispensable for architecture buffs, describing almost every building in the Old Town in a convenient flip-out format.

To arrange for a guided **tour** in English, call 03581/475-713.

Arrival in Görlitz

Görlitz's train station, about a half-mile southwest of the city center, is a sight in itself. Built in 1901, the main hall is a pearl of Prussian *Jugendstil*, while the building itself is Neoclassical. Its opening hours are shorter than those at larger stations, and it's virtually deserted after 21:00. Lockers are in the passage between the tracks and the main hall (€1–2). You'll also find handy WCs (€0.50, deposit coin, then wait for buzzer) and a *Reisezentrum* for train information and tickets (Mon–Fri 7:30–17:30 except Wed closed 13:00–13:45, Sat 8:00–13:00, closed Sun).

To get into town (a 15-min **walk**), exit straight out the front entrance and follow Berliner Strasse. At the first large square *(Postplatz)*, the road veers left, and you'll see the Hertie department store (marking Marienplatz and the start of my self-guided walking tour). You can also take **tram** #2 or #3 to Demianiplatz (departs from the platform on your right as you exit the station; €1.20, 5 min).

Görlitz: A Silesian Brew

Görlitz is a city with an identity crisis, much like the entire region of Silesia. Silesia, which has never been a "nation" of its own, encompasses parts of Germany (where it's called "Schlesien"), Poland ("Śląsk"), and the Czech Republic ("Slezsko"). Silesians are proud of this diversity, and of their pragmatic ability to work and live peacefully with each other despite the borders that separate them. Just like the Silesians themselves, their cuisine, folk art, and customs are a mishmash of German, Polish, and Czech.

After Slavic Sorbs founded Gorelec in 1071, the village—renamed Görlitz—came under the German sphere of cultural influence in the 12th century, and has been predominantly German ever since. For most of its early existence, the city technically belonged to Bohemia, but was ceded to Saxony after the Peace of Prague in 1635. In 1815, Görlitz fell into Prussian hands at the Congress of Vienna and became the largest city in the province of Lower Silesia.

The city's unusual experience in World War II made it the unique place it is today: While Görlitz almost miraculously escaped destruction (only its Old Town Bridge was bombed), it was split in two by the Potsdam Agreement in 1945. This treaty determined the Neisse River—which runs through the center of Görlitz—to be the border between Germany and Poland. The following year, Poland expelled all Germans from its country, which included booting them out of Silesia and, therefore, out of the Polish side of Görlitz.

This expulsion created two ethnically distinct halves: the German town of Görlitz on the west side of the river, and the Polish town of Zgorzelec, which is still part of Poland on the east. Although most German Silesians have long since abandoned any hope of re-establishing their lost homeland, they have gone to great efforts to stress the unity between Silesians of all ethnic backgrounds—Germans, Poles, and Czechs—by re-establishing cultural connections across the rivers and mountains. Czechs and Poles are strong participants at all city festivals. After German, Polish and Czech are the most common languages you'll hear spoken in the streets and see on signs in Görlitz.

In 2004, German Görlitz and Polish Zgorzelec completed the reconstruction of a new pedestrians-only Old Town Bridge (Altstadtbrücke) across the Neisse. Locals like to think this largely symbolic gesture makes Görlitz the most European city in Europe. And now that Poland has joined the open-borders Schengen Agreement, anyone can freely cross the bridge without even having to flash a passport.

Getting Around Görlitz

The communists left little Görlitz with a highly developed and efficient public-transportation system (€1.20/ride, *Einzelfahrt Normal;* €3 day pass, *Tageskarte Normal;* €6.50 pass for up to 5 people, *Kleingruppenkarte*). Tickets are valid on both trams and buses. Buy tickets from bus drivers or the machines on the platforms and trams (coins only), and validate tickets in the little blue box on board. All buses and trams converge at Demianiplatz. The Old Town is compact, so unless you're planning to visit the Holy Sepulcher or go out to the Landeskrone mountain, you'll probably only use public transit to get from the train station into the city center.

Self-Guided Walk

Welcome to Görlitz

The joy of Görlitz is simply wandering the Old Town and appreciating the architecture. Begin this orientation walk at Marienplatz, the small square right outside the former city walls.

Marienplatz

The unique *Jugendstil* **Hertie department store** (completed in 1911) has a richly decorated facade concealing an ornate glass-domed interior with intricate staircases and galleries (Mon–Fri 9:00–19:00, Sat 9:00–18:00, closed Sun).

Behind Hertie is the **Church of our Lady** (Frauenkirche), a 15th-century late-Gothic church built near the hospital and poorhouse outside the city walls. Although this church seems unremarkable, take a moment to step inside (free, Mon–Sat 10:00–18:00, Sun 11:00–18:00; Mon–Fri try to catch the *Mittagsrast* prayer and organ music at 12:00). Imagine being here in the fall of 1989, shortly before the Berlin Wall came down. This church served as a forum for discussions and peace prayers *(Friedensgebete)*. A poster announcing the first prayer meeting was placed in the glass cabinet on the front of the church. Soon, like-minded shopkeepers began to follow suit, and 580 people attended the first meeting. Just two weeks later, 1,300 people showed up, and subsequent meetings swelled to 5,000—so large that they spilled over into other churches. The meetings became a forum for discussing impending political changes, civil rights, and environmental issues. As each participant came forward and voiced their concerns, a candle was blown out until the church was dark. Then, as those who had a hopeful or positive experience came forward, a candle was lit until the church was illuminated once again. The East German secret police, the *Stasi*, stationed plainclothes police in the buildings across the street to document who was participating in these

Görlitz

TO HOLY SEPULCHER

NIKOLAI-TURM

ST. PETER

OLD CITY WALLS

POLAND

PEDESTRIAN OLD TOWN BRIDGE

NEISSE RIVER

END

TOWN HALL

TRAITOR'S PASSAGE

EMPEROR'S KEEP
CULTURAL HISTORY MUSEUM

BAROQUE HOUSE

REICHEN-BACH TOWER

THEATER

UPPER MARKET SQUARE

CHURCH OF THE TRINITY

FISCH-MARKT

ELIZABETH STRASSE

DEMIANI-PLATZ

MARIENPLATZ
START

SYNAGOGUE

HERTIE (JUGENDSTIL DEPT STORE)

CHURCH OF OUR LADY

POST-PLATZ

STADT-PARK

TO TRAIN STATION

TO ZGORZELEC (POLAND)

TO LANDSKRON BREWERY

100 YARDS
100 METERS

→ WALKING TOUR ROUTE

P PARKING

DCH

1 Hotel Bon Apart
2 To Pension Am Stadtpark 8
3 Die Destille Pension/Rest.
4 Hotel und Gasthof Dreibeiniger-Hund
5 Zur Goldenen Sonne Rest.
6 Vierradenmühle Rest.
7 Piwnica Staromiejska Pub
8 Bürgerstübl
9 Lebensmittel Weiss Grocery
10 Farmers' Market
11 Görlitzer Weinachts Haus (Christmas Shop)
12 Schlesische Schatztruhe Shop

GÖRLITZ

"acts of civil disobedience." Many people lost their jobs or were punished. But the hope for democracy and self-determination had already caught on, and today, this church stands as a symbol of peace and solidarity.

To the north, the **Fat Tower** (Dicker Turm) is the second-oldest tower in the city's defensive network. Although the tower itself is Gothic (from 1270), it's topped by a copper Renaissance cupola. The tower was attached to the so-called Women's Gate (Frauen Tor) in 1477. It's decorated with a sandstone relief of the Görlitz city coat of arms, featuring a Bohemian lion and a Silesian black eagle—representing Görlitz as an independent and free city.

• *Walk down the street to the left of the tower (Steinstrasse) and onto the...*

Upper Market Square (Obermarkt)

This square dates from the 13th century, and is lined with mainly Baroque houses. The **Reichenbach Tower** dominates the west-ern end of the square. The tower formed the western city wall and dates from the 13th century, although the cylindrical portion was added in 1485 and is topped with a Baroque cupola from 1782. The tower housed city guards and watchmen—who among other things kept a lookout for fires— until the last "tower family" moved out in 1904. Inside is an impressive collection of armaments, early 20th-century photographs, and an interesting exhibit on the daily lives of the tower's occupants (€1.50, May–Oct Tue–Sun 10:00–17:00, closed Mon and Nov–April, Platz des 17 Juni, tel. 03581/671-355). The view from the top is worth the 165 steps.

In 1490, Görlitz strengthened its city fortifications by build-ing a circular bastion outside Reichenbach Tower. The structure came to be known as the **Emperor's Keep** (Kaisertruz) when the Swedish troops made their last stand against the Imperial Saxon army during the Thirty Years' War. Since then, the Emperor's Keep has been used as an archive, and today houses the Cultural History Museum (closed for renovation until 2011).

• *The tall tower on Obermarkt belongs to the...*

Church of the Trinity (Dreifaltigkeitskirche)

In 1245, Franciscan monks consecrated this church, at the south-east side of Obermarkt. Although originally a Romanesque struc-ture, renovations in 1380 gave the church its current late-Gothic appearance. When the Reformation took hold in Silesia in 1563,

Görlitz Architecture

Although no bombs fell on Görlitz itself during World War II (only on its bridge), the city didn't escape partial destruction during the Thirty Years' War or the ravages of three great city

fires. Each wave of devastation allowed Görlitz to rebuild in the architectural style of the time. The results are an astonishing collection of exemplary buildings from every architectural era: Gothic, Renaissance, Baroque, *Gründerzeit* (late 19th century), and *Jugendstil*. The East German government placed the entire city under a protection order, rescuing it from the bleak communist aesthetic of the late 20th century. More than 3,700 buildings are registered historical monuments. This, combined with energetic reconstruction, makes Görlitz the gem that it is today.

the monks surrendered the keys to the church and monastery—with the condition that the monastery be used as a school. A school operates in the former monastery to this day.

Go inside the church (free, daily 9:00–18:00, tel. 03581/311-311). The interior seems austere, but upon careful inspection it reveals delightful little details. As you enter, go immediately to your left. This is the oldest part of the church. Pillars from the original 13th-century Romanesque chapel are integrated into the walls. The fancy balcony is where the nobility sat. If you've been to Dresden, the high altar will look familiar, as it was built by artists brought from Dresden, and resembles the crown gate of the Zwinger. The swirly clouds identify this as Rococo. The missing crucifix on the left wall (now in Warsaw) is a reminder of the artifacts that were pillaged from this church during various wars, but the choir stalls, carved in the 1430s, are original. As you follow signs to the *Marienaltar*, look up at the vaulted ceiling, and notice how complex it gets as you walk into newer parts of the church.

The church's trophy is the beautiful 15th-century carved triptych, the **Marienaltar.** The simple side was used on regular worship days, while the gilded side—containing an almost life-size carving of the Virgin Mary—was reserved for high feast days. Today, you can usually see it open, and can admire the closed panels via the display on the bench to the right of the altar. (If the altar is closed, ask one of the guides to open it for you.) It's an eyeful—rich with action and symbolism. The symmetry and order of the checked tablecloth is replaced in the other panels by lots of action and purposefully conflicting lines that create energy and tension. Notice the symbolism—there's a turban-wearing Ottoman (archenemy of the time) and Jesus wearing a Franciscan frock (a nod to the church's Franciscan heritage).

Behind you, an exhausted **Jesus,** reminiscent of Auguste Rodin's *The Thinker,* ponders the fate of man. This statue, from 1910, used to sit on the grass outside of the Holy Sepulcher (see page 496)—notice the rotting wood at the base.

The church's **tower** is unusually thin—the locals call it the *Mönch* ("Monk"). The clock doesn't keep very good time, thanks to one in a series of Cloth-Maker Rebellions. In the Middle Ages, Görlitz was run by the powerful guilds of the cloth trade and the brewers, who neglected the rights of their workers and forbade non-members from practicing their trades. Finally, in the early 16th century, the workers rose up against the corrupt city council, which allowed the guilds to continue their unfair practices. The rebels ended their meetings punctually at midnight to avoid the night watchmen, who would be on the other side of town at that hour. But the city council was one step ahead: They ordered the church bell to chime seven minutes before midnight to fool the conspirators out onto the street and into the waiting arms of the guard. Fourteen of the conspirators were executed, and 25 more banished from the city. To this day, the bell chimes seven minutes early.

Across the square is the **Traitor's Passage** (Verrätergasse), a dark, sinister passageway used by the instigators of the rebellion to sneak in and out of the main marketplace. Walk about halfway down and you'll see the letters *DVRT 1527* carved into the stone next to a gate. This was the house where the traitors met and stored their weapons. "DVRT" stands for *"die verräterische Rotte Tor,"* or "The Gate of the Traitorous Gang"—it's a warning.

• *To leave Obermarkt, walk down...*

Brüderstrasse

This street, connecting Obermarkt and Untermarkt, is home to a fine collection of Renaissance houses. These houses were the single-family dwellings of Görlitz's rich tradesmen, who lived on the upper floors and stored their goods on the street level. The orange-and-gray house at the end of Brüderstrasse (#8) claims to be Germany's oldest Renaissance civic building (from 1526) and now houses the **Silesian Museum of Görlitz** (Schlesisches Museum zu Görlitz), a state museum featuring Silesian culture (€4, Tue–Sun 10:00–17:00, closed Mon, Brüderstrasse 8, tel. 03581/87910, www .schlesisches-museum.de).

As you pass Schwarzestrasse, look left. The street's flying buttresses are typical of Görlitz's Old Town—these two are remnants of a series of brick barriers used to keep insurgents out of the inner city during the Cloth-Maker Rebellions.

• *At the end of Brüderstrasse, you'll reach...*

Lower Market Square (Untermarkt)

The remarkably well-preserved Untermarkt is typical of Central European squares: It's built up in the middle to make maximum use of this prime real estate. The square shows just how prosperous the cloth trade made Görlitz.

Ignoring the tall tower (we'll get to it later), take a look around the square. The building at #14 (east end of the square) housed the city **scales** and was one of the most important commercial buildings because, at its peak, more than 1,000 wagons per day entered Görlitz. Everything had to be weighed and duties paid here. The late-Gothic ground floor, which housed the scales, is topped off with three Renaissance levels. The column-topping busts are a virtual Who's Who of the town's masons and scale-masters.

Around the corner from the scales, on the northern edge of the square, the city established a **commodity exchange** at the beginning of the 18th century. The building was also a kind of department store used to drive simple street vendors away from the financial center. With the rabble banished, the Baroque building with its adorning portal was a favored place for merchants to meet and deal.

• *Untermarkt is dominated by the tall Gothic tower of the...*

Town Hall

Görlitz had no town hall until 1350, when the city purchased this building from a prominent citizen. The tower was extended to 195 feet in 1368. A lightning strike blew the top off the tower on July 9, 1742, prompting the addition of the current Baroque turret. The tower houses two clocks: The upper clock measures the day, month, and phase of the moon, while the lower clock tells the time. The warrior's head used to stick out his tongue every hour, but now just seems to open his mouth. The date inscribed on the clock, 1584, commemorates the year when Bartholomäus Sculteus, an astronomer and mathematician, first divided the clock into 12 points. Sculteus also helped develop the Gregorian calendar. The city honored Sculteus, a Görlitz native, by being the first city in Germany to adopt both the new calendar and the clock. The Town Hall stairs represent the height of Görlitz Renaissance sculpture, and lead from the street level to the building's then-main entrance. Local officials used the balcony to make public announcements and decrees. If you look closely at the statue of Justice (1591), she's not blindfolded—in other words, the city is the highest authority.

• For evidence that Görlitz is definitely a Protestant town, head down Neissstrasse to #29. There you'll find the...

Biblical House

Since the Catholic Church had banned religious depictions on secular buildings, the carvings on the Biblical House made it clear that the Reformation was here to stay. The houses in the Neissstrasse had all burned to the ground in 1526. Hanz Heinz, a cloth trader, purchased this house and rebuilt it completely in the Renaissance style. The house is named after the sandstone reliefs decorating the facade between the first- and second-floor parapets. The top level represents the New Testament, with (from left to right) the Annunciation, birth of Jesus, Jesus' baptism, the Last Supper, and the Crucifixion. The bottom row depicts the creation of Eve, the Fall of Man, Isaac's sacrifice, Moses receiving the Ten Commandments, and Moses banishing serpents.

• Next door, step into the...

Baroque House (Barockhaus)

This museum, which is being renovated but may open sometime in 2010, offers a peek at life in the 17th and 18th centuries. There's also an exhibit honoring another of Görlitz's favorite sons (the philosopher Jacob Böhme, who lived here from 1575–1624), and a fascinating library, which is accessible only with an escort (request a viewing when you buy your ticket). This amazing library is still functioning today—for a €2.50 annual fee, you can have access to any of the books three days a week...anyone interested in tax records from 1475? The rest of the exhibit includes elaborately painted farm furniture, formal 18th-century apartments, a glass exhibit, and a unique lab of electrophysical instruments that belonged to a local contemporary of scientist (and "volt" namesake) Alessandro Volta. The natural sciences library holds geological samples, topographic models, and a first edition of a book by Benjamin Franklin—it's in the last room of books, on the shelf to your right by the window, fifth shelf from the bottom (when open: likely €3.50, Tue–Sun 10:00–17:00, closed Mon, little English information but ask for the free explanatory fliers, tel. 03581/671-355, www.museum-goerlitz.de).

• *Backtrack to Untermarkt and hang a right onto...*

Peterstrasse

On the corner of Peterstrasse is the **City Apothecary** (Ratsapotheke). The owner attempted to transform a Gothic building into a Renaissance masterpiece, but ended up only combining the two styles. The two sundials on the southern facade were added in 1550. The left dial (Solarium) displays the time using the Arabic, local, Roman, and Babylonian clocks. The dial on the right (*Arachne*, "spider" in Greek) displays the position of the planets and the signs of the zodiac. The City Apothecary houses one of the city's best cafés, Kretschmer Ratscafé.

Peterstrasse is yet another impressive street. Look inside #14—the staircase seems to hang in mid-air. The house at #6 is a perfect example of renovations gone wrong: The building is Renaissance, with Gothic doors and windows, Ionic columns, and Baroque decorations—the combination doesn't really work, does it?

At the end of Peterstrasse, you can turn either right or left. Left leads to the **Nikolaiturm** (open to the public only on rare occasions), the oldest of Görlitz's towers, which marks the site of the original village of Gorelec. The Nikolaiturm, like all of the city-wall towers, got a facelift in the 18th century that replaced its pointy top with its current round dome. The city walls and gates were destroyed in 1848—the stones were used to build the Jägerkaserne, a barracks off in the distance to the left of the Nikolaiturm. The only remaining section of the city wall is now a pleasant park that curves around from the base of the Nikolaiturm to the back of the Church of St. Peter.

Alternatively, to the right of the park entrance, a small alleyway (Karpfengrund) snakes its way back to the Peterstrasse.

• *If you turn right at the end of Peterstrasse, you'll reach the...*

Church of St. Peter (Peterskirche)

The church was completed—after many setbacks, landslides, and Hussite invasions—in 1457, and renovated after fire destroyed the interior in 1691. The spires were added in 1890. The facade looks like a thousand other Gothic churches, but it's what's inside that counts: The Silesian-Italian Eugenio Casparini's **Sun Organ** (Sonnenorgel) is a spectacular, one-of-a-kind musical instrument and the center of Görlitz's musical life since 1701. The organ gets its name not from the golden sun at the center (which spins when air is pushed through the pipe), but for the circularly arranged pipes that shoot out like the sun's rays. Take in a free concert Thursday or Sunday at noon (Nov–March Sun only). The colorful baptistery, from 1617, is also worth a look.

• *Your walk is finished. Consider visiting some of Görlitz's other sights (described next), or relax with a local Landskron beer.*

More Sights in Görlitz

▲**Holy Sepulcher (Heiliges Grab)**—One of Görlitz's most unusual and interesting sights, this is the only complete and relatively accurate replica of the garden of Gethsemane and the holy places in Jerusalem, as they appeared in the 15th century. It takes a bit longer to visit than other sights in Görlitz, but pilgrims find it well worth ▲▲▲.

After making a pilgrimage to Jerusalem, Georg Emmerich commissioned this site as an offering to those who could not make such a journey themselves (built 1480–1503). The first building is the two-story Chapel of the Holy Cross. Reflecting the traditional belief that Christ was crucified on the site of Adam's grave, the crypt represents the tomb of Adam with the Golgotha Chapel above. Next door is the Salbhaus, a tiny chapel with a statue of Mary anointing Jesus' dead body. Finally, the Church of the Holy Sepulcher is a much smaller version of the original, but nonetheless is an interesting fusion of Middle Eastern and European architecture. This version actually predates the restored Jerusalem site, which was damaged by fire in the 16th century. Medieval pilgrims to this site purchased a *Görlitzer Scheckel*—gold, silver, or pewter, according to their means—as payment to the church and a symbol of their pilgrimage (€1.50, daily April–Sept 10:00–18:00, Oct–March 10:00–16:00, English handout, Heilige-Grab-Strasse 79, tram #1, #2, or #3 to Heilige Grab, www.heiligesgrab-goerlitz.de).

GÖRLITZ

▲**Landskron Brewery**—Beer has been brewed in Görlitz since the 12th century. The last remaining (and best) brewery is Landskron, which brews 11 different beers, including the best *Hefeweizen* (wheat beer) in Germany. It's also one of the last breweries to use open fermentation. The brewery offers tours in German, but the staff tries to be accommodating to English-speakers. In the end, it's all about the taste samples anyway. There are two tour versions: the ".33l Tour" (€6.50, 1.5 hours) or the ".5l Tour" (€9.50, 2.5 hours). Contact the brewery in advance to check the tour schedule and reserve—although it's usually possible to sneak into an already scheduled tour, if you ask nicely (An der Landskronbrauerei 116, tel. 03581/465-121, www.landskron.de, besichtigung@landskron.de). In the summer, the brewery hosts concerts and other events.

▲**Landeskrone**—On the outskirts of the city is a dormant volcano that stretches 1,376 feet above sea level. The city of Görlitz purchased the Landeskrone from the aristocracy and incorporated it into the city in 1440. The mountainside provided wood for building (especially for rebuilding the town after fires) and basalt for cobblestones, and gave the city a commanding view into three countries at once—helping to defend the city against marauding robber-barons. The observation tower on top, built on the ruins of a Bohemian fort, came in the 18th century, and was followed by a small restaurant and hotel in 1844 (the current version was rebuilt in 1951). The entire area is a park, ideal for short hikes. To get here, take tram #2 to the stop Biesnitz/Landeskrone. It's about a 40-minute hike from the tram stop to the top.

Near Görlitz

Three Silesian towns near Görlitz offer an interesting and diverse glimpse into this unique cultural crossroads.

▲**Zgorzelec**—When everything east of the Neisse River (and, farther north, the Oder River) became a part of Poland, Görlitz lost its eastern suburb. By 1946, Poles transplanted from Belarus and Ukraine eliminated all traces of the German past and created the city of Zgorzelec. On both sides of the river, government and citizenry are making great strides to glue the city back together (at least culturally) in a united Europe. And now, since Germany and Poland opened their borders in late 2007, you can stroll freely between the two countries. A walk into Poland is an interesting experience and offers a stark contrast to wonderfully restored Görlitz. Zgorzelec is obviously the less wealthy part of the city, but offers a fine collection of patrician and burgher houses (along ulica Warszawska). Some have been lovingly renovated, but others are in desperate need of repair.

The main part of Zgorzelec is across the Pope John Paul II Bridge (Neissebrücke), south of the Old Town. Once across the bridge, turn to the right and go up the hill to reach the Upper Lusatian Memorial Hall (nowadays the Dom Kultury, or Civic House of Culture), a memorial to Kaiser Wilhelm I. Wander north through Poland, then cross back into Germany at the pedestrian Old Town Bridge, behind the Church of St. Peter.

Zittau and Oybin Castle (Burg Oybin)—Although Zittau is a splendid city in its own right, with pretty squares and a town hall by Karl Friedrich Schinkel, the real reason to come here is to take the narrow-gauge steam railroad to the top of Oybin Mountain to see the castle ruins. Bohemian Emperor Charles IV built the fortress and monastery Burg Oybin in the 14th century. The structure fell into disuse by the 16th century, and was repeatedly struck by lightning in the 18th and 19th centuries. Nineteenth-century painters such as Caspar David Friedrich made the castle famous again. The ruins are huge and fun to poke around, and the views of the unique geological formations of the Zittau Mountains are grand (castle entry-€4, daily April–Oct 9:00–18:00, Nov–March 10:00–16:00, www.burgundkloster -oybin.de).

Bautzen/Budyšin—This town, about halfway between Dresden and Görlitz, is the cultural capital of the Sorbs (or Wends, as they are known in the US). The Sorbs—not to be confused with the Serbs of the former Yugoslavia, much farther south—are of Slavic descent, and still speak a distinct language that's a hybrid of Polish and Czech. About 20,000 Sorbs live in Germany, making up the country's only indigenous ethnic minority.

Bautzen's dual-language signs and slightly Mediterranean feel of spacious squares and public fountains, combined with intact city walls and a tower that's more off-center than Pisa's, make this town a perfect stopover between Dresden and Görlitz. Bautzen is also home to Germany's only Simultaneous Church, a house of worship shared by Catholics on one side and Protestants on the other. Germany's best spicy mustard comes from Bautzen. For lunch, try **Restaurant Wjelbik,** which serves wonderful Sorbian food (Kornstrasse 1). For more information on the town, see www .bautzen.de.

Shopping in Görlitz

Görlitzer Weinachts Haus celebrates Christmas all year long. Stop here for good deals on traditional crafts such as nutcrackers, incense burners shaped like smoking men, and Nativity scenes. Big draws are traditional paper stars from Herrnhut, hand-blown Sorbian glass eggs, and Thuringian glass (Mon–Fri 10:00–18:00, Sat 10:00–17:00, Sun 11:00–16:00 in summer only, otherwise closed Sun, Fleischerstrasse 19, just off Obermarkt—look for the huge nutcracker out front, tel. 03581/649-205).

Schlesische Schatztruhe is one-stop shopping for all your Silesian souvenir needs: books, posters, maps, cookbooks, and more. This is the first place to stop for Silesian ceramics and "Polish pottery" from Bolesławiec (Bunzlau in German). Unfortunately, they don't ship pottery to the US—you'll have to ship or carry it yourself. Their *Streuselkuchen* pastry seems to stay fresh forever (Mon–Fri 9:00–18:00, Sat 10:00–19:00, Sun 10:00–17:00, Brüderstrasse 13, tel. 03581/410-956, www.schlesien-heute.de).

Sleeping in Görlitz

$$ Hotel Bon Apart is a comfortable hotel with an eclectic interior design that can only be described as "Gothic meets Baroque." It's a great value, with the best breakfast buffet in town. The rooms and suites have kitchens, and they brew their own beer (Sb-€80– 90, Db-€95–130, 1-person suite-€130, 2-person suite-€150, family suites-€170–225, Elisabethstrasse 41, tel. & fax 03581/48080, www.bon-apart.de, hotel@bon-apart.de). Owner François also owns the slightly cheaper **Pension Am Stadtpark 8,** a pension with renovated rooms in a gorgeous old building on the edge of the city park, a little farther from the center overlooking the former border crossing (same contact info as above, Am Stadtpark 8).

Sleep Code

(€1 = about $1.40, country code: 49, area code: 03581)
S = Single, **D** = Double/Twin, **T** = Triple, **Q** = Quad, **b** = bathroom, **s** = shower only. Unless otherwise noted, credit cards are accepted, English is spoken, and breakfast is included.

To help you sort easily through these listings, I've divided the rooms into two categories, based on the price for a standard double room with bath:

$$ Higher Priced—Most rooms €85 or more.
$ Lower Priced—Most rooms less than €85.

$ Die Destille ("The Distillery") is a clean, friendly, family-run pension with well-apportioned rooms near the Nikolaiturm. A good breakfast is left in the refrigerator near your room, so you can have breakfast whenever you want. During renovation of the building in the 1990s, workers discovered a *mikveh* (ritual Jewish bath) in the basement (Sb-€50, Db-€68, cash only, restaurant—see next section, Nikolaistrasse 6, tel. & fax 03581/405-302, www.destille-goerlitz.de).

$ Hotel und Gasthof Dreibeiniger-Hund ("Three-Legged Dog"), down the street from Die Destille, is a small, meticulously restored pension offering 13 cozy and romantic rooms in a 14th-century shell (Sb-€63–73, Db-€73–83, cash only, book ahead in summer, restaurant—see next section, Büttnerstrasse 13, tel. 03581/423-980, www.dreibeinigerhund.de).

Eating in Görlitz

Silesians are a hearty people, and their cooking combines German, Polish, and Czech elements into one of Germany's most interesting regional cuisines. The Silesian specialty is *Schlesisches Himmelreich* ("Silesian Heaven"), a mix of pork roast and ham with stewed fruit in a white sauce served with dumplings. For dessert, try Silesian *Streuselkuchen*, a yummy crumb cake available everywhere. Landskron is Görlitz's ubiquitous brew, and one of the best pilsners in Germany. The first two places listed here also rent rooms (described earlier).

Die Destille, literally in the shadow of the Nikolaiturm, is a delightful restaurant oozing comfortable country elegance, with a friendly staff to boot. They excel at extremely traditional Silesian dishes, including the best *Schlesisches Himmelreich* in town. It's small, so come early or be prepared to share a table (€7–13 plates, daily 12:00–22:00, Nikolaistrasse 6, tel. 03581/405-302).

Gasthof Dreibeiniger-Hund has a personal and homey restaurant. Regional cuisine with fresh seasonal specialties makes the "Dog" a must. In summer, sit outside under the sprawling oak tree (€6–12 plates, daily 11:00–23:00, Büttnerstrasse 13, tel. 03581/423-980).

Zur Goldenen Sonne, a favorite among the artsy clientele from the neighboring theater, serves traditional Silesian cuisine as well as exotic meats such as ostrich, bison, and crocodile. Don't worry—you can get a steak or a schnitzel here, too. Or try one of the excellent *Pfannen* dishes, served in a cast-iron skillet. Housed in a former stable, the Sonne has a cozy ambience and reasonable prices, and offers a sunny Mediterranean break from dumplings (€6–18 plates, daily 11:30–14:30 & 17:00–23:00, Demianiplatz 54, tel. 03581/311-609).

Vierradenmühle, Germany's easternmost restaurant, is the perfect place to ponder the division and reunification of Europe. The restaurant sits on top of a water-filtration station and former power plant (with museum) in the Neisse River, so the eastern foundation wall is actually the German-Polish border. The two sides of the border are marked by wooden poles on either side in the colors of the respective country: white and red for Poland, and black, red, and yellow for Germany. The food is mediocre and overpriced, but the location is great—making it the ideal spot to enjoy a cold beer (Mon–Sat 11:00–24:00, Sun 10:00–22:00, at the end of Neissstrasse at Hotherstrasse 20, tel. 03581/406-661).

In Poland: **Piwnica Staromiejska** ("Old Town Pub"), in a former grain mill on the Polish side of the Old Town Bridge, serves traditional eastern Polish specialties. The lively, largely Polish crowd welcomes visitors from both sides of the city, and the friendly and helpful staff will explain the menu. Don't worry about paying with Polish *złoty*—the restaurant accepts euros, and won't cheat you on the exchange (€3–12 plates, *pelmeni* dumplings and a Żywiec beer-€5.50, lavish salads, daily 12:00–22:00, ulica Wrocławska 1, Zgorzelec, from Germany dial 00-48-75-775-2692).

Near the Lower Market Square: Good eateries abound near the Untermarkt. The best are on Peterstrasse, between the market and the Church of St. Peter; and on Neissstrasse, stretching from Untermarkt to the river. Almost every building on Neissstrasse was once a brewery. The pick of the litter is the **Bürgerstübl,** which was recently renovated with the help of the Landskron brewery and has a secret *Biergarten* in the back (€7–10 plates, open daily from 18:00, Sat–Sun also 12:00–14:00, Neissstrasse 27, tel. 03581/879-579).

Picnic Supplies: The only grocery store in the city center is the **Lebensmittel Weiss,** at the corner of Steinstrasse and Obermarkt (Mon–Fri 8:00–18:30, Sat 8:00–16:00, closed Sun). For fresh fruit and produce, try the **Farmer's Market,** on Elisabethstrasse across from Hotel Bon-Apart (Mon–Fri 6:00–18:00, Sat 6:00–12:00, closed Sun).

Görlitz Connections

From Görlitz by Train to: Zittau (hourly, 45 min, not covered by railpass), **Bautzen** (about hourly, 30–45 min; Bautzen-bound trains continue on to Dresden), **Dresden** (hourly, 1.5 hrs), **Berlin** (hourly, 2.5 hrs, transfer in Cottbus to the green-and-yellow ODEG train). Train info: tel. 0180-599-6633 (€0.14/min).

If you are day-tripping from Görlitz to Zittau, your best bet is the **Tageskarte Lausitz** day pass—at the ticket machine, choose *Tageskarte Lausitz,* then *1* (€10); or *Kleingruppenkarte Lausitz,* then *1* (€20 for up to 5 adults).

BERLIN

No tour of Germany is complete without a look at its historic and reunited capital. Over the last two decades, Berlin has been a construction zone. Standing over ripped-up tracks and under a canopy of cranes, visitors witnessed the rebirth of a great European capital. Today, as we enjoy the thrill of walking over what was the Wall and through the well-patched Brandenburg Gate, it's clear that history is not contained in some book, but is an exciting story that we are a part of. Historians find Berlin exhilarating.

Berlin had a tumultuous 20th century. After the city was devastated in World War II, it was divided by the Allied powers: The American, British, and French sectors became West Berlin, and the Soviet sector, East Berlin. In 1948 and 1949, the Soviet Union tried to starve the Western half into submission, but the siege was foiled by the Western Allies' Berlin Airlift, which flew in supplies from Frankfurt. The East-West division was set in stone in 1961, when the East German government boxed in West Berlin by building the Berlin Wall. The Wall stood for 28 years. In 1990, less than a year after the Wall fell, the two Germanys—and the two Berlins—officially became one. When the dust settled, Berliners from both sides of the once-divided city faced the monumental challenge of reunification.

While the work is far from over, a new Berlin has emerged. Berliners joke that they don't need to go anywhere because their city's always changing. Spin a postcard rack to see what's new. A five-year-old guidebook on Berlin covers a different city.

Reunification has had its negative side, and locals are fond of saying, "The Wall survives in the minds of some people." Some

"Ossies" (impolite slang for Easterners) miss their security. Some "Wessies" miss their easy ride (military deferrals, subsidized rent, and tax breaks offered to West Germans willing to live in an isolated city surrounded by the communist world). For free spirits, walled-in West Berlin was a citadel of freedom within the East.

The city government has been eager to charge forward, with little nostalgia for anything that was Eastern. Big corporations and the national government have moved in, and the dreary swath of land that was the Wall and its notorious "death strip" has been transformed. City planners have boldly made Berlin's reunification and the return of the national government a good opportunity to make Berlin a great capital once again.

Today, Berlin feels like the nuclear fuel rod of a great nation. It's so vibrant with youth, energy, and an anything-goes-and-anything's-possible buzz that Munich feels spent in comparison. Berlin is both extremely popular and surprisingly affordable. As a booming tourist attraction, Berlin welcomed more visitors than Rome in 2009. But the city is so spread out, you'll often feel like you have the place to yourself.

Planning Your Time

Because of Berlin's inconvenient location, try to enter and/or leave by either night train or plane. On a three-week trip through Germany, I'd give Berlin at least two days and spend them this way:

Day 1: Begin your day getting oriented to this huge city. Either take the 10:00 "Discover Berlin" guided walking tour offered by Original Berlin Walks or follow my "Do-It-Yourself Orientation Tour" by bus to the Reichstag, then continue by foot down Unter den Linden. Focus on sights along Unter den Linden, including the Reichstag dome (most crowded 10:00–16:00; best to visit 8:00–9:00 or 21:00–22:00), the German History Museum, and Museum Island (with the Pergamon and Egyptian museums). Take a stroll (or boat tour) along the park-like banks of the Spree River from Museum Island to the Chancellery.

Day 2: Concentrate on the sights in central Berlin, and in eastern Berlin south of Unter den Linden. Spend the morning with the paintings at the Gemäldegalerie. After lunch, hike via Potsdamer Platz to the Topography of Terror exhibit and along the surviving Zimmerstrasse stretch of the Wall to the Museum of The Wall at Checkpoint Charlie. If you're not museum-ed out yet, swing by the magnificent Jewish Museum. Finish your day in the lively East—ideally in the once glum, then edgy, now fun-loving and trendy Prenzlauer Berg district.

If you're maximizing your sightseeing, note that the Reichstag dome and the Museum of The Wall are open late.

BERLIN

Berlin Sightseeing Modules

SPREE RIVER

EASTERN BERLIN
New Synagogue
Museum Island
German Hist. Museum
TV Tower
Prenzlauer Berg

CHARLOTTEN-BURG
Charlottenburg Palace
Picasso Museum
Art Nouveau Museum
Surrealist Museum

Reichstag
Brandenburg Gate
Memorial to Murdered Jews
Hauptbahnhof

UNTER DEN LINDEN

BUS 100

Checkpoint Charlie
Museum of the Wall
Jewish Museum

KU-DAMM

WESTERN BERLIN
Zoo Station
Savignyplatz
Hotel Area
Ka De We Dept Store

CENTRAL BERLIN
Tiergarten Park
Potsdamer Platz
Kulturforum
Gemäldegalerie

DCH

Berlin merits additional time if you have it. There's much more in the city. And the concentration camp memorial at Sachsenhausen and the palace at Potsdam are both worthwhile side-trips.

Orientation to Berlin

(area code: 030)

Berlin is huge, with 3.4 million people. But the tourist's Berlin can be broken into four digestible chunks:

1. Eastern Berlin has the highest concentration of notable sights and colorful neighborhoods. Near the landmark Brandenburg Gate, you'll find the Reichstag building, Pariser Platz, and the new Holocaust Memorial. From the Brandenburg Gate, the famous Unter den Linden boulevard runs eastward through the former East Berlin, passing the marvelous German History Museum and Museum Island (Pergamon Museum, Egyptian Museum, and Berlin Cathedral) on the way to Alexanderplatz (TV Tower). The intersection of Unter den Linden and Friedrichstrasse is emerging as the new center of the city. South of Unter den Linden, you'll find the delightful Gendarmenmarkt square, most Nazi sites (including the Topography of Terror exhibit), the Jewish Museum, the best Wall-related sights (Museum of The Wall at Checkpoint Charlie and East Side Gallery), and the colorful Turkish neighborhood of

Kreuzberg. North of Unter den Linden are these worth-a-wander neighborhoods: around Oranienburger Strasse (Jewish Quarter and New Synagogue), Hackescher Markt, and Prenzlauer Berg (several recommended hotels and a very lively restaurant/night-life zone). Eastern Berlin's newest attraction is a stroll along its pedestrian-friendly Spree riverbank.

2. Central Berlin is dominated by the giant Tiergarten park. South of the park are Potsdamer Platz and the Kulturforum museum cluster (including the Gemäldegalerie, New National Gallery, Musical Instruments Museum, and Philharmonic Concert Hall). To the north, the huge Hauptbahnhof (main train station) straddles the former Wall in what was central Berlin's no-man's-land.

3. Western Berlin centers on the Bahnhof Zoo (Zoo train station, often marked "Zoologischer Garten" on transit maps) and the grand Kurfürstendamm boulevard, nicknamed "Ku'damm" (transportation hub, tours, information, shopping, and recommended hotels). The East is all the rage. But the West, while staid in comparison, is bouncing back—with lots of big-name stores and destination restaurants that keep the area buzzing. During the Cold War, this "Western Sector" was the hub for Western visitors. Capitalists visited the West, with a nervous side-trip beyond the Wall into the grim and foreboding East. (Cubans, Russians, Poles, and Angolans stayed behind the Wall and did their sightseeing in the East.) Remnants of this Iron Curtain–era Western focus have left today's visitors with a stronger focus on the Ku'damm and Bahnhof Zoo than the district really deserves.

4. Charlottenburg Palace Area, on the western edge of the city center, is home to a palace and nearby museums (Picasso, Art Nouveau, and Surrealist). This area is of least interest to a visitor on a tight schedule.

Tourist Information

With any luck, you won't have to use Berlin's TIs—they're for-profit agencies working for the city's big hotels, which colors the information they provide. TI branches, appropriately called "info-stores," are unlikely to have the information you need (tel. 030/250-025, www.berlin-tourist-information.com). You'll find them at the **Hauptbahnhof** train station (daily 8:00–22:00, by main entrance on Europaplatz), **Ku'damm** (Kurfürstendamm 21, in the glass-and-steel Neues Kranzler Eck building, Mon–Sat 10:00–20:00, Sun 10:00–18:00, shorter hours in winter), and the **Brandenburg Gate** (daily 10:00–18:00).

Skip the TI's €1 map, and instead pick up any of the walking tour companies' brochures—they include better maps for free (most hotels also provide free city maps). While the TI does sell

BERLIN

Berlin

the three-day Museumspass (described next), it's also available at major museums. If you take a walking tour, your guide is likely a better source of nightlife or shopping tips than the TI. The TI offers a €3 room-finding service (but only for hotels that give them kickbacks—many don't).

Museum Passes: The three-day **Museumspass** (a.k.a. Schaulust MuseenBerlin) gets you into 70 museums, including the national museums and most of the recommended biggies, on three consecutive days for €19. As you'll routinely spend €5–8 per admission, this pays for itself in a hurry. And you'll enjoy the ease of popping in and out of museums that you might not otherwise want to pay for. Buy it at the TI or any participating museum. Note that if a museum is closed on one of the days of your Museumspass, you have access to that museum on a fourth day to make up for lost time. The pass won't, however, enable you to skip lines: Many museums want passholders to stand in line to get a free ticket that lets you through the turnstile. The €12 **Museum Island Pass** (Standortkarte Museumsinsel) covers all the museums on the island (otherwise €8 each) and is a fine value—but for €7 more, the three-day Museumspass gives you triple the days and many more entries. TIs also sell the **WelcomeCard,** a transportation pass that also gives some museum discounts (described later, under "Getting Around Berlin").

Local Publications: Various magazines can help make your time in Berlin more productive (all available at the TI and most at newsstands). *Berlin Programm* is a comprehensive German-language monthly, especially strong in high culture, that lists upcoming events and museum hours (€2, www.berlin-programm .de). *Berlin To Go* is a sketchier German/English TI-produced bimonthly magazine offering timely features on Berlin and a par-tial calendar of events (€1). *Exberliner Magazine,* the only real English monthly (published mostly by expat Brits who love to poke fun at expat Americans), is very helpful for curious travel-ers. It has an edgy, somewhat pretentious, youthful focus and gives a fascinating insider's look at this fast-changing city (€2 but often given away at theaters or on the street, www.exberliner .com).

Arrival in Berlin
By Train

Berlin's newest and grandest train station is **Berlin Hauptbahnhof**
(main train station, a.k.a. simply
"der Bahnhof"). All long-distance
trains now arrive at Europe's biggest, mostly underground train
station. Tracks 1–8 are in the
lowest underground level, while
tracks 11–16 (along with the
S-Bahn) are a floor above ground
level, marked *+1*.

It's a "transfer station"—unique for its major lines coming in
at right angles—where the national train system meets the city's
train system (S-Bahn). It's also the home of 80 shops with long
hours—some locals call the station a "shopping mall with trains"
(daily 8:00–22:00, even Sunday). The Kaisers supermarket (on the
underground shopping level, marked *-1*) is handy for assembling a
picnic for the ride.

Services: The easy way to store your luggage is at the Gepäck
Center, an efficient and secure deposit service (€4/day per bag,
always open, on the upper level directly under track 14). Luggage
lockers (€3–5) are difficult to find since they're in the parking
garage (P-3 level). Look for the garage entrance near Kaisers on
the underground shopping level. The WC Center (public toilets) is
next to the Virgin Megastore.

Train Information: The station has two DeutscheBahn
Reisezentrum information counters (one on the upper level, the
other on the underground shopping level—just follow signs; both
open daily 6:00–22:00). If you're staying in western Berlin, keep
in mind that the info center at the Bahnhof Zoo station is just as
good and much less crowded.

EurAide is an English-speaking information desk with
answers to your questions about train travel around Europe. It
operates from a single counter in the underground shopping level
Reisezentrum (follow signs to tracks 5–6). It's American-run, so
communication is simple. This is an especially good place to make
fast-train and *couchette* reservations for later in your trip. EurAide
also gives out a helpful free city map (April–Sept daily 10:00–
20:00; Oct–March Mon–Fri 11:00–19:00, closed Sat–Sun; www
.euraide.com).

Getting into Town: While taxis and buses await outside the
station, the S-Bahn is probably your best means of connecting to
your destination within Berlin. The crosstown express S-Bahn line
connects the station with my recommended hotels in a few minutes.
It's simple: All S-Bahn trains are on tracks 15 and 16 at the top of the

station. All trains on track 15 go east (toward the Ostbahnhof and Hackescher Markt), and trains on track 16 go west (toward Bahnhof Zoo and Savignyplatz). Your train ticket or railpass into the station covers you on your connecting S-Bahn ride into town (and your ticket out includes the transfer via S-Bahn to the Hauptbahnhof). U-Bahn rides are not covered by tickets or railpasses.

If you're sleeping at my recommended hotels in eastern Berlin, take any train on track 15 two stops to Hackescher Markt, then catch tram #M1 north (see map on page 567).

If you're sleeping at my recommended hotels in western Berlin, catch any train on track 16 to Savignyplatz, and you're a five-minute walk from your hotel (see map on page 570). Savignyplatz is one stop after **Bahnhof Zoo** (rhymes with "toe," a.k.a. Bahnhof Zoologischer Garten), the once-grand train hub now eclipsed by the Hauptbahnhof. Nowadays it's useful mainly for its shops, uncrowded train-information desk, and BVG transit office (outside the entrance, amid the traffic).

The Berlin Hauptbahnhof is not well-connected to the city's U-Bahn (subway) system—yet. The station's sole U-Bahn line—U-55—only goes two stops to the Brandenburger Tor station, and doesn't really connect to the rest of the system. It's part of a planned extension of the U-5 line to Alexanderplatz that's far from completion. But for transit junkies, it is an interesting ride on Europe's newest and shortest subway line.

By Plane

For information on reaching the city center from Berlin's airports, see "Berlin Connections" at the end of this chapter.

Helpful Hints

Medical Help: "Call a Doc" is a non-profit referral service designed for tourists (toll tel. 01804-2255-2362, phone answered 24 hours a day, www.calladoc.com). Payment is arranged between you and the doctor, and is likely far more affordable than similar care in the US. The US Embassy also has a list of local English-speaking doctors (tel. 030/832-9233, www.usembassy.de).

Museum Hours: Some major Berlin museums are closed on Monday. All national museums, including the Pergamon and Gemäldegalerie (plus others, as noted in "Sights in Berlin"), are free for the last four hours on Thursdays (for example, if it closes at 18:00, it's free from 14:00 on; www.museen-berlin.de).

Monday Activities: Since many museums close on Monday, save the day for Berlin Wall sights, the Reichstag dome, my "Do-It-Yourself Orientation Tour" and strolling Unter den Linden, walking/bus tours, the Jewish Museum, churches, the zoo, or shopping (the Kaufhaus des Westens—KaDeWe—department store is a sight in itself). Be aware that when Monday is a holiday—as it is several times a year—museums are open then and closed Tuesday.

Addresses: Many Berlin streets are numbered with odd and even numbers on the same side of the street, often with no connection to the other side (for example, Ku'damm #212 can be across the street from #14). To save steps, check the white street signs on curb corners; many list the street numbers covered on that side of the block.

Internet Access: You'll find Internet access in most hotels and hostels, as well as at small Internet cafés all over the city. The **easyInternetcafé** outlets—generally paired with Dunkin' Donuts (daily 6:00–23:00)—have handy locations, including Hardenbergplatz 2 (across from Bahnhof Zoo, next to McDonald's), Ku'damm 224 (10-min walk from Bahnhof Zoo, near several recommended hotels), and Rathaus-Passagen (on Alexanderplatz). Buy a ticket at the self-service machines and follow the English instructions. Unused time can be used at any branch in Berlin for up to a week.

Bookstore: Berlin Story, a big, cluttered, fun bookshop, has the best selection anywhere in town of English-language books on Berlin. They also have a fascinating free little museum in the back with a model of Unter den Linden from 1930 and a room showing a good 25-minute Berlin history video (in English). The shop has a knowledgeable staff and stocks an amusing mix of knickknacks and East Berlin nostalgia souvenirs (daily 10:00–20:00, Unter den Linden 26, tel. 030/2045-3842, www.berlinstory.de).

Laundry: Schnell und Sauber Waschcenter is a chain of handy launderettes, with a location in western Berlin's Charlottenburg at Kaiserdamm 100 (while waiting, grab a beer at Alt-Berlin, a locals-only pub next door), and another in eastern Berlin at Torstrasse 115, around the corner from the recommended Circus Hostel (€5–9/load wash and dry, daily 6:00–23:00). Also near my recommended hotels in Prenzlauer Berg, try **Eco-Express Waschsalon** (€4–9/load wash and dry, daily 6:00–22:00, self- or full-serve, attached café, Danziger Strasse 7).

Travel Agency: Last Minute Flugbörse can help you find a flight in a hurry (discount flights, no train tickets, in Europa Center near Bahnhof Zoo, Mon–Sat 10:00–20:00, closed Sun, tel. 030/2655-1050, www.lastminuteflugboerse.de). **American Express** is a few blocks off Unter den Linden at Friedrichstrasse 172 (sells train tickets for €4 service fee, Mon–Fri 9:00–19:00, Sat 10:00–14:00, closed Sun, tel. 030/201-7400).

Getting Around Berlin

Berlin's sights spread far and wide. Right from the start, commit yourself to the city's fine public-transit system.

By Subway, Train, Tram, and Bus: Berlin's many modes of transportation are consolidated into one system that uses the same tickets: U-Bahn (*Untergrund-Bahn*, Berlin's subway), S-Bahn (*Schnell-Bahn*, or "fast train," mostly above ground and with fewer stops), *Strassenbahn* (streetcars, called "trams" by locals), and buses. Here are your options:

• A basic ticket *(Einzelfahrschein)* for two hours of travel in one direction on buses or subways—€2.10. It's easy to make this ticket stretch to cover several rides...as long as they're all in the same direction.

• A cheap, short-ride ticket *(Kurzstrecke)* for a single short ride of six bus stops or three subway stations (one transfer allowed)—€1.30.

• A four-trip ticket *(4-Fahrten-Karte)*, four basic tickets at a small discount—€8.

• A day pass *(Tageskarte)* covering zones A and B, the city proper—€6.10 (good until 3:00 the morning after). To get out to Potsdam, you need a ticket that also covers zone C—€6.30. (For longer stays, a 7-day pass—*Sieben-Tage-Karte*—is also available for €26.20, or €32.30 including zone C; or consider the WelcomeCard—good for up to 5 days, and described next.) The *Kleingruppenkarte* lets groups of up to five travel all day for €16.

• If you plan to cover a lot of ground using public transportation during a two- or three-day visit, the **WelcomeCard** (available at TIs) is usually the best deal. For longer stays, there's even a five-day option. It covers all public transportation, and gives you up to 50 percent discounts on lots of minor and a few major museums (including Checkpoint Charlie), sightseeing tours (including 25 percent off the recommended Original Berlin Walks), and music and theater events (www.visitberlin.de /welcomecard). If you plan to stay inside the city, the Berlin-only option works best (covers transit zones A and B, €16.50/48 hrs, €22/72 hrs). If you want to visit Frederick the Great's palaces outside the city and are using Schönefeld Airport, you might want to get the Berlin-with-Potsdam option (zones A, B, and C, €18.50/48 hrs, €25/72 hrs). If you're a museum junkie, consider the **WelcomeCard Museumsinsel** (€24.50/48 hrs, €30/72 hrs), which combines travel in zones A and B with unlimited access to the five museums on Museum Island. Families get an extra price break: The ABC versions are valid for one adult and up to three kids younger than 14.

Buy your U- and S-Bahn tickets from machines at stations. (They are also sold at BVG pavilions at train stations, airports, and the TI, and aboard trams and buses—drivers give change.) *Erwachsener* means "adult"—anyone 14 or older. Don't be afraid of the automated machines: First select the type of ticket you want, then load in the coins or paper bills. As you board the bus or tram, or enter the subway system, punch your ticket in a red or yellow clock machine to validate it (or risk a €40 fine; for an all-day or multi-day pass, stamp it only the first time you ride). Within Berlin, Eurailpasses are good only on S-Bahn connections from the train station when you're arriving, and to the station when you're departing.

The S-Bahn crosstown express is a river of public transit through the heart of the city, in which many lines converge on one basic highway. Get used to this, and you'll leap within a few minutes between key locations: Savignyplatz (hotels), Bahnhof Zoo (Ku'damm, bus #100, walking tour meeting spot), the Hauptbahnhof (all major trains in and out of Berlin), Friedrichstrasse (heart of Unter den Linden), Hackescher Markt (Museum Island, hotels, restaurants, nightlife), and Alexanderplatz (eastern end of Unter den Linden).

Sections of the U- or S-Bahn sometimes close temporarily for repairs. In this situation, a bus route often replaces the train (*Ersatzverkehr,* or "replacement transportation").

Berlin's public transit is operated by BVG (except the S-Bahn, run by DeutscheBahn). Bus schedules are available on the helpful BVG website, www.bvg.de.

By Taxi: Taxis are easy to flag down, and taxi stands are common. A typical ride within town costs €8–10, and a crosstown trip (for example, Bahnhof Zoo to Alexanderplatz) will run you about €15.

Money-Saving Taxi Tip: For any ride of less than two kilometers (about a mile), you can save several euros if you take advantage of the *Kurzstrecke* (short-stretch) rate. To get this rate, it's important that you flag the cab down on the street—not at or even near a taxi stand. Also, you must ask for the *Kurzstrecke* rate as soon as you hop in: Confidently say *"Kurzstrecke, bitte"* (KOORTS-shtreh-keh BIT-teh), and your driver will flip the meter to a fixed €4 rate.

By Bike: Flat Berlin is a very bike-friendly city, but be careful—Berlin's motorists don't brake for bicyclists (and bicyclists don't brake for pedestrians). Fortunately, some roads and sidewalks have special red-painted bike lanes. Just don't ride on the regular sidewalk—it's *verboten.*

In eastern Berlin, **Take a Bike** near the Friedrichstrasse S-Bahn station is owned by a lovely Dutch couple who know a lot about bikes and have a huge inventory (€12.50/day, €19/2 days, slightly cheaper on weekdays, daily 9:30–19:00, 8 Neustädtische Kirchstrasse, tel. 030/2065-4730, info@takeabike.de). To find it, leave the S-Bahn station via the Friedrichstrasse exit, turn right, go through a triangle-shaped square, and hang a left on Neustädtische Kirchstrasse.

In western Berlin, you can rent good bikes at the **Bahnhof Zoo** left-luggage counter, next to the lockers at the back of the station (€10/day, €23/3 days, €35/7 days; bikes come with lock, air pump, and mounted basket; daily 7:00–21:00, there's a limited supply of bikes and they've been known to run out).

Tours in Berlin

▲▲▲Walking Tours

Berlin is an ideal city to get to know with a walking tour. The city is a battle zone of extremely competitive and creative walking-tour companies, all offering employment to American and British expats and students—and cheap, informative tours to visiting travelers. Unlike many other European countries, Germany has no regulations controlling who can give city tours. Berlin is home to a large number of expatriates and academics, and it seems that every year some of them get together and form a new tour company. Some of these upstarts run great tours, but you'll generally get the best quality with one of the more established companies. All give variations on the same themes: general introductory walk, Hitler and Nazi sites walk, communism walk, and day trips to Potsdam and the Sachsenhausen Concentration Camp Memorial. The youth-oriented outfits also do nightly pub crawls. For details, see the various websites.

Original Berlin Walks—This is the most established operation, with tours aiming at a clientele that's curious about the city's history. I've enjoyed the help of O.B.W.'s high-quality, high-energy guides for many years, and routinely hire them when my tour groups are in town. I'm always impressed with founder Nick Gay's ability to assemble guides of such high caliber. Tours generally cost €12 (€9 with WelcomeCard, or €10 if you're under 26). Readers of this book get a €1 discount (off the adult or youth price) per tour in 2010.

There's no need to reserve ahead—just show up. All tours meet at the taxi stand in front of the Bahnhof Zoo, and start at 10:00 unless otherwise noted. The Discover Berlin and Jewish Life tours have a second departure point 30 minutes later opposite eastern Berlin's Hackescher Markt S-Bahn station, outside the Weihenstephaner restaurant; if you're staying in eastern Berlin, save time by meeting the group there.

Discover Berlin, O.B.W.'s flagship introductory walk, covers the birthplace of the city, Museum Island, then heads up Unter den Linden, stops at the Reichstag, and goes on to Checkpoint Charlie (no interior visits, 4 hours, English only, daily year-round, meet at

Berlin at a Glance

▲▲▲**Reichstag** Germany's historic Parliament building, topped with a striking dome you can climb. **Hours:** Daily 8:00–24:00, last entry at 22:00. To avoid long lines, go very early (8:00) or late (after 21:00). See page 520.

▲▲▲**German History Museum** The ultimate swing through the tumultuous history of this country. **Hours:** Daily 10:00–18:00. See page 535.

▲▲▲**Museum of The Wall at Checkpoint Charlie** Moving museum near the former site of the famous border checkpoint between the American and Soviet sectors, with stories of brave escapes during the Cold War and the gleeful days when the Wall fell. **Hours:** Daily 9:00–22:00. See page 543.

▲▲▲**Jewish Museum Berlin** User-friendly museum celebrating Jewish culture, in a highly conceptual building. **Hours:** Daily 10:00–20:00, Mon until 22:00. See page 545.

▲▲▲**Gemäldegalerie** Germany's top collection of 13th- through 18th-century European paintings, featuring Dürer, Van Eyck, Rubens, Titian, Raphael, Caravaggio, and more. **Hours:** Tue–Sun 10:00–18:00, Thu until 22:00, closed Mon. See page 555.

▲▲**Berlin Wall** Mostly gone, but parts of the Wall are still visible—including the East Side Gallery, the Documentation Center on Bernauer Strasse, and a chunk near the Topography of Terror (former SS and Gestapo headquarters). **Hours:** Always open. See page 525.

▲▲**Brandenburg Gate** One of Berlin's most famous landmarks, a massive columned gateway, at the former border of East and West. **Hours:** Always open. See page 526.

▲▲**Memorial to the Murdered Jews of Europe** New Holocaust memorial with almost 3,000 symbolic pillars, plus an exhibition about Hitler's Jewish victims. **Hours:** Memorial always open; information center open Tue–Sun 10:00–20:00, closed Mon. See page 528.

▲▲**Unter den Linden** Leafy boulevard through the heart of former East Berlin, lined with some of the city's top sights. **Hours:** Always open. See page 529.

BERLIN

▲▲**Pergamon Museum** World-class museum of classical antiquities on Museum Island (just off Unter den Linden), featuring the fantastic second-century B.C. Greek Pergamon Altar. **Hours:** Daily 10:00–18:00, Thu until 22:00. See page 537.

▲▲**Egyptian Museum/Neues Museum** Proud new home (on Museum Island) of the exquisite 3,000-year-old bust of Queen Nefertiti. **Hours:** To be announced, may match Pergamon Museum hours. See page 537.

▲▲**Gendarmenmarkt** Inviting square bounded by twin churches (one with a fine German history exhibit), a chocolate shop, and a concert hall. **Hours:** Always open. See page 542.

▲**Deutsche Kinemathek Film and TV Museum** An entertaining look at German film and TV from *Metropolis* to Dietrich, from Hitler through the Communist days. **Hours:** Tue-Sun 10:00–18:00, Thu until 20:00, closed Mon. See page 554.

▲**New Synagogue** Largest prewar synagogue in Berlin, damaged in WWII, with a facade that has since been rebuilt. **Hours:** Generally Sun–Fri 10:00–17:00 or later, closed Sat. See page 547.

▲**Prenzlauer Berg** One of Berlin's most colorful and lively neighborhoods, worth exploring. **Hours:** Always bustling. See page 549.

▲**Potsdamer Platz** The "Times Square" of old Berlin, long a postwar wasteland, now rebuilt with huge glass skyscrapers, an underground train station, and—covered with a huge canopy—the Sony Center mall with eateries. **Hours:** Always open. See page 552.

▲**Kaiser Wilhelm Memorial Church** Evocative destroyed church in the heart of the former West Berlin, with a modern annex. **Hours:** Church open daily 9:00–19:00, Memorial Hall in the bombed tower open Mon-Sat 10:00–16:00, closed Sun. See page 557.

▲**Käthe Kollwitz Museum** The black-and-white art of the Berlin artist who conveyed the suffering of her city's stormiest century. **Hours:** Daily 11:00–18:00. See page 558.

▲**Potsdam's Palaces** Frederick the Great's escapist, *über*-frilly palaces, nestled in a vast leafy park. **Hours:** Sanssouci interior open April–Oct Tue-Sun 10:00–18:00, Nov–March Tue-Sun 10:00–17:00, closed Mon year-round. See page 561.

10:00 at Bahnhof Zoo, April–Oct also daily at 13:30). Other tours include: **Infamous Third Reich Sites** (April–Oct Tue and Thu at 10:00, Sat at 14:30, Sun at 10:00; less frequently off-season—check their website or pick up a flier for the schedule); **Jewish Life in Berlin** (April–Oct Mon at 10:00 at Bahnhof Zoo); **Potsdam** (€15, see page 561); and the newest itinerary, **Nest of Spies** (April–Oct only, Sat at 10:00). Many of the Third Reich and Jewish history sights are difficult to pin down without these excellent walks.

Their ground-breaking six-hour trip to the **Sachsenhausen Concentration Camp Memorial** intends to "provide a challenging history lesson with universal applications" (€15, April–Oct Tue, Thu, Fri, and Sun at 10:00 from Bahnhof Zoo meeting point, also from Hackescher Markt meeting point at 10:00, runs less off-season—check website or flier for details).

You can confirm these starting times at EurAide or by phone with Nick or his wife and business partner, Serena (tel. 030/301-9194, www.berlinwalks.de, info@berlinwalks.de).

New Berlin Tours—This company targets a younger crowd and offers free introductory tours, in which their guides make money off of tips, cross-selling their specialty tours and their hugely successful pub crawls. They offer essentially the same itineraries as O.B.W. The basic introductory city walks leave daily at 11:00, 13:00, and 16:00 (free but tip expected, 3.5 hours, meet at Starbucks at Brandenburg Gate/Pariser Platz, just show up). Their wildly popular €12 pub crawls occur nightly (explained under "Nightlife in Berlin," page 566). Where they excel is their Alternative Berlin Tour, which explores Berlin's gritty counterculture, squats, and urban life (daily at 14:00; €12, €10 for students, €1 discount with this book on any tour in 2010, meet at the Old Post Office on the corner of Oranienburger Strasse and Tucholskystrasse, S-Bahn: Oranienburger Strasse, www.newberlintours.com).

Brewer's Berlin Tours—For a more exhaustive (or, for some, exhausting) walking tour of Berlin, consider Brewer's Berlin Tours. These are run by Terry (retired from the British diplomatic service—he worked at the embassy in East Berlin) and his well-trained and engaging staff (all native English speakers). Their Best of Berlin Tour leaves daily at 10:30 (€12, 3 hours). The All-Day Berlin with Terry tours are legendary for their length, and best for those with a long attention span and a serious interest in Berlin (€12, tour lasts 8 hours or more and covers the entire old center, departs Tue and Fri at 10:30 year-round). All tours depart from the Bandy Brooks ice cream shop at Friedrichstrasse U- and S-Bahn station (tel. 030/2248-7435, mobile 0177-388-1537, www.brewersberlintours.com). Just show up. They also do all-day Potsdam tours (May–Oct Wed and Sun; for details, see page 562).

BERLIN

Berlin Underground Association (Berliner Unterwelten Verein)—Much of Berlin's history lies beneath the surface, and this group has an exclusive agreement with the city to explore and research what is hidden underground. Their one-of-a-kind tour of a WWII air-raid bunker features a chilling explanation of the air war over Berlin (daily April–Oct at 11:00, Nov–March Thu–Mon at 11:00). They also have access to the inside of the Humboldthain air defense tower (April–Oct Thu at 13:00 and Sun at 16:00) and a completely stocked and fully functional nuclear emergency bunker (runs all year Fri–Mon at 13:00). The English tours are usually led by Nick Jackson, one of the best tour guides in the city (all tours cost €9, meet in the hall of the Gesundbrunnen U-Bahn/S-Bahn station, follow signs to Humboldthain/Brunnenstrasse exit and walk up the stairs to their office, tel. 030/4991-0517, www.berlinerunterwelten.de).

Local Guides—Both **Nick Jackson** (from the Berlin Underground Association, mobile 0174-346-4262) and **Lee Evans** (my longtime helper in Berlin and one of my tour guides, mobile 0177-423-5307) enjoy sharing the story of their adopted hometown with visitors. If they are busy, try **Björn Awe** at Humboldt Tours. Björn has put together a crew of excellent, professional guides with an academic bent (mobile 0162-472-6502, www.humboldttoursberlin.com).

Bus Tours

Full-Blown Bus Tours—**Severin & Kühn** offers a long list of bus tours in and around Berlin; their three-hour "Big Berlin Tour" is a good introduction (€19, daily at 10:00, Fri–Sun also at 14:00, two stops: Checkpoint Charlie and Brandenburg Gate, live guides in two languages, departs from Ku'damm 216, buy ticket at bus, tel. 030/880-4190, www.severin-kuehn-berlin.de).

Hop-on, Hop-off City Circle Tours—Several companies cooperate so that you can make a circuit of the city with unlimited hop-on, hop-off privileges (about 14 stops) on buses with boring recorded commentary (€20, 4/hr, daily 10:00–18:00, last bus leaves all stops at 16:00, 2-hour loop). Just hop on where you like and pay the driver. On a sunny day, when some convertible double-decker buses go topless, these are a photographer's delight, cruising slowly by just about every major sight in town. In the winter (Nov–March), the buses come only twice an hour and the last departure is at 15:00.

Bike Tours

Fat Tire Bike Tours—Choose among three different four-hour, six-mile tours (€20 each): City Tour (daily March–April and Oct–Nov at 11:00, May–Sept also at 16:00, Dec–Feb Wed and Sat at 11:00), Berlin Wall Tour (May–Sept Mon, Thu, and Sat at 10:30),

BERLIN

and Third Reich Tour (May–Sept Wed, Fri, and Sun at 10:30). For any tour, meet at the TV Tower at Alexanderplatz—but don't get distracted by the Russians pretending to be Fat Tire (no need to reserve for the Wall or Third Reich tours, tel. 030/2404-7991, www.fattirebiketoursberlin.com, info@fattirebiketoursberlin .com).

New Berlin Tours—The energetic guides who offer New Berlin's free walking tours also give quite good two-hour bike tours (daily at 11:00 and 14:00; €15, €12 students; meet on the corner of Oranienburger Strasse and Tucholskystrasse, S-Bahn: Oranienburger Strasse, no need to reserve, for contact info see page 516).

Boat Tours

Spree River Cruises—Several boat companies offer one-hour €10 trips up and down the river. They used to be boring, but now a relaxing hour on one of these boats can be time and money well-spent. You'll listen to excellent English audioguides, see lots of wonderful new government-commissioned architecture, and enjoy the lively park action fronting the river. Boats leave from various docks that cluster near the bridge at the Berlin Cathedral (just off Unter den Linden). I enjoyed the Historical Sightseeing Cruise from **Stern und Kreisschiffahrt** (mid-March–Nov daily 10:30–18:30, leaves from Nikolaiviertel Dock—cross bridge from Berlin Cathedral toward Alexanderplatz and look right, tel. 030/536-3600, www.sternundkreis.de). Confirm that the boat you choose comes with English commentary.

Self-Guided Tour

Do-It-Yourself Orientation Tour:
Bus #100 from Bahnhof Zoo to the Reichstag

This tour narrates the route of convenient bus #100, which connects my recommended hotel neighborhood in western Berlin with the sights in eastern Berlin. If you have the €20 and two hours for a hop-on, hop-off bus tour, take that instead. But this short €2.10 bus ride provides a fine city introduction. Bus #100 is a sightseer's dream, stopping at Bahnhof Zoo, the Berlin Zoo, Victory Column (Siegessäule), Reichstag, Brandenburg Gate, Unter den Linden, Pergamon Museum, and Alexanderplatz. While you could ride it to the end, it's more fun to get out at the Reichstag and walk down Unter den Linden at your own pace (using my commentary on page 529). When combined with the self-guided walk down Unter den Linden, this tour merits ▲▲▲. Before you take this bus into eastern Berlin, consider checking out the sights in western Berlin (see page 556).

The Tour Begins: Buses start from Hardenbergplatz in front of Bahnhof Zoo (from elsewhere in the city, just take the S-Bahn to Bahnhof Zoo). Buses come every 10 minutes, and single tickets are good for two hours—so take advantage of hop-on-and-off privileges. Climb aboard, stamp your ticket (giving it a starting time), and grab a seat on top. This is about a 15-minute ride. The upcoming stop will light up on the reader board inside the bus.

➋ On your left and then straight ahead you'll see the bombed-out hulk of the **Kaiser Wilhelm Memorial Church,** with its postwar sister church (described on page 557) and the **Europa Center.** This shopping district, once the center of West Berlin, is still a bustling people zone with big department stores nearby. When the Wall came down, East Berliners flocked to this area's department stores (especially KaDeWe, described on page 558). Soon after, the biggest, swankiest new stores were built in the East. Now western Berlin is trying to win those shoppers back by building even bigger and better shopping centers around the Europa Center.

➋ At the stop in front of Hotel Palace: On the left, the elephant gates mark the entrance to the **Berlin Zoo** and its aquarium (described on page 559).

➋ Cruising down Kurfürstenstrasse, you'll pass several Asian restaurants—a reminder that, for most, the best food in Berlin is not German. Turning left, with the huge Tiergarten park in the distance ahead, you'll cross a canal and see the **Bauhaus Archive** behind the trees on the right (hard to see—it's the off-white, blocky building with scoopy roof ducts). The Bauhaus movement ushered in a new age of modern architecture that emphasized function over beauty, giving rise to blocky steel-and-glass skyscrapers in big cities around the world. On the left is Berlin's new embassy row. The big turquoise wall marks the communal home of all five Nordic embassies. This building is "green," run entirely on solar power.

➋ The bus enters a 400-acre park called the **Tiergarten,** packed with cycling paths, joggers, and—on hot days—nude sunbathers. Straight ahead, the **Victory Column** (Siegessäule, with the gilded angel, described on page 550) towers above this vast city park that was once a royal hunting grounds, now nicknamed the "green lungs of Berlin."

➋ A block after leaving the Victory Column (on the left) is the 18th-century late-Rococo **Bellevue Palace.** Formerly the official residence of the Prussian (and later German) crown prince, and at one time a Nazi VIP guest house, it's now the residence of the federal president (whose power is mostly ceremonial—the chancellor wields the real power). If the flag's out, he's in.

➋ Driving along the Spree River, look left for the next sights: This park area was a residential district before World War II. Now it's filled with the buildings of the **national government.** The

BERLIN

huge brick "brown snake" complex was built to house government workers—but it didn't sell, so now its apartments are available to anyone. A metal Henry Moore sculpture entitled *Butterfly* floats in front of the slope-roofed House of World Cultures (Berliners have nicknamed this building "the pregnant oyster"). The modern tower (next on left) is a carillon with 68 bells (from 1987).

○ Leap out at the Platz der Republik stop. (While you could continue on bus #100, it's better on foot from here.) Through the trees on the left you'll see Germany's new and sprawling **Chancellery.** Started during the more imperial rule of Helmut Kohl, it's now considered overly grand. The big open space is **Platz der Republik,** where the Victory Column stood until Hitler moved it. The Hauptbahnhof (Berlin's vast main train station, marked by its tall tower with the *DB* sign) is across the field between the Chancellery and the Reichstag. Watch your step—excavators found a 250-pound undetonated American bomb here.

○ Just down the street stands an old building with a new dome...the **Reichstag.**

Sights in Berlin

Eastern Berlin

I've arranged the following sights in the order of a convenient self-guided orientation walk, picking up where the bus #100 part of my "Do-It-Yourself Orientation Tour" (previous section) leaves off. Allow a comfortable hour for this walk from the Reichstag to Alexanderplatz, including time for lingering (but not museum stops).

Near the Brandenburg Gate

▲▲▲**Reichstag Building**—The parliament building—the heart of German democracy—has a short but complicated and emotional history. When it was inaugurated in the 1890s, the last emperor, Kaiser Wilhelm II, disdainfully called it the "house for chatting." It was placed outside of the city's old walls—far from the center of real power, the imperial palace. It was from here that the German Republic was proclaimed in 1918.

In 1933, this symbol of democracy nearly burned down. While the Nazis blamed a communist plot, some believe that Hitler himself (who needed what we'd call today a "new Pearl Harbor") planned the fire, using it as a handy excuse to frame the communists and grab power. (Dutch

Communist Marinus van der Lubbe, who supposedly set the fire and was eventually guillotined for the crime, was posthumously pardoned by the German government in 2008.) As World War II drew to a close, Stalin ordered his troops to take the Reichstag from the Nazis by May 1 (the workers' holiday). More than 1,500 German soldiers (mostly French SS troops) made their last stand here—extending World War II by two days. On April 30, 1945, after fierce fighting on this rooftop, the Reichstag fell to the Red Army.

It was hardly used from 1933 to 1999. For the building's 101st birthday in 1995, the Bulgarian-American artist Christo wrapped it in silvery-gold cloth. It was then wrapped again—in scaffolding—and rebuilt by British architect Lord Norman Foster into the new parliamentary home of the Bundestag (Germany's lower house, similar to the US House of Representatives). To many Germans, the proud resurrection of the Reichstag symbolizes the end of a terrible chapter in German history.

The **glass cupola** rises 155 feet above the ground. Its two sloped ramps spiral 755 feet to the top for a grand view. Inside the dome, a cone of 360 mirrors reflects natural light into the legislative chamber below. Lit from inside at night, this gives Berlin a memorable nightlight. The environmentally friendly cone also helps with air circulation, drawing hot air out of the legislative chamber (no joke) and pulling in cool air from below.

Cost, Hours, Location: Free, daily 8:00–24:00, last entry at 22:00, most crowded 10:00–16:00, arrive as early as possible or shortly before last entry—see tips below, wait in line to go up—good street musicians, metal detectors, no big luggage allowed, some hour-long English tours when parliament is not sitting, Platz der Republik 1, S- or U-Bahn: Friedrichstrasse or Brandenburger Tor, tel. 030/2273-2152, www.bundestag.de.

Audioguide: The free GPS-driven audioguide explains the building and narrates the view as you wind up the spiral ramp to the top of the dome.

Crowd-Beating Tips: Berlin is now Germany's biggest tourist attraction. Lines at the Reichstag can be terrible. If possible, visit between 8:00 and 9:00 or between 21:00 and 22:00. Pick up the English flier just before the security checkpoint to have something to read as you wait. The skip-the-line entrance is under the grand front porch on the right. If you're here with a child (younger than 8 years old) or a frail person, or have reservations for the Dachgarten rooftop restaurant, you can get in without a wait. To reserve at the restaurant, call 030/2262-9933 (lunch from €15, dinner from €20, outside of meal times you can reserve a table for just a coffee, daily 9:30–16:30 & 18:30–24:00).

○ Self-Guided Tour: As you approach the building, look above the door, surrounded by stone patches from WWII bomb

Eastern Berlin

- - - FORMER COURSE OF THE WALL
U U-BAHN STN. **S** S-BAHN STN.

damage, to see the motto and promise: *Dem Deutschen Volke* ("To the German People"). The open, airy lobby towers 100 feet high, with 65-foot-tall colors of the German flag. See-through glass doors show the **central legislative chamber.** The message: There will be no secrets in government. Look inside. The seats are "Reichstag blue," a lilac-blue color designed by the architect to brighten the otherwise gray interior. Spreading his wings behind the podium is the *Bundestagsadler* (a.k.a. "the fat hen"), a stylized German eagle representing the Bundestag (each branch of government has its own symbolic eagle). Notice the doors marked *Ja* (Yes), *Nein* (No), and *Enthalten* (Abstain)...an homage to the Bundestag's traditional "sheep jump" way of counting votes by exiting the chamber through the corresponding door (although for critical issues, all 669 members vote with electronic cards).

Ride the elevator to the base of the glass **dome.** Pick up the free audioguide and take some time to study the photos and read the circle of captions—an excellent exhibit telling the Reichstag

story. Then study the surrounding architecture: a broken collage of new on old, torn between antiquity and modernity, like Germany's history. Notice the dome's giant and unobtrusive sunscreen that moves as necessary with the sun. Peer down through the skylight to look over the shoulders of the elected representatives at work. For Germans, the best view from here is down—keeping a close eye on their government.

Start at the ramp nearest the elevator and wind up to the top of the **double ramp.** Take a 360-degree survey of the city as you hike: First, the big park is the **Tiergarten,** the "green lungs of Berlin." Beyond that is the **Teufelsberg,** or "Devil's Hill" (built of rubble from the destroyed city in the late 1940s, and famous during the Cold War as a powerful ear of the West—notice the telecommunications tower on top). Knowing the bombed-out and bulldozed story of their city, locals say, "You have to be suspicious when you see the nice, green park." Find the **Victory Column** (Siegessäule). This was moved by Hitler in the 1930s from in front of the Reichstag to its present position in the Tiergarten, as the first step in creating a grandiose axis he envisioned for postwar Berlin. Next, scenes of the new Berlin spiral into your view—**Potsdamer Platz,** marked by the conical glass tower that houses Sony's European headquarters. The yellow building to the right is the Berlin Philharmonic Concert Hall, marking the museums at the Kulturforum. Continue circling left, and find the green chariot atop the **Brandenburg Gate.** The new **Memorial to the Murdered Jews of Europe** stretches south of the Brandenburg Gate. Next, you'll see **former East Berlin** and the city's next huge construction zone, with a forest of 300-foot-tall skyscrapers in the works. Notice the TV Tower (featuring the Pope's Revenge—explained on page 540), the Berlin Cathedral's massive dome, the red tower of the City Hall, the golden dome of the New Synagogue, and the Reichstag's **Dachgarten Restaurant**.

Follow the train tracks in the distance to the left toward Berlin's huge main train station, the **Hauptbahnhof.** Just in front of it, alone in a field, is the Swiss Embassy. It used to be surrounded by buildings, but now it's the only one left. Complete your spin-tour with the blocky **Chancellery,** nicknamed by Berliners "the washing machine." It may look like a pharaoh's tomb, but it's the office and home of Germany's most powerful person, the chancel-lor (currently Angela Merkel). To remind the chancellor who he or she works for, the Reichstag, at about 130 feet, is about six feet taller than the Chancellery.

Memorial to Politicians Who Opposed Hitler—As you leave the Reichstag, look for the row of slate slabs imbedded in the

ground by the park across from the main entry (looks like a fancy slate bicycle rack). This is a memorial to the 96 politicians (the equivalent of our members of Congress) who were murdered and persecuted because their politics didn't agree with Chancellor Hitler's. They were part of the Weimar Republic, the weak and ill-fated attempt at post-WWI democracy in Germany. These were the people who could have stopped Hitler...so they became his first victims. Each slate slab remembers one man—his name, party (mostly KPD—Communists, and SPD—Social Democrats), and date and location of death—generally in concentration camps. (*KZ* stands for "concentration camp.") They are honored here, in front of the building in which they worked.

Spree Riverfront—Before leaving the Reichstag area, circle the building to enjoy the wonderful architecture incorporating the Spree River into the people's world. It's a poignant spot because this river was once a symbol of division—the East German regime put nets underwater to stymie those desperate for freedom who might swim to the West. When kings ruled Prussia, government buildings went right up to the river. But today, the city is incorpo-rating the river thoughtfully into a people-friendly cityscape. From the Reichstag, a delightful riverside path leads around the curve, past "beach cafés," to the Chancellery. For a slow, low-impact glide past this zone, consider one of the river cruises described on page 518 (we'll pass the starting point—on Museum Island—later on this walk).

Let's continue our walk and cross what was the Berlin Wall. Leaving the Reichstag, return to the busy road and walk around the building. At the rear of the building (across the street, at the edge

The Berlin Wall

The 100-mile "Anti-Fascist Protective Rampart," as it was called by the East German government, was erected almost overnight in 1961 to stop the outward flow of people (three million leaked out between 1949 and 1961). The 13-foot-high Wall *(Mauer)* had a 16-foot tank ditch, a no-man's-land (or "death strip") that was 30–160 feet wide, and 300 sentry towers. During the Wall's 28 years, border guards fired 1,693 times and made 3,221 arrests, and there were 5,043 documented successful escapes (565 of these were East German guards).

The carnival atmosphere of those first years after the Wall fell is gone, but hawkers still sell "authentic" pieces of the Wall, flags of the DDR (East Germany), and military para-phernalia to gawking tourists. When it fell, the Wall was liter-ally carried away by the euphoria. What managed to survive has been nearly devoured by a decade of persistent "Wall-peckers."

Americans—the Cold War "victors"—have the biggest appetite for Wall-related sights, and a few bits and pieces remain for us to seek out. Berlin's single best Wall-related sight is the Museum of The Wall at Checkpoint Charlie (see page 543). Stretches of the Wall still standing include the short section at Zimmerstrasse/Wilhelmstrasse (near the Topography of Terror exhibit; see page 544), the longer East Side Gallery (near the Ostbahnhof; see page 546), and at the Berlin Wall Documentation Center along Bernauer Strasse (near S-Bahn: Nordbahnhof; see page 550).

of the park on the corner of Scheidemannstrasse and Ebertstrasse) is a small memorial of white crosses.

Berlin Wall Victims Memorial—This monument commemorates some of the East Berliners who died trying to cross the Wall. Look at the faces of these exceptionally free spirits. Notice that the last person shot while trying to escape was 20-year-old Chris Gueffroy, who was killed nine months before the Wall fell. (He was shot through the heart and died in no-man's-land.) This monument used to stand right on the Berlin Wall behind the Reichstag.

The Wall was built on August 13, 1961. Of these people—many of whom perished within months of the wall's construction—most died trying to swim the river to freedom. In the park just behind this memorial, another memorial is planned. It will remember the Roma (Gypsy) victims of the Holocaust. The Roma, as disdained by the Nazis as the Jews were, lost the same percentage of their population to Hitler. Unfortunately, the project is stalled for lack of a well-funded individual or group to finance it.

The Brandenburg Gate is ahead. Stay on the park side of the street for a better view of the gate. As you cross at the light, notice the double row of **cobblestones**—it goes around the city, marking where the Wall used to stand.

▲▲Brandenburg Gate (Brandenburger Tor)—The historic Brandenburg Gate (1791) was the grandest, and is the last survivor, of 14 gates in Berlin's old city wall (this one led to the neighboring region of Brandenburg). The gate was the symbol of Prussian Berlin...and later the symbol of a divided Berlin. It's crowned by a majestic four-horse chariot with the Goddess of Peace at the reins. Napoleon took this statue to the Louvre in Paris in 1806. After

the Prussians defeated Napoleon and got it back (1813), she was renamed the Goddess of Victory.

The gate sat unused, part of a sad circle dance called the Wall, for more than 25 years. Now postcards all over town show the ecstatic day—November 9, 1989—when the world enjoyed the sight of happy Berliners jamming the gate like flowers on a parade float. Pause a minute and think about struggles for freedom—past and present. (There's actually a special room built into the gate for this purpose—see the sidebar.) Around the gate, look at the information boards with pictures of how much this area changed throughout the 20th century. The latest chapter: The shiny white gate was completely restored in 2002 (but you can still see faint patches marking war damage). The TI within the gate is open daily (10:00–18:00, S-Bahn: Brandenburger Tor).

The Brandenburg Gate, the center of old Berlin, sits on a major boulevard running east to west through Berlin. The western segment, called Strasse des 17 Juni (named for a workers' uprising against the DDR government on June 17, 1953), stretches for four miles from the Brandenburg Gate and Victory Column to the Olympic Stadium. But we'll follow this city axis in the

The Brandenburg Gate, Arch of Peace

Two hundred years ago, the Brandenburg Gate was designed as an arch of peace, crowned by the Goddess of Peace and showing Mars sheathing his sword. The Nazis misused it as a gate of triumph and aggression. Today a Room of Silence, built into the gate, is dedicated to the peaceful message of the original Brandenburg Gate (daily 11:00-18:00). As you consider the history of Berlin in this room—which is carefully not dedicated to any particular religion—you may be inspired to read the prayer of the United Nations:

"Oh Lord, our planet Earth is only a small star in space. It is our duty to transform it into a planet whose creatures are no longer tormented by war, hunger, and fear, no longer senselessly divided by race, color, and ideology. Give us courage and strength to begin this task today so that our children and our children's children shall one day carry the name of man with pride."

opposite direction, east, walking along what is known as Unter den Linden—into the core of old imperial Berlin and past what was once the palace of the Hohenzollern family who ruled Prussia and then Germany. The palace—the reason for just about all you'll see—is a phantom sight, long gone (though the facade—which we'll see later on this walk—is now being partially rebuilt). Alexanderplatz, which marks the end of this walk, is near the base of the giant TV Tower hovering in the distance.

Now cross through the gate, into...

▲**Pariser Platz**—"Parisian Square," so named after the Prussians defeated Napoleon in 1813, was once filled with important government buildings—all bombed to smithereens in World War II. For decades, it was an unrecognizable, deserted no-man's-land—cut off from both East and West by the Wall. But now it's rebuilt, and the banks, hotels, and embassies that were here before the bombing have reclaimed their original places...with a few new additions: a palace of coffee (Starbucks) and the small Kennedys Museum (described later). The winners of World War II enjoy this prime real estate: The American, French, British, and Soviet (now Russian) embassies are all on or near this square.

Face the gate and look to your left. The new **US Embassy** reopened in its historic location in 2008. The building has been controversial: For safety's sake, Uncle Sam wanted more of a security zone around the building, but the Germans wanted to keep Pariser Platz a welcoming people zone. (Throughout the world, American embassies are the most fortified buildings in town.) The compromise: The extra security the US wanted is actually built into the structure. The building is pretty low-key; easy-on-the-eyes barriers keep potential car bombs at a distance, and its front door is on the side farthest from the Brandenburg Gate.

Just to the left, the **DZ Bank building** is by Frank Gehry, the unconventional American architect famous for Bilbao's organic Guggenheim Museum, Prague's Dancing House, Seattle's Experience Music Project, Chicago's Millennium Park, and Los Angeles' Walt Disney Concert Hall. Gehry fans might be surprised at the DZ Bank building's low profile. Structures on Pariser Platz are designed to be bland so as not to draw attention away from the Brandenburg Gate. (The glassy facade of the Academy of Arts, next to Gehry's building, is controversial for drawing attention to itself.) For your fix of the good old Gehry, step into the lobby and check out its undulating interior. It's a fish—and you feel like you're both inside and outside of it. The architect's vision is explained on a nearby plaque. The best view of Gehry's creation is from the Reichstag dome.

The **Academy of Arts** (Akademie der Kunst), with its notorious glass facade, is next door. Its doors lead to a mall (daily 10:00–22:00), which leads directly to the vast...

▲▲Memorial to the Murdered Jews of Europe (Denkmal für die Ermordeten Juden Europas)—This Holocaust memo-

rial, consisting of 2,711 grave-stone-like pillars and completed in 2005, is an essential stop for any visit to Berlin. It is the first formal, German government–sponsored Holocaust memorial. Jewish American architect Peter Eisenman won the competition for the commission (and built it on time and on budget—€27 mil-

lion). It's controversial for the focus—just Jews—but the government promises to make memorials to the other groups targeted by the Nazis.

The pillars are made of hollow concrete, each chemically coated for easy removal of graffiti. (Ironically, the chemical coating was developed by a subsidiary of the former IG Farben group—the company infamous for supplying the Zyklon B gas used in Nazi death camps.) The number of pillars, symbolic of nothing, is simply how many fit on the provided land.

Is it a labyrinth...symbolic cemetery...intentionally disorienting? The meaning is entirely up to the visitor to derive. The idea is for you to spend time pondering this horrible chapter in human history.

BERLIN

The pondering takes place under the sky. For the learning, go under the field of concrete pillars to the state-of-the-art information center (there may be a short line because visitors must go through a security check). This studies the Nazi system of extermination, humanizes the victims, traces stories of individual families and collects vivid personal accounts, and lists 200 different places of genocide (all well-explained in English, free, memorial always open; information center open Tue–Sun 10:00–20:00, closed Mon, last entry 45 min before closing, S-Bahn: Brandenburger Tor or Potsdamer Platz, tel. 030/2639-4336, www.stiftung-denkmal.de). The €3 audioguide augments the experience.

The location—where the Wall once stood—is coincidental. It's just a place where lots of people will experience it. Nazi propagandist Joseph Goebbels' bunker was discovered during the work and left buried under the northeast corner of the memorial. Hitler's bunker is just 200 yards away, under a nondescript parking lot. Such Nazi sites are intentionally left hidden to discourage neo-Nazi elements from creating shrines.

Now backtrack to Pariser Platz (through the yellow building). Across the square, consider dropping into the...

The Kennedys Museum—This crisp private enterprise facing the Brandenburg Gate recalls John F. Kennedy's Germany trip in 1963, with great photos and video clips as well as a photographic shrine to the Kennedy clan in America. It's a small, overpriced, yet delightful experience with interesting mementos—such as JFK's notes with the phonetic "ish bin ein Bear lee ner." Jacqueline Kennedy commented on how strange it was that this was her husband's most quotable quote (€7, €3.50 to a broad array of visitors—dream up a discount and ask for it, daily 10:00–18:00, Pariser Platz 4a, www.thekennedys.de, tel. 030/2065-3570).

Leave Pariser Platz and begin strolling...

▲▲Unter den Linden

The street called Unter den Linden is the heart of former East Berlin. In Berlin's good old days, Unter den Linden was one of Europe's grand boulevards. In the 15th century, this carriage-way led from the palace to the hunting grounds (today's big Tiergarten). In the 17th century, Hohenzollern princes and princesses moved in and built their palaces here so they could be near the Prussian king.

Named centuries ago for its thousand linden trees, this was the most elegant street of Prussian Berlin before Hitler's time, and the main drag of East Berlin after his reign. Hitler replaced the venerable trees—many 250 years old—with Nazi flags. Popular discontent actually drove him to replant linden trees. Today, Unter den Linden is no longer a depressing Cold War cul-de-sac, ar

Eastern Berlin's Unter den Linden

Sights
1. Brandenburg Gate
2. White Crosses Memorial
3. Pariser Platz
4. US Embassy
5. The Kennedys Museum
6. Russian Embassy
7. Berlin Story Bookstore
8. Bebelplatz
9. Humboldt University
10. German State Opera
11. Neue Wache
12. German History Museum
13. Pergamon Museum
14. Egyptian/Neues Museum
15. Old National Gallery
16. Berlin Cathedral
17. Spree River Cruises
18. SAS Radisson & DDR Museum
19. Marien Church
20. TV Tower
21. German Cathedral
22. Fassbender & Rausch
23. To Museum of The Wall at Checkpoint Charlie

BERLIN

S S-BAHN STN. **U** U-BAHN STN.

B BUS STOP --- FORMER COURSE OF THE WALL

Eateries

24 Aufsturz Pub
25 Operncafé & Schinkel Klause Biergarten
26 Bier's Curry und Spiesse
27 Deponie3 & Die Zwölf Apostel
28 Bräuhaus Georgbrau

29 Lutter & Wegner; Maredo Argentine Steak Restaurants
30 Galeries Lafayette Food Circus
31 Hasir Turkish Restaurant
32 Weihenstephaner Bavarian Restaurant

its pre-Hitler strolling café ambience is returning. Notice how it is divided, roughly at Friedrichstrasse, into a business section that stretches toward the Brandenburg Gate, and a culture section that spreads out toward Alexanderplatz. Frederick the Great wanted culture, mainly the opera and the university, closer to his palace, and to keep business (read: banks) farther away, near the city walls.

As you walk toward the giant TV Tower, the big building you see jutting out into the street on your right is the **Hotel Adlon.** It hosted such notables as Charlie Chaplin, Albert Einstein, and Greta Garbo. This was the setting for Garbo's most famous line, "I want to be alone," in the film *Grand Hotel.* And, perhaps fresher in your memory, this is where Michael Jackson shocked millions by dangling his little baby, Blanket, over the railing (second balcony up, center of facade). Destroyed by Russians just after World War II, the grand Adlon was rebuilt in 1996. See how far you can get inside.

Descend into the Brandenburger Tor S-Bahn station ahead of you. It's one of Berlin's former **ghost subway stations.** During the Cold War, most underground train tunnels were simply blocked at the border. But a few Western lines looped through the East. To make a little hard Western cash, the Eastern government rented the use of these tracks to the West, but the stations (which happened to be in East Berlin) were strictly off-limits. For 28 years, the stations were unused, as Western trains slowly passed through, seeing only eerie DDR (East German) guards and lots of cobwebs. Literally within days of the fall of the Wall, these stations were reopened, and today they are a time warp (looking essentially as they did when built in 1931, with dreary old green tiles and original signage). Walk along the track (the walls are lined with historic photos of the Reichstag through the ages) and exit on the other side, following signs to *Russische Botschaft* (the Russian Embassy).

The **Russian Embassy** was the first big postwar building project in East Berlin. It's built in the powerful, simplified Neoclassical style that Stalin liked. While not as important now as it was a few years ago, it's immense as ever. It flies the Russian white, blue, and red. Find the hammer-and-sickle motif decorating the window frames—a reminder of the days when this was the USSR embassy.

Continuing past the Aeroflot airline offices, look across Glinkastrasse to the right to see the back of the **Komische Oper** (Comic Opera; program and view of ornate interior posted in window). While the exterior is ugly, the fine old theater interior—amazingly missed by WWII bombs—survives.

Back on the main drag, at #26, is a great bookstore, **Berlin Story.** In addition to a wide range of English-language books, this shop has a free museum (with a model of 1930s Unter den Linden) and a 25-minute English film about the history of Berlin (daily

10:00–20:00; for more details, see page 509). This is also a good opportunity to pick up some nostalgic knickknacks from the Cold War. The West lost no time in consuming the East; consequently, some are feeling a wave of *Ost*-algia for the old days of East Berlin. In 2006 local elections, nearly half of East Berlin's voters—and 6 percent of West Berliners—voted for the extreme left party, which has ties to the bygone Communist Party.

One symbol of that era has been given a reprieve. As you continue to Friedrichstrasse, look at the DDR-style pedestrian lights, and you'll realize that someone had a sense of humor back then. The perky red and green men—*Ampelmännchen*—were under threat of replacement by the far less jaunty Western signs. Fortunately, after a 10-year court battle, the DDR signals will be kept after all. This communist-era icon has been popping up as far away as Munich—hardly a bastion of sympathy for East German culture.

At **Friedrichstrasse,** look right. Before the war, the Unter den Linden/Friedrichstrasse intersection was the heart of Berlin. In the 1920s, Berlin was famous for its anything-goes love of life. This was the cabaret drag, a springboard to stardom for young and vampy entertainers like Marlene Dietrich. (Born in 1901, Dietrich starred in the first German talkie—*The Blue Angel*—and then headed straight to Hollywood.) Over the last few years, this boulevard—lined with super department stores (such as Galeries Lafayette) and big-time hotels (such as the Hilton and Regent)—is attempting to replace Ku'damm as the grand commerce-and-café boulevard of Berlin. (More recently, western Berlin is retaliating with some new stores of its own. And so far, Friedrichstrasse gets little more than half the pedestrian traffic that Ku'damm gets in the West. Why? Locals complain that this area has no daily life—no supermarkets, not much funky street food, and so on.) Across from Galeries Lafayette is American Express (handy for any train-ticket needs—see page 510). Consider detouring to Galeries Lafayette, with its cool marble and glass waste-of-space interior (Mon–Sat 9:30–20:00, closed Sun; belly up to its amazing ground-floor viewpoint, or have lunch in its basement cafeteria—see page 575).

If you continued down Friedrichstrasse, you'd wind up at the sights listed in "South of Unter den Linden," on page 541—including the Museum of The Wall at Checkpoint Charlie (a 10-min walk from here). But for now, continue along Unter den Linden. You'll notice big, colorful **water pipes** around here, and throughout Berlin. As long as the city remains a gigantic construction zone, it will be laced with these drainage pipes—key to any building project. Berlin's high water table means any new basement comes with lots of pumping out.

The **VW Automobil Forum** shows off the latest models from the many car companies owned by VW (free, corner of Friedrichstrasse and Unter den Linden, VW art gallery in the basement).

Continue down Unter den Linden a few more blocks, past the large equestrian statue of Frederick II ("the Great"), and turn right into the square called **Bebelplatz.** Stand on the glass window in the center.

Frederick the Great—who ruled from 1740 to 1786—established Prussia not just as a military power, but as a cultural and intellectual heavyweight, as well. This square was the center of the "new Athens" that Frederick envisioned. His grand palace was just down the street (explained later).

Look down through the glass you're standing on (center of Bebelplatz): The room of empty bookshelves is a memorial to the notorious Nazi **book burning.** It was on this square in 1933 that staff and students from the university threw 20,000 newly forbidden books (like Einstein's) into a huge bonfire on the orders of the Nazi propaganda minister Joseph Goebbels. A memorial plaque nearby reminds us of the prophetic quote by the German poet Heinrich Heine. In 1820, he wrote, "Where they burn books, at the end they also burn people." The Nazis despised Heine because he was Jewish before converting to Christianity. A century later, his books were among those that went up in flames on this spot.

Great buildings front Bebelplatz. Survey the square counterclockwise:

Humboldt University, across Unter den Linden, is one of Europe's greatest. Marx and Lenin (not the brothers or the sisters) studied here, as did the Grimms (both brothers) and more than two dozen Nobel Prize winners. Einstein, who was Jewish, taught here until taking a spot at Princeton in 1932 (smart guy).

The former **state library** is where Vladimir Lenin studied during much of his exile from Russia. If you climb to the second floor of the library and go through the door opposite the stairs, you'll see a 1968 vintage stained-glass window depicting Lenin's life's work with almost biblical reverence. On the ground floor is Tim's Canadian Deli, a great little café with light food, student prices, and garden seating (€3 plates, Mon–Sat 7:00–20:00, closed Sun, handy WC).

The **German State Opera** was bombed in 1941, rebuilt to bolster morale and to celebrate its centennial in 1943, and bombed again in 1945.

The round, Catholic **St. Hedwig's Church**—nicknamed the "upside-down teacup"—was built by the pragmatic Frederick the Great to encourage the integration of Catholic Silesians after his empire annexed their region in 1742. (St. Hedwig is the patron saint of Silesia, a region now shared by Germany, Poland, and the Czech Republic, and covered in the Görlitz chapter.) When asked what the church should look like, Frederick literally took a Silesian teacup and slammed it upside-down on a table. Like all Catholic churches in Berlin, St. Hedwig's is not on the street, but stuck in a kind of back lot—indicating inferiority to Protestant churches. You can step inside the church to see the cheesy DDR government renovation.

Continue down Unter den Linden. The next square on your right holds the **Opernpalais,** formerly a Prussian royal residence. Preening with fancy prewar elegance, it hosts the pricey Operncafé. With the best desserts and the longest dessert bar in Europe, it's popular with Berliners for *Kaffee und Kuchen* (see page 573).

Cross Unter den Linden to the university side. The Greek-temple-like building set in the small chestnut-tree-filled park is

the **Neue Wache** (the emperor's "New Guardhouse," from 1816). When the Wall fell, this memorial to the victims of fascism was transformed into a new national memorial. Look inside, where a replica of the Käthe Kollwitz statue, *Mother with Her Dead Son,* is surrounded by thought-provoking silence. This marks the tombs of Germany's unknown soldier and the unknown concentration camp victim. The inscription in front reads, "To the victims of war and tyranny." Read the entire statement in English (on wall, left of entrance). The memorial, open to the sky, incorporates the elements—sunshine, rain, snow—falling on this modern-day *pietà.*

After the Neue Wache, the next building you'll see is Berlin's pink-yet-formidable Zeughaus, or arsenal. Dating from 1695, it's considered the oldest building on the boulevard and now houses the...

▲▲▲German History Museum (Deutsches Historisches Museum)—This fantastic museum is a two-part affair: the pink former Prussian arsenal building, and the I. M. Pei–designed annex. The main building (fronting Unter den Linden) houses the permanent collection. Two huge rectangular floors are packed with more than 8,000 artifacts telling the story of Germany—making this the top history museum in town. Historical objects, photographs, and models are intermingled with multimedia stations to help put everything in context. The first floor traces German history from 1 B.C. to 1918, with exhibits on early cultures, the Middle Ages, Reformation, Thirty Years' War, German Empire, and World War I. Exhibits on the ground floor continue with the Weimar Republic, Nazism, World War II, Allied occupation, and a divided Germany, wrapping up with reunification and a quick look at Germany today (€5, daily 10:00–18:00, excellent €3 audioguide has six hours of info for you to choose from, tel. 030/2030-4751, www.dhm.de).

For architecture buffs, the big attraction is the Pei annex behind the history museum, which complements the museum with often-fascinating temporary history exhibits. From the old building (with the Pei glass canopy over its courtyard), take a tunnel to the new wing, emerging under a striking glass spiral staircase that unites four floors with surprising views and lots of light. It's here that you'll experience why Pei—famous for his glass pyramid at Paris' Louvre—is called the "perfector of classical modernism," "master of light," and a magician of uniting historical buildings with new ones. (If the museum is closed, or you don't have a ticket, venture down the street—Hinter dem Giesshaus—to the left of the museum to see the Pei annex from the outside.)

Back on Unter den Linden, head toward the **Spree River.** Just before the bridge, wander left along the canal through a tiny but colorful arts-and-crafts market (weekends only; a larger flea market is just outside the Pergamon Museum). Continue up the riverbank two blocks and cross the Spree at the footbridge, which takes you to...

Museum Island (Museumsinsel)

This island, home of Berlin's first museum, is undergoing a formidable renovation. The grand vision is to integrate the city's major museums with a grand entry and tunnels that will lace the complex together (intended completion date: 2015, www.museumsinsel -berlin.de). The complex was originally built in about 1871, when Germany was newly unified as one nation—and when Berlin was calling itself the "Athens on the Spree River." Today, its imposing Neoclassical buildings host five grand museums: the Pergamon (classical antiquities), the Altes Museum ("Old Museum," archaeological treasures and a huge collection of Celtic goldwork), the newly renovated Neues Museum ("New Museum," housing the Egyptian Museum, with the bust of Queen Nefertiti), the Old National Gallery (19th-century German Romantic painting), and the Bode Museum (European statuary through the ages, coins, and Byzantine art). The museums function as one with the same prices, phone number, and a €12 combo-ticket that's far better than buying individual €8 entries (all are also included in the city's €19 Museumspass; Pergamon, Altes, and Bode museums open daily 10:00–18:00, Thu until 22:00, free on Thu after 18:00; Old National Gallery open same hours except closed Mon; check online for the latest on the Neues Museum hours, tel. 030/2090-5577, www.smb .museum). The nearest S-Bahn station is Hackescher Markt.

Consider visiting any of these museums, and other Museum Island attractions, before continuing our walk. I've described the top attractions below. Once you're finished, skip down to "Museum Island to Alexanderplatz," page 539, to resume the self-guided tour.

▲▲**Pergamon Museum**—This world-class museum, part of Berlin's Collection of Classical Antiquities (Antikensammlung), stars the fantastic Pergamon Altar. From a second-century B.C. Greek temple, the altar shows the Greeks under Zeus and Athena beating the giants in a dramatic pig pile of mythological mayhem. Check out the action spilling onto the stairs. The Babylonian Ishtar Gate (glazed blue tiles from the sixth century B.C.) and many ancient Greek and Mesopotamian treasures are also impressive. The superb "Pergamon in 30 Minutes" audioguide (free with admission, but €4 during free Thu extended hours) covers the museum's highlights and broadens your experience by introducing you to wonders you might not otherwise notice.

▲▲**Egyptian Museum (Ägyptisches Museum) in the Neues Museum**—Showing off one of the world's top collections of Egyptian art, this wonderfully presented museum fills a good chunk of the recently rebuilt Neues Museum. The curator welcomes you on the included audioguide and encourages a broader approach to the museum than just seeing its claim to fame, the bust of Queen Nefertiti. The fine audioguide celebrates new knowledge about ancient Egyptian civilization and offers fascinating insights into workaday Egyptian life as it describes the vivid papyrus collection, slice-of-life artifacts, and dreamy wax portraits decorating mummy cases.

But let's face it: The main reason to visit is to enjoy one of the great thrills in art appreciation—gazing into the still-young-and-beautiful face of 3,000-year-old **Queen Nefertiti,** the wife

of King Akhenaton. This bust of Queen Nefertiti (c. 1340 B.C.) is the most famous piece of Egyptian art in Europe. Discovered in 1912, Nefertiti—with all the right beauty marks: long neck, symmetrical face, and the perfect amount of makeup—is called "Berlin's most beautiful woman." The bust never left its studio, but served as a master model for all other portraits of the queen. (That's probably why the left eye was never inlaid.)

How the Queen arrived in Germany is a tale out of *Indiana Jones.* The German archaeologist Ludwig Borchardt uncovered her in the Egyptian desert in 1912. The Egyptian Department of Antiquities had first pick over all the artifacts excavated on their territory. After the first takings, the rest would be divided up 50-50. When Borchardt presented Nefertiti to the Egyptians, they passed her over, never bothering to examine her closely. Unsubstantiated rumors persist that Borchardt misled the Egyptians in order to keep the bust for himself—rumors that have prompted some Egyptians to call for the return of Nefertiti (just as the Greeks are lobbying the British to return the Parthenon marbles currently housed in the British Museum). Although this bust is not particularly representative of Egyptian art in general, and despite increasing claims that it's a Neoclassical fake, it has become a symbol for Egyptian art by popular acclaim.

Old National Gallery (Alte Nationalgalerie)—This gallery, behind the Egyptian Museum and Altes Museum, is designed to look like a Greek temple. It shows mostly paintings: three floors with French and German Impressionists on the second, and Romantic German paintings (which I find most interesting) on the top (audioguide is free).

Lustgarten—For 300 years, the island's big central square has flip-flopped between being a military parade ground and a people-friendly park, depending upon the political tenor of the time. In 1999, it was made into a park again (read the history posted in corner opposite church). On a sunny day, it's packed with relaxing locals and is one of Berlin's most enjoyable public spaces.

Berlin Cathedral (Berliner Dom)—This century-old church towers over Museum Island (€5 includes access to dome gallery, €8 with audioguide, not covered by Museum Island ticket, Mon–Sat 9:00–20:00, Sun 12:00–20:00, until 19:00 in winter, www.berliner-dom.de; many organ concerts—generally Sat at 20:00, tickets about €10 always available at the door, tel. 030/2026-9136). Inside, the great reformers (Luther, Calvin, and company) stand around the brilliantly restored

dome like stern saints guarding their theology. Frederick I rests in an ornate tomb (right transept, near entrance to dome). The 270-step climb to the outdoor dome gallery is tough, but offers pleasant, breezy views of the city at the finish line (last entry 45 min before closing). The crypt downstairs is not worth a look.

Former Site of the City Palace and the Palace of the Republic—Across Unter den Linden from Berlin Cathedral is a big lawn that once held the decrepit Palace of the Republic—

formerly East Berlin's parliament building/futuristic entertainment complex, and a showy symbol of the communist days. Even earlier, this was the site of the City Palace (Stadtschloss), the grand urban residence of the rulers of Brandenburg and Prussia since the 15th century. Much of the palace actually survived World War II, but was replaced by the communists with a blocky Soviet-style building. The landmark building fell into disrepair after reunification, and was eventually dismantled in 2007. After much debate, the German Parliament decided to construct a building that will include the rebuilt facade of Frederick's original Hohenzollern palace. Investing a huge sum, they will create a huge new public venue to be filled with museums, shops, galleries, and concert halls. All of this is highly controversial, not in the least due to the €1.2 billion price tag. Many Berliners see the reconstruction as a complete waste of money that could be better spent elsewhere, so it is still far from clear if the palace will ever be built. For now, the site of the kings' palace—and the people's palace during communist times—is just a very plain, wide-open grassy park.

Spree River Cruises—If you want a break from our walk, the recommended Spree River boat tours depart from the riverbank near the bridge by the Berlin Cathedral. For details, see page 518.

Museum Island to Alexanderplatz

Continue walking down Unter den Linden. Before crossing the bridge (and leaving Museum Island), look across the river. The pointy twin spires of the 13th-century Nikolai Church mark the center of medieval Berlin. This Nikolaiviertel (*Viertel* means "quarter") was restored by the DDR and was trendy in the last years of communism. Today, it's a lively-at-night riverside restaurant district.

As you cross the bridge, look left in the distance to see the gilded **New Synagogue** dome, rebuilt after WWII bombing (described on page 547).

Across the river to the left of the bridge is the giant **SAS Radisson Hotel** and shopping center, with a huge aquarium in the center. The elevator goes right through the middle of a deep-sea world. (You can see it from the unforgettable Radisson hotel lobby—tuck in your shirt and walk past the guards with the confidence of a guest who's sleeping there.) Here in the center of the old communist capital, it seems that capitalism has settled in with a spirited vengeance.

At the river side of the SAS Radisson Hotel, the little **DDR Museum** offers an interesting peek at a humbler life before capitalism took hold. You'll crawl through a Trabant car, see a DDR kitchen, and be surrounded by former DDR residents reminiscing about the bad old days (steep €5.50 admission, daily 10:00–20:00, Karl-Liebknecht Strasse 1, tel. 030/847-123-731, www.ddr -museum.de).

In the park immediately across the street (a big jaywalk from the Radisson) are grandfatherly statues of **Marx and Engels** (nicknamed by locals "the old pensioners"). Surrounding them are stainless-steel monoliths with evocative photos that show the struggles of the workers of the world.

Walk toward **Marien Church** (from 1270, an artist's render-ing helps you follow the interesting but very faded old "Dance of Death" mural that wraps around the narthex inside the door), just left of the base of the TV Tower. The big red-brick building past the trees on the right is the **City Hall,** built after the revolution of 1848 and arguably the first democratic building in the city.

The 1,200-foot-tall **TV Tower** (Fernsehturm) has a fine view from halfway up (€9.50, daily March–Oct 9:00–24:00, Nov–Feb 10:00–24:00, www.tv-turm.de). The tower offers a handy city orientation and an interesting view of the flat, red-roofed sprawl of Berlin—including a peek inside the city's many courtyards *(Höfe)*. Consider a kitschy trip to the observation deck for the view and lunch in its revolving restaurant (mediocre food, €12 plates, horrible lounge music, reservations smart for dinner, tel. 030/242-3333). It's very retro and somewhat trendy these days, so expect a line for the elevator—but remember: If you can't see the top from the ground, you can't see the ground from the top. Built (with Swedish know-how) in 1969 for the 20th anniversary of the communist government, the tower was meant to show the power of the atheistic state at a time when DDR leaders were having the crosses removed from church domes and spires. But when the sun shined on their tower—the greatest spire in East Berlin—a huge cross was reflected on the mirrored ball. Cynics called it "The Pope's Revenge." East Berliners dubbed the tower the "Tele-Asparagus." They joked that if it fell over, they'd have an elevator to the West.

Farther east, pass under the train tracks into **Alexanderplatz.** This area—especially the Kaufhof department store—was the commercial pride and joy of East Berlin. Today, it's still a land-mark, with a major U- and S-Bahn station. The once-futuristic, now-kitschy "World Time Clock" is nostalgic for old-timers, and has been left here as a reminder of a popular meeting point back in DDR times.

Our orientation stroll or bus ride (this is the last stop for bus #100) is finished. From here, you can hike back a bit to take the riverboat tour, venture into the colorful Prenzlauer Berg neighbor-hood, or consider extending this foray into eastern Berlin to...

Karl-Marx-Allee

The buildings along Karl-Marx-Allee in East Berlin (just beyond Alexanderplatz) were completely leveled by the Red Army in 1945. As an expression of their adoration to the "great Socialist Father" (the "cult of Stalin" was in full gear), the DDR government decided to rebuild the street better than ever (the USSR provided generous subsidies) and made it intentionally one meter wider than the Champs-Elysées. They named it Stalinallee. Today, this street, done in the bold "Stalin Gothic" style so common in Moscow in the 1950s, has been restored, renamed after Karl Marx, and lined with "workers' palaces"— providing a rare look at Berlin's communist days. Distances are a bit long for convenient walking, but you can cruise Karl-Marx-Allee by taxi, or ride the U-Bahn to Strausberger Platz (which was built to resemble an Italian promenade) and walk to Frankfurter Tor, reading the good information posts along the way. Notice the Social Realist reliefs on the buildings and the lampposts, which incorporate the wings of a phoenix (rising from the ashes) in their design. Once a "workers' paradise," the street now hosts a two-mile-long capitalist beer festival the first weekend in August.

The **Café Sibylle,** just beyond the Strausberger Platz U-Bahn station, is a fun spot for a coffee, traditional DDR ice-cream treats, and a look at its free informal museum that tells the story of the most destroyed street in Berlin. While the humble exhibit is nearly all in German, it's fun to see the ear (or buy a €10 plaster replica) and half a moustache from what was the largest statue of Stalin in Germany (the centerpiece of the street until 1961) and a few intimate insights into apartment life in a DDR flat. The café is known for its good coffee and *Schwedeneisbecher mit Eierlikor*—an ice-cream sundae with a shot of egg liqueur, popular among those nostalgic for communism (daily 10:00–20:00, Karl-Marx-Allee 72, at intersection with Koppenstrasse, a block from U-Bahn: Strausberger Platz, tel. 030/2935-2203).

Heading out to Karl-Marx-Allee (just beyond the TV Tower), you're likely to notice a giant colorful **mural** decorating a blocky communist-era skyscraper. This was the Ministry of Education, and the mural is a tile mosaic trumpeting the accomplishments of the DDR's version of "No Child Left Behind."

South of Unter den Linden

The following sights—heavy on Nazi and Wall history—are listed roughly north to south (as you reach them from Unter den Linden).

▲▲Gendarmenmarkt—This delightful and historic square is bounded by twin churches, a tasty chocolate shop, and the Berlin Symphony's concert hall (designed by Karl Friedrich Schinkel, the man who put the Neoclassical stamp on Berlin). In summer, it hosts a few outdoor cafés, *Biergarten*s, and sometimes concerts. Wonderfully symmetrical, the square is considered by Berliners to be the finest in town. The name of the square—part

French and part German (after the *Gens d'Armes*, Frederick the Great's royal guard who were headquartered here)—reminds us that in the 17th century, a fifth of all Berliners were French émigrés, Protestant Huguenots fleeing Catholic France. Back then, tolerant Prussia was a magnet for the persecuted. These émigrés vitalized Berlin with new ideas and know-how.

The German Cathedral (described next) on the square has an exhibit worthwhile for history buffs. The French Cathedral (Französischer Dom) offers a humble museum on the Huguenots (€2, Tue–Sun 12:00–17:00, closed Mon, U-Bahn: Französische Strasse or Stadtmitte). Fun fact: Neither of these churches are true cathedrals, as they never contained a bishop's throne; their German title of *Dom* (cathedral) is actually a mistranslation from the French word *dôme* (cupola).

Fassbender & Rausch, on the corner near the German Cathedral, claims to be Europe's biggest chocolate store. After 150 years of chocolate-making, this family-owned business proudly displays its sweet delights—250 different kinds—on a 55-foot-long buffet. Truffles are sold for about €0.60 each—it's fun to compose a fancy little eight-piece box of your own for about €5 (daily 10:00–20:00, opens Sun at 11:00, corner of Mohrenstrasse at Charlottenstrasse 60, tel. 030/2045-8440). Upstairs is an elegant hot chocolate café with fine views. If this isn't enough to entice you, I have three words: "Erupting Chocolate Volcano."

Gendarmenmarkt is buried in what has recently emerged as Berlin's new "Fifth Avenue" shopping district. For the ultimate in top-end shops, find the corner of Jägerstrasse and Französische Strasse and wander through the **Quartier 206** (Mon–Fri 10:30–19:30, Sat 10:00–18:00, closed Sun, www.quartier206.com).

▲German Cathedral (Deutscher Dom)—This cathedral (not to be confused with the Berlin Cathedral on Unter den Linden) was bombed flat in the war and rebuilt only in the 1980s. It houses the thought-provoking *Milestones, Setbacks, Sidetracks (Wege, Irrwege, Umwege)* exhibit, which traces the history of the

German parliamentary system. The parliament-funded exhibit—while light on actual historical artifacts—is well done and more interesting than it sounds. It takes you quickly from the revolutionary days of 1848 to the 1920s, and then more deeply through the tumultuous 20th century. There are no English descriptions, but you can follow the essential, excellent, and free 1.5-hour English audioguide or buy the wonderfully detailed €10 guidebook. If you think this museum is an attempt by the German government to develop a more sophisticated and educated electorate in the interest of stronger democracy, you're exactly right. Germany knows (from its own troubled history) that a dumbed-down electorate, manipulated by clever spin-meisters and sound-bite media blitzes, is a dangerous thing (free, May–Sept Tue–Sun 10:00–19:00, Oct–April Tue–Sun 10:00–18:00, closed Mon year-round, on Gendarmenmarkt just off Friedrichstrasse, tel. 030/2273-0431).

▲▲▲**Museum of The Wall at Checkpoint Charlie (Mauermuseum Haus am Checkpoint Charlie)**—While the famous border checkpoint between the American and Soviet sectors is long gone, its memory is preserved by one of Europe's most cluttered museums. During the Cold War, the House at Checkpoint Charlie stood defiantly— spitting distance from the border guards—showing off all the clever escapes over, under, and through

the Wall. Today, while the drama is over and hunks of the Wall stand like victory scalps at its door, the museum still tells a gripping history of the Wall, recounts the many ingenious escape attempts (early years—with a cruder wall—saw more escapes), and includes plenty of video coverage of those heady days when people-power tore down the Wall. While dusty, disorganized, and slightly overpriced, with lots of reading, all of that just adds to its borderline-kitschy charm. It's the best place in Berlin to get a handle on the Cold old days (€12.50, assemble 20 tourists and get in for €7.50 each, €3 audioguide, discount with WelcomeCard but not covered by Museumspass, cash only, daily 9:00–22:00, U6 to Kochstrasse or—better from Zoo—U2 to Stadtmitte, Friedrichstrasse 43–45, tel. 030/253-7250, www.mauermuseum .de). If you're pressed for time, this is a decent after-dinner sight. With extra time, consider the "Hear We Go" audioguide about the Wall that takes you outside the museum (€7, 1.5 hours, leave ID as deposit).

Hitler and Third Reich Sites

While many come to Berlin to see Hitler sites, these are essentially invisible. The German Resistance Memorial is in German only and difficult for the tourist to appreciate (see page 551). The Topography of Terror (SS and Gestapo headquarters) is a fascinating exhibit, but all that remains of the building is its foundation. (Both museums have helpful audioguides in English.) Hitler's bunker is completely gone (near Potsdamer Platz). Your best bet for "Hitler sites" is to take the Infamous Third Reich Sites walking tour offered by Original Berlin Walks (see "Tours in Berlin," page 513).

▲▲**Checkpoint Charlie Street Scene**—Where Checkpoint Charlie once stood, notice the thought-provoking post with larger-than-life posters of a young American soldier facing east and a young Soviet soldier facing west. The area has become a Cold War freak show. The rebuilt guard station now hosts two actors playing American guards who pose for photos. Across the street is Snack Point Charlie. The old checkpoint was not named for a person, but because it was checkpoint number three—as in Alpha (at the East–West German border, a hundred miles west of here), Bravo (as you enter Berlin proper), and Charlie (the most famous because it was where most foreigners would pass). A fine photo exhibit stretches down the street with great English descriptions telling the story of the Wall. While you could get this information from a book, it's poignant to stand here in person and ponder the gripping history of this place. A few yards away (on Zimmerstrasse), a glass panel describes the former checkpoint. From there, a double row of cobbles in Zimmerstrasse traces the former path of the Wall. These innocuous cobbles run throughout the city, even through some modern buildings.

Follow the cobbles one very long block to Wilhelmstrasse, a surviving stretch of Wall, and the...

Topography of Terror (Topographie des Terrors)—The park behind the Zimmerstrasse/Wilhelmstrasse bit of Wall marks the site of the command center of Hitler's Gestapo and SS. Because of the horrible things planned here, the rubble of these buildings will always be left as rubble. The SS, Hitler's personal bodyguards, grew to become a state-within-a-state, with its talons in every corner of German society. Amid the excavated foundation of the building, an exhibit tells the story of National Socialism and its victims in Berlin. While you could read this story anywhere, to take this in while standing atop the Gestapo headquarters is a powerful experience (free, info booth open daily May–Sept 10:00–20:00, Oct–April

10:00–18:00 or until dark, tel. 030/2548-6703, www.topographie
.de). Posted information is in both German and English, but the free
English audioguide is helpful (available only until 18:45 in summer).

Across the street (facing the Wall) is the **German Finance
Ministry** (Bundesministerium der Finanzen). Formerly the head-

quarters of the Nazi Luftwaffe
(Air Force), this is the only
major Hitler-era government
building that survived the war's
bombs. The communists used
it to house their—no joke—
Ministry of Ministries. Walk up
Wilhelmstrasse (to the north) to
see an entry gate (on your left)
that looks much like it did when
Germany occupied nearly all of Europe. On the north side of the
building (farther up Wilhelmstrasse, at corner with Leipziger
Strasse) is a wonderful example of communist art. The mural,
Max Lingner's *Aufbau der Republik* (*Building the Republic*, 1953),
is classic Socialist Realism, showing the entire society—industrial
laborers, farm workers, women, and children—all happily singing
the same patriotic song. This was the communist ideal. For the
reality, look at the ground in the courtyard in front of the mural to
see an enlarged photograph from a 1953 uprising here against the
communists...quite a contrast.

▲▲▲**Jewish Museum Berlin (Jüdisches Museum Berlin)**—
This museum is one of Europe's best Jewish sights. The highly
conceptual building is a sight in
itself, and the museum inside—an
overview of the rich culture and
history of Europe's Jewish community—is excellent. The Holocaust
is appropriately remembered, but it
doesn't overwhelm this celebration of
Jewish life. Even though the museum
is in a nondescript residential neighborhood (a 10-min walk from the
Hallesches Tor U-Bahn station or
the Checkpoint Charlie museum),
it's well worth the trip.

Designed by American architect Daniel Libeskind (who is
redeveloping New York City's World Trade Center site), the zinc-
walled building's zigzag shape is pierced by voids symbolic of the
irreplaceable cultural loss caused by the Holocaust. Enter through
the 18th-century Baroque building next door, then go through an
underground tunnel to reach the museum interior.

Before you reach the exhibit, your visit starts with three memorial spaces. Underground, follow the Axis of Exile to a disorienting slanted garden with 49 pillars. Then the Axis of Holocaust leads to an eerily empty tower shut off from the outside world. A detour near the bottom of the long stairway leads to the "Memory Void," a thought-provoking space of "fallen leaves": heavy metal faces that you walk on, making unhuman noises with each step.

Finally, climb the stairs to the top of the museum, from where you stroll chronologically through the 2,000-year story of Judaism in Germany. The exhibit, on two floors, is engaging. Interactive bits (for example, spell your name in Hebrew) make it lively for kids. English explanations interpret both the exhibits and the design of the very symbolic building.

Cost and Hours: €5, covered by Museumspass, discount with WelcomeCard, daily 10:00–20:00, Mon until 22:00, last entry one hour before closing, closed on Jewish holidays. Tight security includes bag check and metal detectors. If you're here in December, be sure to check out their "Hannumas" holiday market. Tel. 030/2599-3300, www.jmberlin.de.

Getting There: Take the U-Bahn to Hallesches Tor, find the exit marked *Jüdisches Museum*, exit straight ahead, then turn right on Franz-Klühs-Strasse. The museum is a five-minute walk ahead on your left, at Lindenstrasse 9.

Eating: The museum has a good, but not kosher, café/restaurant (€9 daily specials, lunch served 12:00–16:00, snacks at other times, tel. 030/2593-9760).

East Side Gallery—The biggest remaining stretch of the Wall is now "the world's longest outdoor art gallery." It stretches for nearly a mile and is covered with murals painted by artists from around the world. The murals are routinely whitewashed so new ones can be painted. This segment of the Wall makes another poignant walk. For a quick look, take the S-Bahn to the Ostbahnhof station (follow signs to Stralauerplatz exit; once outside, TV Tower will be to your right; go left and at next corner look to your right—the Wall is across the busy street). The gallery is slowly being consumed by developers. If you walk the entire length of the East Side Gallery, you'll find a small Wall souvenir shop at the end and a bridge crossing the river to a subway station at Schlesisches Tor (in Kreuzberg). The bridge, a fine example of Brandenburg Neo-Gothic brickwork, has a fun neon "rock, paper, scissors" installment poking fun at the futility of the Cold War.

Kreuzberg—This district—once abutting the dreary Wall and inhabited mostly by poor Turkish guest laborers and their families—is still run-down, with graffiti-riddled buildings and plenty of student and Turkish street life. It offers a gritty look at melting-pot Berlin, in a city where original Berliners are as rare as old buildings. Berlin is the largest Turkish city outside of Turkey itself, and Kreuzberg is its "downtown." But to call it a "little Istanbul" insults the big one. You'll see *döner kebab* stands, shops decorated with spray paint, and mothers wrapped in colorful scarves looking like they just got off a donkey in Anatolia. But lately, an influx of immigrants from many other countries has diluted the Turkishness of Kreuzberg. Berliners come here for fun ethnic eateries. For a dose of Kreuzberg without getting your fingers dirty, joyride on bus #129 (catch it near Jewish Museum). For a colorful stroll, take the U-Bahn to Kottbusser Tor and wander—ideally on Tuesday and Friday between 12:00 and 18:00, when the Turkish Market sprawls along the Maybachufer riverbank.

North of Unter den Linden

While there are few major sights to the north of Unter den Linden, this area has some of Berlin's trendiest, most interesting neighborhoods.

▲**New Synagogue (Neue Synagoge)**—A shiny gilded dome marks the New Synagogue, now a museum and cultural center on Oranienburger Strasse. Only the dome and facade have been restored—a window overlooks the vacant field marking what used to be the synagogue. The largest and finest synagogue in Berlin before World War II, it was desecrated by Nazis on "Crystal Night" (Kristallnacht) in 1938, bombed in 1943, and partially rebuilt in 1990. Inside, past tight security, there's a small but moving exhibit on the Berlin Jewish community through the centuries with some good English descriptions (ground floor and first floor). On its facade, the *Vergesst es nie* message—added by East Berlin Jews in 1966—means "Never forget." East Berlin had only a few hundred Jews, but now that the city is reunited, the Jewish community numbers about 12,000 (€3; March–Oct Sun–Mon 10:00–20:00, Tue–Thu 10:00–18:00, Fri 10:00–17:00, closed Sat; Nov–Feb Sun–Thu 10:00–18:00, Fri 10:00–14:00, closed Sat; Oranienburger Strasse 28/30, S-Bahn: Oranienburger Strasse, tel. 030/8802-8300 and press 1, www.cjudaicum.de).

Cheer things up 50 yards away with every local kid's favorite traditional candy shop—**Bonbonmacherei**—where you can see candy being made the old-fashioned way (at Oranienburger Strasse 32, in another example of a classic Berlin courtyard).

A block from the synagogue, walk 50 yards down Grosse Hamburger Strasse to a little park. This street was known for 200 years as the "street of tolerance" because the Jewish community donated land to Protestants so that they could build a church. Hitler turned it into the "street of death" *(Todes Strasse),* bulldozing 12,000 graves of the city's oldest Jewish cemetery and turning a Jewish nursing home into a deportation center. Because of the small but growing radical Islamic element in Berlin, and a smattering of persistent neo-Nazis, several police officers and an Israeli secret agent keep watch over this park and the Jewish high school nearby.

▲**Oranienburger Strasse**—Berlin is developing so fast, it's impossible to predict what will be "in" from year to year. The area around Oranienburger Strasse is definitely trendy (but is being challenged by hip Friedrichshain, farther east, and Prenzlauer Berg, described later). While the area immediately around the synagogue is dull, 100 yards away things get colorful. The streets behind Grosse Hamburger Strasse flicker with atmospheric cafés, *Kneipen* (pubs), and art galleries. At night (from about 20:00), techno-prostitutes line Oranienburger Strasse. Prostitution is decriminalized here, but there's a big debate about taxation. Since they don't get unemployment insurance, why should they pay taxes?

A good place to watch this part of Berliner life is the pub **Aufsturz**, which serves over 100 different beers and 40 different whiskeys, traditional Berliner pub grub—like nachos—and incredible potato soup for under €5. The traditional Berlin platter for €14 can easily feed three voracious carnivores. Aufsturz is also a hang-out for local tour guides who don't mind if you join them to talk shop (daily from 12:00 until "at least" 2:00, across from the old Imperial Post Office at Oranienburger Strasse 67, tel. 030/2804-7407).

Hackescher Markt—This area, in front of the S-Bahn station by the same name, is a great people scene day and night. The brick trestle supporting the train track is another classic example of the city's Brandenburg Neo-Gothic brickwork. Most of the brick archways are now filled with hip shops, which have official—and newly trendy—addresses such as "S-Bahn Arch #9, Hackescher Markt." Within 100 yards of the S-Bahn station, you'll find Hackesche Höfe (see next), recommended Turkish and Bavarian restaurants, walking-tour and pub-crawl departure points, and tram #M1 to Prenzlauer Berg.

Hackesche Höfe (a block in front of the Hackescher Markt S-Bahn station) is a series of eight courtyards bunny-hopping through a wonderfully restored 1907 *Jugendstil* building. Berlin's apartments are organized like this—courtyard after courtyard leading off the main roads. This complex is full of trendy restaurants (including a good Turkish place, Hasir—see page 575), theaters, and cinemas (playing movies in their original languages). This is a

Stolpersteine (Stumbling Stones)

As you wander through the Hackesche Höfe and Oranienburger Strasse neighborhoods—and throughout Germany—you might stumble over small brass plaques in the sidewalk called *Stolpersteine*. *Stolpern* means "to stumble," which is what you are meant to do. These plaques are placed in front of former homes of residents who were killed during World War II. The *Stolpersteine* serve not only to honor the victims, but also to stimulate thought and discussion on a daily basis (rather than only during visits to memorial sites) and to put an individual's name on the mass horror.

More than 7,500 of these plaques have been installed across Germany. They're made of brass so they stay polished as you walk over them, instead of fading into the sidewalk. On each plaque is the name of the person who lived in that spot, and how and where they died. While some Holocaust memorials formerly used neutral terminology like "perished," now they use words like "murdered"—part of the very honest way in which today's Germans are dealing with their country's past. Ironically, the city of Munich banned *Stolpersteine*, saying that the plaques were insulting and that they were degrading to victims of persecution, who would continue to be trod on by "Nazi boots." Installation of a *Stolperstein* can be sponsored for €95 and has become popular in schools, where the students research the memorialized person's life as a class project.

wonderful example of how to make huge city blocks livable. Two decades after the Cold War, this area has reached the final evolution of East Berlin's urban restoration—this is where Prenzlauer Berg is heading. (These courtyards also serve a useful lesson for visitors: Much of Berlin's charm hides off the street front.)

▲**Prenzlauer Berg**—Young, in-the-know locals agree that "Prenzl'berg" is one of Berlin's most colorful neighborhoods (roughly between Helmholtzplatz and Kollwitzplatz and along Kastanienallee, U-Bahn: Senefelderplatz and Eberswalder Strasse; or take the S-Bahn to Hackescher Markt and catch tram #M1 north). This part of the city was largely untouched during World War II, but its buildings slowly rotted away under the communists. After the Wall fell, it was overrun with laid-back hipsters, energetic young families, and clever entrepreneurs who breathed life back into its classic old apartment blocks, deserted factories, and long-forgotten breweries. Ten years of rent control kept things affordable for its bohemian residents. But now landlords are free to charge what the market will bear, and the vibe is changing. Locals complain that these days the cafés and bars cater to yuppies

BERLIN

wearing Lacoste and sipping prosecco, while the working class and artistic types have been pushed out. While it has changed plenty, I still find Prenzlauer Berg a celebration of life and a joy to stroll through. Though it's a few blocks farther out than the neighborhoods described earlier, it's a fun area to explore and have a meal (see page 575) or spend the night (see page 566).

Natural History Museum (Museum für Naturkunde)—This museum is worth a visit just to see the largest dinosaur skeleton ever assembled. While you're there, meet "Bobby" the stuffed ape. Since its "reconception" in 2008, the museum is a magnet for the city's children, who love the interactive displays, the "History of the Universe in 120 Seconds" exhibit, and the cool virtual-reality glasses that put meat and skin on all of the dinosaur skeletons (€4, Tue–Fri 9:30–17:00, Sat–Sun 10:00–18:00, closed Mon, last entry 30 min before closing, Invalidenstrasse 43, U-Bahn: Zinnowitzer Strasse, tel. 030/2093-8591, www.museum.hu-berlin.de).

Berlin Wall Documentation Center (Dokumentations-zentrum Berliner Mauer)—The last surviving complete "Wall system" (with both sides of its Wall and its no-man's-land, or "death strip," all still intact) is now part of a sober little memorial and "Doku-Center." Though it's directed at German-speakers and far from other sights, it's handy enough to the S-Bahn that any Wall aficionado will find it worth a quick visit. The Documentation Center has a photo gallery and rooftop viewpoint (accessible by elevator), from which you can view the "Wall system." It's poignantly located where a church was destroyed to make way for the Wall; today, a memorial chapel has been built where the church once stood (free, April–Oct Tue–Sun 10:00–18:00, Nov–March until 17:00, closed Mon year-round, Bernauer Strasse 111, tel. 030/464-1030, www.berliner-mauer-dokumentationszentrum.de). Take the S-Bahn to Nordbahnhof and walk 200 yards along Bernauer Strasse, which is still lined with a long chunk of Wall.

Central Berlin
Tiergarten Park and Nearby
Berlin's "Central Park" stretches two miles from Bahnhof Zoo to the Brandenburg Gate.

Victory Column (Siegessäule)—The Tiergarten's centerpiece, the Victory Column, was built to commemorate the Prussian defeat of Denmark in 1864...then reinterpreted after the defeat of France in 1870. The pointy-helmeted Germans rubbed it in, decorating the tower with French cannons and paying for it all with francs received as war reparations. The three lower rings commemorate Bismarck's victories. I imagine the statues of Moltke and other German military greats—which lurk in the trees nearby—goose-stepping around the floodlit angel at night. Originally standing at the Reichstag, in 1938 the tower was moved to this position and given a 25-foot lengthening by Hitler's architect Albert Speer, in anticipation of the planned re-envisioning of Berlin as "Germania"—the capital of a world-wide Nazi empire. Streets leading to the circle are flanked by surviving Nazi guardhouses, built in the stern style that fascists loved. At the memorial's first level, notice how WWII bullets chipped the fine marble columns. More recently, the column has been the epicenter of the Love Parade (Berlin's city-wide techno-hedonist street party) and the backdrop for Barack Obama's summer 2008 visit to Germany as a presidential candidate. (He asked to speak in front of the Brandenburg Gate, but German Chancellor Angela Merkel wanted to save that symbol from "politics.") Climbing its 285 steps earns you a breathtaking Berlin-wide view and a close-up look at the gilded bronze statue of the goddess Victoria (go ahead, call her "the chick on a stick"—everybody here does). You might recognize Victoria from Wim Wenders' 1987 art-house classic *Wings of Desire*, or the *Stay (Faraway, So Close!)* video he directed for U2 (€2.20; April–Sept Mon–Thu 9:30–18:30, Fri–Sun 9:30–19:00; Oct–March daily 9:30–17:30; closes in the rain, WCs for paying guests only, no elevator, bus #100, tel. 030/8639-8560). From the tower, the grand Strasse des 17 Juni leads east to the Brandenburg Gate.

Flea Market—A colorful flea market with great antiques, more than 200 stalls, collector-savvy merchants, and fun German fast-food stands thrives weekends on Strasse des 17 Juni (Sat–Sun 6:00–16:00, right next to S-Bahn: Tiergarten).

German Resistance Memorial (Gedenkstätte Deutscher Widerstand)—This memorial and museum, just south of the Tiergarten, tells the story of several organized German resistance movements and of the more than 42 separate assassination attempts against Hitler. The Bendlerblock was a military headquarters where an ill-fated attempt to assassinate Hitler was plotted (the actual attempt occurred in Rastenburg, eastern Prussia; the event was dramatized in the 2009 Tom Cruise film *Valkyrie*). Claus Schenk Graf von Stauffenberg and several of his co-conspirators were shot here in the courtyard. While posted explanations are in German only and there are no real artifacts, the spirit that haunts the place is multilingual (free, Mon–Fri 9:00–18:00, Thu until 20:00, Sat–Sun 10:00–18:00, free and good English audioguide with passport, €3 printed English translation, no crowds, near Kulturforum at Stauffenbergstrasse 13, enter in courtyard, door on left, main exhibit is on third floor, bus #M29, tel. 030/2699-5000).

Central Berlin

400 YARDS
400 METERS

STRASSE DES 17 JUNI

ENTLASTUNG

TO VICTORY COLUMN

TIER-GARTEN

MUSICAL INSTRUMENTS MUSEUM

PHILHARMONIC CONCERT HALL

ARTS & CRAFTS MUSEUM

SONY CENTER

TIERGARTENSTR.

GEMÄLDEGALERIE

GERMAN RESISTANCE MEMORIAL

STAUFFEN-

SIGISMUND.

New Natl. GALLERY

STRASSE

LIBRARY

PIETERSC

LANDWEHR

REICH-

LÜTZOWUFER

POTSDAMER

CANAL

U U-BAHN STN.
S S-BAHN STN.
★ KULTURFORUM
- - - FORMER COURSE OF THE WALL

DCH

▲Potsdamer Platz

The "Times Square of Berlin," and possibly the busiest square in Europe before World War II, Potsdamer Platz was cut in two by the Wall and left a deserted no-man's-land for 40 years. Today, this immense commercial/residential/entertainment center, sitting on a futuristic transportation hub, is home to the European corporate headquarters of several big-league companies.

The new Potsdamer Platz was a vision begun in 1991, when it was announced that Berlin would resume its position as capital of Germany. Sony, Daimler, and other major corporations have turned the square once again into a center of Berlin.

Like great Christian churches built upon pagan holy grounds, Potsdamer Platz—with its corporate logos flying high and shiny above what was the Wall—trumpets the triumph of capitalism.

While Potsdamer Platz tries to give Berlin a common center, the city has always been—and remains—a collection of towns. Locals recognize 28 distinct neighborhoods that may have grown together but still maintain their historic orientation. While Munich has the single dominant Marienplatz, Berlin will always have Charlottenburg, Savignyplatz, Kreuzberg, Prenzlauer Berg, and so on. In general, Berliners prefer these characteristic neighborhoods to an official city center. They're unimpressed by the grandeur of Potsdamer Platz, and consider it simply a good place for movies, with overpriced, touristy restaurants.

While most of the complex just feels big (the arcade is like any huge, modern, American mall), the entrance to the complex and Sony Center are worth a visit, and German-film buffs will enjoy the Deutsche Kinemathek museum (described later).

For an overview of the new construction, and a scenic route to the Sony Center, start at the Bahnhof Potsdamer Platz (east end of Potsdamer Strasse, S- and U-Bahn: Potsdamer Platz, exit following *Leipziger Platz* signs to see the best view of skyscrapers as you emerge). Find the green hexagonal clock tower with the traffic lights on top. This is a replica of the first automatic traffic light in Europe, which once stood at the six-street intersection of Potsdamer Platz. On either side of Potsdamer Strasse, you'll see enormous cubical entrances to the new underground Potsdamer Platz train station. Near these entrances, notice the slanted glass cylinders sticking out of the ground. The mirrors on the tops of the tubes move with the sun to collect light and send it underground (saving piles of euros in energy costs). A line in the pavement indicates where the Berlin Wall once stood. Notice also the slabs of the Wall re-erected where the Wall once stood. Imagine when the first piece was cut out (see photo and history on nearby panel). These hang at the gate of Fort Capitalism...look up at the towering corporate headquarters: Market forces have won a clear victory. Now descend into one of the train station entrances and follow signs to *Sony Center.*

You'll come up the escalator into the **Sony Center** under a grand canopy (designed to evoke Mount Fuji). At night, multi-colored floodlights play on the underside of this tent. Office workers and tourists eat here by the fountain, enjoying the parade of people. The modern Bavarian Lindenbräu beer hall—the Sony boss wanted a *Bräuhaus*—serves traditional food (€5–16, daily 11:00–24:00, big salads, three-foot-long taster boards of eight different

beers, tel. 030/2575-1280). The adjacent Josty Bar is built around a surviving bit of a venerable hotel that was a meeting place for Berlin's rich and famous before the bombs (expensive, daily 10:00–24:00, tel. 030/2575-9702). CineStar is a rare cinema that plays mainstream movies in their original language (www.cinestar.de).

▲**Deutsche Kinemathek Film and TV Museum**—This exhibit is the most interesting place to visit in the Sony Center. Your admission ticket gets you into several floors of exhibits (third floor is permanent exhibits, first and fourth floor are temporary exhibits) made meaningful by the included (and essential) English audioguide. The film section takes you from the German film industry's beginnings, with emphasis on the Weimar Republic period in the 1920s, when Berlin rivaled Hollywood (*Metropolis* was a 1927 German production). Three rooms are dedicated to

Marlene Dietrich, and another section features Nazi use of film as propaganda. The TV section tells the story of *das Idioten Box* from its infancy (when it was primarily used as a Nazi propaganda tool) to today. The 30-minute kaleidoscopic review—kind of a frantic fast-forward montage of greatest hits in German TV history— is great fun even if you don't understand a word of it (it plays all day long, with 10-minute breaks). Upstairs is a TV archive where you can dial through a wide range of new and classic German TV standards (€6, includes 90-min audioguide, Tue–Sun 10:00–18:00, Thu until 20:00, closed Mon, tel. 030/2474-9888, www.deutsche -kinemathek.de). The Kino Arsenal theater downstairs shows off-beat art-house films in their original language.

Panaromapunkt—Across Potsdamer Strasse from the Film and TV Museum, you can ride what's billed as "the fastest elevator in Europe" to skyscraping rooftop views. You'll travel at nearly 30 feet per second to the top of the 300-foot-tall Kollhoff Tower. Its sheltered but open-air view deck provides a fun opportunity to survey Berlin's ongoing construction from above (€5, likely closed for renovation until March 2010, then open daily 11:00–20:00, last elevator at 19:30, in red-brick building at Potsdamer Platz 1, tel. 030/2529-4372, www .panoramapunkt.de).

Kulturforum

Just west of Potsdamer Platz, with several top museums and Berlin's concert hall—home of the world-famous Berlin Philharmonic orchestra—is the city's cultural heart (admission to all Kulturforum sights covered by a single €8 "Standortkarte Kulturforum" combo-ticket or the Museumspass; phone number for all museums: tel. 030/266-2951). Of its sprawling museums, only the Gemäldegalerie is a must (S- or U-Bahn to Potsdamer Platz, then walk along Potsdamer Platz; or from Bahnhof Zoo, take bus #200 to Philharmonie).

▲▲▲**Gemäldegalerie**—Germany's top collection of 13th-through 18th-century European paintings (more than 1,400 canvases) is beautifully displayed in a building that's a work of art in itself. Follow the excellent free audioguide. The North Wing starts with German paintings of the 13th to 16th centuries, including eight by Albrecht Dürer. Then come the Dutch and Flemish—Jan van Eyck, Pieter Brueghel, Peter Paul Rubens, Anthony van Dyck, Frans Hals, and Jan Vermeer. The wing finishes with

German, English, and French 18th-century art, such as Thomas Gainsborough and Antoine Watteau. An octagonal hall at the end features an impressive stash of Rembrandts. The South Wing is saved for the Italians—Giotto, Botticelli, Titian, Raphael, and Caravaggio (free Thu after 18:00, open Tue–Sun 10:00–18:00, Thu until 22:00, closed Mon, clever little loaner stools, great salad bar in cafeteria upstairs, Matthäikirchplatz 4).

New National Gallery (Neue Nationalgalerie)—This features 20th-century art, with ever-changing special exhibits (Tue–Fri 10:00–18:00, Thu until 22:00, Sat–Sun 11:00–18:00, closed Mon, café downstairs, Potsdamer Strasse 50).

Museum of Arts and Crafts (Kunstgewerbemuseum)— Wander through a thousand years of applied arts—porcelain, fine *Jugendstil* furniture, Art Deco, and reliquaries. There are no English descriptions and no crowds (Herbert-von-Karajan-Strasse 10).

▲Musical Instruments Museum (Musikinstrumenten Museum)—This impressive hall is filled with 600 exhibits from the 16th century to modern times. Wander among old keyboard instruments and funny-looking tubas. There's no English, aside from a €0.10 info sheet, but it's fascinating if you're into pianos (Tue–Fri 9:00–17:00, Thu until 22:00, Sat–Sun 10:00–17:00, closed Mon, low-profile white building east of the big yellow Philharmonic Concert Hall, tel. 030/254-810).

Philharmonic Concert Hall—Poke into the lobby of Berlin's yellow Philharmonic building and see if there are tickets available during your stay (ticket office open Mon–Fri 15:00–18:00, Sat–Sun 11:00–14:00, must purchase tickets in person, box office tel. 030/2548-8132). You can often get inexpensive and legitimate tickets sold on the street before the performance. The interior is famous for its extraordinary acoustics. Even from the outside, this is a remarkable building, designed by a nautical engineer to look like a ship—notice how different it looks from each angle.

Western Berlin

Throughout the Cold War, Western travelers—and most West Berliners—got used to thinking of western Berlin's Kurfürstendamm boulevard as the heart of the city. But those days have gone the way of the Wall. With the huge changes the city has undergone since 1989, the real "city center" is now, once again, Berlin's historic center (the Mitte district, around Unter den Linden and Friedrichstrasse). While western Berlin has long had the best infrastructure to support your visit, and still works well as a home base, it's no longer the obvious base from which to explore Berlin. And after the new Hauptbahnhof essentially put the Bahnhof Zoo out of business in 2006, the area was left with an identity crisis. Now, almost 20 years after reunification, the west side is back and has fully embraced its historical role as a chic, classy suburb. There are a few interesting sights here, all within walking distance of Bahnhof Zoo and the Savignyplatz hotels.

For a detailed map of this area, see page 570.

▲**Kurfürstendamm**—Western Berlin's main drag, Kurfürstendamm boulevard (nicknamed "Ku'damm"), starts at Kaiser Wilhelm Memorial Church and does a commercial cancan for two miles. In the 1850s, when Berlin became a wealthy and important capital, her new rich chose Kurfürstendamm as their street. Bismarck made it Berlin's Champs-Elysées. In the 1920s, it became a chic and fashionable drag of cafés and boutiques. During the Third Reich, as home to an international community of diplomats and journalists, it enjoyed more freedom than the rest of Berlin. Throughout the Cold War, economic subsidies from the West made sure that capitalism thrived on Ku'damm. And today, while much of the old charm has been hamburgerized, Ku'damm is still a fine place to enjoy elegant shops (around Fasanenstrasse), department stores, and people-watching.

▲**Kaiser Wilhelm Memorial Church (Gedächtniskirche)**— This church was originally dedicated to the first emperor of

Germany. Reliefs and mosaics show great events in the life of Germany's favorite *Kaiser*, from his coronation in 1871 to his death in 1888. The church's bombed-out ruins have been left standing as a poignant memorial to the destruction of Berlin in World War II (Breitscheidplatz, S-Bahn and U-Bahn: Zoologischer Garten or U-Bahn: Kurfürstendamm, www.gedaechtniskirche.com).

The church is actually an ensemble of buildings: a new church, the matching bell tower, a meeting hall, and the bombed-out ruins of the old church, with its Memorial Hall.

Under a Neo-Romanesque mosaic ceiling, the **Memorial Hall** features a small exhibit of interesting photos about the bombing and before-and-after models of the church (free, Mon–Sat 10:00–16:00, closed Sun).

After the war, some Berliners wanted to tear down the ruins and build it anew. Instead, it was decided to keep what was left of the old church as a memorial, and stage a competition to design a modern, add-on section. The winning entry—the short, modern building (1961) next to the Memorial Hall—offers a world of 11,000 little blue windows. The blue glass was given to the church by the French as a reconciliation gift. For more information on both churches, pick up the English booklet (€2.60).

BERLIN

As you enter the **church** (free, daily 9:00–19:00), turn immediately right to find a simple charcoal sketch of the Virgin Mary wrapped in a shawl. During the Battle of Stalingrad, German combat surgeon Kurt Reuber rendered the Virgin on the back of a stolen Soviet map to comfort the men in his care. On the right are the words "Light, Life, Love" from the gospel of John; on the left, "Christmas in the cauldron 1942"; and at the bottom, "Fortress Stalingrad." Though Reuber died in captivity a year later, his sketch had been flown out of Stalingrad on the last medical evacuation flight, and post-war Germany embraced it as a symbol of the wish for peace. Copies of the drawing, now known as the *Stalingrad Madonna,* hang in the Berlin Cathedral, in England's Coventry, and in Russia's Volgograd (formerly Stalingrad), as a sign of peaceful understanding between the nations. As another act of reconciliation, every Friday at 13:00 there is a "Prayers for Peace" service held simultaneously with the cathedral in Coventry.

The lively square between the churches and the Europa Center (a once-impressive, shiny high-rise shopping center built as a showcase of Western capitalism during the Cold War) usually attracts street musicians and performers—especially in the summer. Berliners call the funky fountain "the wet meatball."

The Story of Berlin—Filling most of what seems like a department store right on Ku'damm (at #207), this sprawling history exhibit is a business venture making money by telling the stormy 800-year story of Berlin in a creative way. While there are almost no real historic artifacts, the exhibit does a good job of cobbling together many dimensions of the life and tumultuous times of this great city. However, for similar information, the German History Museum on Unter den Linden is a far better use of your time and money (see page 535).

▲**Käthe Kollwitz Museum**—This local artist (1867–1945), who experienced much of Berlin's stormiest century, conveys some powerful and mostly sad feelings about motherhood, war, and suffering through the stark faces of her art. This small yet fine collection (the only one in town of Kollwitz's work) consists of three floors of charcoal drawings, topped by an attic with a handful of sculptures (€5, €1 pamphlet has necessary English explanations of a few major works, daily 11:00–18:00, a block off Ku'damm at Fasanenstrasse 24, U-Bahn: Uhlandstrasse, tel. 030/882-5210, www.kaethe-kollwitz.de).

▲**Kaufhaus des Westens (KaDeWe)**—The "Department Store of the West" has been a Berlin tradition for more than a century. With a staff of 2,100 to help you sort through its vast selection of 380,000 items, KaDeWe claims to be the biggest department store on the Continent. You can get everything from a haircut and train ticket (basement) to souvenirs (third floor). The theater and concert box office on the sixth floor charges an 18 percent booking fee, but they know all your options (cash only). The sixth floor is a world of gourmet taste treats. The biggest selection of deli and exotic food in Germany offers plenty of classy opportunities to sit down and eat. Ride the glass elevator to the seventh floor's glass-domed Winter Garden, a self-service cafeteria—fun but pricey (Mon–Thu 10:00–20:00, Fri 10:00–21:00, Sat 9:30–20:00, closed Sun, S-Bahn: Zoologischer Garten or U-Bahn: Wittenbergplatz, tel. 030/21210, www.kadewe.de). The Wittenbergplatz U-Bahn station (in front of KaDeWe) is a unique opportunity to see an old-time station. Enjoy its interior.

Berlin Zoo (Zoologischer Garten Berlin)—More than 1,400 different kinds of animals call Berlin's famous zoo home...or so the zookeepers like to think. The big hit here is Knut, a young polar bear who first made headlines for being born in captivity, but quickly became an international star after he was abandoned by his mother and raised by zookeepers. Germans also enjoy seeing the pandas at play (straight in from the entrance). I enjoy seeing the Germans at play (€12 for zoo, €12 for world-class aquarium, €18 for both, children half-price, daily mid-March–mid-Oct generally 9:00–19:00, mid-Oct–mid-March generally 9:00–17:00, aquarium closes 30 min earlier; feeding times—*Fütterungszeiten*—posted on map just inside entrance, the best feeding show is the sea lions—generally at 15:30; enter near Europa Center in front of Hotel Palace or opposite Bahnhof Zoo on Hardenbergplatz, Budapester Strasse 34, tel. 030/254-010, www.zoo-berlin.de).

Erotic Art Museum—This offers two floors of graphic art (especially East Asian), old-time sex-toy knickknacks, and a special exhibit on the queen of German pornography, the late Beate Uhse. This amazing woman, a former test pilot for the Third Reich and groundbreaking purveyor of condoms and sex ed in the 1950s, was the female Hugh Hefner of Germany and CEO of a huge chain of porn shops. She is famously credited with bringing sex out of the bedroom, and onto the kitchen table, "where it belonged" (€6, Mon–Sat 9:00–24:00, Sun 13:00–24:00, last entry at 23:00, hard-to-beat gift shop, at corner of Kantstrasse and Joachimstalerstrasse, a block from Bahnhof Zoo, tel. 030/8862-6613). If you just want to see sex, you'll see much more for half the price in a private video booth next door.

Charlottenburg Palace Area

The Charlottenburg district—with a cluster of museums across the street from a grand palace—is an easy side-trip from downtown. The palace isn't much to see, but if the surrounding museums appeal to you, consider making the trip. To get here, ride U2 to Sophie-Charlotte Platz and walk 10 minutes up the tree-lined boulevard

Charlottenburg Palace Area

GARDENS

Ⓑ BUS STOP

N

ENTRY

PALACE

#M45

SAMOVAR
■ RUSSIAN
REST.

↖ KNOBELSDORFF
WING

🔲 BRÄUHAUS
LEMKE

SPANDAUER   DAMM

Ⓑ

BERGGRUEN
COLLECTION ↗

SCHLOSS STR.

SCHARF-
GERSTENBERG
COLLECTION

#M45

Ⓑ

OTTO SUHR ALLEE

BRÖHAN
MUSEUM

SCHLOSS
STR.

TO
BAHNHOF
ZOO
STATION

DCH

↓ TO U-BAHN

Schlossstrasse (following signs to *Schloss*), or—much faster—catch bus #M45 (direction Spandau) direct from Bahnhof Zoo.

Eating near Charlottenburg Palace: For a Charlottenburg lunch, the **Bräuhaus Lemke** is a comfortable brewpub restaurant with a copper and woody atmosphere, good local microbeers (*dunkles* means "dark," *helles* is "light"), and traditional German grub (€8–15 meals, daily 9:00–24:00, fun for groups, across from palace at Luisenplatz 1, tel. 030/3087-8979). Or consider lunching like the Russians, who have been part of Charlottenburg ever since Frederick the Great invited them in the 18th century. Small **Samovar** serves traditional Russian specialties in a comfortable, intimate setting (€6–12 meals, €3.40 Russian tea, daily 11:00–22:00, just past Bräuhaus Lemke at Luisenplatz 3, tel. 030/341-4154).

▲**Charlottenburg Palace (Schloss Charlottenburg)**—If you've seen the great palaces of Europe, this Baroque palace, also known as the Altes Schloss, comes in at about number 10 (behind Potsdam, too). It's the largest former residence of the royal Hohenzollern family in Berlin, and contains the largest collection of 17th-century French fresco painting outside of France (€10, includes audioguide, Tue–Sun 10:00–18:00, closed Mon, last entry at 17:30, tel. 030/320-911, www.spsg.de).

The Neue Flügel (a.k.a. the Knobelsdorff Wing) features a few royal apartments. Go upstairs and take a substantial hike through restored-since-the-war gold-crusted white rooms (€6, more during special exhibitions, free English audioguide, Wed–Mon 10:00–17:00, closed Tue, last entry at 16:30, when facing the palace walk toward the right wing, tel. 030/3209-1442).

▲**Berggruen Collection: Picasso and His Time**—This tidy little museum is a pleasant surprise. Climb three floors through a fun and substantial collection of Picassos. Along the way, you'll see plenty of notable works by Henri Matisse. Enjoy a great chance to meet Paul Klee (€6, covered by Museumspass, free Thu after 14:00, open Tue–Sun 10:00–18:00, closed Mon, Schlossstrasse 1, tel. 030/326-9580, www.smb.museum).

▲**Bröhan Museum**—Wander through a dozen beautifully furnished *Jugendstil* and Art Deco living rooms, a curvy organic world of lamps, glass, silver, and posters. English descriptions are posted on the wall of each room on the main floor. While you're there, look for the fine collection of Impressionist paintings by Karl Hagemeister (€6, covered by Museumspass excluding special exhibits, Tue–Sun 10:00–18:00, closed Mon, Schlossstrasse 1A, tel. 030/3269-0600, www.broehan-museum.de).

▲**Scharf-Gerstenberg Collection**—Opened in 2008, this small museum houses a collection of more than 250 works of Surrealist and pre-Surrealist art. The *Surreal Worlds* exhibit shows just how freaky and weird the world looked to artists like Salvador Dalí, Paul Klee, and Francisco de Goya. Be sure to check out Dalí's film of his birth from an egg on the beach (€8, covered by Museumspass, free Thu after 14:00, open Tue–Sun 10:00–18:00, closed Mon, Schlossstrasse 70, tel. 030/3435-7315, www.smb.museum).

▲Near Berlin: Potsdam's Palaces

Featuring a lush park strewn with the escapist whimsies of Frederick the Great, the sleepy town of Potsdam has long been Berlin's holiday retreat. Frederick's super-Rococo Sanssouci Palace is one of Germany's most dazzling. His equally extravagant New Palace, built to disprove rumors that Prussia was running out of money after the costly Seven Years' War, is on the other side of the park (it's a 30-minute walk between palaces). Potsdam's much-promoted Wannsee boat rides are exceedingly dull.

Getting to Potsdam: Potsdam is easy to reach from Berlin (17 min on direct Regional Express/RE trains from Hauptbahnhof, Bahnhof Zoo, or Friedrichstrasse every 30 min; round-trip covered by €6.30 transit day pass with zones A, B, and C; any train to Brandenburg or Magdeburg stops in Potsdam). Once in Potsdam, bus #695 runs from the Potsdam train station to the palaces, and is invariably packed (3/hr, 20 min, leaves from lane 4; April–Oct bus #X15 runs the same route on weekends). A less-crowded option is to take tram #91 to Luisenplatz (3/hr, 11 min, leaves from lane 1), then walk 20 minutes through the park and enjoy a classic view of Sanssouci Palace. The tram is also the better option if you're taking the Potsdam TI's tour (see "Tours at Potsdam," later). Use the same bus #695 to shuttle between the sights in the park.

Orientation and Information: Unless you're planning on spending time exploring the town of Potsdam itself, skip the Potsdam **TI** (April–Oct Mon–Fri 9:30–18:00, Sat–Sun 9:30–16:00; Nov–March Mon–Fri 10:00–18:00, Sat–Sun 9:30–14:00; tel. 0331/275-580, Brandenburger Strasse 3, www.potsdam tourismus.de) and head straight to the **palace information office** (across the street from windmill near Sanssouci entrance, helpful English-speaking staff, daily April–Oct 8:30–17:00, Nov–March 9:00–16:00, tel. 0331/969-4202, www.spsg.de; clean WC in same building, €0.30). To supplement the English tour handouts, consider picking up the gray "official guide" booklets (available for all of the sights, €3 each at palace information office and gift shop).

Tours at Potsdam: The Potsdam TI offers a bus tour of Potsdam sights, plus the interior of Sanssouci Palace. This normally wouldn't be worth the time...except that it's the only way to get into Sanssouci with a live, English-speaking guide (often with some German, too; €26 covers tour, palace, and park; Sun–Tue at 11:00, no tours Mon, 3.5 hrs, departs from TI at Luisenplatz, reserve by phone, in summer reserve at least 2 days in advance, tel. 0331/275-5850).

Tours from Berlin: Original Berlin Walks, Brewer's Tours, and New Berlin Tours all offer inexpensive all-day tours from Berlin through Potsdam (small groups, English-language only, no reservations necessary, admissions and public transportation not included, doesn't actually go into Sanssouci Palace). These tours are the best way to get the most out of Potsdam, and can help you avoid a lot of stress. **Original Berlin Walks'** tour leaves from the taxi stand outside Berlin's Bahnhof Zoo at 9:50 every Sunday, April through October (also on Thu June–Aug; €15, meet at taxi stand at Bahnhof Zoo, tel. 030/301-9194). The guide takes you to Cecilienhof Palace (site of postwar Potsdam conference attended by Churchill, Stalin, and Truman), through pleasant green landscapes to the historic heart of Potsdam for lunch, and finishes outside Sanssouci Palace. The **Brewer's** tour is similar (€12, Wed and Sun, May–Oct only, leaves at 9:30 from Bandy Brooks ice cream shop at Friedrichstrasse U- and S-Bahn station, call to confirm and hold a spot, tel. 030/2248-7435, mobile 0177-388-1537, www.brewersberlintours.com). **New Berlin**'s entertaining tour leaves daily at 11:00 from their starting point in front of Starbucks on Pariser Platz (€14, tel. 030/5105-0030, www.newberlintours.com).

Sanssouci Palace—Visits to this palace include an interesting audioguide. *Sans souci* means "without a care," but for the most stress-free visit, arrive early: In the summer, if you arrive by 10:00, you'll get right in; if you arrive after 11:00, plan on a wait (€12 with audioguide, April–Oct Tue–Sun 10:00–18:00, Nov–March Tue–Sun 10:00–17:00, closed Mon year-round).

Greater Berlin

New Palace (Neues Palais)—This palace's apartments are underwhelming and frustrating for non-German speakers (€6, includes audioguide, April–Oct Sat–Thu 10:00–18:00, Nov–March Sat–Thu 10:00–17:00, closed Fri year-round). If you also want to see the king's apartments, you must take a required 45-minute tour in German (included in entrance fee, offered May–Oct daily at 10:00, 11:00, 14:00, and 16:00). Off-season (Nov–April), the king's apartments are closed, and you can visit the rest of the New Palace only on a German tour (€5); it can take up to an hour for enough people to gather.

Bornstedt Royal Estate (Krongut Bornstedt)—Designed to look like an Italian village, this warehouse-like complex once provided the royal palaces with food and other supplies. Today the estate houses the Bornstedt Buffalo brewery and distillery, which delivers fine brews and schnapps, as it has since 1689. The restaurant is a good place for lunch, serving local specialties (€6–12 plates). The grounds also house a wood-fired bakery with fresh bread and pastries. You can watch hatmakers, candle makers, coopers, potters, and glassmakers produce (and sell) their wares using traditional techniques (free except during special events, daily 10:00–19:00, restaurant serves until 21:30, from Sanssouci walk toward the windmill and follow the street An der Orangerie about 500 yards to Ribbeckstrasse 6, toll tel. 01805-766-488, www .krongut-bornstedt.de).

Cecilienhof—The former residence of Crown Prince William and the site of the 1945 Potsdam Conference is a short bus ride away

(€6, April–Oct Tue–Sun 10:00–18:00, Nov–March Tue–Sun 10:00–17:00, closed Mon year-round; take bus #695 from Sanssouci Palace to Reiterweg, then transfer to bus #692; tel. 0331/969-4224). If you're hungry at Cecilienhof, try the brewery called **Meierei** ("Creamery"). Its nice beer garden offers spectacular views of the lake, solid German food, and great homemade beer. When you walk down the hill into the restaurant, note the big open field to the right—it used to be part of the Berlin Wall (€6–15 meals, daily 11:00–22:00, follow *Meierei* signs to Im Neuen Garten 10, tel. 0331/704-3211).

Nightlife in Berlin

Berlin is a happening place for nightlife—whether it's nightclubs, pubs, jazz music, cabaret, hokey-but-fun German variety shows, theater, or concerts.

Sources of Entertainment Info: *Berlin Programm* lists a non-stop parade of concerts, plays, exhibits, and cultural events (€2, in German, www.berlin-programm.de); *Exberliner Magazine* (€2, www.exberliner.com) and the TI-produced *Berlin To Go* (€1) have less information, but are in English (all sold at kiosks and TIs). For the young and determined sophisticate, *Zitty* and *Tip* are the top guides to alternative culture (in German, sold at kiosks). Also pick up the free schedules *Flyer* and *030* in bars and clubs. Visit KaDeWe's ticket office for your music and theater options (sixth floor, 18 percent fee but access to all tickets; see page 558). Ask about "competitive improvisation" and variety shows.

Western Berlin Jazz—To enjoy live music near my recommended Savignyplatz hotels in western Berlin, consider **A Trane Jazz Club** (all jazz, great stage and intimate seating, €7–18 cover depending on act, opens at 21:00, live music nightly 22:00–2:00 in the morning, Bleibtreustrasse 1, tel. 030/313-2550) and **Quasimodo Live** (mix of jazz, rock, and blues, €5–12 cover, Tue–Sat from 22:00, closed Sun–Mon, Kantstrasse 12A, under Delphi Cinema, tel. 030/312-8086, www.quasimodo.de).

Berliner Rock and Roll—Berlin has a vibrant rock and pop scene, with popular venues at the Spandau Citadel and at the outdoor Waldbühne ("Forest Stage"). Check out what's playing on posters in the U-Bahn, in *Zitty,* or at any ticket agency. Great Berlin bands include Wir Sind Helden, The Beatsteaks, Jennifer Rostock, and the funky ska band Seeed.

Cabaret—**Bar Jeder Vernunft** offers modern-day cabaret a short walk from the recommended hotels in western Berlin. This variety show—under a classic old tent perched atop a modern parking lot—is a hit with German speakers, but can still be worthwhile for those who don't speak the language (as some of the music shows are in a sort of "Denglish"). Even some Americans perform here

BERLIN

periodically. Tickets are generally about €20, and shows change regularly (performances start Mon–Sat at 20:30, Sun at 20:00, Wed is non-smoking, seating can be a bit cramped, south of Ku'damm at Schaperstrasse 24, tel. 030/883-1582, www.bar-jeder -vernunft.de).

German Variety Show—To spend an evening enjoying Europe's largest revue theater, consider "Qi—A Palace Fantasy" at the **Friedrichstadt Palast**. It's a visual spectacle that would be at home in Vegas, exploding with scantily clad showgirls, high-stepping chorus lines, acrobats, and more sequined feathers than you can count (€21–94, Tue–Sat at 19:30, Sat–Sun also at 15:30, no shows Mon, U-Bahn: Oranienburger Tor, tel. 030/2326-2326, www .friedrichstadtpalast.de).

The Friedrichstrasse area around the Palast and to the south has been synonymous with entertainment for at least 200 years. The East German government built the current Palast in 1984 on the ruins of an older theater, which itself was a horse barn for the Prussian Army. The current exterior is meant to mimic the interior design of the older theater.

Nightclubs and Pubs—Oranienburger Strasse's trendy scene (page 548) is being eclipsed by the action at Friedrichshain (farther east). To the north, you'll find the hip Prenzlauer Berg neighborhood, packed with everything from smoky pubs to small art bars and dance clubs (best scene is around Helmholtsplatz, U-Bahn: Eberswalder Strasse; see page 549).

Dancing—Cut a rug at **Clärchens Ballhaus,** an old ballroom that's been a Berlin institution since 1913. At some point everyone in Berlin comes through here, as the dance hall attracts an eclectic Berlin-in-a-nutshell crowd of grannies, elegant women in evening dresses, yuppies, scenesters, and hippies. The music (swing, waltz, tango, or cha-cha) changes every day, with live music on Friday and Saturday (daily from 10:00 until the last person goes home, in the heart of the Auguststrasse gallery district at Auguststrasse 24, S-Bahn: Oranienburger Strasse, tel. 030/282-9295, www.ballhaus .de). Dancing lessons are also available (€8, Mon–Tue and Thu at 19:00, 90 min). The restaurant serves decent food and good pizzas.

Art Galleries—Berlin, a magnet for new artists, is a great city for gallery visits. Galleries—many of which stay open late—welcome visitors who are "just looking." The most famous gallery district is in eastern Berlin's Mitte neighborhood, along **Auguststrasse** (branches off from Oranienburger Strasse at the Tacheles building). Check out the Berlin outpost of the edgy-yet-accessible art of the New Leipzig movement at **Galerie Eigen+Art** (Tue–Sat 11:00–18:00, closed Sun–Mon, Auguststrasse 26, tel. 030/280-6605, www.eigen-art.com). The other gallery area is in western Berlin, along **Fasanenstrasse.**

Pub Crawl—New Berlin Tours offers a popular €12 pub crawl. "The New Berlin Pub Crawl" starts at 20:15 from the Oranienburger Strasse S-Bahn station, with free beer until 21:00. Organizers are fairly adamant about their slogan, "Our mission: To show you Berlin's great nightlife...not to hospitalize you." The (unrelated) binge-drinking death of a 16-year-old teenager in Berlin a few years ago has reinforced the tour's strict 18-year-old minimum age limit. The pub crawl generally visits four bars and two clubs, and provides a great way to drink it up with new friends from around the world while getting a peek at Berlin's bar scene... or at least how its bars look when invaded by 50 loud tourists.

Sleeping in Berlin

When in Berlin, I used to sleep in the former West, on or near Savignyplatz. But now the focus of Berlin is moving farther east. If you're interested in staying in a lively, colorful district in the heart of the *Kiez* (literally "gravel," meaning a homey, homogenous neighborhood in Berlin), I've listed some suggestions in eastern Berlin's youthful and increasingly popular Prenzlauer Berg neighborhood.

Berlin is packed and hotel prices go up on holidays, including Green Week in mid-January, Easter weekend, the first weekend in May, Ascension weekend in May, German Unity Day (Oct 3), Christmas, and New Year's. Keep in mind that many hotels have limited staff after 20:00, so if you're planning to arrive after that, let the hotel know in advance.

In Eastern Berlin: Prenzlauer Berg

If you want to sleep in the former East Berlin, set your sights on the youthful, colorful, and fun Prenzlauer Berg district (or "Prenzl'berg" for short). After decades of neglect, this corner of eastern Berlin has quickly come back to life. Gentrification has brought Prenzlauer Berg great hotels, tasty ethnic and German eateries (listed later, under "Eating in Berlin"), and a happening nightlife scene. Think of all the graffiti as just some people's way of saying they care. The huge and impersonal concrete buildings are now enlivened with a street fair of fun little shops and eateries. Prenzlauer Berg is about a mile and a half north of Alexanderplatz, roughly between Kollwitzplatz and Helmholtzplatz, and to the west, along Kastanienallee (known affectionately as "Casting Alley" for its extra share of beautiful people). The closest U-Bahn stops are Senefelderplatz at the south end of the neighborhood and Eberswalder Strasse at the north end. Or, for less walking, take the S-Bahn to Hackescher Markt, then catch tram #M1 north.

Prenzlauer Berg Neighborhood

1 Myer's Hotel

2 Hotel Jurine

3 Hotel Kastanienhof

4 Hotel Transit Loft

5 EastSeven Hostel

6 Karlito Apartmenthaus

7 Gugelhof Restaurant

8 Metzer Eck

9 Prater Biergarten

10 Zum Schusterjungen Speisegaststätte & Launderette

11 La Bodeguita del Medio Cuban Bar Restaurant

12 Konnopke's Imbiss

13 Kauf Dich Glücklich

14 Original Berlin Walks Departure Point

15 To Berlin Wall Documentation Center, Nordbahnhof S-Bahn & Natural History Museum

$$$ Myer's Hotel is a boutique-hotel splurge renting 52 simple, small, but elegant rooms. The gorgeous public spaces include a patio and garden. Details done right and impeccable service set this place apart. This peaceful hub—off a quiet courtyard and tree-lined street, just a five-minute walk from Kollwitzplatz or the nearest U-Bahn stop (Senefelderplatz)—makes it hard to believe you're in a capital city (Sb-€79–139, Db-€99–189, price depends on size of room, Metzer Strasse 26, tel. 030/440-140, fax 030/4401-4104, www.myershotel.de, info@myershotel.de).

$$ Hotel Jurine (yoo-REEN) is a pleasant 53-room business-style hotel whose friendly staff aims to please. Enjoy the breakfast buffet surrounded by modern art, or relax in the lush backyard (Sb-€82, Db-€99, Tb-€152, extra bed-€37, prices can zoom up during conventions, check website for discounts in July–Aug, parking garage-€13/day, Schwedter Strasse 15, 10-min walk to U-Bahn: Senefelderplatz, tel. 030/443-2990, fax 030/4432-9999, www.hotel-jurine.de, mail@hotel-jurine.de).

$$ Hotel Kastanienhof is a basic, less-classy hotel offering 35 sleepable but slightly overpriced rooms (Sb-€79, Db-€105, reception closed 22:00–6:30, 40 yards from the #M1 tram stop at Kastanienallee 65, tel. 030/443-050, fax 030/4430-5111, www.kastanienhof.biz, info@kastanienhof.biz).

$ Hotel Transit Loft is technically a hostel, but feels more like an upscale budget hotel. Located in a refurbished factory, it offers clean, bright, modern, new-feeling, mostly blue rooms with an industrial touch. The reception—staffed by friendly, hip Berliners—is open 24 hours, with a bar serving drinks all night long (4- to 6-bed dorms-€21/bed, Sb-€62, Db-€72, Tb-€96, includes sheets and breakfast, no age limit, cheap Internet access, fully wheelchair-accessible, Emmanuelkirchstrasse 14A, U-Bahn: Alexanderplatz then tram #M4 to Hufelandstrasse and walk 50 yards, tel. 030/4849-3773, fax 030/4405-1074, www.transit-loft.de, loft@hotel-transit.de).

$ EastSeven Hostel rents the best cheap beds in Prenzlauer Berg. It's sleek and modern, with all the hostel services and more: 24-hour reception, inviting lounge, fully equipped guests' kitchen, lockers, garden, and bike rental. Children are welcome. While most hostels—especially in Prenzlauer Berg—are annoyingly youthful to people over 30, easygoing people of any age are comfortable here (S-€37, D-€50, T-€63, €17 for a bed in a 4-, 5-, or 6-bed dorm, bathrooms always down the hall, one-time €3 fee for sheets, free Internet access and Wi-Fi, laundry-€5, 100 yards from U-Bahn: Senefelderplatz at Schwedter Strasse 7, tel. 030/9362-2240, www.eastseven.de, info@eastseven.de).

$ Karlito Apartmenthaus offers nine well-located, modern, and comfortable apartments near Hackescher Markt (Sb-€62, Db-€77, Tb-€93, Qb-€107, cash only, up to 2 children under

---

Sleep Code

(€1 = about $1.40, country code: 49, area code: 030)
S = Single, **D** = Double/Twin, **T** = Triple, **Q** = Quad, **b** = bathroom,
s = shower only. Unless otherwise noted, credit cards are accepted, English is spoken, and breakfast is included.

To help you sort easily through these listings, I've divided the rooms into three categories, based on the price for a standard double room with bath:

$$$ Higher Priced—Most rooms €125 or more.
$$ Moderately Priced—Most rooms between €85–125.
$ Lower Priced—Most rooms €85 or less.

---

13 sleep free with 2 paying adults, fully equipped as if you live there, breakfast in Café Lois-€4, Linienstrasse 60—enter on Gormannstrasse, 350 yards from S-Bahn: Hackescher Markt, even closer to U-Bahn: Rosenthaler Platz, mobile 0179-704-9041, www.karlito-apartments.de, info@karlito-apartments.de.

In Western Berlin:
Near Savignyplatz and Bahnhof Zoo

While Bahnhof Zoo and Ku'damm are no longer the center of the action, this western Berlin neighborhood is still a comfortable and handy home base (thanks to its easy transit connections to the rest of the city, and proximity to the starting point of many good walking tours). The streets around the tree-lined Savignyplatz (a 10-min walk behind the station) have a neighborhood charm—simple, small, friendly, good-value places abound here. The area has an artsy aura going back to the cabaret days in the 1920s, when it was the center of Berlin's gay scene. The hotels and pensions I list below—which are all a 5- to 15-minute walk from Bahnhof Zoo and Savignyplatz (with S- and U-Bahn stations)—are generally located a couple of flights up in big, run-down buildings. Inside, they're clean and spacious enough so that their well-worn character is actually charming. Asking for a quieter room in back gets you away from any street noise. Of the accommodations listed here, Pension Peters offers the best value for budget travelers.

$$ Hotel Askanischerhof is the oldest B&B in Berlin, posh as can be with 16 sprawling, antique-furnished living rooms you can call home. Photos on the walls brag of famous movie-star guests. Frau Glinicke offers Old World service and classic Berlin atmosphere (Sb-€105, Db-€117, extra bed-€25, elevator, free parking, Ku'damm 53, tel. 030/881-8033, fax 030/881-7206, www.askanischer-hof.de, info@askanischer-hof.de).

BERLIN

Western Berlin

BERLIN

1 Hotel Askanischerhof
2 Hecker's Hotel
3 Hotel Astoria
4 Hotel Carmer 16
5 Hotel-Pension Funk
6 Hotel Bogota
7 Hotel Pension Alexandra
8 Pension Peters
9 Restaurant Marjellchen
10 Die Zwölf Apostel Restaurant
11 Zillemarkt Restaurant
12 To Genazvale Restaurant
13 Technical University Mensa
14 Ullrich Supermarkt
15 Schleusenkrug Beer Garden
16 A Trane Jazz Club
17 Quasimodo Live

$$ Hecker's Hotel is an ultra-modern four-star business hotel with 69 rooms and all the sterile Euro-comforts (Sb-€110, Db-€120, all rooms €200 during conferences but generally only €100 July–Aug, breakfast-€16, non-smoking rooms, elevator, parking-€12–18/day, between Savignyplatz and Ku'damm at Grolmanstrasse 35, tel. 030/88900, fax 030/889-0260, www.heckers-hotel.com, info@heckers-hotel.com).

$$ Hotel Astoria is a friendly three-star business-class hotel with 32 comfortably furnished rooms and affordable summer and weekend rates (Db-€94–118; check their website for deals; breakfast-€10 extra, non-smoking floors, elevator, Internet access, parking-€5/day, around corner from Bahnhof Zoo at Fasanenstrasse 2, tel. 030/312-4067, fax 030/312-5027, www.hotelastoria.de, info@hotelastoria.de).

$$ Hotel Carmer 16, with 30 bright and airy (if a bit dated) rooms, is both business-like and homey, and has an inviting lounge and charming balconies (Db-€95–160, ask for Rick Steves discount, extra person-€20, some rooms have balconies, elevator and a few stairs, Carmerstrasse 16, tel. 030/3110-0500, fax 030/3110-0510, www.hotel-carmer16.de, info@hotel-carmer16.de).

$$ Hotel-Pension Funk, the former home of a 1920s silent-movie star, is delightfully quirky. Kind manager Herr Michael Pfundt offers 14 elegant old rooms with rich Art Nouveau furnishings (S-€42, Ss-€60, Sb-€72, D-€72, Ds-€85, Db-€105, extra person-€23, cash preferred, a long block south of Ku'damm at Fasanenstrasse 69, tel. 030/882-7193, fax 030/883-3329, www.hotel-pensionfunk.de, berlin@hotel-pensionfunk.de).

$$ Hotel Bogota is a once-elegant old slumbermill renting 115 rooms in a sprawling maze of a building that used to house the Nazi Chamber of Culture. Today, pieces of the owner's modern-art collection lurk around every corner (S-€44, Ss-€72, Sb-€98, D-€69, Ds-€77, Db-€98, extra bed-€22, children under 12 free, elevator, 10-min walk from Savignyplatz at Schlüterstrasse 45, tel. 030/881-5001, fax 030/883-5887, www.bogota.de, info@hotel-bogota.de).

$$ Hotel Pension Alexandra has 11 pleasant rooms on a tree-lined street between Savignyplatz and Ku'damm. Expect the usual high ceilings and marble entryway found in these turn-of-the-century buildings, but with added touches—most rooms and the elegant breakfast room are decorated with original antique furniture (Ss-€69, Sb-€89, Ds-€95, Db-€105–120, lower prices off-season, extra bed-€35, Wielandstrasse 32, tel. 030/881-2107, fax 030/885-77818, www.hotelalexandra.de, info@hotelalexandra.de, Frau Kuhn and Mariane).

$ Pension Peters, run by a German–Swedish couple, is sunny and central, with a cheery breakfast room and a super-friendly staff that goes out of their way to help their guests. Decorated sleek Scandinavian, with each of its 37 rooms renovated, it's a good choice. Some of the ground-floor rooms are a bit dark—and cheaper for the inconvenience (Sb-€55, D-€51, Db-€78, extra bed-€10, family room-€83, these special prices offered only with this book in 2010—mention when you reserve, up to 2 kids under 13 free with 2 paying adults, cash preferred, Internet access, 10 yards off Savignyplatz at Kantstrasse 146, tel. 030/3150-3944, fax 030/312-3519, www.pension-peters-berlin.de, info@pension -peters-berlin.de, Annika and Christoph).

More Hostels

Berlin is known among budget travelers for its fun, hip hostels. Here are some good bets. The first one is south of Bahnhof Zoo, the next two are in Prenzlauer Berg, and the last is in Friedrichshain.

$ Studentenhotel Meininger 10 (€14/bed in 8-bed dorms, D-€48, includes sheets, no curfew, elevator, free parking, near City Hall on JFK Platz, Meininger Strasse 10, a 200-yard walk from U-Bahn: Rathaus Schöneberg, tel. 030/7871-7414, www .meininger-hostels.de).

$ Circus is a brightly colored, well-run place with 230 beds, a Dylanesque ambience, and a bar downstairs (€19/bed in 4- to 8-bed dorms, S-€40, Sb-€50, D-€56, Db-€70, T-€75, Q-€92, 2-person apartment with kitchen-€85, 4-person apartment-€140, breakfast-€5, no curfew, Internet access; Weinbergsweg 1a, U-Bahn: Rosenthaler Platz, tel. 030/2839-1433, www.circus-berlin.de, info@circus-berlin.de).

$ Mitte's Backpacker Hostel (€18/bed in 32-bed dorms, S-€32–36, D-€50–58, Db-€60–68, T-€66, Q-€92, sheets-€2.50, no breakfast, could be cleaner, no curfew, Internet access, English newspapers, laundry, bike rental, Chauseestrasse 102, U-Bahn: Zinnowitzer Strasse, tel. 030/2839-0965, fax 030/2839-0935, www.backpacker.de, reservation@backpacker.de).

$ Ostel is a fun retro-1970s-DDR apartment building that re-creates the lifestyle and interior design of a country relegated to the dustbin of history. All the furniture and room decorations have been meticulously collected and restored to their former socialist glory—only the psychedelic wallpaper is a replica. Guests buy ration vouchers (€3.50 per person) for breakfast in the attached restaurant. Kitschy and tacky, sure—but also clean and memorable (€9 for a bed in a 4- or 6-bed "Pioneer Camp" room, S-€33, Sb-€40, D-€54, Db-€61, 4-person apartments-€120, Wi-Fi, free bike rental, free parking, free collective use of the people's own barbeque, right behind Ostbahnhof station on the corner of Strasse der Pariser Kommune at Wriezener Karree 5, tel. 030/2576-8660, www.ostel.eu, contact@ostel.eu).

BERLIN

Eating in Berlin

Don't be too determined to eat "Berlin-style." The city is known only for its mildly spicy sausage. Still, there is a world of restaurants to choose from in this ever-changing city. Your best approach may be to select a neighborhood, rather than a particular restaurant.

Colorful pubs—called *Kneipen*—offer light, quick, and easy meals and the fizzy local beer, *Berliner Weiss*. Ask for it *mit Schuss* for a shot of fruity syrup in your suds. Germans—especially Berliners—consider their food old-school; when they go out to eat, they're not usually looking for the "traditional local fare" many travelers are after. Nouveau German is California cuisine with scant memories of wurst, kraut, and pumpernickel. In 2008, Berlin banned smoking in restaurants.

If the kraut is getting the wurst of you, try one of the many Turkish, Italian, and Balkan restaurants. Eat cheap at *Imbiss* snack stands, bakeries (sandwiches), and falafel/kebab counters. Train stations have grocery stores, as well as bright and modern fruit-and-sandwich bars.

In Eastern Berlin
Along Unter den Linden
These eateries are listed as you'll reach them as you walk along Unter den Linden from west to east (see map on page 531 for locations).

At the Opera House (Opernpalais): The **Operncafé** is perhaps the classiest coffee stop in Berlin, with a selection of 50—count 'em: 50—different decadent desserts (daily 8:00–24:00, across from university and war memorial at Unter den Linden 5, tel. 030/202-683). The **Schinkel Klause Biergarten** serves good €9–14 meals on its shady terrace with a view of the Unter den Linden scene when sunny, or in its cellar otherwise (daily 11:30–24:00. tel. 030/2026-8450).

Cheap Eats on Friedrichstrasse: **Bier's Curry und Spiesse**, under the tracks at the Friedrichstrasse S-Bahn stop, is a great, greasy, cheap, and generous place for an old-fashioned German hot dog. This is the local favorite near Unter den Linden for *Currywurst*. Experiment with variations (the *Flieschspiess* is excellent) and sauces—and don't hold the *Zwiebeln* (fried onions). While you'll likely munch standing at a counter, the people-watching is great.

Near the Pergamon Museum: Georgenstrasse, a block behind the Pergamon Museum and under the S-Bahn tracks, is lined with fun eateries filling the arcade of the train trestle—close to the sightseeing action but in business mainly for students from nearby Humboldt University. **Deponie3** is a trendy Berlin *Kneipe* usually filled with students. Garden seating in the back is nice if you don't mind the noise of the S-Bahn passing directly above you. The interior is a cozy, wooden wonderland of a bar with several inviting spaces. They serve basic sandwiches, salads, traditional Berlin dishes, and hearty daily specials (€3–7 breakfasts, €5–11 lunches and dinners, open daily from 9:00, sometimes live music, Georgenstrasse 5, tel. 030/2016-5740). A branch of **Die Zwölf Apostel** is nearby (daily until 24:00, described earlier, under "Near Savignyplatz").

In the Heart of Old Berlin's Nikolai Quarter: The *Nikolaiviertel* marks the original medieval settlement of Cölln, which would eventually become Berlin. The area was destroyed during the war, but rebuilt for Berlin's 750th birthday in 1987. The whole area has a cute, cobbled, and characteristic old town...Middle Ages meets Socialist Realism. Today, the district is pretty soulless by day, but is a popular restaurant zone at night. **Bräuhaus Georgbrau** is a thriving beer hall serving homemade suds on a picturesque courtyard overlooking the Spree River. Eat in the lively and woody but mod-feeling interior, or outdoors with fun riverside seating—thriving with German tourists. It's a good place to try one of the few typical Berlin dishes: *Eisbein* (boiled ham hock) with sauerkraut and mashed peas with bacon (€9.99 with a beer and schnapps). The statue of St. George once stood in the courtyard of Berlin's old castle—until the Nazis deemed it too decadent and not "German" enough, and removed it (€9–13 plates, three-foot-long sampler board with a dozen small glasses of beer, daily 10:00–24:00, 2 blocks south of Berlin Cathedral and across the river at Spreeufer 4, tel. 030/242-4244).

South of Unter den Linden, near Gendarmenmarkt

The twin churches of Gendarmenmarkt seem to be surrounded by people in love with food. The lunch and dinner scene is thriving with upscale restaurants serving good cuisine at highly competitive prices to local professionals (see map on page 531 for locations). If in need of a quick-yet-classy lunch, stroll around the square and along Charlottenstrasse.

Lutter & Wegner Restaurant is well-known for its Austrian cuisine (*Schnitzel* and *Sauerbraten*) and popular with businesspeople. It's dressy, with fun sidewalk seating or a dark and elegant interior (two-course lunch with wine—€15 Mon–Fri, €20 Sat–Sun; €34 fixed-price gourmet dinner, daily 11:00–24:00, Charlottenstrasse 56, tel. 030/202-9540). They have a second location at Oranienburger Strasse 52, near the New Synagogue.

Maredo Argentine Steak Restaurant, a family-friendly chain restaurant, is generally a good value with a fine €6.20 salad bar that can make a healthy and cheap meal (behind French Cathedral at Gendarmenmarkt, at Charlottenstrasse 57, tel. 030/2094-5230).

Galeries Lafayette Food Circus is a French festival of fun eateries in the basement of the landmark department store (Mon–Sat 10:00–20:00, closed Sun, U-Bahn: Französische Strasse, tel. 030/209-480).

Turkish and Bavarian Cuisine at Hackescher Markt

Hasir Turkish Restaurant is your chance to dine with candles, hardwood floors, and happy Berliners as snappy Turkish waiters bring plates piled high with meaty Anatolian specialties. As Berlin is the world's largest Turkish city outside of Asia Minor, it's no wonder you can find some good Turkish restaurants here. But while most locals think of Turkish food as fast and cheap, this is a dining experience. The restaurant, in a courtyard next to the Hackesche Höfe shopping complex (see page 548), offers indoor and outdoor tables filled with an enthusiastic local crowd (€14 plates, huge and splittable portions, daily from 11:30 until late, a block from the Hackescher Markt S-Bahn station at Oranienburger Strasse 4, tel. 030/2804-1616).

Weihenstephaner Bavarian Restaurant serves upmarket Bavarian traditional food for around €15 a plate, offers an atmospheric cellar and a busy people-watching street-side terrace, and, of course, has excellent beer (daily 11:00–24:00, Neue Promenade 5 at Hackescher Markt, tel. 030/2576-2871).

In Prenzlauer Berg

Prenzlauer Berg is packed with fine restaurants—German, ethnic, and everything in between. (For more on this district, see page 549, and for restaurant locations, see page 567.) Before making a choice, I'd spend half an hour strolling and browsing through this bohemian wonderland of creative eateries. **Kollwitzplatz** is an especially good area to prowl for dinner—this square, home of the DDR student resistance in 1980s, is now trendy and upscale. With its leafy playground park in the center, it's a good place for upmarket restaurants. Walk the square and choose. Just about every option offers sidewalk seats in the summer—these are great on a balmy evening. Nearby **Helmholtzplatz** (especially Lychener Strasse) is a somewhat younger, hipper, and edgier place to eat and drink.

Gugelhof, right on Kollwitzplatz, is the Prenzlauer Berg stop for visiting dignitaries. It's an institution famous for its Alsatian German cuisine. You'll enjoy French quality with German proportions. It's highly regarded with a boisterous and enthusiastic local crowd filling its minimalist yet classy interior (€25 three-course meal, daily from 16:00, reservations required during peak times, where Knaackstrasse meets Kollwitzplatz, tel. 030/442-9229).

Metzer Eck is a time-warp *Kneipe* with a family tradition dating to 1913 and a cozy charm. It serves cheap basic typical

Berlin food with Czech Budvar beer on tap (€5–7 meals, daily from 18:00, Metzer Strasse 33, on the corner of Metzer Strasse and Strassburger Strasse, tel. 030/442-7656).

Prater Biergarten offers two great eating opportunities: a rustic restaurant indoors and a mellow, shady, super-cheap, and family-friendly beer garden outdoors—each proudly pouring Prater's own microbrew. In the beer garden—Berlin's oldest—you step up to the counter and order (simple €3–5 plates and an intriguing selection of beer munchies). The restaurant serves serious traditional *Biergarten* cuisine and good salads (€8–14 plates, Mon–Sat 18:00–24:00, Sun 12:00–24:00, cash only, Kastanienallee 7, tel. 030/448-5688).

Zum Schusterjungen Speisegaststätte ("The Cobbler's Apprentice") is a classic old-school, German-with-attitude eatery that retains its circa-1986 DDR decor. Famous for its schnitzel and filling €7–8 meals, it's a no-frills place with quality ingredients and a strong local following. It serves the eating needs of those Berliners lamenting the disappearance of solid traditional German cooking amid the flood of ethnic eateries (small 40-seat dining hall, daily 11:00–24:00, corner of Lychener Strasse and Danziger Strasse 9, tel. 030/442-7654).

La Bodeguita del Medio Cuban Bar Restaurant is purely fun-loving Cuba—Christmas lights, graffiti-caked walls, Che Guevara posters, animated staff, and an ambience that makes you want to dance. Come early to eat or late to drink. This restaurant has been here for more than a decade—and in fast-changing Prenzlauer Berg, that's an eternity. Cuban ribs and salad for €7 is a hit. Main dishes are big enough to split. There's live Cuban music on Wednesdays, and you can puff a Cuban cigar any day (€4–10 tapas, struggle with a menu in German and Spanish, daily 17:00–24:00, 1 block from U-Bahn: Eberswalder Strasse at Lychener Strasse 6, tel. 030/4171-4276).

Konnopke's Imbiss, a super-cheap German-style sausage stand, has been a Berlin institution for over 70 years—it was family-owned even during DDR times. Berliners say Konnopke's cooks up the city's best *Currywurst* (grilled bratwurst with curry-infused ketchup, €2). There are a few tables under a nearby tent for sit-down wurst-munching (Mon–Sat 6:00–20:00, closed Sun; Kastanienallee dead-ends at the elevated train tracks, and under them you'll find Konnopke's at Schönhauser Allee 44A). Don't be fooled by the Currystation at the foot of the stairs coming out of the station; Konnopke's is actually across the street, under the tracks.

For Dessert: **Kauf Dich Glücklich** makes a great capper to a Prenzlauer Berg dinner. It serves an enticing array of sweet Belgian waffles and ice cream (best pistachio ice cream in Berlin) in a candy-sprinkled, bohemian, retro setting under WWII bullet holes on a great Prenzlauer Berg street (daily until late, indoor and outdoor seating, Oderberger Strasse 44—it's the only un-renovated building on the street, tel. 030/4435-2182).

In Western Berlin
Near Savignyplatz

Many good restaurants are on or within 100 yards of Savignyplatz, near my recommended western Berlin hotels (see map on page 570 for locations). Take a walk and survey these; continue your stroll along Bleibtreustrasse to discover many trendier, more creative little eateries.

Restaurant Marjellchen is a trip to East Prussia. Dine in a soft, jazzy elegance in one of two six-table rooms. While it doesn't have to be expensive (€25 for two courses), plan to go the whole nine yards here, as this can be a great Prussian experience with caring service. The menu is inviting, and all the recipes were brought to Berlin by the owner's mother after being expelled from East Prussia. The Königsberg meatballs are the specialty. Reservations are smart (daily 17:00–23:30, family-run, Mommsenstrasse 9, tel. 030/883-2676).

Dicke Wirtin is a pub with traditional old-Berlin *Kneipe* atmosphere, six good beers on tap, and good, solid home cooking at reasonable prices—such as their famously cheap *Gulaschsuppe* (€3.40). Their interior is fun and pubby; their streetside tables are also inviting (€5 daily specials, open daily from 12:00 with dinner served from 18:00, just off Savignyplatz at Carmerstrasse 9, tel. 030/312-4952).

Die Zwölf Apostel ("The Twelve Apostles") is trendy for good Italian food. Choose between indoors with candlelit ambience, outdoors on a sun-dappled patio, or overlooking the people-parade on its pedestrian street. A dressy local crowd packs this restaurant for excellent €10 pizzas and €15–30 meals (daily 7:00–1:00 in the morning, cash only, immediately across from Savignyplatz S-Bahn entrance, Bleibtreustrasse 49, tel. 030/312-1433).

Zillemarkt Restaurant, which feels like an old-time Berlin *Biergarten,* serves traditional Berlin specialties in the garden or in the rustic candlelit interior. Their *Berliner Allerlei* is a fun way to sample a bit of nearly everything (cabbage, pork, sausage, potatoes and more for a minimum of two people...but it can feed up to five). They have their own microbrew (€10 meals, daily 12:00–24:00, near the S-Bahn tracks at Bleibtreustrasse 48A, tel. 030/881-7040).

Genazvale ("Best Friends") serves traditional fare from the Republic of Georgia, and is popular with Charlottenburg's immigrant Russian community. Sample some Georgian wines— virtually impossible to find in North America—and try their warm *catchapuri* (cheese bread) or a delicious plate of *chinkali* (cheese dumplings). The best way to enjoy Georgian food is to order several appetizers and split a main dish, which is usually grilled meat or stew (€8–15 main dishes, daily 15:00–23:00, live music and dancing on Georgian holidays, on the corner of Kantstrasse at Windscheidstrasse 14, tel. 030/4508-6026).

Technical University Mensa, a student cafeteria with impossibly cheap prices, puts you in a modern university scene with fine food and good indoor or streetside seating (€3–5 meals, Mon–Fri 11:00–15:30, closed Sat–Sun, general public entirely welcome but pay the highest of the three prices, cheap coffee bar downstairs with Internet access, just north of Uhlandstrasse at Hardenbergstrasse 34).

Ullrich Supermarkt is the neighborhood grocery store (Mon–Sat 9:00–22:00, Sun 11:00–22:00, Kantstrasse 7, under the tracks near Bahnhof Zoo). There's plenty of fast food near Bahnhof Zoo and on Ku'damm.

Near Bahnhof Zoo

Schleusenkrug beer garden is hidden in the park between the Bahnhof Zoo and Tiergarten stations. Choose from an ever-changing self-service menu of huge salads, pasta, and some German dishes. English breakfast is served until 15:00 (€7–12 plates, €3–5 grill snacks, daily 10:00–24:00, Müller-Breslau-Strasse; standing in front of Bahnhof Zoo, turn left and follow the path into the park between the zoo and train tracks; tel. 030/313-9909).

Self-Service Cafeterias: The top floor of the famous department store, **KaDeWe,** holds the Winter Garden Buffet view cafeteria, and its sixth-floor deli/food department is a picnicker's nirvana. Its arterials are clogged with more than 1,000 kinds of sausage and 1,500 types of cheese (Mon–Fri 10:00–20:00, Sat 9:30–20:00, closed Sun, U-Bahn: Wittenbergplatz). **Wertheim** department store, a half-block from Kaiser Wilhelm Memorial Church, has cheap food counters in the basement and a city view from its self-service cafeteria, Le Buffet, located up six banks of escalators (Mon–Sat 9:30–20:00, closed Sun, U-Bahn: Kurfürstendamm). **Marche,** a chain that's popped up in big cities all over Germany, is another inexpensive self-service cafeteria within a half-block of Kaiser Wilhelm Memorial Church (Mon–Thu 8:00–22:00, Fri–Sat 8:00–24:00, Sun 10:00–22:00, plenty of salads, fruit, made-to-order omelets, Ku'damm 14, tel. 030/882-7578).

Berlin Connections

Trains

Berlin used to have several major train stations. But now that the Hauptbahnhof has emerged as the single, massive central station, all the others have wilted into glorified subway stations. Virtually every long-distance train passes through the Hauptbahnhof—

ignore the other stations.

EurAide is an agent of the German Railroad that sells reservations for high-speed and overnight trains, with staff that can answer your travel questions in English (located in the Hauptbahnhof; see "Arrival in Berlin," on page 508).

From Berlin by Train to: Dresden (every 2 hrs, more with a transfer in Leipzig, 2.25 hrs), **Frankfurt** (hourly, 4 hrs), **Bacharach** (hourly, 6–7 hrs, 1–3 changes), **Rothenburg** (hourly, 5–6 hrs, 2 changes), **Würzburg** (hourly, 4 hrs, change in Fulda or Hannover), **Nürnberg** (hourly, 4.5 hrs), **Munich** (1–2/hr, 6–6.75 hrs, every 2 hrs direct, otherwise a change in Göttingen), **Köln** (hourly, 4.75 hrs), **Amsterdam** (6/day direct to Amsterdam Zuid, 6.5 hrs), **Budapest** (3/day, 13 hrs; these go via Czech Republic and Slovakia, for an overnight you need to go to Vienna and then change), **Copenhagen** (5/day, 6.5 hrs, reservation required, change in Hamburg; also consider the direct overnight train-plus-ferry route to Malmö, Sweden, which is just 20 min from Copenhagen—covered by a railpass that includes Germany or Sweden), **London** (5/day, 10–11.5 hrs, 2 changes—but you're better off flying cheap on easyJet or Air Berlin, even if you have a railpass), **Paris** (5/day, 8–9 hrs, 1 change in Köln—via Belgium—or in Mannheim, 1 direct 12-hr night train), **Zürich** (hourly, 8.5 hrs, 1 direct 12-hr night train), **Prague** (6/day, 4.5–5 hrs, no overnight trains), **Warsaw** (3/day, 6 hrs, 1 night train; reservations required on all Warsaw-bound trains), **Kraków** (1/day direct, 2 more with transfer in Warsaw, 10 hrs), **Vienna** (8/day, most with 1 change, 9.5 hrs, some via Czech Republic; the Berlin–Vienna via Passau train avoids Czech Republic—nightly at 20:55—as do connections with a change in Nürnberg or Munich). It's wise but not required to reserve in advance for trains to or from Amsterdam or Prague. Train info: tel. 0180-599-6633 (€0.14/min). Before buying a ticket for any long train ride from Berlin (over 7 hours), consider taking a cheap flight instead (buy it well in advance to get a super fare).

There are **night trains** from Berlin to these cities: Munich, Frankfurt, Köln, Paris, Vienna, Warsaw, Malmö (Sweden, near Copenhagen), Basel, and Zürich. There are no night trains from Berlin to anywhere in Italy or Spain. A *Liegeplatz,* or *couchette* berth (€13–36), is a great deal; inquire at EurAide at the Hauptbahnhof for details. Beds generally cost the same whether you have a first- or second-class ticket or railpass. Trains are often full, so reserve your *couchette* a few days in advance from any travel agency or major train station in Europe.

Berlin's Two Airports

Tegel Airport handles most flights from the United States and Western Europe (4 miles from center, no subway trains, catch the faster bus #X9 to Bahnhof Zoo, or bus #109 to Ku'damm and Bahnhof Zoo for €2.10; bus #TXL goes between Tegel Airport, the Hauptbahnhof, and Alexanderplatz in eastern Berlin; taxi from Tegel Airport costs €15 to Bahnhof Zoo, €25 to Alexanderplatz; taxis from Tegel levy a €0.50 surcharge).

Flights from the east and discount airlines usually arrive at **Schönefeld Airport** (12.5 miles from center). It's just a three-minute walk to the train station, where you catch a regional express train into the city (ignore the S-Bahn, as there are no direct S-Bahn trains to the city center). The Airport Express RE and RB trains go direct to Ostbahnhof, Alexanderplatz, Friedrichstrasse, Hauptbahnhof, and Bahnhof Zoo (€2.60, every 30 min, take trains in the direction of Nauen or Dessau, railpass valid). A taxi to the city center costs about €35.

The central toll telephone number for both airports is 01805-000-186. For British Air, toll tel. 01805-266-522; Delta, toll tel. 01803-337-880; SAS, toll tel. 01805-117-002; Lufthansa, toll tel. 01803-803-803.

Berlin, the New Discount Airline Hub: Berlin's Schönefeld Airport is now the continental European hub for discount airlines such as easyJet (with lots of flights to Spain, Italy, Eastern Europe, the Baltics, and more—book long in advance to get the incredible €30-and-less fares, www.easyjet.com). Ryanair (www.ryanair.com) and German Wings (www.germanwings.com) are also making the London–Berlin trip (and other routes) dirt-cheap, so consider this option before booking an overnight train. Consequently, British visitors to the city are now outnumbered only by Americans. But not every budget line uses Schönefeld; Air Berlin flies out of Tegel (www.airberlin.com). For more on cheap flights, see page 617.

Warnemünde Cruise Ship Port

The closest cruise ship terminal to Berlin is 150 miles north, at Warnemünde on the Baltic Sea. Train connections run about hourly between the dock (Warnemünde Werft) and the Berlin train station (Hauptbahnhof); the trip takes about three hours. To get to Berlin, board the local S-Bahn at the dock (direction Rostock Hauptbahnhof) and change at the Rostock train station. If you are leaving Berlin for the cruise ship terminal, take the train to Rostock and transfer to the S-Bahn (direction Warnemünde) to get to your ship. While you could buy tickets in advance, you shouldn't reserve if you're unsure of your boat's arrival time. It's easy to buy tickets at the station with either euros or a credit card. For more about German rail tickets and passes, see www.rick steves.com/rail.

BERLIN

GERMAN HISTORY

There was no Germany before 1871, but the cultural heritage of the German-speaking people (of modern-day Germany and Austria) stretches back 2,000 years.

Romans (A.D. 1-500)

German history begins in A.D. 9, when Roman troops were ambushed and driven back by the German chief Arminius. For the next 250 years, the Rhine and Danube rivers marked the border between civilized Roman Europe (to the southwest) and "barbarian" German lands (northeast). While the rest of Western Europe's future would be Roman, Christian, and Latin, Germany would follow its own pagan, *Deutsch*-speaking path.

Rome finally fell to the Germanic chief Theodoric the Great (a.k.a. Dietrich of Bern, A.D. 476). After that, Germanic Franks controlled northern Europe, ruling a mixed population of Romanized Christians and tree-worshipping pagans.

Charlemagne and the Franks (A.D. 500-1000)

For Christmas in A.D. 800, the pope gave Charlemagne the title of Holy Roman Emperor. Charlemagne, the king of the Franks, was the first of many German kings to be called *Kaiser* ("emperor," from "Caesar") over the next thousand years. Allied with the pope, Charlemagne ruled an empire that included Germany, Austria, France, the Low Countries, and northern Italy.

Charlemagne (Karl der Grosse, or Charles the Great, r. 768–814) stood a head taller than his subjects, and his foot became a standard measurement. The stuff of legend, Charles the Great had five wives and four concubines, producing descendants with names like Charles the Bald, Louis the Pious, and Henry the Quarrelsome. After Charlemagne died of pneumonia (814),

Why We Call Deutschland "Germany"

Our English name "Germany" comes from the Latin *Germania*, the Roman name for the lands north of the Alps where "barbarian" tribes lived. The French and Spanish call it *Allemagne* and *Alemania*, respectively, after the Alemanni tribe. Italians call the country *Germania*, but in Italy the German language is known as *tedesco*. Completely confused by all this, the Slavic peoples of Eastern Europe simply throw up their hands and call Germany *Německo* (Czech), *Niemcy* (Polish), or other variations of a word that basically means "people who can't speak right." The Hungarians borrowed this word from the Slavs and call anything German *német*.

To Germans, their country is *Deutschland*, their language is *Deutsch*, and they themselves are *Deutsche*. A few hundred years ago, this word was spelled *Teutsch* (later, the "t" changed to a "d"). The English word Teutonic, the Italian *tedesco*, and the Scandinavian *tysk* all come from this earlier form. *Alles klar?*

his united empire did not pass directly to his oldest son but was divided into (what would become) Germany, France, and the lands in between (Treaty of Verdun, 843).

The Holy Roman Empire (1000–1500)

Chaotic medieval Germany was made up of more than 300 small, quarreling dukedoms ruled by the Holy Roman Emperor. The title was pretty bogus, implying that the German king ruled the same huge European empire as the ancient Romans. In fact, he was "Holy" because he was blessed by the Church, "Roman" to recall ancient grandeur, and the figurehead "Emperor" of only a scattered kingdom.

Germany's emperors had less hands-on power than other kings around Europe. Because of the custom of electing emperors by nobles and archbishops, rather than bestowing the title through inheritance, they couldn't pass the crown father to son. This system gave nobles great power, and the peasants huddled close to their local noble's castle for protection from attack by the noble next door. There were no empire-wide taxes and no national capital.

When Emperor Henry IV (r. 1056–1106) tried to assert his power by appointing bishops, he was slapped down by the nobles, and forced to repent to the pope by standing barefoot in the alpine snow for three days at Canossa (in northern Italy, 1077).

Emperor Frederick I Barbarossa (1152–1190), blue-eyed and red-bearded (hence *barba rossa*), gained an international reputation as a valiant knight, gentleman, bon vivant, and lover of poetry and women. Still, his great victories were away in Italy and Asia (on the Third Crusade, where he drowned in a river), while back home nobles wielded real power.

This was the era of Germany's troubadours *(Meistersingers)*, who traveled from castle to castle singing love songs *(Minnesang)* and telling the epic tales of chivalrous knights (Tristan and Isolde, Parzival, and the Nibelungen) that would later inspire German nationalism and Wagnerian operas.

While France, England, and Spain were centralizing power around a single ruling family to create modern nation-states, Germany remained a decentralized, backward, feudal battle-ground.

Medieval Growth

Nevertheless, Germany was located at the center of Europe, and trading towns prospered. Several northern towns (especially Hamburg and Lübeck) banded together into the Hanseatic League, promoting open trade around the Baltic Sea. To curry favor at election time, emperors granted powers and privileges to certain towns, designated Free Imperial Cities. Some towns, such as Köln, Mainz, Dresden, and Trier, held higher status than many nobles, as hosts of one of the seven Electors of the emperor.

Textiles, mining, and the colonizing of eastern lands made Germany an economic powerhouse with a thriving middle class. In towns, middle-class folks (burghers), not the local aristocrats, began running things. In about 1450, Johann Gutenberg of Mainz invented moveable type for printing, a creation that would allow the export of a new commodity: ideas.

Religious Struggles and the Thirty Years' War (1500–1700)

Martin Luther—German monk, fiery orator, and religious whistle-blower—sparked a century of European wars by speaking out against the Catholic Church (see sidebar).

Luther's protests ("Protestantism") threw Germany into a century of turmoil, as each local prince took sides between Catholics and Protestants. In the 1525 Peasant Revolt, peasants attacked their feudal masters with hoes and pitchforks, fighting for more food, political say-so, and respect. The revolt was brutally put down.

The Holy Roman Emperor, Charles V (r. 1519–1556), sided with the pope. Charles was the most powerful man in Europe, having inherited an empire that included Germany and Austria, plus the Low Countries, much of Italy, Spain, and Spain's New World possessions. But many local German nobles took the opportunity to go Protestant—some for religious reasons, but also to seize Church assets and powers.

Martin Luther
(1483–1546)

One of the most influential Germans of all time was Martin Luther, who defied the Catholic Church and forever divided its congregation. Luther was born on November 10, 1483, in Eisleben, south of Berlin. His dad owned a copper smelter, affording Luther a middle-class upbringing—a rarity in the medieval hierarchy of nobles, clergy, and peasants. At the University of Erfurt, Luther earned a liberal-arts degree, entered law school, and earned himself two nicknames—"the philosopher" for his wide-ranging mind, and "the king of hops" for his lifelong love affair with beer.

In 1505, while riding back to school after a trip home, a bolt of lightning knocked him to the ground. Terrified, he vowed to become a monk. By age 23, he was ordained a priest in Erfurt Cathedral, and was on the fast track to become a professor of theology.

Luther soon got a teaching job at a brand-new university in Wittenberg—the progressive city that would be his home for the rest of his life. Luther taught theology and mingled with the town's brightest thinkers and artists; he also spent hours alone in his cell (living quarters) in the Augustinian monastery. Consumed with the notion that he was a sinner, he devoured the Bible, looking for an answer and finding it in Paul's letter to the Romans. Luther realized that God makes sinners righteous through their faith in Jesus Christ, not by earning it through good deeds. As this concept of grace took hold, Luther said, "I felt myself to have been born again."

Energized, he began a series of Bible lectures at Wittenberg's twin-towered St. Mary's City Church. The pews were packed as Luther quoted passages directly from the Bible. Speaker and audience alike began to see discrepancies between what the Bible said and what the Church was doing.

Coincidentally, a representative of the pope arrived in Wittenberg to raise money by selling letters of indulgence promising "full forgiveness for all sins." Luther was outraged at the idea that God's grace could be bought, and thought the subject should be debated openly. On October 31, 1517, Luther approached Wittenberg's Castle Church and nailed 95 "theses"—or topics for discussion—to the door, which was then used as a public bulletin board. The theses questioned indulgences and other Church practices and beliefs. Luther's propositions were printed and circulated from Wittenberg's newfangled presses (some of Europe's first). It was the talk of Germany, and Luther became famous—or infamous—almost overnight.

The pope ordered Luther's writings to be burned and sent a letter excommunicating the rebellious monk. Luther was branded a heretic and ordered to Rome to face charges, but he refused to go. Finally, the most powerful man in Europe, Emperor Charles V, stepped in to arbitrate, calling an Imperial Diet (congress) at Worms (1521). Luther made a triumphal entry into Worms, greeted by cheering crowds.

The Diet convened, and Luther took his place in the center of the large hall, standing next to a stack of his books. Inquisitors grilled him while the ultra-Catholic Charles looked on from his throne. Luther refused to disavow his beliefs or books. "Here I stand," he told the assembly, "I can do no other. So help me God. Amen."

Given a few days to reconsider, Luther disappeared. Rumor was he was kidnapped, but in fact he'd escaped to safety in Wartburg Castle, overlooking his teenage home of Eisenach. Protected by a German prince opposed to Rome, he spent a year fighting depression and translating the New Testament from Greek into German. This "German King James Version" was revolutionary, bringing the Bible to the masses and shaping the modern German language. Finally, wearing a fake beard and disguised as a knight, Luther returned home to Wittenberg.

In 1525, 41-year-old Luther met 25-year-old Katherine von Bora, and within months, the ex-monk married the ex-nun in St. Mary's City Church. He and "Katie" moved from the monastery to their own house. Martin and Katherine had six children and raised four orphans.

Though living in Wittenberg under the protection of German princes, Luther traveled, spreading the Protestant message. In 1529, at Marburg Castle just north of Frankfurt, he attended a summit of leading Protestants to try and forge an alliance against Catholicism (1529). They agreed on everything except a single theological point: whether Christ was present in the wine and bread of Communion in a physical sense (according to Luther) or symbolic sense (per Ulrich Zwingli). The disagreement doomed the Protestant movement to splinter into dozens of sects.

In his 50s, Luther's health declined and he grew bitter, a fact made clear in such writings as "Against the Papacy at Rome Founded by the Devil" and "Of the Jews and Their Lies." He died on February 18, 1546, and was buried in Wittenberg. To this day, pilgrims bring flowers.

The 1555 Peace of Augsburg allowed each local noble to decide the religion of his realm. In general, the northern lands became Protestant, while the south (today's Bavaria, along with Austria) remained Catholic.

Unresolved religious and political differences eventually expanded into the Thirty Years' War (1618–1648). This Europe-wide war, fought mainly on German soil, involved Denmark, Sweden, France, and Bohemia (in today's Czech Republic), among others. It was one of history's bloodiest wars, fueled by religious extremism and political opportunism, and fought by armies of brutal mercenaries who worked on commission, and were paid in loot and pillage.

By the war's end (Treaty of Westphalia, 1648), a third of all Germans had died, France was the rising European power, and the Holy Roman Empire was a medieval mess of scattered feudal states. In 1689, France's Louis XIV swept down the Rhine, gutting and leveling its once-great castles, and Germany ceased to be a major player in European politics until the modern era.

Austria and Prussia (1700s)

The German-speaking lands now consisted of three "Germanys": Austria in the south, Prussia in the north, and the rest in between.

Prussia—originally colonized by celibate ex-Crusaders called Teutonic Knights—was forged into a unified state by two strong kings. Frederick I (the "King Sergeant," r. 1701–1713) built a modern state around a highly disciplined army, a centralized government, and national pride. His grandson, Frederick II "The Great" (r. 1740–1786), added French culture and worldliness, preparing militaristic Prussia to enter the world stage. A well-read, flute-playing lover of the arts and liberal ideals, Frederick also ruled with an iron fist—the very model of the "enlightened despot."

Meanwhile, Austria thrived under the laid-back rule of the Habsburg family. Habsburgs gained power in Europe by marrying it. They acquired the Netherlands, Spain, Bohemia, and Hungary that way—a strategy that didn't work so well for Marie-Antoinette, who wed the king of France.

In the 1700s, the Germanic lands became a cultural power-house, producing musicians (Bach, Haydn, Mozart, Beethoven), writers (Goethe, Schiller), and thinkers (Kant, Leibniz). But politically, feudal Germany was no match for the modern powers.

After the French Revolution (1789), Napoleon swept through Germany with his armies, deposing feudal lords, confiscating church lands, and forcing the emperor to hand over his crown (1806). After a thousand years, the Holy Roman Empire (or *Reich*) was dead.

Germany Before Unification

German Unification (1800s)

Napoleon's invasion helped unify the German-speaking peoples by rallying them against a common foreign enemy. After Napoleon's defeat, the Congress of Vienna (1815), presided over by the Austrian Prince Metternich, realigned Europe's borders. The idea of unifying the three Germanic nations—Prussia, Austria, and the German Confederation, a loose collection of small states in between—began to grow. By mid-century most German-speaking people favored forming a modern nation-state. The only question was whether the confederation would be under Prussian or Austrian dominance.

Economically, Germany was becoming increasingly modern, with a unified trade organization (1834), railroads (1835), mechanical-engineering prowess, and factories booming on a surplus of labor.

Energetic Prussia took the lead in unifying the country. Otto von Bismarck (served 1862–1890), the strong minister of Prussia's weak king, used cunning politics to engineer a unified Germany under Prussian dominance. First, he started a war with Austria,

GERMAN HISTORY

Castle Architecture

A castle is a fortified residence for a medieval noble. Castles come in all shapes and sizes, but knowing a few general terms will help you understand them.

The Keep (or Donjon): A high, strong stone tower in the center of the castle complex that was the lord's home and refuge of last resort.

Great Hall: The largest room in the castle, serving as throne room, conference center, and dining hall.

The Yard (or Bailey or Ward): An open courtyard inside the castle walls.

Loopholes: Narrow slits in the walls (also called embrasures, arrow slits, or arrow loops) through which soldiers could shoot arrows at the enemy.

Towers: Tall structures serving as lookouts, chapels, living quarters, or the dungeon. Towers could be square or round, with either crenellated tops or conical roofs.

Turret: A small lookout tower projecting up from the top of the wall.

Moat: A ditch encircling the wall, often filled with water.

Wall Walk (or Allure): A pathway atop the wall where guards could patrol and where soldiers stood to fire at the enemy.

Parapet: Outer railing of the wall walk.

Crenellation: A gap-toothed pattern of stones atop the parapet.

Hoardings (or Gallery or Brattice): Wooden huts built onto the upper parts of the stone walls. They served as watch towers, living quarters, and fighting platforms.

Machicolation: A stone ledge jutting out from the wall, fitted with holes in the bottom. If the enemy was scaling the walls, soldiers could drop rocks or boiling oil down through the holes and onto the enemy below.

Barbican: A fortified gatehouse, sometimes a stand-alone building located outside the main walls.

Drawbridge: A bridge that could be raised or lowered, using counterweights or a chain-and-winch.

Portcullis: A heavy iron grille that could be lowered across the entrance.

Postern Gate: A small, unfortified side or rear entrance used during peacetime. In wartime, it became a "sally-port" used to launch surprise attacks, or as an escape route.

Church Architecture

History comes to life when you visit a medieval church. Knowing a few simple terms will enrich your experience. Note that not every church will have every feature, and a "cathedral" isn't a type of church architecture, but rather a governing center for a local bishop.

Aisles: The long, generally low-ceilinged arcades that flank the nave.

Altar: The raised area with a ceremonial table (often adorned with candles or a crucifix), where the priest prepares and serves the bread and wine for Communion.

Apse: The space beyond the altar, generally bordered with small chapels.

Choir: A cozy area, often screened off, located within the church nave and near the high altar where services are sung in a more intimate setting.

Cloister: A square-shaped series of hallways surrounding an open-air courtyard, traditionally where monks and nuns got fresh air.

Facade: The outer wall of the church's main (west) entrance, viewable from outside and generally highly decorated.

Groin Vault: An arched ceiling formed where two equal barrel vaults meet at right angles. Less common usage: term for a medieval jock strap.

Narthex: The area (portico or foyer) between the main entry and the nave.

Nave: The long, central section of the church (running west to east, from the entrance to the altar) where the congregation stood through the service.

Transept: The north–south part of the church, which crosses (perpendicularly) the east–west nave. In a traditional Latin cross-shaped floor plan, the transept forms the "arms" of the cross.

West Portal: The main entry to the church (on the west end, opposite the main altar).

Germany During World War II
(1939-1945)

1939 Soldiers singing *"Muss ich denn, Muss ich denn"* ("I must leave, I must leave my happy home") march off to war. On September 1, Germany invades Poland, sparking World War II. Germany, Italy, and Japan (the Axis) would eventually square off against the Allies—Britain, France, the United States, and the Soviet Union.

1940 The Nazi *Blitzkrieg* (lightning war) quickly sweeps through Denmark, Norway, the Low Countries, France, Yugoslavia, and Greece. With fellow fascists ruling Italy (Mussolini), Spain (Franco), and Portugal (Salazar), all of the Continent is now dominated by fascists, creating a "fortress Europe."

1941 Hitler invades his former ally, the USSR. Bombastic victory parades in Berlin celebrate the triumph of the Aryan race over the lesser peoples of the world.

1942 Allied bombs begin falling on German cities. That autumn and winter, German families receive death notices from the horrific Battle of Stalingrad. On the worst days, 50,000 men died (by comparison, America lost 58,000 total in Vietnam). Back home, Nazi officials begin their plan for the "final solution to the Jewish problem"— systematic execution of Europe's Jews in specially built death camps.

ensuring that any united Germany would be under Prussian control. (The Austrian Empire would remain a separate country.) Next, Bismarck provoked a war with France (Franco-Prussian War, 1870–1871). This action united Prussia and the German Confederation against their common enemy, France.

Fueled by hysterical patriotism, German armies swept through France and, in the Hall of Mirrors at Versailles, crowned Prussia's Wilhelm I as Emperor *(Kaiser)* of a new German Empire uniting Prussia and the German Confederation (but excluding Austria). This Second Reich (1871–1918) featured elements of democracy (an elected *Reichstag*, or parliament), offset by a strong military and an emperor with veto powers.

A united and resurgent Germany was suddenly flexing its muscles in European politics. With strong industry, war spoils, overseas colonies, and a large and disciplined military, it sought its rightful place in the sun. *Volk* art flourished (Wagner's operas, Nietzsche's essays), fueled by nationalist fervor, reviving medieval German myths and Nordic gods. The rest of Europe saw Germany's rapid rise and began arming themselves to the teeth.

1943 Germany has to fight a two-front war: against tenacious Soviets on the chilly Eastern Front, and against Brits and Yanks advancing north through Italy on the Western Front. Germany's industrial output tries desperately to keep up with the Allies'. The average German suffers through shortages, rationing, and frequent trips to the bomb shelter.

1944 Hitler's no-surrender policy is increasingly unpopular, and he narrowly survives being assassinated by a bomb planted in an office. After the Allies reach France on D-Day, Germany counterattacks with a last-gasp offensive (the Battle of the Bulge) that slows but does not stop the Allies.

1945 Soviet soldiers approach Berlin from the east, and Americans and Brits advance from the west. Adolf Hitler commits suicide, and families lock up their daughters to protect them from rapacious Soviet soldiers. When Germany finally surrenders on May 8, the country is in ruins, occupied by several foreign powers, divided into occupation zones, and viewed by the world as an immoral monster.

In the war's aftermath, German citizens are faced with the scope of the mass killings and atrocities committed by their leaders. Over 11 million people have been systemically murdered—six million Jews as well as hundreds of thousands of disabled people, homosexuals, prisoners of war, political dissidents, and ethnic minorities.

World War I and Hitler's Rise (1914–1939)

When Archduke Franz Ferdinand, the heir to the Austro-Hungarian Empire, was assassinated in 1914, all of Europe took sides as the political squabble quickly escalated into World War I. Germany and Austria-Hungary attacked British and French troops in France, but were stalled at the Battle of the Marne. Both sides dug defensive trenches, then settled in for four years of bloodshed, boredom, mud, machine-gun fire, disease, and mustard gas.

Finally, at 11:00 in the morning of November 11, 1918, the fighting ceased. Germany surrendered, signing the Treaty of Versailles in the Hall of Mirrors at Versailles. The war cost the defeated German nation 1.7 million men, precious territory, colonies, their military rights, reparations money, and national pride.

A new democratic government called the Weimar Republic (1919) dutifully abided by the Treaty of Versailles, and tried to maintain order among Germany's many divided political parties. But the country was in ruins, its economy a shambles, and the war's victors demanded heavy reparations. Communists rioted in the streets, fascists plotted coups, and a loaf of bread cost a billion inflated Marks.

War vets grumbled in their beer about how their leaders had sold them out. All Germans, regardless of their political affiliations, were fervently united in their apathy toward the new democracy. When the worldwide depression of 1929 hit Germany with brutal force, the nation was desperate for a strong leader with answers.

Adolf Hitler (1889–1945) was a disgruntled vet who had spent the post–World War I years homeless, wandering the streets of Vienna with sketchpad in hand, hoping to become an artist. In Munich, he joined other disaffected Germans to form the National Socialist (Nazi) party. In stirring speeches, Hitler promised to restore Germany to its rightful glory, blaming the country's current problems on communists, foreigners, and Jews. After an unsuccessful coup attempt (the Beer Hall Putsch in Munich, 1923), Hitler was sent to jail, where he wrote an influential book of his political ideas, called *Mein Kampf (My Struggle)*.

By 1930, the Nazis—now wearing power suits and working within the system—had become a formidable political party in Germany's democracy. They won 38 percent of the seats in the *Reichstag* in 1932, and Hitler was appointed chancellor (1933). Two months later, the *Reichstag* building was mysteriously set on fire— an apparent act of terrorism with a September 11–size impact— and a terrified Germany gave Chancellor Hitler sweeping powers to preserve national security.

Hitler wasted no time in using this Enabling Act to jail opponents, terrorize the citizenry, and organize every aspect of German life under the watchful eye of the Nazi party. Plumbers' unions, choral societies, school teachers, church pastors, filmmakers, and artists all had to account to a Nazi Party official about how their work furthered the Third Reich.

For the next decade, an all-powerful Hitler proceeded to revive Germany's economy, building the autobahns and rebuilding the military. Defying the Treaty of Versailles and world opinion, Hitler occupied the Saar region (1935) and the Rhineland (1936), annexed Austria and the Sudetenland (1938), and invaded Czechoslovakia (March 1939). The rest of Europe finally reached its appeasement limit, and World War II began (see sidebar on previous spread).

Two Germanys (1945–1990)

After World War II, the Allies divided occupied Germany into two halves, split down the middle by an 855-mile border that Winston Churchill called an "Iron Curtain." By 1949, Germany was officially two separate countries. West Germany (the Federal Republic of Germany) was democratic and capitalist, allied with the powerful United States. East Germany (the German Democratic

Benedict XVI, the German Pope

When Josef Ratzinger became the 265th pope in 2005, he introduced himself as "a simple, humble worker in the vineyard of the Lord." But the man has a complex history, a reputation for intellectual brilliance, a flair for the piano, a penchant for controversy for his unbending devotion to traditional Catholic doctrine...and a Bavarian accent.

Born in 1927 in the small Bavarian town of Marktl am Inn (southeast of Munich), young Josef went to school in nearby Traunstein, studying in the seminary. When Hitler took power, he lived life under Nazi rule as many Germans did—outwardly obeying leaders while inwardly conflicted. Like many Germans, he joined the Hitler Youth, was drafted into the Army, sprayed flak from anti-aircraft guns (guarding a BMW plant), and saw Jews transported to death camps. Near the war's end, he deserted, and subsequently spent a brief time in an American POW camp near Ulm.

After the war, Ratzinger became a priest and a professor of theology, first at Munster, then at the University of Tübingen. Originally a voice of liberal Catholicism, he became increasingly convinced that Church tradition was needed to offset the growing chaos of the world.

In 1977, he was made Archbishop of Munich. Ratzinger became Pope John Paul II's closest advisor and good friend. Every Friday afternoon for two decades, they met for lunch, intellectual sparring, and friendly conversation.

Under John Paul II, Ratzinger served as the Church's "enforcer" of doctrine, earning the nickname "God's Rottweiler." He spoke out against ordaining women, chastised Latin American priests for fomenting class warfare, reassigned bishops who were soft on homosexuality, reaffirmed opposition to birth control, and wrote thoughtful papers challenging the secular world's moral relativism.

The name of "Benedict" recalls both Pope Benedict XV (who healed World War I's divisions) and Europe's patron St. Benedict (c. 480–543), who symbolizes Europe's Christian roots.

Republic, or DDR) was a socialist state under Soviet control. The former capital, Berlin, sitting in East German territory, was itself split into two parts, allowing a tiny pocket of Western life in the Soviet-controlled East. Armed guards prevented Germans from crossing the border to see their cousins on the other side.

In 1948, Soviet troops blockaded West Berlin. The Allies responded by airlifting food and supplies into the stranded city, forcing the Soviets to back off. In 1961, the East Germans erected a 12-foot-high concrete wall through the heart of Berlin. The Berlin

Wall—built at the height of the Cold War between the United States and the USSR—was designed to prevent the westward flow of East German citizens. It came to symbolize divided Germany.

In West Germany, Chancellor Konrad Adenauer (who had suffered imprisonment under the Nazis) tried to restore Germany's good name, paying war reparations and joining international organizations of nations. Thanks to US aid from the Marshall Plan, West Germany was rebuilt, democracy was established, and its "economic miracle" quickly exceeded pre-WWII levels. Adenauer was succeeded in 1969 by the US-friendly Willy Brandt.

East Germany was ruled with an iron fist by Walter Ulbricht (who had been exiled by the Nazis). In 1953, demonstrations and protests against the government were brutally put down by Soviet—not German—troops. Erich Honecker (having endured a decade of Nazi imprisonment) succeeded Ulbricht as ruler of the East in 1971. Honecker was a kinder, gentler tyrant.

Throughout the 1970s and 1980s, both the US and the Soviet Union used divided Germany as a military base. West Germans debated whether US missiles aimed at the Soviets should be placed in their country. Economically, West Germany just got stronger while East Germany stagnated.

On November 9, 1989, East Germany unexpectedly opened the Berlin Wall (see "The Berlin Wall" sidebar, page 525). Astonished Germans from both sides climbed the Wall, hugged each other, shared bottles of beer, sang songs, and chiseled off souvenirs. At first, most Germans—West and East—looked forward to free travel and better relations between two distinct nations. But before the month was out, negotiations and elections to reunite the two Germanys had already begun. October 3, 1990, was proclaimed German Unification Day, and Berlin re-assumed its status as German capital in 1991.

Germany Today (1990–present)

Differences between "Ossies" (rude slang for former East Germans) and "Wessies" remain, but they're diminishing as the two economies seek equilibrium. Germany remains a major economic and political force in Europe. The country spent a decade under a center-right government led by Chancellor Helmut Kohl, followed by a decade under the center-left Chancellor Gerhard Schroeder. Elections in 2005 resulted in no clear victory, and both major parties formed a "Grand Coalition," sharing power equally under Germany's first woman chancellor, Angela Merkel. After strengthening her position in the country's 2009 elections, Merkel formed a big-business-friendly, center-right coalition with the conservative Liberal Democrats. German-American relations suffered when the US invaded Iraq (Germany opposed the invasion), but the relationship remains fundamentally strong. Germany is fully integrated into the international community as a member of the European Union—an organization whose chief aim was to avoid future wars with an aggressive Germany by embracing it in the economic web of Europe.

APPENDIX

Contents

Tourist Information

Tourist Information Offices

Germany's national tourist information office **in the US** is a wealth of information. They have maps, Rhine boat schedules, and information on festivals, castles, biking, genealogy, cities, and regions. Most materials can be downloaded from their website; if you want tourist materials sent to you, a small donation is requested (tel. 800-651-7010, www.cometogermany.com).

In Germany, your best first stop in every town is generally the tourist information office—abbreviated TI in this book. Throughout Germany, you'll find TIs are usually well-organized and have English-speaking staff. A TI is a great place to get a city map, advice on public transportation (including bus and train schedules), walking-tour information, tips on special events, and recommendations for nightlife. Many TIs have information on the entire country or at least the region, so try to pick up maps for destinations you'll be visiting later in your trip. If you're arriving in town after the TI closes, call ahead or pick up a map in a neigh-boring town.

As national budgets tighten, many TIs have been privatized. This means they have become sales agents for big tours and hotels, and their "information" is unavoidably colored. While TIs are eager to book you a room, you should use their room-finding service only as a last resort. TIs can as easily book you a bad room as a good one—they are not allowed to promote one place over another. It's better to book direct, using the listings in this book.

Communicating

Telephones

Smart travelers use the telephone daily to book or reconfirm rooms, get tourist information, reserve restaurants, confirm tour times, or phone home. This section covers dialing instructions, phone cards, and types of phones.

Generally, the cheapest way to go is to buy an international phone card in Germany and make your calls from hotel-room phones or mobile phones, but not pay phones. The handiest—though pricier—way to make calls is by using a mobile phone (brought from home or purchased in Germany).

How to Dial

Calling from the US to Europe, or vice versa, is simple—once you break the code. The European calling chart in this chapter will walk you through it.

Dialing Domestically Within Germany

Germany, like much of the US, uses an area-code dialing system. If you're calling within the same area code, you just dial the local number to be connected; but if you're calling outside your area code, you have to dial both the area code (which starts with a 0) and the local number. You'll find area codes listed throughout this book, or you can get them from directory assistance (tel. 11833).

For example, Munich's area code is 089 and the number of one of my recommended Munich hotels is 545-9940. To call the hotel within Munich, you'd dial 545-9940. To call it from Frankfurt, you'd dial 089/545-9940.

Don't be surprised if local phone numbers in Germany have different numbers of digits within the same city or even the same hotel (for example, a hotel can have a 6-digit phone number and an 8-digit fax number).

Be aware that some numbers, typically those that start with 018 (including some train and airline information numbers), are actually premium toll calls, costing more than a regular land-line

Hurdling the Language Barrier

German—like English, Dutch, Swedish, and Norwegian—is a Germanic language, making it easier on most American ears than Romance languages (such as Italian and French). These tips will help you pronounce German words: The letter *w* is always pronounced as "v" (e.g., the word for "wonderful" is *wunderbar*, pronounced VOON-der-bar). The vowel combinations *ie* and *ei* are pronounced like the name of the second letter—so *ie* sounds like the letter *e* (as in *hier* and *Bier*, the German words for "here" and "beer"), while *ei* sounds like the letter *i* (as in *nein* and *Stein*, the German words for "no" and "stone"). The vowel combination *au* is pronounced "ow" (as in *Frau*). The vowel combinations *eu* and *äu* are pronounced "oy" (as in *neu, Deutsch,* and *Bräu,* the words for "new," "German," and "brew"). To pronounce *ö* and *ü,* purse your lips when you say the vowel; the other vowel with an umlaut, *ä,* is pronounced the same as *e* in "men." (In written German, these can be depicted as the vowel followed by an *e*—*oe, ue,* and *ae,* respectively.) The letter *Eszett (ß)* represents *ss.* Written German always capitalizes all nouns.

Though most young or well-educated Germans—especially those in the tourist trade, and in big cities—speak at least some English, you'll get more smiles if you learn and use the German pleasantries. Study the German Survival Phrases on page 629. Give it your best shot. The locals will appreciate your efforts.

call. The per-minute charge should be listed in small print next to the phone number. Mobile phone numbers start with 015, 016, or 017, and cost much more to call than land lines.

Dialing Internationally to or from Germany
To make an international call, follow these steps:

1. Dial the international access code (00 if you're calling from Europe, 011 from the US or Canada).

2. Dial the country code of the country you're calling (see the European calling chart).

3. Dial the area code (without its initial 0) and the local number.

Calling from the US to Germany: To call the recommended Munich hotel from the US, dial 011 (the US's international access code), 49 (Germany's country code), 89 (Munich's area code without the initial 0), then 545-9940 (the hotel's number).

Calling from Germany to the US: To call from Germany to my office in Edmonds, Washington, I dial 00 (Europe's international access code), 1 (US country code), 425 (Edmonds' area code), and 771-8303.

European Calling Chart

Just smile and dial, using this key:
AC = Area Code, LN = Local Number.

European Country	Calling long distance within ...	Calling from the US or Canada to ...	Calling from a European country to ...
Austria	AC + LN	011 + 43 + AC (without the initial zero) + LN	00 + 43 + AC (without the initial zero) + LN
Belgium	LN	011 + 32 + LN (without initial zero)	00 + 32 + LN (without initial zero)
Bosnia-Herzegovina	AC + LN	011 + 387 + AC (without initial zero) + LN	00 + 387 + AC (without initial zero) + LN
Britain	AC + LN	011 + 44 + AC (without initial zero) + LN	00 + 44 + AC (without initial zero) + LN
Croatia	AC + LN	011 + 385 + AC (without initial zero) + LN	00 + 385 + AC (without initial zero) + LN
Czech Republic	LN	011 + 420 + LN	00 + 420 + LN
Denmark	LN	011 + 45 + LN	00 + 45 + LN
Estonia	LN	011 + 372 + LN	00 + 372 + LN
Finland	AC + LN	011 + 358 + AC (without initial zero) + LN	999 + 358 + AC (without initial zero) + LN
France	LN	011 + 33 + LN (without initial zero)	00 + 33 + LN (without initial zero)
Germany	AC + LN	011 + 49 + AC (without initial zero) + LN	00 + 49 + AC (without initial zero) + LN
Gibraltar	LN	011 + 350 + LN	00 + 350 + LN
Greece	LN	011 + 30 + LN	00 + 30 + LN
Hungary	06 + AC + LN	011 + 36 + AC + LN	00 + 36 + AC + LN
Ireland	AC + LN	011 + 353 + AC (without initial zero) + LN	00 + 353 + AC (without initial zero) + LN
Italy	LN	011 + 39 + LN	00 + 39 + LN

European Country	Calling long distance within ...	Calling from the US or Canada to ...	Calling from a European country to ...
Montenegro	AC + LN	011 + 382 + AC (without initial zero) + LN	00 + 382 + AC (without initial zero) + LN
Morocco	LN	011 + 212 + LN (without initial zero)	00 + 212 + LN (without initial zero)
Netherlands	AC + LN	011 + 31 + AC (without initial zero) + LN	00 + 31 + AC (without initial zero) + LN
Norway	LN	011 + 47 + LN	00 + 47 + LN
Poland	LN	011 + 48 + LN (without initial zero)	00 + 48 + LN (without initial zero)
Portugal	LN	011 + 351 + LN	00 + 351 + LN
Slovakia	AC + LN	011 + 421 + AC (without initial zero) + LN	00 + 421 + AC (without initial zero) + LN
Slovenia	AC + LN	011 + 386 + AC (without initial zero) + LN	00 + 386 + AC (without initial zero) + LN
Spain	LN	011 + 34 + LN	00 + 34 + LN
Sweden	AC + LN	011 + 46 + AC (without initial zero) + LN	00 + 46 + AC (without initial zero) + LN
Switzerland	LN	011 + 41 + LN (without initial zero)	00 + 41 + LN (without initial zero)
Turkey	AC (if no initial zero is included, add one) + LN	011 + 90 + AC (without initial zero) + LN	00 + 90 + AC (without initial zero) + LN

- The instructions above apply whether you're calling a land line or mobile phone.
- The international access codes (the first numbers you dial when making an international call) are 011 if you're calling from the US or Canada, or 00 if you're calling from virtually anywhere in Europe (except Finland, where it's 999).
- To call the US or Canada from Europe, dial 00, then 1 (the country code for the US and Canada), then the area code and number. In short, 00 + 1 + AC + LN = Hi, Mom!

Note: You might see a + in front of a European number. When dialing the number, replace the + with the international access code of the country you're calling from (00 from Europe, 011 from the US or Canada).

Public Phones and Hotel-Room Phones

To make calls from public phones, you'll need a prepaid phone card. There are two different kinds of phone cards: international and insertable. (Coin-op phones are virtually extinct.)

International Phone Cards: These are the cheapest way to make international calls from Europe—with the best cards, it costs literally pennies a minute. They also work for local calls.

To use the card, you'll dial a toll-free access number, then type in your scratch-to-reveal PIN number. You can use international phone cards from any type of phone, including the one in your hotel room (but ask at the front desk if there are any fees for toll-free calls). Avoid using international phone cards at pay phones, however. Because the German phone company slaps on hefty surcharges, you'll get far fewer minutes for your money (for example, 10 minutes instead of 100 on a €5 card) than if you call from your hotel room or a mobile phone.

The cards are sold at small newsstand kiosks and hole-in-the-wall long-distance shops. Ask the clerk which of the various brands has the best rates for calls to America. Because cards are occasionally duds, avoid the more expensive denominations. Some shops also sell cardless codes, printed right on the receipt. Certain international phone cards work in multiple countries—if traveling to both Germany and Austria, try to buy a card that will work in both places.

Remember that you don't need the actual card to use a card account. You can write down the access number and PIN code in your notebook and share it with friends. Give the number of a still-live card to another traveler if you're leaving the country.

Insertable Phone Cards: This type of card can be used only at pay phones. It's handy and affordable for local and domestic calls, but more expensive than "code cards" for international calls. To use the card, physically insert it into a slot in the pay phone. They're sold in denominations starting at about €5 at TIs, tobacco shops, post offices, and train stations.

While you can use these cards to call anywhere in the world, it's only a good deal for making quick local calls from a phone booth. Note that insertable phone cards don't work outside of Germany.

Hotel-Room Phones: Phoning from your room can be cheap for local calls (ask for the rates at the front desk first), but is often a rip-off for long-distance calls ($1–2/minute unless you use an international phone card, explained earlier). Incoming calls are free, making this a cheap way for friends and family to stay in touch (provided they have a good long-distance plan for calls to Europe—and a list of your hotels' phone numbers). Even small hotels in Germany tend to have a direct-dial system, so callers can reach you in your room without going through reception. Ask the staff for your room's specific telephone number.

US Calling Cards: These cards, such as the ones offered by AT&T, Verizon, or Sprint, are the worst option. You'll nearly always save a lot of money by using a local phone card instead.

Mobile Phones

Many travelers enjoy the convenience of traveling with a mobile phone (if you need more in-depth information than we provide below, see www.ricksteves.com/phones).

Using Your Mobile Phone: Your US mobile phone works in Europe if it's GSM-enabled, tri-band or quad-band, and on a calling plan that includes international calls. It's convenient, but pricey. For example, with a T-Mobile phone, you'll pay $1 per minute for calls and about $0.35 for text messages.

You can save money if your phone is electronically "unlocked" —then you can simply buy a **SIM card** (a fingernail-sized chip that stores the phone's information) in Europe. SIM cards, which give you a European phone number, are sold at mobile-phone stores and some newsstand kiosks for about $5–15. On my last trip, I bought a German T-Mobile SIM card for €10, which included €10 of calling time—so the card itself was effectively free. Simply insert the SIM card in your phone (usually in a slot behind the battery), and it'll work like a European mobile phone. When buying a SIM card, always ask about fees for domestic and international calls, roaming charges, and how to check your credit balance and buy more time. You can top up with more prepaid calling time as needed; just buy vouchers at newsstands or mobile-phone shops, then punch the number into your phone.

Many **smartphones**, such as the iPhone or BlackBerry, work in Europe—but beware of sky-high fees, especially for data downloading (checking email, browsing the Internet, watching videos, and so on). Ask your provider in advance how to avoid unwittingly "roaming" your way to a huge bill. Some applications allow for cheap or free smartphone calls over a Wi-Fi connection (see "Calling over the Internet," later).

Using a European Mobile Phone: Local mobile-phone shops all over Europe sell basic phones for around $50–100. Look for deals (e.g., $40 for a basic, unlocked phone) at electronics stores such as MediaMarkt. You'll also need to buy a SIM card (explained above) and prepaid credit for making calls. If you remain in the phone's home country, domestic calls are reasonable, and incoming calls are free. You'll pay more if you're "roaming" in another country. If your phone is "unlocked," you can swap out its SIM card for a new one when you travel to other countries.

Calling over the Internet

Some things that seem too good to be true...actually are true. If you're traveling with a laptop, you can make calls using VoIP (Voice over Internet Protocol). With VoIP, two computers act as the phones, and the Internet-based calls are free (or you can pay a few cents per minute to call from your computer to a telephone). The major providers are Skype (www.skype.com) and Google Talk (www.google.com/talk).

Useful Phone Numbers

Emergency Needs
Police and Ambulance: tel. 112.

Directory Assistance
National: tel. 11833.
International: tel. 11834.
Train info: tel. 0180-599-6633 (€0.14/min); ask for an English speaker.
German Tourist Offices: Dial the local code, then 19433.

Embassies
US Embassy in Berlin: Neustädtische Kirchstrasse 4–5, tel. 030/83050; consular services at Clayallee 170, Mon–Fri 8:30–12:00, closed Sat–Sun, tel. 030/832-9233—Mon–Fri 14:00–16:00 only, www.usembassy.de, consberlin@state.gov.
Canadian Embassy in Berlin: Leipziger Platz 17, tel. 030/203-120, www.berlin.gc.ca.

Travel Advisories
US Department of State: US tel. 202/647-5225, www.travel.state.gov.
Canadian Department of Foreign Affairs: Canadian tel. 800-267-6788, www.dfait-maeci.gc.ca.
US Centers for Disease Control and Prevention: US tel. 800-CDC-INFO (800-232-4636), www.cdc.gov/travel.

The Internet

The Internet can be an invaluable tool for planning your trip (researching and booking hotels, checking bus and train schedules, and so on). It's also useful to get online periodically as you travel—to reconfirm your trip plans, check the weather, catch up on email, blog or post photos from your trip, or call folks back home (explained earlier, under "Calling over the Internet").

Some hotels offer a computer in the lobby with Internet access for guests. Smaller B&Bs may sometimes let you sit at their desk for a few minutes just to check your email, if you ask politely. If you're traveling with a laptop, see if your hotel has Wi-Fi (wireless Internet access) or a port in your room where you can plug in a cable to get online. Most hotels offer Internet access and/or Wi-Fi for free; others charge a fee.

If your hotel doesn't have access, ask your hotelier to direct you to the nearest place to get online. Most of the towns where I've listed accommodations in this book also have Internet cafés. Many libraries offer free access, but they also tend to have limited opening hours and restrict your online time to 30 minutes, and may require reservations.

Mail

Get stamps at the neighborhood post office, newsstands within fancy hotels, and some mini-marts and card shops. Avoid standing in line at the post office by using the handy yellow stamp *(Briefmarke)* machines found just outside the building. Warning: These machines give change only in stamps, not in coins. A postcard stamp to the US or Canada costs €1.

While you can arrange for mail delivery to your hotel (allow 10 days for a letter to arrive), phoning and emailing are so easy that I've dispensed with mail stops altogether.

Transportation

By Car or Train?

Cars are best for three or more traveling together (especially families with small kids), those packing heavy, and those scouring the countryside. Trains and buses are best for solo travelers, blitz tourists, and city-to-city travelers. While a car gives you the ultimate in mobility and freedom, enables you to search for hotels more easily, and carries your bags for you, the train zips you effortlessly from city to city, usually dropping you in the center and near the tourist office. A car is a worthless headache in cities such as Munich, Berlin, and Frankfurt.

Trains

German trains are speedy, comfortable, non-smoking, and fairly punctual, with synchronized connections. They cover cities and small towns well, but some frustrating schedules make a few out-of-the-way recommendations (such as Bavaria's Wieskirche) not worth the time and trouble for the less determined. If you have a railpass,

Public Transportation

you can hop on any train without much forethought (though for a small fee, you can reserve a seat on a fast train). Without a rail-pass, you can save a lot of money by understanding the difference between fast trains and cheaper "regional" trains. Trains are operated by the German Railway (Deutsche Bahn, or DB).

Types of Trains

There are big differences in price, speed, and comfort between Germany's three levels of trains. ICE trains (white with red trim and streamlined noses) are the fastest, zipping from city to city in air-conditioned comfort, and costing proportionately more. Red regional trains (mostly labeled RB, RE, and IRE on schedules) are the slowest—the milk-run RB trains stop at every small station—but cost much less. Mid-level IC and EC trains are white with red trim but look older than the ICEs. If you have a railpass, take the fastest train available—railpass-holders don't pay a supplement for the fast ICE trains (with one exception, the "ICE Sprinter"). If you're buying point-to-point tickets, taking a slower train can save a lot of money.

Schedules

Schedules change by season, weekday, and weekend. Verify train times listed in this book at http://bahn.hafas.de/bin/query.exe/en. At staffed train stations, attendants will print out a step-by-step itinerary for you, free of charge. You can also produce an itinerary yourself by using the computerized trackside machines marked *Fahrkarten* (usually silver, red, and blue). The touch-screen display gives you an English option; choose "Timetable Information," indicate your point of departure and destination, and then hit "Print" for a personalized schedule, including transfers and track numbers.

If all else fails, call Germany's train information number from anywhere in the country: tel. 0180-599-6633 (€0.14/min). Ask for an English-speaker.

Railpasses

The German Pass is a great value for rail travel within Germany. If you're traveling in a neighboring country, two-country Eurailpasses allow you to pair Germany with Austria, Switzerland, France, the BeNeLux region, Denmark, Poland, or the Czech Republic. The Eurail Selectpass gives you more travel in three, four, or five adjacent countries (but some Eastern European countries—like Poland—are not eligible). If you're planning a whirlwind tour of Europe, another possibility is the 21-country Eurail Global Pass. These passes are available in a Saverpass version, which gives a 15 percent discount on railpasses for two or more companions travel-

ing together. For specifics, check the railpass chart on the next page and visit www.ricksteves.com/rail.

Railpass travelers should know what extras are covered by their pass: for example, travel on any German buses marked "Deutsche Bahn" or "DB" (run by the train company)

Railpasses

Prices listed are for 2009 and are subject to change. **For the latest prices, details, train schedules, and easy online ordering, see my comprehensive Guide to Eurail Passes at www.ricksteves.com/rail.** See Web site for more passes, including France-Germany, Germany-Poland, and Germany-Czech passes.

"Saver" prices are per person for two or more people traveling together. "Youth" means under age 26. All passes for Germany cover KD Line boats on the Rhine and Mosel, 20% off Romantic Road bus ride.

GERMAN PASS

	Indiv. 1st Cl.	Indiv. 2nd Cl.	Twin 1st Cl.	Twin 2nd Cl.	Youth 2nd Cl.
4 days in 1 month	$340	$260	$267	$195	$216
Extra rail days (max. 6)	43-47	29-32	30-32	21-24	14-17

Twin prices are per person for two traveling together. The fare for children 6–11 is half the individual fare. Kids under age 6 travel free. Five and ten-day versions available at some stations in Germany.

Map key:

Approximate point-to-point one-way second-class rail fares in US dollars. First class costs 50 percent more. Add up the approximate ticket costs for your trip to see if a railpass will save you money.

SELECTPASS

This pass covers travel in three adjacent countries. For four- and five-country options, please visit www.ricksteves.com/rail.

	Individual 1st Class	Saver 1st Class	Youth 2nd Class
5 days in 2 months	$468	$398	$305
6 days in 2 months	517	441	339
8 days in 2 months	613	524	398
10 days in 2 months	711	601	460

Selectpass diagram key:

A **Selectpass** can be designed to connect a "chain" of any three, four, or five countries in this diagram linked by direct lines. (Examples that qualify: Norway-Sweden-Germany or Germany-Austria-Switzerland.) "Benelux" is considered one country.

GERMANY–AUSTRIA PASS

	Indiv. 1st Cl.	Indiv. 2nd Cl.	Saver 1st Cl.	Saver 2nd Cl.	Youth 2nd Cl.
5 days in 2 months	$419	$357	$357	$306	$306
6 days in 2 months	461	392	392	338	338
8 days in 2 months	548	466	466	400	400
10 days in 2 months	637	542	542	466	466

The fare for children 4–11 is half the adult individual fare or Saver fare. Kids under age 4 travel free.

GERMANY–SWITZERLAND PASS

	Individual 1st Class	Saver 1st Class	Youth 2nd Class
5 days in 2 months	$442	$377	$311
6 days in 2 months	488	416	343
8 days in 2 months	577	493	405
10 days in 2 months	668	570	469

The fare for children 4–11 is half the adult individual or Saver fare. Kids under age 4 travel free.

BENELUX–GERMANY PASS

	Indiv. 1st Cl.	Indiv. 2nd Cl.	Saver 1st Cl.	Saver 2nd Cl.	Youth 2nd Cl.
5 days in 2 months	$436	$328	$328	$266	$266
6 days in 2 months	483	363	363	291	291
8 days in 2 months	570	429	429	343	343
10 days in 2 months	663	498	498	399	399

The fare for children 4–11 is half the adult individual fare or Saver fare. Kids under age 4 travel free.

DENMARK–GERMANY PASS

	Indiv. 1st Cl.	Indiv. 2nd Cl.	Saver 1st Cl.	Saver 2nd Cl.	Youth 2nd Cl.
4 days in 2 months	$355	$291	$291	$224	$224
5 days in 2 months	399	328	328	253	253
6 days in 2 months	442	363	363	276	276
8 days in 2 months	533	437	437	318	318
10 days in 2 months	641	488	488	360	360

The fare for children 4–11 is half the adult individual fare or Saver fare. Kids under age 4 travel free.

GERMANY RAIL & DRIVE PASS

Any 2 rail days and 2 car days in 1 month.

Car Category	1st Class	2nd Class	Extra Car Day
Economy	$228	$185	$53
Compact	237	194	62
Intermediate	245	202	70
Small automatic	263	220	88

Prices are per person, two traveling together. Extra rail day $65 in 1st Class, $48 in 2nd Class (max. 2).

SELECTPASS RAIL & DRIVE

Any 3 rail days and 2 car days in 2 months within 3 adjoining countries.

Car Category	1st Class	Extra Car Day
Economy	$364	$54
Compact	384	72
Intermediate	392	82
Small Automatic	415	104

Prices are per person, two traveling together. Extra rail days (max. 2) about $40 each. 2-rail-day version also available. Third and fourth persons sharing car get a 3-day out of 2-month railpass for approx. $326 (kids 4-11: $163). A fourth or fifth country each adds about $45 to these prices. Longer durations available for five countries.

To order a Rail & Drive pass, call your travel agent or Rail Europe at 800-438-7245. *These passes are not sold by Europe Through the Back Door.*

and travel on city S-Bahn systems (except in Berlin, where only S-Bahn lines between major train stations are covered). Railpasses also cover or discount boats on the Rhine, Mosel, and Danube rivers, and give you a 20 percent discount on the Romantic Road bus. Flexipass-holders should note that discounted trips don't use up a flexi-day, but fully covered ("free") trips do. The "used" flexipass day can also cover your train travel on that day (but if you're not planning to travel more that day, it makes sense to pay for, say, a short boat ride rather than use up a day of your pass for it).

Because it's so close to the border, traveling to or from Salzburg, Austria, on the main line from Munich counts as traveling within Germany, as far as your railpass is concerned.

When choosing how many flexi-days you need for your railpass, note that it's not worth buying an extra day to cover short trips on regional trains—for instance, from Würzburg to Rothenburg, or a day trip from Cochem to Burg Eltz. Buy point-to-point tickets instead.

Point-to-Point Tickets

Ticket fares are shown on the map on page 608 and at http://bahn.hafas.de/bin/query.exe/en (no fare information for trains outside Germany). The German Railway can charge a wide variety of fares for the same journey, depending on the time of day, how far ahead you purchase the ticket, and other considerations. Know your options to get the best deal.

First Class vs. Second Class: First-class tickets usually cost 50 percent more than second-class tickets. While first-class cars are always a bit more spacious and quiet than second class, the main advantage of a first-class ticket is the lower chance that the train will fill up. Riding in second class, however, gets you there at the same time, and with the same scenery. As second-class seating is still comfortable and quiet, most of my readers find the extra cost of first class isn't worth it—Germans themselves tell me they never ride in first class unless someone else is paying for it.

Full-Fare Tickets: The most you'll ever have to pay for a journey is the unrestricted *Normalpreis*. This full-fare ticket allows you to easily change your plans and switch to an earlier or later train, without paying a penalty. (If you buy a *Normalpreis* ticket for a slower train, though, you can't use it on a fast one without paying extra.)

Discount Fares: If you reserve round-trip travel at least three days in advance and are comfortable committing to particular trains, you can usually save 25 to 50 percent on long-distance round trips. But these tickets are more restrictive; changing one of these discounted tickets usually costs at least €15.

You can also save money on point-to-point tickets if you're

willing to skip Germany's high-speed trains (IC, EC, and ICE). This is especially the case with discount deals such as the Länder-Tickets and the Schönes-Wochenende-Ticket.

With a **Länder-Ticket,** five people traveling together get unlimited travel in second class for one day for a very cheap price (€26–28, depending on area; a Länder-Ticket Single covers one person for about €20). The catch: A Länder-Ticket only covers travel within a certain *Land* (Germany's version of a US state, such as Bavaria or Rheinland-Pfalz). Also, these tickets don't cover travel on weekdays before 9:00, and only work on slower regional trains (labeled RB, RE, IRE, S, TR, or ALX). For example, it takes about two hours on regional trains to travel between Munich and Nürnberg, versus one hour on an express train; but for a family, the Länder-Ticket price is such a steal that the extra travel time might be worthwhile. The Länder-Ticket is also valid on local transport. For example, a Bayern-Ticket (the Bavarian version) not only gets you from Munich to Füssen, but also covers the bus from Füssen to Neuschwanstein and back. The Rhineland-Pfalz-Ticket makes sense for day trips around the Rhine and the Mosel (for example, from Bacharach to Burg Eltz).

The **Schönes-Wochenende-Ticket** (€37) works much the same way, except that it's good for two days (Sat–Sun only), and covers regional trains all over Germany (rather than limiting you to one *Land).* It, too, is valid for up to five adults, but unlike the Länder-Tickets, doesn't cover buses and urban transport.

Kids 6–14 travel free with a parent or grandparent, but the ticket needs to list the number of children (except if purchased from a regional-train ticket machine). Kids under 6 don't need tickets. Those staying longer in Germany can get additional discounts for a full year by purchasing one of several BahnCards (starting at €57; see www.bahn.de).

Buying Tickets

At the Station: Major German stations have a handy *Reisezentrum* (travel center) where you can ask questions and buy tickets (with a small markup for the personal service). Many smaller stations are unstaffed, so you'll have to buy tickets from the silver, red, and blue touch-screen machines (marked *Fahrkarten,* which means "tickets"). These generally user-friendly machines sell short- and long-distance train tickets, and print schedules for free (described earlier, under "Schedules"). You can pay with bills, coins, or credit cards.

You'll also see the older, silver ticket machines with smaller screens and plenty of buttons; at some smaller stations, these machines are the only ticket-buying option. They sell same-day-only tickets to nearby destinations. In cities, they also sell local public transport tickets. To buy a ticket, press the flag button until it gives you a screen in English. Then look for your destination on the long list of towns on the left side of the machine. If your destination isn't on the list (because it's too far away), you can buy the ticket on board (let the conductor know where you boarded and you won't even have to pay the small markup for buying a ticket on the train). If your destination *is* on the list, note its four-digit code and enter it on the number pad. The machine will automatically issue you a ticket for a one-way *(Einfache)* second-class fare, but you can alter that with the buttons below the keypad (press *Hin- und Rückfahrt* if you want a round-trip ticket, and *1./2. Klasse* for first class; also note the buttons for *Länder-Karte* day passes and children's tickets). Feed the machine cash (small bills are okay, but it won't take your non-European credit card), then collect your ticket and change. *Gut gemacht!* (Well done!)

In the Rhineland, you'll see a new generation of these regional ticket machines, which are yellow and have touch screens, but still sell only same-day tickets.

On the Train: You can buy a ticket on board from the conductor for a long-distance journey (by paying a small markup), but if you're riding a local (short distance) train, you're expected to board with a valid ticket...or you can get fined.

Online: You can buy German train tickets online and print them out yourself or (for a fee) have them delivered by mail; you'll need to visit http://bahn.hafas.de/bin/query.exe/en and create a login and password. If you print out your own ticket, the conductor will also ask to see your credit card (usually the one that you used to buy the ticket).

Getting a Seat

As you board or exit a train, you'll usually have to push a button or flip a lever to open the door. Watch and imitate.

It costs €2 extra per person to reserve a seat. German trains generally offer ample seating, but can fill up on popular routes, especially on holiday weekends. If your itinerary is set, and you don't mind the small fee, seat reservations can be worth it for the peace of mind—and a few fast trains require reservations (slower regional trains, however, don't accept them). With rare exceptions, it doesn't make sense to reserve seats in advance of your trip (as reservations made through US agents cost a lot more); just do it at a German station.

If you're traveling without a reservation and are looking for a free seat, watch for the slips of paper that mark reserved seats. For seats in compartments, you'll find these slips tucked into slots near each compartment's door (*Gang* = aisle, *Fenster* = window); for open-seat cars, slips are stuck into the top of each reserved seat. If you have a hard time finding an unreserved seat, take a closer look at the reservations—if you find a seat that's reserved for a leg of the journey that doesn't overlap with yours, you're free to take the seat. For example, if you're traveling from Frankfurt to Würzburg on a Munich-bound train, and you find a seat reserved only from Nürnberg to Munich, it's all yours—you'll be getting off the train before the reservation-holder boards in Nürnberg.

Bikes on Board

Your bike can travel with you for €4.50 per day on regional trains or €9 per trip on fast trains. Deutsche Bahn's helpful website even has a list of bike rental shops that are in or near train stations. Rentals usually run about $10 a day, and some rental outfits offer easy "pick up here and drop off there" plans.

Renting a Car

To rent a car in Germany, you likely have to be 21 years old (most companies will not rent to anyone under that age), and restrictions and "underage fees" can apply if you're 21–24. There's generally not a maximum age limit, but if you are 70 or older, it's smart to ask. If you're considered too young or old, look into leasing (explained later), which has less-stringent age restrictions. An International Driving Permit is recommended, but not required, if your driver's license has been renewed within the last year ($15 through your local AAA, plus two passport photos, www.aaa.com); however, I've frequently rented cars in Germany and traveled problem-free with just my US license.

Research car rentals before you go. It's cheapest to arrange most car rentals from the US. Call several companies, and look online to compare rates, or arrange a rental through your home-town travel agent. Two reputable companies among many are Auto Europe (www.autoeurope.com) and Europe by Car (www .ebctravel.com). For the best deal, rent by the week with unlimited mileage (but for long trips, consider leasing). To save money on gas, ask for a diesel car.

I normally rent the smallest, least-expensive model with a stick-shift (like a Ford Fiesta). For a bigger, roomier, more powerful but inexpensive car, move up to a Ford Focus or VW Polo. Minibuses are a great budget way to go for 5–9 people. Almost all rentals are manual by default, so if you need an automatic, you must request one in advance; beware that these cars are usually larger models (not as maneuverable on narrow, winding roads). You'll pay about 40 percent more to rent a car with an automatic instead of a manual transmission.

Expect to pay about $800 per person (based on 2 people sharing) for a small economy car for three weeks with unlimited mileage, including gas, parking, and insurance. Consider leasing to save money on insurance and taxes.

If you drop the car off early or keep it longer, you'll be credited or charged at a fair, prorated price. But keep your receipts in case any questions arise about your billing.

When picking up the car, check it thoroughly and make sure any damage is noted on your rental agreement. Find out how your car's lights, turn signals, wipers, and gas cap function. When you return the car, make sure the agent verifies its condition with you.

Car Insurance Options

When you rent a car, you are liable for a very high deductible, sometimes equal to the entire value of the car. Limit your financial risk in case of an accident by choosing one of these three options: Buy Collision Damage Waiver (CDW) coverage from the car-rental company, get coverage through your credit card (free, if your card automatically includes zero-deductible coverage), or buy coverage through Travel Guard.

While each rental company has its own variation, basic **CDW** costs $15–25 a day (figure roughly 25 percent extra) and reduces your liability, but does not eliminate it. When you pick up the car, you'll be offered the chance to "buy down" the basic deductible to zero (for an additional $10–30/day; this is often called "super CDW").

If you opt for credit-card coverage, there's a catch. You'll technically have to decline all coverage offered by the car-rental company, which means they can place a hold on your card (can be up to the full value of the car). In case of damage, it can be time-consuming to resolve the charges with your credit-card company. Before you decide on this option, quiz your credit-card company about how it works and ask them to explain the worst-case scenario.

Finally, you can buy CDW insurance from Travel Guard ($9/day plus a one-time $3 service fee covers you up to $35,000, $250 deductible, tel. 800-826-4919, www.travelguard.com). It's valid everywhere in Europe except the Republic of Ireland, and some Italian car-rental companies refuse to honor it. Residents of Washington state aren't eligible for this coverage.

For more fine print about car-rental insurance, see www.rick steves.com/cdw.

APPENDIX

Leasing

For trips of two and a half weeks or more, leasing (which automatically includes zero-deductible collision and theft insurance) is the best way to go. By technically buying and then selling back the car, you save lots of money on tax and insurance. Leasing provides you a new car with unlimited mileage and a 24-hour emergency assistance program. You can lease for as little as 17 days to as long as six months. Car leases must be arranged from the US. One of many reliable companies offering affordable lease packages is Europe by Car (US tel. 800-223-1516, www.ebctravel.com).

Driving

Remember to bring your driver's license. Seat belts are mandatory, and two beers under those belts are enough to land you in jail. You're required to use low-beam headlights if it's overcast, raining, or snowing.

Use good local maps and study them before each drive. Learn which exits you need to look out for, which major cities you'll travel toward, where the ruined castles lurk, and so on. Every long drive between my recommended destinations is via the autobahn (super-freeway), and nearly every scenic backcountry drive is paved and comfortable.

Learn the universal road signs (explained in charts in most road atlases and at service stations). To get to the center of a city, follow signs for *Zentrum* or *Stadtmitte*. Ring roads go around a city. For parking, you can pick up a cardboard clock (*Parkscheibe,* available free at gas stations, police stations, and *Tabak* shops). Display your arrival time on the clock and put it on the dashboard, so parking attendants can see you've been there less than the posted maximum stay.

The Autobahn: The shortest distance between any two points is the autobahn (no speed limit, toll-free). Blue signs direct you to the autobahn. To understand the complex but super-efficient autobahn, look for the *Autobahn Service* booklet

STOP AND LEARN THESE ROAD SIGNS

Speed Limit (km/hr) — Yield — No Passing — End of No Passing Zone

One Way (EINBAHNSTRASSE) — Intersection — Main Road — Freeway

Danger — No Entry — No Entry for cars — All Vehicles Prohibited

Parking — No Parking — Customs (ZOLL DOUANE) — Peace

Driving: Distance and Time

To Flensburg (DANISH BORDER)
95m • 1.25h

Hamburg

POLAND

NETH.

GERMANY

265m • 4.25h

180m • 3h

Berlin

60m • 1.25h
Frankfurt an der Oder

To Amsterdam
165m • 2.5h

360m • 5.5h

120m • 2.25h

70m • 1.25h
Görlitz

40m
.75h

335m • 5.5h

305m • 4.5h

Dresden

Köln

350m • 5.5h

95m • 3h

Aachen
30m
.5h

55m • .75h

25m
.5h

Koblenz
60m • 1h

195m • 3h

Frankfurt

190m • 3h

Prague

Cochem

60m • 1h

Würzburg

CZECH

REPUBLIC

Bacharach
55m • 1h

135m • 1.5h

40m
.5h

Nürnberg

105m • 2.25h

185m • 3.25h

Trier
175m • 2.5h

70m • 1h

100m • 1.5h

Roth-
enburg

70m
1.25h

100m • 1.75h

240m • 4h

Český
Krumlov

Vienna

FRANCE

135m • 2h

Baden-Baden

150m
2h

Munich

135m
2.5h

140m
3.25h

Melk

55m
1.25h

60m • 1.25h

200m • 3.25h

Freiburg

260m • 4h

70m
1.5h

80m • 1.25h

125m • 2h

Salzburg

AUSTRIA

175m • 3.75h

95m
2.25h

100m • 1.5h

110m • 2h

95m • 1.75h

Zurich

Füssen

70m
1.75h

Innsbruck
20m • .25h

Bern

70m
1.25h

55m
1h

Appenzell

Brenner Pass

SWITZ.

ITALY

SLOVENIA

m = miles
h = hours

Note: Your times may vary based on traffic, construction, and road conditions.

CROATIA

at any autobahn rest stop (free, lists all stops, services, road symbols, and more). Learn the signs: *Dreieck* ("three corners") means a Y-intersection; *Autobahnkreuz* is where two expressways cross. Exits are spaced about every 20 miles and often have a gas station (*bleifrei* means "unleaded"), a restaurant, a mini-market, and sometimes a tourist information desk. Exits and intersections refer to the next major city or the nearest small town. Peruse the map and anticipate which town names to look out for. Know what you're looking for—miss it, and you're long autobahn-gone. When navigating, you'll see *nord, süd, ost,* and *west*.

Autobahns in Germany generally have no speed limit, but you will commonly see a recommended speed posted. While no one gets a ticket for ignoring this recommendation, exceeding this speed means your car insurance no longer covers you in the event of an accident. Don't cruise in the passing lane; stay right. Obstructing traffic on the autobahn is against the law—so running out of gas is not only dangerous, it can earn you a big ticket. In fast-driving Germany, the backed-up line caused by an insensitive slow driver is called an *Autoschlange,* or "car snake." What's the difference between a car snake and a real snake? According to locals, "On a real snake, the ass is in the back."

Driving in Austria: If you side-trip by car into Austria, bring your US driver's license and get an International Driving Permit (explained on page 613). Austria charges drivers who use their major roads. You'll need to have a *Vignette* sticker stuck to the inside of your rental car's windshield (buy at the border crossing, big gas stations near borders, or a rental-car agency). The cost is €8 for 10 days, or €22 for two months. Dipping into the country on regular roads—such as around Reutte in Tirol—requires no special payment. In Austria, green signs direct you to the autobahn, and autobahn speed limits are enforced.

Cheap Flights

If you're visiting one or more cities on a longer European trip, consider intra-European airlines. While trains are usually the best way to connect places that are close together, a flight can save both time and money on longer journeys.

One of the best websites for comparing inexpensive flights is www.skyscanner.net. Other comparison search engines include www.mobissimo.com and www.wegolo.com.

Airlines offering inexpensive flights include easyJet (www.easyjet.com) and Ryanair (www.ryanair.com). Those based in Germany are Air Berlin (www.airberlin.com), Germanwings (www.germanwings.com), and TUIfly (www.tuifly.com).

Be aware of the potential drawbacks of flying on the cheap: nonrefundable and nonchangeable tickets, rigid baggage restrictions (and fees if you have more than what's officially allowed), trekking to airports far outside of town, tight schedules that can mean more delays, little in the way of customer assistance if problems arise, and, of course, no frills. Read the small print—especially baggage policies—before you book.

Resources

Resources from Rick Steves

Rick Steves' Germany 2010 is one of more than 30 titles in a series of **books** on European travel, which includes country guidebooks, city and regional guidebooks, and my budget-travel skills handbook, *Rick Steves' Europe Through the Back Door.* My phrase books—for German, French, Italian, Spanish, and Portuguese—are practical and budget-oriented. My other books are *Europe 101* (a crash course on art and history, newly expanded and in full color), *Travel as a Political Act* (a travelogue sprinkled with advice for bringing home a global perspective), *European Christmas* (on traditional and modern-day celebrations, including Germany's and Austria's), and *Postcards from Europe* (a fun memoir of my travels over 25 years). For a complete list of my books, see the inside of the last page of this book.

My **TV series**, *Rick Steves' Europe,* covers European destinations in 100 shows, with four episodes on Germany. My weekly public radio show, *Travel with Rick Steves,* features interviews with travel experts from around the world, including several hours on Germanic culture. All the TV scripts and radio shows (which are easy and free to download to an iPod or other MP3 player) are at www.ricksteves.com.

If your travels take you beyond Germany to France, Italy, or Great Britain, take advantage of my free, self-guided **audio tours** of the major sights in Paris, Florence, Rome, Venice, and London. Simply download them from www.ricksteves.com or iTunes (search for "Rick Steves' tours" in the iTunes Store), then transfer them to your iPod or other MP3 player.

Maps

The black-and-white maps in this book, drawn by Dave Hoerlein, are concise and simple. Dave, who is well-traveled in Germany, has designed the maps to help you locate recommended places and get to local TIs, where you can pick up more in-depth maps of towns or regions (free or cheap). Better maps are sold at newsstands—before you buy a map, look at it to be sure it has the level of detail you want.

European bookstores, especially in touristy areas, have good selections of maps. For drivers, I'd recommend a 1:200,000- or 1:300,000-scale map. Train travelers usually manage fine with the freebies they get with the train pass and from the local tourist offices.

Other Guidebooks

If you're like most travelers, this book is all you need. But if you're heading beyond my recommended destinations, $40 for extra maps and books is money well spent. Note that none of the following

Begin Your Trip at www.ricksteves.com

At our travel website, you'll find a wealth of free information on European destinations, including fresh monthly news and helpful tips from thousands of fellow travelers. You'll also find my latest guidebook updates (www.ricksteves.com/update) and my travel blog.

Our **online Travel Store** offers travel bags and accessories specially designed by Rick Steves to help you travel smarter and lighter. These include my popular carry-on bags (roll-aboard and rucksack versions), money belts, totes, toiletries kits, adapters, other accessories, and a wide selection of guidebooks, planning maps, and DVDs.

Choosing the right **railpass** for your trip—amidst hundreds of options—can drive you nutty. We'll help you choose the best pass for your needs, plus give you a bunch of free extras.

Rick Steves' Europe Through the Back Door travel company offers **tours** with more than two dozen itineraries and about 300 departures reaching the best destinations in this book...and beyond. We offer a 14-day tour of Germany, Austria, and Switzerland. You'll enjoy great guides, a fun bunch of travel partners (with small groups of generally about 28), and plenty of room to spread out in a big, comfy bus. You'll find European adventures to fit every vacation length. For all the details, and to get our Tour Catalog and a free *Rick Steves Tour Experience* DVD (filmed on location during an actual tour), visit www.ricksteves.com or call the Tour Department at 425/608-4217.

guidebooks is updated annually; check the publication date before you buy.

Lonely Planet's guide to Germany is thorough, well-researched, and packed with good maps and hotel recommendations for low- to moderate-budget travelers. The similar Rough Guide is written by insightful British researchers.

Students and vagabonds like the highly opinionated Let's Go series, which is updated by Harvard students. Let's Go is best for backpackers who have railpasses, stay in hostels, and are interested in the youth and nightlife scene.

The popular skinny green Michelin Guides are excellent, especially if you're driving. Michelin Guides are known for their city and sightseeing maps, dry but concise and helpful information on all major sights, and good cultural and historical background. English editions are sold in Europe at gas stations and tourist shops.

Recommended Books and Movies

To get a feel for Germany past and present, consider these books and films.

Non-Fiction

Germany: A New History (Schulze) is a one-volume compendium covering 2,000 years. Albert Speer's *Inside the Third Reich,* based on 1,200 manuscript pages, is an authoritative account of 1933 through 1945. *Stasiland: True Stories from Behind the Berlin Wall* (Funder) relays the secrets of the Stasi, the East German Ministry for State Security.

Germany and the Germans (Ardagh) is interesting if you'd like to know more about the 1990s reunification. For more on modern Germany, including cultural insights, pick up *Culture Shock! Germany* (Lord), *When in Germany, Do as the Germans Do* (Flippo), and *Of German Ways* (Rippley). Gourmets may want to grab *The Marling Menu-Master for Germany.*

Memoirs: Günter Grass stirred up controversy with his 2007 memoir, *Peeling the Onion,* which revealed he was a soldier in the dreaded Waffen-SS. *A Time of Gifts* (Fermor) tells of the author's walking tour of Europe—and Germany—in the 1930s. In *A Tramp Abroad,* Mark Twain recounts his amusing European adventures, including some in Germany.

Fiction

Classics of German fiction include the works of Thomas Mann (*Buddenbrooks* and *The Magic Mountain*) and Hermann Hesse (*Narcissus and Goldmund* and *Siddhartha*).

Some of the best modern German literature has wrestled with

the country's warmongering past. *All Quiet on the Western Front*, a classroom classic by Erich Maria Remarque, speaks with eloquence about World War I. First published before World War II, *Address Unknown* (Kathrine Kressman Taylor) is a novella with a cautionary tone about what would follow. In *The Tin Drum*, Günter Grass broke the post-WWII silence, creating a landmark work of literature in the process. *The Silent Angel* is a complex love story set after the war (by Nobel Prize winner Heinrich Böll).

A book of science fiction and time travel, *1632* (Flint) sends West Virginians back to 17th-century Germany. *The Good German* (Kanon), set during the postwar years, is part thriller, part historical fiction. *Berlin Noir* (Kerr) is filled with stories of secrets and crime.

For a recently written read, consider the following books, published since the mid-1990s. Esther Freud, the daughter of artist Lucien Freud, set *Summer at Gaglow* during the Great War. *Stones from the River*, the story of a dwarf in Nazi Germany, and *Floating in My Mother's Palm*, which takes place in a small town on the Rhine, have brought Ursula Hegi accolades. Told by a sympathetic narrator, *The Reader* (Schlink) challenges readers to think, "What if my loved ones had been Nazis?" *Saints and Villains* (Giardina) is the fictionalized account of Dietrich Bonhoeffer, a Protestant theologian who protested against Hitler's rise. *Marrying Mozart* (Cowell) reveals a more intimate side of the famous composer.

Films

Leni Riefenstahl's *Triumph of the Will* (1935) is infamous Nazi propaganda turned film classic. Orson Welles infuses *The Third Man* (1949, actually shot in a bombed-out and Soviet-occupied Vienna) with noir foreboding. *The Tin Drum* (1979) is based on Günter Grass' seminal novel (described earlier).

Other meditations on the war years—films filled with allegory and metaphor about the Nazis' rise to power—include *Mephisto* (1981) and Rainer Werner Fassbinder's *The Marriage of Maria Braun* (1979). *Downfall* (2004) tells of the Führer's final days. *Schindler's List* (1993)—about a factory owner's inspirational efforts to save his Jewish employees from deportation to concentration camps—won Steven Spielberg the Best Picture and Best Director Oscars.

Shoah (1985) is a 9.5-hour Holocaust documentary that includes no wartime footage, only interviews with those who lived through it. The well-respected *Das Boot* (1981) has a strong pacifist message, as do the films about the students who defied Hitler—and were ultimately sentenced to die: *The White Rose* (1982) and the beautiful, devastating *Sophie Scholl: The Final Days* (2005).

But German film is not composed of only dramatic, war-themed movies. *Cabaret* (1972, about the crazy Berlin scene in the late 1920s) made Liza Minnelli a star. Set in Berlin, *Wings of Desire* (1987) is Wim Wenders' best film, showing an angel who falls in love and falls to earth. *Amadeus* (1984) made Mozart into a flesh-and-blood man (who giggles), as did *Immortal Beloved* (1994) for Beethoven. *Run Lola Run* (1998) was an art-house phenomenon, combining action, love, and mobsters. Jewish refugees settle in 1930s Kenya in *Nowhere in Africa* (2001). *Good Bye, Lenin!* (2003) is a funny, poignant look at a son's struggle to re-create long-gone Eastern Europe for his mother, while the former GDR's harsh secrets are exposed in *The Lives of Others* (2006).

Holidays and Festivals

This is a partial list of holidays and festivals. Some dates have yet to be set. Before planning a trip around a festival, make sure you verify the dates by checking the festival's website. For more information, contact the tourist information office (tel. 800-651-7010, www.cometogermany.com). Salzburg has music festivals nearly every month.

Jan	Perchtenlaufen (winter festival, parades), Tirol and Salzburg, Austria
Jan–Feb	Fasching (carnival season, balls, parades), throughout Germany
April 2	Good Friday
April 4	Easter; Easter Festival, Salzburg
May 1	May Day with maypole dances, throughout Austria and Germany
May 29–June 6	Spring Horse Races (www.baden-galopp.de), Baden-Baden
May 21–24	Meistertrunk Show (medieval costumes, parties in the Biergartens, www.meistertrunk.de), Rothenburg
May 24	Pentecost Monday (Pfingstmontag), southern Germany
June 3	Corpus Christi (Fronleichnam), southern Germany
Late June	City Festival (www.elbhangfest.de), Dresden; Frankfurt Summertime Festival (arts); Midsummer Eve Celebrations, Austria
July 17	Lichter Festival (fireworks and music, www.koelner-lichter.de), Köln
Late July	Kinderzeche Festival, Dinkelsbühl (www.kinderzeche.de)
Late July–Aug	Salzburg Festival (music)

2010

JANUARY
S	M	T	W	T	F	S
					1	2
3	4	5	6	7	8	9
10	11	12	13	14	15	16
17	18	19	20	21	22	23
24/31	25	26	27	28	29	30

FEBRUARY
S	M	T	W	T	F	S
	1	2	3	4	5	6
7	8	9	10	11	12	13
14	15	16	17	18	19	20
21	22	23	24	25	26	27
28						

MARCH
S	M	T	W	T	F	S
	1	2	3	4	5	6
7	8	9	10	11	12	13
14	15	16	17	18	19	20
21	22	23	24	25	26	27
28	29	30	31			

APRIL
S	M	T	W	T	F	S
				1	2	3
4	5	6	7	8	9	10
11	12	13	14	15	16	17
18	19	20	21	22	23	24
25	26	27	28	29	30	

MAY
S	M	T	W	T	F	S
						1
2	3	4	5	6	7	8
9	10	11	12	13	14	15
16	17	18	19	20	21	22
23/30	24/31	25	26	27	28	29

JUNE
S	M	T	W	T	F	S
		1	2	3	4	5
6	7	8	9	10	11	12
13	14	15	16	17	18	19
20	21	22	23	24	25	26
27	28	29	30			

JULY
S	M	T	W	T	F	S
				1	2	3
4	5	6	7	8	9	10
11	12	13	14	15	16	17
18	19	20	21	22	23	24
25	26	27	28	29	30	31

AUGUST
S	M	T	W	T	F	S
1	2	3	4	5	6	7
8	9	10	11	12	13	14
15	16	17	18	19	20	21
22	23	24	25	26	27	28
29	30	31				

SEPTEMBER
S	M	T	W	T	F	S
			1	2	3	4
5	6	7	8	9	10	11
12	13	14	15	16	17	18
19	20	21	22	23	24	25
26	27	28	29	30		

OCTOBER
S	M	T	W	T	F	S
					1	2
3	4	5	6	7	8	9
10	11	12	13	14	15	16
17	18	19	20	21	22	23
24/31	25	26	27	28	29	30

NOVEMBER
S	M	T	W	T	F	S
	1	2	3	4	5	6
7	8	9	10	11	12	13
14	15	16	17	18	19	20
21	22	23	24	25	26	27
28	29	30				

DECEMBER
S	M	T	W	T	F	S
		1	2	3	4	
5	6	7	8	9	10	11
12	13	14	15	16	17	18
19	20	21	22	23	24	25
26	27	28	29	30	31	

Aug 15	Assumption (Mariä Himmelfahrt), Munich
Aug 28–Sept 5	Summer Horse Races (www.baden-galopp.de), Baden-Baden
Sept	Berlin Festwochen (arts festival, www.berlinerfestspiele.de)
Sept 3–5	Reichsstadt Festival (fireworks), Rothenburg
Sept 18–Oct 3	Oktoberfest (www.oktoberfest.de), Munich
Oct 3	German Unity Day (Tag der Deutschen Einheit), Germany
Oct 22–24	Fall Horse Races (www.baden-galopp.de), Baden-Baden
Nov 1	All Saints' Day (Allerheiligen), southern Germany

Nov	Berlin Jazz Festival; St. Martin's Day Celebrations (feasts), Bavaria
Dec	Christmas markets throughout Germany, particularly in Nürnberg, Munich, Rothenburg, and Freiburg
Dec 6	St. Nicholas Day (Nikolaustag; parades), throughout Germany
Dec 24	Christmas Eve (Heilige Abend), when Germans celebrate Christmas
Dec 25	Christmas
Dec 31	New Year's Eve (Silvester; fireworks), throughout Germany, particularly Berlin

Conversions and Climate

Numbers and Stumblers

- Europeans write a few of their numbers differently than we do. 1 = 1, 4 = 4, 7 = 7.
- In Europe, dates appear as day/month/year, so Christmas is 25/12/10.
- Commas are decimal points and decimals commas. A dollar and a half is 1,50, and there are 5.280 feet in a mile.
- When counting with fingers, start with your thumb. If you hold up your first finger to request one item, you'll probably get two.
- What Americans call the second floor of a building is the first floor in Europe.
- On escalators and moving sidewalks, Europeans keep the left "lane" open for passing. Keep to the right.

Metric Conversions (approximate)

A kilogram is 2.2 pounds, and 1 liter is about a quart, or almost four to a gallon. A kilometer is six-tenths of a mile. I figure kilometers to miles by cutting them in half and adding back 10 percent of the original (120 km: 60 + 12 = 72 miles, 300 km: 150 + 30 = 180 miles).

1 foot = 0.3 meter	1 square yard = 0.8 square meter
1 yard = 0.9 meter	1 square mile = 2.6 square kilometers
1 mile = 1.6 kilometers	1 ounce = 28 grams
1 centimeter = 0.4 inch	1 quart = 0.95 liter
1 meter = 39.4 inches	1 kilogram = 2.2 pounds
1 kilometer = 0.62 mile	32°F = 0°C

Clothing Sizes

When shopping for clothing, use these US-to-European compari-sons as general guidelines (but note that no conversion is perfect).
- Women's dresses and blouses: Add 30 (US size 10 = European size 40)
- Men's suits and jackets: Add 10 (US size 40 regular = European size 50)
- Men's shirts: Multiply by 2 and add about 8 (US size 15 collar = European size 38)
- Women's shoes: Add about 30 (US size 8 = European size 38½)
- Men's shoes: Add 32–34 (US size 9 = European size 41; US size 11 = European size 45)

Climate

The first line is the average daily high; the second line, the aver-age daily low. The third line shows the average number of days without rain. For more detailed weather statistics for destinations throughout Germany (as well as the rest of the world), check www.worldclimate.com.

J	F	M	A	M	J	J	A	S	O	N	D
GERMANY • Berlin											
35°	37°	46°	56°	66°	72°	75°	74°	68°	56°	45°	38°
26°	26°	31°	39°	47°	53°	57°	56°	50°	42°	36°	29°
14	13	19	17	19	17	17	17	18	17	14	16
GERMANY • Munich											
35°	38°	48°	56°	64°	70°	74°	73°	67°	56°	44°	36°
23°	23°	30°	38°	45°	51°	55°	54°	48°	40°	33°	26°
15	12	18	15	16	13	15	15	17	18	15	16

Temperature Conversion:
Fahrenheit and Celsius

For Weather   For Health

Europe takes its temperature using the Celsius scale, while we opt for Fahrenheit. For a rough conversion from Celsius to Fahrenheit, double the number and add 30. For weather, remember that 28°C is 82°F—perfect. For health, 37°C is just right.

APPENDIX

Essential Packing Checklist

Whether you're traveling for five days or five weeks, here's what you'll need to bring. Remember to pack light to enjoy the sweet freedom of true mobility. Happy travels!

- ❑ 5 shirts
- ❑ 1 sweater or lightweight fleece jacket
- ❑ 2 pairs pants
- ❑ 1 pair shorts
- ❑ 1 swimsuit (women only—men can use shorts)
- ❑ 5 pairs underwear and socks
- ❑ 1 pair shoes
- ❑ 1 rainproof jacket
- ❑ Tie or scarf
- ❑ Money belt
- ❑ Money—your mix of:
  - ❑ Debit card for ATM withdrawals
  - ❑ Credit card
  - ❑ Hard cash in US dollars ($20 bills)
- ❑ Documents (and back-up photocopies)
- ❑ Passport
- ❑ Printout of airline e-ticket
- ❑ Driver's license
- ❑ Student ID and hostel card
- ❑ Railpass/car rental voucher
- ❑ Insurance details
- ❑ Daypack
- ❑ Sealable plastic baggies
- ❑ Camera and related gear
- ❑ Empty water bottle
- ❑ Wristwatch and alarm clock
- ❑ Earplugs
- ❑ First-aid kit
- ❑ Medicine (labeled)
- ❑ Extra glasses/contacts and prescriptions
- ❑ Sunscreen and sunglasses
- ❑ Toiletries kit
- ❑ Soap
- ❑ Laundry soap
- ❑ Clothesline
- ❑ Small towel
- ❑ Sewing kit
- ❑ Travel information
- ❑ Necessary map(s)
- ❑ Address list (email and mailing addresses)
- ❑ Postcards and photos from home
- ❑ Notepad and pen
- ❑ Journal

If you plan to carry on your luggage, note that all liquids must be in three-ounce or smaller containers and fit within a single quart-size baggie. For details, see www.tsa.gov/travelers.

APPENDIX

Hotel Reservation

To: _____ _____
                hotel   **email or fax**

From: _____ _____
                name   **email or fax**

Today's date: _____ / _____ / _____
                      day   **month**   **year**

Dear Hotel _____ ,
Please make this reservation for me:

Name: _____

Total # of people: _____ # of rooms: _____ # of nights: _____

Arriving: ____ / ____ / ____   My time of arrival (24-hr clock): _____
              day month year   (I will telephone if I will be late)

Departing: ____ / ____ / ____
                day month year

Room(s): Single___ Double ___ Twin___ Triple ___ Quad___

With: Toilet ____ Shower____ Bath ___ Sink only___

Special needs: View___ Quiet___ Cheapest ___ Ground Floor___

Please email or fax confirmation of my reservation, along with the type of room reserved and the price. Please also inform me of your cancellation policy. After I hear from you, I will quickly send my credit-card information as a deposit to hold the room. Thank you.

_____
Name

_____
Address

_____
City   **State**   **Zip Code**   **Country**

Before hoteliers can make your reservation, they want to know the information listed above. You can use this form as the basis for your email, or you can photocopy this page, fill in the information, and send it as a fax (also available online at www.ricksteves.com/reservation).

German Survival Phrases

When using the phonetics, pronounce ī as the long I sound in "light."

English	German	Phonetics
Good day.	Guten Tag.	**goo**-tehn tahg
Do you speak English?	Sprechen Sie Englisch?	**shprehkh**-ehn zee **ehng**-lish
Yes. / No.	Ja. / Nein.	yah / nīn
I (don't) understand.	Ich verstehe (nicht).	ikh fehr-**shtay**-heh (nikht)
Please.	Bitte.	**bit**-teh
Thank you.	Danke.	**dahng**-keh
I'm sorry.	Es tut mir leid.	ehs toot meer līt
Excuse me.	Entschuldigung.	ehnt-**shool**-dig-oong
(No) problem.	(Kein) Problem.	(kīn) proh-**blaym**
(Very) good.	(Sehr) gut.	(zehr) goot
Goodbye.	Auf Wiedersehen.	owf **vee**-der-zayn
one / two	eins / zwei	īns / tsvī
three / four	drei / vier	drī / feer
five / six	fünf / sechs	fewnf / zehkhs
seven / eight	sieben / acht	**zee**-behn / ahkht
nine / ten	neun / zehn	noyn / tsayn
How much is it?	Wieviel kostet das?	**vee**-feel **kohs**-teht dahs
Write it?	Schreiben?	**shrī**-behn
Is it free?	Ist es umsonst?	ist ehs oom-**zohnst**
Included?	Inklusive?	in-kloo-**zee**-veh
Where can I buy / find...?	Wo kann ich kaufen / finden...?	voh kahn ikh **kow**-fehn / **fin**-dehn
I'd like / We'd like...	Ich hätte gern /	ikh **heh**-teh gehrn /
	Wir hätten gern...	veer **heh**-tehn gehrn
...a room.	...ein Zimmer.	īn **tsim**-mer
...a ticket to ___.	...eine Fahrkarte nach ___.	ī-neh **far**-kar-teh nahkh
Is it possible?	Ist es möglich?	ist ehs **mur**-glikh
Where is...?	Wo ist...?	voh ist
...the train station	...der Bahnhof	dehr **bahn**-hohf
...the bus station	...der Busbahnhof	dehr **boos**-bahn-hohf
...tourist information	...das Touristen-	dahs too-**ris**-tehn-
	informationsbüro	in-for-maht-see-**ohns-bew**-roh
...toilet	...die Toilette	dee toh-**leh**-teh
men	Herren	**hehr**-rehn
women	Damen	**dah**-mehn
left / right	links / rechts	links / rehkhts
straight	geradeaus	geh-**rah**-deh-ows
When is this	Um wieviel Uhr ist hier	oom **vee**-feel oor ist heer
open / closed?	geöffnet / geschlossen?	geh-**urf**-neht / geh-**shloh**-sehn
At what time?	Um wieviel Uhr?	oom **vee**-feel oor
Just a moment.	Moment.	moh-**mehnt**
now / soon / later	jetzt / bald / später	yehtst / bahld / **shpay**-ter
today / tomorrow	heute / morgen	**hoy**-teh / **mor**-gehn

In the Restaurant

I'd like / We'd like...	Ich hätte gern / Wir hätten gern...	ikh **heh**-teh gehrn / veer **heh**-tehn gehrn
...a reservation for...	...eine Reservierung für...	ī-neh reh-zer-**feer**-oong fewr
...a table for one / two.	...einen Tisch für ein / zwei.	ī-nehn tish fewr īn / tsvī
Non-smoking.	Nichtraucher.	**nikht**-rowkh-er
Is this seat free?	Ist hier frei?	ist heer frī
Menu (in English), please.	Speisekarte (in Englisch), bitte.	**shpī**-zeh-kar-teh (in **ehng**-lish) **bit**-teh
service (not) included	Trinkgeld (nicht) inklusive	**trink**-gehlt (nikht) in-kloo-**zee**-veh
cover charge	Eintritt	**īn**-trit
to go	zum Mitnehmen	tsoom **mit**-nay-mehn
with / without	mit / ohne	mit / **oh**-neh
and / or	und / oder	oont / **oh**-der
menu (of the day)	(Tages-) Karte	(**tah**-gehs-) **kar**-teh
set meal for tourists	Touristenmenü	too-**ris**-tehn-meh-**new**
specialty of the house	Spezialität des Hauses	shpayt-see-ah-lee-**tayt** dehs **how**-zehs
appetizers	Vorspeise	**for**-shpī-zeh
bread	Brot	broht
cheese	Käse	**kay**-zeh
sandwich	Sandwich	**zahnd**-vich
soup	Suppe	**zup**-peh
salad	Salat	zah-**laht**
meat	Fleisch	flīsh
poultry	Geflügel	geh-**flew**-gehl
fish	Fisch	fish
seafood	Meeresfrüchte	**meh**-rehs-**frewkh**-teh
fruit	Obst	ohpst
vegetables	Gemüse	geh-**mew**-zeh
dessert	Nachspeise	**nahkh**-shpī-zeh
mineral water	Mineralwasser	min-eh-**rahl**-vah-ser
tap water	Leitungswasser	**lī**-toongs-vah-ser
milk	Milch	milkh
(orange) juice	(Orangen-) Saft	(oh-**rahn**-zhehn-) zahft
coffee	Kaffee	kah-**fay**
tea	Tee	tay
wine	Wein	vīn
red / white	rot / weiß	roht / vīs
glass / bottle	Glas / Flasche	glahs / **flah**-sheh
beer	Bier	beer
Cheers!	Prost!	prohst
More. / Another.	Mehr. / Noch ein.	mehr / nohkh īn
The same.	Das gleiche.	dahs **glīkh**-eh
Bill, please.	Rechnung, bitte.	**rehkh**-noong **bit**-teh
tip	Trinkgeld	**trink**-gehlt
Delicious!	Lecker!	**lehk**-er

For more user-friendly German phrases, check out *Rick Steves' German Phrase Book and Dictionary* or *Rick Steves' French, Italian & German Phrase Book*.

INDEX

INDEX

MAP INDEX

Rick Steves

EUROPEAN TOURS

ADRIATIC • ATHENS & THE HEART OF GREECE • BARCELONA & MADRID • BELGIUM & HOLLAND • BERLIN, VIENNA & PRAGUE BEST OF EUROPE • BEST OF ITALY BEST OF TURKEY • BULGARIA • EASTERN EUROPE • ENGLAND • FAMILY EUROPE GERMANY, AUSTRIA & SWITZERLAND HEART OF ITALY • IRELAND • ISTANBUL LONDON • PARIS • PARIS & HEART OF FRANCE • PARIS & SOUTH OF FRANCE PORTUGAL • PRAGUE & BUDAPEST • ROME SAN SEBASTIAN & BASQUE COUNTRY SCANDINAVIA • SCOTLAND • SICILY SOUTH ITALY • SPAIN & MOROCCO ST. PETERSBURG, TALLINN & HELSINKI VENICE, FLORENCE & ROME • VILLAGE FRANCE • VILLAGE ITALY • VILLAGE TURKEY

VISIT **TOURS.RICKSTEVES.COM**

Great guides, small groups, no grumps

▸ Plan Your Trip

Browse thousands of articles and a wealth of money-saving tips for planning your dream trip. You'll find up-to-date information on Europe's best destinations, packing smart, getting around, finding rooms, staying healthy, avoiding scams and more.

▸ Eurail Passes

Find out, step-by-step, if a rail pass makes sense for your trip—and how to avoid buying more than you need. Get a bunch of free extras!

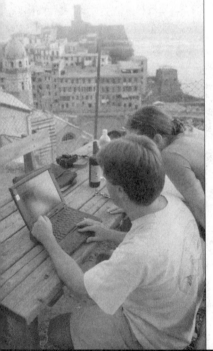

▸ Graffiti Wall & Travelers' Helpline

Learn, ask, share—our online community of savvy travelers is a great resource for first-time travelers to Europe, as well as seasoned pros.

Rick Steves' Europe Through the Back Door, Inc.

turn your travel dreams into affordable reality

NOW AVAILABLE

RICK STEVES APPS FOR THE iPHONE OR iPOD TOUCH

With these apps you can:

▸ Spin the compass icon to switch views between sights, hotels, and restaurant selections—and get details on cost, hours, address, and phone number.

▸ Tap any point on the screen to read Rick's detailed information, including history and suggested viewpoints.

▸ Get a deeper view into Rick's tours with audio and video segments.

Go to iTunes to download the following apps:

Rick Steves' Louvre Tour

Rick Steves' Historic Paris Walk

Rick Steves' Orsay Museum Tour

Rick Steves' Versailles

Rick Steves' Ancient Rome Tour

Rick Steves' St. Peter's Basilica Tour

Once downloaded, these apps are completely self-contained on your iPhone or iPod Touch, so you will not incur pricey roaming charges during use overseas.

Rick Steves books and DVDs are available at bookstores and through online booksellers.

Rick Steves guidebooks are published by Avalon Travel, a member of the Perseus Books Group.

Rick Steves apps are produced by Übermind, a boutique Seattle-based software consultancy firm.

Credits

Researchers
To help update this book, Rick relied on...

Ian Watson
Ian has worked with Rick's guidebooks since 1993, after starting out with Let's Go and Frommer's guides. Originally from upstate New York, Ian speaks several European languages, including German, and makes his home in Reykjavík, Iceland.

Lee Evans

Lee Evans left his Eastern Washington home on a Congress-Bundestag Scholarship and never looked back. After completing his studies in Florence and Prague, he finally found his home in the greatest city on the planet: Berlin. His beautiful wife and daughter tolerate his historical ranting and frequent absences as a tour guide.

Cameron Hewitt

Cameron writes and edits guidebooks for Rick Steves, specializing in Eastern Europe. To update and expand this book's Black Forest chapter, Cameron scoured the land of cuckoo clocks, mineral baths, and cream cakes. When he's not traveling, Cameron lives in Seattle with his wife Shawna.

Contributor
Gene Openshaw

Gene is the co-author of seven Rick Steves books. For this book, he wrote material on art, history, and contemporary culture. When he's not traveling, Gene enjoys composing music, recovering from his 1973 trip to Europe with Rick, and living everyday life with his daughter.

Acknowledgements
Thanks to my wife, Anne, for her support. Thanks to Gene Openshaw for writing the tour of Munich's Alte Pinakothek; to Cameron Hewitt for writing the original versions of the Dresden and Nürnberg chapters; and to Lee Evans for writing the original version of the Görlitz chapter.

Images

Location	Photographer
Introduction: Füssen	Rick Steves
Munich: Marienplatz	Rick Steves
Bavaria and Tirol: Neuschwanstein Castle	Dominic Bonuccelli
Salzburg and Berchtesgaden: Salzburg Overview	Dominic Bonucelli
Baden-Baden and the Black Forest: Baden-Baden	Cameron Hewitt
Rothenburg and the Romantic Road: Rothenburg	David C. Hoerlein
Würzburg: Residenzplatz	Ian Watson
Frankfurt: Frankfurt Scene from Bridge	Rick Steves
Rhine Valley: Bacharach and the Rhine	Dominic Bonuccelli
Mosel Valley: Beilstein	Cameron Hewitt
Trier: Trier	Ian Watson
Köln and the Unromantic Rhine: Köln's Cathedral	Cameron Hewitt
Nürnberg: Market Square	Rick Steves
Dresden: Zwinger	Cameron Hewitt
Görlitz: Church of St. Peter	Lee Evans
Berlin: Gendarmenmarkt	Cameron Hewitt